A MANUAL OF
CARPENTRY AND
JOINERY

BY

J. W. RILEY

LECTURER IN DESCRIPTIVE GEOMETRY, BUILDING CONSTRUCTION,
AND CARPENTRY AND JOINERY, AT THE MUNICIPAL
TECHNICAL SCHOOL, ROCHDALE

WITH 923 ILLUSTRATIONS

1905

Copyright © 2013 Read Books Ltd.
This book is copyright and may not be
reproduced or copied in any way without
the express permission of the publisher in writing

British Library Cataloguing-in-Publication Data
A catalogue record for this book is available from the
British Library

Woodworking

Woodworking is the process of making items from wood. Along with stone, mud and animal parts, wood was one of the first materials worked by early humans. There are incredibly early examples of woodwork, evidenced in Mousterian stone tools used by Neanderthal man, which demonstrate our affinity with the wooden medium. In fact, the very development of civilisation is linked to the advancement of increasingly greater degrees of skill in working with these materials.

Examples of Bronze Age wood-carving include tree trunks worked into coffins from northern Germany and Denmark and wooden folding-chairs. The site of Fellbach-Schmieden in Germany has provided fine examples of wooden animal statues from the Iron Age. Woodworking is depicted in many ancient Egyptian drawings, and a considerable amount of ancient Egyptian furniture (such as stools, chairs, tables, beds, chests) has been preserved in tombs. The inner coffins found in the tombs were also made of wood. The metal used by the Egyptians for woodworking tools was originally copper and eventually, after 2000 BC, bronze - as ironworking was unknown until much later. Historically, woodworkers relied upon the woods native to their region, until transportation and trade innovations made more exotic woods available to the craftsman.

Today, often as a contemporary artistic and 'craft' medium, wood is used both in traditional and modern styles; an excellent material for delicate as well as forceful artworks. Wood is used in forms of sculpture, trade, and decoration including chip carving, wood burning, and marquetry, offering a fascination, beauty, and complexity in the grain that often shows even when the medium is painted. It is in some ways easier to shape than harder substances, but an artist or craftsman must develop specific skills to carve it properly. 'Wood carving' is really an entire genre itself, and involves cutting wood generally with a knife in one hand, or a chisel by two hands - or, with one hand on a chisel and one hand on a mallet. The phrase may also refer to the finished product, from individual sculptures to hand-worked mouldings composing part of a tracery.

The making of sculpture in wood has been extremely widely practiced but survives much less well than the other main materials such as stone and bronze, as it is vulnerable to decay, insect damage, and fire. It therefore forms an important hidden element in the arts and crafts history of many cultures. Outdoor wood sculptures do not last long in most parts of the world, so we have little idea how the totem pole tradition developed. Many of the most important sculptures of China and Japan in particular are in wood, and the great majority of African sculptures and that of Oceania also use this medium. There are various forms of carving which can be utilised; 'chip carving' (a style of carving in which knives or chisels are used to remove small chips of the material), 'relief carving' (where figures are carved in a flat panel of wood), 'Scandinavian flat-plane' (where figures are carved in large flat planes, created primarily using a carving knife - and rarely rounded or sanded afterwards) and 'whittling' (simply carving shapes using just a knife). Each of these techniques will need slightly varying tools, but broadly speaking, a specialised 'carving knife' is essential, alongside a 'gouge' (a tool with a curved cutting edge used in a variety of forms and sizes for carving hollows, rounds and sweeping curves), a 'chisel' and a 'coping saw' (a small saw, used to cut off chunks of wood at once).

Wood turning is another common form of woodworking, used to create wooden objects on a lathe. Woodturning differs from most other forms of woodworking in that the wood is moving while a stationary tool is used to cut and shape it. There are two distinct methods of turning wood: 'spindle turning' and 'bowl' or 'faceplate turning'. Their key difference is in the orientation of the wood grain, relative to the axis of the lathe. This variation in orientation changes the tools and techniques used. In spindle turning, the grain runs lengthways along the lathe bed, as if a log was mounted in the lathe. Grain is thus always perpendicular to the direction of rotation under the tool. In bowl turning, the grain runs at right angles to the axis, as if a plank were mounted across the chuck. When a bowl blank rotates, the angle that the grain makes with the cutting tool continually changes between the easy cuts of lengthways and downwards across the grain to two places per rotation where the tool is cutting across the grain and even upwards across it. This varying grain angle limits some of the tools that may be used and requires additional skill in order to cope with it.

The origin of woodturning dates to around 1300 BC when the Egyptians first developed a two-person lathe. One person would turn the wood with a rope while the other used a sharp tool to cut shapes in the wood. The Romans improved the Egyptian design with the addition of a turning bow. Early bow lathes were also developed and used in Germany, France and Britain. In the Middle Ages a pedal replaced hand-operated turning, freeing both the craftsman's hands to hold the woodturning tools. The pedal was usually connected to a pole, often a straight-grained sapling. The system today is called the 'spring pole' lathe. Alternatively, a two-person lathe, called a 'great lathe', allowed a piece to turn continuously (like today's power lathes). A master would cut the wood while an apprentice turned the crank.

As an interesting aside, the term 'bodger' stems from pole lathe turners who used to make chair legs and spindles. A bodger would typically purchase all the trees on a plot of land, set up camp on the plot, and then fell the trees and turn the wood. The spindles and legs that were produced were sold in bulk, for pence per dozen. The bodger's job was considered unfinished because he only made component parts. The term now describes a person who leaves a job unfinished, or does it badly. This could not be more different from perceptions of modern carpentry; a highly skilled trade in which work involves the construction of buildings, ships, timber bridges and concrete framework. The word 'carpenter' is the English rendering of the Old French word *carpentier* (later, *charpentier*) which is derived from the Latin *carpentrius;* '(maker) of a carriage.' Carpenters traditionally worked with natural wood and did the rougher work such as framing, but today many other materials are also used and sometimes the finer trades of cabinet-making and furniture building are considered carpentry.

As is evident from this brief historical and practical overview of woodwork, it is an incredibly varied and exciting genre of arts and crafts; an ancient tradition still relevant in the modern day. Woodworkers range from hobbyists, individuals operating from the home environment, to artisan professionals with specialist workshops, and eventually large-scale factory operations. We hope the reader is inspired by this book to create some woodwork of their own.

PREFACE.

IN writing this book the needs of carpenters and joiners who are studying the scientific principles of their work have been borne in mind throughout. Students who are attending classes at Technical Institutes to prepare for the examinations of the City and Guilds of London Institute in Carpentry and Joinery will find that the following chapters have the same aims as their syllabus, inasmuch as they are intended to develop an appreciation of general principles rather than to encourage empirical methods of work. In fact, the educational ideal underlying the syllabus of the City and Guilds of London Institute has constantly guided the author.

The simplest types of construction have been dealt with most fully, and the principles they embody have been emphasised continually. Without going into great detail, these rules have then been applied to more complicated examples; for a long experience has convinced the author that a student who has grasped the fundamental facts of a subject requires a minimum of guidance in more advanced work.

Unusual prominence has been given to the elementary parts of geometry, mensuration, and mechanics, because students of Carpentry and Joinery constantly begin their work without this necessary preliminary knowledge. Among other special features of the book are the chapters on tools and woodworking machinery as well as the large number of pictorial diagrams of details of construction.

It is hoped that in addition to its use by students of technical classes the book will be of service to practical men in the workshop and to schoolmasters framing courses of manual training.

Summaries are given at the ends of the chapters, and ample material for testing the knowledge of the student will be found in the questions—chiefly derived from past examination papers of the City and Guilds of London Institute—which immediately follow the summaries.

Acknowledgement is gladly made of indebtedness to Messrs. William Marples & Sons, Ltd., Sheffield, and to Messrs. Joseph Gleave & Son, Manchester, for permission to use illustrations of tools from their catalogues; also to Messrs. Thomas Robinson & Sons, Ltd., of Rochdale, for all the photographs of wood-working machines which illustrate Chapter VI. Thanks are gratefully tendered to Mr. E. Holden, Principal of the Municipal Technical School, Newry, Co. Down, for reading the proofs and making many valuable suggestions during the passage of the work through the press.

It is a great pleasure to acknowledge, in conclusion, the generous help which has been received, throughout the whole period of preparation of the book, from Prof. R. A. Gregory and Mr. A. T. Simmons, B.Sc. Their kindly criticism and advice, and the advantage of their wide experience have very materially lessened the difficulties of the author's task.

J. W. RILEY.

ROCHDALE.

CONTENTS.

	PAGE
CHAPTER I.	
TIMBER,	1
CHAPTER II.	
PLANE GEOMETRY,	21
CHAPTER III.	
SOLID GEOMETRY,	49
CHAPTER IV.	
MENSURATION OF CARPENTRY AND JOINERY,	85
CHAPTER V.	
TOOLS,	107
CHAPTER VI.	
WOODWORKING MACHINERY,	129
CHAPTER VII.	
JOINTS AND FASTENINGS,	158
CHAPTER VIII.	
WOODEN FLOORS,	193
CHAPTER IX.	
WOODEN ROOFS,	215

CONTENTS

CHAPTER X.
PARTITIONS AND WOODEN FRAMED BUILDINGS, - - - 259

CHAPTER XI.
MISCELLANEOUS CARPENTRY CONSTRUCTIONS, - - - 274

CHAPTER XII.
MECHANICS OF CARPENTRY, - - - - - - - 306

CHAPTER XIII.
DOORS AND OTHER PANELLED FRAMING, - - - - 346

CHAPTER XIV.
WINDOWS, - - - - - - - - - 381

CHAPTER XV.
ROOF-LIGHTS AND CONSERVATORIES, - - - - 412

CHAPTER XVI.
STAIRCASE WORK AND HANDRAILING, - - - - - 430

CHAPTER XVII.
WORKSHOP PRACTICE AND SPECIAL CONSTRUCTIONS, - - 460

TECHNOLOGICAL EXAMINATION PAPERS, 1905, - - 483

ANSWERS, - - - - - - - - 491

INDEX, - - - - - - - - - 492

A MANUAL OF CARPENTRY AND JOINERY.

CHAPTER I.

TIMBER.

The Source of Timber.—The wood used by the carpenter and joiner is obtained from the plants known as **trees**. In tropical countries palms and grasses (*e.g.* bamboo) grow to great size, but the stems of these plants are unsuitable for timber. In temperate climates most forest trees are of a quite different type, belonging either to the class which includes the oak, ash, beech, birch, etc., or to that known as the conifers, among which are the pines and firs. It is such trees alone which yield the timber used by wood-workers.

The Structure of the Stem of the Oak.—If a branch or young stem of an oak tree be cut across, it will be seen to consist of (*a*) a central pith; (*b*) layers of wood; (*c*) bark, consisting of an outer part composed of corky and dead layers, and an inner part of bast which can be torn off in shreds; and (*d*) a thin layer between the bast and the wood called **cambium** which, by dividing, forms new layers of wood on its inner side and new layers of bast on its outer side. The cambium is most active in spring and early summer, and the new wood then formed is of open texture. As autumn approaches the activity of the cambium decreases, and the wood it forms is close in texture and small in amount. In the winter the division of the cambium stops altogether, to be renewed in spring by the formation of more open-textured wood. The difference in the appearance of the autumn wood of one year and the spring wood of the next is so marked that it is easy to distinguish the

2   A MANUAL OF CARPENTRY AND JOINERY.

limits of the wood formed in one year. The layer of wood formed in one year is called an **annual ring**. The bast is soft and becomes squeezed up under the bark so that it is not at all conspicuous.

In such a cross section as that described may be seen, stretching from the pith to the bark, a number of radial lines of tissue

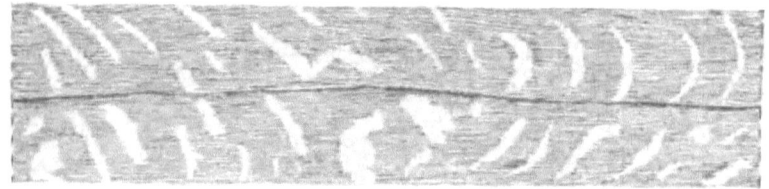

FIG. 1.—Sketch showing the appearance of silver grain in a radial longitudinal section of Oak.

which are called **medullary rays**. A comparison of such a transverse section with wood cut in other directions shows that the medullary rays are really thin lath-like plates arranged radially. In a radial longitudinal section of the wood (Fig. 1) the

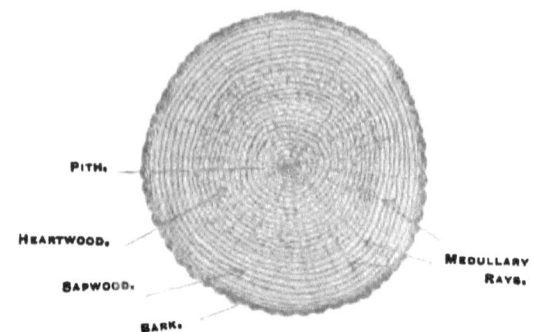

FIG. 2.—Cross section of the trunk of an Oak tree.

medullary rays show as silvery patches on the surface, giving the appearance known as *silver grain*. In most kinds of wood the medullary rays—though really present—are not distinguishable by the naked eye; they are most clearly seen in the oak and the beech. In a section of an older oak (Fig. 2) it will be seen that the wood consists of two well-marked parts: an inner **heartwood**, dark in colour and hard; and an outer **sapwood**, lighter in colour and of somewhat spongy texture. Their difference is explained by the fact that the heartwood is dead and of no use to the tree except as a mechanical support; while the sapwood is still actively alive and conveying up the trunk the water and mineral food which the roots take up from the soil.

The heartwood, although dead so far as the life of the tree is concerned, is the only part of the tree which is suitable for use for constructional purposes.

Fig. 3.—Cross section of a Larch stem showing annual rings.

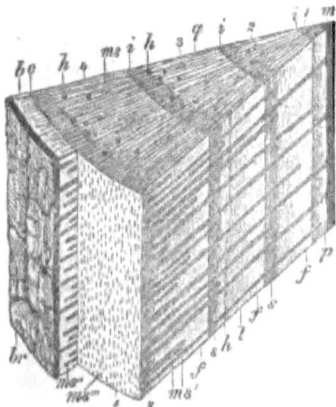

Fig. 4.—Portion of a four-year-old stem of the Pine, cut in winter. 1, 2, 3, 4, the successive annual rings of the wood; b, bast; br, bark; c, cambium; r, spring wood; h, resin canals; i, junction of wood of successive years; m, pith; ms, medullary rays; s, autumn wood. (Four times natural size.)

When a tree begins to decay, the heartwood, being the oldest, is naturally the first to suffer. Trees cut down before they have attained maturity are likely to have an over-abundance of sapwood.

Sapwood is unsuitable for use on account of its soft spongy texture, and its liability to absorb moisture.

The Timber of other Trees. —Although the above description of the oak applies also, in its general features, to other timber-producing trees, there are many respects in which a marked difference is observable. In the pines, firs, and larches (Fig. 3), the annual rings are more clearly defined, and the wood is perforated with small canals which contain resin (Fig. 4). Compared with oak the

4 A MANUAL OF CARPENTRY AND JOINERY.

wood of these conifers is open-textured and soft. The difference is so constant that these trees are generally called the **soft-wood** trees in contra-distinction to **hard-wood** trees such as oak, ash, elm, birch, beech, mahogany, walnut, etc. The soft-wood trees (the conifers) are easily distinguished by their needle-shaped leaves.

Among the hard-wood trees the oak is pre-eminent for the distinctness of its annual rings. In some others, *e.g.* the box, the wood is so close and compactly formed that the separate rings are only distinguished with difficulty. Such woods are in general heavier and more difficult to work than soft-woods.

Felling.—Trees vary considerably in their period of growth, and if left to grow after they have attained maturity begin to decay. Although, strictly speaking, this fact does not directly concern the carpenter and joiner—as he generally purchases his timber from the merchant—it is desirable to have some idea of the age at which trees ought to be cut down in order to obtain the best results.

It is generally considered that the oak and most hard-wood trees are best cut down at an age of from 120 to 200 years. Soft-wood trees, such as the firs and pines, are ready for felling after from 70 to 100 years growth. The proper time of the year to cut down a tree is in the early winter, when the sap is at rest. If the tree is felled during the spring, summer, or early autumn, the sap which is then flowing will affect the durability of the wood.

Converting.—As an average tree when cut down contains from 25 to 40 per cent. of moisture, it should be at once so sawn or "converted" that the shrinkage upon drying will not split the wood. If the tree is left unsawn the outer layers dry first and cause splitting to take place in a radial direction. The method of converting depends upon the character of the wood, the purpose for which it is to be used, and possibly upon the country from which it is obtained. It must be remembered that wood shrinks least in the radial direction, that is, in a direction at right angles to the annual rings, therefore the method of conversion will materially affect the amount of shrinkage that takes place. It is also of some importance to know that the outer, or bark, side of a plank or board will wear better and be less likely to "shell" than the inner, or heart, side; for example, the plank of Fig. 14 will shrink less in width than that of Fig. 13, while in Fig. 13 it would be better to expose the side X rather than the side Y. In order to obtain the beautiful marking known as silver grain in oak, it is necessary to convert the log so that all the saw cuts are radial. This result is obtained by first cutting the tree into quarterings, that is, sawing by two radial cuts at right angles to each other, as shown in Fig. 5. This also allows the wood to shrink without the danger of splitting. Other hardwoods are sometimes cut in a similar manner.

Soft-wood trees are generally cut into planks and boards of marketable sections. The exact way depends upon the size of the tree, but in all cases care should be taken not to have the

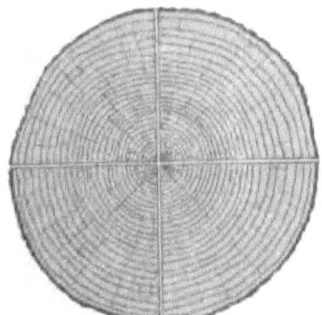 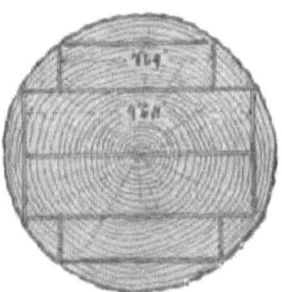

FIG. 5.—Method of quartering a log.   FIG. 6.—Method of converting a soft-wood log.

pith in the inside of a plank. Fig. 6 shows how such trees are usually cut. As most of the timber used in this country is imported from abroad, the question of conversion seriously affects the mode and cost of conveyance. It is economical to send across the sea the better qualities of material only, and to have these in the most compact form for stacking during transport. In order to render this possible, large saw-mills exist, as near as convenient to the forests where the trees grow. At these saw-mills the trees are sawn into the various marketable sections, and only the better quality of material is shipped.

Seasoning.—As previously explained, a large percentage of moisture is present in timber when the tree is felled. As this moisture dries out, the wood contracts. It is therefore necessary that the timber be seasoned by exposure to the air for some time before it can be used satisfactorily for constructional purposes.

It should be clearly understood that in many woods shrinkage is more in the direction of the annual rings than in that of their thickness; the thickness of the annual rings and the density of

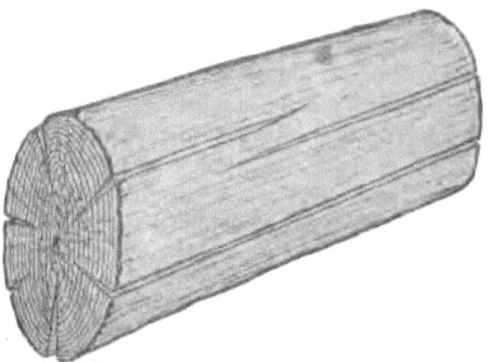

FIG. 7.—Effect of shrinkage upon a log left unsawn.

the wood have also a decided influence upon the amount of shrinkage that takes place during seasoning. Fig. 7 shows the effect of leaving the trunk of a tree unsawn for a long period. Fig. 8 shows how each of the planks into which a balk is cut will be likely to be affected by seasoning. Figs. 9 and 10 show respectively how a quarter of a log, and a rectangular piece, each cut so that one corner contains the pith, will be affected by being seasoned.

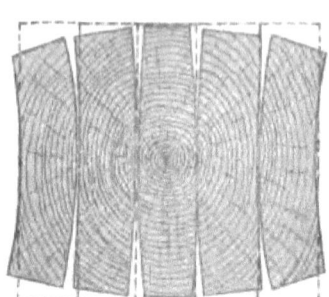

FIG. 8.—Effect of shrinkage of a balk sawn into planks.

The best method of seasoning wood is to stack it in such a manner that the air can circulate freely all round each piece. This is done in a variety of ways according to the available space in the timber, or storage, yard. The ground used for storage purposes should be dry, and free from grass or other vegetation.

A shed with open sides and ends, where the roof is carried on pillars, is a particularly suitable place for stacking wood during the seasoning process, as the timber is thus protected from the direct rays of the sun and also from the rain, while the open sides allow of a free circulation of air.

When space is limited, a method of stacking often resorted to, especially with wide boards, is to arrange the boards horizontally over each other with short thin laths, called "skids," across and between the boards. These skids are placed in vertical rows about 3 feet apart, great care being taken to have

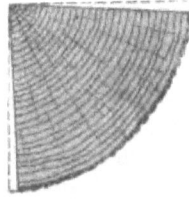
FIG. 9.—Effect of shrinkage upon a quarter of a log.

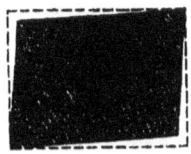
FIG. 10.—Effect of shrinkage upon a rectangular block.

them exactly over each other to prevent the lower boards being bent by the weight of those above. This method is called "skidding." Rough wooden frames are often constructed into which the planks and boards are placed on edge at a little distance apart; or, where space will allow, the boards are arranged on end on perches—horizontal timbers, at heights to suit the length of boards, supported upon posts across which the upper ends of the boards cross each other. The object in each case is to expose as much of the surface of the board as possible to fresh air, as well as to enable any particular piece to be withdrawn easily. Strips of iron or wood are often nailed across the ends of wide boards to prevent them from splitting.

This plan is known as **natural seasoning**, and although it requires a considerable time—varying with the thickness and nature of the material—it yields the best results.

Timber is considered sufficiently seasoned for carpenters' work when it has lost about one-fifth its weight; for joiners' work a loss of one-third is necessary. Wood used for joiners' or other finished work is much improved by a **second seasoning**. This is effected by allowing the framing, or material, to remain in an unfinished state for some time before the work is completed finally.

8   A MANUAL OF CARPENTRY AND JOINERY.

Hot-air Seasoning or Desiccating.—Hot-air seasoning is effected by stacking the wood in an artificially heated room where the hot air quickly dries out the moisture. This method has an advantage over natural seasoning in that it can be completed in a comparatively short time. The disadvantages of its use are:

(1) it can only be satisfactorily applied to small pieces; if used for large pieces the heat dries the outside before the inside is affected, and therefore tends to split the wood;

(2) if applied to newly sawn wood it is very liable to cause shakes (cracks) in the wood;

(3) wood so seasoned is not fit for outside work, as it will be affected by varying changes in the atmosphere, absorb moisture, swell in damp weather, and contract in hot dry weather;

(4) it reduces the strength of the wood and also affects the colour of some of the better varieties.

Water Seasoning.—The sap in wood can quickly be got rid of by immersing the wood in a running stream of water, and afterwards stacking it in the air, where the water which has taken the place of the sap is easily dried out. The timber being treated in this manner should be immersed completely, and should have the end of the wood to the flow, with the butt, or lower, end against the stream. This process, like the hot air process, has the advantage of being quickly performed, but it reduces the elasticity and durability of the wood, and also makes it brittle.

Boiling and Steaming.—Wood can also be seasoned either by immersion in boiling water or by exposure to steam. These methods can only be adopted on a small scale owing to the expense incurred in the operation.

The trouble and expense involved in the seasoning of wood has led to numerous experiments being performed with a view of changing the character of the sap, so that it is solidified and rendered practically unshrinkable, while at the same time the strength of the wood is not affected. These have however, as yet, not become extensively applied.

Defects.—The quality of timber is seriously affected by accidents to the growing tree. These may be caused by lightning, high winds, the unskilful lopping off of branches, etc. **Knots** are the bases of side branches and may be divided into two classes, (a) *loose* or *dead* knots, which are the remains

TIMBER.

of decayed, or broken, branches, and (*b*) good, sound knots. Whenever a knot occurs in wood, the grain is thereby diverted from the straight, and the resulting timber is called *cross-grained*. If the knot is small and sound it does not affect the value of the material seriously unless such is to be used for carrying purposes. A super-abundance of knots generally indicates that the wood is obtained from the upper end of the tree. Knots cause extra labour in working, are objectionable in superior finished work, and are a source of weakness in beams.

Heart shakes (Fig. 11) are defects that occur in the growing tree and are liable to exist in almost every kind of wood. They are radiating clefts in the middle of the tree.

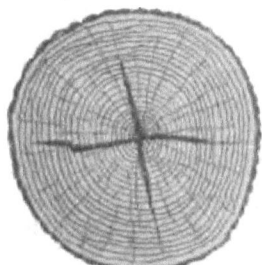   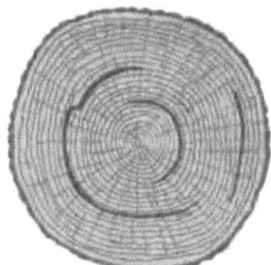

FIG. 11.—Heart shakes.   FIG. 12.—Cup shakes.

Star shakes are similar to heart shakes, and often extend almost through the tree.

Cup shakes are those that follow the path of the annual rings (Fig. 12). These shakes often seriously interfere with the amount of material obtainable from the tree during the conversion into planks and boards. Their cause is attributed to strong winds swaying the tree, to the action of excessive frost upon the moisture present in the tree, or to the tree being struck by lightning when growing.

Twisted fibres are caused by a branch having been cut off and its stump covered by subsequent growth. The result is that the fibres become diverted from the straight. Twisted fibres may also be caused by exceptional storms and strong winds affecting trees in exposed situations.

Druxiness is caused by a branch having been torn off and the rain, or frost, thus getting into the tree. It is indicated by a white or yellowish stain.

Doatiness is a speckled staining found in some kinds of hard wood.

Rindgalls are caused by the bark, and possibly some of the fibres underlying it, being damaged by a blow, or by a branch being lopped off.

Upsets are places where the continuity of the fibre has been interfered with by crushing.

Foxiness is a disease affecting the timber through overgrowth. In this disease the fibres of the wood assume a yellow, or reddish, colour.

Wet Rot is a decomposition of the fibres of the wood and may take place while the tree is growing. It is induced by the wood becoming thoroughly saturated with water. It is also often found when the timber has been stacked in a damp, or wet, situation without air.

Dry Rot is one of the most troublesome of timber diseases. It attacks unseasoned timber in positions where there is not a free access of air. The disease is caused by a fungus-growth which reduces the fibres of the wood to a powder. Dry rot may be prevented almost entirely by taking care to use only thoroughly seasoned timber which is entirely free from sapwood, and by providing for an abundance of fresh air, especially at the ends. The conditions most favourable to the growth of dry rot are found in the lower floors of buildings where a warm and moist atmosphere exists, and where the ends of joists are built into the walls in such a manner that a free circulation of air cannot take place around them. Dry rot can be recognised by the white or brown mushroom-like fungus which covers the surface of the attacked wood. At first such timber becomes brown in colour, and brittle like charred wood; at a later stage it falls to a powder. Dry rot spreads very rapidly, and will travel over brick or stonework, and even affect plaster. When once contracted, this disease is very difficult to exterminate.

Injury caused by Animals.—Timber is very subject to destruction by various mites, ants, etc., especially in certain positions. They destroy it by boring their way through the wood. This does not affect timber used for carpentry and joinery to such an extent as it does that used in shipbuilding, dockyard, and harbour construction.

The **Teredo navalis**, commonly called the *shipworm*, is a worm-shaped, greyish-white mollusc, often twelve inches long and half-an-inch in diameter, which bores its way through the wood and thus destroys it. The ravages made by this animal in many dockyards are notorious. It attacks most kinds of woods and destroys them quickly. Many attempts have been made with varying success to prevent the depredations of these animals; the expedients adopted include coating the piles and other woodwork with sheet-copper, driving flat-headed nails close together into the timber, saturating the wood with creosote, etc.

Termites (white ants), and various other organisms also attack many kinds of wood and quickly destroy them. As wood attacked by these animals is recognised easily by the forester or timber merchant, it rarely comes under the notice of the wood-worker; a detailed description of the injury is therefore unnecessary here.

Preservation.—In order that wood may be durable it must be perfectly free from sapwood, shakes, and other defects, have been properly seasoned, and be well ventilated.

Paint is perhaps one of the best preservatives for finished woodwork that has to be exposed to the weather, as it not only renders the surface impervious to wet and other atmospheric influences, but also lends itself to decoration. For inside work, painting, varnishing, or polishing is resorted to, as much for cleanliness and decoration, as for preservation. For rough outside work, tarring is often adopted, and is a good substitute for painting.

Timber which is buried in the ground—for example, posts for hoardings, rail fencings, etc.—may be preserved either by **tarring** or **charring** the surface of the part that has to be buried.

Charring consists of burning the whole of the outer surface so that it is covered with a layer of charcoal. The charcoal acts as a preservative and protects the interior of the timber from parasitic growths. It should, however, be understood that painting, tarring, or charring will not preserve unseasoned or imperfectly seasoned wood. On the contrary, by closing the pores it may prevent the escape of the sap from the wood, and thus induce a state favourable to decay.

Creosote oil, a coal tar product, which is a powerful antiseptic, is perhaps the most extensively used of all timber preservatives. It is forced into the pores of the wood under pressure after the sap has been removed by previous seasoning. The process is briefly as follows: The seasoned timber is placed in a wrought iron cylinder connected with an air pump. The air pump is worked until the pressure inside the cylinder is from one-sixth to one-eighth that of the outside air. By this means the air is almost entirely withdrawn from the pores of the wood. Creosote oil, at a temperature of about 110° F., is then admitted into the cylinder and is sucked up by the air-exhausted pores of the wood. After the timber has taken up as much oil as it can under these conditions, more creosote is forced into the cylinder at a pressure of from 8 to 10 atmospheres. The timber is thus made to take up more oil, and the process is continued until the pores of the wood are impregnated thoroughly with the preservative. In this way some of the softer woods may be made to absorb 10 lbs. of creosote oil per cubic foot. Creosote is the best known preservative against the attack of destructive organisms. Its more general use as a preservative is prevented by the obnoxious smell which the timber permanently retains.

Other preservatives, which consist of chemicals dissolved in water, have been used to a limited extent for saturating the timber, but have been found either very costly, of poisonous character, or liable to affect the strength or colour of the timber, and have therefore not become adopted generally. Among these chemical methods are:

Kyan's process, which consists of impregnating the timber with a solution in which 1 lb. of corrosive sublimate (bichloride of mercury) is dissolved in 10 gallons of water;

Burnett's process, in which zinc chloride, in the proportion of 1 lb. to 4 gallons of water, is forced by pressure into the pores of the wood;

Boucherie's system, where 1 lb. of copper sulphate dissolved in about 12 gallons of water is used as the preservative, and is forced into the timber.

The **Noden-Bretenneau process** of **Electric seasoning** is a recent invention for seasoning and preserving timber for which much is claimed. It consists of replacing the sap in the pores of the wood by solid matter, which is insoluble and aseptic. The wood is placed in a vat containing the solution, and a sheet of lead connected to the positive pole of a dynamo is placed under it, a second sheet of lead connected to the negative pole is placed in a shallow wooden tray on the top of the material being treated. By electro-capillary attraction the sap is drawn out and rises to the surface, being replaced by the preserving solution. The process takes from five to eight hours, after which a fortnight's seasoning in good weather renders the wood fit for use.

Qualities of Good Timber.—From the foregoing considerations it will be seen that defects and diseases are very prevalent in timber; it must be borne in mind also that the quality and durability depend largely upon the nature of the soil in which the tree grows, the treatment of the tree during growth, the method of conversion, the care taken to effect proper seasoning, and the method of preservation.

For constructional purposes wood should be straight-grained, free from large, loose, or dead knots, and from sapwood. The annual rings should be of even thickness; the closer they are together the stronger is the timber; and as a rule the darker the colour of naturally-coloured woods, the better. The timber should be sweet-smelling, and when planed it should have a firm, bright, silky lustre. A disagreeable smell, a woolly surface, or a chalky appearance, indicates decay. The timber should be a good conductor of sound and, however long the piece, the ticking of a watch, or the scratching of one end, should be distinctly heard by anyone listening at the other end. When used for framing, less danger of shrinkage, and better results in other respects, are obtained if all the pieces are cut so that their width is perpendicular to the annual rings, with the heart edge inwards. When possible a second seasoning after framing before finally finishing off the work should take place.

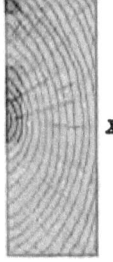 

FIG. 13. FIG. 14.

For carrying purposes, a beam which has the annual rings vertical when in position (Fig. 13) is stronger than when the annual rings are horizontal as shown in Fig. 14, in the proportion of about 8 to 7. Floor boards shrink less and wear longer when cut with the annual rings at right angles to the exposed surface; if they are to be cut with the rings parallel to the surface they should, to prevent shelling, have the heart side down when placed in position.

Varieties of Timber.—Most of the timber used in this country is imported. As previously mentioned, it is classed as "soft-wood" and "hard-wood." For carpenters' and joiners' work the soft-woods are extensively used, both on account of their abundance, their small cost as compared with many hard-woods, and the ease with which they can be worked. Hard-woods are, however, employed where strength is necessary, or where a superior finish is desirable. The soft-woods in most general use are *red deal, white deal, yellow pine*, and *pitch pine*.

Red Deal, Yellow Deal, Red or Yellow Fir, Northern Pine, and **Scotch Fir** are different names given to the wood obtained from the same species of tree (*Pinus sylvestris*). As a very large quantity of this timber is exported from the ports on the Baltic Sea it is often described as *Baltic fir*. It is the product of one of the conifers which flourishes best in exposed mountainous districts in a dry sandy soil. The annual rings are very distinctly marked, and vary in thickness from $\frac{1}{8}$ to $\frac{1}{20}$ of an inch. The wood varies considerably both in texture and appearance, the closer-grained wood being very even and of a yellowish colour, while the more quickly grown timber, with coarse annual rings, yields a wood which is rich in resin and of a reddish colour. This resinous character renders it very durable, especially for outside work. The sap-wood, which varies much in quantity, is of a bluish-colour; while the knots are of a hard transparent nature.

Red Deal is one of the strongest and most durable of soft-woods, the best qualities comparing favourably with many hard-woods. It is one of the most extensively used of soft-woods for outside work, beams for carrying purposes, floor and roof timbers, etc., and weighs when dry from 32 to 35 lbs. per cub. foot.

It grows in abundance in Russia, Prussia, Norway, Sweden, and Scotland. The best qualities are obtained from St. Petersburg, Onega, Dantzic, Archangel, Gefle, and Soderhamm.

White Deal or **Spruce** is the wood of the spruce fir (*Picea excelsa*). In appearance it is of a brownish-white colour, with annual rings fairly distinct. It is inferior in strength to red deal. It is more liable to shrink and warp during seasoning, and the poorer qualities contain hard glassy knots which increase the difficulty of working it. The sapwood is scarcely distinguishable from the heartwood. It is used for scaffold poles and planks for temporary constructional work, and being cheap as compared with most other woods, it is used in many parts of the country for such work in buildings as floor joists, roof timbers, floor boards, etc. It is also in much demand for packing cases, telegraph poles, fencing, etc. It weighs from 30 to 35 lbs. per cub. foot when dry.

It is obtained from Russia, Norway, Sweden, and North America. The best qualities are shipped from Onega, St. Petersburg, Riga, and Christiania.

Yellow Pine (*Pinus strobus*) is an American timber. It is known in America as the white pine. It is very soft, of uniform texture, of a honey-yellow, or straw, colour, and is easily worked. The annual rings are not so distinct as those of the red or white deal, and the sapwood is distinguished easily by its bluish colour. The wood is fairly durable in dry situations, but very liable to dry rot when used in damp unventilated positions. It is used extensively for internal joiners'-work, for pattern-making, and by the cabinet-maker for the cheaper kinds of furniture.

Yellow pine is not so strong as red deal, nor does it warp like white deal. Its weight when dry is from 24 to 28 lbs. per cub. foot. It grows in North America and in Canada. Some of the best yellow pine is shipped at Quebec.

Pitch Pine is a heavy resinous timber which grows in the Southern part of North America. There are several trees the wood of which receives this name, among which are the long-leafed pine (*P. palustris* or *P. Australis*), the short-leaved pine (*P. echinata* or *P. mitis*), the loblolly pine (*P. taeda*) and the Cuban pine (*P. Cubensis*). Although each of these trees differs in some of its characteristics from the others, the wood from them is scarcely distinguishable, and the result is that it is mixed indiscriminately, and classed in this country as pitch pine.

Pitch pine is noted for its straight grain, freedom from large loose knots, and for the large amount of resin it contains. It may be described as of resinous appearance. The annual rings are very distinct and regular, while the sap-wood, being of a bluish colour, is easily distinguishable from the heart-wood.

Pitch pine is chiefly imported into this country in the balk, and being obtainable in large sizes—up to 70 feet in length and 20 inches square in section—it is in much demand for heavy beams for engineering structures, heavy scaffolding, gantries, shoring and strutting, for roof trusses, wooden girders, and the heavy beams of carpenters' work generally. It is also used for the finished woodwork of such public buildings as schools, churches, etc., where the resinous appearance and grain of the wood lend themselves to varnishing instead of painting. Some of the trees yield a wood that has a wavy, or curly, grain. This wood, which has a beautiful appearance, is much sought after for panels and other decorative work.

Pitch pine weighs from 38 to 44 lbs. per cub. foot when dry. The chief ports from which it is shipped are Pensacola, Savannah, and Darien.

Canadian Red Pine is the product of a tree (*Pinus resinosa*) which grows in North America and Canada. In appearance this wood is similar to the lighter kinds of pitch pine, and is often substituted for it. It compares favourably with red deal, the best quality being very clean and free from defects. It is not in great demand in this country.

Oregon Pine, known as the Douglas pine, is the product of one of the largest of the American pines, or, to be more correct, fir trees (*Pseudotsuga Douglasii*). It is found in the Western part of N. America. This wood is of a reddish-white colour, fairly strong, straight grained, of quick growth, and can be obtained of very large size. It is sometimes used as a substitute for red deal or yellow pine in buildings.

Sequoia or **Californian Redwood** is an American timber obtained from a tree (*Sequoia sempervirens*) which often grows to a height of 400 feet, and a diameter varying from 12 to 30 feet. The wood is of a dark brownish-red colour, with coarse annual rings, and is liable to be brittle and lacking in strength. It is obtainable in very large pieces, but is not much used in the construction of buildings.

Larch (*Larix Europaea*) is a native of the European Alps, and also grows abundantly in Russia and Siberia. It is a light, tough, coarse-grained wood (Fig. 3), red or yellowish-white in colour, and has an excessive tendency to shrink and warp. Its coarse grain and warping tendencies prevent its general use for finished work of importance. It can be used with advantage for scaffolding poles, rough boarding, piles, etc.

Hard Woods. Oak.—Many different varieties of oak grow both in this and in other countries. *Quercus robur pedunculata* (the common oak) and *Quercus robur sessiliflora* are the two varieties most common in the British Isles.

British oak is regarded as one of the strongest and most durable of woods. It is generally taken as the standard when comparisons are made with other woods. It is tough, hard, strong and very elastic, the grain is of even texture, and it contains a powerful acid which rapidly corrodes iron fastenings, and leaves a blue stain in the wood. British oak is of a light-brown colour, and when cut in a plane perpendicular to the annual rings shows silvery patches (silver grain).

It is used for all kinds of engineering structures, by ship-builders, wheelwrights, coach-builders and coopers; cabinet-makers consider it one of their most valuable woods, while the builder uses it where great strength and durability are required, as well as in important buildings for decorative work, where advantage is taken of the beautiful marking of the silver grain.

American oak, many varieties of which exist, is not so strong, nor so hard as the British oak. It has a coarse grain, is of a reddish-brown colour, and is much used as a substitute for British oak.

The oak also grows in Russia, Norway, and other European countries, and is imported into this country in the log or balk. Each kind has its peculiar characteristic, distinguishable only by the expert, and as the supply of British oak is not equal to the demand, foreign oak, being more plentiful and consequently cheaper, is often substituted. Oak weighs from 45 to 60 lbs. per cub. foot when dry.

Teak (*Tectona grandis*) is found in Central and Southern India. It is a heavy, strong, straight-grained wood containing an aromatic resinous oil which tends to preserve iron fastenings and also acts as a preservative against worms, ants, etc. It is a very durable wood, of a greenish-brown colour, not so liable to shrink and warp as some woods, and is suitable for use in floors which are subject to heavy traffic, in treads of stairs, wooden sills, and where great strength is required. It is much used by the ship-builder and for railway stock.

Mahogany (*Mahogani swietenia*) is obtained from Central America and from Cuba, and other West Indian islands. Mahogany may be divided into two classes:

(1) **Spanish**, or **Cuba**, **Mahogany** is hard, compact, of even texture, of a reddish-brown colour, with chalk-like lines showing on the surface. It often shows a beautifully marked grain, it is not liable to twist, and is capable of being wrought to a highly

finished surface which polishes readily, and thus shows the grain to great advantage.

This wood is used for the best class of superior joiners'-work, hand-rails for staircases, etc., and is also much in demand by the cabinet-maker.

(2) **Honduras** or **Bay Mahogany**, obtained from Central America, has some of the characteristics of the former variety. It is, however, much softer, more easily worked, and is not so rich in colour, nor does it possess the beautiful grain of Spanish mahogany. It is much used as a cheaper substitute for that wood.

Walnut (*Juglans regia*) grows in Southern Europe, in Asia, America, and also in this country. It is a hard wood, brown in colour, close grained, has a beautiful figure, and when wrought will take a fine polish. The best kind comes from Italy. It is used in superior joiners'-work and also for furniture.

Many other kinds of timber are used to a limited extent for special purposes by the carpenter and joiner. A detailed description of these is beyond the scope of this book. The following, however, call for casual reference :

Ash is a light-coloured wood with annual rings very distinct, and is noted for its elasticity and its toughness. It is used by the coachbuilder, the wheelwright, the cabinet maker, and for agricultural implements.

Beech is of hard, even grain, of a reddish colour, and is used for furniture, wood-turning, and by wood-working toolmakers.

Birch is very hard, liable to excessive shrinkage and warping, it makes good flooring for heavy wear, and is much used by the cabinet-maker and wood-turner.

Chestnut being of a brownish colour resembles oak, excepting that it has no visible medullary rays. It is used for piles, and occasionally as a substitute for oak.

Elm is a coarse-grained wood which is very durable in damp situations.

Maple has a clean, white, satin-like appearance, with a hard close grain which is not liable to splinter. It is a very suitable wood for superior flooring.

Sycamore, which is allied to the maple, has a close compact grain, with a clean appearance, and is used by the wood-turner for domestic requirements, and also in the fittings of butchers' shops by reason of its clean appearance.

TIMBER.

The ash, beech, birch, chestnut, elm, maple and sycamore are all trees that grow in a temperate climate, and are consequently found in this country, most European countries, and in America.

Canary Wood.—There are two or three kinds of wood which are indiscriminately mixed and known as canary wood: American white wood, bass wood, and tulip-tree wood. All kinds grow in America, are of a light yellowish-green colour, not very hard, easily worked, and can be obtained in large size. Canary wood is often used for panels, and also for furniture.

Greenheart is obtained from South America and the West Indies. It is of dark greenish colour, heavy, even-grained, and of oily nature. It is used for heavy engineering work, piles, dock gates, bridge construction, etc.

Jarrah wood is obtained from Western Australia, and has a reddish-brown appearance very much like mahogany. Being a very hard, close-grained wood, it is used for heavy engineering work, for piles, for street paving, and the best qualities for furniture.

Rosewood is obtained from Southern India and Brazil. It is of a rich dark colour, hard and even texture, and possesses a beautiful grain. It is capable of a high polish, and is used by the cabinet-maker and occasionally for superior joiners'-work

Summary.

Trees used for **timber** are classified as:
(a) Hard wood, e.g. oak, ash, beech, birch, mahogany, walnut, etc.; usually have broad leaves; non-resinous.
(b) Soft wood, e.g. red deal, white deal, yellow pine, pitch pine, etc.; markedly resinous; leaves needle shaped.

The wood of timber consists of concentric bands called **annual rings**: each ring represents a year's growth.

The **medullary rays** are radial strips of tissue reaching from the pith to the bark. In some trees they are not easily seen.

Trees should be cut down in the early winter, and should be so **converted** into quartering or planks that the shrinkage during seasoning will be uniform.

Seasoning is the process of drying to which wood is subjected to make it fit for use. The commonest methods are "natural" seasoning and hot-air seasoning.

The principal defects of timber are due to mechanical **shakes**, various diseases set up by **fungi**, and injury by insects and other **animals.**

Timber is **preserved** by painting, charring, and various methods of chemical treatment.

Good timber is free from disease, shakes, dead knots, and sapwood, and should be straight grained. The smell and the power of conducting sound are valuable tests. The suitability for various purposes is affected by the manner of sawing the log.

Most of the timber used in this country is **imported**.

The **soft woods** most commonly used are obtained from the pines and firs, amongst which are red or yellow deal, white deal or spruce, yellow pine, and pitch pine.

The **hard woods** used include oak, teak, mahogany, walnut, ash, beech, birch, elm, sycamore, etc.

Questions on Chapter I.

1. Describe the method of growth of the wood of some common tree. What is the cause of the formation of annual rings?

2. Draw a cross section through the trunk of an oak tree, about 40 years old, naming the various parts shown. Describe the appearance of a radial longitudinal section of the same tree trunk, and explain the cause of the marking known as "silver grain."

3. What is the difference between heartwood and sapwood? How is the difference produced, and how does it affect the value of the wood?

4. At what time of the year is it best to cut down trees, and why? What is meant by "converting," what is its object, and how is it carried out in (a) oak; (b) white deal?

5. Why should timber be seasoned? What effect has seasoning upon its weight and size? What will be the result if unseasoned timber is used in (a) carpenters'; (b) joiners' work?

6. Describe the chief methods of seasoning timber, and compare their advantages.

7. What are the chief defects to be found in timber, and how are they produced?

8. Describe the difference between dry rot and wet rot. State how these diseases originate, and how they may best be combated.

9. Describe the various methods of preserving timber.

10. Enumerate the chief points to be looked for in the selection of timber of good quality.

11. Give a description of the following soft woods: white deal, red or yellow deal, yellow pine, pitch pine. State the distinguishing features of each, the chief sources of supply, and the purposes for which each is most suitable.

12. Describe the principal varieties of hard wood, and state for what purposes each kind is specially suitable.

CHAPTER II.

PLANE GEOMETRY.

A STUDENT can neither prepare nor properly understand the working drawings necessary before the varied work of Carpentry and Joinery can be successfully undertaken, unless he has some preliminary knowledge of Practical Geometry. As it is unlikely that this preliminary knowledge is possessed by all readers of this book, it will be necessary at the outset to deal briefly with some of the more essential principles of the subject.

The student is, however, strongly recommended to make a systematic study of Practical, Plane, and Solid Geometry, as the space here available is insufficient for more than a consideration of a few fundamental principles.

Drawing Instruments.—The student will require a drawing-board, Tee-square, set squares, dividers, compasses, pencils, india-rubber, etc. For ordinary class work the drawing-board (preferably of yellow pine) may conveniently be 23" long and 16" wide. It will then be suitable for use with half an imperial sheet of drawing paper. The Tee-square, which may have either a tapering or parallel blade, should be slightly longer than the board. To allow the set square to slide over the stock of the Tee-square, it is better to have the blade screwed on to the stock rather than let in flush. Two set squares, one with angles of 90, 60, and 30 degrees, and the other with angles of 90, 45, and 45 degrees are required. These may be of hardwood, but are better of celluloid. The accuracy and ease with which drawings can be made depends largely upon the quality of the instruments used. Inexperienced students would do well, therefore, to seek advice before purchasing such instruments as compasses, dividers, etc., as many cheap but almost worthless sets are put upon the market. HB pencils are used for taking notes, but harder pencils are necessary for drawing; H or HH are the most suitable. Cheap pencils of poor quality should not be used. The method of sharpening pencils deserves attention. Figs. 15 and 16 show a pencil sharpened with a chisel point. A point formed in this manner will last longer, when used for drawing, than the rounded pencil-point shown in Fig. 17.

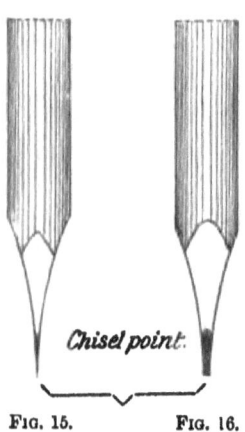
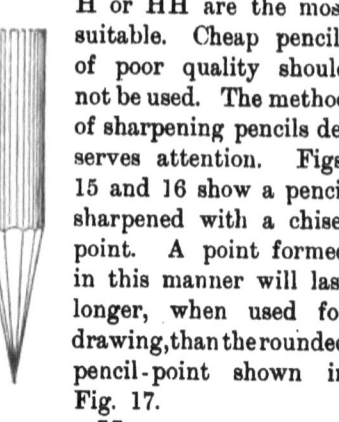

FIG. 15. FIG. 16. FIG. 17.

Measurement of Length.—In this country linear measurements are usually made in yards, feet, inches, and fractions of an inch. The usual sub-divisions of the inch are eighths, tenths, and twelfths. The sub-divisions of the inch generally employed by carpenters and joiners are powers of two, giving ½″, ¼″, ⅛″, etc. In geometry, however, the subdivisions are often given in decimals, and the inch is then divided into tenths.

In many continental countries the **metric system** is adopted. The unit of measurement in the metric system is the **metre**, equal to 39·37 English inches. This is divided into 10 **decimetres**; the decimetre is divided into 10 **centimetres**; and the centimetre is divided into 10 **millimetres**.

Measurement of Angles.—DEFINITION. *An angle is the inclination of two lines which meet at a point in a plane.* An angle may, in familiar language, be said to be "the size of the corner." It ought to be noticed that an angle does not in any sense depend on the length of the lines "containing" it. If two lines AB and CB meet at the point B (Fig. 18) the angle contained by AB and CB is referred to as "the angle ABC." If two straight lines be drawn to cross each other so that the four resulting angles are equal (Fig. 19), the lines are said to be **perpendicular**[1]

---

[1] In ordinary work it will generally be found convenient to draw perpendicular lines with the aid of Tee and set squares.

PLANE GEOMETRY. 23

to each other and the angles are **right angles**. A right angle is divided into 90 equal parts which are called **degrees** (written °).

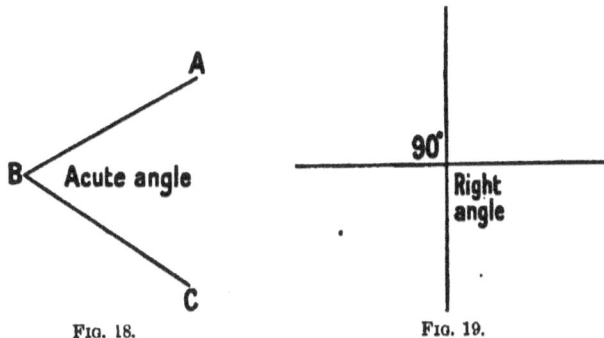

Fig. 18.   Fig. 19.

It follows that the sum of all angles which meet at a point in a plane (*i.e.* in a flat surface) is $4 \times 90° = 360°$.

Several methods are adopted for measuring angles, but possibly the easiest and the most common is by means of the **protractor**.

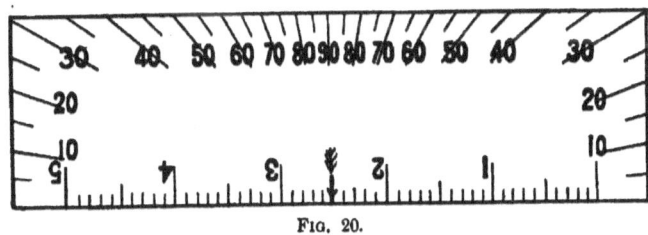

Fig. 20.

Fig. 20 shows a rectangular protractor with the main divisions indicated thereon.

PRELIMINARY DEFINITIONS.

Parallel lines are everywhere the same distance apart, and therefore never meet however far they are produced.

An **acute angle** is one which is smaller than a right angle (Fig. 18).

An **obtuse angle** is one that is greater than a right angle (Fig. 21).

A **circle** is a plane figure contained by one curved line which is called the **circumference**; the line is such

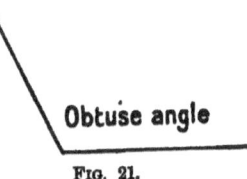

Fig. 21.

that all points in it are equidistant from a point within the circle called the **centre** (Fig. 22).

The **radius** of a circle is a straight line drawn from the centre to the circumference. It follows from the definition

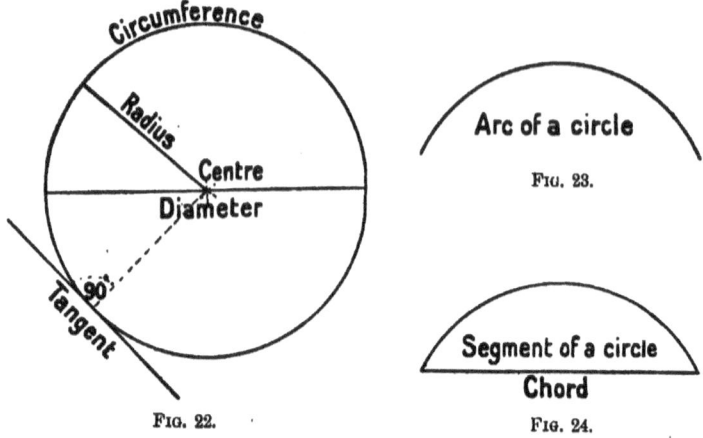

Fig. 22.

Fig. 23.

Fig. 24.

of the circle that all radii of the same circle are equal in length.

A **diameter** of a circle is a straight line passing through the centre and terminated at both ends by the circumference: it is equal in length to twice the radius.

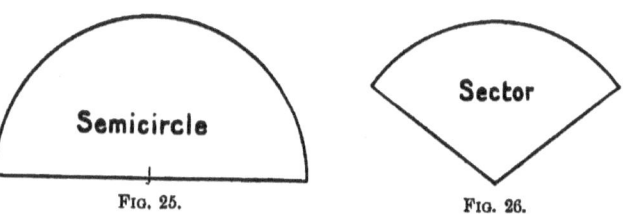

Fig. 25.

Fig. 26.

An **arc** of a circle is part of the circumference of a circle (Fig. 23).

A **chord** is a straight line joining any two points in the circumference of a circle (Fig. 24).

A **segment** (Fig. 24) is a portion of a circle contained by any arc and the chord between the extremities of the arc. If the chord is a diameter the arc is half the circumference, and the segment is called a **semicircle** (Fig. 25).

PRELIMINARY DEFINITIONS. 25

A **sector** is a portion of a circle contained by any two radii and the arc between their outer ends (Fig. 26).

A **tangent** is a straight line touching, but not cutting, the circumference of a circle (Fig. 22). It is always at right angles to the radius drawn to the point of contact.

Concentric circles are circles having the same centre (Fig. 27). Their circumferences are therefore parallel to each other. The **periphery** of a circle is the length of the circumference.

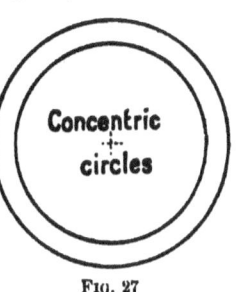

FIG. 27

SIMPLE EXERCISES INVOLVING THE USE OF STRAIGHT LINE, ANGLES, AND CIRCLES.

EXAMPLE 1.—*To bisect a given straight line, i.e. to divide it into two equal parts.*

Let AB (Fig. 28) be the given straight line. Take a pair of compasses and with centre A (*i.e.* placing the steel point on the point A) and radius greater than one half AB (*i.e.* separating the legs of the compasses to any distance greater than one half of AB) draw the arc CD. With the same radius (that is, keeping the compasses open to the same extent) and with centre B, draw the arc EF intersecting the arc CD at the points G and H. Join GH (*i.e.* draw a straight line from G to H). The point K where the line GH cuts AB bisects AB (*i.e.* divides it into two equal parts). The line GH is perpendicular to the line AB, that is at right angles to it.

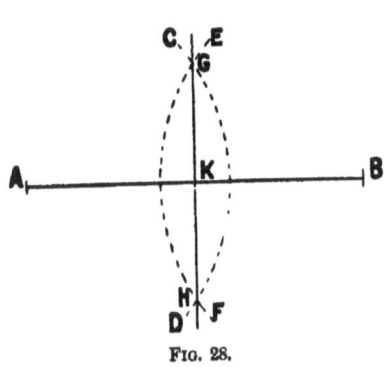

FIG. 28.

EXAMPLE 2.—*To divide a given straight line into any number of equal parts* (say 5).

Take any straight line AB (Fig. 29); from A draw a second straight line AC, of indefinite length, making an acute angle with *AB*. Along *AC* mark off 5 equal parts and number them. Join the point 5 to the point *B*, and through the points 1, 2, 3, 4, —by means of the set squares—draw lines parallel to 5*B*. These parallel lines divide *AB* into the required number (5) of equal parts. The divisions of the inclined line should be such that the parallel lines are nearly at right angles to the given line.

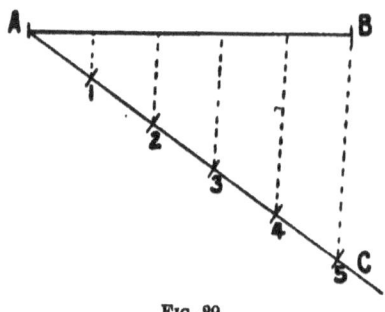

Fig. 29.

EXAMPLE 3.—*To draw a circle which shall pass through three given points not in the same straight line.*

Let *A*, *B* and *C* (Fig. 30) be the given points. Join *AB* and *BC*. Bisect *AB* and *BC* as in Example 1 by straight lines

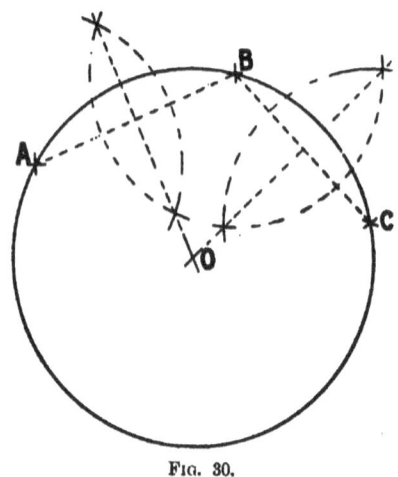

Fig. 30.

at right angles to *AB* and *BC* respectively. The point of intersection, *O*, of the bisectors is the centre of the required circle.

EXAMPLE 4.—*To bisect a given angle.*

Let *ABC* (Fig. 31) be the given angle. With *B* as centre and any radius describe an arc cutting *BA* and *BC* in the points

SIMPLE EXERCISES.

D and E respectively. With centres D and E and any—the same—radius, describe arcs intersecting at G. The straight line BG bisects the angle ABC, the angle ABG being equal to the angle CBG.

EXAMPLE 5.—*To draw a perpendicular to a given straight line, from a given point in the line.*

Let AB (Fig. 32) be the given line and C the given point. With centre C and any radius describe arcs intersecting AB in D and E. With D and E respectively as centres and any radius greater than CD draw arcs intersecting at F. The straight line FC is perpendicular to AB.

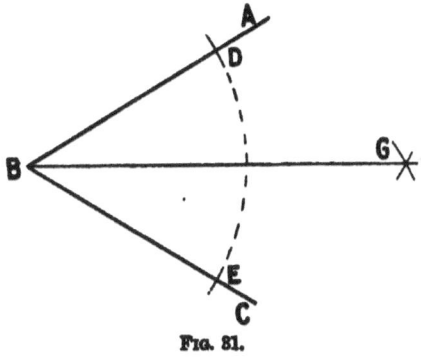

Fig. 31.

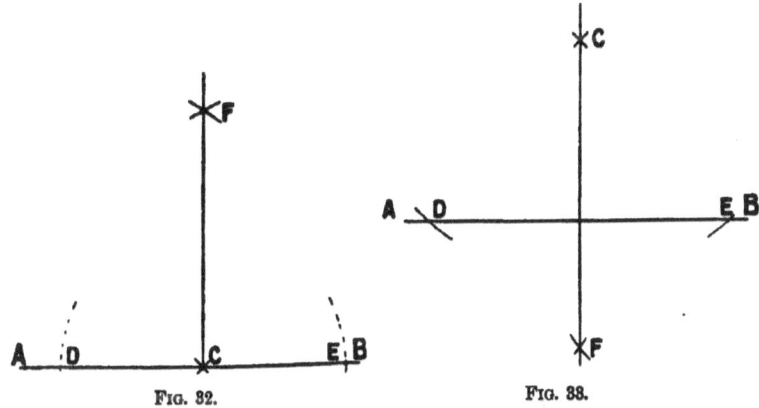

Fig. 32.   Fig. 33.

EXAMPLE 6.—*To draw a perpendicular to a given straight line, from a given point outside the line.*

Let AB (Fig. 33) be the given straight line and C the given point. With centre C and any radius greater than the perpendicular distance from C to AB, draw the arcs intersecting AB at D and E. With D and E as centres, and with any—the same—radius draw arcs intersecting at F. The straight line CF is perpendicular to AB.

TRIANGLES.

A triangle is a plane figure having three sides. Triangles are named according to their shape. The sum of the angles in any triangle is **always** equal to two right angles (180°). A triangle may therefore have three acute angles (Fig. 34), but it can only

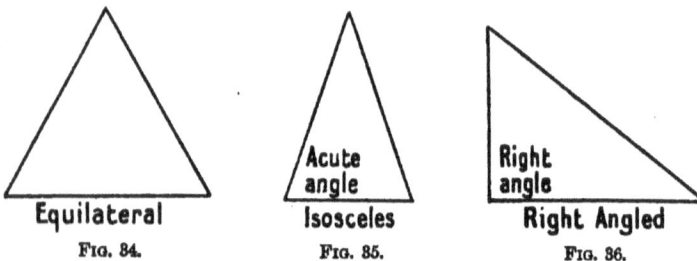

Fig. 84.   Fig. 85.   Fig. 86.

contain one right angle, or one obtuse angle (as an obtuse angle is greater than a right angle). An **equilateral** triangle is one that has all its sides of equal length, and all its angles equal.

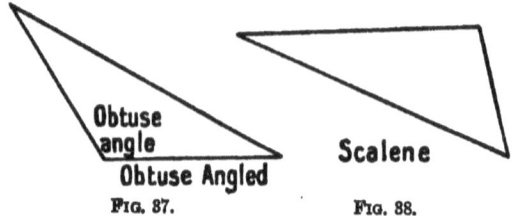

Fig. 87.   Fig. 88.

An **isosceles** triangle is one that has two sides of equal length. A **scalene** triangle has three sides of unequal length.

Figs. 34 to 38 show these different kinds of triangles with the name of each appended.

EXAMPLE 1.—*To construct an equilateral triangle of given side.*

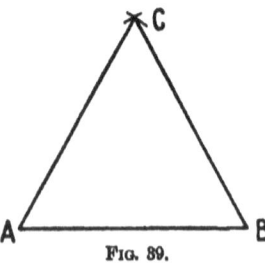

Fig. 89.

Let AB (Fig. 39) be the given side. With A as centre and AB as radius draw an arc of a circle. With B as centre and the same radius draw a second arc intersecting the first at C. Join AC and BC. ABC is the required triangle. It will be found by measurement that each angle of an equilateral triangle equals 60°.

TRIANGLES.

EXAMPLE 2.—*To construct a triangle whose sides are in the proportion of* 3, 4, 5.

Let the line AB (Fig. 40) have a length of $3+4+5=12$ units. Divide AB in the required proportions as shown. With C as centre and radius equal to CA (3 units) draw the arc AE.

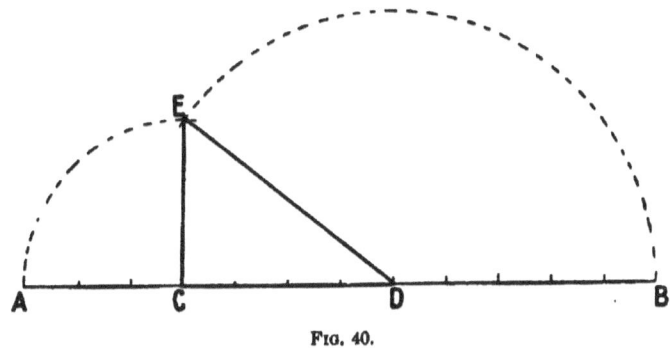

FIG. 40.

With D as centre and DB (5 units) as radius, draw BE intersecting AE at E. Join CE and DE. CDE is the required triangle.

The solution of many examples in the construction of triangles is simplified by a knowledge of the fact that *all the*

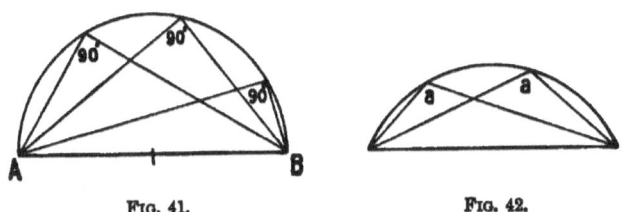

FIG. 41.   FIG. 42.

angles opposite the chord of the same segment of a circle are of equal magnitude. For example, in a semicircle (Fig. 41) the angle contained by any two lines drawn from A and B to any point in the arc is a right angle. When the segment is smaller than a semicircle (Fig. 42), all the angles contained by any two lines drawn from the extremities of the chord to any point in the arc are *obtuse* angles (a, a), and are of equal magnitude. If the segment is greater than a semicircle, the apex-angle (the one opposite the chord) is an *acute* angle (Fig. 43, a, a, a), all the angles of the same segment being equal.

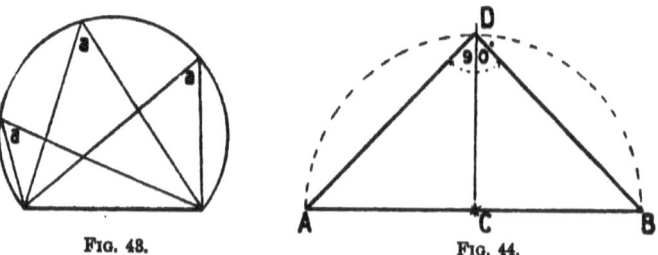

FIG. 43.   FIG. 44.

EXAMPLE 3.—*To construct a right-angled isosceles triangle having a given length of hypotenuse (the side opposite the right angle).*

Let AB (Fig. 44) be the given hypotenuse. On the line AB construct a semicircle. Then the angle contained by any two lines drawn from A and B to a point in this semicircle will be a right angle. As an isosceles triangle is in this case required, it will be necessary to erect a perpendicular line passing through the centre C of the semicircle and intersecting the arc at D. Join DA and DB. ADB is the required triangle, for AD is equal to BD and the angle ADB is in a semicircle and therefore equals 90 degrees.

EXAMPLE 4.—*On a given base to construct an isosceles triangle having a vertical angle of* 70°.

Let AB (Fig 45) be the given base. Draw CD perpendicular to and bisecting AB. From A draw a line making with AB an angle of 90° minus the apex angle—*i.e.* 90° − 70° = 20°. The intersection of this line with CD gives the centre O. With OA as radius complete the segment of the circle. Join AD and BD. ABD is the required triangle.

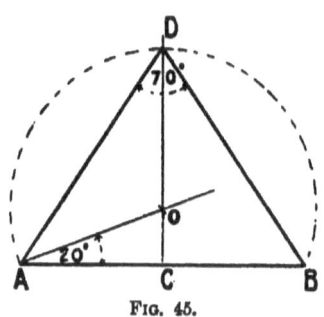

FIG. 45.

EXAMPLE 5.—*To construct a triangle containing an angle of* 110° *and having its two longer sides in the proportion of* 4 *and* 3.

First, determine the segment of a circle which will contain an angle of 110°. Let AB (Fig. 46) be the longest side of the triangle. From A draw AO (below AB) making an angle with AB of $110° - 90° = 20°$ (the difference between the required angle and a right angle). The centre O of the segment is the point where this line intersects the bisector CD of the line AB. Then any two lines drawn from A and B to any point in the arc will contain the required angle $110°$. Next divide AB into 4 equal parts.

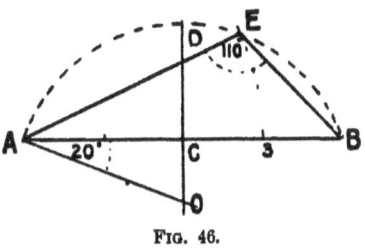

Fig. 46.

With A as centre and $A3$ as radius draw the intersecting arc $3E$. Join AE and BE. ABE is the required triangle, since AE is to AB as 3 is to 4, and the angle AEB equals $110°$.

EXAMPLE 6.—*At a given point in a given straight line, to draw an angle equal to a given angle.*

Let MON (Fig. 47) be the given angle, and A the given point on the line AB. On AB with A as centre make AG equal

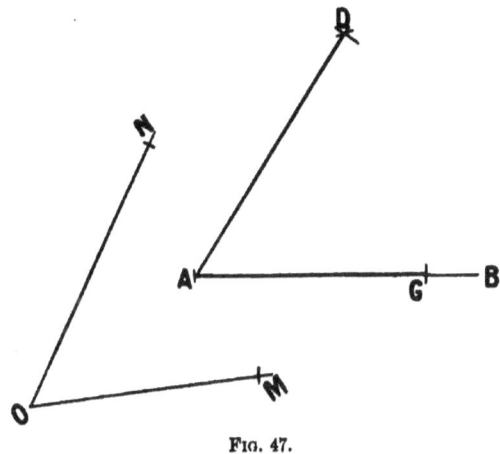

Fig. 47.

to OM. With A as centre and ON as radius draw an arc D. With G as centre and radius MN draw the arc intersecting at D. Join AD. Then the angle GAD is equal to MON and is therefore the required angle.

32 A MANUAL OF CARPENTRY AND JOINERY.

EXAMPLE 7.—*Given an arc of a circle, the centre of which is inaccessible, to continue the curve.*

Take any three points A, B, C, in the given arc and join AB, BC. From any point A' draw the chord $A'B'$ equal to AB and

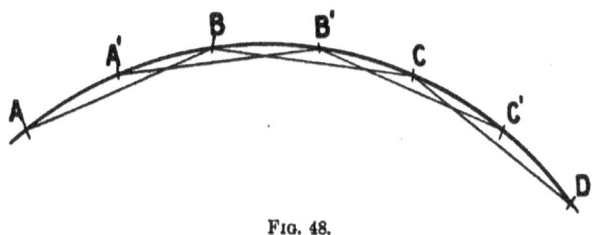

FIG. 48.

from B' draw $B'C'$ such that the angle $A'B'C'$ is equal to the angle ABC and $B'C'$ equal to BC. C' is a further point in the curve. Obtain other points in the same manner and join them by an even curve.

QUADRILATERAL FIGURES.

A **quadrilateral figure** is one which is contained by four straight lines. The straight lines joining opposite angles of a quadrilateral figure are called **diagonals**. Figs. 49 to 54 show different quadrilateral figures with their names appended.

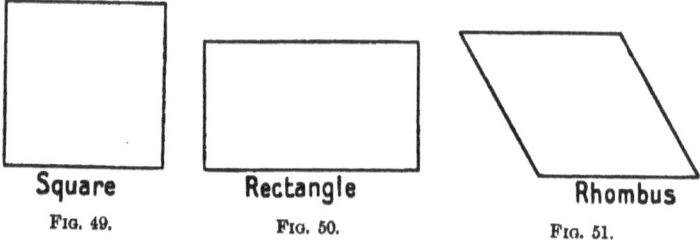

FIG. 49.   FIG. 50.   FIG. 51.

The sum of the angles of any quadrilateral figure is always equal to four right angles.

A **parallelogram** is a quadrilateral figure which has two pairs of parallel sides.

A **rectangular** figure is one having all its angles right angles. The two diagonals of any rectangular figure are always equal in length.

QUADRILATERAL FIGURES.

A **square** (Fig. 49) has all its sides of equal length and all its angles equal (right angles).

A **rectangle** or **oblong** (Fig. 50) has the opposite sides of equal length, and contains four right angles.

A **rhombus** (Fig. 51) has all the sides of equal length, but the angles are not right angles. It may be described familiarly as a square pushed out of shape.

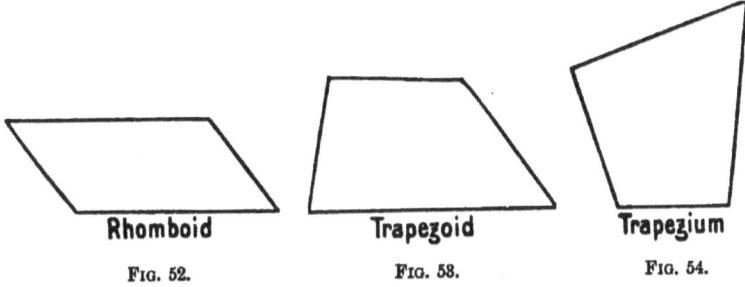

Fig. 52. Fig. 53. Fig. 54.

A **rhomboid** (Fig. 52) has the opposite sides of equal length but its angles are not right angles.

A **trapezoid** (Fig. 53) has two sides parallel but of different lengths.

A **trapezium** (Fig. 54) has none of its sides parallel.

In all quadrilateral figures except the square and the rectangle it is necessary to know either the lengths of the diagonals, or the magnitudes of the angles, in addition to the lengths of the sides, before the figure can be constructed.

POLYGONS.

A **polygon** is the name given to any plane figure which is bounded by straight lines. Usually the name is not applied to triangles and quadrilateral figures, but only to figures bounded by more than four straight lines.

A **regular polygon** has all its sides of equal length and its angles are of equal magnitude.

If the sides are not equal the polygon is said to be **irregular**.

Polygons are named according to the number of their sides, as pentagon (5 sides), hexagon (6 sides), heptagon (7 sides), octagon (8 sides), nonagon (9 sides), decagon (10 sides), undecagon (11 sides), duo-decagon (12 sides), etc.

EXAMPLE 1.—*To construct a regular hexagon of given side.*

Let AB (Fig. 55) be the length of the given side. On AB construct an equilateral triangle AOB. With centre O and radius OA draw a circle passing through A and B. With the same radius and starting from A, mark intersecting arcs on the circumference of this circle. It will be found that six equal lengths are thus obtained. By joining these points by straight lines, the required hexagon is completed. The angle between any two sides of a regular hexagon measures 120°. This figure can also be drawn easily with the aid of the 60° set square.

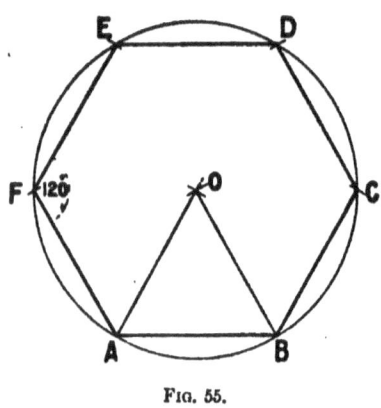

Fig. 55.

EXAMPLE 2.—*To construct a regular pentagon of given side.*

(*First method.*) Let AB (Fig. 56) be the length of the required side. Produce AB to C. With A as centre and AB as radius draw a semicircle. Divide this semicircle (by trial) into 5 equal parts. Through the point 2 (always point 2, whatever the number of sides of the polygon) draw the straight line $2A$. Bisect $2A$ and AB by lines at right angles to them. The point O where these bisecting lines meet is the centre of the circle which will contain the required figure. Starting from A with radius AB, mark off lengths on the circumference of the circle. Join the points $B, C, D, 2, A$. Then $ABCD2$ is the required pentagon.

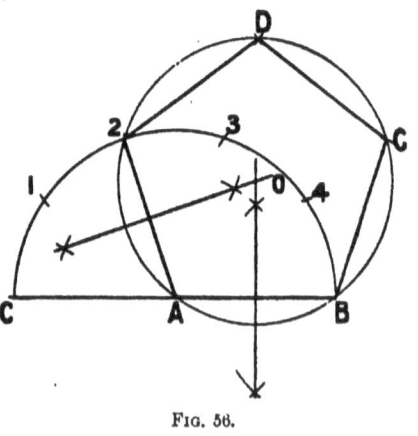

Fig. 56.

POLYGONS.

If any other regular polygon is required, the same construction is applicable; care must be taken to divide the semicircle into as many equal parts as the number of sides of the required polygon, and to work from the second division.

(*Second method.*) Let AB (Fig. 57) be the given side. On AB construct the square $ABCD$ and also the equilateral triangle $AB6$. Draw the diagonals of the square. These intersect at 4, the centre of a circle which, if drawn with $4A$ as radius, will pass through the angles of the **square** $ABCD$. The point 6 is the centre of a circle which with $6A$ as radius will contain a **six**-sided figure (Ex. 1). By bisecting the distance between 6 and 4 a point 5 is obtained, which is the centre of the circle containing the required **pentagon**. With centre 5 and radius $5A$ draw the circle passing through A and B. Take AB as radius, and with A as starting point "stride" round the circumference of the circle. By joining the points B, E, F, G, A, the required pentagon is obtained. This method is applicable to the construction of any polygon. If a heptagon is required, a distance 6, 7 equal to 5, 6 is measured above the point 6 as shown. The point 7 is the centre of a circle which with radius $7A$ will contain a regular **heptagon**, as shown in dotted lines in Fig. 57.

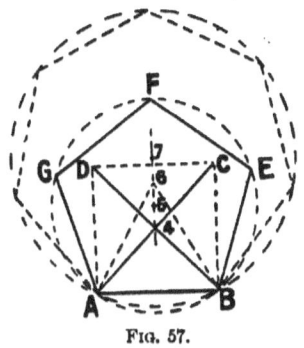

Fig. 57.

An **octagon** can be easily drawn with the aid of the 45° set square as shown in Fig. 58.

Any regular polygon can be drawn by directly measuring, with the protractor, the angles between the sides. The angle required in each case is obtained by reasoning as follows: Every regular polygon consists of a number of equal isosceles triangles. The sum of the angles of a triangle is equal to 180°. If a heptagon (Fig. 59) is required, the apex angles of 7 equal isosceles

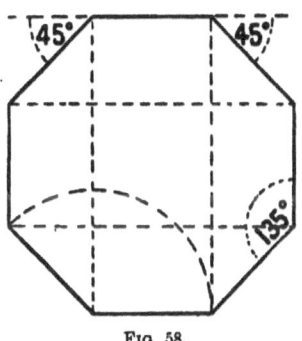

Fig. 58.

triangles meet at the centre of the figure. As the sum of the angles between all the lines drawn through a point equals 360°, the apex-angle of each of these triangles equals $\frac{360}{7} = 51\frac{3}{7}°$. Each of the other two angles of each triangle is therefore equal to $\frac{180° - 51\frac{3}{7}°}{2} = 64\frac{2}{7}°$. As two of these are at the angle between any two sides of a heptagon, then $64\frac{2}{7}° \times 2 = 128\frac{4}{7}°$ is the required angle.

Similarly the apex angle for a pentagon is $\frac{360}{5} = 72°$. The base angle of each isosceles triangle is $\frac{180° - 72°}{2} = 54°$, and therefore the angle between any two sides of the pentagon is $54° \times 2 = 108°$.

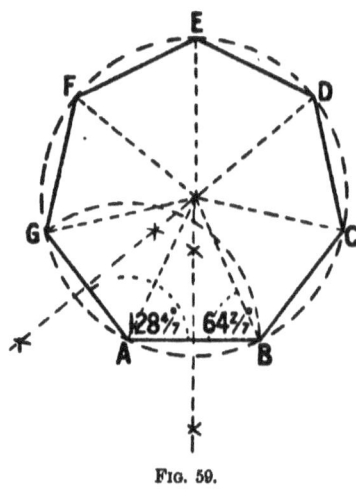

FIG. 59.

For an octagon the apex angle of each of the eight triangles composing it is $\frac{360}{8} = 45°$. The base angle of each of these triangles is $\frac{180° - 45°}{2} = 67\frac{1}{2}°$: therefore the angle between any two sides is $67\frac{1}{2}° \times 2 = 135°$.

For the construction of irregular polygons, the lengths of the sides, and either the lengths of the diagonals or the magnitude of the various angles are required.

INSCRIBED AND CIRCUMSCRIBED FIGURES.

An **inscribed figure** is one that is contained by a larger figure, and—if an angular one—has its sides terminated by the sides or the circumference of the larger or circumscribing figure. If the inscribed figure is a circle, the sides of the circumscribing figure are tangents to the circle. Thus, a circle which is contained by a triangle and touches each side of the triangle is named the inscribed circle, while a circle drawn to pass through the three angular points of the triangle is the circumscribing circle of the triangle.

INSCRIBED AND CIRCUMSCRIBED FIGURES.

EXAMPLE 1.—*In a given triangle to draw the inscribed circle* (i.e. *to draw a circle which shall touch each side of the triangle*).

Let *ABC* (Fig. 60) be the given triangle. Bisect any two of the angles as *ABC* and *BAC*. The point *O* where these bisecting lines intersect is the centre of the required circle. With *O* as centre, and radius equal to the perpendicular distance to any side of the triangle, draw the circle. This is the inscribed circle required.

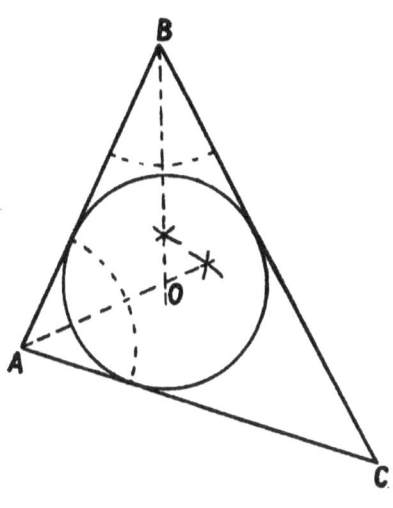

FIG. 60.

EXAMPLE 2.—*About a given triangle to draw the circumscribing circle.*

Let *ABC* (Fig. 61) be the given triangle. Bisect any two sides *AB* and *AC* by lines at right angles to them.

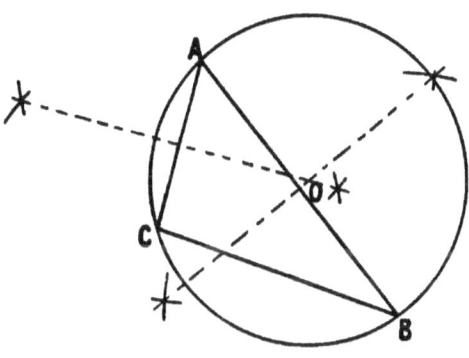

FIG. 61.

The point *O* where these two intersectors meet is the required centre, and is equidistant from the points *A*, *B* and *C*. With *O* as centre, and *OA* as radius, draw the required circle.

38   A MANUAL OF CARPENTRY AND JOINERY.

EXAMPLE 3.—*In a given square to place four equal circles each touching two sides of the square and two other circles.*

Let *ABCD* (Fig. 62) be the given square. Bisect the sides of the square in the points *E, F, G, H* and join *EG* and *FH*.

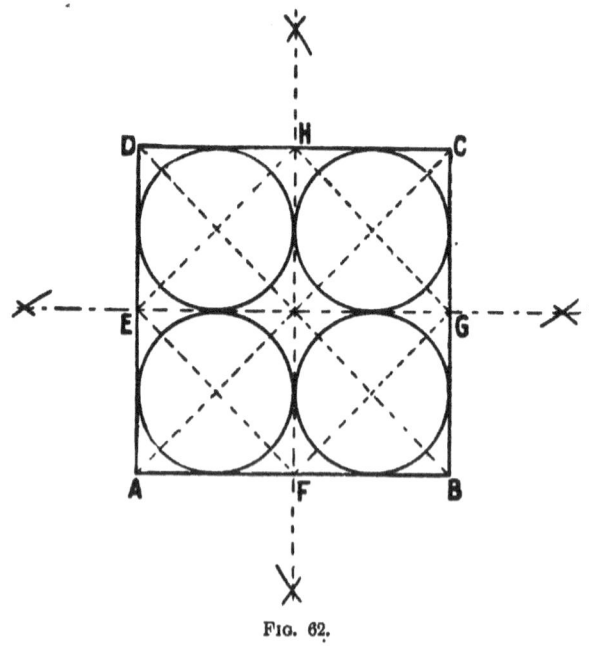

FIG. 62.

Draw the diagonals of each of these smaller squares. The intersections of the diagonals give the centres of the required circles as shown in the figure.

EXAMPLE 4.—*In a given square to place four equal circles, each touching one side of the square and two circles.*

Let *ABCD* (Fig. 63) be the given square. Draw the diagonals *AC* and *BD* intersecting in *O*. In each of the four triangles thus obtained place the inscribed circle as in Example 1.

EXAMPLE 5.—*In a regular hexagon to place six equal circles, each touching two sides of the hexagon and two other circles.*

Let *ABCDEF* (Fig. 64) be the given hexagon. Bisect the sides of the figure in the points 1, 2, 3, 4, 5, 6. Join 1 to 4, 2

INSCRIBED AND CIRCUMSCRIBED FIGURES. 39

to 5, 3 to 6. In the quadrilateral figure 1*A*2*O*, bisect any two angles as shown. The intersection *M* of these bisecting lines

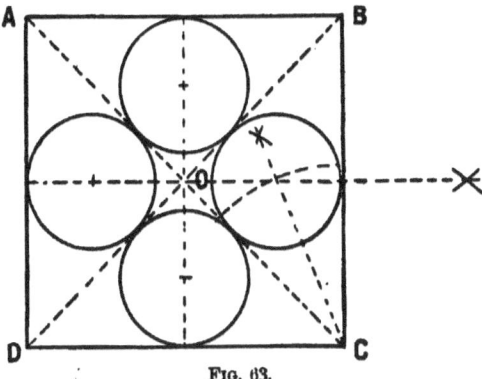

Fig. 63.

gives the centre of one of the required circles. In each of the six quadrilateral figures place a similar circle.

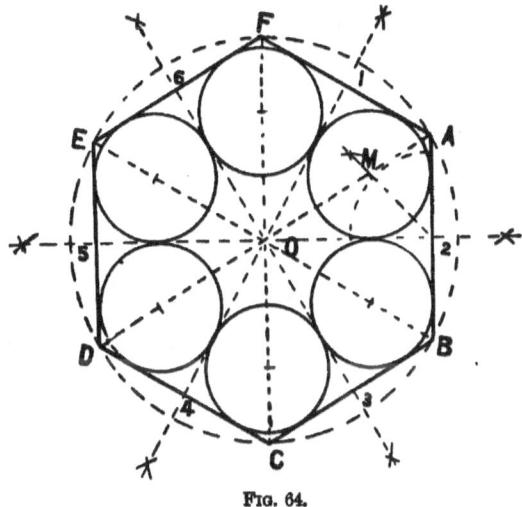

Fig. 64.

EXAMPLE 6.—*In a given triangle to draw the inscribed square.*
Let *ABC* (Fig. 65) be the given triangle. From *C* draw *CD* perpendicular to *AB*. Draw *CE* parallel to *AB* and equal to

CD. Join *AE*, intersecting *BC* at *F*. Draw *FG* parallel to *AB*, and *GH* and *FJ* perpendicular to *AB*. *FGHJ* is the required square.

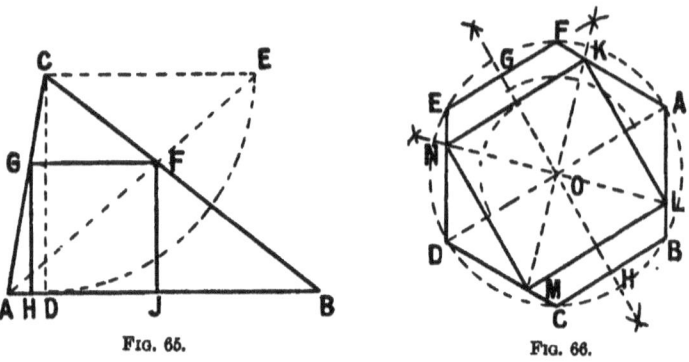

Fig. 65.   Fig. 66.

EXAMPLE 7.—*In a regular hexagon to draw the inscribed square.*

Let *ABCDEF* (Fig. 66) be the given hexagon. Join *AD* and draw *GH* perpendicular to and bisecting *AD*. Through *O* draw straight lines bisecting the right angles thus obtained. The points where these lines intersect the sides of the hexagon as *K, L, M, N* are the angular points of the square.

EXAMPLE 8.—*In a given circle to place two given smaller unequal circles which touch each other and the given circle.*

Let *A* (Fig. 67) be the centre and *AB* the radius of the given circle. Draw the diameter *BC*. On *BC* make *BD* equal to the radius of one of the small circles. With *D* as centre, and *DB* as radius, draw this circle. On *CB* make *CE* equal to the radius of the second small circle. From centre *A* with radius

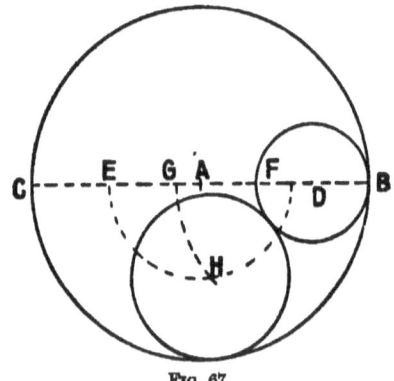

Fig. 67.

AE draw an arc. With the same radius measure off from *F* on *BC* the distance *FG*. With *D* as centre, and *DG* as radius, draw the intersecting arc *GH*. Then *H* is the required centre of the second circle.

PROPORTION.

Definitions.—If one quantity bears to a second quantity the relation which a third bears to a fourth, the four quantities are said to be in proportion; thus 2 bears to 3 the same relation which 4 does to 6; and 2, 3, 4, and 6 are said to be in proportion, a statement which is expressed thus 2 : 3 :: 4 : 6. The same fact may be expressed as 2 : 4 :: 3 : 6 and as 6 : 4 :: 3 : 2 etc. In the proportion 2 : 3 :: 4 : 6, 6 is said to be the fourth proportional of 2, 3, and 4. In general terms, if $A : B :: B : C$, then B is said to be the mean proportional of A and C, and C is the third proportional of A and B. If $A : B :: C : D$ then $A \times D = B \times C$. Similarly if $A : B :: B : C$ then $A \times C = B \times B$. The product of the first and fourth quantities of a proportional is always equal to the product of the second and third.

FIG. 68

EXAMPLE 1.—*To determine the fourth proportional to three given straight lines.*

This problem depends upon the arrangement of the proportion. Let A, B, and C be the given lines and let the proportion be $A : B :: C : X$, X being the straight line required. Draw two straight lines (Fig. 68) containing an acute angle, as at O. On ON measure OA' equal to A, and OC' equal to C, and on OM measure OB' equal to B. Join $A'B'$ and through C' draw $C'X$ parallel to $A'B'$. Then OX is the fourth proportional required.

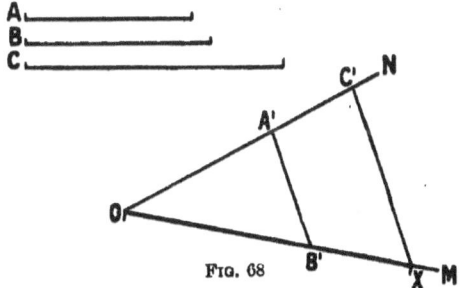

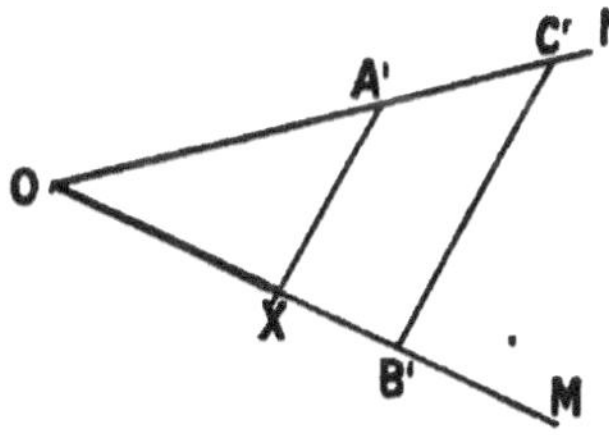

FIG. 69.

If $C : B :: A : X$ then the result will be quite different. This is shown in Fig. 69. Here OX represents the fourth proportional to C, B, and A.

EXAMPLE 2.—*To determine a third proportional to two given straight lines.*

Let A and B be the given lines, and let the proportion be $A : B :: B : X$.

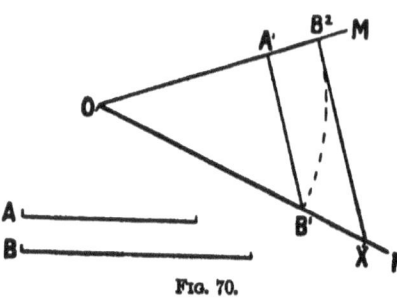

Fig. 70.

Draw the two lines OM and ON meeting at an acute angle. On OM measure OA' equal to A, and OB^2 equal to B. On ON measure OB' also equal to B. Join $A'B'$ and through B^2 draw B^2X parallel to $A'B'$. Then OX is the required third proportional.

EXAMPLE 3.—*To find a mean proportional to two given straight lines.*

Let A and B (Fig. 71) be the given lines. Draw a straight line and measure upon it OA' equal to A, and OB' equal to B. Bisect $A'B'$ at C. With C as centre, and CA' as radius, construct a semicircle. From O erect a perpendicular to $A'B'$ cutting the semicircle at X. Then OX is the mean proportional required.

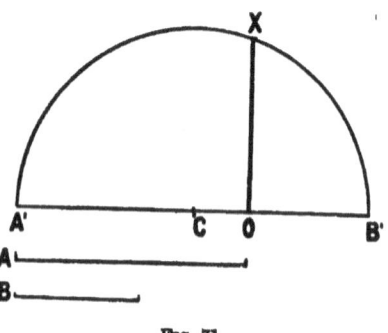

Fig. 71.

SCALES.

As very few details in working drawings can be made of full size, some definite scale must be adopted to show the necessary proportions. The scale used varies according to the nature of the drawing, as well as to the country in which the work is done. Thus, the drawings required to illustrate a complete building are made to a small scale, usually one-eighth of an inch to the foot in this country; while the constructional details require to be shown to a much larger scale. Graduated rules of boxwood,

SCALES.

or paper, may be obtained, on which are marked scales of $\frac{1}{8}$, $\frac{1}{4}$, $\frac{3}{8}$, $\frac{1}{2}$, $\frac{3}{4}$, 1, 1$\frac{1}{2}$, 3, etc. inches to the foot. Although these scales are sufficient for ordinary use, it is occasionally necessary to use other scales, and the student must know how to construct these for himself.

EXAMPLE 1.—*To construct a scale of one-seventh the full size, to read to feet and inches.*

Draw a straight line AC (Fig. 72) and mark off AB one inch long. From A draw AE at any angle (preferably about 30°).

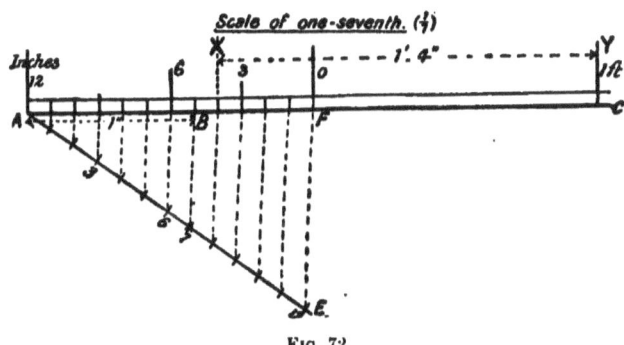

FIG. 72.

On AE mark off any 12 equal divisions, and number them. Join the *seventh* point to B, and through each of the other points on AE draw lines parallel to $B7$, and cutting AC. The length AB (1″) is thus divided into seven equal parts, each measuring one-seventh of an inch. As the scale is one-seventh full size, each division represents one inch, and the distance AF (twelve divisions) represents one foot. Mark the point F zero, and number the scale as shown. Then XY, *e.g.* represents a distance of 1′ 4″.

EXAMPLE 2.—*To construct a scale of one-thirtieth full size, so that one inch represents two feet six inches.*

On AC (Fig. 73) make AB equal to one inch, and on AE mark off ten equal parts. Join the *tenth* point to B, and through the other points on AE draw lines parallel to $B10$, and cutting AB as shown. Then each of the smaller divisions on AB is one-tenth of an inch long, and therefore represents three inches. Mark the fourth division from A zero, and number as shown in Fig. 73. *AF* represents one foot, and *AB* two feet six inches.

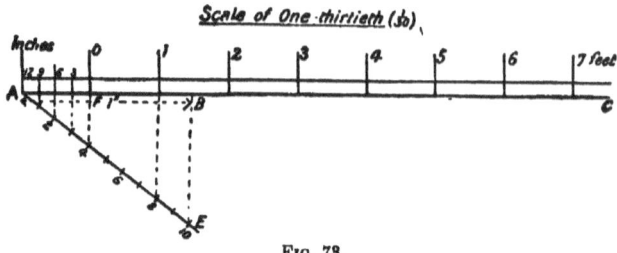

Fig. 73.

EXAMPLE 3.—*To convert an English scale of 3 inches to the foot into a scale upon the Metric system.*

A scale of 3 inches to the foot is one-fourth full size. By dividing the length of a decimetre into four equal parts it will be found that each of the divisions is one-fourth of a decimetre, or a decimetre to a scale of one-fourth full size. By again dividing each of these divisions into ten equal parts a scale is obtained of metric measurements to one-fourth full size, *i.e.* in the proportion of 3 inches to the foot.

EXAMPLE 4.—*A French working drawing represents one metre by a length of 40 millimetres. Convert this into an English scale showing feet and inches.*

40 millimetres represent one metre. As there are 1000 millimetres in a metre the representative fraction will be

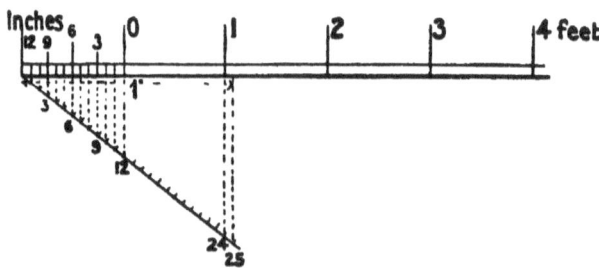

Fig. 74.

$\frac{40}{1000} = \frac{1}{25}$. The scale is therefore $\frac{1}{25}$ full size. By drawing a scale in which one inch represents 25 inches (Fig. 74) the required scale is obtained.

Diagonal Scales.—These are used when very minute divisions are required. When constructing a scale to represent $\frac{1}{100}$

SCALES.   45

part of an inch, it would be both difficult and unsatisfactory to sub-divide a length of one inch into 100 equal parts in the manner

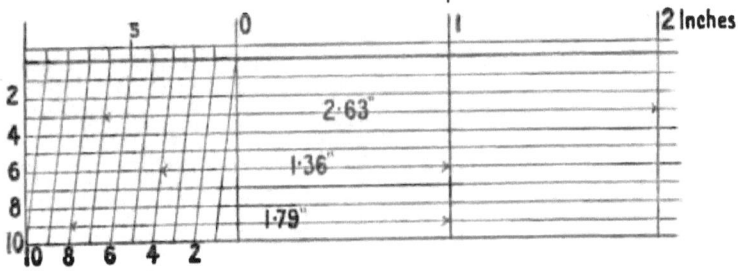

Fig. 75.

already shown. Fig. 75 shows how such a diagonal scale is constructed. Ten horizontal lines, parallel to the given lines, are first drawn, at any—the same—distance apart, and vertical lines erected which divide these into one inch divisions. The length of one inch is then divided into 10 equal parts. By drawing the slanting lines as shown in Fig. 75, a scale is obtained, from which any dimension to the second decimal place of an inch can be measured.

EXAMPLE 5.—*To construct a scale of one-ninth, to read feet, inches, and eighths of an inch.*

The scale of one-ninth is first drawn with the division of inches at the left-hand side. Eight additional horizontal lines

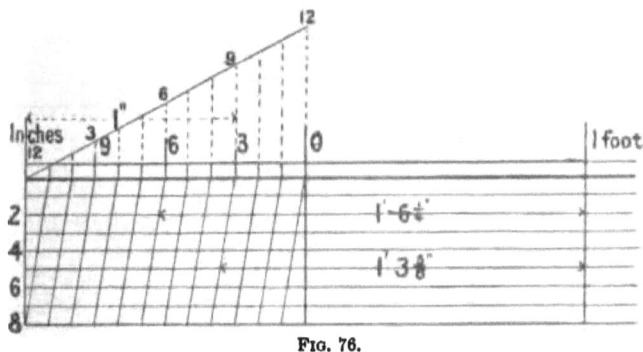

Fig. 76.

will be required in this example, as the inches have to be divided into eighths. By drawing the slanting lines as shown in Fig. 76 and numbering, the scale is completed.

46   A MANUAL OF CARPENTRY AND JOINERY.

Enlarging and Diminishing Figures.—Figs. 77 to 80 are examples which show how similar figures in definite proportion to each other may be drawn easily. Fig. 77 shows two similar triangles ABC and $AB'C'$, the lengths of the sides of which are in the proportion of 2 and 1. By bisecting AB in B', and drawing $B'C'$ parallel to BC, the line AC is bisected in C'', and $B'C'$ is one half the length of BC.

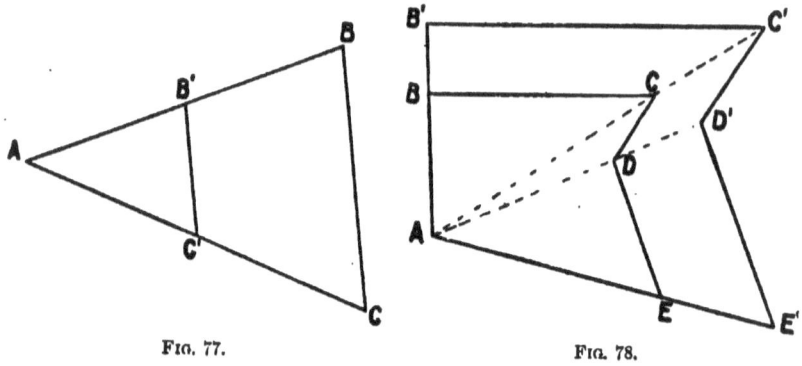

Fig. 77.   Fig. 78.

Fig. 78 shows how, by a similar method, a small irregular figure may be enlarged in any desired proportion. It is required to draw a figure similar to $ABCDE$, the sides of which are to

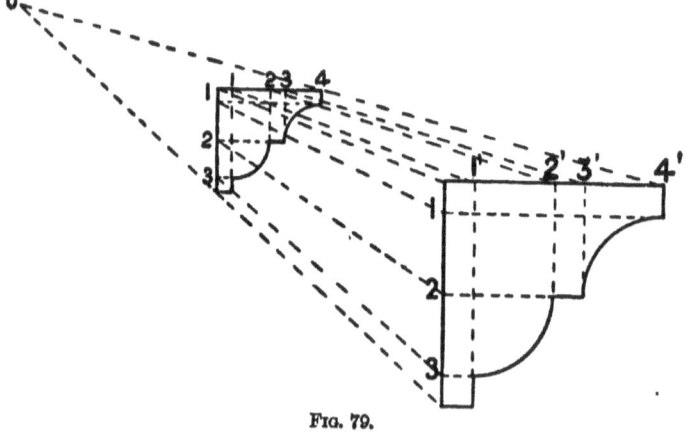

Fig. 79.

the corresponding sides of $ABCDE$ as 3 is to 2. AB, AC, AD, AE are produced. AB' is made one and a half times AB, and the figure is completed by drawing parallels.

ENLARGING AND DIMINISHING FIGURES.

In Fig. 79, which is the section of a common form of moulding, vertical and horizontal lines 1, 2, 3, and 1', 2', 3', are first drawn. Radiating dotted lines are then drawn, from the points in which these ordinates intersect the straight sides of the

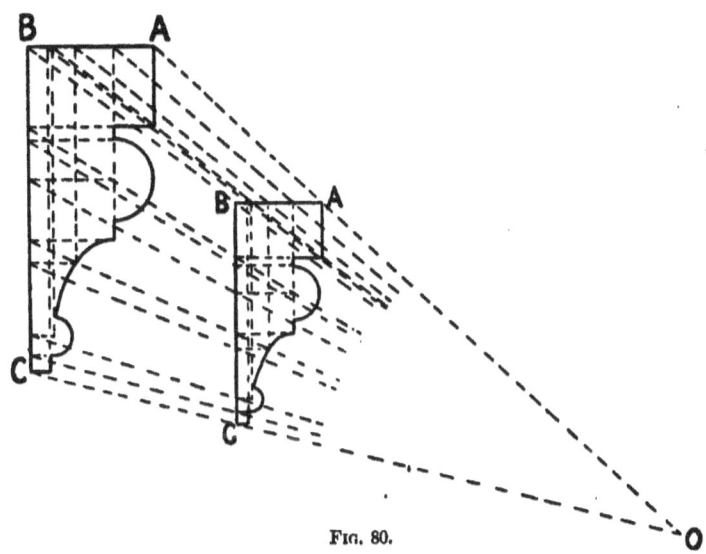

Fig. 80.

moulding, to a convenient point outside the figure. The proportion required is measured on one of these lines, and the diminished or enlarged figure is then obtained by drawing lines which intersect the radiating lines, and are parallel to corresponding lines of the given figure. Fig. 80 shows a somewhat more complicated moulding drawn out in a similar manner.

Questions on Chapter II.

1. In measuring the angle of a building, lengths of 7 ft. and 8 ft. respectively are measured along the walls from the corner; the distance between the two points obtained is 9 ft. What is the inclination (in degrees) of the walls to each other?

2. A segmental arch over an opening 5 ft. wide has a rise in the middle of 1 ft. 3 in. Determine the radius of the curve.

3. The two parallel walls of a building 14 ft. wide (outside measurement) have a difference in height of 6 ft. What is the length of the common rafters required for the roof?

48   A MANUAL OF CARPENTRY AND JOINERY.

4. Construct a square having a diagonal 4 in. long.

5. Construct a regular pentagon of 1·25 in. side.

6. Construct an octagon within a square of 2 in. side. Construct a heptagon of 1 in. edge. (C. and G. Prel. 1900.)

7. Determine the length of the side of a square inscribed in a circle 2·5 in. in diameter.

8. Draw the circumscribing circle about a rectangle having a diagonal 3 in. long, and one side 1·25 in. long.

9. An arch with a rise of 3 in. and 4 ft. span is the segment of a circle. Show the method of obtaining this curve without using the centre of the circle. (C. and G. Prel. 1904.)

10. Draw a triangle the sides of which are in the proportion of 3, 4, and 6, the perimeter being 7 in. Draw the inscribed and circumscribing circles.

11. About a circle 1·2 in. radius, draw a triangle the sides of which are in the ratio of 3, 4, and 5.

12. Describe the method of inscribing in a circle any regular polygon. On a given line 2 inches long construct a pentagon. (C. and G. Prel. 1898.)

13. Within a circle of 1 in. radius construct a regular pentagon. (C. and G. Prel. 1901.)

14. Find graphically a number which bears the same proportion to 8 which 5 bears to 4; also a number which bears the same proportion to 13 that 13 does to 9.

15. Two upright posts 16 ft. apart, fixed on a level site, are respectively 10 ft. and 5 ft. high. Determine graphically the length of two other posts placed between these at 4 ft. and 9 ft. distances respectively from the shorter post, so that the upper ends of all the posts are in line.

16. Make a plane scale to read $2\frac{1}{4}$ in. to 1 ft., not less than 3 ft. to be shown. (C. and G. Prel. 1903.)

17. Construct a plain scale of $1\frac{1}{4}$ in. to 1 ft., long enough to measure 4 ft. (C. and G. Prel. 1904.)

18. Construct a diagonal scale of $\frac{1}{10}$ full size to read feet, inches, and eighths of an inch.

19. Copy Fig. 78, $A'B'C'D'E'$, p. 46, to the size given, and construct a similar figure, the sides of which are 1·75 times the size of those given.

20. Copy, to the same size, the section of moulding given in Fig. 80, p. 47. Draw a similar section to one and a half times the size.

CHAPTER III.

SOLID GEOMETRY.

Methods of Projection.—It is difficult to represent, or *project*, on the surface of a flat sheet of paper the true shape of a solid object, and various methods have been devised to overcome this difficulty.

A **perspective drawing** (Fig. 81) represents the object as seen from one point of view, and the result is a picture such as

FIG. 81.—A perspective drawing.   FIG. 82.—An isometric drawing.

might be obtained by photography. As a *working drawing*, the object of which is to furnish the workman with all details of construction, such a view is unsatisfactory.

An **isometric** drawing (Fig. 82), which attempts to combine pictorial effect with correct proportion, is possibly better than a perspective sketch, but it is also of limited application.

The only really satisfactory method is to make, from several different points of view, *separate* drawings which represent the details of the object in accurate proportion. This last method is known as orthographic projection. Three views are generally represented; that view which shows the appearance as seen directly from above is called a **plan**; those which represent views from positions on a level with the object are called **elevations**; and those which show internal details, obtained by supposing the object cut through in various directions by planes, are called **sections**.

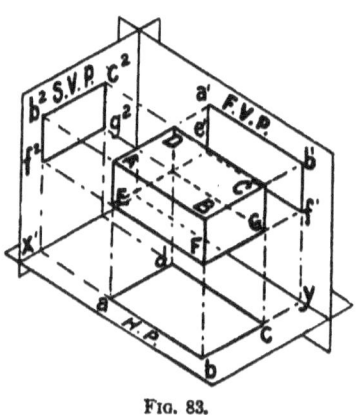

Fig. 83.

In orthographic projection, the views are supposed to be "projected" from the object, on to planes called *co-ordinate planes*. Thus, in Fig. 83, which is a pictorial (isometric) view of these planes and a solid object, F.V.P. is a **vertical plane**, and H.P. is a **horizontal plane**. Suppose straight lines drawn (projected) from each angle of the object and at right angles to the two planes. The figure $a'b'e'f'$ is the projection on F.V.P. It is called the elevation, and $abcd$ is the projection on the H.P.; it is the plan. The two projections represent what would be seen by any observer looking at the object from the front and from above respectively. The intersection of these two reference planes is called the **ground line**, and is usually lettered xy. Similarly, an elevation of the object may be projected upon a third plane, S.V.P.

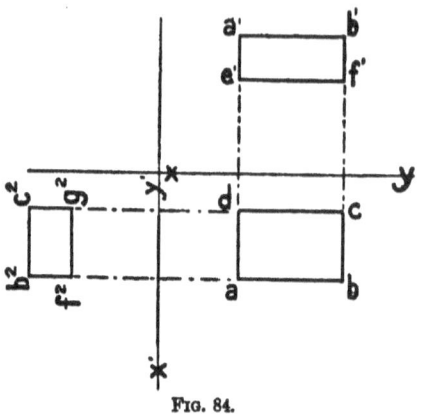

Fig. 84.

It follows that while, with the object in any given position, only one plan can be drawn, any number of elevations may be

SOME SIMPLE SOLIDS

obtained; the only stipulation is that the vertical plane of projection shall be at right angles to the direction of the view.

The three planes with their projections are represented on one surface by supposing the vertical planes to be revolved back on their base lines as hinges, until they are in the same plane as the H.P. The part below xy then represents the H.P., and the part above xy the V.P. A comparison of Fig. 83 and Fig. 84 will show how this takes place. The dotted lines drawn from one projection to another are always perpendicular to xy and are called *projectors*. A uniform system of lettering is always adopted in solid geometry, and a careful attention to the lettering will aid in the solution of the questions. The capital letter (A) indicates the point (or corner) of an object in space, the same letter in italics with a dash (a') is used for the elevation of the point, and the same letter without the dash (a) for its plan. Additional elevations of the point may be indicated with the same letter with a numeral (a^2).

Some Simple Solids.—The study of solid geometry is best commenced by projecting some of the simpler geometrical solids such as the cube, prism, pyramid, cone, cylinder, etc. After this it will be necessary to consider the projection of straight lines

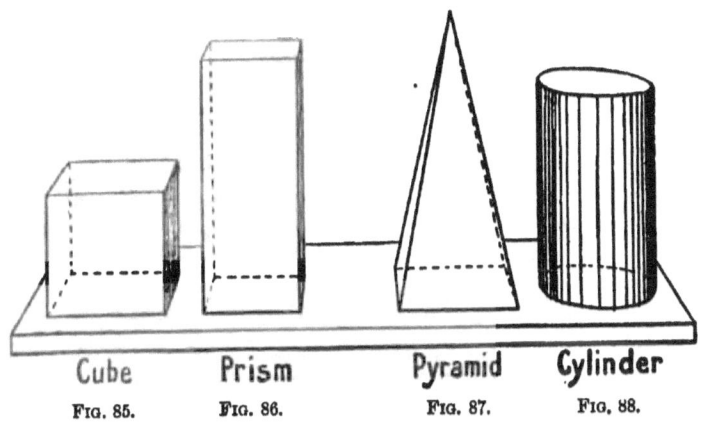

Cube   Prism   Pyramid   Cylinder
FIG. 85.   FIG. 86.   FIG. 87.   FIG. 88.

in different positions; and then inclined and oblique planes—that is, planes inclined to the rectangular planes—must be considered.

A **cube** is a solid figure bounded by six square faces (Fig. 85).
A **prism** (Fig. 86) is a solid figure whose two ends are of the

same shape and size and lie in parallel planes. An imaginary straight line joining the centres of the ends is called the *axis*.

A **pyramid** (Fig. 87) is bounded by a base and a number of triangular faces meeting at a point called the *apex*.

Both the prism and the pyramid are named according to the shape of the base; they may be either *triangular, square, rectangular,* or *polygonal*. A *right* prism or pyramid is one that has the base at right angles to the axis. If the base is not at right angles to the axis the prism or pyramid is said to be *oblique*.

A **cylinder** (Fig. 88) is a prism which has a circular base.

A **cone** (Fig. 89) is a pyramid with a circular base. A conical surface may be supposed to be developed by revolving a right angled triangle around one of the sides containing the right

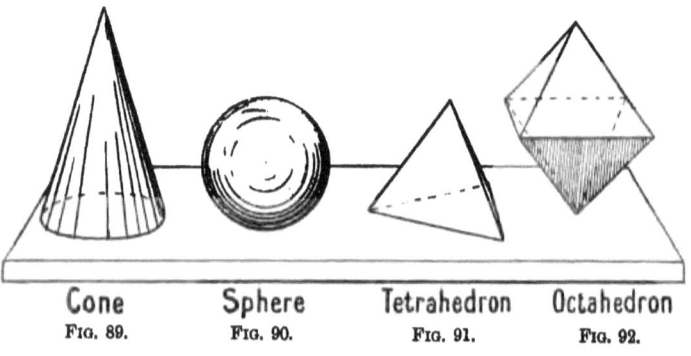

Cone   Sphere   Tetrahedron   Octahedron
Fig. 89.   Fig. 90.   Fig. 91.   Fig. 92.

angle. Any straight line joining the apex to any point on the circumference of the base is called a *generator* of the cone.

A **sphere** (Fig. 90) is generated by a semi-circle revolving upon its diameter. Every part of the surface is equidistant from the centre.

A **tetrahedron** (Fig. 91) is a solid having four equal faces all of which are equilateral triangles. It is a particular kind of triangular pyramid.

An **octadedron** is a solid having eight equal faces all equilateral triangles (Fig. 92).

When working the following examples it is very advisable to be provided with the necessary geometrical solids, and also a piece of stiff paper or cardboard, with the xy line drawn across the middle of it. By folding this paper along xy a model of the co-ordinate planes is obtained, and the student can with the

PROJECTION OF SOLIDS.

aid of this and the solids get a clear conception of the projections required. Much depends upon the position in which the solid is to be drawn; perhaps the plan will have to be drawn first, though sometimes the plan can only be obtained after the elevation has been drawn; while it frequently happens that neither the plan nor the elevation can be drawn at once in the required position. In this case, supplementary drawings must be made first, and from these the necessary projections are obtained. In the projection of lines, a pencil or a straight piece of wire can be used advantageously; while for inclined and oblique planes the set square, or a triangular piece of cardboard, is useful for purposes of illustration.

EXAMPLE 1.—*To draw the plan and elevation of a cube when one face is in the H.P. and a second face inclined to the V.P. at 30°. Draw a new elevation of the cube on any new xy.*

Fig. 93 shows the plan and elevation required. It will be seen that the plan is a square, and as all the vertical faces of the solid are inclined to the vertical plane, it is first necessary to draw the plan, and then project the elevation from it. The projectors must always be at right angles to *xy*. For the second elevation, let $x'y'$ be the ground line. Project from the plan (at right angles to $x'y'$) and measure the height of a^2, b^2, c^2, d^2, equal to the height of a', b', c', d', respectively.

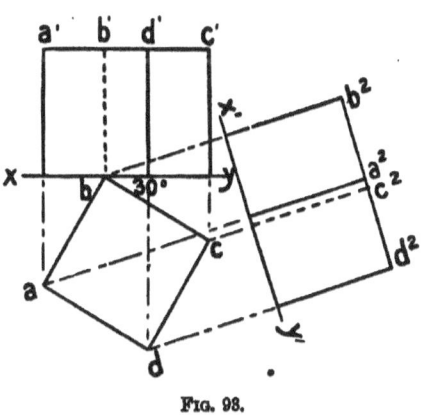

FIG. 93.

EXAMPLE 2.—*To draw the plan and elevation of a square-based pyramid, when the base lies in the H.P. and one edge of the base is inclined to the V.P. at 45°. Draw a new elevation on any vertical plane not parallel to either a diagonal or a side of the base.*

Fig. 94 shows the required projections. In this example it is first necessary to draw the plan, and from it to draw projectors which give the position of the elevation. The new elevation is obtained by first drawing $x'y'$ and then projecting from the points in plan at right angles to $x'y'$, marking the height of the apex the same as in the first elevation.

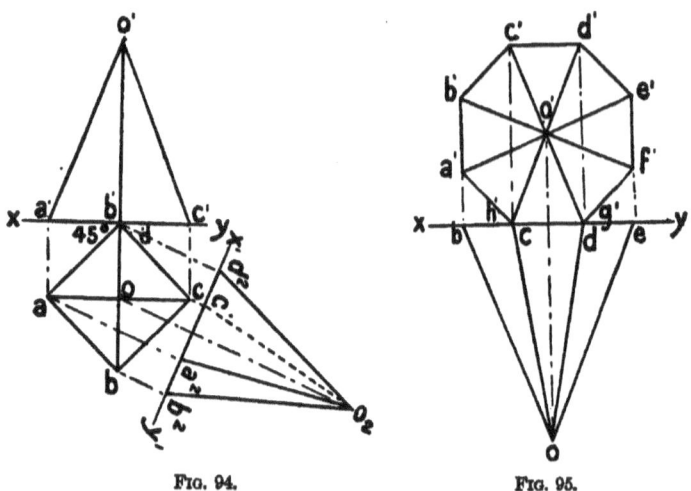

Fig. 94.   Fig. 95.

EXAMPLE 3.—*To draw the plan and elevation of a right octagonal pyramid, when the axis is horizontal, the base in the V.P. and one edge of the base vertical.*

In this example it will be necessary to draw the elevation before the plan. Fig. 95 shows the completed projections.

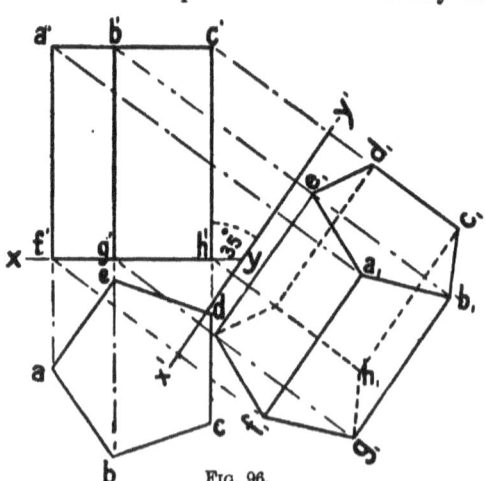

Fig. 96.

EXAMPLE 4.—*To draw the plan and elevation of a right pentagonal prism, when the long edges are parallel to the V.P., inclined to the H.P. at 35°, and one edge of the base is horizontal.*

Here it is impossible to obtain

the required projections without first drawing an auxiliary view. Fig. 96 shows the projections of the prism in an upright position, and with the base in the horizontal plane. A new $x'y'$ is then drawn at an angle of 35° to the elevation of one rectangular face; the projectors drawn at right angles to $x'y'$ will then contain the angular points of a second plan which, with the elevation already drawn, will give the projections required. These points, a, b, c, etc., lie on the projectors at distances from $x'y'$ equal to the distances from xy of the corresponding points in the plan abc, etc. Join these points and complete the required plan in the manner shown in the figure.

EXAMPLE 5.—*To draw the projections of a right heptagonal pyramid when* (1) *one triangular face lies in the H.P.*, (2) *one triangular face is vertical and perpendicular to the V.P.*

This example also involves the use of additional ground lines, as the required projections cannot be drawn direct from the data given (Fig. 97). First draw the plan and elevation of the pyramid when the base lies in the H.P., and one triangular face is at right angles to V.P. $a'o'b'$ and aob are the projections of that triangular face which is at right angles to the vertical plane. Draw a second ground line $x'y'$ through $a'o'$. Draw projectors from the elevation at right

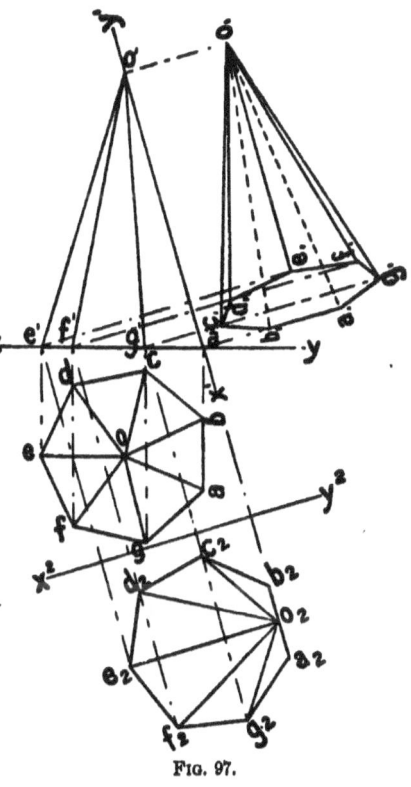

FIG. 97.

angles to $x'y'$, and measure the points for the plan as in the previous example, thus obtaining the plan a, b, c, d, e, f, g, o. This

56 A MANUAL OF CARPENTRY AND JOINERY.

plan and the elevation are the projections of the pyramid when one triangular face (OAB) lies in the H.P. To obtain the projections of the figure when one triangular face is vertical, draw another ground line x^2y^2 at right angles to $a'o'$. By projecting from the elevation, another plan $a_2b_2c_2d_2e_2f_2g_2o_2$ is obtained which gives, with the elevation, the projections of the pyramid with one triangular face (OAB) vertical.

EXAMPLE 6.—*To draw the projections of a cylinder when* (1) *the axis is vertical,* (2) *the axis is horizontal and parallel to the V.P.,* (3) *the axis is horizontal, and inclined to the V.P. at* 45°.

Fig. 98 shows the projections of this solid when the axis is vertical; either the plan or the elevation may be drawn first.

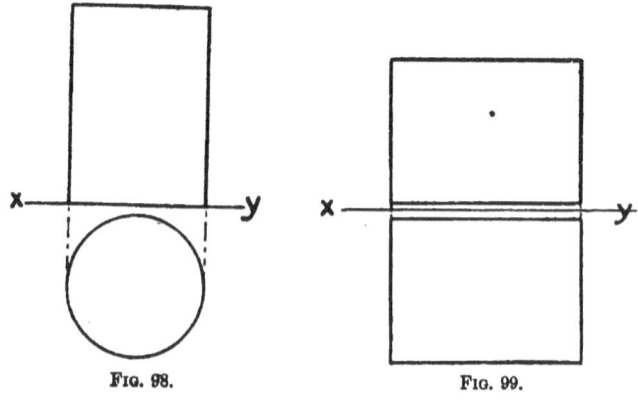

FIG. 98.   FIG. 99.

Fig. 99 gives the projections when the axis is horizontal and parallel to the vertical plane. It will be seen that in this case the plan and the elevation are of the same size and shape. In the third case (Fig. 100), as the axis is horizontal, the plan—which is a rectangle—is drawn first. As the ends of the cylinder are neither parallel nor perpendicular to the vertical plane, the shape of their elevation will be a curved line. This particular kind of curved line (the appearance of a circle seen obliquely) is named an *ellipse*. After drawing the plan, project from it an elevation on a vertical plane parallel to the ends of the cylinder. This elevation is a circle. Through the centre of this circle draw the line $a'b'$ parallel to $x'y'$, and the perpendicular lines $c'c'$, $d'd'$, etc. Project the plans of these lines on to the plan of the cylinder. The required elevation can now be drawn by projecting from

PROJECTION OF SOLIDS. 57

the points *aa*, *bb*, *cc*, *dd*, etc., and measuring the heights above *xy* equal to the heights of the same points above *x'y'* as shown. Even curves drawn through the points give the two ellipses required. To understand these examples clearly, the method of lettering must be carefully followed and adopted.

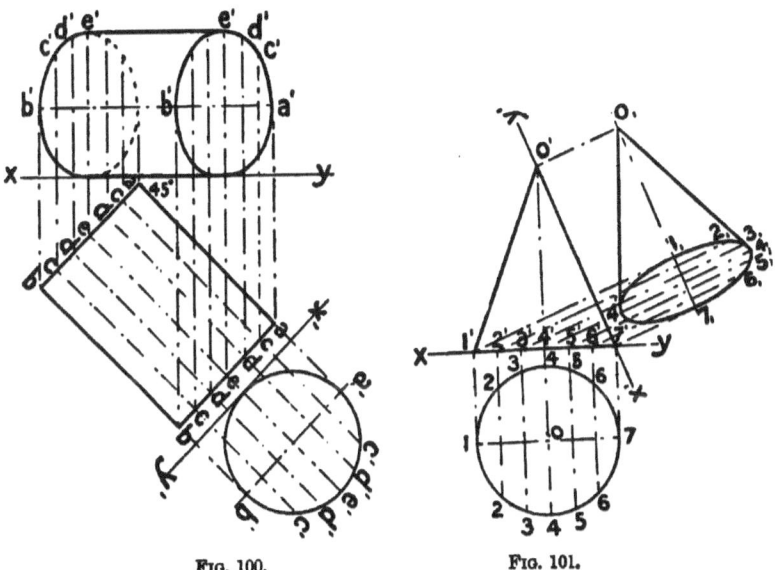

Fig. 100. Fig. 101.

EXAMPLE 7.—*To draw the plan and elevation of a right cone when (1) the base is in the horizontal plane, (2) a generator (a straight line drawn from the apex to a point in the circumference of the base) lies in the H.P., and the axis is parallel to the V.P.*

Fig. 101 shows the projections of the cone when the base is in the H.P. The second position—using the elevation already drawn—can be obtained by drawing a new *x'y'* through one of the sides *o'7'* of the elevation and projecting from it a new plan, the distances of the points in it from *x'y'* being equal to the distances from the same points on the first plan drawn. In order to get the ellipse which is now the plan of the base, points 1, 2, 3, 4, 5, 6, 7 are fixed in the first plan, projected to the elevation, and then to the required second plan as shown in the figure.

PROJECTION OF LINES.

Lines.—When a line is parallel to both planes of projection, its **true** length is shown in both plan and elevation (Fig. 102). When a line is parallel to one plane of projection only, its projection upon that plane shows its true length. Figs. 103 and 104 show two examples of a line inclined to the H.P. and parallel to the V.P. The length of the plan of this line depends upon its

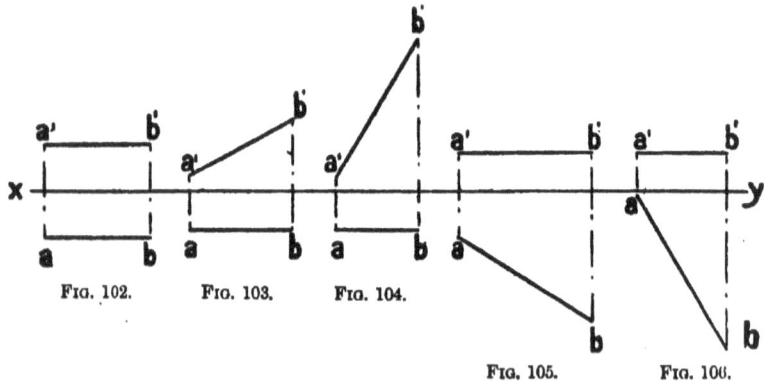

FIG. 102.   FIG. 103.   FIG. 104.   FIG. 105.   FIG. 106.

inclination to the H.P. If the line is vertical then its plan is a point. Fig. 105 shows a line which is parallel to the H.P. and is inclined to the V.P. The length of the plan of a horizontal line is always **equal** to the length of the line, while the length of the elevation varies according to the **inclination** of the line to the V.P. (Figs. 105 and 106).

More difficulty is found in determining the projections of lines which are parallel to neither plane of projection. Neither the plan nor the elevation gives the true length of the line. As already explained in the case of solids, auxiliary construction is necessary in such circumstances. It is here impossible to consider more than a few of the various ways in which lines may be placed. It is, however, necessary to know that the sum of the inclinations of a line to the two planes cannot be together greater than 90°. The traces of a line are the points where the line intersects the co-ordinate planes, the **horizontal trace** (H.T.) being the point where the line meets the H.P., and the **vertical trace** (V.T.) where it meets the V.P.

PROJECTION OF LINES.

EXAMPLE 1.—*To draw the projections of a straight line of given length which is inclined to the H.P. at 45° and to the V.P. at 20°.*

From a point O in xy (Fig. 107), draw OA (above xy) of the required length and inclined to xy at 45°. From A, draw the projector Aa. Then Oa is the length of the plan of any line of this length and inclination. From O draw OB (below xy) also the real length of the line and inclined at 20° to xy. A projector from B to xy gives Ob as the length of the elevation of this line. If the two extremities of the line are in the coordinate planes then one end is at the height A in the v.p. and the other end is in a horizontal line on H.P., which is at a distance from xy equal to the distance Bb.

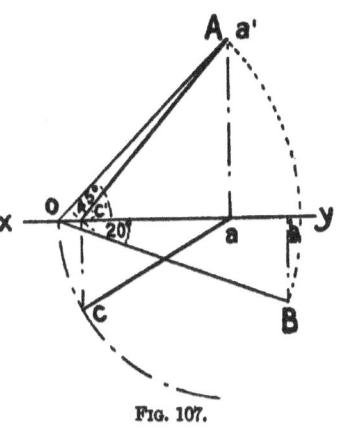

FIG. 107.

What is now required is to arrange these lines in the same projectors and in their proper position. Taking the length of the plan Oa as radius, and with a as centre, draw the semicircle. The plan of the required line will be a radius of this semicircle. Now take the length of the elevation Ob as radius, and with A as centre draw the arc intersecting xy at c'. Join Ac' and draw a projector from c' to intersect the semicircle in c. Re-letter the point A as a', then $a'c'$ is the elevation and ac the plan of the given line.

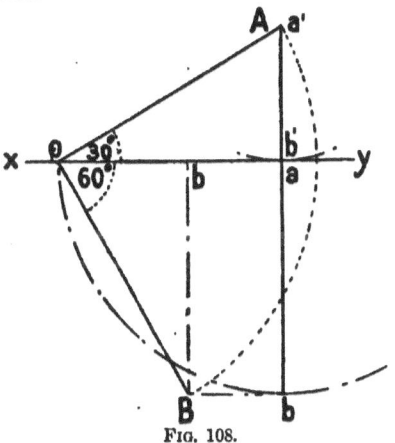

FIG. 108.

EXAMPLE 2.—*To draw the projections of a straight line of given length which is inclined to the H.P. at 30° and to the V.P. at 60°.*

From a point O in xy (Fig. 108), draw OA inclined at 30°, and OB at 60° to xy, both being of length equal to the length of the line. Projectors drawn from A and B to xy give the lengths of the plan and the elevation respectively. With a as centre and radius aO draw the semicircle, a radius of which is the required plan. With A as centre and the length of the elevation (Ob) as radius, draw the arc which just reaches to yx at a. Had the sum of the inclinations been less than 90°, this length of elevation would have intersected xy somewhere between O and a as it did in the previous example. As the elevation is perpendicular to xy, the plan will also be perpendicular to xy; that is, will be a continuation of the same line as shown in the figure; $a'b'$ is the elevation and ab the plan of the given line.

EXAMPLE 3.—*Given the plan and elevation of a straight line, to determine its length and inclination to both planes of projection.*

Let $a'b'$ and ab be the given projections (Fig. 109). With b as centre and ba as radius turn the length of plan into xy as at A.

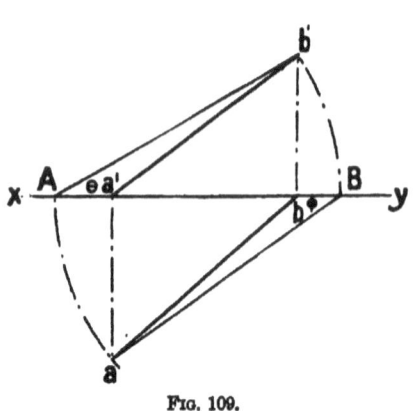

FIG. 109.

Join Ab'. Then Ab' is the true length of the line, and the angle $b'Ab$ (usually marked θ) gives the inclination to the H.P. With a' as centre and $a'b'$ as radius, turn the elevation into xy as at B. Join aB, then aB is also the true length of the line, and the angle aBa' (usually marked ϕ) is the inclination to the V.P.

Another method of working this example is shown in Fig. 110. Let $a'b'$ and ab be the given projections. At the ends a and b of the line draw perpendicular lines as shown. On the perpendicular from a measure a length aA equal to the height of a' above xy, and on the line from b measure a length bB equal to the height of b' above xy. Join AB and produce it until it meets ab produced at H. Then AB is the true length of the line, and the angle BHb (θ) gives the inclination to the horizontal plane. To obtain the inclination to the vertical plane, draw perpendicular lines from a' and b', and measure on each of

PROJECTION OF LINES. 61

these the distance that the corresponding point is in front of the vertical plane (its distance below xy). Join $A'B'$ and produce it until it meets $a'b'$ in V. The line $A'B'$ is the real length of the line, and the angle $A'Va'$ (ϕ) is the inclination to the vertical plane. The points V and H are the vertical and horizontal traces of the line. If this example (Fig. 110) is drawn, and then the triangle $a'A'V$ is cut to fold upon $a'V$, and the triangle bBH is cut to fold upon Hb, by turning these triangles at right angles to the planes and folding the co-ordinate planes at right angles to each other upon xy, the lines AB and $A'B'$ come together as illustrated in Fig. 111.

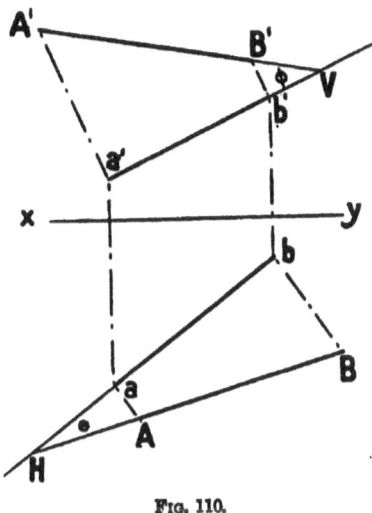

FIG. 110.

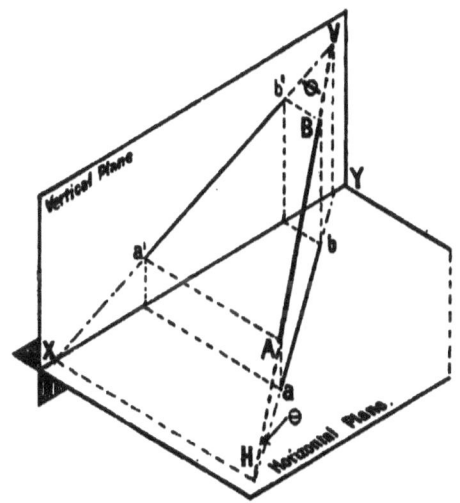

FIG. 111.

62 A MANUAL OF CARPENTRY AND JOINERY.

INCLINED AND OBLIQUE PLANES.

In addition to the co-ordinate planes, **inclined** and **oblique** planes are to be considered. In orthographic projection these can only be shown by their lines of intersection with the rectangular co-ordinate planes. The intersecting lines are called *traces*; that which intersects the vertical plane is called the **vertical trace** (V.T.), and the one which intersects the horizontal plane is the **horizontal trace** (H.T.). Two planes always intersect in a straight line, and three planes may intersect in a straight line or in a point. If the plane is perpendicular to one plane of projection, and inclined to the other, it is usually named an **inclined plane**. If it makes an acute angle with both planes of projection it is termed an **oblique plane**.

The method of determining the inclination of these planes to the planes of projection is to suppose them cut through at right angles to their line of intersection.

The **cone** is used extensively in solving questions on oblique planes. By drawing the projections of a cone having its base

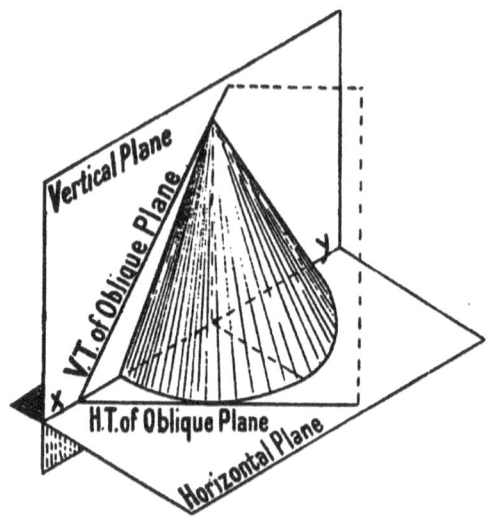

Fig. 112.

on the H.P. and a generator (p. 52) in the oblique plane (Fig. 112), the base angle of the cone gives the angle between the

INCLINED AND OBLIQUE PLANES.

two planes. A cone placed with its base in the vertical plane, and a generator in an oblique plane (Fig. 113), has a base angle equal to the inclination of the plane to the V.P. Oblique planes can be easily converted into simple inclined planes by alteration of ground line, *i.e.* by placing *xy* at right angles to the H.T. The sum of the inclinations cannot be greater than 180° nor less than 90°.

Figs. 114 and

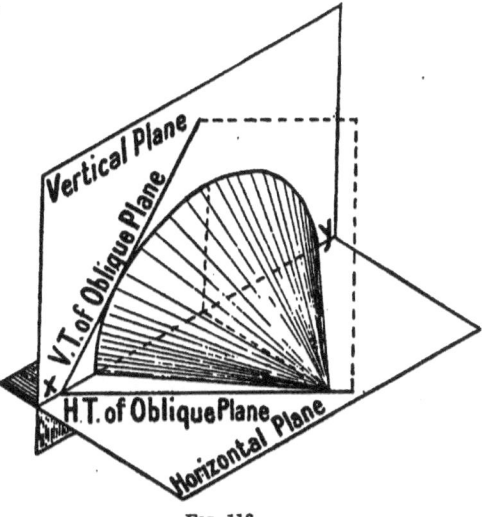

FIG. 113.

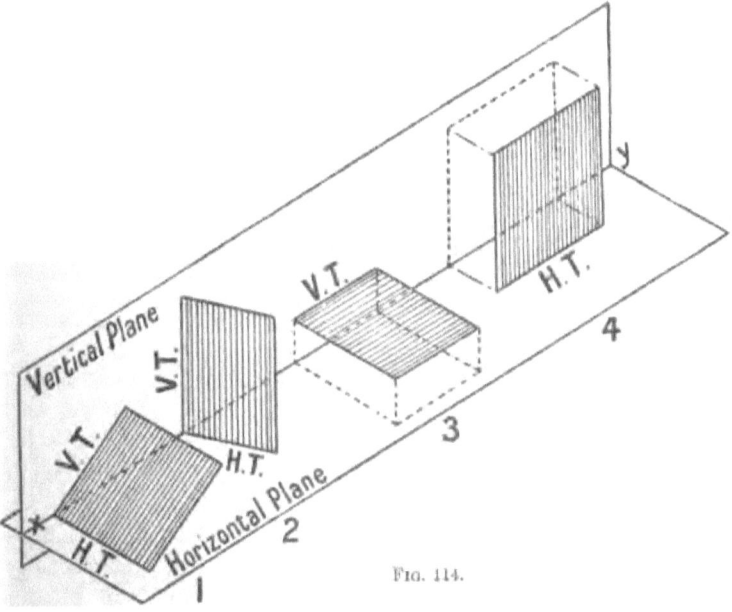

FIG. 114.

116 show some of the different positions in which inclined and oblique planes can be placed. Figs. 115 and 117 show the geometrical projections of the same. Fig. 115 (1) is an

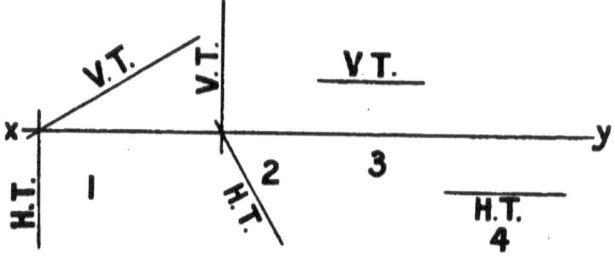

FIG. 115.

inclined plane which is perpendicular to the vertical plane. Fig. 115 (2) is a vertical plane which is inclined to the vertical plane. Fig. 115 (3) is a horizontal plane, and has therefore only

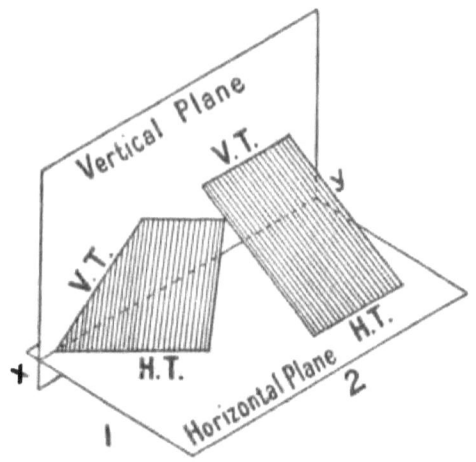

FIG. 116.

one—a vertical—trace; while in Fig. 115 (4) a vertical plane which is parallel to the v.p. is shown; as will be seen, it has only one—a horizontal—trace. Figs. 116 and 117 show oblique planes, and it is these which usually present the most difficulty to the student of geometry. Fig. 117 (2) shows an oblique

INCLINED AND OBLIQUE PLANES.

plane, the traces of which are parallel to *xy*. It should be noticed that when the traces of a plane intersect, they always do so in the ground line.

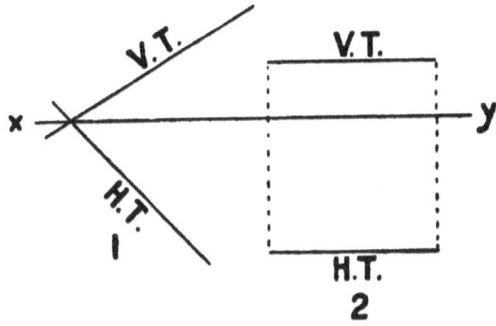

Fig. 117.

EXAMPLE 1.—*To determine the traces of a plane which is inclined to the H.P. at 40°, and is perpendicular to the V.P.*

The solution of this example is very simple, as it only consists of two straight lines in addition to *xy*. One is drawn

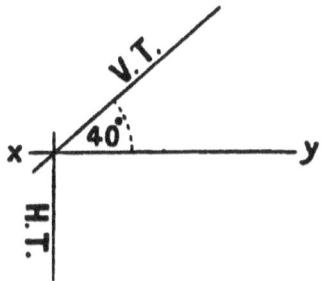

Fig. 118.

above *xy* at an angle of 40° to it, and the other one is drawn perpendicular to *xy* so that the two intersect on *xy* as shown in Fig. 118.

EXAMPLE 2.—*A rectangular chimney shaft penetrates a sloping roof, the inclination of which is 60°. Determine the true shape of the hole in the roof.*

The roof surface can be considered as a plane to be shown by its traces. In Fig. 119 let V.T. and H.T. be the traces of the plane, and *abcd* the plan of the chimney shaft. Draw the elevation of the shaft, showing it cut by the plane. Suppose the plane of the roof, with the section of the shaft, to be revolved

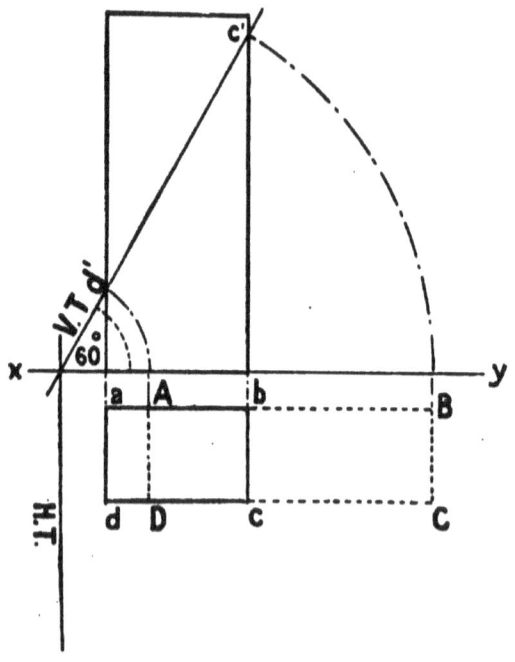

Fig. 119.

upon the H.T. into the H.P.; *ABCD* gives the shape of the hole. It will be seen that the greater the inclination, the longer will be the rectangular hole in the roof.

EXAMPLE 3.—*Given the traces of an oblique plane, to determine the inclination of the plane to both the H.P. and the V.P.*

Let V.T. and H.T. (Fig. 120) be the traces of the given plane. Draw the projections of a semi-cone having its axis $a'b'$ in the vertical plane, the apex a' in the given V.T. and its base (a semi-circle) *ced* in the H.P. and lying tangentially to the given H.T. Then the base angle (θ) of the cone gives the inclination of the plane to the H.P. To determine the inclination of the plane to the V.P., draw the projections of a second

INCLINED AND OBLIQUE PLANES. 67

semi-cone, having the axis mn in the H.P., and the apex m in the given H.T., while the base is in the V.P. and tangential to the V.T. The base angle (ϕ) of this cone gives the inclination to the V.P.

EXAMPLE 4.—*Given the traces of an oblique plane, to convert it into a simple inclined plane, and determine its inclination to the H.P.*

Let V.T. and H.T. (Fig. 121) be the given traces. Draw any new ground line ($x'y'$) at right angles to the H.T. Draw the plan of

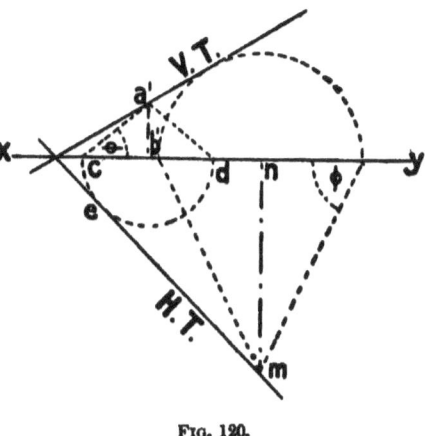

FIG. 120.

a horizontal line at any height (say 1″) on this plane. The plan of a horizontal line lying on a plane is always parallel to the

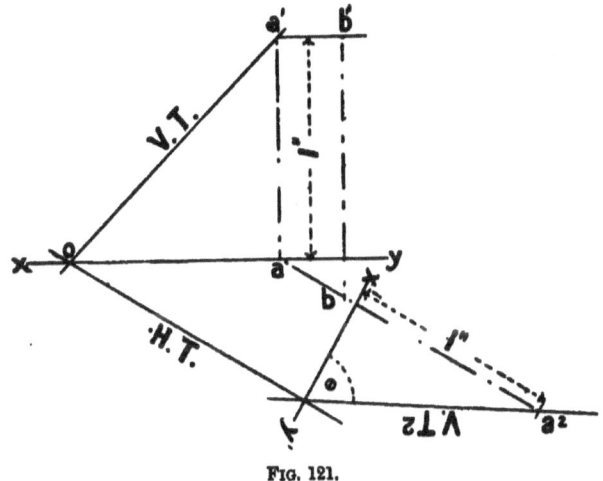

FIG. 121.

H.T. of the plane containing it. To draw this line, first draw a line $a'b'$ parallel to xy at a height of 1″ above it. Where this line cuts the V.T., as at a', drop a projector to xy. Draw ab

parallel to H.T. This is the plan of the line. Produce ab beyond $x'y'$ and make a^2 equal in height to a' (1"). This gives a point in the new vertical trace. As the traces of a plane always meet in the ground line, the V.T. is drawn through the points a^2 and the intersection of H.T. as shown. The angle (θ) which this line makes with $x'y'$ gives the inclination of the plane to the H.P.

EXAMPLE 5.—*Determine the traces of a plane which is inclined to the H.P. at 45° and to the V.P. at 65°.*

To solve this example it is necessary to suppose two cones, one with a base angle equal to the inclination to the H.P., and the

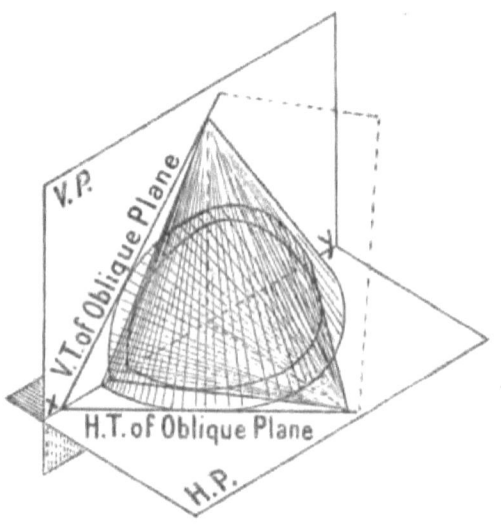

FIG. 122.

other with a base angle equal to the inclination to the V.P., each cone to envelop one---the same---sphere (Fig. 122). On any point O in xy (Fig. 123) draw a circle (any radius) as shown. This circle is the plan and elevation of a quarter of a sphere having its centre in the ground line. Draw the plan and elevation of a semi-cone having a base angle of 45°, its base being on the H.P., its axis in the V.P., and of such size that it just envelops the quarter-sphere. Draw a second semi-cone with the base in the V.P., the axis on H.P., with a base angle of 65°, and also

INCLINED AND OBLIQUE PLANES.

enveloping the quarter-sphere. The required traces are then drawn—one through the apex of the first cone and tangential to the base of the second; the other through the apex of the second and tangential to the base of the first, as shown in Fig. 123, which is the geometrical solution of the example.

SECTIONS.

The section of a drawing is the representation of a cut part. Many of the details of construction can only be shown by means of a section. As an illustration of this, Fig. 124 is the plan of a simple carpenters'

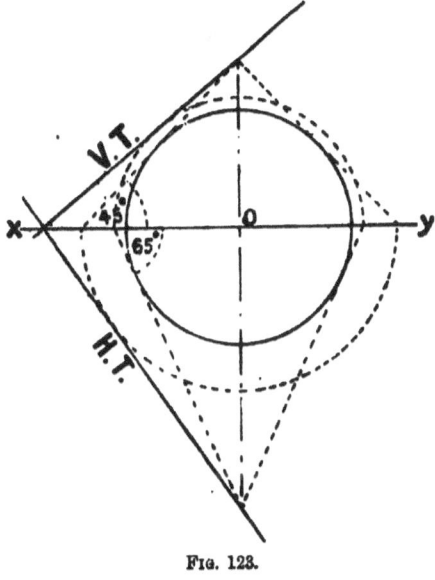

Fig. 123.

joint. From this plan alone it is not possible to determine the exact kind of joint. Figs. 125 to 128 show sections, in the

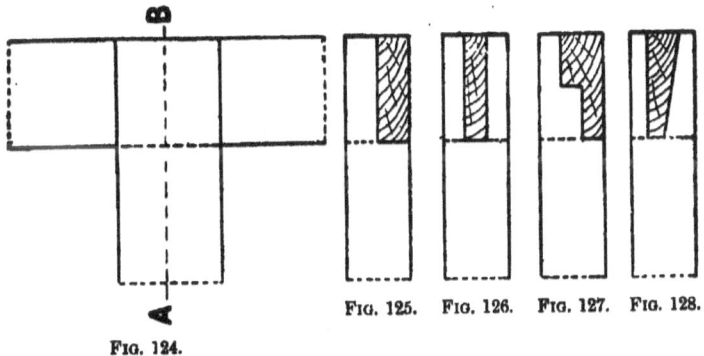

Fig. 124. Fig. 125. Fig. 126. Fig. 127. Fig. 128.

plane AB, of four different kinds of joint, of each of which Fig. 124 may be the plan.

70   A MANUAL OF CARPENTRY AND JOINERY.

EXAMPLE 1.—*Fig.* 129 *shows a section of a piece of moulding. To determine the section made when the moulding is cut at an angle of 45° with the long edges.*

Draw *xy* and also the plan of a short length of the moulding. Show by its trace the vertical plane cutting the

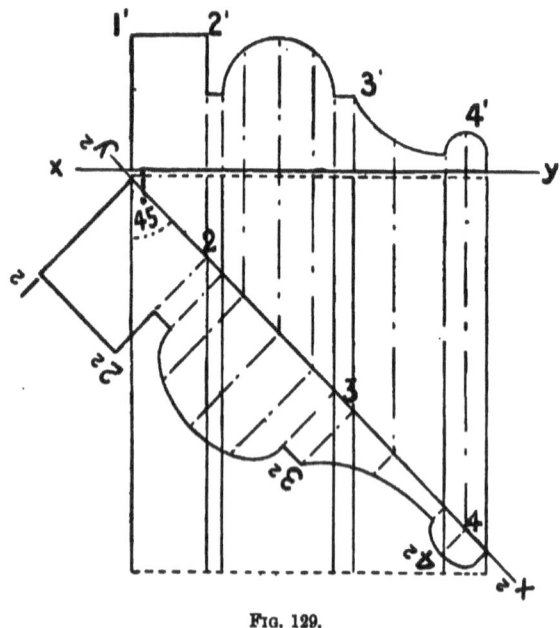

FIG. 129.

moulding at an angle of 45° with the long edges. By assuming this H.T. to be a new ground line (x^2y^2), projectors drawn through the plans of the edges of the moulding at right angles to the H.P. give the increased width required. As the cutting plane is vertical, the heights of the points above *xy* are transferred to these projectors, and the section is completed as shown.

EXAMPLE 2.—*To determine the section made by a horizontal plane cutting through a given triangular-based pyramid.*

Let $a'b'c'o'$ and $abco$ (Fig. 130) be the projections of the given pyramid. Draw V.T. the vertical trace of the cutting plane. Draw projectors from $d'e'f'$, the points where the cutting plane

SECTIONS. 71

passes through the elevation of the inclined edges of the solid, to meet the plans of the same lines, as at d, e, f. By joining def the required section is obtained.

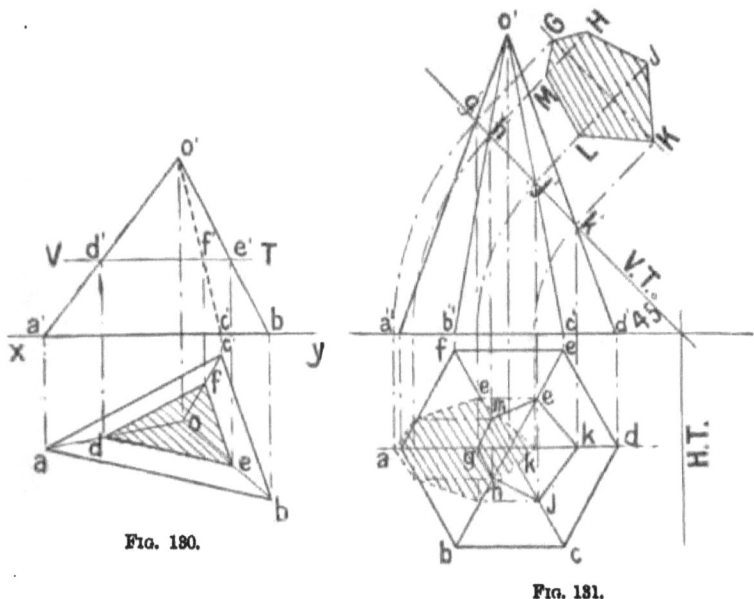

Fig. 130.

Fig. 131.

EXAMPLE 3.—*Given a hexagonal pyramid, to draw the section made by a plane inclined at 45° cutting through it.*

Let Fig. 131 be the projections of the pyramid. Draw the traces V.T. and H.T. of the cutting plane as shown. Letter the figure as indicated. Draw projectors from $g'h'j'k'l'm'$ to the plan, thus obtaining $ghjklm$. The required section is obtained by using H.T. as a hinge, and turning the points $g'h'j'k'l'm'$ into xy, and then projecting them at right angles to xy until they meet lines drawn through the corresponding points in the plan and parallel to xy.

An alternative method of drawing this section is shown in the figure. In this the V.T. is considered as a new ground line, and projectors are drawn from the points where V.T. cuts the elevation, at right angles to it. The distances of the points below xy are transferred to these projectors, thus giving the true shape of the section.

72 A MANUAL OF CARPENTRY AND JOINERY.

EXAMPLE 4.—*To determine the section made by a plane cutting a cylinder at an angle of* 30° *to the axis.*

Let Fig. 132 be the projections of the cylinder, which is horizontal, and H.T. the horizontal trace of the vertical cutting plane. This section—which is an ellipse—is obtained by

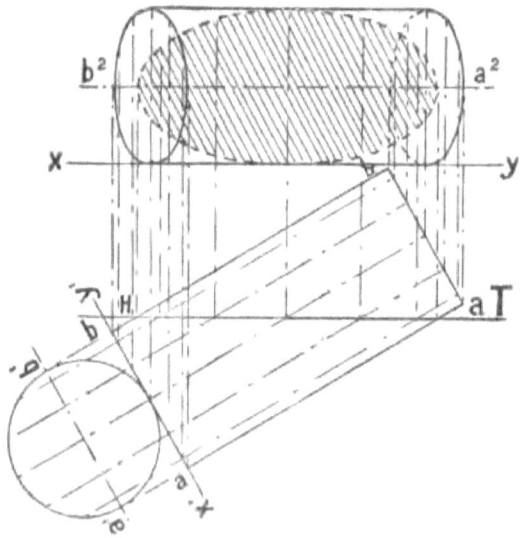

FIG. 132.

marking on the surface of the cylinder a number of horizontal lines as nearly equidistant as possible, and projecting these as shown in the figure.

Sections of the Cone.—The consideration of the sections of the cone is of some importance. The sections obtained are known as **conic sections**. The shape of the section depends upon the way the cone is cut. Any section of the cone taken at right angles to the axis is a **circle**. If the cutting plane passes through the apex the shape of the section is an **isosceles triangle**. If the cut is other than at right angles to the axis, and passes through opposite generators of the cone, the section is an **ellipse**; when the section is obtained by a plane parallel to a generator the section is a **parabola**; while the section made by a plane cutting the cone parallel to the axis is called a **hyperbola**.

SECTIONS.

Fig. 133 shows in plan the circular section made by a horizontal cutting plane at right angles to the axis. The size of the section is determined by the size of the cone, the apex angle, and by the distance that the cutting plane is from the apex of the cone. In the elevation of the same figure is shown the section of the cone when cut by a vertical plane *MN*, which passes through the axis. The shape of the section is an isosceles triangle.

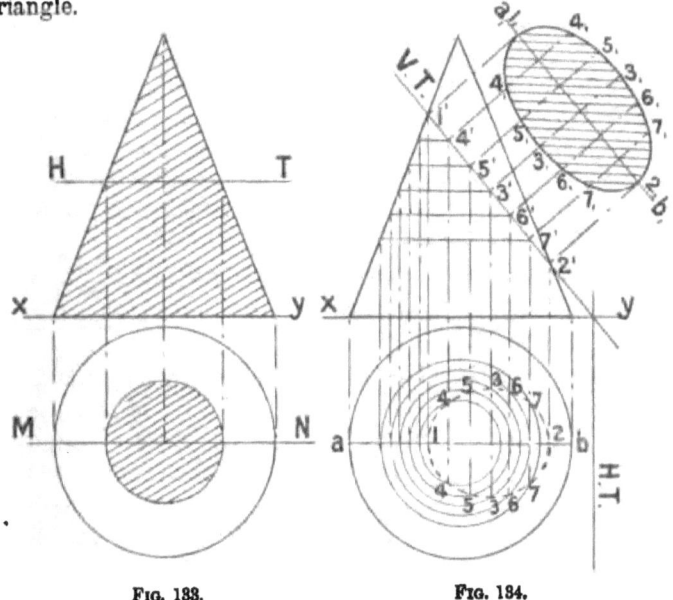

FIG. 133.   FIG. 134.

The outline of some of these conic sections may also be considered as having been traced by a point moving along a curved path, and having a fixed relationship to a given line, the *directrix*, and a given point, the *focus*, or to two given points, the *foci*.

The Ellipse has two axes which bisect each other at right angles: the **major**, or **transverse** axis which is the longer; and the **minor** or **conjugate** axis. Two points on the major axis are called **foci**, and an important property of this figure is that **the sum of any two straight lines drawn from the foci to any point in the curve is equal to the length of the major axis.**

(*a*) **The ellipse considered as a conic section.**—Fig. 134 shows the elliptical section of the cone obtained by projection. V.T. and H.T. are the traces of the cutting plane. The dotted ellipse shown in the plan is the plan of the section, and gives the lengths of a number of horizontal lines in the section, *i.e.* of the lines of intersection of the cutting plane and horizontal sections taken at different heights. To obtain the true shape of the section draw a,b, parallel to v.т. and at a distance from v.т. equal to the distance of ab below xy. The length of the major axis is determined by drawing projectors from 1' and 2' at right angles to v.т. until they meet a,b, in 1,2,. To obtain the length of the minor axis, bisect 1'2' in 3', project from this point, measure the length of 3 3 in plan, and transfer to the section being drawn as at 3,3,. The two axes are now in position. Other points through which the curve is drawn are obtained by projecting from 4', 5', 6', 7', then obtaining the length of the horizontal line through these points as shown in the plan at 4 4, 5 5, 6 6, 7 7, and transferring these lengths to the required section as indicated in the figure.

(*b*) **The ellipse curve considered as the path of a moving point.**

(I.) EXAMPLE.—*To construct the curve of an ellipse, the lengths of the axes being given.*

Let AB and CD (Fig. 135) be the given major and minor axes respectively. With the point of intersection of the two axes as centre, draw two concentric circles having radii equal to OA and OC respectively. Draw equidistant diameters EE, FF, GG, HH, as shown. Where these lines meet the large and small circles draw lines parallel to CD and AB respectively, until they intersect as at $efgh$, etc. A freehand curve drawn evenly through the points gives the required curve.

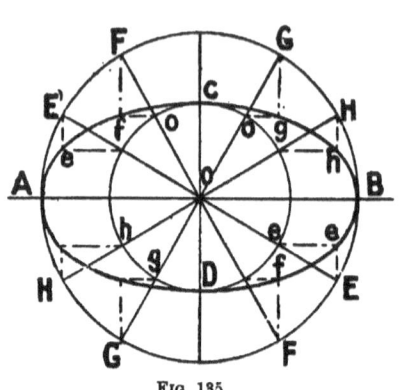

FIG. 135.

(II.) EXAMPLE.—*Given the axes of an ellipse, to determine the foci and draw the curve.*

Let AB and CD (Fig. 136) be the given axes. Draw these so that they bisect each other at right angles at O. With C as centre and AO as radius, draw the arcs intersecting AB at F and F_1. These points are the foci of the required ellipse.

The sum of any two straight lines drawn from the foci to any point in the curve is equal to the length of the major axis. Take any number, say 3, of points between F and O (nearest together at F) and number them 1, 2, 3. With $A1$ as radius and with F and F_1 as centres

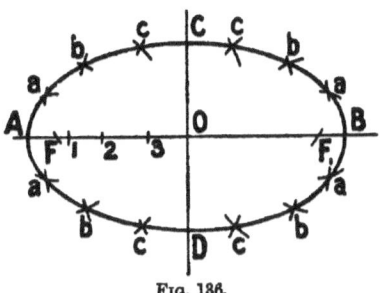

Fig. 136.

draw arcs on each side of AB. With $B1$ as radius and F and F_1 as centres draw the arcs intersecting at a, a, a, a; repeat the construction, having $A2$ and $B2$ as radii and F and F_1 as centres; and again with $A3$ and $B3$ as radii draw more intersecting arcs. Through the points thus obtained draw the curve of the ellipse.

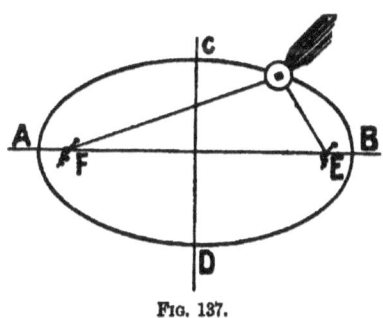

Fig. 137.

(III.) The workshop method of applying this construction is to get a length of fine string and fasten one end to a pin at F, twist it round another pin at E with the intervening length stretched to C. Place the pencil to move along the string as shown in Fig. 137. The moving pencil point traces out the elliptical curve.

(IV.) EXAMPLE.—*To construct an elliptical curve by means of a trammel.*

Take two laths of wood or other material, having a groove along the middle of the length of each, and fix them so that they are at right angles to each other. Obtain another lath of wood having near one end a hole through which a lead pencil is placed. Place two small pegs in holes in this rod, such that the distances from the pencil to these pegs are equal to the lengths of half the major and half the minor axes respectively. On moving this rod so that the pegs slide in the grooves as shown in Fig. 138, the pencil traces out the elliptical curve.

A modification of the trammel method of drawing an ellipse is to use a strip of paper. Mark, on one edge, OM equal to the length of half the major axis, and ON equal to half the minor

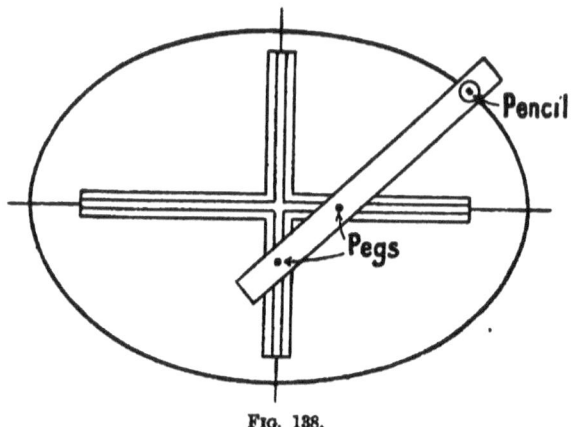

FIG. 138.

axis. Draw the axes of the ellipse at right angles to each other. On moving the strip so that the point M is constantly on the minor axis line, and N on the major axis line, the point O traces the elliptical curve.

The Parabola.—The section obtained when the cone is cut by a plane parallel to a generator is named a **parabola**. Unlike the circular or elliptical sections the curve of the parabola is not a closed curve, but extends indefinitely unless terminated by the base of the cone. In Fig. 139 V.T. and H.T. are the traces of a plane cutting the cone so that the resulting section obtained by projection is a parabola. Draw $a,b,$ parallel to V.T. and at a distance from it equal to the distance of ab from xy. Circular horizontal sections are drawn in the plan, and the lengths of the horizontal lines of intersection of these planes with the inclined cutting plane are obtained as shown at bb, cc, etc. Projectors from a', b', c', etc., at right angles to V.T. are drawn, and the lengths bb, cc, etc. transferred to the new projectors as shown at $b,b,$ $c,c,$ etc. An evenly drawn curve through these points gives a parabola.

The Hyperbola.—Fig. 139 also shows the section made by a

DEVELOPMENTS OF SOLIDS. 77

plane cutting the cone parallel to the axis. Its construction is exactly similar to that described for the parabola, and will be

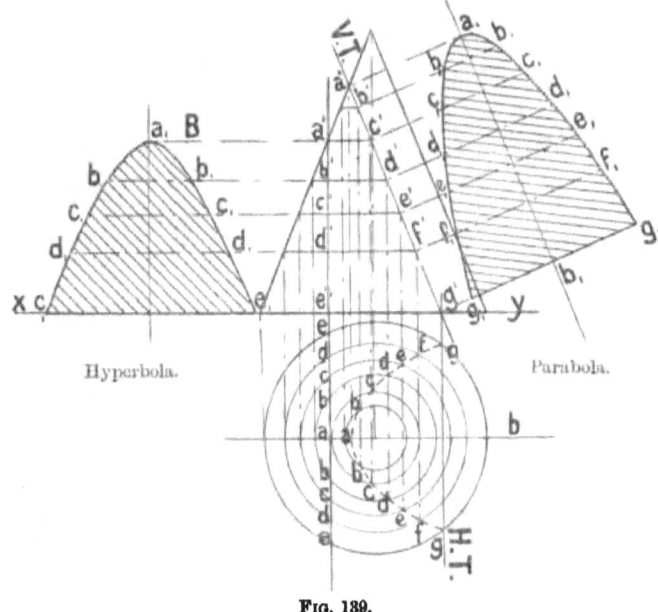

Fig. 139.

easily understood by reference to the lettering of Fig. 139. It is known as the **hyperbola.**

DEVELOPMENTS OF SOLIDS.

This is a branch of geometry which is specially important to the carpenter and joiner. It consists of unfolding or spreading-out surfaces so that the exact shape of the covering material may be ascertained. Figs. 140 to 142 show the **development** of the cube, a pentagonal pyramid, and a cone respectively.

In the **cube** six squares are drawn to touch each other as shown, and are

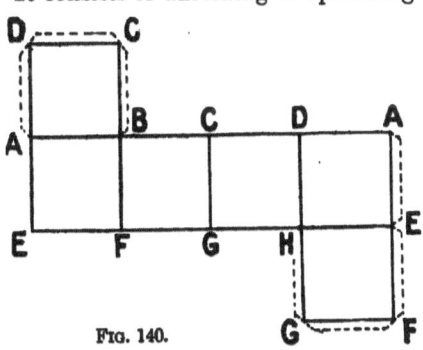

Fig. 140.

78   A MANUAL OF CARPENTRY AND JOINERY.

then folded on the lines. If such a solid is made out of stiff paper or cardboard, it is best to leave narrow strips on some of the sides, as shown by the dotted lines, for gumming purposes.

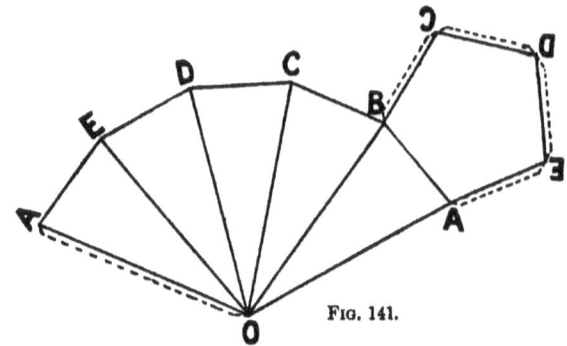

Fig. 141.

In the **pyramid**, the base, which is a pentagon, is first drawn, and on one side of this is constructed an isosceles triangle the lengths of the sides of which are equal to the slant edges of the required pyramid. With O as centre, and radius OA, draw the arc as shown, and measure BC, CD, DE, and EA, each equal to AB. The pyramid can be made by folding the figure on the various lines, so that the corresponding letters come together. The dotted lines indicate narrow strips by which the pyramid may be gummed together.

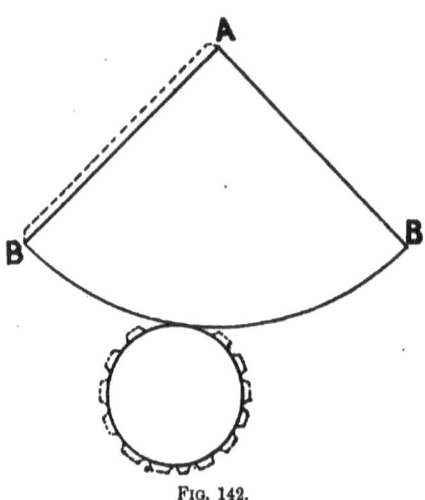

Fig. 142.

The **cone** is made out of stiff paper by first drawing the circle of diameter equal to the required base, and then marking out the arc of another circle of radius equal to the length of a generator of the cone, and a length of arc equal to the circumference of the base. The teeth-like projections around the circle are for gumming purposes.

DEVELOPMENTS OF SOLIDS.

EXAMPLE 1.—*To draw the development of a square prism when one end is cut obliquely.*

The method of construction will be clear from an examina-

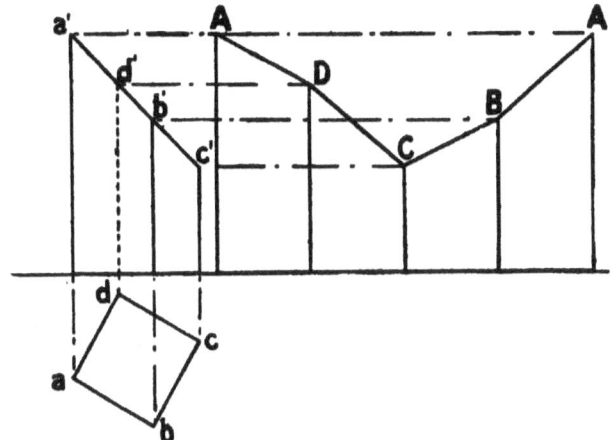

FIG. 143.

tion of Fig. 143, in which the corresponding points of plan, elevation, and developed surface are similarly lettered.

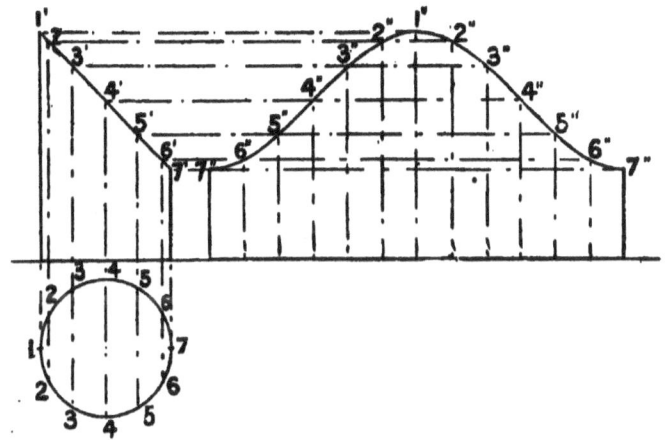

FIG. 144.

EXAMPLE 2.—*To draw the development of a cylinder when one end is cut off at an oblique angle with the axis.*

Fig. 144 shows the projections of the cylinder. In this

example the "stretch-out" is equal to the length of the circumference of the circle, the lower end is a straight line, while the upper end is represented by a curved line, the shape of which is obtained by assuming a number of vertical lines on the surface, and determining the length of each of these and transferring it to the developed surface as shown in the figure.

EXAMPLE 3.—*To draw the development of a truncated hexagonal pyramid, the top being cut off at an oblique angle with the axis.*

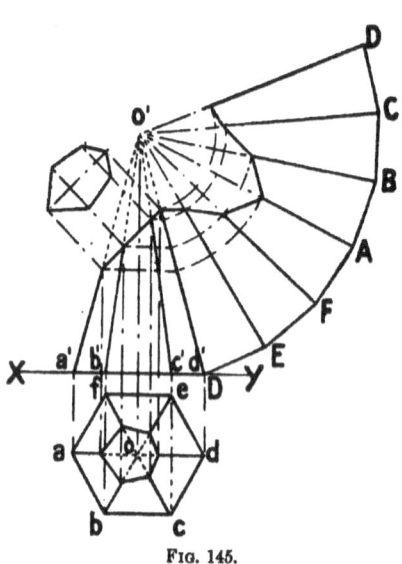

FIG. 145.

Let Fig. 145 be the projections of the pyramid, the part shown dotted being supposed to be removed. The base is a regular hexagon, of size given in the plan. The six isosceles triangles representing the inclined faces are obtained as shown in Fig. 145, with the exception that the apex angle of each is cut off, the exact length of each edge being obtained by treating each edge as a line, and finding its true length. The top end is obtained by finding the true shape of the section cutting the solid, in the manner indicated.

EXAMPLE 4.—*To draw the development of a truncated right cone.*

Let Fig. 146 be the plan and elevation of the cone. The base, which is of course a circle, is first drawn. Develop the conical surface as shown in Fig. 146. On the plan and elevation, draw a number (say 6) of equidistant generators, determine the length of each of these by turning it into, or parallel to, the V.P., and transfer these lengths to the developed surface. A freehand curve drawn through the points will give the upper end of the developed surface. The upper end of the truncated

DEVELOPMENT OF SOLIDS.

cone is of elliptical shape, and can be obtained as previously explained (Fig. 146.)

The application of this work to the determination of the covering of peculiarly-shaped roof surfaces is illustrated in the following examples, which may be taken as typical :

Fig. 147 shows a roof, the plan, *abcd*, of which is a square, and the vertical sections, through both *AB* and *CD*, are semicircles. In such a roof the *hips* (p. 216) will be elliptical in outline. The shape of the developed covering surface is obtained by dividing the semicircle (elevation) into a number of equal parts as shown. Draw the plan of each of the

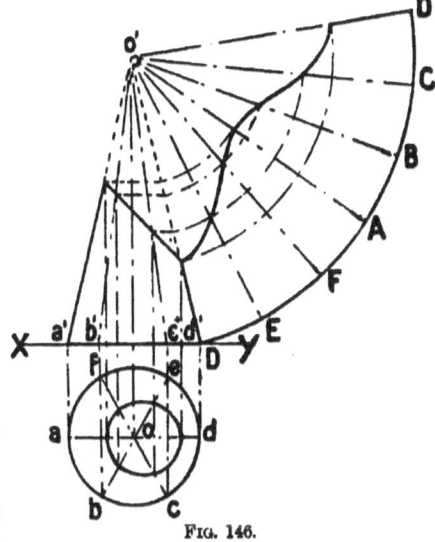

FIG. 146.

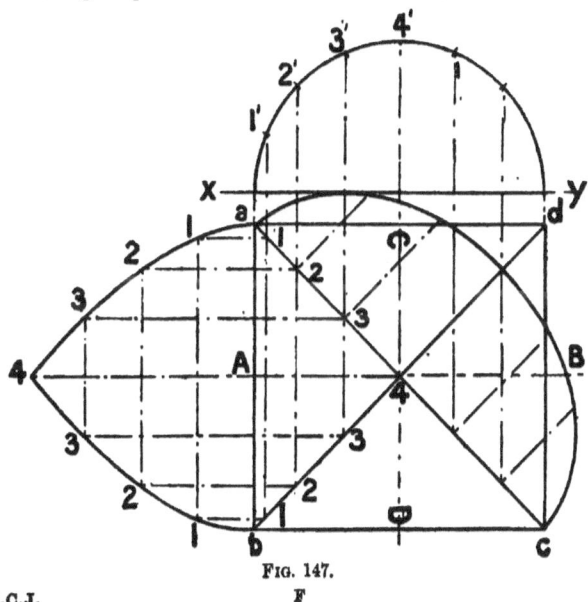

FIG. 147.

M.C.J. F

horizontal lines, of which these points are elevations, and thus obtain the lengths across the surface at these places. Stretch out, on one side of the plan, a length equal to the distance along the curve of the elevation from A to 4, and place these horizontal lines on this stretch-out as shown, projecting the length from the plan. Draw a freehand curve through the points thus obtained. Fig. 147 shows one quarter of the roof surface developed; as the plan is a square, and the sections taken either way are the same in this example, the remaining three sides are of exactly the same shape as the one shown.

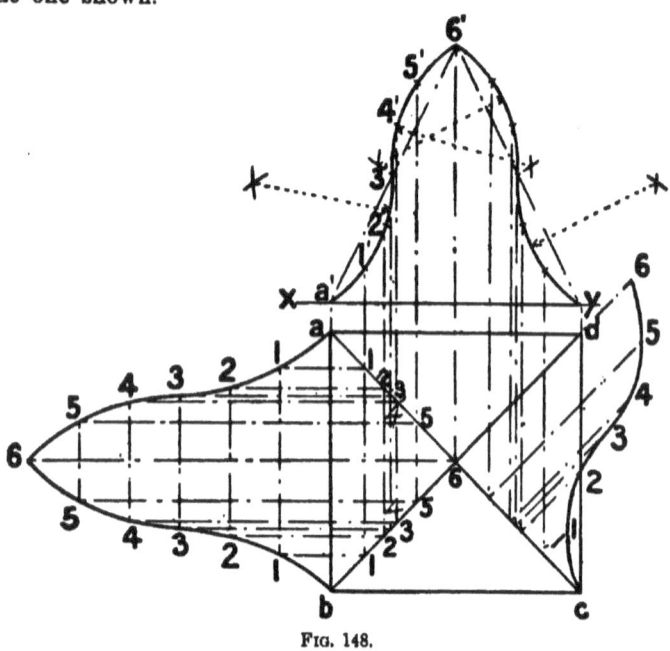

Fig. 148.

Fig. 148 shows a roof, the plan of which is a square, and the elevation a curved surface known as an *ogee*. The development is obtained in exactly the same manner as in the preceding example. It is necessary to take a number of horizontal lines, as shown in the figure by their plans and elevations, and then to obtain the stretch-out of the curved surface as in Fig. 147. As the drawing is numbered, an examination of it will make the method clear.

Questions on Chapter III.

1. Draw the plan and elevation of a square prism, of 3 in. edge, and 1·75 in. high, when the base is inclined at 30° to the H.P. and one edge of the base is in the H.P., and perpendicular to the V.P. Draw a second elevation upon a vertical plane which is parallel to the horizontal edges of the solid.

2. Draw the plan and elevation of a right pentagonal pyramid (edge of base 1·25 in., length of axis 3 in.) when the base is on the H.P., and one triangular face is perpendicular to V.P. Draw a second plan of the solid, which will, with the elevation, be the projections of the solid when a triangular face is on H.P.

3. Draw the projections of a cylinder (base 2·5 in. diameter, axis 1 in. long) when the axis is inclined to the H.P. at 45° and is parallel to the vertical plane.

4. Draw the projections of a straight line 3 in. long in each of the following positions:
   (a) inclined to the H.P. at 45°, and parallel to the V.P.:
   (b) parallel to the H.P., and inclined to the V.P. at 30°:
   (c) parallel to the H.P., and inclined to the V.P. at 60°:
   (d) inclined to the H.P. at 30°, and inclined to the V.P. at 45°:
   (e) inclined to the H.P. at 20°, and inclined to the V.P. at 70°.

5. The plan of a line 4 in. long is 2·5 in. What is its inclination to the H.P.?

6. One end of a line is 3 in. from both planes of projection, and the other end is in xy. The length of the line is 5 in. Draw the plan and elevation, and determine its inclination to the H.P.

7. A sloping surface has an inclination of 45°. It is cut by a vertical plane the plan of which makes an angle of 45° with the horizontal edges of the sloping surface. Determine the inclination of the line of intersection of the sloping surface and the vertical plane.

8. A square chimney shaft of 3 ft. side penetrates a roof surface which is inclined at 30°. One diagonal of the shaft is parallel to the ridge. Determine the shape and size of the hole in the roof.

9. The H.T. of a plane is inclined at 60° to xy. The plane is inclined to the H.P. at 45°. Determine the vertical trace, and convert the plane into a simple inclined plane.

10. The traces of a plane are parallel to xy. Assuming the V.T. to be 2 in. above xy, and the inclination of the plane to be 30° to the H.P., determine the distance of the H.T. from xy.

11. Draw the plan and elevation of a hexagonal prism of 1½ in. edge at ends, and 3 in. axis, when the axis is horizontal but inclined to the plane of elevation at 40°. Make the section of this prism, when cut by a plane, parallel to the plane of elevation. (C. and G. Prel., 1898.)

12. A hexagon 1¼ in. side is the base of a pyramid, the axis of which is 3 in. in height. Draw the plan and elevation, also a section parallel to the axis and ½ inch from it. (C. and G. Prel., 1904.)

13. Draw the plan and elevation of a right hexagonal pyramid, axis 4 in. in length and base of 3 in. side; also draw the section cut by a plane passing through one of the sides of the base, and inclined at 60° to the axis. (C. and G. Prel., 1901.)

14. Show by sketches, the manner in which the several conic sections are obtained from a cone. Give rules for approximately setting out an ellipse. (C. and G. Prel., 1897.)

15. Construct an ellipse, having its major and minor axes 3 in. and 1½ in. long respectively. (C. and G. Prel., 1903.)

16. Draw the plan and elevation of a cone. The diameter of the base is to be 3 in., the length of the axis 4½ in. Make a section parallel to the axis, and a section which is an ellipse, whose major axis is 2½ in. long. (C. and G. Prel., 1902.)

CHAPTER IV.

MENSURATION OF CARPENTRY AND JOINERY.

Calculations.—It is constantly necessary for the carpenter and joiner to make calculations from the given dimensions of the sizes of the materials used, the areas of surfaces, and the volumes, or cubical contents, of solids. Although most of the methods used involve only an elementary knowledge of arithmetic, it will be advisable to work out in full a few typical examples which are constantly occurring in practical work.

Units of length.—The British system of measurement is in yards, feet, inches, and sub-divisions of the inch. These sub-divisions may be given in decimals or in duo-decimals. In the decimal system the unit is either multiplied or divided by tens, and the working of such calculations is easily accomplished by the use of the decimal point. Duo-decimal measurement is expressed in feet, inches, and lines, the ratio of increase or decrease being in twelfths.

In most continental countries the metric system is in general use. This system is gradually increasing in favour in our own country. In the metric system the unit of length is the metre, approximately equal to 39·37 inches. This unit is divided into ten decimetres, the decimetre is divided into ten centimetres, and the centimetre is divided into ten millimetres.

The multiples of the metre are :
10 Metres = 1 Dekametre = 393·7 inches = 32′ 9″
10 Dekametres = 1 Hectometre = 3937 inches = 328′ 1″
10 Hectometres = 1 Kilometre = 39370 inches = 3280′ 10″
10 Kilometres = 1 Myriametre = 393700 inches = 32808′ 4″.

86 A MANUAL OF CARPENTRY AND JOINERY.

The sub-divisions of the metre are:

1 millimetre =	0·03937	inches
10 millimetres = 1 centimetre =	0·3937	inches
10 centimetres = 1 decimetre =	3·937	inches
10 decimetres = 1 metre =	39·37	inches 3' 3⅓".

It is frequently found necessary to convert the measurements of one system to equivalent distances in the other. This is done as follows:

EXAMPLE 1.—*How many millimetres* (mm.) *are there in 12 inches?*
In 39·37 inches there are 1000 mm.: in 12 inches there are:
$$\frac{1000 \times 12}{39\cdot 37} = 304\cdot 8 \text{ mm.}$$

EXAMPLE 2.—*What is the metric equivalent of 16 inches?*
$$\frac{1000 \times 16}{39\cdot 37} = 406\cdot 4 \text{ mm.} = 40\cdot 64 \text{ cm.} = 4\cdot 064 \text{ dcm.} = 0\cdot 4064 \text{ metre.}$$

The calculations to be made will include the use of **linear** or length measure, **square** or surface measure, and **cubic** or solid measure.

LONG MEASURE.	SQUARE MEASURE.
12 inches = 1 foot.	(12 × 12) = 144 square inches = 1 square foot.
3 feet = 1 yard.	(3 × 3) = 9 square feet = 1 square yard.

CUBIC MEASURE.
(12 × 12 × 12) = 1728 Cubic inches = 1 Cubic foot.
(3 × 3 × 3) = 27 Cubic feet = 1 Cubic yard.

In the metric system 10 decimetres = 1 metre:
10 × 10 = 100 square dcm. = 1 square metre.
10 × 10 × 10 = 1000 cubic dcm. = 1 cubic metre.

British and Metric Units.—Figs. 149 to 152 show the

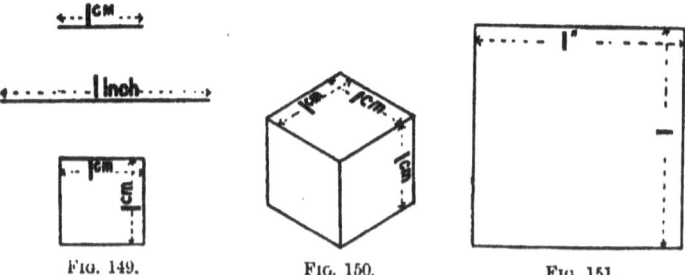

FIG. 149.   FIG. 150.   FIG. 151.

comparative size of the inch and the centimetre both as regards linear, square, and cubic measurement. It will be seen

MENSURATION OF CARPENTRY AND JOINERY.

that the inch is just over two and a half (2·54) times as long as the centimetre. In square measure, which involves the multiplication of a length by a breadth, the area of the square inch is 6·45 times the area of the square centimetre; while in cubic measurement there are 16·38 cubic centimetres in a cubic inch.

A consideration of Fig. 153 will serve to illustrate further the difference between linear, square, and cubic measurement. First, it must be noticed that every solid has three dimensions, namely length (in this example 24 inches), breadth (12"), and thickness (6"). To obtain the area (surface measure) of one of the largest faces, multiply the length by the breadth,

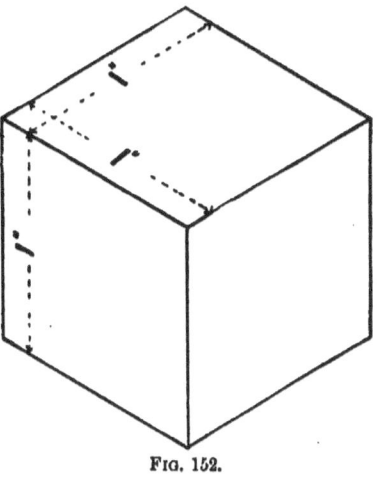

FIG. 152.

i.e. 24 × 12 = 288 sq. inches, or 2 sq. feet.

The area of one of the edges is obtained by multiplying the length by the thickness—24 × 6 = 144 sq. inches, or 1 sq. foot.

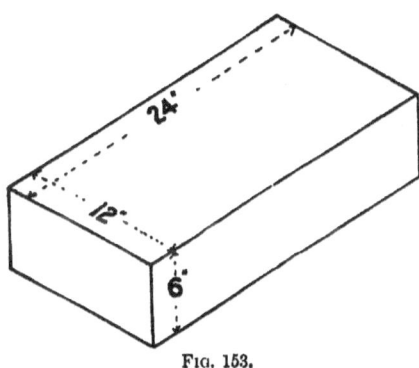

FIG. 153.

The cubic content is obtained by multiplying the three dimensions together thus:

24 × 12 × 6 = 1728 cub. ins.

or if the measurements are in feet, the cubic content is

2 × 1 × $\frac{1}{2}$ = 1 cub. foot.

Care must be taken to have all the measurements in the same units —either feet or inches.

When making calculations it is always advisable to take a mental survey of what is required and try to obtain an approximate result which may serve as a guide and possibly prevent errors in the subsequent calculation.

88 A MANUAL OF CARPENTRY AND JOINERY.

Squares and Square Root.—The *square* of a number is obtained by multiplying the number by itself; thus:
$2^2 = 2 \times 2 = 4$. $10^2 = 10 \times 10 = 100$. $24^2 = 24 \times 24 = 576$.

The *square root* of a number (indicated by the sign $\sqrt{\ }$) is that quantity which when multiplied by itself is equal to the number; thus $\sqrt{36} = 6$; $\sqrt{64} = 8$.

The rule for finding the square root of a number is as follows:

EXAMPLE.—*To find the square root of 529.*—Mark off the number 529 into periods of two figures as indicated, beginning with the units figure. The nearest square to 5 is 4, the square root of which is 2. Put 2 in the answers place. Square 2, place the result 4 under 5 and subtract. Bring down the next period 29; place the double of 2 in the left column. Divide all except the right-hand figure of 129 by 4, this gives 3. Place 3 in the answer place and also to the right of 4. Multiply 43 by 3 and place the result 129 under 129 and subtract. As there is no remainder the work is completed and 23 is the square root of 529. Test this by multiplying 23 by 23, the result is 529.

```
2 ) 5̂2̂9̂ ( 23
    4
43 | 129
     129
     ...
```

A knowledge of square root as well as of the following theorem is very necessary to a successful working of a large number of the questions to be considered. *In a right angled triangle the square on the side (the hypotenuse) opposite the right angle is equal in area to the sum of the squares on the sides containing the right angle.* [Euclid I. 47.]

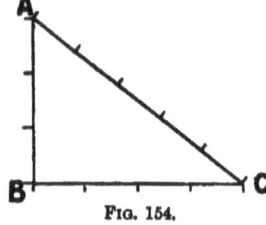

Fig. 154.

Thus, in Fig. 154, which is a right angled triangle,
$$AC^2 = AB^2 + BC^2.$$
Assuming the sides to be 5″, 4″, and 3″ long respectively, then
$$5 \times 5 = (4 \times 4) + (3 \times 3),$$
$$25 = 16 + 9.$$

This example and the proportions of the sides of the triangle are of some importance, since by an application of the proportions in it the setting out of right angles can be easily and accurately determined or tested without the aid of special appliances.

EXAMPLE 1.—*What is the length of the diagonal of a rectangular room whose sides are 12′ and 9′ long respectively?*

The length of the required diagonal is the square root of the

MENSURATION OF CARPENTRY AND JOINERY.

sum of the squares of the lengths of two adjacent sides of the rectangle. As the lengths of the sides are 12′ and 9′ respectively, that of the diagonal is:

$$\sqrt{(12 \times 12)+(9 \times 9)} = \sqrt{144+81} = \sqrt{225} = 15 \text{ feet.}$$

EXAMPLE 2.—*What is the length of the diagonal of a square of 8 feet side?*

As the two sides are at right angles to each other it will be necessary to square them both, add the result, and extract the square root. Then the length of the diagonal is

$$\sqrt{8^2+8^2} = \sqrt{64+64} = \sqrt{128} = 11\cdot31 \text{ feet.}$$

EXAMPLE 3.—*The diagonal of a square room is 18′, what is the length of side?*

Let x equal the length of the required side; then

$$2x^2 = 18^2; \therefore x = \sqrt{\tfrac{324}{2}} = \sqrt{162} = 12\cdot72 \text{ feet} = 12′\ 8\tfrac{3}{3}″.$$

EXAMPLE 4.—*What is the perpendicular height of an equilateral triangle of 12 feet side?*

The height of the triangle (Fig. 155) is obtained by squaring the side AB; squaring BD (half the base BC); subtracting BD^2 from AB^2 and extracting the square root.

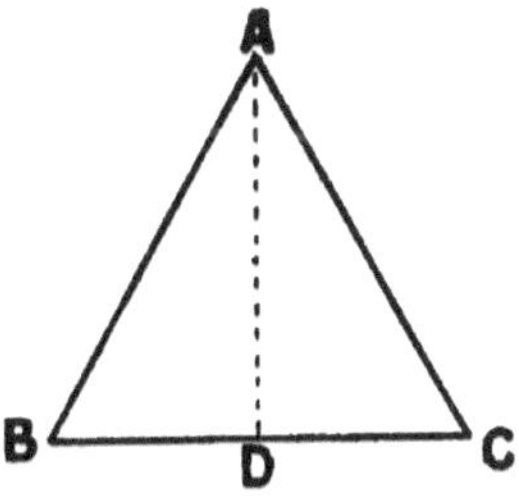

Let x equal the required height of the triangle then:

FIG. 155.

$$x^2 = (AB^2 - BD^2) = (12 \times 12) - (6 \times 6) = 144 - 36 = 108$$
$$\therefore x = \sqrt{108} = 10\cdot39 \text{ feet} = 10′\ 4\tfrac{2}{3}″.$$

EXAMPLE 5.—*A building 24 feet wide (outside measurement) is roofed to slope both ways. The ridge, which is in the centre, is 8 feet above the level of the walls. What will be the length of the common rafters?*

This example is solved by finding the length of the hypotenuse of a right-angled triangle, the known sides being the height of the ridge (8′), and half the width of the building (12′).

Let x equal the required length of the rafters, then

$$x = \sqrt{(8 \times 8)+(12 \times 12)} = \sqrt{64+144} = \sqrt{208}$$
$$= 14\cdot42 \text{ feet} = 14′\ 5\tfrac{1}{2\tfrac{1}{5}}″.$$

EXAMPLE 6.—*An inclined spur against a vertical post is* 20 *feet long. The lower end rests upon the ground* 12 *feet distant from the foot of the post. At what height from the ground is the upper end of the spur?*

Let x be the height required, then :
$$x = \sqrt{20^2 - 12^2} = \sqrt{(20 \times 20) - (12 \times 12)} = \sqrt{400 - 144} = \sqrt{256}$$
$$x = \sqrt{256} = 16 \text{ feet.}$$

AREAS.

Square and Rectangular Figures.—The areas of these figures are found by multiplying the length by the breadth.

EXAMPLE 1.—Let $ABCD$ (Fig. 156) be a rectangular surface, a floor for example, the length and breadth of which are respectively 18′ and 8′. As

$$18 \times 8 = 144,$$

the area of the room is 144 square feet.

If the room were square and of the same area, it would be necessary to find the number which multiplied by itself equals 144, that is 12. Therefore a room 12′ × 12′ will have the same area as a room 18′ × 8′, namely 144 square feet.

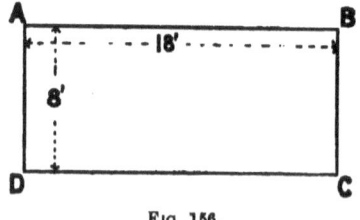

Fig. 156.

EXAMPLE 2.—*A square room has an area of* 1296 *sq. feet; what is the length of the side of the room?*

Find the square root of 1296. This is found to be 36. Therefore the length of the side of the room is 36 feet.

EXAMPLE 3.—*A rectangular room is* 14′ 6″ *long and* 12′ 9″ *wide, what area is the floor surface?*

This example, which involves fractions of the foot easily expressed in both measurements, may be worked in either fractions and decimals.

IN FRACTIONS :
14′ 6″ = $14\frac{1}{2}$′.
12′ 9″ = $12\frac{3}{4}$′.
Area = $14\frac{1}{2} \times 12\frac{3}{4}$
$= \dfrac{29}{2} \times \dfrac{51}{4} = \dfrac{29 \times 51}{8} = \dfrac{1479}{8} = 184\frac{7}{8}$ sq. ft.

IN DECIMALS :
14′ 6″ = 14·5′.
12′ 9″ = 12·75′.
14·5 × 12·75 = 184·875 sq. ft.

The area is $184\frac{7}{8}$ sq. ft. or 184 sq. ft. 126 sq. in.

AREAS.

EXAMPLE 4.—*What is the length of one side of a square room, the floor of which contains 1000 sq. feet area?*

The square root of 1000 is 31·622, therefore this is the length in feet of the side of the room.
$$31·622 \text{ feet} = 31' \ 7\tfrac{1}{2}''.$$
For practical purposes it is seldom necessary to work out these results beyond the second place of decimals.

EXAMPLE 5.—*What is the length in metres of the side of a square room of 50 square metres area?*

$$\sqrt{50} = 7·071 \text{ metres} = 7 \text{ m. } 0 \text{ dcm. } 7 \text{ cm. } 1 \text{ mm.}$$
$$= 70·71 \text{ dcm.}$$
$$= 707·1 \text{ cm.}$$
$$= 7071 \text{ mm.}$$

EXAMPLE 6.—*What is the length of the side of the room in Ex. 5 in feet?*

$$1 \text{ metre} = 39·37 \text{ inches} = \frac{39·37}{12} \text{ feet.}$$

$$7·071 \text{ metres} = \frac{39·37 \times 7·071}{12} = \frac{278·385}{12} = 23' \ 2\tfrac{1}{3}''.$$

EXAMPLE 7.—*A flat roof 20' by 12' has in the centre a raised lantern light the outside dimensions of which are 10' by 6'. How many sq. feet of square-edged boarding will be required to cover the flat roof surface?*

Area of the whole surface = $20 \times 12 = 240$ sq. feet.
Deduct for lantern light $\quad 10 \times 6 \ = 60.\quad$ „
Quantity of boarding required
$$= 240 - 60 = 180 \text{ sq. feet.}$$

Triangles.—The **area of a triangle** can be obtained by multiplying the length of the base by half the perpendicular height, that is,
$$\text{area} = \text{base} \times \frac{\text{perpendicular height}}{2}.$$

The shape of the triangle does not affect the result, as all triangles on the same base and between the same parallels are equal in area.

The area of a triangle can also be determined by the following formula: $\sqrt{s(s-a)(s-b)(s-c)}$ = area of triangle, when
$$s = \text{half the perimeter, and}$$
a, b, c, are the lengths of the sides of the triangle.

92 A MANUAL OF CARPENTRY AND JOINERY.

EXAMPLE.—*To find the area of a triangle the sides of which are 5″, 6″, and 7″ long respectively.*

$$\sqrt{s(s-a)(s-b)(s-c)} = \sqrt{9(9-5)(9-6)(9-7)} = \sqrt{9 \times 4 \times 3 \times 2}$$
$$= \sqrt{216} = 14\cdot7 \text{ sq. inches nearly.}$$

Graphical Solutions.—Many examples in the determination of the areas and sides of triangles can be more easily solved by graphic construction than by arithmetical methods. Graphic methods are also to be employed by preference in cases where the arithmetic is laborious. In the following examples only the simpler ones are worked by arithmetic.

EXAMPLE 1.—*A triangle has a base of 8′ and a perpendicular height of 10′. What is its area?*

$$\text{Area} = \frac{8 \times 10}{2} = 40 \text{ sq. feet.}$$

EXAMPLE 2.—*What is the area of an equilateral triangle of 12′ edge?*

$$\text{Area} = \sqrt{s(s-a)(s-b)(s-c)}$$
$$= \sqrt{18(18-12)(18-12)(18-12)}$$
$$= \sqrt{18 \times 6 \times 6 \times 6} = \sqrt{3888} = 62\cdot35 \text{ sq. feet.}$$

EXAMPLE 3.—*A triangle has a perpendicular height of 50 cm. and an area of 30 sq. dcm. What is the length of the base of the triangle?*

$$\text{Base} = \frac{\text{area} \times 2}{\text{perpen. height}}.$$

As the area is in decimetres and the height is in centimetres the base $= \dfrac{30 \times 100 \times 2}{50} = 120$ cm. $= 12$ dcm.

EXAMPLE 4.—*A triangle with a base 16 dcm. in length has an area of 12 sq. feet. Find the height and the length of the base in feet, the perpendicular height of the triangle in cm., and also the area in sq. dcm.*

As 1 dcm. $= 3\cdot937$ inches, the length of the base of the triangle will be $16 \times 3\cdot937 = 62\cdot992$ inches $= 5\cdot25$ feet;

the height of the triangle in feet
$$= \frac{\text{area} \times 2}{\text{length of base}} = \frac{12 \times 2}{5\cdot25} = 4\cdot57 \text{ feet;}$$

the height in dcm. $= \dfrac{4\cdot57 \times 12}{3\cdot937} = 13\cdot93 = 139\cdot3$ cm.;

the area of the triangle in sq. dcm. $= \dfrac{16 \times 13\cdot93}{2} = 111\cdot44.$

AREAS.

Triangles and parallelograms on the same base and between the same parallels are equal in area. Thus, in Fig. 157 the triangles ABC, DBC, and EBC, all being upon the same base BC and between the same parallels BC and DE, are equal in area. As previously explained, the area of a square or rectangular figure may be obtained by multiplying the length by

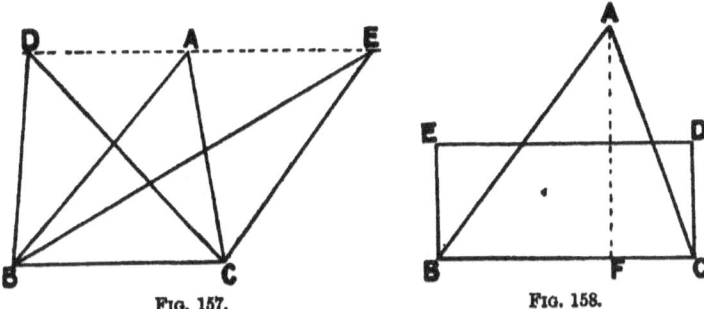

FIG. 157.   FIG. 158.

the breadth. The area of a triangle is equal to a rectangle upon the same base and of half the altitude, or, what is the same thing, to a rectangle having half the base and the same altitude. The rectangle $BCDE$ (Fig. 158) is equal in area to the triangle ABC when the height BE is equal to $\frac{AF}{2}$. By drawing to scale any triangle the length of the sides of which are given, the area can thus be easily obtained.

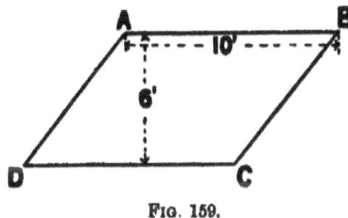

FIG. 159.

EXAMPLE 1.—*To find the area of the parallelogram $ABCD$.* (Fig. 159).

Multiply the length by the breadth. The fact that the angles are not right angles does not affect the result. Care must however be taken to measure the breadth at right angles to the long sides. As the length is 10′ and the breadth is 6′ the area is $10 \times 6 = 60$ sq. feet.

EXAMPLE 2.—*Determine a square equal in area to a given rectangle.*

Let $ABCD$ (Fig. 160) be the given rectangle. Produce DC and make CE equal in length to BC. Bisect DE at O and with OD as radius and O as centre draw the semicircle DFE. Produce CB to intersect the semicircle at F. Then CF is the length of the side of the square, because CF multiplied by itself is equal to $DC \times BC$. This example shows how square root can be worked graphically.

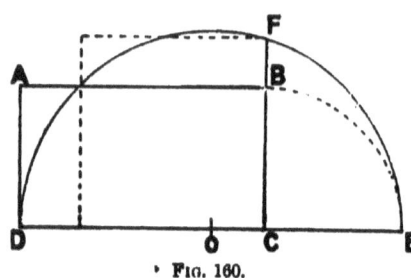

Fig. 160.

Areas of Polygons and Irregular Figures.—An easy way of determining the areas of polygons and of irregular figures which are bounded by straight lines is to sub-divide them into triangles, find the areas of these separately, and then add the results together. This can be done either by arithmetic or graphically, the latter by preference.

A rule applicable for finding the **area of any regular polygon** is to multiply half the perimeter by the perpendicular from the centre to any side. (The perimeter is the sum of the lengths of the lines bounding the figure.)

EXAMPLE 1.—*To find the area of any given regular polygon,* (*e.g. a regular hexagon of 3' side*).

(1) *Arithmetically.*—A regular hexagon consists of six equal equilateral triangles, in this case of 3' side. The area of each triangle is:

$$\sqrt{s(s-a)(s-b)(s-c)}.$$

Area of hexagon $= 6 \times \sqrt{4 \cdot 5 (4 \cdot 5 - 3)(4 \cdot 5 - 3)(4 \cdot 5 - 3)}$,
$= 6 \times \sqrt{4 \cdot 5 \times 1 \cdot 5 \times 1 \cdot 5 \times 1 \cdot 5}$,
$= 6 \times \sqrt{15 \cdot 1875}$,
$= 6 \times 3 \cdot 897 = 23 \cdot 38$ sq. feet.

(2) *Graphically.*—Let $ABCDEF$ (Fig. 161) be the given hexagon drawn to scale. The area of this figure is equal in area to the

AREAS.

rectangle $AEHG$, since the triangle AFE is deducted from the hexagon, and the two triangles BGC and CDH which are together equal in area to AFE are added. By measuring the sides of this rectangle and multiplying them together the area of the polygon is obtained.

EXAMPLE 2.—*To find the area of a regular pentagon of 4' side.*

This is one of those examples where it is difficult to apply arithmetic only in the solution of the question. By drawing the pentagon to scale,

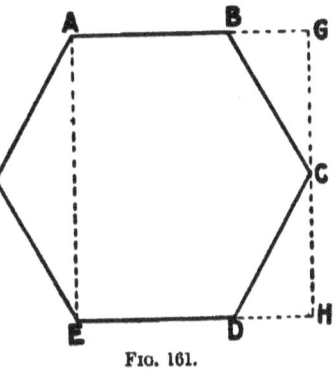

FIG. 161.

the perpendicular distance from any side to the centre is obtained easily. Then the area of the figure is obtained by multiplying the $\frac{\text{perimeter}}{2}$ by the length of this perpendicular distance.

Area of pentagon $= \frac{\text{perimeter} \times 2\cdot 76}{2} = \left(\frac{5 \times 4}{2}\right) \times 2\cdot 76 = 27\cdot 6$ sq. ft.

EXAMPLE 3. *To find the area in sq. inches of a regular octagon of 6" side.*

The area of this figure may be obtained by drawing it to scale, measuring the perpendicular distance from any one side to the centre point, and multiplying this by half the perimeter of the figure.

Another method is to find the square which contains the figure, find its area, and from this to deduct the area of a smaller square on the side BC (Fig. 162). This smaller square is equal in area to the sum of the four triangular corners which must be deducted from the large square to obtain the octagon.

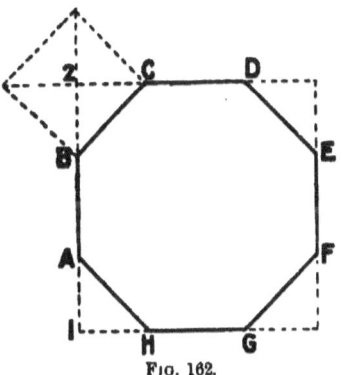

FIG. 162.

This question provides a good arithmetical example. It is first necessary to find the length of side of the large square which encloses the figure.

To find the length of the side of a square whose diagonal is 6″. Let $x=$ the side $B2$ in the figure, then $2x^2 = BC^2$;

$$\therefore 2x^2 = 6 \times 6 = 36,$$
$$x^2 = \tfrac{36}{2} = 18,$$
$$x = \sqrt{18} = 4\cdot 24 \text{ inches.}$$

The length of side of the large square is therefore
$$= 4\cdot 24 + 6 + 4\cdot 24 = 14\cdot 48''.$$

Area of the large square - - $= 14\cdot 48 \times 14\cdot 48 = 209\cdot 67$ sq. in.
Area of small square which must
be deducted for the corners is 6×6 = 36   sq. in.
Leaves the area of the octagon equal to   173·67 sq. in.

EXAMPLE 4.—*To find the area of a given irregular figure.*

Let $ABCDE$ (Fig. 163) be the given figure. The easiest solution is to work it graphically, finding a rectangle of equal area.

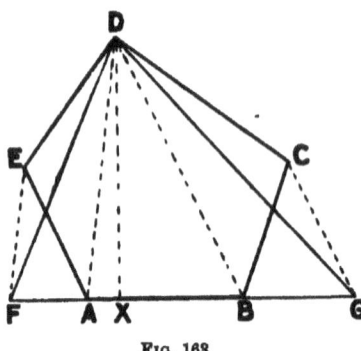

FIG. 163.

This is done by an application of the fact that triangles on the same base and between the same parallels are equal in area (Fig. 157, p. 93). Produce AB and join AD. Through E draw EF parallel to DA; then the triangles AFD and AED are equal, as they are between the same parallels AD and EF and on the same base AD. Join DB and through C draw CG parallel to DB. Join DG. Then DCB and DGB being on the same base BD and between the same parallels BD and GC are of equal area. Thus, the triangle FDG is equal in area to the pentagon $ABCDE$. A rectangle whose length is FG and height $\dfrac{DX}{2}$ gives the required area.

Generally the shape of the figure decides the method which it is advisable to adopt in the calculation of areas. If the surface is of irregular shape with straight sides, the area can be obtained by sub-dividing the whole space into rectangles and triangles, calculating these separately, and then adding them together.

AREAS.

EXAMPLE 5.—*To find the number of square yards of flooring required to cover the floor of the room* (Fig. 164).

Find the area of each of the lettered spaces separately and then add them together.

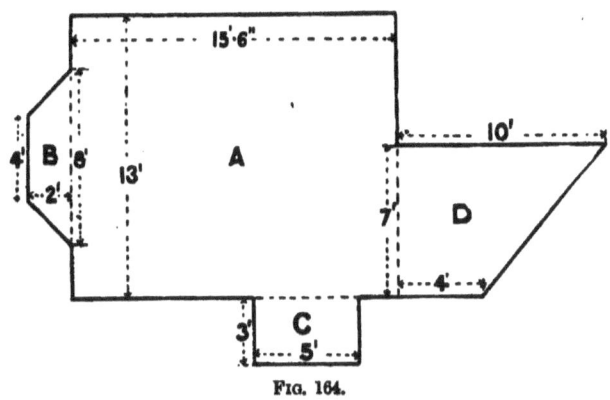

Fig. 164.

Area of space $A = 15'\ 6'' \times 13' = 201\frac{1}{2}$ sq. ft.
$\phantom{\text{Area of space }}B = 6 \times 2 = 12$,,
$\phantom{\text{Area of space }}C = 5 \times 3 = 15$,,
$\phantom{\text{Area of space }}D = 7 \times 7 = 49$,,
$\phantom{\text{Area of space AAAAA}}$ total area $= \overline{277\frac{1}{2}}$ sq. ft.

Circles and other Figures bounded by Curved Lines.—The radius of a circle is equal to one half the diameter, and the **length of the circumference** is obtained by multiplying the diameter by 3·1416, which is approximately 3⅐. This number is represented by the Greek letter π. Thus, the radius of a circle of 3″ diameter is 1·5 inches, and the circumference is $3 \times 3\cdot 1416 = 9\cdot 4248$ inches.

EXAMPLE 1.—*What is the length of the circumference of a circle of 4 feet radius?*

Circumference $= 2\pi r$
$\phantom{\text{Circumference }}= \text{radius} \times 2 \times 3\cdot 1416$
$\phantom{\text{Circumference }}4' \times 2 \times 3\cdot 1416 = 25\cdot 1328$ feet.

EXAMPLE 2.—*The girth at the middle of the length of the trunk of a tree, which is circular in section, is 10 feet. What is the radius?*

$$\text{Radius} = \frac{10}{3\cdot 1416 \times 2} = 1\cdot 591 \text{ feet.}$$

M.C.J.

The **radius of any segment of a circle,** or circular arc, may be obtained by squaring half the chord, dividing by the rise, adding the rise, and dividing by two; or (Fig. 165)

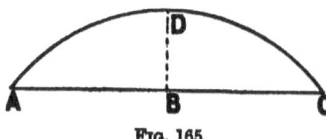

Fig. 165.

$$\text{radius} = \frac{(AB^2 \div BD) + BD}{2}.$$

EXAMPLE.— *What is the radius of a circle the chord of which is 8' and the rise in the centre 2'?*

$$\text{Radius} = \frac{(AB^2 \div BD) + BD}{2} = \frac{\left(\frac{AB^2}{BD}\right) + BD}{2} = \frac{\frac{4 \times 4}{2} + 2}{2} = \frac{\frac{16}{2} + 2}{2}$$

$$= \frac{8 + 2}{2} = \frac{10}{2} = 5 \text{ feet.}$$

The **area of a circle** is obtained by squaring the radius and multiplying the result by 3·1416, or, area $= \pi r^2$.

EXAMPLE 1.— *What is the area of a circle of 4' diameter?*
$$2 \times 2 \times 3\cdot1416 = 12\cdot566 \text{ feet.}$$

EXAMPLE 2.—*A circle has an area of 3 square feet, what is the radius?*

$$\text{Radius} = \sqrt{\frac{3}{3\cdot1416}} = \sqrt{0\cdot9549} = 0\cdot97 \text{ feet.}$$

EXAMPLE 3.—*The circumference of a circle is 12 inches. What is its area?*

$$\text{Diameter} = \frac{12}{\pi}; \quad \therefore \text{radius} = \frac{6}{\pi}; \quad \therefore \text{area} = \frac{\pi \times 6^2}{\pi^2} = \frac{6^2}{3\cdot1416}$$
$$= 11\cdot4 \text{ sq. inches.}$$

EXAMPLE 4.— *What is the area of a semicircular surface the radius of which is 8 feet?*

The area is half that of a circle of the same radius.
$$\text{Area} = \frac{\pi r^2}{2} = \frac{3\cdot1416 \times 8 \times 8}{2} = 100\cdot53 \text{ sq. feet.}$$

EXAMPLE 5.— *What is the area of a quadrant (a quarter of a circle) the radius of which is 6 inches?*

Area of circle $= 6 \times 6 \times 3\cdot1416 = 36 \times 3\cdot1416.$

Area of quadrant $= \dfrac{36 \times 3\cdot1416}{4} = 9 \times 3\cdot1416 = 28\cdot27$ sq. inches.

AREAS.

EXAMPLE 6.—*What is the area of an annulus (ring) the larger diameter of which is 10 feet and the smaller diameter 5 feet.*
Area of annulus = area of large circle − area of small circle.
$= [(5 \times 5) - (2.5 \times 2.5)] \times 3.1416$
$= (25 - 6.25) \times 3.1416 = 18.75 \times 3.1416 = 58.905$ sq. feet.

EXAMPLE 7.—*One side of the interior of a room is 12 feet long, and 10 feet high, and contains a window-opening with a semicircular head. The width of this opening is 4' 6", and the total height of the window is 7' 3". What is the exact area of the wall surface on this side of the room.*
Area of the side of the room = $12 \times 10 = 120$ sq. feet.
Area of rectangular part of window opening
$= 5 \times 4.5 = 22.5$ sq. ft.
Area of semicircular part of window opening $= \dfrac{(2.25)^2 \times 3.1416}{2} = 8.0$
Total area of window opening $= 30.5$
Required area of wall surface $120 - 30.5 = 89.5$ sq. feet.

The approximate **area of an ellipse** (near enough for all practical purposes) is obtained by multiplying the product of the two axes by 0·7854.

EXAMPLE 1.—*An ellipse has axes of 16 feet and 10 feet. How many square feet does it contain?*
Area of ellipse $= 16 \times 10 \times 0.7854 = 125\frac{3}{5}$ sq. feet.

EXAMPLE 2.—*The inclined roof surface on one side of a building is 20 feet long, and 16 feet wide measured from eaves to ridge. In the roof surface is a rectangular skylight 5' 3" long, by 3' 3" wide, and also a circular shaft passes through it which requires an elliptical space 4' by 3'. What is the area of the roof surface to be covered allowing for these voids?*
Total area of roof surface $= 20 \times 16 = 320$ sq. ft.
Rectangular space for roof light $= 5.25 \times 3.25 = 17.06$ „
Elliptical space for circular shaft $= 4 \times 3 \times 0.7854 = 9.42$ „
Total area to be deducted $= 17.06 + 9.42 = 26.48$ „
∴ Area of roof surface to be covered $= 320 - 26.48 = 293.52$ „

To measure the **area of irregular surfaces** which have curved boundaries, sub-divide them into rectangles or triangles of approximately the same size, find the areas of these, and add them together.

CUBIC OR SOLID MEASURE.

Cubic, or solid measure, is involved in the calculations of quantities of timber, stone, etc., excavations of earth, sizes of rooms, buildings, and in any questions affecting mass. An illustration of the difference between surface and solid measure is seen by considering the various measurements of a lead-lined wooden cistern. Such a cistern is usually employed to hold water or other liquid substance, and the size will be regulated by the volume required to be stored. It may be that there are limitations as to length, or breadth, or the depth of such a cistern, any of which will affect the other dimensions in obtaining the required capacity. Suppose the cistern to be 10 feet long, 6 feet wide, and 3 feet deep, inside measure. The cubic content or the volume of water it will hold when full is obtained by multiplying together the length, the breadth, and the thickness, thus $10 \times 6 \times 3 = 180$ cubic feet. On the other hand, if the quantity of sheet lead required for lining this cistern, not allowing for joints, must be obtained, it is necessary to find the surface measurement of the inside.

That is : two sides each 10 feet by 3 feet = 60 sq. feet
two ends each 6 feet by 3 feet = 36 ,, ,,
one bottom 10 feet by 6 feet = 60 ,, ,,
∴ Total quantity required = 156 sq. feet.

The amount of timber required for the above cistern can be obtained only when the thickness of the material, and the kind of joints to be used in the construction, are known.

Mode of calculating Timber.—In the buying and selling of timber the calculations of quantity are governed by trade custom. Logs, balks, and heavy beams are usually estimated in cubic feet, while planks and boards may be reckoned by the square foot of specified thickness, or lineal foot of given width and thickness. The following standards are in general use :

A **Petersburg standard** (which is the one chiefly used in timber calculations) of timber contains 165 cubic feet.
This is equivalent to 660 square feet of 3" thick,
or 1980 ,, ,, 1" ,,
or 220 ,, yards of 1" ,,

CUBIC OR SOLID MEASURE.

A **London standard**, which is equivalent to the **Dublin standard**, contains 270 cubic feet,
or 1080 square feet of 3" thick,
or 120 pieces each 12' long, 9" wide, and 3" thick.
A load of sawn or hewn timber contains 50 cubic feet.
A load of unhewn „ „ 40 „
A square of flooring contains 100 square feet or 10' × 10'.

EXAMPLE 1.—*A square balk of timber is 24 feet long, 24 inches wide, and 24 inches thick. How many cubic feet of wood does it contain?*

Content in cubic feet = 24 × 2 × 2 = 96 cubic feet.

EXAMPLE 2.—*What will be the price of a balk of timber 30 feet long by 16" × 16" at 2s. per cubic foot?*

Content in cubic feet = 30 × $1\frac{1}{3}$ × $1\frac{1}{3}$ = 30 × $\frac{4}{3}$ × $\frac{4}{3}$ = $\frac{160}{3}$ = $53\frac{1}{3}$.
Price at 2s. per cubic foot = $53\frac{1}{3}$ at 2s. = £5. 6s. 8d.

EXAMPLE 3.—*The dimensions of the different scantlings in a king-post roof truss are as follows: one tie-beam, 22' × 12" × 5"; two principal rafters each 13' × 6" × 5"; one king-post, 7' × 8" × 5"; two struts each 6' × 3" × 5". How many cubic feet of timber does the above truss contain and how much will it cost at 2s. 2d. per cubic foot?*

Quantity of timber = 22' × 1' × 5" = 22 square feet of 5" thick.
26' × $\frac{1}{2}$' × 5" = 13 „ „
7' × $\frac{2}{3}$' × 5" = $4\frac{2}{3}$ „ „
12' × $\frac{1}{4}$' × 5" = 3 „ „

$42\frac{2}{3}$ × $\frac{5}{12}$ = $17\frac{3}{4}$ cubic feet.

Cost at 2s. 2d. per cubic foot = $17\frac{3}{4}$ × 2s. 2d. = £1. 18s. 6d.

EXAMPLE 4.—*How many floor joists each 16' × 9" × 3" are there in a Petersburg standard?*

The cubic content of each joist 16' × $\frac{3}{4}$' × $\frac{1}{4}$' = 3 cubic feet.
Number of joists, $\frac{165}{3}$ = 55.

EXAMPLE 5.—*A Petersburg standard of 1" flooring consists of boards all of which are 18' long and 6" wide. What is the number of boards?*

Each board contains 18 × $\frac{1}{2}$ = 9 square feet;
∴ number of boards = 1980 ÷ 9 = 220 boards.
Each board has an area of one square yard.

102 A MANUAL OF CARPENTRY AND JOINERY.

EXAMPLE 6.—*A warehouse is* 70' *long and* 30' *wide, inside measure, and three storeys high. The first and second floors are of timber; wooden binders, each* 14" *deep and* 8" *thick placed* 10' *apart carry* 7" *by* 3" *floor joists placed at* 15" *centres, on the top of which rest* 1½" *rebated and filleted boards for the first floor; and* 1" *grooved and tongued boards on the second floor. Calculate the quantity and the cost of the material required for these floors, assuming pitch pine for the beams at* 1s. 9d. *per cubic foot, and white deal for the joists and floor boards at* £11. *per Petersburg standard.*

A plan of one of these floors will show that with the binders placed 10' apart each floor will require six in number, and assuming a wall hold of 9" at each end, each binder will require to be 31' 6" long. The plan will also show that with the joists placed at 15" centres 24 rows will be required, the joists in the end bays being 11' long to allow one end to rest on the end walls.

Timber required :
12 beams each 31' 6" × 14" × 8" = 294 cubic feet at 1s. 9d.
$\qquad$ = £25. 14s. 6d.

Floor joists in both floors :
10 bays each containing 24 joists 10' long × 7" × 3"
$\qquad$ = 10 × 24 × 10 = 2400 lin. ft.
4 bays each containing 24 joists 11' long × 7" × 3"
$\qquad$ = 4 × 24 × 11 = 1056 lin. ft.;
$\qquad\qquad\qquad\qquad\qquad$ 3456 lin. ft.

$$\therefore \frac{3456 \times 7}{12} = 2016 \text{ square feet of 3" stuff}$$

$\qquad$ = 3 standards + 36 sq. feet.

$\qquad$ 3 standards at £11 = £33 0 0
$\qquad$ 36 feet at 4d.   =   0 12 0
$\qquad\qquad\qquad\qquad\qquad$ £33 12 0

Area of lower floor $\qquad$ = 70 × 30 = 2100 square feet.
Add $\frac{1}{24}$ for the shrinkage }
$\quad$ of square-edged boards } = $\qquad$ 87½ $\quad$ „ $\quad$ „

$\qquad\qquad\qquad\qquad\qquad \frac{2187\frac{1}{2}}{9} = 243\frac{1}{18}$ sq. yds.

£11 per standard = 1s. 6d. per sq. yd. of 1½" thick.
$\therefore$ 243$\frac{1}{18}$ sq. yds. of 1½" boards at 1s. 6d. = £18. 4s. 7d.

CUBIC OR SOLID MEASURE.

Area of upper floor $= 70' \times 30' = 2100$ sq. feet.
Add $\frac{1}{12}$ for loss of width and shrinkage $\Big\} = \underline{175}$,, ,,

$2275 = 252\frac{7}{9}$ sq. yards.

£11 per standard = 1s. per sq. yd. of 1" thick.
∴ $252\frac{7}{9}$ at 1s. = £12. 12. 9d.

Summary: Cost of beams = £25 14 6
,, joists = 33 12 0
,, 1½" boards = 18 4 7
,, 1" boards = 12 12 9
Total £90 3 10

Prism and Cylinder.—The content of a prism or a cylinder is obtained by multiplying the area of the base by the length.

EXAMPLE 1.—*A roughly hewn trunk of a tree is of octagonal shape. The length is 30 feet and the length of side of the octagon is 12". What number of cubic feet does it contain?*

First obtain the area of the octagon by the method explained on p. 95, Ex. 3. This gives the side of a square containing the octagon as 29" long, and the area of the octagon as $4\frac{5}{8}$ square feet.

Cubic content of the balk $= 4\frac{5}{8} \times 30 = 145$ cubic feet.

EXAMPLE 2.—*The hewn trunk of a tree, octagonal in section, is 3' across (from side to side), and 18' long. Find the number of square feet of 3" stuff it will yield.*

It will be necessary first to find the length of the side of an octagon in a square of 3' side, Ex. 3, p. 95.

This gives a length of side of octagon as 1·24 feet.

The area of the octagon is 7·45 square feet.

The cubic content of the balk $= 7·45 \times 18 = 134·1$ cubic feet, and it will yield $134·1 \times 4 = 536·4$ square feet of 3" stuff if no allowance is made for the waste, inevitable in such a polygonal section.

EXAMPLE 3.—*A balk of timber which is square in section is 27 feet long, and contains 48 cubic feet. What is the size of the section?*

Area of the end in square feet $= \dfrac{48}{27} = \dfrac{16}{9}$;

∴ length of side $= \dfrac{\sqrt{16}}{\sqrt{9}} = \dfrac{4}{3} = 1\frac{1}{3}$ feet.

104   A MANUAL OF CARPENTRY AND JOINERY.

EXAMPLE 4.—*Find the cubic content of a circular tank* 10′ *deep and* 8′ *in diameter.*

Area of end $= 4 \times 4 \times 3\cdot1416 = 50\cdot265$ square feet.

Cubic content of tank $= 50\cdot265 \times 10 = 502\cdot65$ cubic feet.

When measuring and calculating the contents of balks of timber that are smaller at one end than the other, with a gradual taper, the usual practice is to take a mean of the breadth and the thickness, and multiply together this and the length. This result does not, however, give the exact content, but it is considered sufficiently near for all practical purposes.

EXAMPLE 1.—*A rectangular balk of timber is* 26′ 6″ *long,* 18″ *by* 16″ *at one end, and* 14″ *by* 12″ *at the other. What number of cubic feet does it contain?*

$$\text{Mean breadth,} \quad \frac{18+14}{2} = \frac{32}{2} = 16'' = 1\tfrac{1}{3}',$$

$$\text{Mean thickness,} \quad \frac{16+12}{2} = \frac{28}{2} = 14'' = 1\tfrac{1}{6}';$$

$$\therefore\ 26\tfrac{1}{2} \times 1\tfrac{1}{3} \times 1\tfrac{1}{6} = \frac{53}{2} \times \frac{4}{3} \times \frac{7}{6} = \frac{371}{9} = 41\tfrac{2}{9} \text{ cubic feet.}$$

EXAMPLE 2.—*The trunk of a tree* 30′ *long is* 2′ 6″ *in diameter at one end and* 1′ 6″ *at the other. How many cubic feet does it contain?*

$$\text{Mean diameter,} \quad \frac{30'' + 18''}{2} = 24'' = 2'.$$

Area of section $= 1 \times 1 \times 3\cdot1416 = 3\cdot1416$ square feet.

Cubic content $= 3\cdot1416 \times 30' = 94\cdot248$ cubic feet.

Pyramid and Cone.—The cubic content of a pyramid or cone is obtained by dividing the area of the base by one-third of the vertical height, *i.e.*

$$\text{content} = \frac{\text{area of base} \times \text{height}}{3}.$$

EXAMPLE 1.—*An equilateral-triangular-based pyramid of* 6″ *edge is* 9″ *high. How many cubic inches does it contain?*

Area of base

$$= \sqrt{s(s-a)(s-b)(s-c)} = \sqrt{9 \times 3 \times 3 \times 3} = \sqrt{243} = 15\cdot58 \text{ sq. ins.};$$

$$\therefore\ \text{content} = \frac{15\cdot58 \times 9}{3} = 46\cdot74 \text{ cubic inches.}$$

CUBIC OR SOLID MEASURE.

EXAMPLE 2.—*A hexagonal pyramid of 4' side is 10' high. Calculate the cubic content.*

Area of $\frac{1}{6}$ of base (an equilateral triangle of 4' side)
$$= \sqrt{s(s-a)(s-b)(s-c)} = \sqrt{6 \times 2 \times 2 \times 2} = \sqrt{48}.$$

Cubic content of pyramid
$$= \frac{6 \times \sqrt{48} \times 10}{3} = 20 \times 6{\cdot}92 = 138{\cdot}4 \text{ cubic feet.}$$

EXAMPLE 3.—*A cone has a base 12" in diameter and is 16" high. What is the cubic content?*

Area of base $= 6^2 \times 3{\cdot}1416.$

Content of cone $= \dfrac{6 \times 6 \times 3{\cdot}1416 \times 16}{3} = 603{\cdot}18$ cubic inches.

Sphere.—To find the cubic content of a sphere, multiply the cube of the diameter by one-sixth of $3{\cdot}1416$, *i.e.*
$$\text{content} = d^3 \times \frac{3{\cdot}1416}{6} = d^3 \times 0{\cdot}5236.$$

EXAMPLE.—*What is the cubic content of a sphere of 6" diameter?*
$6 \times 6 \times 6 \times 0{\cdot}5236 = 113{\cdot}09$ cubic inches.

A ready and accurate method of finding the volume or **cubic content of any irregular solid** of small size is totally to immerse the solid in water, using for the purpose a receptacle, the capacity of which can be easily measured. The volume of water displaced will be equal to the cubic content of the solid.

Questions on Chapter IV.

1. (*a*) What is the difference between the English and the metric system of measurement? (*b*) What is the metric equivalent of 14 in. ? (C. and G. Prel., 1899.)

2. What is the metric equivalent of 4 square feet? (C. and G. Prel., 1900.)

3. Determine the square root of (*a*) 289; (*b*) 3721; (*c*) 69696.

4. Find the length of the diagonal of a square of 12 ft. side.

5. A 20 ft. ladder when in position just reaches to the top of a 19 feet wall. How far is the foot of the ladder from the foot of the wall ?

6. Buildings which are 12 ft., 16 ft., 30 ft., and 43 ft. wide (outside measurement) respectively have central ridges at heights of

106   A MANUAL OF CARPENTRY AND JOINERY.

4 ft., 7 ft., 14 ft., and 20 ft. respectively above the wall levels. Find in each case the length of the common rafters.

7. What is the area in English measurement of a rectangle 5 metres long and 3 metres wide ? (C. and G. Prel., 1904.)

8. What is the area of a triangle having a base 4 metres long and an altitude of 3 metres ? (C. and G. Prel., 1903.)

9. Describe a hexagon within a circle of $\frac{7}{8}$ of an inch radius, and find how many feet superficial that hexagon would represent to a scale of $\frac{3}{4}$ of an inch to 1 ft. (C. and G. Prel., 1902.)

10. A room is 25 ft. 6 in. long, 13 ft. 6 in. wide at one end, and 18 ft. 4 in. at the other. What is its area? (C. and G. Prel., 1901.)

11. (a) What is the area of an octagon having a side 3 ft. long ?
(b) Make an irregular pentagon, and construct an oblong of equal area. (C. and G. Prel., 1899.)

12. Make an irregular heptagon and reduce the same to an oblong of equal area. (C. and G. Prel., 1898.)

13. The chord of a circle is 12 feet; the rise in the segment is 2 feet. Find the radius of the circle by figures. (C. and G. Prel., 1898.)

14. A window is 5 ft. 6 in. wide, and the head rises 10 in. from the springing line; the curve is the segment of a circle. Find the length of the radius by arithmetic. (C. and G. Prel., 1901.)

15. It is required to make a cylindrical framing for a tank which is 5 ft. 9 in. in diameter; the framing is to be 3 in. from the tank and 7 feet high. Find the superficial area of the framing. (C. and G. Prel., 1902.)

16. What is the cubic content of a balk of timber 4 ft. square at one end, and 2 ft. 6 in. square at the other end, and 10 ft. long ? (C. and G. Prel., 1900.)

17. A balk of timber is 20 feet long, 15 inches by 15 inches at one end, and 12 inches by 12 inches at the other. What would be its price at 2s. per foot cube ? (C. and G. Prel., 1897.)

18. Find the cubical content of a hexagonal prism of 10 ft. axis and 2 ft. side. (C. and G. Prel., 1901.)

19. What is the cubic content of a hexagonal prism of 3 ft. edge and 7 ft. long? (C. and G. Prel., 1899.)

20. What is the cubical content of half a regular hexagonal pyramid of 2 feet edge and 5 feet high ? (C. and G. Prel., 1898.)

CHAPTER V.

TOOLS.

General Remarks.—The tools used by the carpenter and joiner are of so varied a character that a special consideration of the manner of using them, and of the means of sharpening and otherwise keeping them in order is necessary. It is of the greatest importance, as all experienced craftsmen know, to have tools of the best material, and to use them with the greatest care, so that they can be relied upon for durability and accuracy. All edged tools should be of evenly tempered steel, so that they will retain for a reasonable time the sharp edge required for use.

Machinery is now extensively used in the preparation of the timber for all kinds of wood work. Besides facilitating working, this renders unnecessary many tools and appliances which were formerly in use.

The Training of the Eye.—One of the first objects of the intelligent workman should be to train his eye to estimate dimensions and to judge whether lines are straight and surfaces are truly plane. This power can only be obtained by careful and conscientious practice.

MEASURING AND TESTING TOOLS.

The **one-, two-** and **three-foot** rule, the *tape* or *chain measure* and *wooden staves* or *rods* of various lengths, are the usual means by which measurements are made. The two-foot rule used by the wood-worker generally has the inches sub-divided into eighths and sixteenths. In work of large dimensions, carefully graduated rods (which can be made by the workman himself) are preferable to either the rule or tape measure, as by their employment more accurate results are obtained. In preparing such a rod of, say, 12 feet in length, it is best to lay two-foot rules end to end (using two rules) instead of using only one rule and marking with a pencil.

The Measurement of Angles.—In the measurement of angles, or irregular surfaces, it is best to divide the surface into triangles, and to measure the sides with the graduated rods mentioned above.

Testing Tools.—Testing tools may be considered under two headings: those used in the workshop in the preparation of all kinds of framing and other benchwork; and those employed on the building or in the erection of any structure. The *straight-edge, winding strips, try-square, sliding bevel, marking gauge*, and *compasses* are amongst the testing tools used in the bench work. The object of these is to test for straightness, size, and accuracy the material employed.

The **straight-edge.**—The best material for short straight-edges is steel. Wooden straight-edges—made from straight-grained wood that does not twist, preferably yellow pine or mahogany—are, however, generally used.

Winding strips are also made of wood that is not likely to twist. They are from 18 to 30 inches long, 2 to 3 inches wide, and about ½ inch thick; they have parallel edges, and are used when "trueing-up" the surface of the wood with the plane.

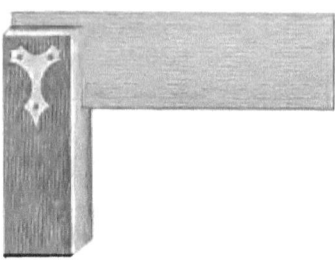

FIG. 166.—Try-square.

The **try-square** (Fig. 166) is used for testing whether surfaces are at right angles to each other, as well as for drawing "square" lines (*i.e.* at right angles) for setting-out purposes.

The **sliding bevel** (Fig. 167) is similar in character to the try-square, but has a loose blade. It is used when surfaces or lines not at right angles to each other are required.

Different kinds of gauges are used: the **marking gauge** (Fig. 168), which has only one marking point, is employed for marking lines parallel to the edge of the wood which is to be worked. A **mortise-gauge** (Fig. 169) has two adjustable marking points, and is used when two parallel lines are required, as in

MEASURING AND TESTING TOOLS.

the setting out of framing with mortise and tenon joints. The **cutting gauge** has a cutting blade instead of a marking point.

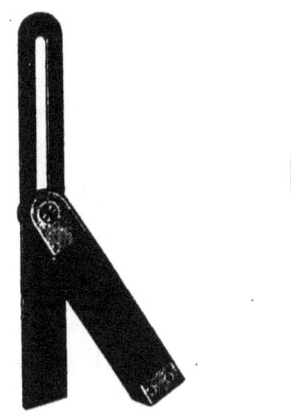

FIG. 167.—Sliding Bevel. FIG. 168.—Marking Gauge. FIG. 169.—Mortise-Gauge.

A **thumb** or **set gauge** can easily be made by the workman when a repetition of similar lines is necessary.

For curved work the **compasses** are necessary. Fig. 170 shows a pair of compasses fitted with a radial arm or wing, of use to connect the two legs to prevent their slipping during use.

FIG. 170.—Compasses.

For larger work a pair of **trammel pins** is needed (Fig. 171). The length of the rod used is determined by the radius of the curves required. A simple though crude substitute for the trammel pins, or compasses, may be made by fixing two bradawls at the ends of a rod of wood.

The testing tools used by the carpenter for fixing framing include (in addition to those above described) the *spirit level*, the *plumb-rule*, *plumb-line*, and *chalk-line*.

The **spirit level** (Fig. 172) consists of a small sealed glass tube containing spirit. It is so made that the enclosed bubble of

FIG. 171.—Trammel Pins.

air occupies a certain position only when the instrument is

Fig. 172.—Spirit Level.

placed horizontally. It is usually mounted in a wooden frame from 8 to 12 inches long, and is generally used in conjunction with a long parallel straight edge, to determine whether surfaces are level.

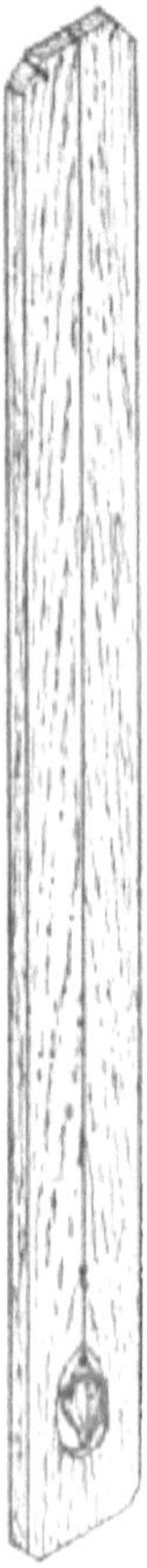

The **plumb-line** (Fig. 173) is of assistance to determine whether walls or upright timbers are vertical. It consists of a string, at the lower end of which is a metal weight, generally lead, called a **plumb-bob** (Fig. 174). For convenience in practice, the string or plumb-line is fastened at the upper end to a parallel straight-edge which is from 4 to 6 feet long and 3 to 5 inches wide. This straight-edge is marked with a centre line down its length, and has a hole cut near the bottom, in which the bob swings. A straight-edge so fitted is called a **plumb-rule**. During the fixing of carpenters' and joiners' work, the spirit level, straight-edge, and plumb-rule, are indispensable testing tools.

The **chalked line** is useful for a variety of purposes. When a long straight line is required between two points and the straight-edge is either not available or is too short, a straight line may be obtained by chalking a length of string, fixing it on two points, pulling tight, and then raising the string and sharply letting go. The line is also used as a guide and aid in many fixing operations.

Fig. 173.—Plumb-rule and -line.

Fig. 174.—Plumb-bob.

Geometrical Tests.—Many simple geometrical principles are

CUTTING TOOLS.

applied in workshop tests. Amongst them may be mentioned the following:

To obtain a right angle, it is only necessary to draw a triangle whose sides are in the proportion of 3, 4, and 5 (p. 88); the angle opposite the longest side is a right angle.

Again, to test whether a piece of framing is truly rectangular (or in workshop phrase "square") measure the lengths of the diagonals; if they are equal, the corners are right angles.

CUTTING TOOLS.

The Saw.—It is very necessary that the blades of all saws be of the best spring steel, of uniform hardness, evenly tempered, and slightly thinner at the back than at the cutting edge.

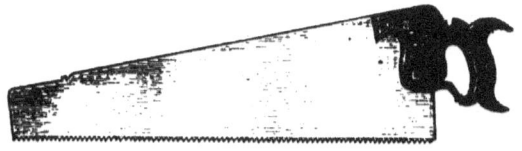

FIG. 175.—Hand Saw.

The **rip saw**, used for cutting with the grain, that is, in the direction of the fibres of the wood; the **cross-cut saw**, for cutting across the grain (at right angles to the fibres); and the **panel saw**, used for fine work, are all of the shape shown in Fig. 175. The chief difference in these saws lies in the shape and size of the teeth on the cutting edge.

FIG. 176.—Rip Saw Teeth.

The **rip saw**, usually 28″ long, has the teeth points from $0''{\cdot}3$ to $0''{\cdot}4$ apart, or about 8 teeth to 3″ of length of blade. The shape of the tooth is shown in Fig. 176. The front of the tooth is at right angles to the cutting edge of the blade.

The **cross-cut** saw is usually 26" long; the teeth are smaller than in the rip saw—about 4 points to the inch—the front of the tooth being inclined at an angle (from 65° to 75°) to

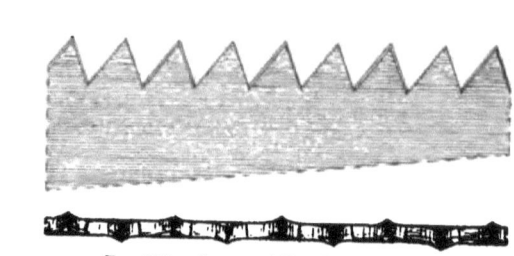

FIG. 177.—Cross-cut Saw Teeth.

the cutting edge, as shown in Fig. 177. Many modifications in the shape of the tooth of the cross-cut saw are to be found, such as the *peg-tooth* (Fig. 178) and the *lance-tooth* (Fig. 179). While these teeth may produce better results, and cut more easily in soft wood, or when used with dry timber, the ordinary tooth

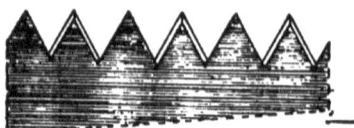

FIG. 178.—Peg-teeth.

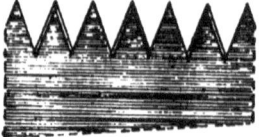

FIG. 179.—Lance-teeth.

(Fig. 177) may be considered the most satisfactory for all-round work.

The **panel saw** has teeth similar in shape to those of the cross-cut saw, but much smaller in size,—from 6 to 8 points to the inch.

The "set" on a saw.—If the teeth were exactly in the plane of the blade, the friction or "binding" against the fibres of the wood would render the free working of the saw almost impossible.

To lessen the friction between the wood and the blade, the points of the teeth are bent slightly outwards, alternately to one side and then to the other, so that the resulting cut is wider than the thickness of the blade and thus gives "clearance" in working. The distance which the points project beyond the

CUTTING TOOLS.

plane of the blade is called the **set**. The amount of set required depends upon the kind of material to be operated upon. The bending (setting) is done either by means of a nail punch and hammer upon a block of hard-wood, or with a special appliance named a "saw-set." Figs. 180 and 181 show two different types of saw-set.

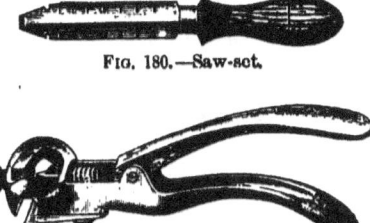

Fig. 180.—Saw-set.

Fig. 181.—Saw-set.

The rip saw requires less set than the cross-cut saw owing to the fibres of the wood being parallel to the direction of the saw cut, while the saw used in the workshop—generally upon dry material—does not require so much set as the saw employed by the carpenter on rough and sometimes unseasoned timber. The less set there is on the saw—providing it will clear—the more easily the saw will work. The set on each side should never exceed half the thickness, so that at the most the width of cut is not more than twice the thickness of the blade.

The **back or tenon saw** (Fig. 182) has a thinner blade than the "hand" saws above described. The blade is 12″ to 16″ long,

 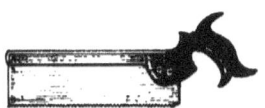

Fig. 182.—Tenon Saw.   Fig. 183.—Dovetail Saw.

3″ to 4″ wide, has about ten tooth-points to the inch, and has the back edge of the blade stiffened by an iron or brass back, the blade being thus kept rigid. The shape of the tooth is intermediate between that of the rip and the cross-cut saws, as the tenon saw is chiefly used for fine bench work, which consists of cutting both with and across the grain, as well as in oblique directions.

The **dovetail saw** (Fig. 183) is similar to the tenon saw, but is of smaller size, and has smaller teeth. Its use is confined to very fine work.

The **bow or turning saw** (Fig. 184) has a thin narrow blade held in tension by a wooden frame and string. It is used for cutting curved surfaces, its narrow blade allowing for the necessary turning movements.

The **compass saw** (Fig. 185), and the **pad saw** (Fig. 186), have narrow tapering blades, and are used for curved surfaces in circumstances where the bow saw would be inapplicable.

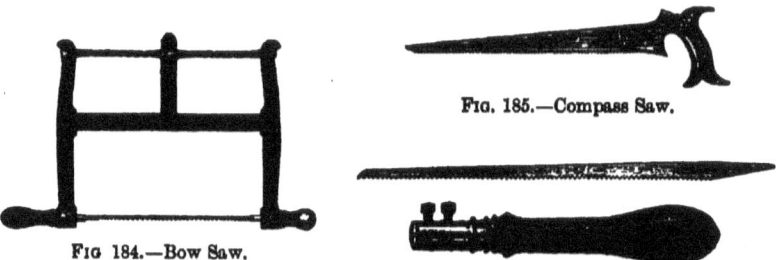

FIG 184.—Bow Saw.

FIG. 185.—Compass Saw.

FIG. 186.—Pad Saw and Handle.

A **two-handled saw** (Fig. 187) for cross-cutting large balks of timber, has a blade from 4 to 7 feet long, 5 to 8 inches wide, with large teeth of shape shown in Fig. 178.

The sharpening of saws.—Saws for hand use are sharpened with triangular files of size varying with the size of the teeth. The ease and accuracy with which a saw cuts depends largely upon the care bestowed on the setting and sharpening. Some

FIG. 187.—Two-handled Cross-cut Saw.

experience is required to obtain satisfactory results. All the teeth should be set evenly, be of uniform size, and have their points in a perfectly regular line. Rough usage of saws often causes them to be strained or buckled. These defects can be remedied by careful hammering. It is very advisable, however, that this process be deputed to the expert, as any unskilled attempt may ruin the tool.

Planes.—A plane is a tool which derives its name from its use in the preparation of plane surfaces.

A wooden plane consists of the following parts—a **rectangular**

CUTTING TOOLS. 115

stock (generally of beech wood by reason of its even grain and freedom from warping tendency), the face or *sole* of which must be accurately plane (true). Fixed by means of a **wedge**, and guided by the stock, is a steel cutter (**plane-iron**) (Fig. 188) which projects slightly beyond the sole, and makes an angle of about 45° with it. When planing cross-grained, or knotty wood, where the fibres of the wood are not parallel to the surface being operated upon, the cutter has a tendency to "pluck up" the grain. This plucking tendency is lessened by a guard called a **back-** or **cap-iron** which is fixed, by means of a screw, to the *face* of the plane-iron. The back-iron is the same width as the plane-iron, and capable of adjustment to different distances from the cutting edge, according to the kind of work and the character of the material. By setting the back-iron very close (*e.g.* $\frac{1}{64}$″) to the cutting edge, the plucking tendency is reduced to a minimum. In addition to this, the back iron stiffens the cutting iron and thereby lessens vibration or "chattering"; it also serves to break the shaving as it enters the mouth of the plane and thus prevents choking.

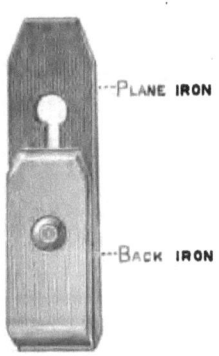

Fig. 188.—Cutting Iron for Wooden Plane.

In planes used for working hard wood it is advisable to have the plane-iron set into the stock at a steeper pitch than for soft wood, usually about 55° to the sole of the plane.

Fig. 189.—Jack Plane.

The constant wear of the sole of a wooden plane necessitates an occasional trueing-up of its surface. The result of this is to increase the size of the mouth, and produce a less effective guiding of the shavings as they are removed.

The **jack plane** (Fig. 189), about 16″ long, the **trying plane**

116   A MANUAL OF CARPENTRY AND JOINERY.

(Fig. 190), 22" long, and the **smoothing plane** (Fig. 191), 9" long are the usual bench planes. Of these the jack plane is used

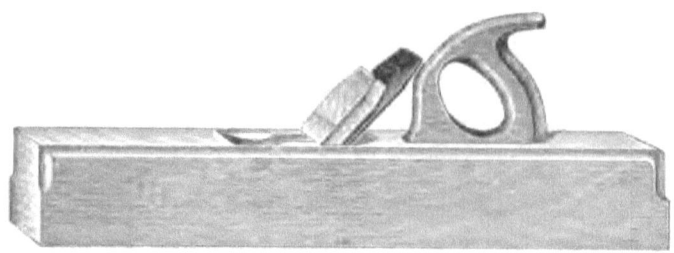

FIG. 190.—Trying Plane.

for roughing off; the trying plane for trueing up; and the smoothing plane is used for finishing the surface.

FIG. 191.—Smoothing Plane.

The accuracy and smoothness of planed surfaces depend upon the condition in which the plane-iron is kept. Plane-irons are from 2" to 2¾" wide, the cutting edge is ground at an angle of from 20° to 25° with the face, and the sharpening angle varies from 25° to 40°. The jack plane-iron should have the cutting edge slightly convex, as shown in Fig. 192; the result of this is that the plane takes off shavings that are thicker in the middle than at the edges,

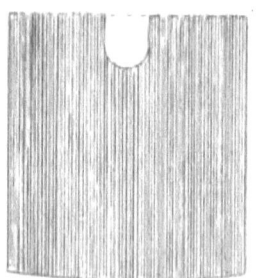

FIG. 192.—Cutting Iron for Jack Plane.

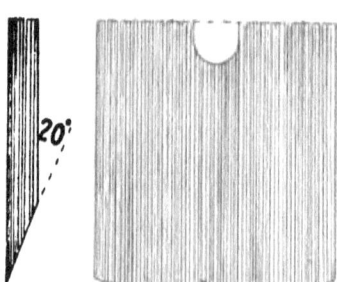

FIG. 193.—Cutting Iron for Trying or Smoothing Plane.

and the corners of the iron do not plough into the wood. The irons of the trying and smoothing planes should be square across, excepting at the corners, which must be slightly rounded

CUTTING TOOLS.

as in Fig. 193. If the cutting edge of these is curved as in the jack plane, the finished planed surface will have a wavy appearance and show in an objectionable manner when the surface is painted or varnished.

Iron planes, or combination iron and wooden planes, are now supplementing wooden planes to a large extent. The advantage of these planes over wooden ones lies in the fact that the sole of the plane does not wear, and therefore does not get "out of truth"; the mouth of the plane consequently always remains the same size. Again, in these planes the cutter is held in position by means of either a screw or a lever, and the adjustment is therefore easier and more accurate.

Fig. 194.—Iron Plane.

The cutters of iron planes are thinner than those used in wooden planes and thus a saving of time in both the grinding and sharpening is effected by their use.

For the best class of work, iron planes are decidedly better and capable of giving more accurate results than wooden planes. Disadvantages lie in the fact that they are heavier, and when used in the multifarious work required by the carpenter when fixing, they will not bear the rough usage to which wooden planes are subjected. Fig. 194 is a typical example of an iron plane.

The **panel plane** is intermediate in size between a jack plane and a smoothing plane.

A **jointing plane** is an extra long trying plane, chiefly used when great accuracy is required, as in jointing the edges of boards which have to be glued together.

Fig. 195.—Compass Plane.

The **compass plane** (Fig. 195) is used for working concave or hollow surfaces, and therefore has, in the direction of its length,

118   A MANUAL OF CARPENTRY AND JOINERY.

a convex sole. Fig. 196 shows an iron adjustable circular plane which is an improvement upon the wooden compass plane, as it can be adjusted readily to any required curve.

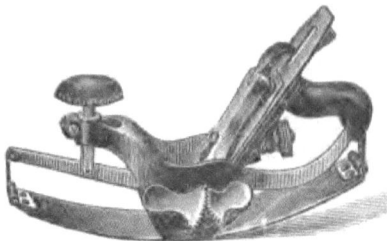

FIG. 196.—Adjustable Compass Plane.

The **rebate plane** (Fig. 197) has a cutter equal in width to the width of the plane. The cutter is placed at an oblique angle with the edge of the sole of the plane, the cutting edge being straight. Its use is confined to the planing of sunk surfaces such as rebates. The length of this plane is about 9" and its width varies from ½" to 2".

A **plough** (Fig. 198) is a plane used for making grooves in the direction of the grain of the wood. This is a somewhat

FIG. 197.—Rebate Plane.

FIG. 198.—Plough.

complicated tool and consists of a stock which holds the cutter, and a movable fence which is secured to the stock by means of two arms. These arms are either screwed or held with wedges. The cutter, which varies in size according to the size of the groove required, is held in position by means of a wedge. A second iron fence, used to govern the depth of groove required, works with an adjustable screw against the stock.

The **bullnose plane** (Fig. 199) is a small plane having the cutter as near the front end of the sole as possible.

Other planes such as the *sash-fillister* (Fig. 200), *chariot* (Fig. 201), *router* (Fig. 202), *bead* (Fig. 203), *ovolo*, *tonguing*, and

CUTTING TOOLS.

grooving and almost innumerable moulding planes, are used for special purposes in hand work.

FIG. 199.—Bullnose Plane.

FIG. 201.—Chariot Plane.

FIG. 200.—Sash Fillister.

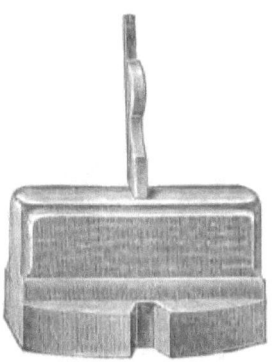

FIG. 202.—Router or "Old Woman's Tooth."

The **spokeshave** (Fig. 204) is a special kind of small hand plane used for finishing curved surfaces.

Sharpening. The cutting edge of the plane-iron or chisel is

FIG. 203.—Bead Plane.

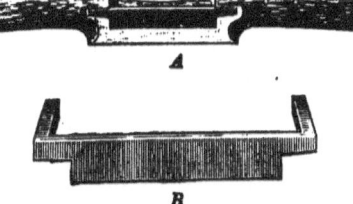

FIG. 204.—*A*, Spokeshave; *B*, Spokeshave Iron.

obtained by first **grinding**, and afterwards rubbing upon an **oil-stone**. The oil-stone is of even texture, should not be too hard, and as its name implies is kept lubricated with oil. "Washita" and "Arkansas" are among the different kinds of

120 A MANUAL OF CARPENTRY AND JOINERY.

oil-stones in general use. The grinding angle of the cutter is from 20° to 25°; the sharpening angle varies from 25° to 40°, becoming slightly greater each time the tool is sharpened.

Small oil-stones called "slips" are used for sharpening the concave (hollow) cutting edges that are found in bead and hand moulding plane cutters, the spokeshave, and other tools with curved cutting edges.

Chisels.—These may be divided into *firmer*, *paring* and *mortising chisels*, and *gouges*. Chisels are made in all sizes from

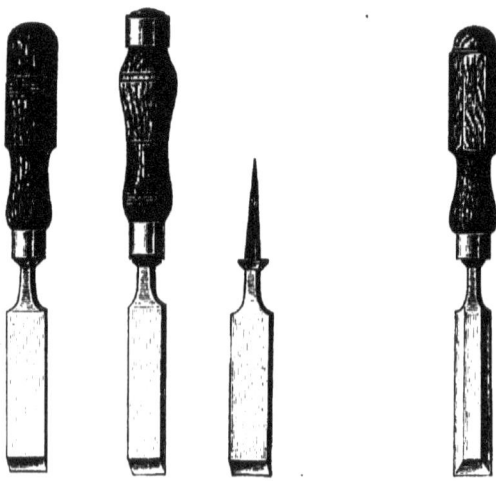

FIG. 205.—Types of Firmer Chisels.   FIG. 206.—Paring Chisel.

one-sixteenth of an inch to 2 inches in width. They consist of a steel blade with the cutting edge at one end, and a "tang," on to which the wooden handle is fitted, at the other end. The **firmer** and **paring** chisels are similar in shape (Figs. 205 and 206), the only difference being that the firmer chisels are a little stronger than the paring chisels to withstand rough usage and the occasional use of the mallet.

Paring chisels often have bevel edges as shown in Fig. 206.

Mortise chisels (Fig. 207) are much stronger than firmer chisels, as they are subjected to more rough usage in the making of mortises.

Gouges (Fig. 208), are chisels with curved cutting edges; the

CUTTING TOOLS.

cutting edge may be ground on the hollow or on the rounded surface. The grinding angle as well as the sharpening angle of chisels are the same as in the plane irons (p. 116).

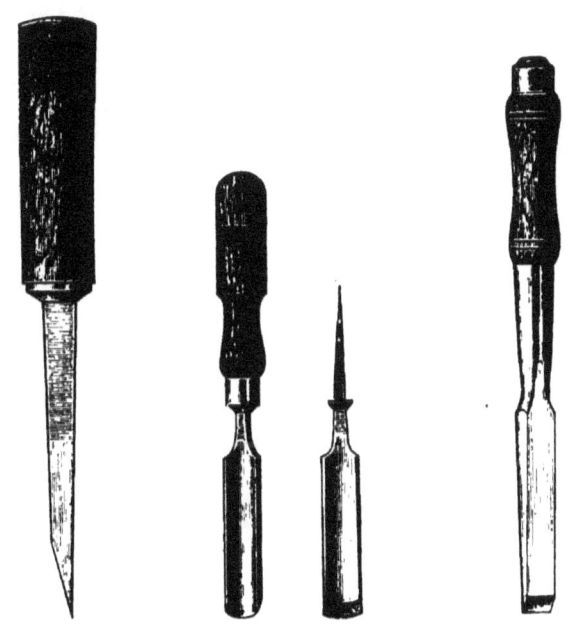

FIG. 207.—Mortise Chisel.   FIG. 208.—Gouge.   FIG. 209.—Socketed Chisel.

The slip is used for sharpening gouges.

Socketed chisels (Fig. 209) instead of having a tang, are provided with a socket, into which the handle fits, at the upper end.

The **handles** are of hard wood: box, beech, and ash being used. A brass ferrule is usually put on the lower end of the chisel handle to prevent it from splitting. Handles of chisels that have to be used for very heavy work with the mallet are often hooped at both ends.

Other cutting tools, such as the *axe*, *adze*—used chiefly by ship-builders—and the *draw-knife* (a tool used by coach-builders), need no detailed description.

BORING TOOLS.

Brad-awl and Gimlet.—The brad-awl and gimlet are two of the simplest kinds of boring tools. The method of their use also illustrates the principle of most boring bits. The brad-awl (Fig. 210) has a wedge-shaped cutter, and requires the exertion of pressure during its use. Care must be exercised to have the cutting edge across the fibres, or it will be liable to split the wood. The gimlet (Fig. 211) has a screw feed, and therefore, instead of a pressure a rotary movement is necessary.

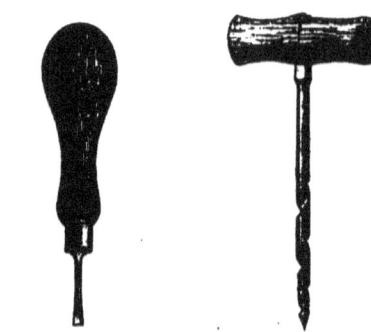

FIG. 210.—Brad-awl.   FIG. 211.—Gimlet.

Brace and Brace-bits.—Boring is, however, generally performed by the **brace**, and **brace-bits**. By means of the brace, the principle of the lever is applied to exert an increased force

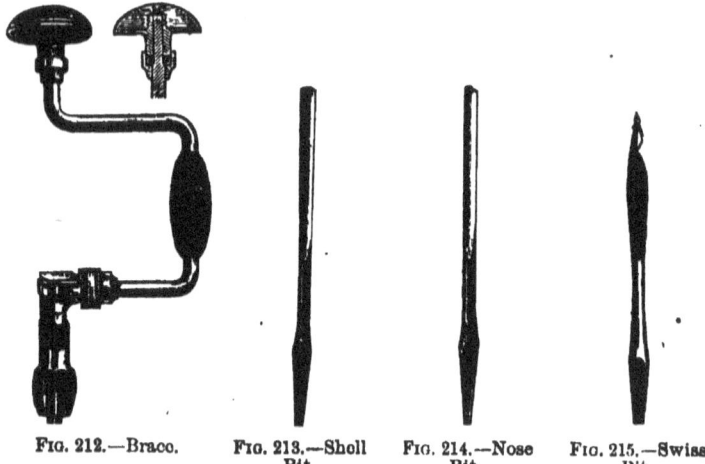

FIG. 212.—Brace.   FIG. 213.—Shell Bit.   FIG. 214.—Nose Bit.   FIG. 215.—Swiss Bit.

whereby the brace bit is easily forced into the wood. Many different types of brace are in use; perhaps one of the best is the ratchet brace (Fig. 212) in which the turning movement

BORING TOOLS. 123

may be effected by a rack. This brace enables boring to be done in corners, and other awkward positions where the ordinary circular movement of a brace could not be applied.

The **shell** (Fig. 213) and **nose bits** (Fig. 214) are very similar; in the latter, a projecting nose assists in clearing the hole. The nose-bit is specially suitable for boring holes 2" to 3" deep in the direction of the grain of the wood. The **Swiss-bit** (Fig. 215) has a spiral point. These three bits are chiefly used for boring for nails and screws; their diameters are from $\frac{1}{16}$" to $\frac{1}{2}$".

Fig. 216.—Centre Bits.   Fig. 217.—Auger or twisted Bit.

The **centre bit** (Fig. 216) has three separate cutting parts. Its boring diameter varies from $\frac{1}{8}$" to $1\frac{1}{2}$". It is a clean-cutting tool, but requires pressure during the operation, and if the holes to be bored are more than 2" deep it is liable to become choked unless the accumulating chips are frequently removed.

The **auger bit** (Fig. 217) exists in many forms. Its helical shape renders it suitable for most work, except in very hard woods. Its central guide point has a spiral screw feed; this renders boring across the grain possible with very little pressure. When boring with an auger bit in the direction of the grain of the wood, pressure is required, as the screw feed alone is not

124 A MANUAL OF CARPENTRY AND JOINERY.

strong enough to draw the bit into the wood. The "Forstner" bit (Fig. 218) is useful for flat bottom or angular boring.

Expanding brace bits (Fig. 219) are also to be obtained. These

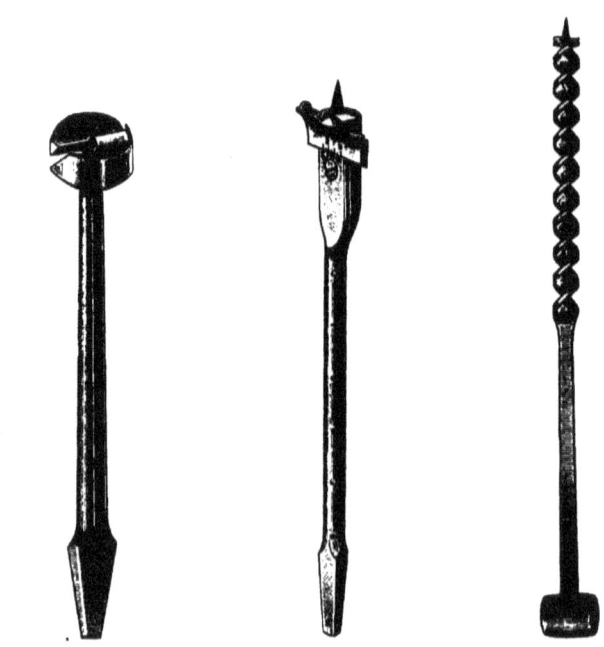

FIG. 218.—Forstner Bit. FIG. 219.—Expansion Brace-bit. FIG. 220.—Auger Bit.

are capable of adjustment within certain dimensions, and prove very useful tools.

Other brace bits, such as the *screw driver bit, countersink bit* (for iron and wood), *rimers*, etc., are also used. For heavy work, *auger* bits with long stems are used (Fig. 220); they are provided with wooden handles for turning purposes.

VICES AND CRAMPS.

Bench Vice.—The woodworker's bench is usually provided with a vice for holding the material being worked. This vice is fixed against the side of the bench at the left hand end. Many different kinds of vice are in general use, some of these being

VICES AND CRAMPS.

of antiquated and primitive character. Others, of more recent invention, are valuable time-saving appliances. The wooden screw, which is about 3″ in diameter, is one of the old type. A steel threaded screw is sometimes used instead of the wooden screw. In either case, the screw passes through the wooden jaw of the vice. Many patent vices are now on the market. Some of these are called "instantaneous-grip," because they are fitted with a ratchet that allows the jaw of the vice to be drawn out; when the spring is released the screw comes into action. It is reasonable to expect that a good bench-vice will in a short space of time repay its cost as compared with that of the old-fashioned wooden screw-vices that are still in use in some workshops.

FIG 221.—Floor Cramp.

Cramps.—Cramps, as the name implies, are used for holding together framing, such as sashes, doors,

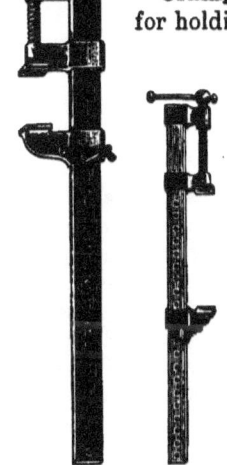

FIG. 222.   FIG. 223.
Types of Sash Cramps.

FIG. 224.—Floor Cramp.

etc.; for cramping floor boards; for holding down work on the bench; and for many other purposes. Figs. 222 and 223 show two kinds of *sash cramp*. Each consists of a steel bar with an adjustable shoe at one end, and a jaw attached to a screw-threaded shaft for tightening up as required. Sash cramps are made in a large variety of sizes and strengths to suit their different applications in the fixing together of structures. Figs. 221 and 224 show two types of *floor cramp*. This

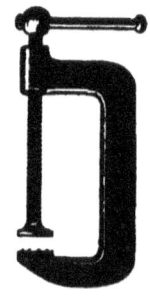

FIG. 225.—G-Cramp.

FIG. 226.—Bench Holdfast.

appliance is so constructed that it will clip on the edge of the floor joist, and force the boards into position. Other cramps, such as the *G-cramp* (Fig. 225) and the *bench holdfast* (Fig. 226) are too well known to require description.

SUMMARY.

Tools should not only be of the best materials, but should be kept constantly in good order.

The commonest **measuring** tools are the *rule*, *tape* or *chain measure*, and *graduated rods*. For testing the straightness and accuracy of work, the *straight edge*, *try square*, *sliding bevel*, *gauges*, *compasses*, *spirit-level*, *plumb rule*, *chalked line*, etc., are used.

Among **cutting** tools are the various types of *saws*, *planes*, and *chisels*. Saws require the teeth to be "set" to obtain clearance in cutting. They are sharpened with a triangular file. Planes and chisels are first ground to an angle of 20° to 25°, and afterwards repeatedly sharpened upon the oil-stone, the cutting angle varying from 25° to 40°.

Boring tools include the *brad-awl*, *gimlet*, *brace* and *brace bits*, and *auger*. There are many types of brace bit.

For holding in position the material which is being worked, and as an aid in putting together framed structures, **vices** and **cramps** are indispensable.

Questions on Chapter V.

1. Make sketches of a try-square, a sliding bevel, and a mortise gauge. State for what each of these tools is used.

2. Give a description of the teeth of a rip saw, and of a dovetail saw, and state the reason for their shapes. Make a sketch of a plough, and state the purposes for which it may be used. (C. and G. Ord., 1900.)

3. What is meant by the set on a saw? What will be the effect of using a saw without set? Show by sketches the amount of set required for (a) a hand cross-cut saw when cutting rough unseasoned timber; (b) a rip saw for cutting dry stuff.

4. Make sketches, and describe the following tools and their uses: tenon saw, spokeshave, and smoothing plane. (C. and G. Prel., 1900.)

5. (a) Make a sketch of a jack plane. What is the object of the cap or back iron? (b) Describe the sharpening of a centre bit, and its cutting action. (C. and G. Prel., 1899.)

6. Make sketches and describe the uses of the following tools:
  (1) Trying plane.
  (2) Smoothing plane.
  (3) Beads.
State why (2) is sometimes fitted with an iron face, and how (3) are used and sharpened. (C. and G. Prel., 1902.)

7. Show by sketches the cutting edge of (a) a jack plane iron, (b) a smoothing plane iron, (c) a firmer chisel. State approximately the grinding and the sharpening angle.

8. Describe fully with sketches the cutting edges of the following tools, and explain the proper method of sharpening each: firmer chisel, mortising chisel, gouge, one kind of carving tool, trying plane, rebate plane, rip saw, spokeshave. (C. and G. Ord., 1895.)

9. State for what purposes the following tools are used: firmer chisel, back saw, jack plane, router, side fillister, chariot plane. (C. and G. Ord., 1897.)

10. State for what purposes the following tools are used: chisel, tenon or back saw, gouge, jack plane, smoothing plane, trying plane, rebate plane, old woman's tooth, plough, sash fillister, trammel. (C. and G. Ord., 1893.)

11. Describe the following tools and their uses. Give sketches:
  (1) Brace and different forms of bits.
  (2) Bow saw.
  (3) Firmer chisels and gouges. (C. and G. Prel., 1901.)

12. Describe the form and use of ten ordinary kinds of bit for use with a hand brace. (C. and G. Ord., 1896.)

13. Give a short description of six ordinary tools used by the carpenter and joiner. (C. and G. Prel., 1897.)

14. State the difference between a sash cramp and a floor cramp. Make a sketch of each kind.

15. Describe the tools in your possession, their uses, and the special advantages of any not in every-day use. (C. and G. Hon., 1895.)

CHAPTER VI.

WOODWORKING MACHINERY.

General.—The use of woodworking machinery is now so extensive and so general that many of the hand tools required by the craftsman of thirty years ago have become obsolete, and are unknown to many workmen of the present day. The demand for labour-saving appliances has led to the making of machines which are capable of performing almost every operation necessary in woodworking. Sawing by reciprocal frame, by circular and by band saws; planing—either one, two, or all four sides at the same time; moulding in almost every conceivable design, in either straight or curved work; mortising, tenoning, dovetailing, trenching, even sandpapering, as well as box nailing, are all operations capable of being performed with machinery at the present time. Indeed, machines called "general joiners" are to be obtained which are capable of several different operations.

The very great variety of woodworking machinery prevents more than a casual reference to some of the most important types.

SAWING.

Vertical Log Frame.—The vertical log frame saw is a very heavy machine, capable of sawing logs up to 50″ in diameter. It has a movable carriage which carries the material to be sawn, and is provided with a feed motion. This carriage works through a strong iron frame into which the saws are fixed. The saws work with a reciprocal—up and down—motion. Many of these machines are capable of holding as many as forty saws at once, and thus of converting the log into this number of boards at one feed. Of course, a frame with a large number of saws requires a considerable amount of driving power, and entails a slow feed; still, these are compensated for by the advantage of converting a large log at one operation. Fig. 227

FIG. 227.—Vertical Log Frame Saw.

shows a type of vertical log frame said to be *underdriven*; that is, the crank which works the saws, and consequently all the driving part of the machine, is below the saws and the carriage. Fig. 228 shows a similar machine having the driving gear at the top.

Deal Frame.—A much lighter machine of a similar type to the vertical log frame, known as a *deal frame*, is used for cutting deals and planks into thinner boards. The use of this machine is considered more economical than that of the circular saw, both as regards production and economy of material when the timber is being cut into several boards; for, in the first place, a number

Fig. 228.—Vertical Log Frame Saw.

of saws work together, and, secondly, the saws, being in tension, are thinner than the average circular saw, and thus entail less waste of wood. Many different types of this machine exist, and Figs. 229 and 230 are good examples. The main feature is that a strong frame carries a number of vertical saws which have a reciprocal motion. Fig. 229 illustrates a *double deal frame*—that is, one in which two deals can be sawn at the same time,

132   A MANUAL OF CARPENTRY AND JOINERY.

Fig. 230 shows a *single deal frame*, a machine which only allows of one deal being passed through the machine at once. The feed of these machines—that is, the means adopted for drawing the

FIG. 229.—Double Deal Frame Saw.

material into the machine—is obtained by geared rollers which grip the material to be sawn and draw it into the machine.

Horizontal Log Frame.—The horizontal log frame consists of a frame holding a reciprocating saw which works to and fro in a horizontal direction. Occasionally two saws are used at the same time. This machine is also provided with a movable carriage, upon which the log to be cut is placed. This carriage

SAWING.   133

is fitted with a feed motion capable of being regulated to suit the travelling speed of the material towards the saw. Figs. 231 and 232 illustrate this class of machine. In Fig. 232 two saws are shown in position. An advantage claimed for this machine over the vertical type is that it always allows of the log being examined during the cutting, and therefore of regulating the

FIG. 230. Single Deal Frame Saw.

thickness of each board according to the quality of the timber. It is well known that defects which would not impair the value of planks three inches thick might prove detrimental in boards under one inch in thickness, especially when sawing up choice hardwood logs for panels, furniture, etc.

Cross-cut Saw.—A reciprocating cross-cut saw used for cross-cutting large logs and balks of timber is illustrated in Fig. 233. It is specially adapted for use in the timber yard, or engineering

Fig. 231.—Horizontal Log Frame Saw.

Fig. 232.—Horizontal Log Frame Saw.

works, where much cross-cutting is done. The saw has a reciprocating motion and cuts with the inward stroke.

FIG. 233.—Reciprocating Cross-cut Saw.

Band Saws.—Band saws are endless saws running on two (sometimes three) pulleys, placed some distance apart, which

FIG. 234.—Heavy Band Saw for cutting Logs and Balks.

hold the saw in tension. Fig. 234 shows a very strong type of band saw and frame used for the conversion of heavy balks and logs of timber. This illustration shows the saw cutting in a vertical position, the log being carried upon a movable carriage. In some of these machines the pulleys are fixed on either side of the machine, so that the saw runs horizontally and cuts horizontal slices off the top of the log. The saws used in this class of machine are from 6" to 8" in width. As they run at a very rapid rate and are continuously cutting they get through the work more quickly than the log frame saw. Fig. 235

FIG. 235.—Band Saw with Geared Roller Feed.

illustrates a band saw and frame, fitted with a geared roller feed; it is used for sawing deals into boards.

Lighter band saws are very largely used for cutting curved work of almost every conceivable design; the saws vary considerably in width and may be as narrow as one-eighth of an inch. Such band saws have heavy cast-iron frames to carry the pulleys around which the saw runs. Figs. 236 and 237 show two types, one of which is provided with a motor for driving

Fig. 236.—Band Saw with Motor.

Fig. 237.—Band Saw.

purposes. The feeding of the material in these saws is done by hand, and in most cases the table, which is from 3 to 4 feet square, is capable of being tilted.

FIG. 238.—Circular Saw Shaft and Bearings.

Circular Saws.—Circular saws are more extensively used than any others for the mass of ordinary sawing. The general arrangement is to have a heavy cast iron frame, the top (table) of which is smooth and perfectly plane, and a short shaft (as

FIG. 239.—Circular Saw Bench.

illustrated separately in Fig. 238) which runs in bearings underneath the table. The circular saw is fixed upon this shaft and runs in a slot in the table. In most cases either the shaft carrying the saw, or the top of the table, is constructed so that it can be adjusted—raised and lowered. This allows of accurate setting for any depth of saw cut that may be required, and is of

SAWING.

the greatest importance for general work. The size of the frame is proportionate to the size of the saw used and the character of the work to be executed. Circular saws vary in size from 7 feet to a few inches in diameter. With the larger saws the frames require to be very heavy.

As the amount of power required for driving a circular saw is considerable and increases with an increase in the size of the saw, it is always advisable to use the smallest size of saw that is capable of performing the work required.

FIG. 240.—Circular Saw Bench with Radial Arm Roller Feed.

The speed at which saws are driven varies with the size of the saw; the circumferential velocity should not be less than 9000 feet per minute. For example, a circular saw of 12 inches in diameter should make about 3000 revolutions per minute.

On the top of the table is arranged a movable fence against which the timber slides when the machine is being used for dimension sawing. The face of this fence, which is from two to three feet long, is parallel to the blade of the saw, and the fence is adjustable, generally by means of a screw and hand wheel. This is shown in Fig. 239, which illustrates a type of circular saw bench in general use. The fence is arranged generally so

140 A MANUAL OF CARPENTRY AND JOINERY.

that it can be tilted for sawing the edges of timber at other than right angles. In the heavier machines the fence as well as the top of the table are often provided with rollers pro-

FIG. 241.—Circular Saw Bench with Rope Feed.

jecting slightly beyond the surface to lessen the friction. The fence is often provided with an appliance in the shape of a lever and weights, whereby the material is held against the fence during the sawing, as shown in Fig. 240.

FIG. 242.—Circular Saw Bench with Movable Table.

In the conversion of heavy material with circular saws, some mechanical feeding arrangement is necessary. Several different devices are in use; among these is a radial arm carrying fluted rollers which are driven with chain gear (Fig. 240); a rope or chain drag as shown in Fig. 241, which also shows loose carriages for supporting the ends of long timbers; while in

SAWING. 141

some of the heavier machines the table is of considerable length and runs upon rollers as illustrated in Fig. 242.

Saw Teeth.—In both frame and circular saws, the saws used vary in thickness according to their size and the nature of the material being operated upon. As the frame saws are held in tension they are usually thinner than the larger circular saws.

The size and shape of the teeth of saws used in machine work are also regulated by the kind of material to be cut and

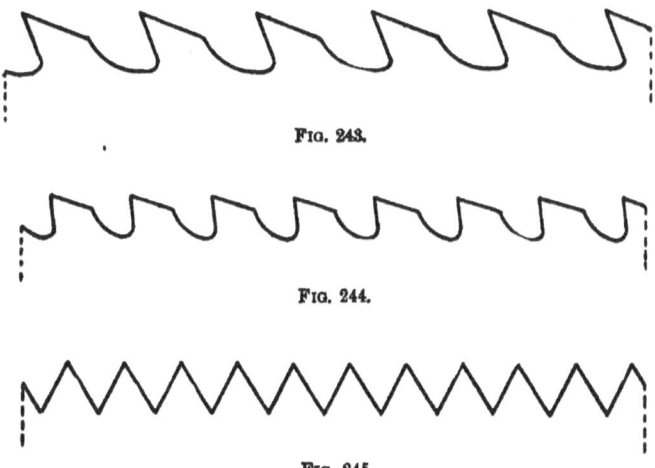

FIG. 243.

FIG. 244.

FIG. 245.

Types of Saw Teeth.

the manner in which it has to be cut. The larger the teeth, the rougher are the cut surfaces, especially if any attempt is made to force the work through the machine. Fig. 243 shows a typical shape of tooth used for cutting soft wood such as pine and deal. For hard wood such as oak, birch, walnut, etc., a tooth with less hook, as shown in Fig. 244, is more suitable; while for cross-cutting, the shape of the tooth more nearly approaches that of the hand saw (Fig. 245). Many variations from these shapes are in common use, and are the subject of considerable differences of opinion among experts.

As explained in the remarks upon hand saws (Chap. V.), the teeth of saws require to be "set" in order to give the necessary clearance in cutting. This is done either with the pene hammer and block, or with the saw-set. There are one or two types of circular saw however, that do not require setting. The **swage saw** is a type of circular saw which is used for sawing very thin boards. This saw is much thicker at the centre than at the circumference, and has one face of the saw perfectly true.

FIG. 246.—Type of Saw Sharpening Machine.

The result is that the saw-cut is very thin, and consequently the waste of material is very little, and the clearance is effected by the giving way of the thin board which is cut off. Such a saw does not require any set; it cannot be used for cutting thick pieces of timber.

Another type of circular saw that does not require setting is the **hollow-ground saw**, a saw which is chiefly used for crosscutting purposes and for other special work. This saw is thicker at the circumference than at the centre.

SAWING. 143

The teeth of frame and circular saws are sharpened either with the file or with the emery wheel. When sharpened with the file, the teeth require periodically gulleting (re-cutting to the proper shape), as the point only of the tooth is filed during sharpening. When the emery wheel is used, the size of the teeth is kept constant, and no gulleting is necessary. Figs. 246

FIG. 247. – Type of Saw Sharpening Machine.

to 248 show three different types of emery wheel used for saw sharpening. The emery wheel is also used for sharpening the cutters of planing and moulding machines.

Large circular saws require considerable skill in their manipulation in order to obtain the best results. The "packing" of a circular saw in the slot in which it works is a necessary operation, and requires great care and judgment. The packing consists of hempen cord folded around a piece of wood, and must be exactly of the required thickness to prevent any straining of the saw. Frequent oiling of the packing also serves as a lubricant to the saw.

FIG. 248.—Type of Saw Sharpening Machine.

PLANING MACHINES.

Planing machines are used to convert the sawn material into the exact sizes required, and to make the surfaces smooth and true. To attain this result, steel cutters are mounted in strong cast iron frames, either as stationary cutters, or so that they revolve at a very rapid rate. The revolving cutters are mounted upon square or specially shaped steel blocks, which are either part of the shaft itself or are fitted accurately upon the shaft. The cutters must be secured firmly with bolts, and arranged so that they accurately balance each other, as they revolve at a very rapid rate, and exert a considerable centrifugal force. It is very essential that the bearings of such machines be of the best material, and that they be kept lubricated constantly.

Surface Planer.—The simplest kind of planing machine (Fig. 249) is one that has cutters bolted upon a revolving spindle, and projecting slightly above the top surface of the table. The speed of this shaft is from 3000 to 4000 revolutions per minute, and the material is slid along the top of the table until it is brought in contact with the cutters. Such a machine is called a **surface planer**; it has two cutters varying from 12 to 18 inches long, which balance each other, and are secured with

FIG. 249.—Surface Planer.

bolts to the shaft. In some machines these cutters are straight, and work at right angles to the edge of the table; in others the cutters are so arranged on the block that they have a helical cutting action. In Fig. 249 the top of the table is adjustable by means of the inclined slides, and is regulated with the hand screws to govern the thickness of the shaving to be taken off. In some machines the shaft carrying the cutters is adjustable for the same purpose. A movable fence which can, if necessary, be tilted at other than a right angle, is arranged on the top of the table, and by its aid surfaces either at right angles to each other, or at any other angle (greater than a right angle), can be readily planed. Although this machine is perhaps the most effective for surface planing, and is useful for rebating and chamfering, it is not economical when used for large quantities of material requiring to be finished of exactly the same size. The feeding of such a machine is generally done by hand.

Panel Planer.—A heavier machine named a **panel planer** has revolving cutters capable of taking a width of 30", and working in a heavy cast iron frame. This machine has a mechanical feed arrangement in the shape of fluted rollers which are fixed almost directly above the cutters, and are geared to regulate the speed of the feed.

Thicknessing Machines.—Fig. 250 shows a machine having superposed tables, one of which is placed below the cutter

FIG. 250.—Surface Planer and Thicknessing Machine.

block and one above it. The former is used for carrying the timber to be planed to a definite thickness, and can be raised or lowered to suit the thickness required. The timber is fed under the cutter block by means of feed rollers placed before and behind the cutter block. The upper table is used for surface planing, and is fed by hand. It is capable of taking material up to 24" in width and 6" in thickness.

Figs. 251 and 252 show two types of a heavier and more complicated machine, which is capable of planing all four sides of the same piece at one operation. The cutters that plane the edges are mounted on vertical spindles. Such machines are provided with gear-driven fluted rollers, which draw the material into the machine and force it through. This class of machine will take in material up to 24" by 6", and is used

PLANING MACHINES.

FIG. 251.—Planing Machine.

FIG. 252.—Planing and Moulding Machine.

extensively for preparing floor and match boards with either square, grooved and tongued, or rebated edges; and skirting boards, etc.

Many of these machines have stationary cutters fixed in the machine; these produce a better finished surface than the revolving cutters. This is especially the case with machines constantly used in the preparation of floor and match boarding. Such machines are capable of producing this class of work at the rate of from 80 to 100 feet per minute.

Moulding Machines.—Moulding machines are planing machines in which the cutters are shaped so that the planed

FIG. 258.—Vertical Spindle Circular Moulding Machine.

material passing through them is of ornamental design. The shape and design of the moulding produced is only limited by the impossibility of preparing "undercut" mouldings by this means. It is often advisable, in order to save material, that the timber used for mouldings should be sawn to other than rectangular shape, and, also for economical reasons, it is often desirable to build up large mouldings by preparing them in two or more separate pieces. Many such machines (Fig. 252) are made with the top cutters carried upon a canting spindle. This allows of the cutters being fixed upon the blocks, so that they do not have an unnecessary leverage or projection from the block.

A **vertical spindle** moulding machine consists of a stand or

PLANING MACHINES. 149

Fig. 254.—Circular Moulding, Trenching, Housing, etc., Machine.

Fig. 255.—Tenoning Machine.

150 A MANUAL OF CARPENTRY AND JOINERY.

table, upon which is arranged a vertical shaft which carries the cutters. With such machines the material requires to be previously planed to the required size, and only one surface can be moulded at one time. An advantage of this class of machine is that curved surfaces of almost any radii can be treated as easily as straight ones. Such machines are, as a rule, hand fed, and have a reversible motion to suit the grain of the wood. Fig. 253

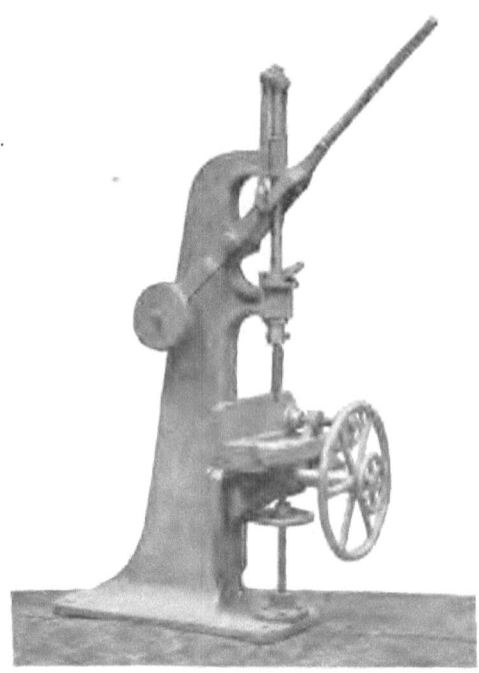

FIG. 256.—Lever Mortising Machine.

is an illustration of this class of machine. Fig. 254 shows a machine that can be used for either moulding—straight or circular—housing, trenching, therming, recessing, etc. It is specially applicable to such work as the trenching of the stringboards of stairs, the preparation of raised panels, of rectangular or polygonal shaped stair-balusters, and other similar work.

Tenoning Machines.—As most framing is held together with mortise and tenon joints, both tenoning and mortising machines are largely used. The tenoning machine (Fig. 255) consists of a frame which holds two sets of cutters working opposite each other, and capable of adjustment to suit varying thicknesses of tenons. The cutters are mounted on blocks, so that they have a helical-cutting action. Additional small cutters are also fixed upon the blocks which cut through the fibres at the shoulders. The table upon which the material is held by means of a lever is provided with a lateral motion, and is fitted with guides.

FIG. 257.—Mortising and Boring Machine.

A **Mortising Machine** is used for making rectangular holes (mortises) in framing. Fig. 256 shows a type of hand mortising machine, in which a strong chisel is given a reciprocal—up and down—motion by means of the lever. The table is fitted with a hand wheel for holding the material, and works in slides which allow both a longitudinal and a lateral movement. Fig. 257 shows another machine, which is fitted with boring apparatus in addition to the mortise chisel. Fig. 258 shows a power mortising machine, where the motion of the chisel is obtained by means of a crank. Boring apparatus is also fitted to this machine.

152 A MANUAL OF CARPENTRY AND JOINERY.

Another type of power mortising machine is shown in Fig. 259. This consists of an endless link chain of cutters which has a continuous motion. The cutters are brought down to the work, which is fastened upon the table, by means of a foot lever. Fig. 260 shows a boring and slot-mortising machine, in which the boring bit works in a horizontal position. An examination

FIG. 258.—Power Mortising Machine.

of the illustration will show the various movements of which this machine is capable.

Combination Machines.—A class of machine very suitable for small workshops where a variety of work—but not sufficient in quantity to warrant separate machines for each kind of work—is executed, is known as a **general joiner**. Figs. 261 and 262 show two different views of such a machine. It is capable of dimension sawing to 6" deep, surface planing to 12" wide, thicknessing "small stuff," variety moulding, tenoning, boring, and

Fig. 259.—Chain Cutter Mortising Machine.

Fig. 260.—Boring and Slot Mortising Machine.

slot mortising. The circular saw table is held in slides against the stand, and is provided with a screw and hand wheel for raising and lowering. The table is fitted with loose plates, so that upon their removal it can be lowered beneath the spindle or shaft which carries the saw. This shaft is so arranged that the saw can be taken off, and either cutter block and cutters for thickness planing, moulding cutters and block for moulding, or tenoning block for cutting one side only of a tenon, can be

FIG. 261.—Combination Machine (General Joiner).

fixed. A fluted roller feed is fixed on the bench, and springs and guides are used for thicknessing or moulding, while a special apparatus is used for cutting tenons. Appliances are also supplied to act as guides in cross-cutting.

The surface planer has the cutters fixed by bolts upon the shaft that carries the saw, and the table of this is raised and lowered upon inclined slides by hand wheels. It is provided with a movable fence which can be set at any angle (greater than a right angle) with the surface of the table. By using this fence, and lowering the front table, "rebating" of any reasonable dimensions can be done. The left hand end of the

GENERAL JOINER.

FIG. 262.—General Joiner.

FIG. 263.—General Joiner.

spindle is drilled and provided with auger bits for boring. Another table having a raising and lowering movement, and both a longitudinal and transverse movement, holds the material to be bored. Special bits are provided whereby slot mortises with circular ends can be made.

Another type of general joiner is illustrated in Fig. 263. The saw spindle in this machine is capable of being raised and lowered, and the machine will carry a saw of any size up to 20" in diameter, and cutting 7" deep. Tenons can be cut by placing two equal-sized saws upon the spindle at the same time, and having a washer between them to gauge the thickness of the tenon. The shoulders of the tenons are cut by two small circular saws carried on vertical adjustable spindles which can also be arranged for carrying cutter blocks and cutters for circular moulding, or they can be removed easily when not in use. The planing is done with revolving cutters; the machine will take in material up to 11" wide and 4" thick; it can be used for moulding; it is provided with a rising and falling table for thicknessing, and it has a self-acting roller feed. Boring and mortising appliances are also fitted as shown, a table being provided to hold the material being operated upon.

Summary.

Handwork in carpentry and joinery has been largely superseded by the use of machinery.

Sawing is done with: the *log frame saw*, which is arranged to cut either horizontally or vertically; *band saws* for cutting curved surfaces; and *circular saws* for the mass of ordinary work. The saws are best *sharpened* with the emery wheel.

Planing machines are classed as *surface planers*, *thicknessing machines*, and *moulding machines*. They are provided usually with revolving cutters, and are self-feeding.

Among other useful wood-working machines are the *tenoning* and *mortising* machines and the *general joiner*.

Questions on Chapter VI.

1. Compare the advantages and disadvantages of using a vertical and a horizontal log frame saw in the conversion of logs into boards.

2. Describe the different types of band saw, and state the purposes for which each type is most suitable.

QUESTIONS ON CHAPTER VI.

3. What is the advantage claimed for the band saw over the log frame saw in the cutting of logs into planks?

4. Make a sketch of the ordinary type of circular saw bench. What are the most important points to examine when selecting such a machine?

5. Describe the special differences to be found in the feeding arrangements of different types of circular saw bench.

6. What should be the speed of the shaft carrying a circular saw when the diameter of the saw is (a) 15 inches; (b) 3 feet?

7. Make sketches showing the shape of the teeth of circular saws to be used when cutting (a) softwood, in the direction of the grain; (b) hardwood, in the direction of the grain; (c) softwood, across the grain. Describe how the teeth are sharpened.

8. What is meant by a "surface planer"? What disadvantages has this machine when compared with other types of planing machine?

9. Describe the general arrangement of the cutters and the feeding apparatus of a planing or moulding machine suitable for use in the preparation of floor boards, skirting boards, etc.

10. Describe the construction, and the general working, of a vertical moulding machine. State the special advantages claimed for this machine.

11. Describe the different types of hand and power mortising machine.

12. Describe briefly the construction, and fully the uses of, what you consider the most valuable machine in a joiner's shop. (C. and G. Hon., 1897.)

13. Give the names and uses of any machines used for saving labour in a joiner's shop with which you are acquainted, and describe fully the one you consider the most valuable. (C. and G. Hon., 1893.)

14. Describe the construction and all the different uses of a general joiner, and state how many men can work at it at the same time; *or*,

Describe the construction and uses of a planing machine and of a spindle machine. N.B. *One alternative half of this question only to be taken.* (C. and G. Hon., 1894.)

CHAPTER VII.

JOINTS AND FASTENINGS.

One of the most important duties of the carpenter and joiner is the fitting together of timber in such a manner that the completed structure may have the greatest possible strength, and be as little liable to shrinkage as the nature of the materials permit. The methods used vary considerably, but they fall naturally into groups according to the underlying principles of construction. When the connection is effected entirely by means of the timbers fitted together, it is called a **joint**. Most commonly, however, the joint is strengthened and secured by **fastenings**, such as *iron dogs, bolts, iron straps, coach-screws, keys, wedges, wooden pins, screws, nails, paint, glue,* etc.

Principles Governing the Construction of Joints.—The principles governing the construction of joints have been laid down by Professor Rankine[1] as follows:

I. To cut the joints and arrange the fastenings so as to weaken the pieces of timber that they connect as little as possible.

II. To place each abutting surface in a joint as nearly as possible perpendicular to the pressure which it has to transmit.

III. To proportion the area of each abutting surface to the pressure which it has to bear, so that the timber may be safe against injury under the heaviest load which occurs in practice; and to form and fit every pair of surfaces accurately, in order to distribute the stress uniformly.

IV. To proportion the fastenings, so that they may be of equal strength with the pieces which they connect.

---

[1] *A Manual of Civil Engineering*, by Prof. Rankine. (C. Griffin & Co.)

JOINTS AND FASTENINGS.

V. To place the fastenings in each piece of timber so that there shall be sufficient resistance to the giving way of the joint by the fastenings shearing or crushing their way through the timber.

In nearly all cases simple joints are more effective than complicated ones. The latter are not only difficult to fit, but are very liable to be affected by the shrinkage of the timber. As fully explained in Chap. I., timber shrinks more in a direction tangential to the annual rings that radially, while in the direction of the length the shrinkage is so small as to be negligible.

Classification of Joints.—Joints may be classified in a general way as follows :

I. Those used (chiefly in the carpenter's heavier work) for the lengthening of beams and other timbers. These differ in arrangement according to the stresses (p. 160) to which they are to be subjected; they include *lapped, halved, fished,* and *scarfed.*

II. Those used for joining timbers not in the same straight line. This class embraces a very wide range of joints, including those used in such heavy carpentry structures as gantries, temporary scaffolding, roof and other trusses and floors, as well as the joints of door and window-sash construction, panelled framing, drawer construction, etc. These joints include *lap, mortise and tenon, bridled, notched, cogged, housed, trenched, mitred, keyed, dovetailed,* etc.

III. Those used for connecting boards in the same plane, such as floor- and match-boarding; they include *edges-shot, grooved and tongued, grooved and filleted, rebated, dowelled,* etc.

Beside the above there are quite a number of joints which are suited to special circumstances; many of these can best be considered with the construction to which they are specially applicable.

The above joints can best be studied in detail under the heading of (1) Carpentry Joints, (2) Joinery Joints, although many of them are equally applicable to both branches.

Carpentry may be considered to embrace the framing together of the rougher and heavier timbers used in the construction of buildings, or other timber structures such as bridges, spectators' stands, centres, etc.

Joinery includes the work done at the bench, in the preparation of the finished woodwork of buildings, such as panelled work (including doors), window-frames, staircases, cupboards, partitions, etc. The distinction between the two, if one need be drawn, lies in the fact that the carpenter does not in general require to use the plane in his work, whereas the joiner works almost entirely in wrought or planed stuff. The timber used for joiners' work obviously requires to be more thoroughly seasoned than is necessary with that used for carpentry. Timber is considered sufficiently seasoned for carpenters' work when it has lost one-fifth its weight; for joiners' work a one-third loss is necessary.

Stresses in Beams and Framed Structures.—Beams and framed structures when loaded are subject to various stresses, which must be taken into account in arranging the joints connecting the members. The methods of determining the amount of stress in the various members of a framed structure will be explained in Chap. XII.

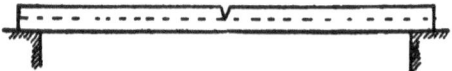

FIG. 264.—Beam cut to illustrate Stresses.

Stress and Strain.—When a weight, or any other force, acts upon a beam, it tends to change the shape or size of the beam. The force is technically called a **stress**, while the change in shape or size is called a **strain**. When a beam, or girder, supported at both ends, is loaded, the upper part is compressed and tends to shorten. The lower part, on the other hand, is in a state of tension, as it tends to stretch. The force acting on the upper part of such a beam is therefore a *compression stress*; that on the lower is a *tension stress*.

The existence of these stresses may be made very apparent either by making a saw-cut across, or by actually cutting out a wedge-shaped piece from, the middle of a beam of wood for half its depth, as shown in Fig. 264. On resting the beam on two supports with the cut edge uppermost, and then loading it, it will be seen that the saw-cut closes. This shows that the fibres on the upper side are in a state of compression. If the same piece is now turned over so that the saw-cut is on the lower side, and again loaded, the tendency is for the cut to open, thus showing that the fibres on the lower side are in a

JOINTS AND FASTENINGS.   161

state of tension. Fig. 265 gives another illustration of tension and compression stresses; it shows three pieces of timber such as might be used in a simple roof truss. It will be readily seen that when a weight is placed at *A* the two members *AB*

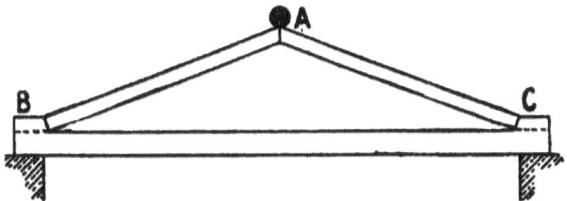

Fig. 265.—Truss to illustrate Stresses.

and *AC* are in a state of compression caused by the weight, and tend to shorten, while the tie *BC* prevents the lower ends of *AB* and *AC* from spreading, therefore *BC* is in tension and has a tendency to stretch.

Shearing Stresses.—A shearing stress is one where the fibres of the wood exhibit a tendency to slide over one another. An

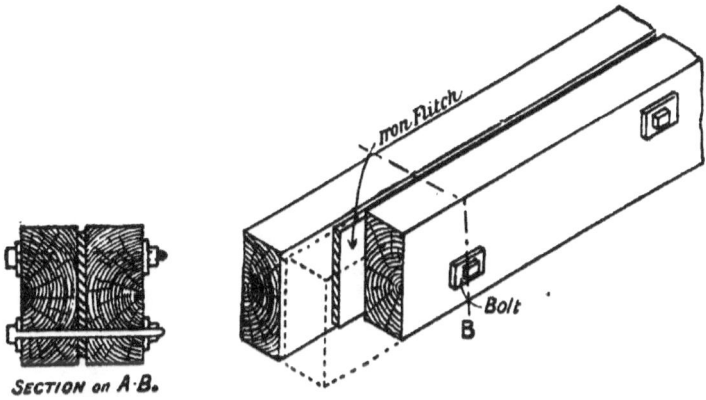

SECTION on A·B.
Fig. 266.   Fig. 267.—Flitched Girder.

example of this is shown in Fig. 265, where the tendency of the rectangular piece forming the abutment of the joint to split off in the direction of the grain is shown at *B* and *C* by the dotted lines. Shearing may take place with or across the grain; thus, wooden pins driven through joints, or bolts used for connecting joints together, are subjected to shearing stresses.

M.C.J.   L

162 A MANUAL OF CARPENTRY AND JOINERY.

Wooden Beams and Girders.—A beam which spans an opening and is supported at each end is known as a **girder** or **bressummer**. Wooden beams may be used as girders and are often put in as "whole timbers." It is better, however, in order to make the girder of uniform strength to proceed as follows :

(1) Saw the beam lengthwise down the middle ;
(2) turn both pieces so that the sawn surfaces are outside ;
(3) reverse one of the pieces lengthwise so that the *butt end* of one half is against the *top end* of the other.

The reasons for (1) and (2) are that they allow of inspection of the inside of the beam, and the detection of any defect that may exist ; and (3) that timber is stronger at the lower or butt end of the tree than at the top end. The two pieces should

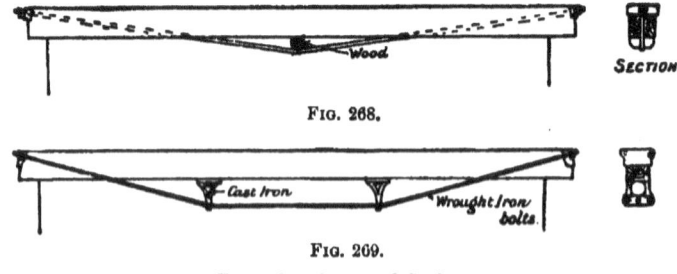

FIG. 268.

FIG. 269.

Examples of Trussed Girders.

then be bolted together at intervals of from 2 to 3 feet, with packing pieces between them, the bolts being placed near the upper and lower edges alternately.

Flitched Girders.—A girder of the kind described in the last paragraph is frequently strengthened by inserting a wrought iron or steel plate called a **flitch** between the two pieces and bolting the whole together. The flitch should be at least half an inch narrower than the wooden beams, in case any shrinkage takes place in the latter. Such a combination is named a **flitched girder** (Figs. 266 and 267). To prevent indentations being made by the bolts in the wooden beams, there should be large plate washers under both the head and nut as shown in Fig. 267.

Trussed Girders.—When space will allow, a girder is often constructed of several pieces joined to form a framework called

JOINTS AND FASTENINGS. 163

a truss. Wooden beams are also strengthened in various ways by means of wrought-iron bolts and plates of wrought or cast

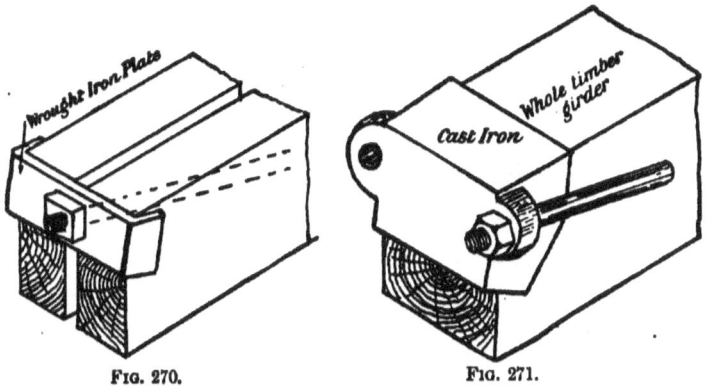

Details of the Ends of Trussed Girders.

iron, and by wooden or cast-iron compression members called **struts**. Such beams are also called **trussed girders**. Figs. 268 to 273 are examples of different types of trussed girders. In Figs.

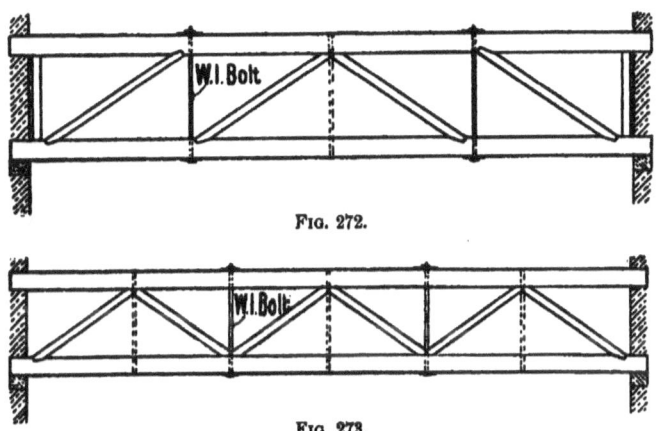

Examples of Trussed Girders.

272 and 273 the bolts shown by dotted lines would be required if the load were placed upon the lower member.

Lengthening of Beams.—It often happens that wooden beams are required longer than they can be obtained in

164 A MANUAL OF CARPENTRY AND JOINERY.

single pieces. The joint used for lengthening such beams varies according to the purpose for which they are to be used, as well as according to the stresses—tension, compression, or shearing—to which they are to be subjected.

A **lapped** joint is formed when one beam overlaps the other for a certain distance. If the beams are to be subjected to a

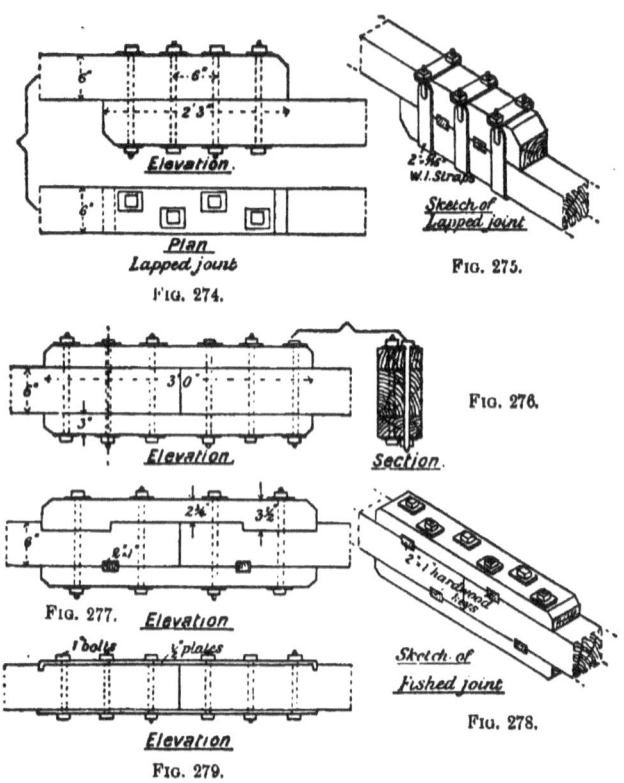

Fig. 274.—Lapped joint.
Fig. 275.
Fig. 276.
Fig. 277.
Fig. 278.
Fig. 279.

compression stress, or are liable to a cross strain, iron straps may be used for connecting them (Fig. 275). If the beam, when in position, will be under the influence of a tension stress, then bolts are preferable (Fig. 274).

When two beams abut end to end, the joint is named a **fished** joint and the cover plates are called fish-plates. With beams "in tension" the fish-plates of wood may be sunk, or *tabled*, into the main beam, as on the upper edge of Fig. 277, or they

JOINTS AND FASTENINGS.   165

may have hard-wood "keys" driven into trenches cut into both beams and plates as shown in Fig. 278, and on the lower edge of Fig. 277. If iron fish-plates are used, the ends of the plate may be turned into the wooden beam for a short distance. This lessens the stress on the bolts, but reduces the strength of the beam. Care should always be taken that the indentations in the beam are not opposite each other.

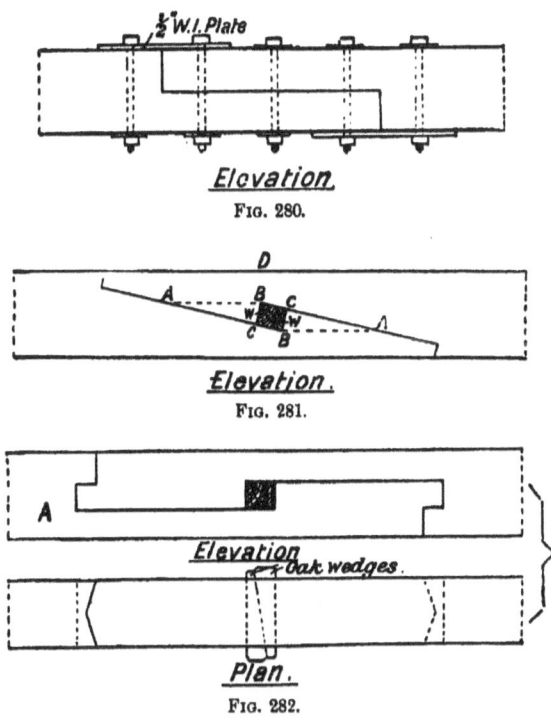

Elevation.
FIG. 280.

Elevation.
FIG. 281.

Elevation.
Plan.
FIG. 282.

Scarfed Joints.

The joints just described are all clumsy in appearance, and in many positions would appear very unsightly. The **scarfed joint** is much neater, though not so strong. Figs. 280 to 287 show different forms of the scarfed joint. In the simplest (Fig. 280) each piece is cut away for half the depth and is secured by bolts. Fig. 281 shows a very common form of scarfed joint used for beams, which when in position will be in tension. The **wedges** w, w, of hard wood are used to tighten up the joint, thus rendering bolts unnecessary. The weakness of this joint lies in the tendency of the triangular pieces ABC to shear off. The maximum strength is secured when the length of AB is about seven times that of DB. Stronger scarfed joints are shown in Figs. 282 and 285. Such scarfed joints are suitable for beams which are to be subjected either to tension or to compression stresses. The length of the scarf will depend upon the material used; the length may be diminished, and the

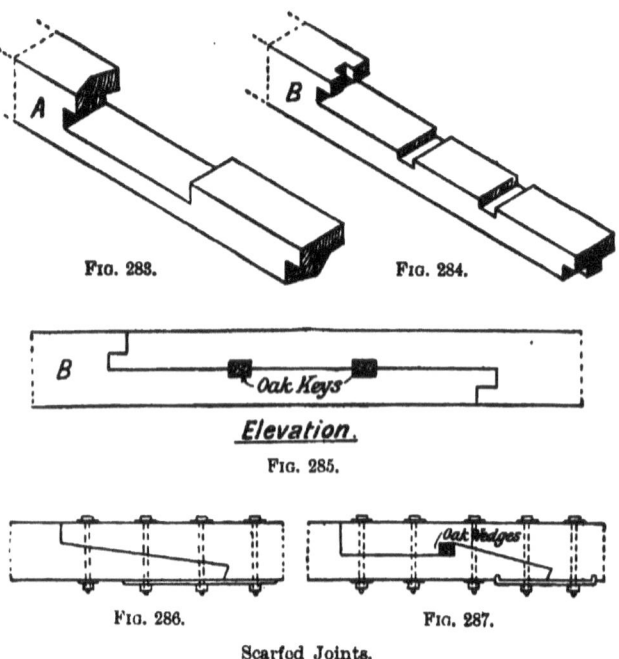

Fig. 283.   Fig. 284.

Fig. 285.

Fig. 286.   Fig. 287.

Scarfed Joints.

strength of the joint increased, by using fish-plates and bolts. Fig. 283 is a sketch of the cut end of one beam of the joint shown in elevation in Fig. 282. Fig. 284 is a corresponding sketch of Fig. 285. Scarfed joints of a design suitable for resisting cross-stress and tension are shown in elevation in Figs. 286 and 287.

Halving.—Halving consists of cutting the ends of each piece to half the depth and securing with either bolts, nails, screws, or wooden pegs. A halved joint is one of the simplest, and is

JOINTS AND FASTENINGS.

very suitable for connecting beams that have to be jointed on the top of a post, or that have some other means of support; for cross rails meeting on a post or other support; for wall-plates resting on the wall; for long ridge-pieces, etc. Figs. 291 and 293 show typical examples.

FIG. 288.—"Built-up" Beam.

Keying.—Wooden keys are pieces of hard wood used either to connect two pieces together, or with bolts to prevent the pieces from sliding over each other. Although very long wooden beams are now seldom used for carrying purposes, having been largely superseded by iron or steel girders, it is—as has been

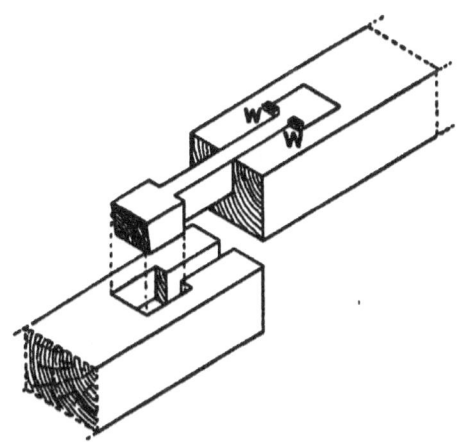

FIG. 289.—"Hammer-headed" Keyed Joint.

said—occasionally necessary to construct beams of greater length than can be obtained in one piece. Fig. 288 shows the elevation of a beam which is built up of four pieces connected by bolts and having hard-wood keys inserted to prevent the pieces from sliding over each other. Fig. 289 illustrates what is known as a *hammer-headed key*. This key is tightened up with small wedges (W, W) as shown.

168 A MANUAL OF CARPENTRY AND JOINERY.

Joints for connecting Timbers meeting at an Angle.—This class of joint requires to be arranged so that the abutment is as nearly as possible at right angles to the pressure. It embraces all the joints in roof and other truss construction, and although many of these can best be considered in detail with the particular

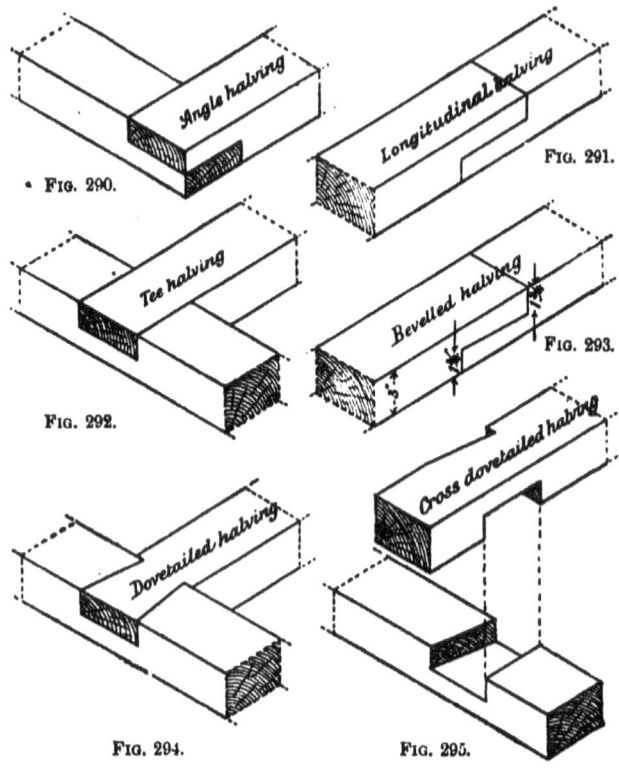

structures with which they are connected, some typical examples will now be explained.

Halving.—Halved joints are used also for connecting timbers at an angle. Figs. 290 to 295 are examples with the distinctive name of each appended. A halved joint may be secured with either bolts, nails, screws, or wooden pins.

Housing.—Housing consists of letting bodily into one piece the end of the other piece which has to be connected to it. Fig. 296 shows in elevation the lower end of a post housed into a cross rail. This joint is also sometimes called a **notched joint**, especially when light pieces are thus connected to a heavy beam. The ceiling joists of a room usually are notched to the main girders of a floor above. The ends of a wooden cistern are often housed into the sides.

Lapping.—Beams are often built up of a number of thicknesses of material with the joints across each other. This is especially the case with the curved ribs of a roof truss, or the curved ribs of a wooden centre. Such built-up beams are secured with either nails, screws, bolts, or wooden pegs. They will be more fully explained in a later chapter.

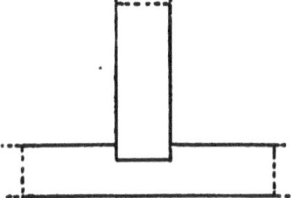

Fig. 296.—Housed Joint.

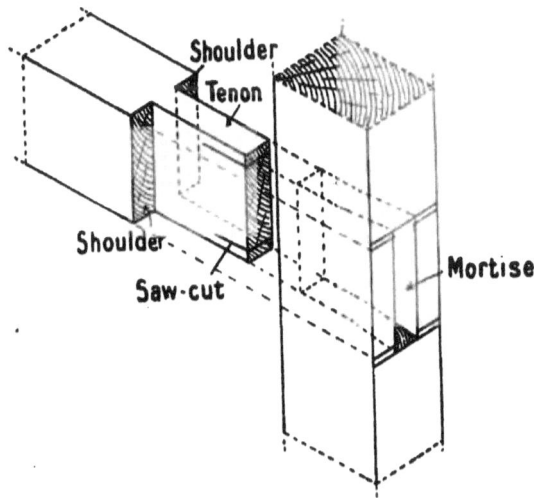

Fig. 297.—Mortise and Tenon Joint.

Mortise and tenon joint.—In its varied forms this joint is used perhaps more extensively than any other. In carpenters' work the mortise and tenon may be the only means by which the two parts are connected, or they may be used simply for the purpose of keeping the joint in position.

The proportions and the shape of the tenon vary considerably, but when used wholly for connecting, the tenon is from one-

170 A MANUAL OF CARPENTRY AND JOINERY.

fourth to one-third the thickness of the material, and the bearing power of the joint depends upon the accuracy with which the shoulders fit the piece containing the mortise. Fig. 297 shows a sketch of a mortise and tenon joint with the names of the different parts given. A joint of this description, when used for connecting purposes, should have a width of tenon of not more than five times the thickness; and the outer side of the mortise should be a little longer than the inner or shoulder side, to allow of wedges being driven into the end of the tenon to fasten it securely. Such joints are often fastened by driving the wedges into the

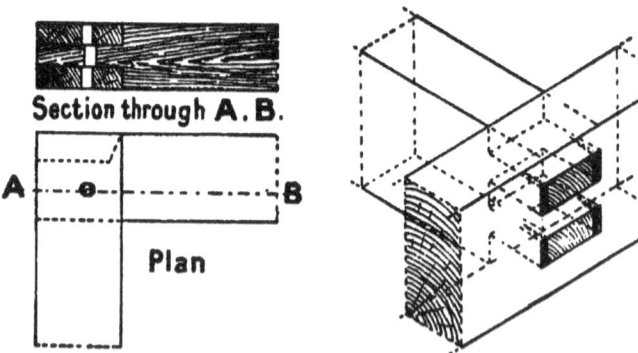

FIG. 298.—Haunched Tenon Joint.   FIG. 299.—Double Mortise and Tenon Joint.

space left between the edge of the tenon and the end of the mortise. This method, however, has a tendency to make the tenon narrower at the outer end, and to some extent to defeat the object aimed at; if two saw-cuts, one near each edge, are made in the tenon before it is put into position (Fig. 297), and the wedges are driven into these saw-cuts, they spread the outer end of the tenon, making it wider, and thus securely fixing it in position. When a tenon is reduced in width, either by cutting off one or both edges, or by cutting a part out of the middle, or—as is the case when a mortise and tenon joint is used where two pieces meet at an angle (Fig. 298)—it is called a *haunched tenon*. Figs. 642 and 643 show types of the haunched tenon.

A *barefaced tenon* is one that has the tenon flush with one side of the material (Fig. 642), and has therefore only one shoulder.

JOINTS AND FASTENINGS.   171

In many kinds of framing, the thickness of the material is so great that a single tenon of the usual proportion would unnecessarily weaken the piece containing the mortise, and therefore two tenons are arranged side by side as shown in Fig. 299. Such tenons are known as *double tenons*.

Another type of mortise and tenon joint used in carpenters' work, arranged to weaken the timbers as little as possible, is the *tusk tenon* joint. This joint is much used in floor and roof construction. The tenon—which usually has a thickness of one-sixth the width of the material—is strengthened at the root by projections left on at the shoulder. These projections, known as the tusk, are of the proportions shown in Fig. 300, which should be noticed carefully. In some cases (as for example the joints of floor joists) the tenon projects through and beyond the surface, and is secured with a wedge which passes through a small mortise made in the tenon, as shown. When this joint is used with large beams the mortise extends about halfway through, and a wooden pin is driven through the tenon.

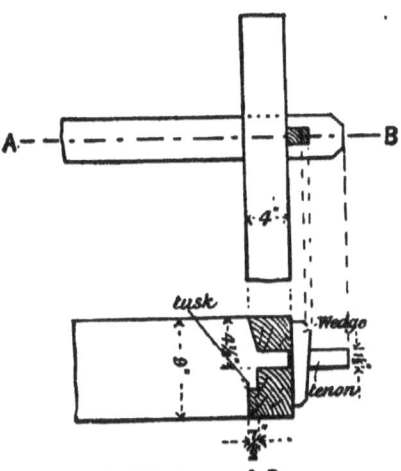

SECTION through A·B.
FIG 300.—Tusk Tenon Joint.

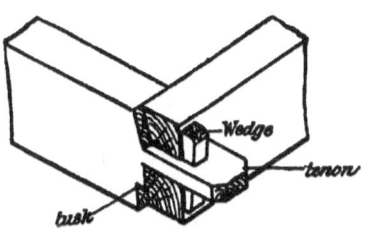

FIG. 301.—Sketch of a Tusk Tenon Joint.

In addition to the tenon, the joint in Fig. 302 has what is known as a *cross-tongue* on each shoulder. This method of strengthening the joint may be used in all cases where the tenon cannot be conveniently of the usual proportions. Cross-tongues are cut out of hard wood in such a way that the grain of the tongue runs in the same direction as that of the tenon.

172 A MANUAL OF CARPENTRY AND JOINERY.

In order to give additional strength to the joint, the end of the piece bearing the tenon is itself frequently sunk (housed)

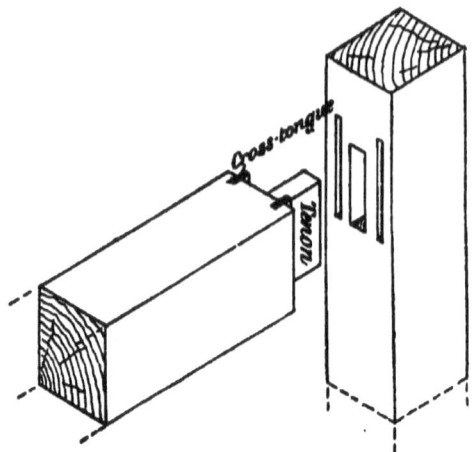

FIG. 302.—Mortise and Tenon Joint with Cross-tongues.

into the other piece for a short distance. This arrangement is known as a *mortised and housed* joint (Figs. 303 and 304).

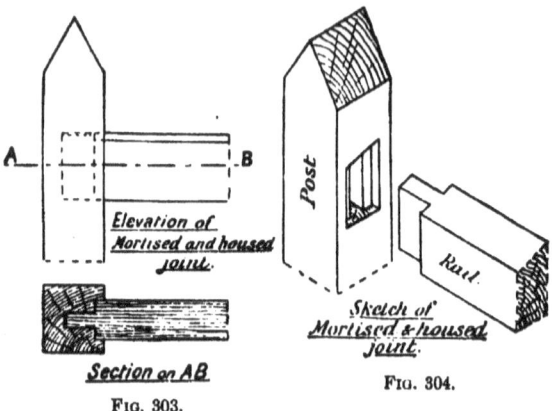

FIG. 303.

FIG. 304.

Fox-wedging is a device adopted for securing a mortise and tenon joint where the joint cannot be wedged from the outside, or where the tenon does not go through the piece, as, for example, in the case of a post fixed against a wall, or of a sill resting on a floor. In these and similar contingencies the length

JOINTS AND FASTENINGS.

of the mortise is greater inside, that is, the ends are cut sloping, and saw-cuts are made in the end of the tenon. When the joint is being put together, wedges are carefully inserted in the saw-

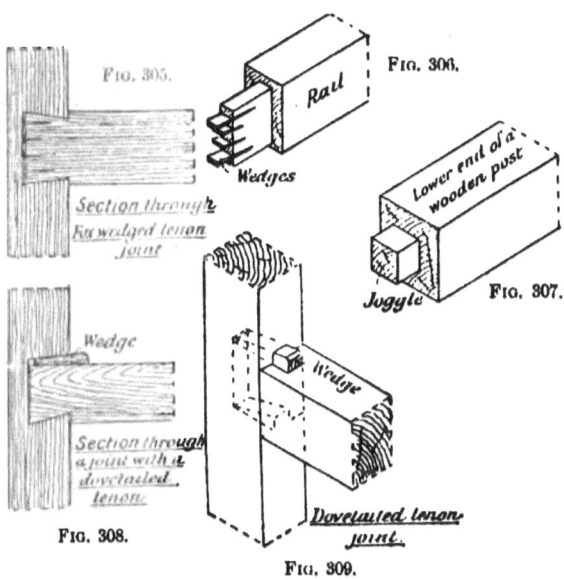

FIG. 308.
FIG. 309.

cuts, and when the joint is forced together the wedges spread the outer ends of the tenon (Figs. 305 and 306).

This method of fox-wedging is also suitable for superior work, where the appearance of the end of the tenon on the edge of the framing would be considered objectionable.

In the *dovetailed tenon* one edge of the tenon is cut obliquely (*splayed*), and the length of the mortise is made a little greater than the width of the tenon. The joint is secured with a wedge which is driven into the space left on the straight side of the tenon (Figs. 308 and 309).

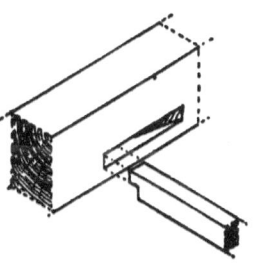

FIG. 310.—Chase Mortising.

A *chase mortise* is used at one side when a cross-piece has to be inserted and fixed with mortise and tenon joints between two beams already fixed. Fig. 310 shows the mortise chased out so that the cross-piece can be pushed into position.

174 A MANUAL OF CARPENTRY AND JOINERY.

A *stump or stub tenon* is a short tenon usually employed more for the sake of keeping the joint in position than as a means of connection. It is used extensively for the joints in large and heavy trusses, as will be seen by referring to Chapter IX., dealing with them.

Bridle Joint.—The bridle joint is the converse of the mortise and tenon joint. In bridle joints the middle part of one member is cut out so that it will fork on to the other member, which is suitably cut to receive it. Generally the bridle joint can be fitted more accurately, weakens the material less, and makes a stronger joint; it is therefore preferable in heavy carpenters' framing—where the members meet at an acute angle, as in Fig. 432,—to the stump tenon, although the latter is possibly more generally used.

Joggle Joint.—In a joggle joint, a projection—the *joggle*—is left on the end of a wooden post which is intended to fit into a stone or wooden sill (Fig. 307). The sill itself contains a suitable mortise cut to receive the joggle.

Cogged Joint.—A cogged joint is one where two pieces are partly sunk into each other in order to minimise space. Examples are to be seen in floor construction, where the floor joists are cogged on to the binders or on to the wall plates; or in roof construction, where the purlins (p. 216) are cogged on to the backs of the principal rafters. It will be seen from an examination of Figs. 390 and 391 that in the cogged joint each piece is cut in such a way that the material is not appreciably weakened.

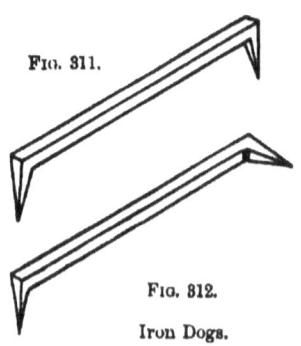

FIG. 311.

FIG. 312.

Iron Dogs.

Fastenings for Carpenters' Joints. — Much heavy carpentry consists of the building of such temporary structures as scaffolding, shoring, gantries, temporary wooden buildings, spectators' stands, bridges, and the like. As the timber in these is after use still a marketable commodity, and as the connections or joints are best made as simple as possible, the *iron dog* and the *cleat* are both much used. A **dog** is a wrought-iron fastening of varying length, having the ends pointed and shaped as shown in Figs. 311 and

JOINTS AND FASTENINGS.

312. It is very necessary to have the pointed ends at an angle a little greater than a right angle, so that as they are driven into the material they will tend to draw the joint together. By their use the need to make either mortise and tenon, or bridle joints, is largely reduced, as the dogs prevent the members from moving laterally. **Cleats** are short pieces of wood which are either bolted or nailed against heavy timbers to assist in forming an abutment for a joint. They may, in addition to being bolted, be housed for a short distance into the beam to which they are fastened.

Bolts are made of the best wrought iron. They have a head of variable shape at one end, the other end being threaded and fitted with a nut for tightening-up purposes. Square bolts are better than round ones for joints in tension. To prevent the nut from sinking into the fibres of the wood when tightening up, washers—small plates of wrought iron—are placed between the nut and the material. In heavy structures, washers should also be placed under the head of the bolt. Small circular washers are used generally, but it is better to use larger plate washers having a thickness of one half times the diameter of the bolt.

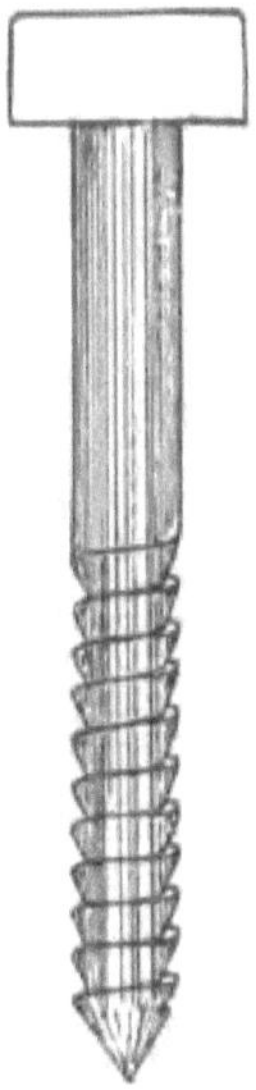

Straps.—Bolts may be used alone or they may be used along with wrought-iron plates, or *straps*, for connecting joints in timber structures. The straps may be of almost any shape: straight, bent, three-way, or four-way, and are generally used in pairs, one being placed on each side of the joint to be connected. They are pierced by a number of holes through which the bolts are passed. It frequently happens that the straps are made to clip the material and are therefore U-shaped, as in the case of the fastening of the lower end of a king post with a strap and gibs and cotters (Fig. 434). Straps may be secured with coach-screws instead of bolts. **Coach-screws** (Fig. 313) are of wrought iron, with a square flat head, and have a coarse screw-thread which passes between the fibres of the wood. When bolts are used, the holes in the material

FIG. 313.—Coach-screw.

should be as nearly as possible of the same size as the bolt; but with coach screws the holes should be a little less than the diameter of the screw, to enable the screw to hook into the fibres and thus get firm hold of the material.

Joint bolts are another type of bolt used for connecting the joints of wooden structures. They are chiefly used where two pieces meet at a right angle, and where a strap would be unsightly or in the way. A joint bolt is circular, has a square flat head, and is screw-threaded for a much greater distance than an ordinary bolt for the purpose of drawing the joint together. The threaded end is also pointed to enable it more readily to catch the nut, which is of rectangular shape, larger than the nut of the ordinary bolt, and requires letting into one of the pieces to be connected (Fig. 439). Another type of joint bolt used for connecting the ends of two pieces together is threaded at both ends, one end being provided with a rectangular nut, and the other with a circular nut with grooves in its edge. Joint bolts are sometimes provided with an extra long thread which is screwed into the end of the material like a coach screw, the nut being dispensed with.

It is a wise precaution in heavy carpentry—the joints of which are connected with bolts—to examine the structure some time after it has been completed, and tighten up where necessary, as the wood of such structures is not always properly seasoned at the time of framing together.

To preserve iron fastenings from oxidation they may be galvanised, dipped while hot into pitch, or they may be painted with oxide-paint. If iron fastenings are used for unseasoned oak, the gallic acid contained in the oak will cause rapid oxidation, and discolour the wood. It is therefore occasionally necessary to use copper or other metal fastenings with such wood.

Wedging and pinning.—As already explained in the description of the mortise and tenon joint, wedges play an important part in fastening the joints of woodwork. The wood from which they are made should be dry, straight-grained, and fairly hard, and the wedges themselves should not have too much taper.

Wooden pins should be of hard wood, straight-grained, dry, and should be split rather than sawn to the required size. Square or rectangular pins are not so liable to become loose, and are therefore better than circular ones. If properly fixed, they may be made a very secure means of connecting a joint. A good method of fixing a wooden pin to connect a mortise and tenon, or a bridle joint is to bore the hole in the centre piece a little distance nearer the shoulder, so that the pin in being driven into position will, by pressing against the fibres (Fig. 298), draw the joint together. This method is named

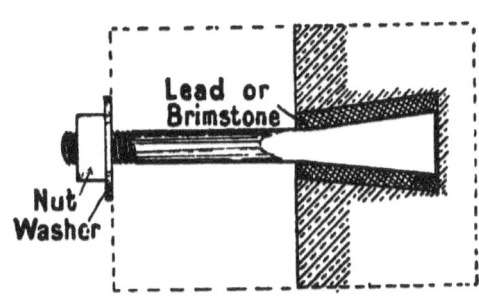

Fig. 314.—Lewis- or Rag-bolt.

draw boring. Large wooden pins are sometimes called *trenails.*

Framing exposed to the weather is preserved, and the wedges, pins, or other wooden fastenings adhere better, if a paint consisting of white and red lead and linseed oil, mixed to the consistency of thick cream, is used as a coating for all parts of the joint which are in contact.

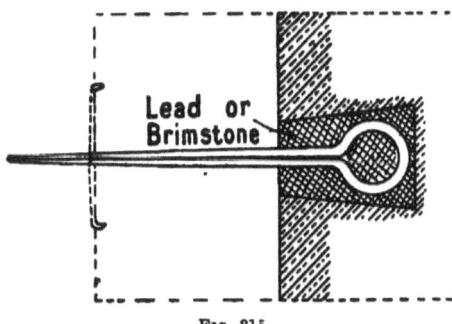

Fig. 315.

For fixing woodwork against stone or brick-work many expedients are employed. A **lewis-** or **rag-bolt** is often used. This consists of a bolt which has a specially shaped head, let into a dovetail-shaped hole made in the stone, and fastened thereto by means of lead or brimstone (Fig. 314). The other end of the bolt is screw-threaded and provided with a nut and washer.

Fig. 316.—Split-bill.

Split-bills, known also as snipe-bills, are iron holdfasts

178 A MANUAL OF CARPENTRY AND JOINERY.

(Fig. 316) let into the stone work at the head end, the points, which pass through the wood work to be secured, being "clenched." Iron holdfasts of many other shapes are also used.

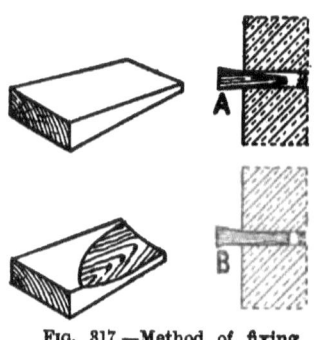

Fig. 317.—Method of fixing Wooden Wedges.

These are driven into the joints of the stone or brick work only; or, which is preferable, wooden plugs are first driven into the joints and the holdfasts are driven into these.

Wooden plugs should be cut out of dry straight-grained wood, and they hold more securely if cut with the axe, with a little twist on each surface (Fig. 317, B), than if they are cut with the saw with straight surfaces (A). The hole into which a plug has to fit should be first made and then the plug cut so that the small end will just fit the hole. The plug should fit the hole accurately for at least two inches (Fig. 317, B).

Nails are too well known to need more than a brief description. Nails may be obtained in any length from 14 inches down to ½ inch. The

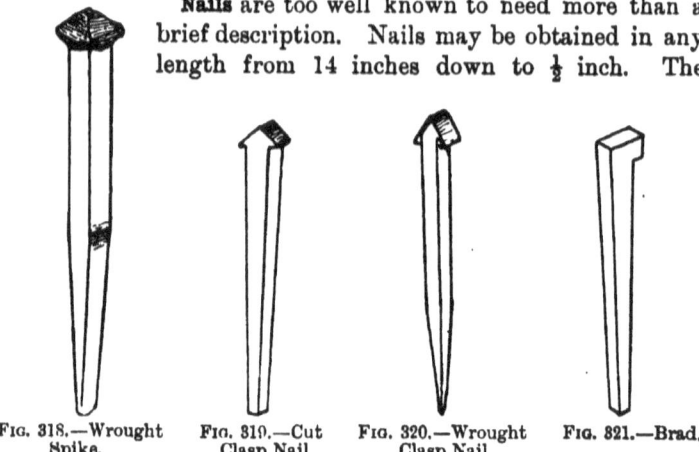

Fig. 318.—Wrought Spike.   Fig. 319.—Cut Clasp Nail.   Fig. 320.—Wrought Clasp Nail.   Fig. 321.—Brad.

larger ones, often called spikes, are only used in very heavy work to a limited extent, as anything that requires a nail longer than six inches will be better fastened with a bolt or a coach screw. Spikes should be forged out of the best wrought iron, and be of the shape shown in Fig. 318.

Clasp nails are of size from six inches downwards, and may

JOINTS AND FASTENINGS. 179

be cut or wrought. "Cut clasp" are those which are cut out of sheet metal and are of shape shown in Fig. 319. "Wrought clasp" are tougher than the cut nails; they are used where the nail passes through both the pieces to be connected, and the points are folded over (clenched). The head of each kind of nail is shaped so that it can be driven readily below the surface.

Brads are cut nails of shape shown in Fig. 321 ; the shape of the head is such that when the nail is driven below the surface the resulting hole is very small. Brads are used for securing floor boards, and the smaller varieties—called *sprigs*—for securing mouldings, etc., in position.

Wire nails are much used in fixing woodwork. They are

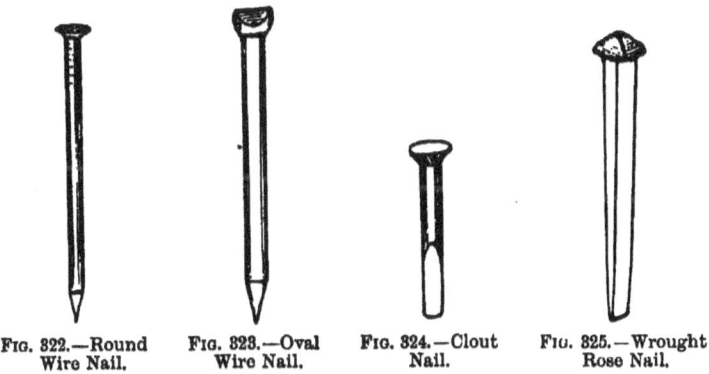

FIG. 322.—Round Wire Nail.   FIG. 323.—Oval Wire Nail.   FIG. 324.—Clout Nail.   FIG. 325.—Wrought Rose Nail.

made in a variety of shapes, and in all sizes from six inches to half an inch in length. The round ones with flat heads (Fig. 322) are used for such purposes as packing-case making, fencing, hoardings, and all kinds of rough carpentry. The oval shaped (Fig. 323) are much used instead of the cut clasp for the mass of ordinary work. Wire nails square in section are also obtainable, but are not so much used as the other varieties.

Clout nails are wrought, and have round heads. They are used for securing sheet metal, hoop iron, roofing-felt, etc., to wood.

Wrought nails of shape shown in Fig. 325 are extensively used by the coach-builder and ship-builder; they are stronger than the ordinary cut nail, but are seldom used by the carpenter.

Tacks are small nails pointed at one end, and have a round, flat head.

180 A MANUAL OF CARPENTRY AND JOINERY.

Screws.—Screws are used more by the joiner than by the carpenter. They may be of wrought iron or of brass. Figs. 326 and 327 show typical screws with flat and round heads respectively. The heads of screws are of various forms, such as flat, round-headed, square, hexagon, and of many ornamental designs. For securing woodwork the flat headed is mostly used. The other shapes are used chiefly for securing metal fastenings to wood work, and to give them an ornamental appearance. Screws are obtainable in all sizes, of both length and diameter, to six inches long. When screws are used for securing removable wood work, they should be provided with sockets which are let into the wood.

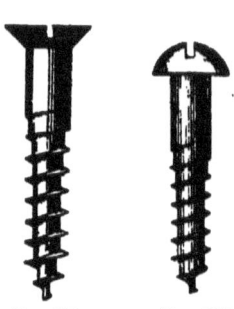

FIG. 326.   FIG. 327.
Types of Screw.

JOINERY.

Although the work of carpentry and of joinery differs enough to justify a separate classification of the joints used in the framing together of the various structures, it is impossible entirely to separate them, even if it were thought advisable to do so. In the same way no hard and fast distinction can be drawn between the work of the carpenter and that of the joiner. It is true that in large works some men are exclusively confined to joinery as "bench hands," while others are engaged as "fixers" on the building, or are employed in setting up carpenters' work. It is advisable, however, that the workman should have a good all-round knowledge of both branches of the work, as it is only in large workshops that such specialisation can be attempted.

Many of the remarks in the early part of this chapter will apply to the joints in joinery, especially those relating to the **mortise and tenon joint**, as the bulk of the panelled framing of doors, partitions, cupboards, etc., as well as the joints of such framing as sashes, are of this type.

The timber used for joiners' work requires to be more thoroughly seasoned than is necessary with that used for carpentry. Greater care is also necessary in arranging the joints, so that any slight shrinkage shall not be visible. Much of the material for joiners' work is now prepared by machinery.

JOINERY. 181

In the joints of door and sash framing many special modifications of the mortise and tenon joint are necessary. In panelled framing, for example, the groove into which the panel fits reduces the width of the tenon; while in sashes the rebate for the glass, and the moulding of the arrises, affect the shape of the shoulder. These points will be considered in detail along with the constructions to which they respectively refer.

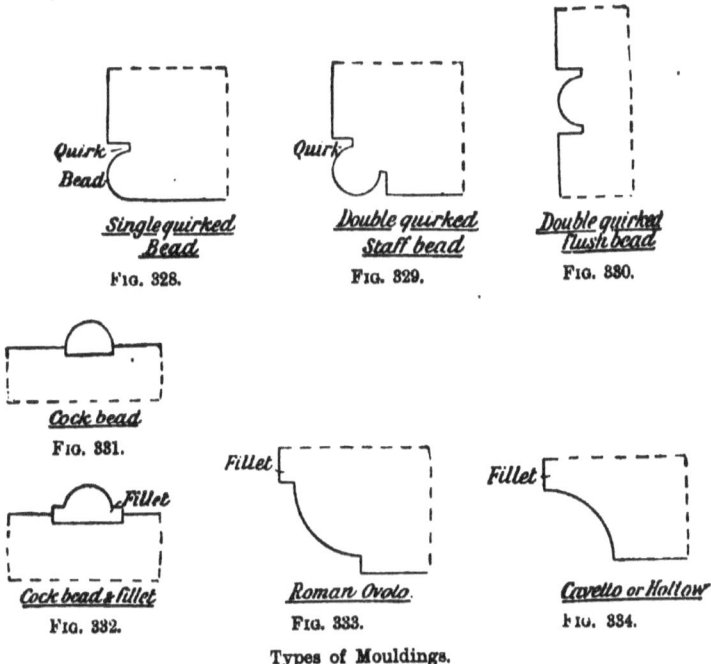

Types of Mouldings.

Mouldings.—The arrises of joiners' work are often ornamented by mouldings. It is necessary to consider these since they influence the making of the joint. The curves in Roman mouldings are segments of circles, while in Greek mouldings parabolic and elliptical curves predominate. Roman mouldings are built up from the types shown in Figs. 333 to 337. The distinctive name is in each case indicated on the sketch.

Bead or astragal.—Various forms of this moulding are shown in Figs. 328 to 332. The difference between the *quirked* bead (Fig. 328) and *double-quirked* or *staff* bead (Fig. 329) and between the *flush* bead (Fig. 330) and the *cock* bead (Fig. 331) should be particularly noticed. The bead is extensively used at the joints of boarding, to counteract the unsightly appearance that might be caused by any slight shrinkage. It is also much used as an angle moulding. When a number of flush beads are worked together on the same surface, as in Fig. 342, a *reeded* moulding is obtained. *Fluting* (Fig. 341) is the converse of reeding.

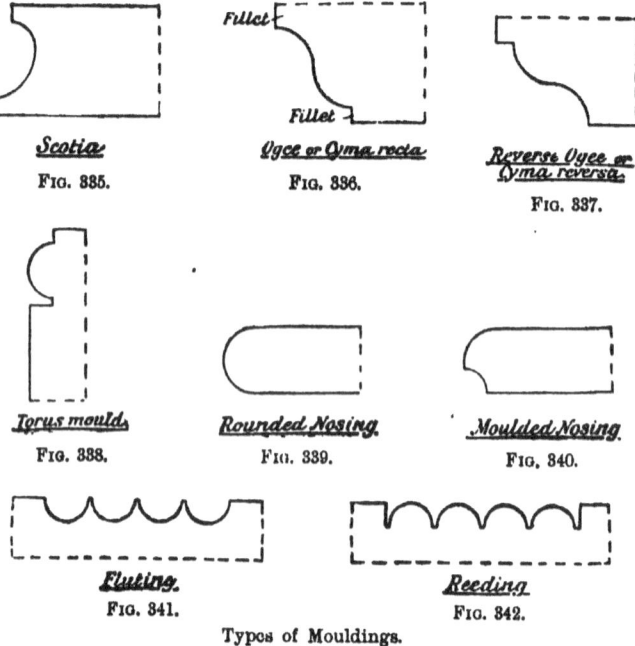

Types of Mouldings.

Torus.—In this moulding (Fig. 338) the diameter of the bead is vertical. It is surmounted by a flat projecting part called a *fillet*.

Lengthening joints.—This class of joint is not required to the same extent in joinery as in carpentry. It is seldom that the scarfed joints are resorted to, and lapped and fished joints are still less frequently used. The halved joint may be used with advantage sometimes, while the hammer headed key (Fig. 368) is very suitable for securing curved ribs that form the head of a semicircular door-frame or large

JOINERY. 183

window-frame, or any other circular framing of like nature. Such joints may be strengthened by inserting either *cross-tongues* of hard wood as shown in Fig. 368, or short wooden *dowels*. The splayed joint is used for connecting the ends of mouldings, skirting boards, etc., which are in long, straight lengths. Other lengthening joints are shown in the chapter

Butt joint.   Tongued joint.   Rebated & beaded.   Rebated with return bead.
FIG. 343.   FIG. 344.   FIG. 345.   FIG. 346.

Housed or trenched joint.   Tongued trenched joint.   Dovetailed trenched joints.
FIG. 347.   FIG. 348.   FIG. 349.   FIG. 350.

Mitred Angle joints.
FIG. 351.   FIG. 352.   FIG. 353.   FIG. 354.

on floors, where floor boards meet on a floor joist. Such joints are called **heading joints**; they may be square-edged, rebated, splayed, tongued and grooved, or forked, although the difficulty of construction in the last-named is not compensated for by the additional advantage it possesses. A form of joint used in connecting hand-rails, is a *butt-joint*; in forming it two hard wood dowels are inserted, and a small *joint-bolt* with a nut at each end, as shown in Fig. 892, is used; such a bolt is called a *handrail* bolt.

184　A MANUAL OF CARPENTRY AND JOINERY.

Angle Joints.—Fig. 343 is the simplest joint for connecting together two boards meeting at an angle. Figs. 344 to 346 show

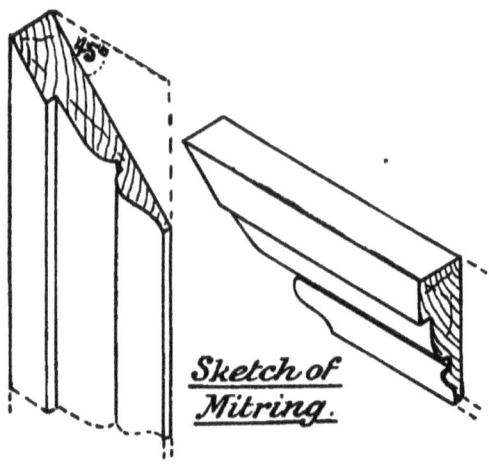

Fig. 355.

variations of this form of joint. Figs. 347 to 350 are sections through different forms of trenched joints. The first of these might also be called a *housed* joint; it is the one used in staircase construction where the steps are housed into the notch boards.

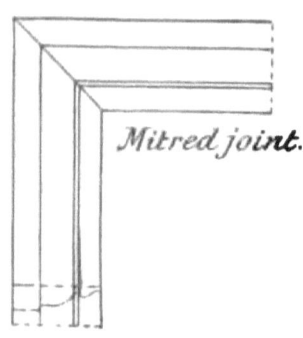

Fig. 356.

Mitring and Scribing.—In cases where it is undesirable to show the end grain of the wood, *mitring* is employed. Figs. 351 to 354 are sections through various kinds of mitred joints. When two lengths of the same moulding meet at an angle, as, for example, at the corners of an architrave surrounding a door or a window opening, or in any mouldings meeting at an angle, the joint always bisects the angle, and is called a mitred joint (Fig. 356). Under certain conditions it is better to cut the end of one moulding to fit the profile of the other as shown in Fig. 357. This plan is called *scribing*. Other examples of these two joints are found in the skirting board that runs round a room. The external angles are mitred; the internal angles are best scribed. The method of cutting the lower edge of a skirting board to fit the slight irregularities of the floor (instead of tonguing the board to the floor) is also known as scribing.

Cross-grooving—The joint shown in section in Fig. 344 may also be applied in the manner shown in the sketch (Fig. 358), as, for example, at the corners of boxes or cisterns. The

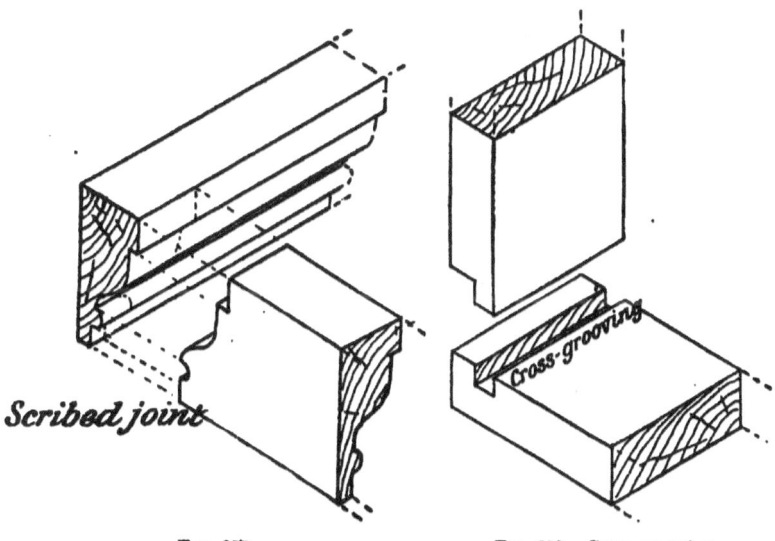

FIG. 357.   FIG. 358.—Cross-grooving.

grooves into which the tongue fits is, when it runs across the grain of the wood, an example of cross-grooving.

Dovetailing.—Figs. 349 and 350 are sections of dovetailed joints. Fig. 359 is a sketch of the common form of *angle dovetail* joint where two boards meet at an angle. This is the strongest kind of angle dovetailed joint. It can only be used, however, when there is no objection to the end grain of the wood being visible. The *lap dovetail* (Fig. 360) is so arranged that the joint on one face is not visible. It is useful in such work as the construction of drawers. The *mitred* or *secret dovetail* joint (Fig. 361) is not so strong as either of the others, but is used when it is desired to hide the joint completely.

186 A MANUAL OF CARPENTRY AND JOINERY.

Edge Joints.—Boards having their edges planed straight and true are said to have their **edges shot**.

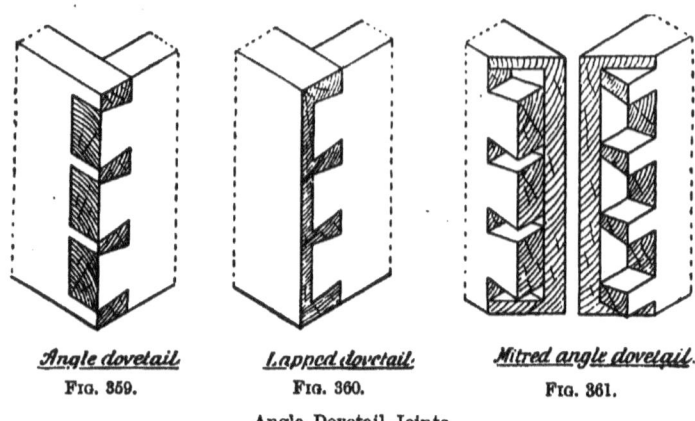

Angle dovetail.
FIG. 359.

Lapped dovetail.
FIG. 360.

Mitred angle dovetail.
FIG. 361.

Angle Dovetail Joints.

Match-boarding.—Timber, however well seasoned, has always a greater or less tendency to shrink; and this renders it inadvisable to use wide boards in covering surfaces of large area. In superior work, panelled framing is extensively adopted. A convenient alternative method is, however, to use boards of batten width, with square, grooved and tongued, or rebated edges. This class of boarding is known as *match-boarding*. In Fig. 363, which is a cross-section of such tongued-and-grooved battens, the tongued edge of each batten is beaded. This serves the double purpose of destroying the monotony of the surface, and of hiding any slight shrinkage that may take place in the boards. It is evident that if some

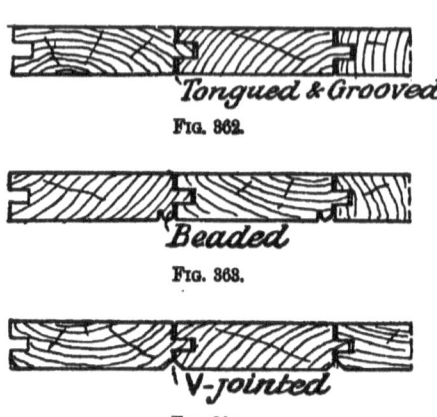

Tongued & Grooved
FIG. 362.

Beaded
FIG. 363.

V-jointed
FIG. 364.

Sections of Match-boarding.

JOINERY. 187

such means of treating the joint were not adopted, as is the case in Fig. 362, any shrinkage would produce an unsightly appearance. Instead of being beaded, the edges are often chamfered, as in Fig. 364. This treatment is known as

FIG. 365.—Glued Joints to obtain Wide Boards.

V-jointing. Examples of the use of match-boarding are seen in wainscotting, and also in boarded ceilings. Wide panels in framing are often constructed of match-boarding.

Edge Joints for wide boards.—If a wide board is required, the tendency to warping is diminished if it is composed of several pieces so jointed together that the heart sides of alternate pieces

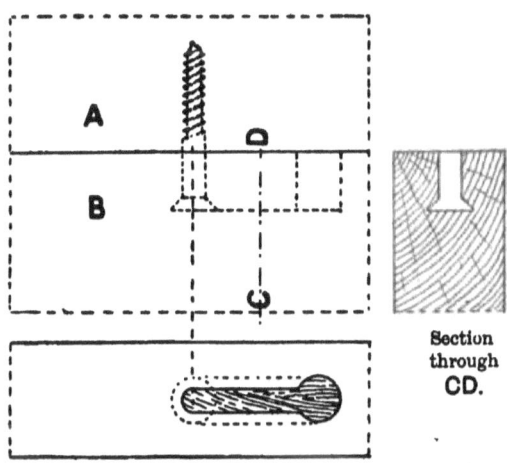

FIG. 366.—Secret Screwed Joint.

are reversed (Fig. 365). If glue is used and the work is for a dry position, the edge joints may be square. Alternative methods are to tongue and groove the edges, to groove both edges and insert a lath or fillet of hard wood (grooved and filleted joint), or to dowel the joint by inserting wooden pegs of hard wood at intervals of 12" to 18" apart.

Another method—although it is not applicable to very thin boards—is to turn strong screws into the edge of one piece, and after boring holes into the edge of the other piece, to make chases to allow the head of the screw to hook between the fibres and thus hold the joint together. These screws may be placed anywhere from one to two feet apart. Fig. 366 illustrates this joint.

Table or Rule Joint.—Fig. 367 is a section of a rule joint. This joint is used, along with hinges, where the edges of two boards move upon each other through an angle. Good examples are found in some types of window shutters (Fig. 793), the leaves of a folding table, etc.

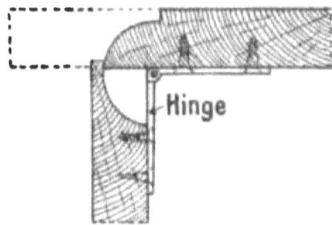

FIG. 367.—Table or Rule Joint.

Keying and Clamping.—The panels used in framing, as well as thin wide boards which are liable to warp, are sometimes strengthened by the insertion of tapering **dovetailed keys** of hard wood. These are placed at right angles to the grain of the wood of the boards, as shown in Fig. 369. **Clamping** serves the same purpose as keying. It consists of arranging narrow pieces along each end of the board, so that the grain shall be at right angles to the grain of the boards, as shown in Fig. 370. The clamp may either have a tongued and grooved, a dowelled, or a square joint, or it may be made with

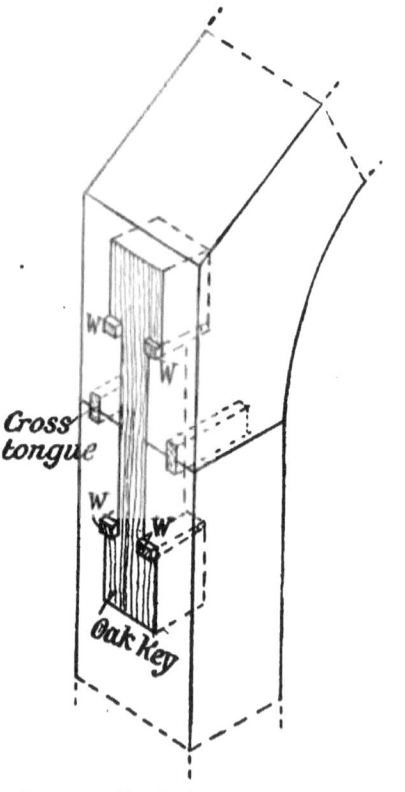

FIG. 368.—Sketch showing Hammer-headed Key.

mortise and tenon joints. Fig. 370 shows one of the clamped ends mitred.

Glue and Glue-blocks.—Glue is used by the joiner as an aid in securing joints. Glue is made by boiling, straining, and reboiling the skins and bones of animals. After being thus treated the material is cut into cakes and dried. Glue made from skins is stronger than that made from bones. Its quality also depends largely upon the care bestowed in the boiling and straining. The appearance of dark blotches in the cakes is a sign of poor quality. Freshly mixed glue is by far the best; repeated heating decreases its strength. Glue should be used as hot

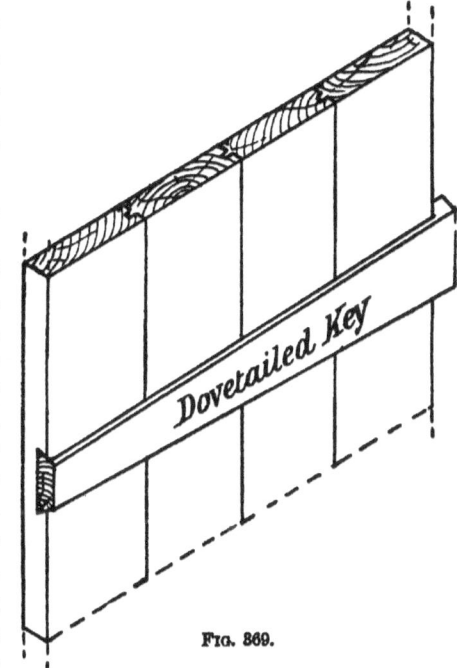

FIG. 369.

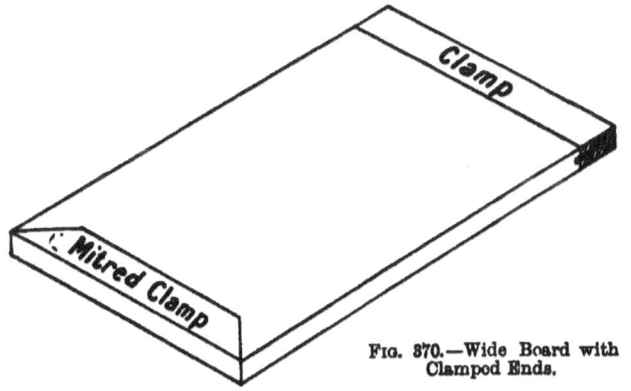

FIG. 370.—Wide Board with Clamped Ends.

as possible, and the surfaces to which it is applied should be perfectly dry and even warmed. Glue should not be too thick;

190 A MANUAL OF CARPENTRY AND JOINERY.

the thinner the layer applied, so long as the whole surface is covered, the better will it adhere.

When preparing glue, it is best to break up the cake into small pieces, place them in a jar with just sufficient water to cover them, and soak for several hours. The glue is afterwards melted by being placed in the upper pan of the glue pot, the lower pan of which is filled with water. The glue is softened by the heat from the water in the lower pan, sufficient *clean* hot water being added to the glue to render it of the right consistency. It is ready for use when it runs freely off the glue brush without breaking into drops. Glue capable of withstanding the weather may be made by adding powdered chalk to ordinary glue.

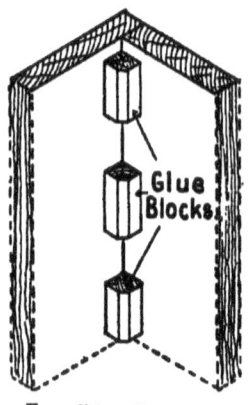

Fig. 371.—Example of Glue-blocks.

Glue-blocks are short pieces of wood that are glued into the angles to aid in strengthening joints. They are much used by both the joiner and the cabinet-maker. Fig. 371 shows an example of glue-blocks in position.

Summary.

The main principles underlying the construction of **joints** are :

To have each abutting surface at right angles to the pressure upon it, and of area proportional to the pressure :

To arrange fastenings so that they cannot weaken the pieces they connect.

Joints are most commonly used for connecting

(1) beams in the same straight line ;
(2) beams making an angle with each other ;
(3) boards in the same plane.

A **stress** is any force producing a change of shape or size ; the change of shape or size produced by a stress is called a **strain.**

A **girder** or **bressummer** is a beam spanning an opening and supported at both ends. Girders may be of wood only (solid and rectangular) ; flitched with an iron plate ; or trussed.

Beams are **lengthened** by *lapped, scarfed, halved,* or *keyed* joints.

SUMMARY.

Timbers at an **angle** are connected by *halved, housed, lapped, mortised* and *tenoned, bridle,* or *cogged* joints.

Fastenings for joints include *iron dogs, cleats, bolts, wrought iron straps, joint bolts, coach screws, wedges, pins, nails, screws,* and *glue.*

Woodwork is fastened to brick or stone work by nails driven into *wooden-plugs,* or by *lewis* or *rag-bolts,* by *split bills,* etc.

In Roman **mouldings** the curves are segments of circles; in Greek mouldings parabolic and elliptical curves predominate.

Other forms of **angle joints** more common in joinery are *rebated, tongued* and *grooved, mitred, scribed,* and *dovetailed.*

The **edge joints** of boards in the same plane may be *grooved and tongued, rebated,* or *grooved and filleted.*

Boards may be strengthened across the grain by *keying* and *clamping.*

Questions on Chapter VII.

1. What is meant by cambering beams? Why is it done? Describe flitching and trussing girders, and illustrate your answer by sketches. Draw six forms of scarfed joints, and state the purposes for which they are used. (C. and G. Ord., 1901.)

2. A fir beam 9 in. by 6 in. and 14 ft. between supports, is insufficient to carry the load upon it. Explain and sketch three various ways in which it might be strengthened. (C. and G. Ord., 1896.)

3. It is required to lengthen three beams (each 10 in. by 6 in.), one of which (a) is to be used in compression, one (b) in tension, and the other (c) in cross strain. Draw, one-quarter full size, the methods of scarfing you would adopt. (C. and G. Ord., 1894.)

4. Show by sketches the different methods of scarfing, and state which are adapted for the different strains. (C. and G. Ord., 1898.)

5. Make isometric, or oblique, projections of one of the following joints; (a) dovetail halving; (b) simple mortise and tenon. (C. and G. Ord., 1899.)

6. Draw the oblique or isometric projections of the following joints :

(a) Bare faced tenon joint.
(b) Double tenon joint.
(c) Common dovetail joint.
(d) Dovetail tongue and groove joint. (C. and G. Prel., 1904.)

7. (a) Make sketches of a tusk tenon joint. Timbers 9 in. by 3 in. Mark on the dimensions of the several parts. (b) What proportion should the tenon bear to the thickness of the material used in joiners' work? (C. and G. Ord., 1899.)

8. Under what conditions are haunched tenons used? State the usual proportions of the width and the thickness of the tenon in a mortise and tenon joint. Mention, and state the reasons for, any exceptions to the usual proportions.

9. Make a sketch of each of the following types of mortise and tenon joint, and show in each case how the joint is fastened: haunched, dovetail, tusk, and stump or stub.

10. Make a sketch of an iron dog. Give an illustration of the use of iron dogs and cleats as a suitable means of fastening timbers together.

11. Make sketches to illustrate three different methods of fastening a vertical wooden post to a stone wall.

12. Make sketches of the following mouldings: Cyma-recta (Roman and Greek), Astragal torus (Roman and Greek), Cavetto (Roman and Greek), Ovolo (Roman and Greek). These drawings must be large enough to show the geometrical construction, and the working lines should be left in. (C. and G. Ord., 1898.)

13. Draw 6 different joints used by joiners, and give their names and uses. (C. and G. Ord., 1902.)

14. Draw the isometric or the oblique projections of the following joints:

(1) Lapped dovetailing joint for drawer front.

(2) Haunched mortise and tenon joint. (C. and G. Prel., 1902.)

15. (1) Make a sketch of a secret dovetail joint, and (2) show two methods of securing and finishing the exterior angle of dado framing. (C. and G. Ord., 1903.)

16. A wide board, $1\frac{1}{2}$ in. thick, has to be constructed (with glued joints) out of three separate boards. Show by sketches three different suitable methods of making the edge joints.

17. State the precautions necessary to observe when preparing and using glue. How would you judge its quality? Give an illustration to show the use of glue-blocks.

CHAPTER VIII.

WOODEN FLOORS.

Types of Wooden Floors.—Wooden floors are constructed by placing on edge, planks, deals, or battens called **joists**, from 12″ to 15″ apart, and on the top of these securing the boards which form the surface of the floor. In upper floors, the joists carry on their undersides either the lath-and-plaster ceiling, or the ceiling joists to which the laths and plaster are fixed. When the distance between the walls which support the ends of the floor joists is not more than 16 feet the joists may be placed so that they stretch from wall to wall without intermediary support. A floor so arranged is named a **single floor**. With spans of greater distance than 16′ it would be essential, in order to obtain the necessary rigidity of such a floor, to have unwieldy joists of large section. Besides involving a waste of material, such joists, not being of the usual marketable sizes, are more expensive and difficult to obtain. It is therefore more economical to use lighter joists, and support them with cross-beams. Floors so arranged are named **double** or **framed floors**, according to the arrangement of the timbers.

Dimensions of Joists.—The carrying strength of a joist, or other beam, is proportional to the fraction $\frac{d^2 \times b}{L}$ where d is the depth in inches, b the breadth in inches, and L the length in feet. From this expression it will be seen that of two joists of the same length and sectional area, the one of greater depth will be the stronger. For example, the relative strengths of two joists 12″ deep by 2″ broad, and 8″ deep by 3″ broad respectively (*i.e.* of the same sectional area, 24 square inches), will be as $12 \times 12 \times 2 = 288$, and $8 \times 8 \times 3 = 192$, that is as 3 : 2.

194 A MANUAL OF CARPENTRY AND JOINERY.

In practice, a limit is set upon the narrowness by the necessity of nailing boards to the joists without splitting the latter, and it is usual to have the depth from three to four times the breadth. To prevent the buckling of narrow joists, strutting is employed.

Dwelling-house floors are made strong enough to carry about 1¼ cwts. per square foot of floor surface; while the floors of

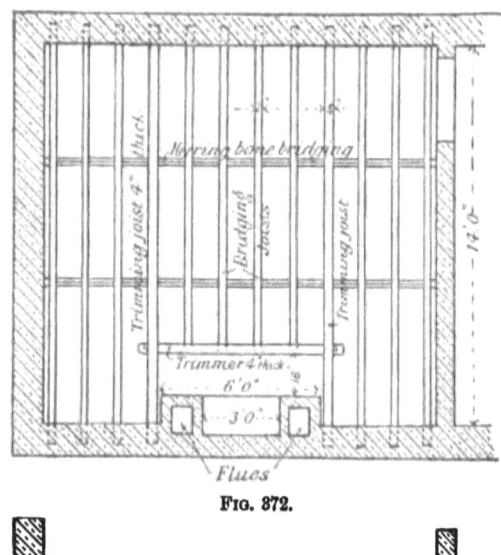

FIG. 372.

FIG. 373.

Plan and Section of a Single Floor.

warehouses, etc., subject to heavy loads, are capable of bearing from 1½ to 3 cwts. per square foot. The calculations necessary to determine the size of the timbers are dealt with in Chapter XII., but a useful rule, generally applicable to dwelling-houses, is to have the depth of the joists (in inches) equal to half the span (in feet) *plus* 2.

Single Floors.—As already explained, single floors are those the joists of which—called **bridging joists**—stretch from wall to wall. Single floors are generally suitable for dwelling-houses,

WOODEN FLOORS. 195

the division walls serving to support the ends of the joists. It is obvious that the strongest floor is obtained by placing the joists across the shortest way of any room which is not square in plan, although the joists should by preference have the ends resting on the outer walls rather than upon the party walls that divide one house from another. Figs. 372 and 373 show plan and section of a single floor.

Instead of having the plasterers' laths nailed to the underside of the joists, floors are sometimes constructed which have every third or fourth joist about 2" deeper than the rest; and smaller joists, called **ceiling joists**, about 3" or 4" by 2", are fixed to the underside of these. These ceiling joists carry the plaster ceiling, and act as a sound-preventive from one room to another. When wooden floors are used as ground floors, and there is no basement or cellar underneath, it is essential that an air space of at least 1' 6" be left under the floor, and that the ground under such a floor be covered with a layer of concrete from 4" to 6" thick. In a floor of this description the depth of the joists may be materially reduced by supporting them at intervals of 5' or 6' by sleeper walls of brick or stone (Fig. 374).

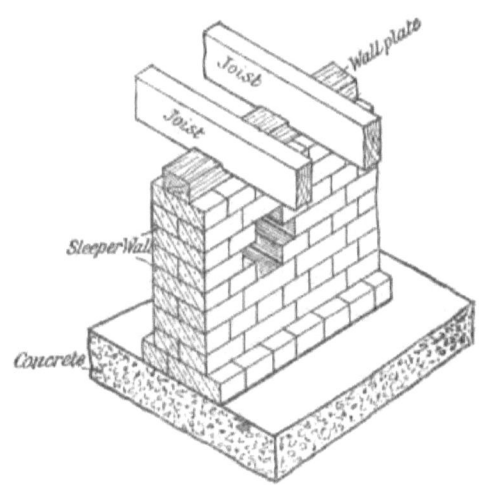

FIG. 374.—Sketch of part of a Brick Sleeper Wall.

Ground floors constructed of wood are liable to the disease known as *dry rot* unless precautions are adopted to have the space well ventilated between the underside of the floor and the ground, and the floor joists well seasoned before being fixed in position.

Wall-plates.—The ends of floor joists may rest on wall-plates, which are lengths of timber about 4½" wide and 3" thick. Wall-plates should also be used at any intermediate points of support, such as those of sleeper walls. As a preferable substitute for a wall-plate when joists are built into the wall, an iron bar 2½" wide and ½" thick may be laid in the wall for the ends of the joists to rest upon. This bar is not so liable to be destroyed, by damp or other agency, as a wooden wall-plate.

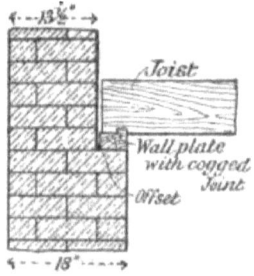

Fig. 375.—Section showing Floor Joists carried on Offset.

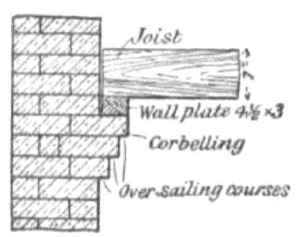

Fig. 376.—Section showing Floor Joists carried on Brick Corbelling.

How the ends of Joists should rest.—The ends of joists, in basement floors, should not be built into the wall, but should rest on **offsets**, which are formed by having the walls thicker below the ground floor. These offsets are frequently obtained in buildings several storeys high by diminishing the thickness of the wall at the floor levels (Fig. 375). Where offsets are inconvenient, an alternative method of carrying joists is obtained by building projecting courses of bricks, as shown in Fig. 376. These are named **over-sailing courses**, and the arrangement is known as **corbelling**. The projection required, about 4½", is obtained in three or more courses, and supports the wall-plate. The same object can be attained by using stone corbels built into the walls at horizontal distances of 2' to 3' apart, and, if necessary, using thicker wall-plates (Fig. 377).

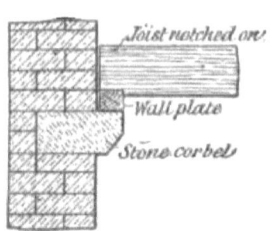

Fig. 377.—Section showing Floor Joists carried on Stone Corbels.

Although offsets and corbelling cannot generally be used for supporting the upper floors of dwelling-houses, it is especially advisable to adopt one of these methods for carrying the upper wooden floors of large warehouses, workshops, etc.; otherwise,

WOODEN FLOORS. 197

in case of fire, the middle part of the floor might be first destroyed, and the remainder would then act as a lever, when there would be considerable danger of the walls being overthrown. The joists may rest on the wallplates, as in Fig. 376; be *notched on*, as in Fig. 377; or they may be *cogged*, as shown in Fig. 375.

When joists are built into the wall, an air space of at least half an inch should be left along the sides and above each joist, to prevent decay.

Trimming. — No bearing timber should be placed nearer than six inches to a chimney flue. This necessitates an arrangement of framing the floor joists which is named *trimming*. In trimming, the bridging joists which would abut against the flue, are supported by a cross piece called a **trimmer**. The joists which carry the ends of the trimmer are called **trimming joists**. It is

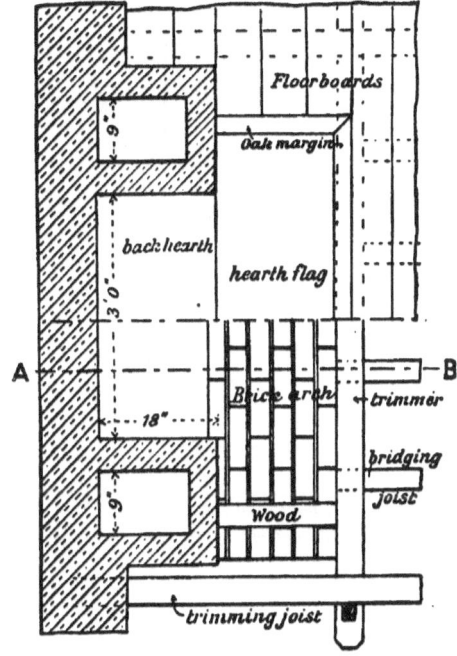

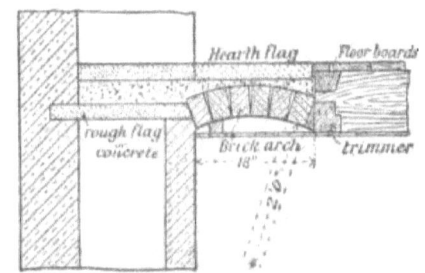

Fig. 378.—Brick Trimmer Arch, Hearth Flag, etc.

usual to have both the trimmer and the trimming joists thicker than the bridging joists by $\tfrac{1}{8}''$ for every bridging joist carried. Fig. 378 shows the trimming of the joists around a fireplace. Trimming is also necessary for staircase wells, trap-doors, or any opening in a floor which is wider than the space between two joists.

Joints used in Trimming.—The form of joint mostly used in trimming is the **tusk-tenon joint.** This joint is specially designed to prevent unnecessary weakening of the timbers. As explained on p. 171, the thickness of the tenon is one-sixth the depth of the joist, and the lower surface of the tenon is in the centre of the depth. The tusk (Figs. 379 and 380) extends into the joist for a distance equal to one-fifth the thickness of the joist. The joint is secured by allowing the tenon to project through the mortise, and inserting a wedge into a small mortise made in the tenon. These are omitted where they would be in the way, as in the joint between the trimmer and bridging joists.

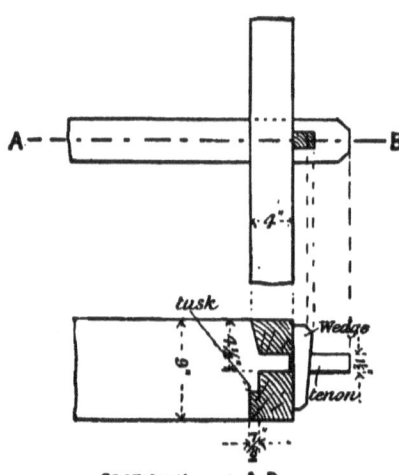

FIG. 879.—Tusk-tenon Joint.

The ordinary mortise and tenon joint, with a thickness of tenon about one-fourth the depth of the joist, is often used and secured with wedges, but is not so strong as the tusk-tenon joint. **Housed joints,** as shown in Figs. 381 and 382, are alternative methods often adopted. These are usually secured with spikes (large nails).

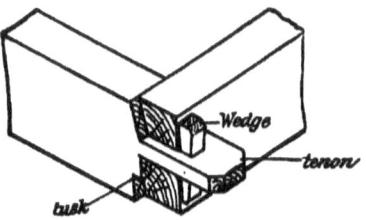

FIG. 380.—Sketch of a Tusk-tenon Joint.

Hearth-Flags and Trimmer Arches.—When a fireplace occurs in an upper room, it is necessary to have a hearth-flag from 3' 6" to 5' long, and projecting at least 18" from the front of the fireplace. The flag may be supported by a **concrete slab** built into the brickwork, and projecting so as to fill the space left between the trimmer and the brickwork; or by a brick arch known as

WOODEN FLOORS. 199

a **trimmer arch**, which springs on one side from the brickwork and on the other from the trimmer. Fig. 378 shows plan and a

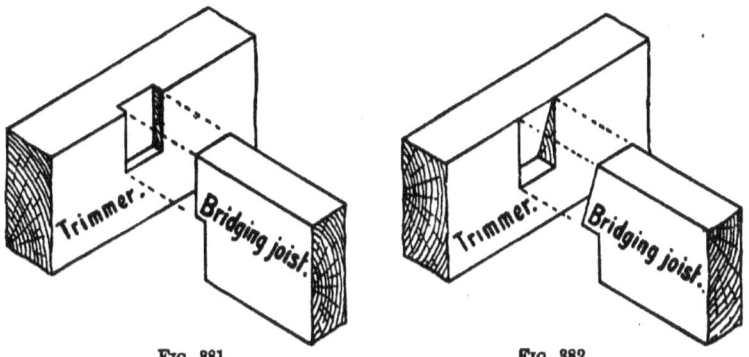

Fig. 381. Fig. 382.
Housed Joints used for Trimming.

vertical section of a fireplace, the hearth-flag of which is carried by a brick trimmer arch. The upper half of the plan shows the

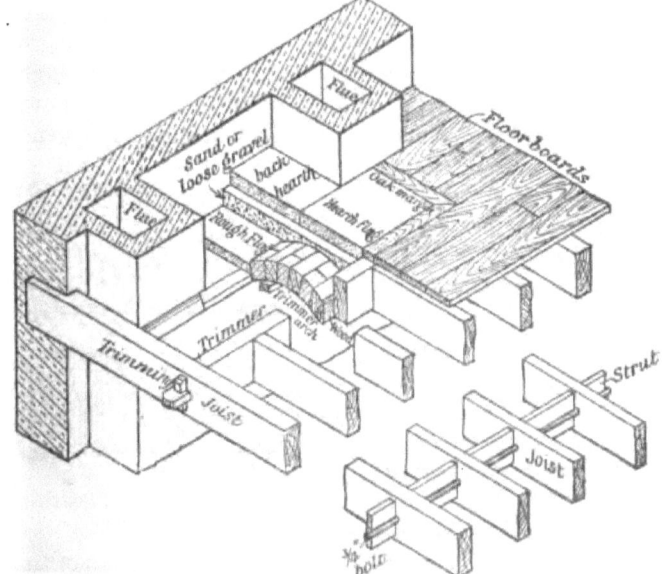

Fig. 383.—Sketch of a Brick Trimmer Arch, Hearth Flag, Joists, Floor Boards, etc.

hearth-flag, floor-boards, etc., in position; in the lower part of the plan the trimmer arch and joists are shown. Such an arch is named a *coach-headed* trimmer arch. Fig. 383 is a sketch of the same fireplace, showing the construction still more clearly. As an alternative, the trimmer arch may abut square on the trimmer, as shown in section in Fig. 384. This is necessary when the joists are not more than seven inches deep. When the bridging joists are placed parallel to the fireplace, as shown in Fig. 392, the trimming joist, which is the one against which the arch will abut, is strengthened, and prevented from yielding by the insertion of two bolts, which hook into the brickwork at one end and pass through the middle of the depth of the trimming joist as shown in Figs. 384 and 392. A narrow margin, often of oak, is generally mitred around the three sides of the hearth-flag; against it the floor-boards abut. Tiles of various kinds are often substituted for a hearth-flag.

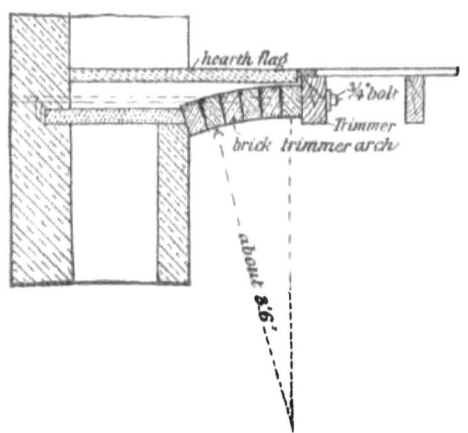

FIG. 384.—Section through Brick Trimmer Arch.

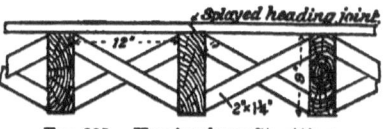

FIG. 385.—Herring-bone Strutting.

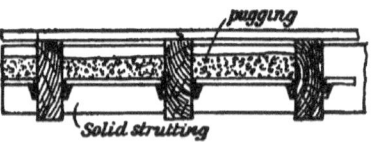

FIG. 386.—Sound Boarding, Pugging, and Solid Strutting.

Bridging and Strutting.—Wooden floors are strengthened by placing rows of *herring-bone bridging* or *strutting* at right angles to the direction of the joists, and at distances of 4' to 5' apart. This strutting is formed by pieces of timber, about 2" by 1½", crossing each other, and nailed to the joists in the manner shown in Figs. 373 and 385. An alternative plan is that known as *solid strutting*. Solid strutting consists of fixing rows of short boards on edge tightly between the joists

WOODEN FLOORS.

(Fig. 386.) Such boards are one inch narrower than the depth of the joists and from 1" to 1½" thick. When solid strutting is adopted, the floor may be further strengthened—

(a) By passing a three-quarter-inch bolt through the centre of the depth of the joists, close against the strutting, thus binding the whole together (Fig. 383);

(b) by nailing hoop iron (1½" to 2" wide, and one-sixteenth of an inch thick) along the top and bottom edges of the joists where the strutting is fixed, and then tightening up the struts by means of wedges.

Sound-boarding and Pugging.—This name is given to a device adopted to prevent the passage of sound from a room to the one below. It consists of laying a floor of rough short boards about half-way down the depth of the joists, and resting on fillets, shaped as in Fig. 387, which are nailed on both sides of each joist. These boards carry rough mortar, often mixed with ashes or sawdust (Fig. 386); or a layer of silicate cotton or slag wool to a

FIG. 387.

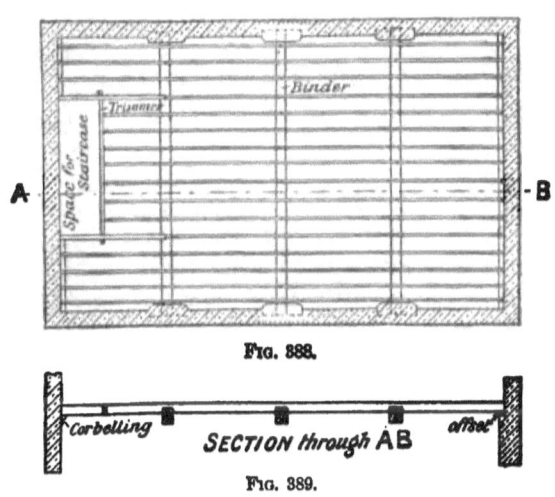

Plan and Section of a Double Floor.

depth of 2" or 3" may be substituted. The rough mortar, etc., is named *pugging*.

Double Floors.—Double floors have beams or **binders** placed from 6' to 10' apart. On these rest the bridging joists which carry the floor boards. In double and framed floors the weight of the whole floor is concentrated on a few points, namely, the ends of the binders and girders. This may be an advantage when there are many window openings, or where the wall can be strengthened by piers; but, since the floor timbers help to bind the walls together, a single floor does this more effectively, as the joists distribute the weight more equally on the walls. Again, double floors take up a greater depth than single floors, and thus, by requiring higher walls for the same height of rooms, increase the cost of buildings. Double floors are, however, most suitable for rooms from 16' to 24' wide. Figs. 388 and 389 show plan and section of a double floor.

In order to reduce the depth of the double floor without materially affecting its strength, the joists are usually *cogged* on to the binders, as shown in Figs. 390 and 391. The distance that the joists are cogged on to the binders may be anything up to two-thirds the depth of the joist. As the upper edge only of the binder is cut and the joists fit tightly into this, and as there is a full bearing for the end of the joist, it will be seen that a little extra depth of cogging does not seriously weaken the joint.

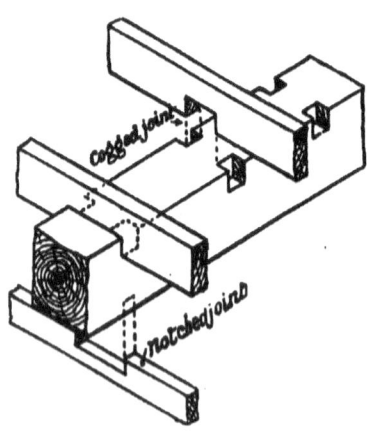

FIG. 390.—Sketch showing Cogged and Notched Joints.

Ceiling Joists.—When a plastered ceiling is required on the underside of a double or framed floor, the plasterers' laths may be nailed to the underside of the bridging joists, and the beams either wrought and their arrises moulded, or be "firred out" for the plasterers' laths: that is, have strips of wood 2" by ¾" nailed at distances of from 12" to 15" apart on the three sides that require to be plastered.

If it is desirable that the beams be hidden so that the ceiling shall be in one plane, ceiling joists 3" to 4" deep, and 2" thick may be fixed in one of the following ways:

(*a*) be notched to the underside of the binder as in Fig. 390;

WOODEN FLOORS.

(*b*) be cut to fit between the binders, and rest upon strips of wood named *fillets* (Fig. 391);

(*c*) have short tenons formed on the ends of the ceiling joists with corresponding mortises cut in the binders. When this method is adopted the binders are "chased out" at one side to allow one end of the ceiling joists to be placed into position after the binders are fixed (Fig. 391). Mortises so cut are named *chase mortises* and are seldom used.

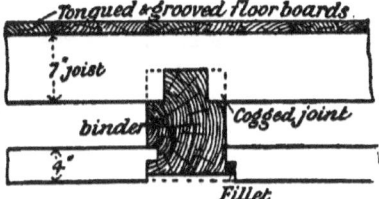

FIG. 391.—Section through a Binder in a Double Floor.

Framed Floors.—Framed floors are occasionally used where the distance between the walls is over 24′ and it is not desirable to have any pillars in the room. A framed floor consists of girders, binders, bridging joists, floor boards, and—when a plaster ceiling is required—ceiling joists.

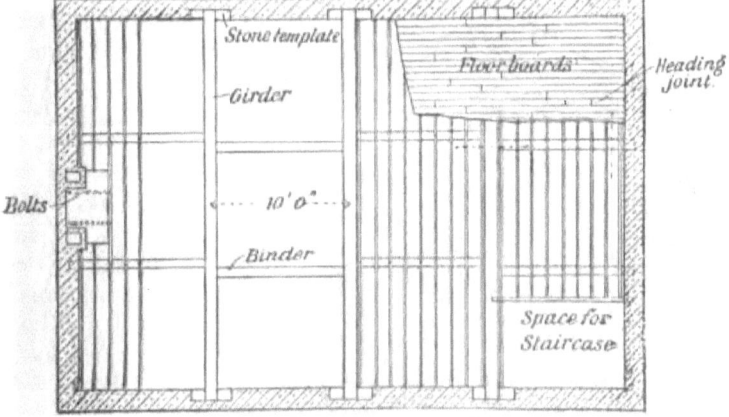

FIG. 392.—Plan of a Framed Floor.

Fig. 392 shows the plan of a framed floor with part of its surface covered with floor boards. Many of the bridging joists are omitted in this illustration for the sake of clearness. The trimming of the joists for a fireplace and for a staircase well is shown. In the fireplace-trimming, the trimming joist is shown to have two bolts connecting it to the brick work to assist the abutment of the arch.

The bridging joists of a double or a framed floor are stronger if they are long enough to span two or three bays, although all joints must be on binders. When this class of floor is framed

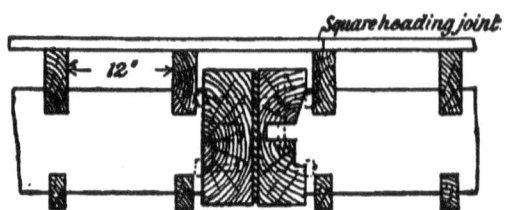

Fig. 393.—Section through a Wooden Girder, showing Tusk-tenon Joint between Binder and Girder.

entirely with wooden beams, the binders which are carried by the girders are tusk-tenoned into them, as shown in Fig. 393. Such a joint, however, weakens the girder considerably, and a stronger connection can be made by resting the binder in a cast-iron shoe or stirrup, having a small projection behind, which is let into the beam. The stirrup itself is secured to the girder with coach screws. Fig. 395 shows a cast-iron stirrup in position on a girder. Wrought iron is also often used for stirrups; Fig. 396 is an example. It remains to be mentioned that flitched and trussed girders (Figs. 266 to 273) are often used as the heavy beams of framed floors.

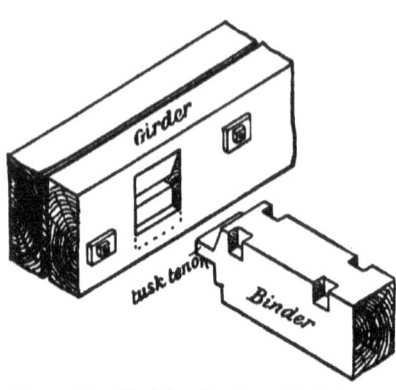

Fig. 394.—Sketch showing Tusk-tenon Joint between Binder and Girder.

Pillars or Columns.—A modification of the framed floor just described is often adopted for buildings of large span. This consists in arranging the floors in bays of from 8' to 12' wide, the ends of the bridging joists of each bay being cogged on to the girders, which have intermediate supports—in the shape of pillars (columns) of wood, cast iron, or steel—when more than 25' long. By using columns in this manner the size of the girders is reduced.

Cast iron columns, which are most frequently used, are hollow cylinders, with a thickness of metal of from $\frac{3}{4}''$ to $1\frac{1}{2}''$. The lower

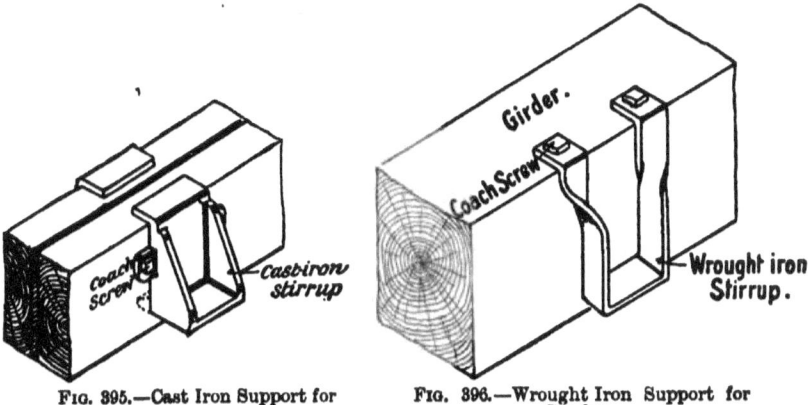

Fig. 395.—Cast Iron Support for Binder.

Fig. 396.—Wrought Iron Support for Binder.

ends of these columns rest either on large foundation stones or upon a base of concrete, and the upper ends have a head or

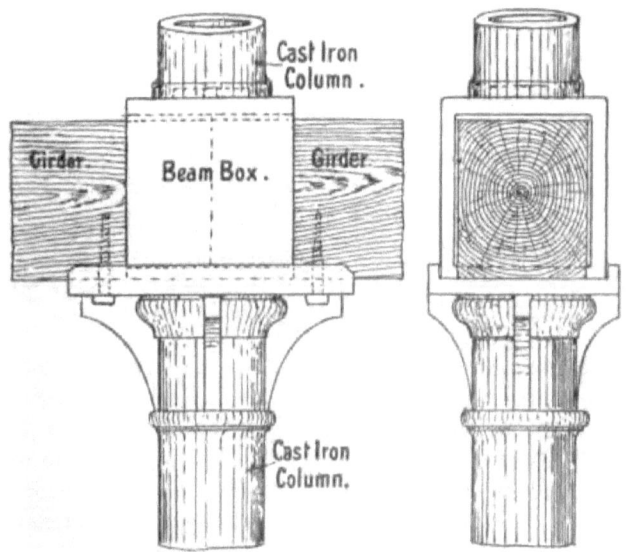

Fig. 397.—Cast Iron Column supporting Wooden Girders.

seating upon which the ends of the beams rest. If the building is two or more storeys high, and necessitates the use of columns vertically over each other, a cast iron beam-box, which spans the beam, may be used to support the lower end of the upper column. Another plan is to allow the upper column to fit into the upper end of the lower one, the head or seating of the lower column being large enough to support the floor girders.

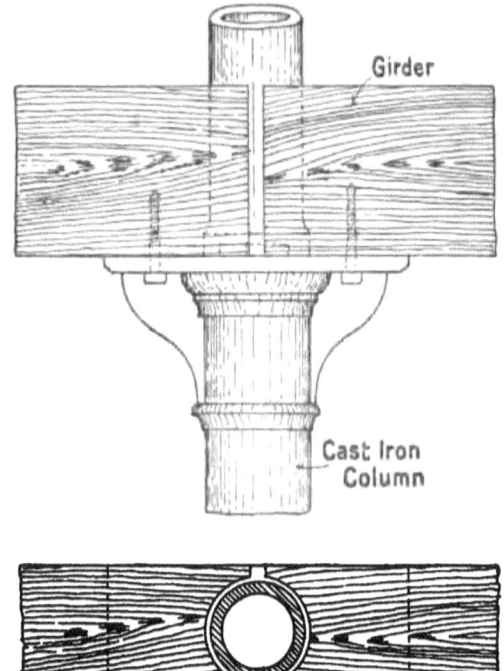

FIG. 398.—Cast Iron Column supporting Wooden Girders.

Figs. 397 and 398 show examples of the heads of columns supporting floor girders.

The Use of Wrought-Iron and Steel Girders in Floor Construction.—Wrought iron and steel girders have in recent years largely superseded heavy wooden beams for floor construction. Although the former are stronger, and not so liable to decay as the latter, experience has shown that they have serious disadvantages. This is especially the case if a building takes fire, when the expansion that occurs, and the tendency to warp and buckle up, are often the cause of overturning the

WOODEN FLOORS.

walls and prove destructive both to life and property. A heavy wooden beam will often burn only until the whole of the outer surface is charred, and it does not expand materially with heat. Wooden beams are therefore to be recommended in preference to iron ones unless the latter are encased in some fire-resisting material.

When iron girders are used to support wooden joists, the joists may rest on the upper flange of the girder, as shown in Fig. 399; or on pieces of timber resting on the bottom flange of the girder, and bolted through its web (Fig. 400); or again, if the joists are deep enough, they may themselves rest on the lower flanges of the iron girder itself. The unsightly appearance of iron girders when constructed as in Fig. 399 may be entirely avoided by encasing them in wood or plaster.

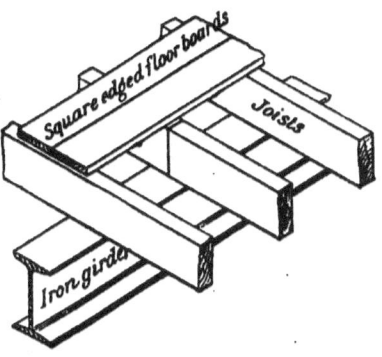

FIG. 399.—Joists resting on Upper Flange of Iron Girder.

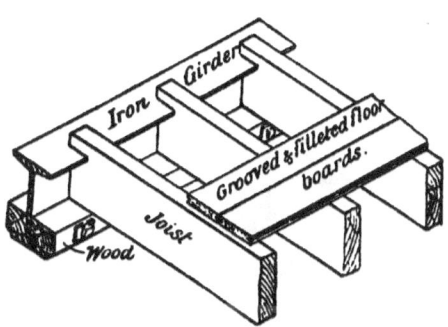

FIG. 400.—Joists carried by Iron Girder.

Stone Templates.—The ends of all beams used in floor and roof construction should either rest on stone templates (padstones) or should fit into cast iron beam boxes which are built into the wall. The reason for this is to allow a firm seating for the beam, and to distribute the weight carried over a large surface of the wall. Stone templates are blocks of hard stone, from 2' to 3' long, 9" to 12" wide, and 4" to 6" thick. The openings, or pockets, into which the beams requiring stone templates rest, should be at least $1\frac{1}{2}$" wider than the breadth of the beam, to allow for an air-space on each side of it. An air-space, which may be closed by a brick arch (Fig. 401) or by a stone lintel, should also be provided on the top of the beam.

Cast iron beam-boxes, made large enough to allow of a circulation of air around the end of the beam, are made with sides from 1" to 1½" thick, and often have a longer base plate to obtain a longer bearing surface on the wall.

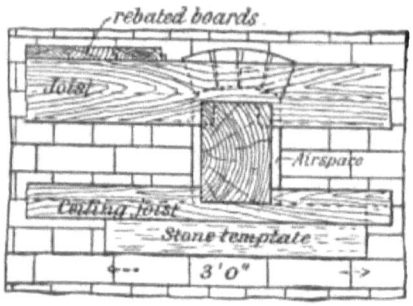

FIG. 401.—Vertical Section through Binder showing Air-space or Pocket in Elevation.

Encasing of Girders.—Plain wooden casings formed out of ¾" tongued, grooved and beaded match-boarding, secured to rough "firring" pieces nailed to every second joist, as shown at A in Fig. 402, may be used. Framed and panelled linings are a superior alternative means of encasing girders. This is shown at B in Fig. 402. When the encasing is effected by laths and plaster, the rough packing pieces (firrings) which are required to carry the plasterers' laths are nailed against every joist.

Fire-resisting Floors.—A very effective fire-resisting floor constructed of wood is made by spiking together battens or deals placed on edge, so as to get a solid wooden slab of thickness equal to the depth of the deals used. The floor is improved by "grouting" the joists with liquid plaster of Paris. The upper surface may consist of the upper edges of the deals planed smooth, or a layer of floor boards may be laid on the top.

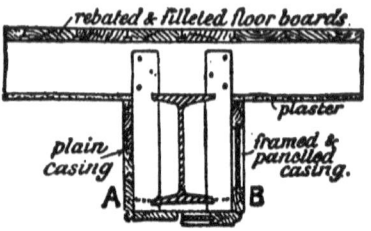

FIG. 402.—Alternative Methods of encasing Iron Girders.

A fire-resisting floor may also be constructed with iron or steel girders, on which rest smaller steel joists placed from 18" to 2' apart. The space between these joists is filled with **cement concrete** to a depth of 6" to 8", a temporary sheeting of planks being fixed on the underside to support the concrete

WOODEN FLOORS.

until it sets. Other methods of constructing fire-resisting floors are by building **brick arches** which spring from heavy iron girders, or by a combination of iron girders and specially constructed **fire-clay blocks**, supported by the girders.

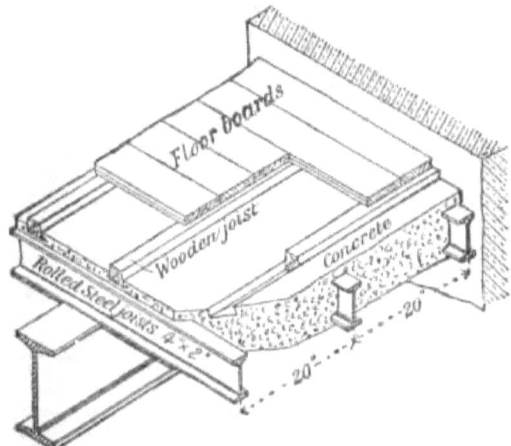

Fig. 403.—Sketch of part of a Fire-resisting Floor, composed of Steel Joists and Concrete.

When a wooden floor is required on the upper surface of any of the above floors, wooden joists about 3" by 3" are laid on the top of the fire-resisting material, or if this is of concrete, are partly embedded into it (Fig. 404) when the concrete is being

Fig. 404.

Fig. 405.—As used in Wooden Block Floors.

laid. The joists are often cut obliquely as shown in Fig. 404. The floor boards are nailed to the joists in the usual manner.

Instead of using joists and boards on the upper surface of a concrete floor, **wooden blocks** of shape shown in Fig. 405 may be used. The blocks are from 6" to 12" long, 3" wide, and from $1\frac{1}{4}$" to 2" thick. They are secured together and in position by being

210 A MANUAL OF CARPENTRY AND JOINERY.

first dipped in a hot composition, of which pitch or tar forms the basis. A decided advantage may be claimed for a block floor, in that, in schools, libraries, and where the floor cannot well be carpeted, it is noiseless as compared with the joist and boarded floors.

Dimensions of Floor Boards.—Floor boarding, like all timber, however well seasoned, is liable to shrinkage. To minimise this as much as possible, floor boards are cut into narrow widths, and in the best class of floors they are seldom

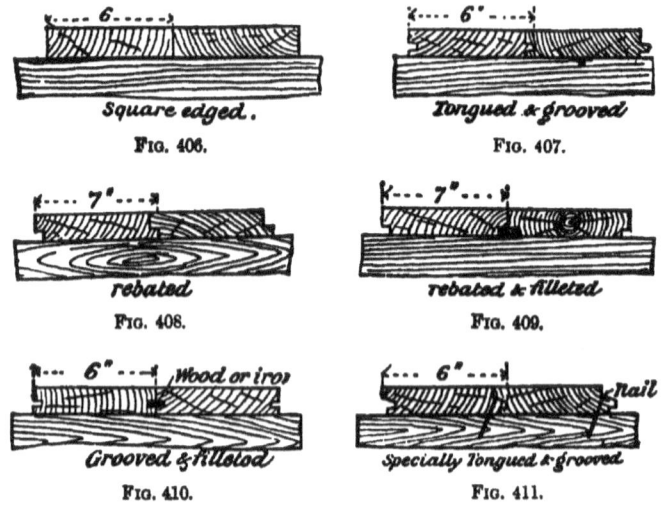

Floor Board Joints.

more than 4" to 5" wide. Ordinarily, however, they vary from 4" to 7" in width, and from $\frac{7}{8}$" to $1\frac{1}{8}$" in thickness. It is not uncommon in warehouses, or where heavy traffic exists, to use wrought battens or deals, the thickness of which is $2\frac{1}{2}$" and 3".

Floors are frequently laid with two thicknesses of boards, the lower one consisting of rough boards about $\frac{3}{4}$" thick. The top layer may be conveniently left until the plastering is finished and the building fairly dry, there is then less liability of the finished floor surface being affected by dampness.

Floor Board Joints.—The edges of floor boards, or floor battens, as they are also called, are prepared in many different ways. The joints most commonly used are the *square-edged* (Fig. 406) and the *tongued and grooved* (Fig. 407). Figs. 408 to

411 show other less-frequently employed joints with their distinctive names appended. Fig. 411 shows a form of joint used in the construction of superior floors. With such a joint each board must be nailed and laid separately to the joists, the object being to obtain a finished floor surface free from unsightly nail-holes.

Heading Joints.—Heading joints are those formed by joining the ends of boards together. A heading joint must always be over a joist. The ends of the boards may be cut square—a *square heading* joint— (Fig. 393); cut obliquely through the thickness as shown in Fig. 385 (a *splayed heading* joint); or a *tongued and grooved* joint may be made (Fig. 412). Another joint, named a *forked heading* joint, and illustrated in Fig. 413, is sometimes used. For ordinary work, the labour involved in the making of this last-named joint is not compensated for by any advantage in its use over those previously described.

Tongued heading joint
Fig. 412.

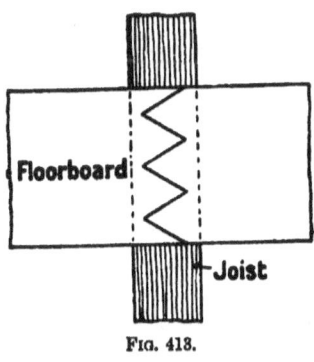
Fig. 413.

Materials used, and Methods of Laying Floors.—Several different kinds of timber are used for floor construction. Perhaps that in most general use, and applicable either to beams or girders, floor joists, ceiling joists, and floor boards is **red** or **yellow deal** (*Pinus sylvestris*). It is one of the strongest of soft woods. **Spruce or white deal** (*Picea excelsa*) is also largely used for joists and floor boards. **Pitch pine** is very suitable for the girders and binders. Pitch pine, birch, maple, and oak are often used for floor boards.

The nails used for nailing down the floor boards are named **brads.** They have, as Fig. 321 shows, a small head, which when driven below the surface of the board leaves only a small hole visible on the floor surface.

The heavy timbers such as the girders and binders, as well as the floor joists, are placed in position as the building proceeds. When wall plates are used these are laid level at the proper height; the necessary joints are made for the trimming for hearths, staircase wells, and any other openings that may require to be provided for; and then the joists are placed in position as required. These timbers serve as a tie for the walls; they are also an aid to the builder in carrying up the higher parts of the building, as they to some extent take the place of scaffolding.

For ordinary dwelling houses it is usual to lay the floor boards directly the building is covered in. There are disadvantages in this plan, inasmuch as, if the boards are well seasoned, the damp state of the building, along with the dampness caused by the plastering of the walls and ceilings, causes the floor boards to swell, and often to rise from the joists. When the building becomes dry the boards again shrink and open joints result. The narrower the boards the less the shrinkage that takes place in each one. Again, as previously explained, wood shrinks more tangentially than radially to the annual rings, therefore a material difference will result from the way the boards are cut from the log.

When two thicknesses of boards are used, the lower layer can be laid and used as the floor, and the upper layer need not be laid until the building is dry and the plasterers' work is finished. With this class of floor the square-edged joints are generally used. With floors laid with only one thickness of boards, the tongued and grooved joint is to be preferred. The heading joints of a floor are usually very numerous. They should always be on a joist, and should not all meet on the same joist; nor should they be in straight lines.

Floor cramps are used for cramping the joints of floor boards together when being laid in position. Many different types are obtainable, especially for use with single layers of boards. Figs. 221 and 224 are types which clip the joist when being used. For the upper layer of a double-boarded floor, **iron dogs** are often driven over the middle of joists into the floor previously laid; and the floor boards are forced into position by folding **wedges** of hard wood bearing against the edges and the dogs.

Another plan is to "buckle" the floor boards into position. This may be done by securely nailing the outermost of five or six boards, and then "folding" or "buckling" the intermediate boards into the space left for them.

Summary.

Wooden floors are known as *single*, *double*, or *framed*, according to the arrangement of the timbers composing them. They consist of *joists*, *binders*, *girders*, *floor boards*, and *ceiling joists*.

In floor joists the usual ratio of depth to breadth is 3 to 1.

Joists ought, whenever possible, to rest upon *offsets* or *corbels* in preference to being built into the wall. When a *joist*, *binder*, or *girder* is built into a wall, an air-space should be left around it to prevent decay of the timber. All binders and girders should rest on *stone templates*. Around staircase openings and fireplaces the joists are *trimmed*; the best joint for trimming is the *tusk tenon* joint.

Floors are strengthened by *herring-bone bridging*, or by *solid strutting*. Joists and binders are connected by a *cogged* joint. Binders and girders may be connected either by a *tusk tenon joint*, or by means of an *iron stirrup*.

Iron and steel girders are much used in floor construction. The heavy beams of large floors are often supported in addition by intermediate *cast iron columns*. Floor boards may have their edges *square*, *tongued and grooved*, *grooved and filleted*, *rebated*, *rebated and filleted*, or *tongued and grooved* for secret nailing. It is often an advantage to have two thicknesses of boards on the same floor.

Small rectangular *wooden blocks*, laid upon *concrete*, are often used instead of joists and boards.

The **timber** used for floor boards may be red deal, *white deal*, *pitch pine*, *oak*, *birch*, or *maple*. For joists generally, *red* or *white deal*, and for heavy girders, binders, etc., *red deal* or *pitch pine* is employed. Specially devised *cramps* are used in the laying of floor boards.

Questions on Chapter VIII.

1. Define the difference between a single, a double, and a framed floor. In what circumstances should each kind be used?

2. How far apart should floor joists be placed? What should be the sizes of floor joists for a single floor of 8 ft., 12 ft., and 14 ft. span respectively?

3. Draw, to a scale of $1\frac{1}{2}$ in. to one foot, vertical cross-sections through the wall supporting the joists of a wooden floor, showing three different methods of carrying the ends of the joists other than by building them into the wall.

4. Shew the method of "trimming" round a fireplace, and make a dimensioned sketch of any joints you would use. Give sketches illustrating herring-bone and solid strutting. (C. and G. Ord., 1900.)

5. Draw a plan and a section showing how you would trim round a fireplace. (C. and G. Ord., 1902.)

6. Show by sketches three different methods of stiffening a floor by strutting. Explain what is meant by sound-boarding and pugging. What is pugging composed of, and why is it used?

7. Draw, to a scale of $1\frac{1}{2}$ in. to one foot, two sections showing the cogged joint between the floor joist and the binder of a double floor.

8. Show by sketches, one-quarter full size, how you would tenon a common joist (9 in. by 3 in.) into a girder (9 in. by 6 in.), carefully marking the relative proportions of the various parts. (C. and G. Ord., 1894.)

9. Draw to scale of $\frac{1}{4}$ inch to a foot, plan and section of a framed floor to a room 20 ft. by 14 ft., with fireplace in the long side, and give two details of joints, one-eighth full size. (C. and G. Ord., 1895.)

10. A warehouse floor, 24 ft. by 32 ft., has an iron girder across the middle. Show to scale $\frac{1}{4}$ inch to a foot, how you would construct the floor; and give detail $\frac{1}{4}$ full size of the connection of your work with the girder. (C. and G. Hon., 1896.)

11. Show by sketches one-quarter full size, and explain, three methods of fixing fir joists to iron girders. (C. and G. Ord., 1895.)

12. Give $\frac{1}{4}$ full-size sections of different joints of floor boards, including heading joints. (C. and G. Ord., 1896.)

13. Describe, as it would appear in a carefully-worded specification, the flooring you would recommend, regardless of cost, for a ground-floor library, and similarly describe other cheaper forms of flooring, including an ordinary yellow deal floor laid straight joint, and explain the technical terms used in your description. (C. and G. Hon., 1900.)

14. Describe the most suitable timber for general use in floor construction for: girders, floor joists, floor boards.

15. (a) Make a sketch of a floor cramp, and describe the method of using it. (b) Make a sketch of a floor brad. (c) Describe and sketch the appliances suitable for use in cramping the upper layer of boards in a floor having two thicknesses of floor boards.

CHAPTER IX.

WOODEN ROOFS.

Slope of Roof.—The arrangement of the timbers used in the construction of the roof of a building varies according to circumstances. Many considerations, such as the class of building, the style of architecture, the size of rooms, the material to be used for covering, the climatic conditions, etc., must be taken into account. Slates and tiles are most frequently used as coverings in this country, but other materials—such as thatch, corrugated iron, asphalted felt, copper, zinc, lead, and concrete —are often used.

With copper, zinc, lead, etc., the roof surface may be laid nearly horizontal, but slates and tiles require a sloping roof, the inclination of which varies from twenty-five degrees (25°) to sixty-five degrees (65°) for slates; and from thirty-five degrees (35°) to sixty-five degrees (65°) for tiles. A common **pitch**, when slates are used, is one-fourth ($\frac{1}{4}$) or one-third ($\frac{1}{3}$) the span, which means that the vertical distance from the level of the top of the walls to the highest point of the roof, when it slopes equally both ways, is respectively one-quarter or one-third the width of the building.

Parts of a Roof.—The highest part of a roof sloping both ways is named the **ridge**; the horizontal piece of timber forming the ridge is called the **ridge piece** or **ridge tree**. The timbers placed in the direction of the slope of the roof are named **spars** or **common rafters**. The common rafters, which are from 3" to $4\frac{1}{2}$" deep, and 2" to 3" thick, should, even with the larger size, be supported at intervals of not more than 8'. The lower edges of a sloping roof are called the **eaves**. Wall-plates, to which the lower ends of the common rafters are nailed, should be bedded on the wall at the eaves. Intermediate horizontal timbers, which support the common rafters, are known as **purlins**. In dwelling houses the walls serve to carry the purlins, but with large buildings, **framed trusses** are required for this purpose. Distinctive names are given to the different types of roof truss according to their size and shape. A **hip** is an angle made when a building, instead of having a gable as at A (Fig. 414) has the roof returned round the end of the building as at B. A **valley** is formed when two roof surfaces meet together and form an internal angle. Hips and valleys are constructed with strong timbers placed on edge; they are carried by the walls or roof trusses. The timbers are named **hip** or **valley rafters**, and carry the common rafters that abut against them. Such short common rafters are known as **jack rafters**.

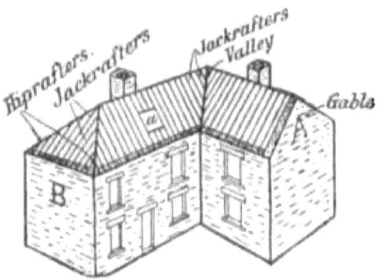

FIG. 414.—Sketch showing Gable, Hipped Roof, Hip and Valley Rafters, etc.

Lean-to Roof.—The simplest kind of sloping roof is that where one wall is carried up sufficiently higher than the other to give the required slope to the roof. Such a roof is called a **lean-to roof** (Fig. 415). In all cases where the length of the common rafter is more than eight feet, one or more purlins should be inserted.

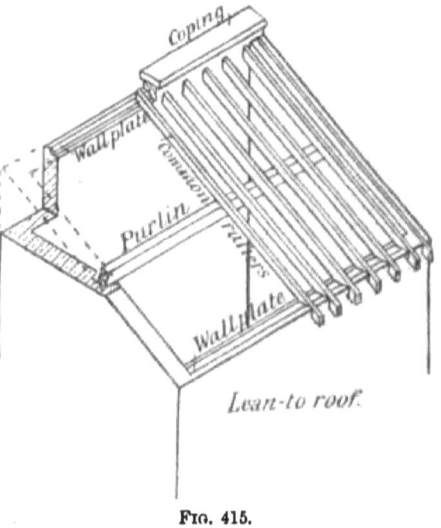

FIG. 415.

Couple Roof.—A couple roof is one in which the common rafters slope upwards from opposite walls and meet a ridge

WOODEN ROOFS. 217

piece in the middle. The common rafters are securely nailed to the ridge piece and to the wall-plate on each wall. The common rafters have no tie or other support in this class of roof, therefore the tendency is for the walls to be thrown over by the

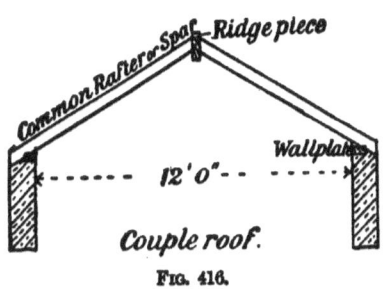

Fig. 416.

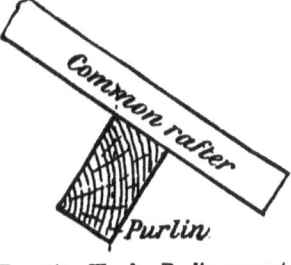

Fig. 417.—Wooden Purlin supporting Common Rafter.

weight of the roof. Such couple roofs are only used on small buildings, where the span is not more than 12′ (Fig. 416).

How Common Rafters are Fixed.—In cottages and dwelling-houses generally, the inside walls of which are carried up to the roof, the common rafters are nailed to the ridge piece, to the

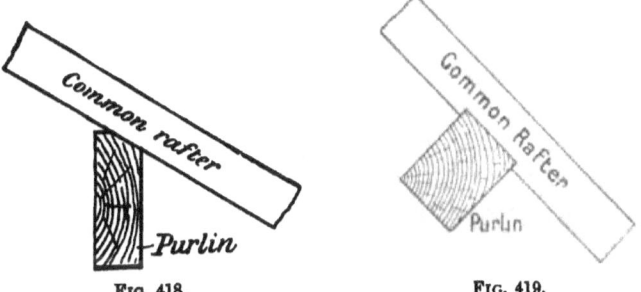

Fig. 418. Fig. 419.

Wooden Purlins supporting Common Rafters.

wall-plates, and to purlins which extend from wall to wall. The size of the purlins depends upon the distance between the walls of support; the purlins may be placed either with one side vertical and with the top corner cut off to the slope of the roof (Fig. 418), or, as shown in Fig. 417, with one side at right angles to the slope of the roof. When the purlins are placed as in Fig. 417, the proportion of the width to the thickness

218 A MANUAL OF CARPENTRY AND JOINERY.

should be adjusted so that, when in position, a diagonal of the cross section is vertical. When the slope of the roof is steep, the common rafters are often notched on to the upper edge of the purlin for about three-quarters of an inch (Fig. 419).

When the walls which support the purlins are more than about 16′ apart, and it is not desirable to insert a framed truss of the usual type, the purlins may be trussed as explained in Chap. VII., and illustrated in Figs. 268 to 273; or rolled steel or wrought-iron girders may be used as purlins. These iron purlins, however, require "lining up" with pieces of timber, which are bolted on the top of the upper flange, and to which the common rafters are nailed (Fig. 420).

FIG. 420.—Iron Girder supporting Common Rafter.

Ceiling.—The ceiling under the roof of a dwelling-house is obtained by fixing the ceiling joists, which are to carry the laths and plaster, level with the top of the side walls; or, to

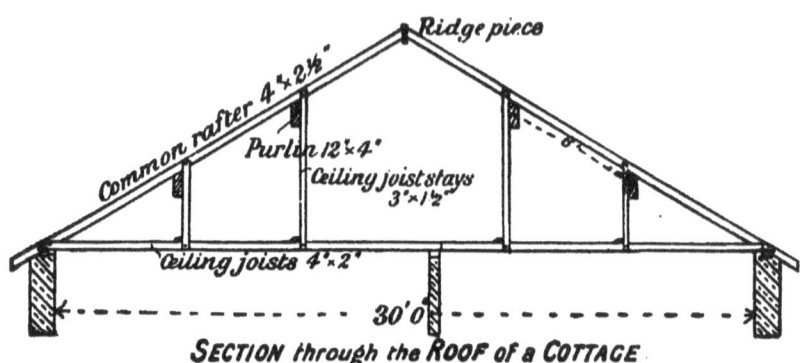

SECTION through the ROOF of a COTTAGE
FIG. 421.

obtain additional height in the rooms, the ceiling joists may be placed part of the way up the slope of the roof. When securely nailed together and to the common rafters, these ceiling joists form a tie which strengthens the roof. To stiffen them further they are secured together and to the purlins with pieces of quartering, named **stays**, about 3″ by 1½″ in section (Fig. 421).

WOODEN ROOFS. 219

Collar-beam Roof.—For spans between 12′ and 18′ the collar-beam roof is used extensively. Its construction is effected

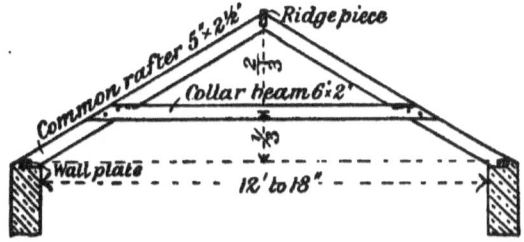

FIG. 422.—Elevation of Collar-beam Roof.

by framing each pair of common rafters into a light truss, and connecting them by means of a horizontal tie named a **collar-**

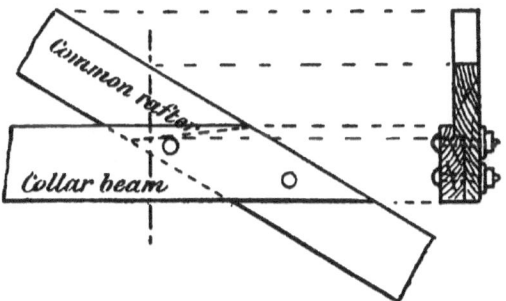

FIG. 423.—Joint between Collar-beam and Common Rafter.

beam. The height of the collar-beam is determined by the amount of room required ; the lower it is placed, the stronger

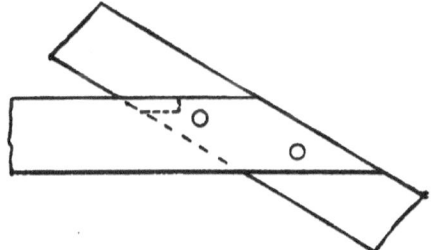

FIG. 424.—Joint between Collar-beam and Common Rafter.

is the roof. It is usually fixed at one-third or one-half the vertical height from the wall to the ridge. The joint connecting the collar-beam to the roof may be a dovetail-halved-joint (Fig. 423), or a halved and cogged joint (Fig. 424). Both these joints require further securing with bolts.

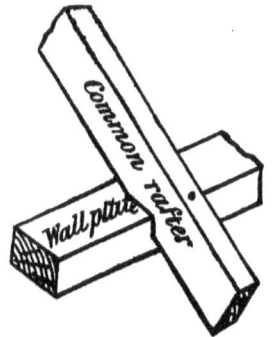

FIG. 425.—Bird's-mouth Joint at Foot of Rafter.

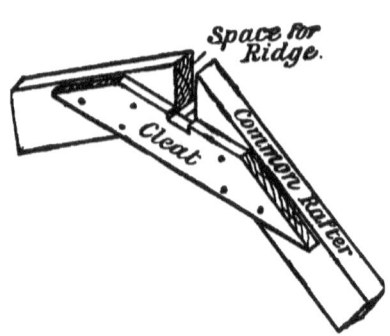

FIG. 426.—Joint at Head of Rafters in a Collar-beam Roof.

The lower ends of common rafters are cut and nailed to the wall-plate as in Fig. 427 ; or, if the ends of the rafters overhang the wall, they are cut as shown in Fig. 425. Both these joints are known as *bird's-mouth joints*.

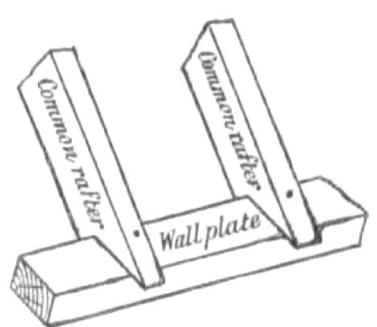

FIG. 427.—Bird's-mouth Joint at Foot of Rafters.

Each pair of common rafters is connected at the upper end by means of a *cleat*, leaving a slot to receive the ridge piece (Fig. 426).

Framed Roof Trusses.— When the span exceeds 18′ and there are no inside cross walls to carry the purlins, framed structures known as **roof trusses** are used for the purpose.

Such trusses should be so constructed that when complete they are as rigid as possible. With this end in view the timbers (members) of each truss are arranged to form a series of triangles. A guiding principle should be that each purlin is directly supported by a member of the truss in such a way that the members are subjected to direct tension or compression stresses only, and not to cross stresses.

WOODEN ROOFS.

This principle, along with the fact that purlins should never be more than 8' apart, decides the shape of the truss for a given span. The joints of all wooden roof trusses should be arranged,

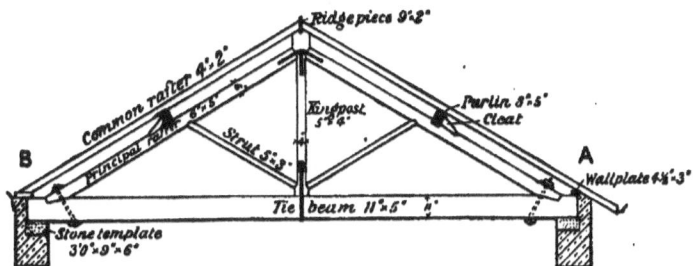

Fig. 428.—Elevation of a King-post Roof Truss.

as far as possible, at right angles to the grain of the wood, so that they will be least affected by shrinkage.

The distance between the trusses is influenced by the position of window and other openings; no truss should be fixed directly over such an opening. It is not economical to place trusses much further apart than 10', on account of the increased size of the purlins required.

King-post Truss.—Fig. 428 shows the elevation of a King-post truss with the names of the different members appended. As will be noticed, the truss derives its name from the central upright, called the **King-post**. The horizontal **tie-beam** prevents the **principal rafters** from spreading. The **struts** are arranged to support

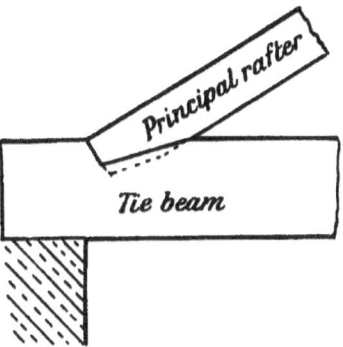

Fig. 429.—Joint at Foot of Principal Rafter.

the principal rafters at points beneath the purlins. Up to spans of 28', with a pitch of not more than one-third the span, it is sufficient to have one purlin on each side. In such a case a King-post truss is most suitable.

Joint at Foot of Principal Rafter.—This joint should be directly over the wall, as shown in Fig. 429, or if it be necessary to have it some distance from the wall, as in Fig. 430, a stronger tie beam will be required, since additional stress is in such a case put on that member. Figs. 431, 432, and 433 show three different ways of making this connection between the tie-beam and

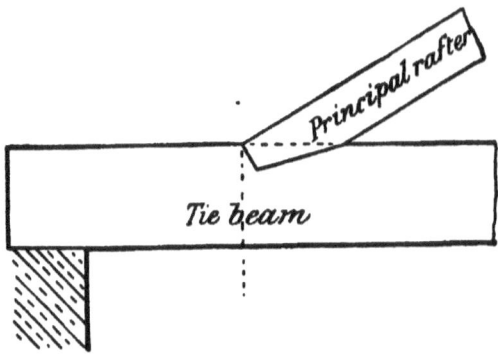

FIG. 430.—Incorrect Position of Joint in a Roof Truss.

principal rafter. In each case the end of the principal rafter is cut at right angles to the grain of the wood for half its width. In Fig. 431 a stump tenon is cut on the end of the principal rafter, and a corresponding mortise made in the tie-beam; in Figs. 432 and 433 a bridle joint is formed. An **iron bolt** may be used to secure the joint (Fig. 428), or **wrought iron straps**, arranged in a variety of ways, may be employed (Figs. 433 and 438).

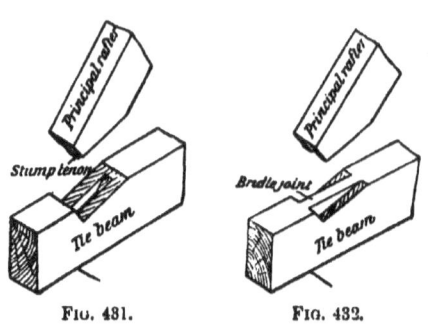

FIG. 431.   FIG. 432.

Sketches of Joints at foot of Principal Rafter.

Joint at Head of King-post.—Fig. 433 shows the elevation of the joint between the upper ends of the principal rafters and the King-post. Each principal rafter is stump tenoned into the King-post—which is made wider at each end to obtain a square abutment—the joint being secured by a wrought iron strap placed on each side and bolted through each member as shown in the illustration.

WOODEN ROOFS. 223

Joint at Ends of Strut.—The strut has the upper end either bridled or stump tenoned into the lower edge of the principal rafter, and the lower end stump tenoned into the lower end of the King-post, which is mortised to receive it, as shown in Fig. 433.

Joint between King-post and Tie-beam.—The lower end of the

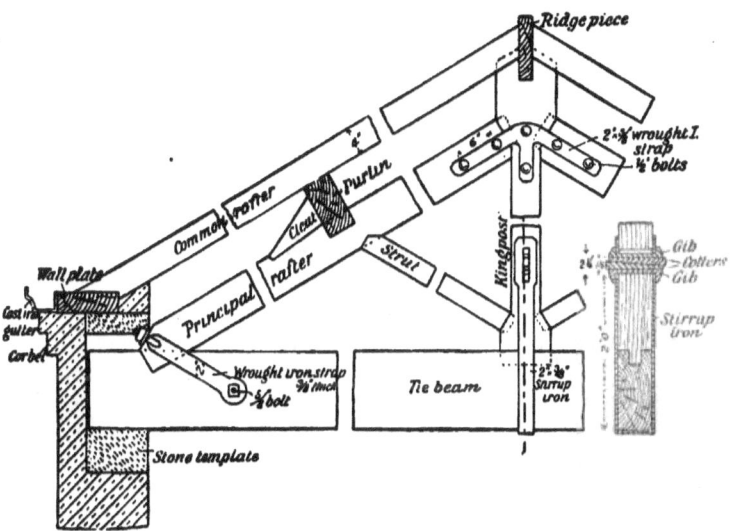

Fig. 488.—Details of the Joints of a King-post Roof Truss.

King-post is stump tenoned into the upper edge of the tie-beam for a distance of about 2″, and is secured with either :

(a) A stirrup iron and gibs and cotters ;
(b) A joint bolt ;
(c) A wrought iron strap and bolts.

In the construction of the truss, the joint between the King-post and tie-beam is left about one inch slack, and by using as the fastening either the stirrup iron and the gibs and cotters, or a joint bolt, all the joints of the truss are drawn close, and a camber (arching) of about $\frac{1}{2}$″ in 10′ is given to the tie-beam to prevent it from sagging when it is placed in position and loaded.

A **stirrup iron** is a U-shaped wrought iron strap, which embraces the tie-beam and the lower end of the King-post, and is fastened with two iron clips called **gibs**, and iron wedges called **cotters.** The length of the stirrup iron, to the holes through which the gibs and cotters pass, is about double the depth of the tie-beam. Fig. 434 shows a sketch of this mode of fastening, where two gibs and two cotters are in position ready for tightening up. It is advisable to note carefully the spaces left for tightening up the joint. These are shown in Fig. 433 where the lower gib rests on the wooden King-post, and brings it down towards the joint; the upper gib bears against the iron stirrup, and in this way draws the tie-beam towards the joint; so that when the cotters are driven tight they may draw the joint together.

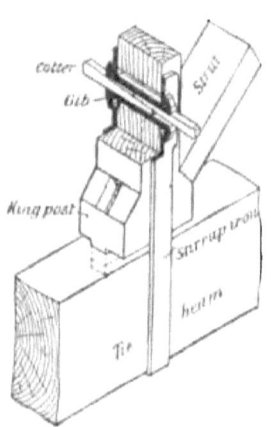

FIG. 484.—Sketch of Joint at Foot of King-post showing Stirrup Iron with Gibs and Cotters.

A **joint bolt,** as has been explained previously (p. 176), is a bolt with a flat square head, and a pointed end which is threaded for a distance of 3" or 4"; it is provided with a flat nut which is in this case let into the King-post. The length of the joint bolt is about twice the depth of the tie-beam; its diameter is from $\tfrac{5}{8}$" to 1"·

In fixing, a hole is bored for the required distance through the tie-beam and into the end of the King-post. The flat nut is let into the King-post in a line with the hole thus bored, so that the end of the joint bolt will pass into the nut. It is tightened up by turning the joint bolt with a spanner. In Fig. 439 a $\tfrac{3}{4}$" joint bolt at the lower end of a Queen-post is shown.

Figs. 435 and 436 show a U-shaped **wrought iron strap,**

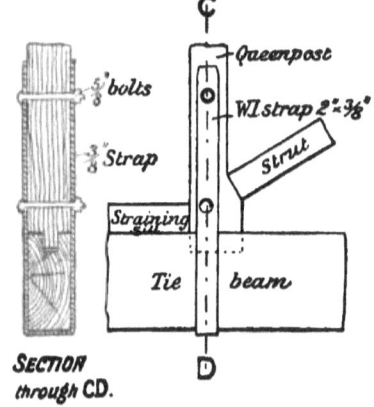

FIG. 435. FIG. 436.

Foot of Queen-post showing Wrought Iron Straps and Bolts.

bent to clip the tie-beam and King-post, and held in position by **bolts.** Although often adopted, this arrangement does not allow of tightening up the joints of the truss, and is therefore not so good a means of securing the joint as either of the two previously described.

The ends of all tie-beams should rest on stone templates and have air-spaces around them as described for floor girders (p. 207).

Joint between Purlin and Principal Rafter.—The best construction is effected by resting the purlin on the upper edge (back) of the principal rafter, with a cogged joint (p. 202) and obtaining additional support by housing a cleat into the principal rafter on the lower side of the purlin. This arrangement

Fig. 437.—Section through Wooden Purlin.

is shown in Fig. 433. The carrying power of the purlins is increased if each is long enough to pass over two bays. Another plan is to tusk-tenon the end of the purlins into the side of the principal rafter—so that the upper edges of the purlin and rafter are in the same plane—securing the joint with a wedge; or, if the tenon only goes into the mortise for about

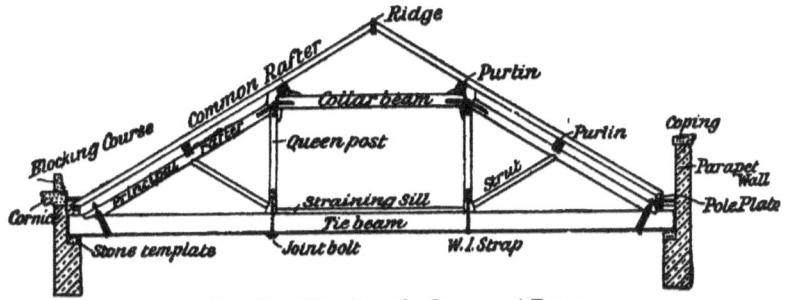

Fig. 438.—Elevation of a Queen-post Truss.

half the thickness of the principal rafter, it may be secured with a joint bolt.

Queen-post Truss.—A Queen-post truss is arranged to support a roof which has *two* purlins on each side of the ridge. Spans of ordinary pitch, of not more than 40′, allow of this truss being used. A Queen-post truss is shown in elevation in Fig. 438, with the names of the different members indicated. This truss differs from a King-post truss in having two vertical members (**Queen-posts**) the upper ends of which are placed

M.C.J.   P

between the upper ends of the **principal rafters** and the ends of a horizontal **collar** or **straining beam**. Another member, which is not found in the King-post truss, is the **straining sill**. It rests upon the **tie-beam**, between the Queen-posts, and counteracts the thrust of the **struts**.

The joints of this truss are made similar to those described for the King-post truss, with the exception of the **joint at the head of the Queen-post**. This joint is shown in elevation in Fig. 439, where the ends of the principal rafter and the collar beam are stump-tenoned into the Queen-post, and secured with wrought-iron straps and bolts. The Queen-post, like the King-post, is wider at each end to provide a better abutment for the principal rafter and the lower end of the strut, which is stump-tenoned into it as shown in Fig. 439.

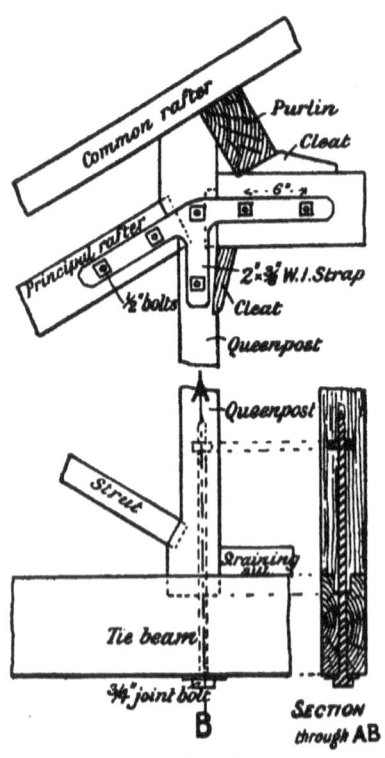

FIG. 439.—Details of Joints at Upper and Lower Ends of Queen-post.

The joint at the lower end of the Queen-post is secured with a joint bolt, and the straining-sill counteracts the thrust caused by the strut.

Other Wooden Roof Trusses.—The King- and Queen-post roof trusses just described are typical examples of truss construction for roofs of ordinary pitch. An almost endless number of modifications is however to be found, even in trusses built of wood only; while with a combination of wood and iron still further scope for modification is available. Figs. 440 to 442 illustrate some of the chief variations from the types already explained. Figs. 440 and 441 show in elevation trusses having *three* purlins on each side and therefore suitable for spans to about 52'. In Fig. 441 the Queen-posts are so placed as to support the middle purlin on each side, and a King-post is added with struts in order to support the ridge and upper purlins. In Fig. 440 smaller posts are added on either side of the Queen-posts; these are called *Princess-posts*, and provide the

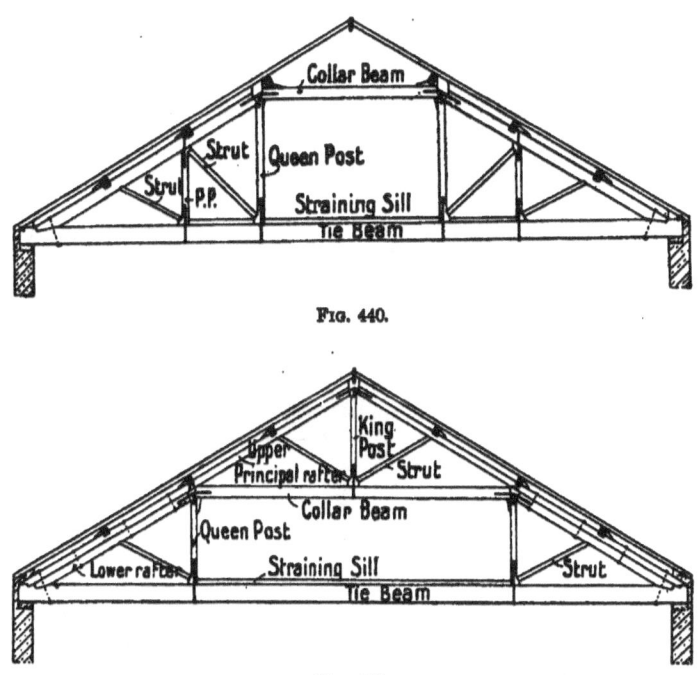

Fig. 440.

Fig. 441.

Roof Trusses for Span up to 50 feet.

abutment for the lower ends of the short struts that support the lower purlins.

Fig. 442 is a diagram of a still larger truss, one which supports *four* purlins on each side. With such a truss there are often two principal rafters—one extending to the Queen-post only (called a *cushion rafter*); the other, which rests on the top of this, and extends to the ridge, being bolted at intervals to the lower one. It might be difficult, in a truss of this size, to obtain a tie-beam long enough in one piece. A tie-beam in two lengths should have the lengthening joint (which is generally a scarfed joint) between the Queen-posts, with the straining sill to act as a fish-plate or cleat.

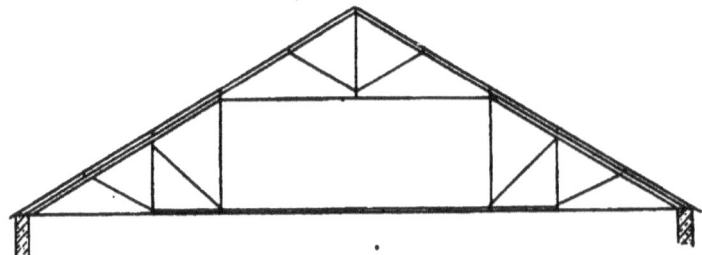

FIG. 442.—Line Diagram of a Roof Truss with four Purlins on each side.

Such large trusses require very heavy timbers in their construction; and as the roofs they support have a wide surface, the wind has, in stormy weather, a considerable effect upon

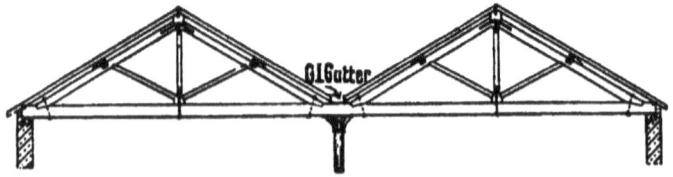

FIG. 443.—Elevation of a Roof in two Bays.

them—a fact which must be taken into account in their construction. In large sheds or buildings of wide span where it is no inconvenience to place pillars of cast iron, the roof may with

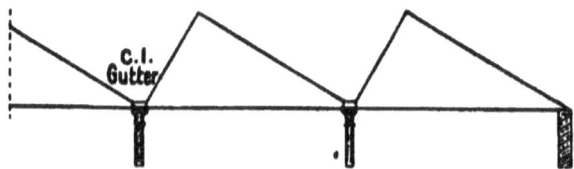

FIG. 444.—Line Diagram of a Shed-Roof.

advantage be constructed in bays. Fig. 443 shows a roof of this description having two bays. The same principle may be applied to any larger building and any number of bays. Fig. 444 shows in line diagram a cross section of a shed-roof where the light of the room is entirely obtained from the roof.

WOODEN ROOFS.

In this example the side of the roof containing the lights—preferably facing the north—is of greater inclination than the one covered with slates.

Combined Wood and Iron Trusses.—Roof trusses are often constructed with a combination of wood and iron. In such trusses the members in *tension* are of iron; those in *compression* are of wood. Iron members in roof trusses impart an appearance of lightness without sacrifice of strength, and when used with iron connections also make it practicable to employ simpler joints. The main objection to this class of truss is that while the iron is affected by varying temperatures and expands with heat, the wood is practically not affected. This

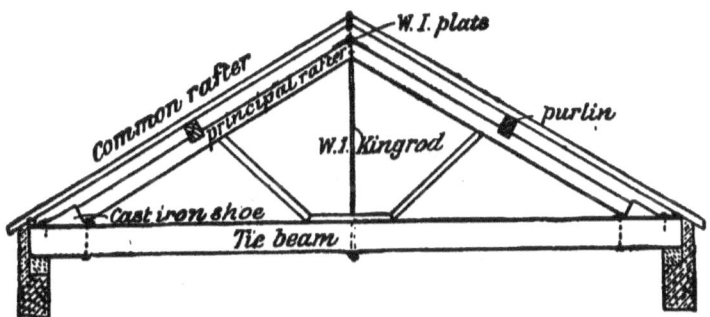

FIG. 445.—Elevation of a Roof Truss with an Iron King-rod.

difference of behaviour renders the truss liable to be overstrained in parts. Again, plaster ceilings cannot conveniently be secured when an iron tie-rod takes the place of the tie-beam.

A truss suitable for a roof having one purlin on each side is shown in Fig. 445. In this truss an iron **King-bolt** takes the place of the wooden King-post. The lower ends of the principal rafters fit into cast-iron shoes which are secured to the tie-beam with bolts and coach screws.

Fig. 446 shows a modified form of collar-beam truss with tension rods instead of the tie-beam, and with a king-rod replacing the king-post. In this example the collar-beam is placed so that it directly supports the lower purlin, and the truss supports two purlins on each side. By placing the collar-beam higher, and dispensing with the strut, this type of truss could be used instead of a King-post truss.

230 A MANUAL OF CARPENTRY AND JOINERY.

Fig. 447 shows part elevation of a modified Queen-post truss, the only alteration being in the substitution of bolts for the

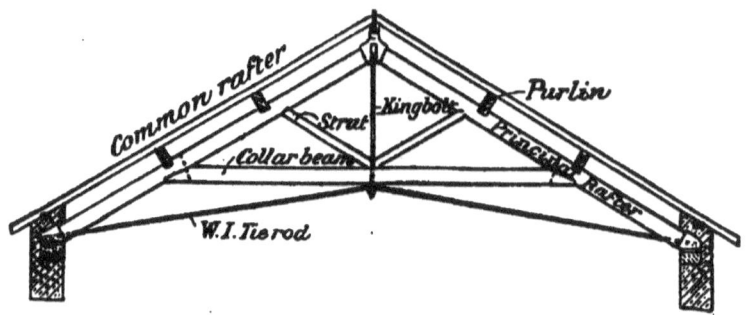

FIG. 446.—Elevation of a Roof Truss with Iron King-rod and Wrought-iron Tie-rods.

Queen-posts, with a consequent simplifying of the joints. Trusses for larger spans are shown in Figs. 448 to 450. Fig. 451 shows an ornamental cast-iron strut for a roof truss, the only wooden members of which are the principal rafters.

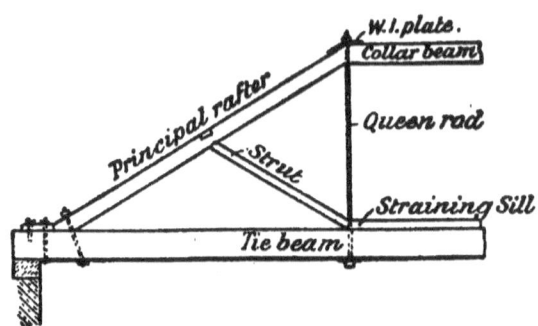

FIG. 447.—Part Elevation of a Roof Truss with Iron Queen-rods.

Cast-iron connections are often used in order to simplify the joints of both wooden and combination trusses. Figs. 452 and 453 show in detail two different connections at the foot of the principal rafter. Fig. 454 is a sketch of the cast-iron head used at the upper end of the principal rafters in Fig. 446. When long wrought-iron bolts are used as in Figs. 449 and 450, they are best if both ends are threaded and provided with nuts which should bind against large plate washers when tightened.

WOODEN ROOFS.

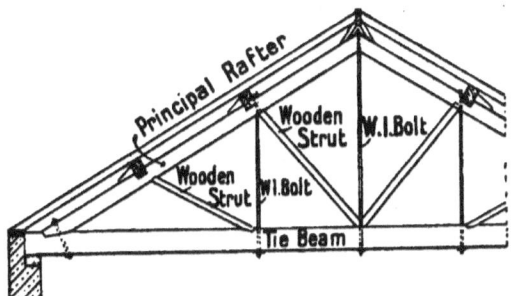

Fig. 448.

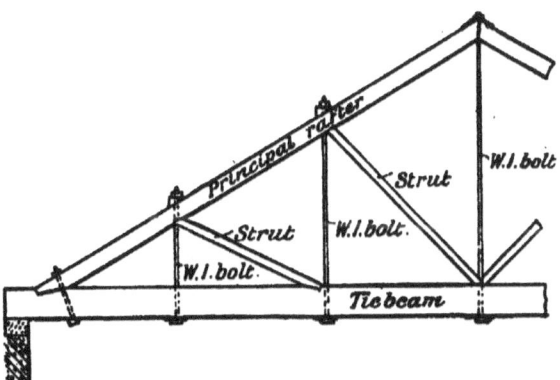

Fig. 449.

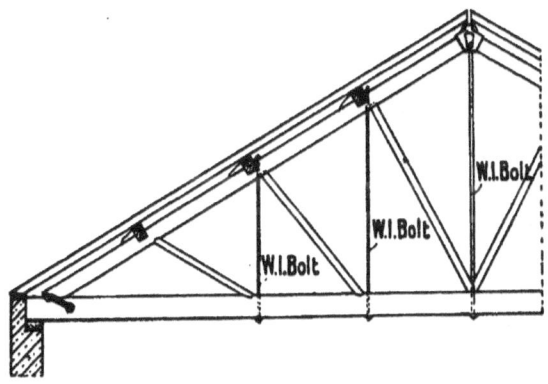

Fig. 450.

Types of Composite Roof Trusses.

232 A MANUAL OF CARPENTRY AND JOINERY.

Ceiling Joists.—When wooden roof trusses are used, and a horizontal plaster ceiling is required, the ceiling joists may:

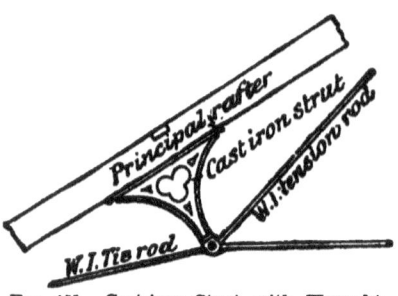

Fig. 451.—Cast-iron Strut with Wrought-iron Tension and Tie-rods.

(a) be notched and nailed to the under sides of the tie-beams;

(b) rest on wooden fillets nailed to the sides of the tie-beams so as to come either level with the under side or part way up the beams;

(c) rest on the top of the tie-beams and be nailed down to them.

Ceiling joists cannot be conveniently fixed to iron tie-rods.

Eaves of Roof.—The finish at the eaves depends upon whether:

(a) the roof finishes practically in a line with the vertical surface of the wall;

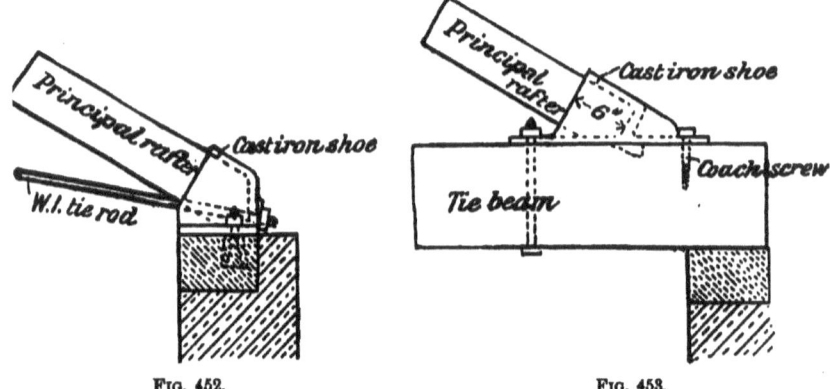

Fig. 452.   Fig. 453.

Alternative Arrangements of Cast-iron Shoes at the Foot of the Principal Rafter.

(b) the roof overhangs the wall for some distance;

(c) the wall is continued above the eaves, with the rain-water gutter in the angle between the wall and the roof surface.

Where the roof finishes flush with the surface of the wall, as in Fig. 433, the lower ends of the common rafters are cut to fit the wall-plate, and the **eaves gutter** lies partly on the

WOODEN ROOFS.

wall, being secured to the wall-plate: or, it may rest on projecting brick, or stone, *corbels* placed from two or three feet apart.

Overhanging Eaves.—Fig. 428, *A*, shows the eaves overhanging the wall; this method affords a means of protecting the wall from the weather. The projection varies considerably, and may be anything from 4" to 2'. The lower ends of the common rafters may be wrought and moulded, with the eaves gutter carried by wrought-iron straps nailed or screwed to

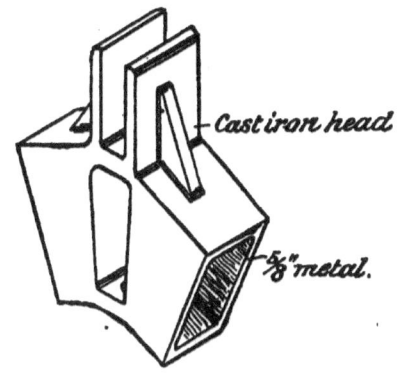

Fig. 454.—Sketch of Cast-iron Connection at Upper Ends of Principal Rafters and King-rod.

every second or third rafter; or a wide vertical board, named a **fascia board**, may be nailed to the ends of the common rafters.

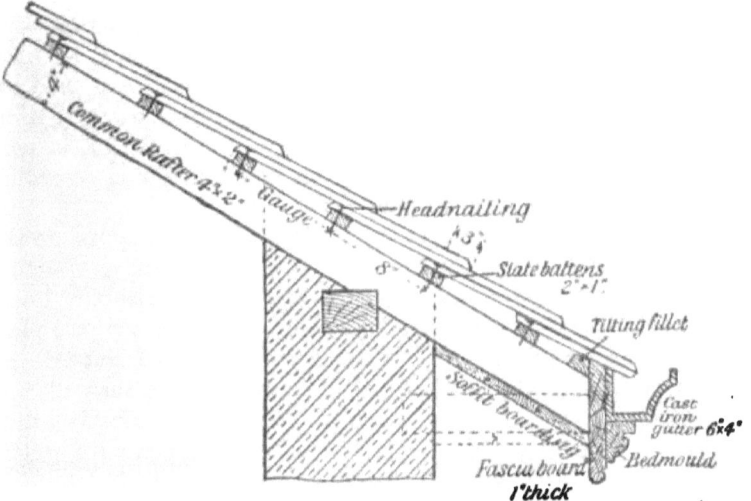

Fig. 455.—Section through the Overhanging Eaves of a Roof, showing Fascia Board, Cast-iron Gutter, Soffit Boarding, etc.

In Fig. 455, which is a section through the eaves, the fascia board is shown with a bed mould secured to it and supporting the eaves gutter. The boarding on the under side of the common rafters—which may either be nailed to the lower sides as shown, or fixed horizontally, as indicated by dotted lines—is named **soffit boarding**.

Gutters behind Parapet Wall.—Fig. 438 shows on its right side a wall reduced in thickness, and continued above the roof surface. Such a wall is known as a parapet wall. In these circumstances the rain-water gutter is formed in the angle behind the wall. Several different types of gutter are used; and as the arrangement of the timbers is governed by the type of gutter, it will be necessary to describe it in detail.

When the gutter is of **cast iron**, as shown in section in Fig. 456, and the wall is diminished in the manner indicated, the lower ends of the common rafters may rest on the wall-plate as shown.

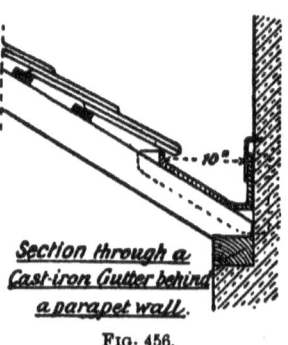

Section through a Cast-iron Gutter behind a parapet wall.

Fig. 456.

Cast-iron gutters are made in long lengths, and have the advantage of not requiring so great a fall as **lead** gutters. The joints are made with a cement obtained by mixing cast-iron borings with sal-ammoniac and water. When **lead** is used for the gutter it may be either a **parallel, box**, or **trough** gutter, that is, of the same width throughout its length; or, it may be a **tapering** gutter, *i.e.* one which varies in width according to the length and the amount of fall.

Parallel gutters are from 9" to 13" wide, and require, on the roof side of the gutter, a horizontal beam similar in size to a roof purlin, and called a **pole plate**, which carries the lower ends of the common rafters. The space between the pole plate and the wall is prepared for carrying the lead gutter. As sheet lead cannot well be laid in longer lengths than 10', and requires a fall of at least one inch in ten feet, the boarding which carries the lead must be laid accordingly. All gutter boards must be firmly supported, must have their length in the direction of the flow, and must be free from all sharp edges or arrises. To obtain these conditions it is necessary to have gutter bearers, to which the gutter boards are nailed, placed from 15" to 18" apart. Fig. 457 is a vertical cross-section

WOODEN ROOFS.

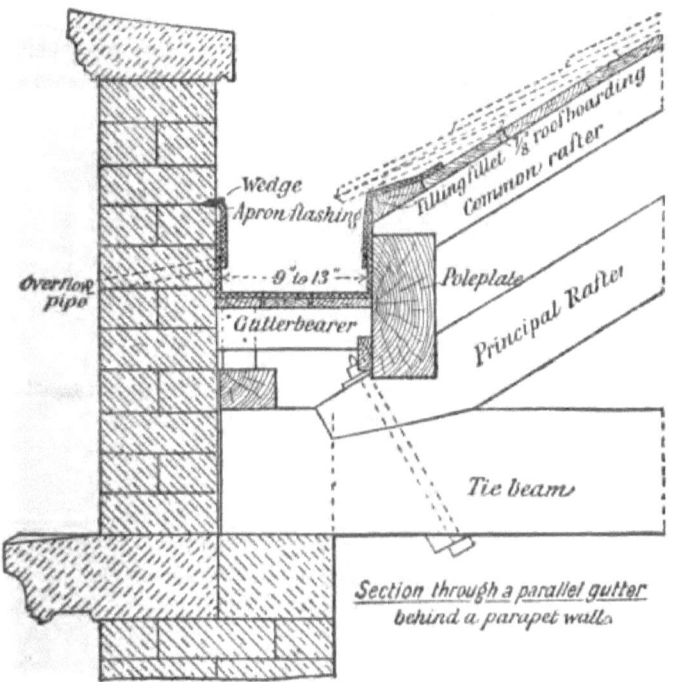

Fig. 457.

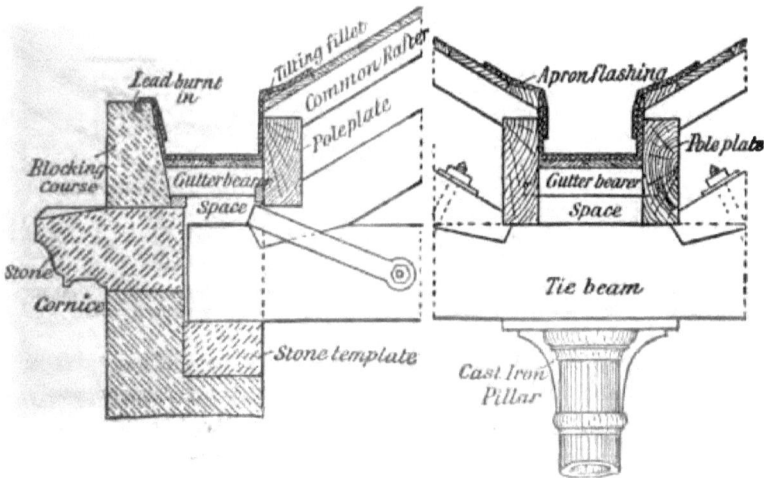

Fig. 458.—Section through a Parallel Gutter behind a Stone Cornice.

Fig. 459.—Section through a Parallel Gutter between two Sloping Roofs.

of a parallel gutter behind a parapet wall, and Fig. 458 is a section of a similar gutter behind a stone cornice, where the arrangement of the roof timbers is similar to that behind a parapet wall.

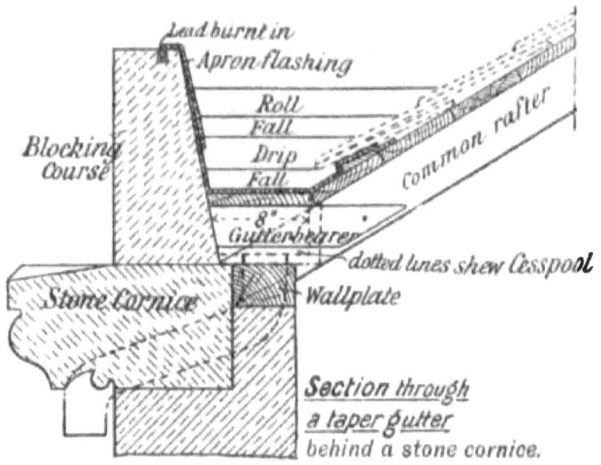

FIG. 460.

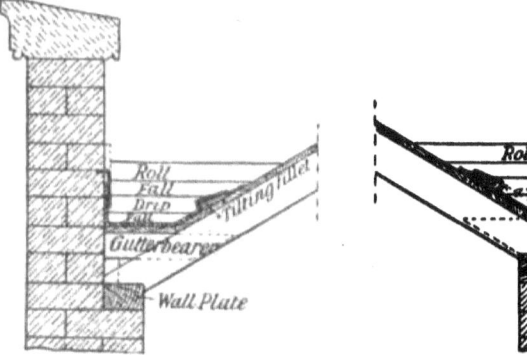

FIG. 461.—Section through a Taper Gutter behind a Parapet Wall.

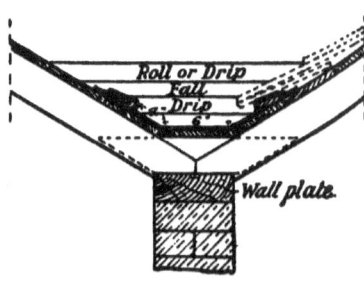

FIG. 462.—Section through a Taper Gutter between two Sloping Roofs.

In Figs. 460 and 461 cross-sections are shown through **taper** gutters behind a stone cornice and parapet wall respectively. With a taper gutter the common rafters may be supported by a wall plate: a pole plate being dispensed with. A taper gutter is applicable to any place where a parallel gutter can be used. To secure the necessary fall, bearers of gradually

WOODEN ROOFS. 237

increasing length are nailed to the sides of the common rafters. Such a gutter is of necessity widest at the highest point. The shape of the plan of the gutter depends on the slope of the

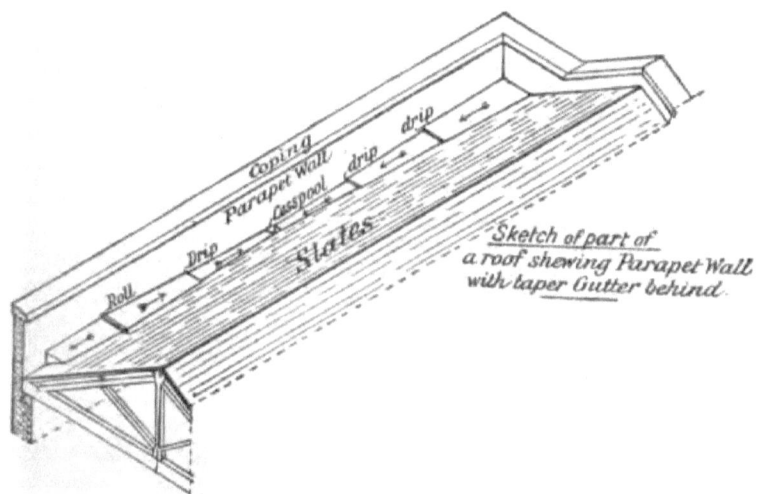

Fig. 463.

Fig. 464.

Fig. 465.

roof and the position of the outlets. The flatter the roof, the wider is the highest part of the gutter, as will be seen by referring to Figs. 463, 464 and 465.

A gutter between **two sloping** roofs that meet may be of cast iron as in Fig. 466, in which case flanges on the outer sides

238   A MANUAL OF CARPENTRY AND JOINERY.

serve to carry the lower ends of the common rafters. Fig. 459 shows a parallel gutter lined with lead, where a pole plate is required on each side to carry the common rafters. Fig. 462 is the section of a taper gutter between two sloping roofs. Instead of the wall which is shown carrying the common rafters in Fig. 462, a beam or trussed girder might be used.

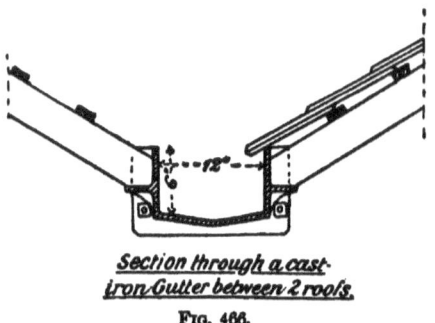

Section through a cast-iron Gutter between 2 roofs.
FIG. 466.

Roll and Drip.—The joints which are used for connecting the sheets of lead together, and for which, in gutters and lead flats, the carpenter has to

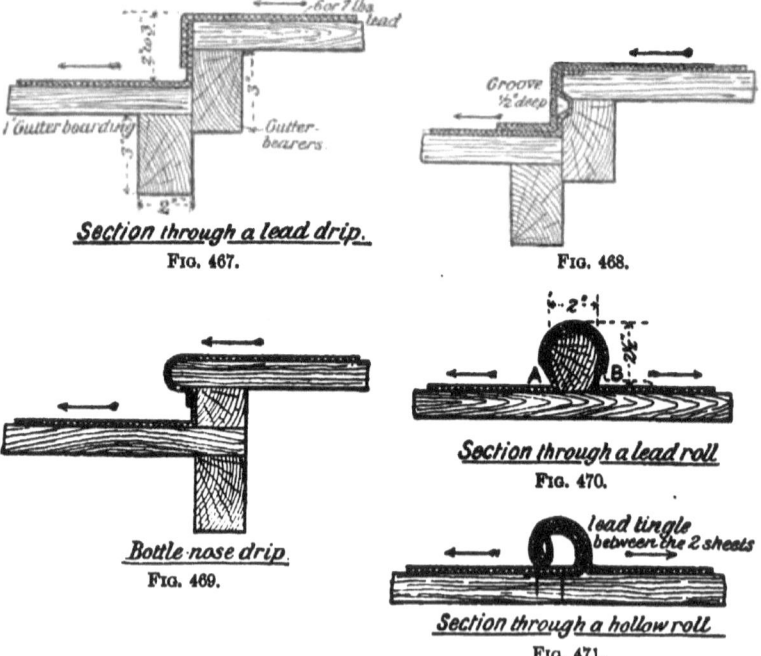

Section through a lead drip.
FIG. 467.

FIG. 468.

Bottle-nose drip.
FIG. 469.

Section through a lead roll.
FIG. 470.

Section through a hollow roll.
FIG. 471.

make provision, are the roll and drip. Typical examples of these are shown in Figs. 467 to 471. It ought to be noticed

WOODEN ROOFS.

that the upper part of the roll is circular, and has a height of a little more than the width.

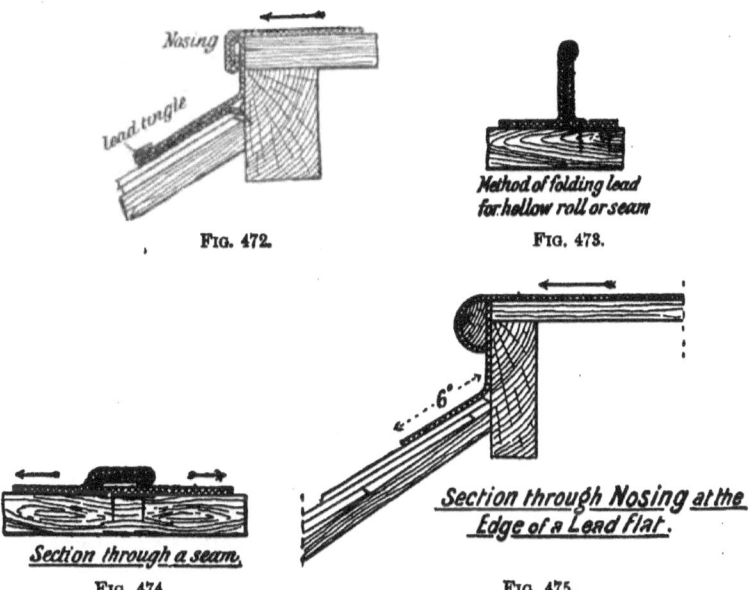

Fig. 472.

Fig. 473.

Fig. 474.—Section through a seam.

Fig. 475.—Section through Nosing at the Edge of a Lead flat.

Cesspool.—A cesspool is a lead-lined wooden box placed at the lowest part of a lead gutter. Into it runs the water, to be afterwards conveyed by means of the rain-water pipes to the drains. The outlet at the bottom of the cesspool should have a rose or perforated covering to prevent dirt, dead leaves, etc., from entering and choking the rain-water pipe.

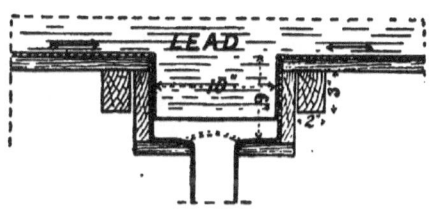

Fig. 476.—Longitudinal Section through a lead-lined Cesspool.

Fig. 476 is a longitudinal section through a cesspool.

Gutters behind Chimneys.—Gutters behind chimneys are seldom of such length that they require drips. If the length exceeds four feet it may be advisable to place a roll in the middle and arrange the gutter boards to fall each way. Fig. 477 is a cross-section through such a gutter.

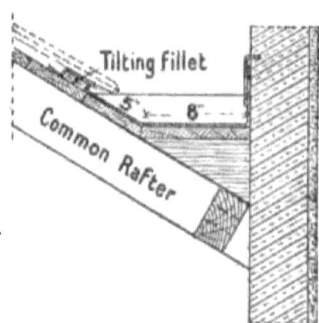

Fig. 477.—Section through a Lead Gutter behind a Chimney or Wall of a higher Building.

Snow Boards.—To prevent the damming-up and consequent leakage resulting from accumulations of snow, dead leaves, etc., in the lead gutters above described, rough frames of wood are usually laid over them. They also serve to protect the lead.

Gables.—With roofs that have overhanging eaves, it is quite a usual method of construction to arrange the roof to overhang the gables, and to hide the common rafters and the ends of the slates with sloping boards called **barge boards**, and shown in Figs. 521 and 522. Great variety of style of barge boards exists, from the plain board about 7" wide, with a simple capping on the top, to the framed structure that almost completely hides the gable. In all cases care should be taken to have thoroughly seasoned timber entirely free from sap wood, to have well-made joints so arranged that the weather cannot affect them, and to have them painted and properly secured. The capping on barge boards should be wide enough to overlap the joint between the slates and the board.

Trimming.—When roof-lights, chimney shafts, large ventilators, etc., occur on a roof, the common rafters around them require framing in order to support the ends of the short rafters. The joint used is the mortise and tenon secured with wedges or nails, and the method of framing is called **trimming**.

Roofs to be covered with Lead or Zinc.—Roofs of this description have their surfaces nearly horizontal and are covered with boards, care being taken to nail down the edges of the boards so that there is no warping nor projecting arrises. The preparation of the necessary drips and rolls for the plumber is the work of the carpenter, and he must know that sheet lead ought not to be laid in longer lengths than 10 feet, nor in wider sheets than 3 feet.

WOODEN ROOFS. 241

The boarded surfaces are carried on rafters that require to be stronger than the ordinary rafter; if the span is great they are supported by girders of wood or iron.

Such roofs are often covered with vulcanite or other bituminous substance, which, when there is no traffic over it, makes a good covering material. A roof surface covered with this material requires an inclination of about 1 in 40; no rolls or drips are needed.

Latticed Trusses.—A type of truss much used for temporary structures, the roofs of which are covered with boards and roofing felt, is a **latticed** or **bowstring** truss shown in elevation in Fig. 478.

It is built up of small scantling, and has a rise in the centre of about one-eighth the span. It is applicable to roofs of any

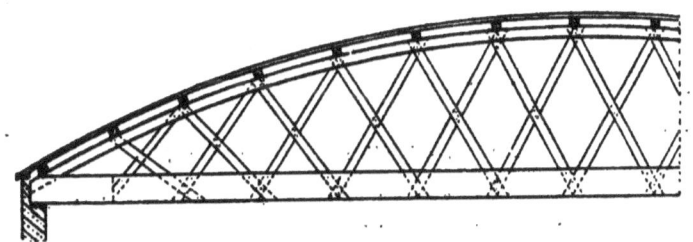

FIG. 478.—Elevation of part of a Latticed or Bow-string Truss.

span, the size of the timbers naturally increasing with the width of the span. The tie-beam is composed of two thicknesses, between which the braces or lattices are fixed. The trusses are from six to ten feet apart. The purlins, which are much lighter than the ordinary roof purlins, are about two feet apart, and rest on the top of the curved ribs; they are directly supported by the upper ends of the braces.

The covering boards are laid either at right angles to or diagonally with the purlins, and, as the roof is curved, they require bending when being placed in position.

This type of truss is also often used when the roof covering is of corrugated iron.

It is necessary, in the construction of a number of similar latticed trusses, that the outline be set out on the floor, and each truss put together according to the same outline. The joints, which are too simple to need description, are secured

242 A MANUAL OF CARPENTRY AND JOINERY.

by being well nailed together in the smaller trusses; in larger trusses, bolts may in addition be used.

Mansard Truss.—Fig. 479 shows the elevation of what is called a curb or Mansard roof truss. This truss is used with

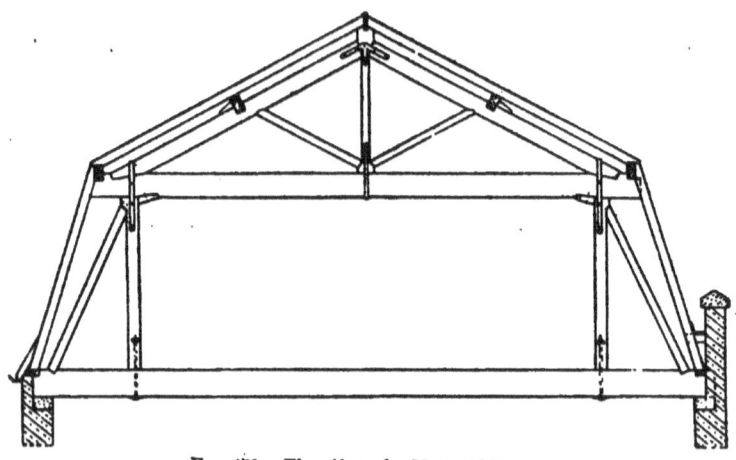

FIG. 479.—Elevation of a Mansard Truss.

advantage when it is desired to have an additional attic or an upper room in a building without the expense of carrying up the walls to accommodate the ordinary type of truss. A suitable method for determining the outlines of the truss is shown in Fig. 480. The semicircle is divided into five equal parts. The points 1 and 4, and the centre of the arc 2—3, give the angular points of the outline of the truss. Many modifications of this shape are adopted to suit the size of the room required, the roof-covering used, etc.

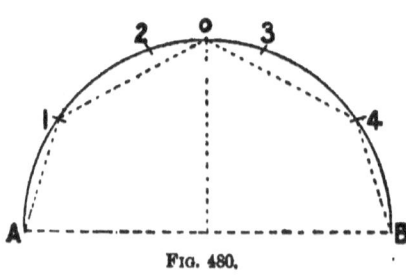

FIG. 480.

Gothic Roof Trusses.—In public buildings of importance, such as churches, schools, assembly rooms, etc., it is very usual to have a roof of high pitch, and to make a special feature of its construction and decoration. When the pitch is steeper than forty-five degrees (45°) the style tends towards the Gothic

WOODEN ROOFS.

style of architecture, with its pointed arches and windows, and its distinctive mouldings. Trusses supporting roofs of this description are styled Gothic roof trusses. The members of such trusses are subjected to more stress than are those of flatter roofs, as they present larger surfaces to be affected by high winds.

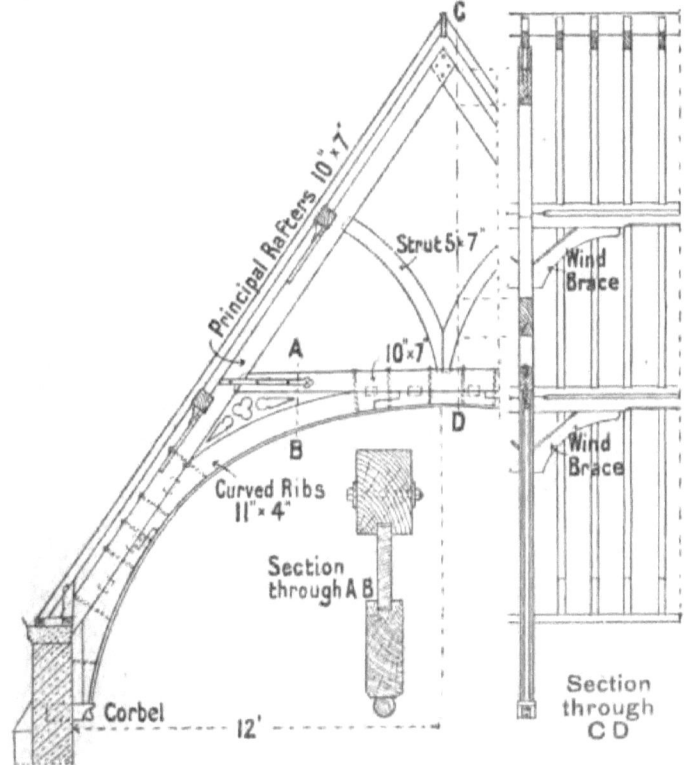

Fig. 481.—Gothic Roof Truss.

All roof trusses are stronger when provided with a tie-beam or tie-rod at the eaves level. As a general rule, however, such cross ties are absent in Gothic roof trusses, and the roof timbers are consequently of large section. The general style is on the lines of the collar-beam truss, the angular parts (spandrel) under the collar being filled in with curved ribs. To throw the weight as low as possible on the wall, these curved ribs often terminate at from three to six feet below the eaves level.

The walls carrying Gothic roof trusses are generally strengthened by buttresses placed opposite the position occupied by the trusses.

Fig. 481 shows an elevation of a little more than one half of a Gothic roof truss with the main dimensions indicated. The curved ribs may be cut out of one thickness, with spliced

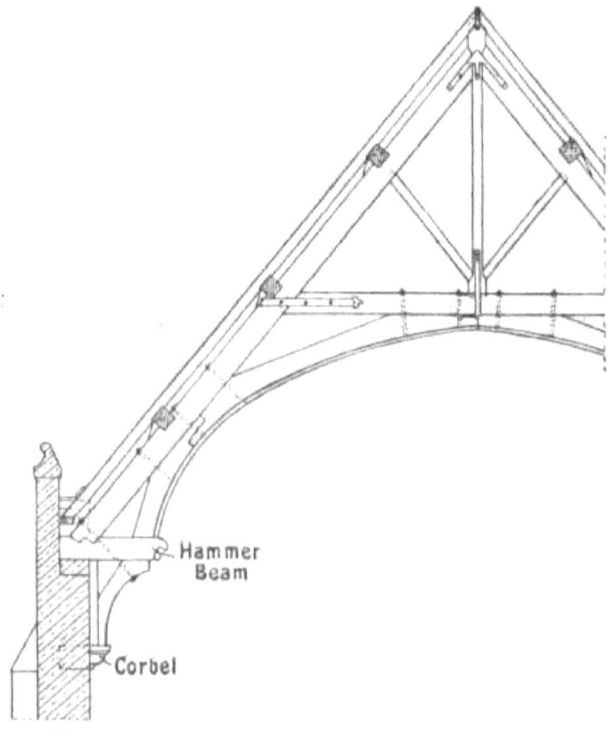

Fig. 482.—Elevation of part of Hammer-beam Roof Truss.

joints as shown in Fig. 481 ; or they may be built up of two or three thicknesses, with overlapping joints, and nailed, screwed, or pegged together. The joints are secured with iron straps or bolts, or with bolts passed through them as shown.

Magnificent examples of Gothic roof trusses are to be found in many of the cathedrals of the country, as well as in other important buildings, and the student of carpentry would do well to examine some of these in detail.

Hammer Beam Trusses.—When a Gothic roof truss has, at the eaves level, a short horizontal member to support the curved ribs above it, this member is called a **hammer beam**, and the truss is known as a hammer beam truss. Fig. 482 shows in elevation a hammer beam truss, and Figs. 483 and 484 are line diagrams of other types of a similar truss. It will be noticed that judicious use is made of bolts to support the outer ends of the hammer beams.

The hammer beam truss, in its many and varied forms, lends itself to elaborate decoration and ornamentation. The triangular spaces are often filled with Gothic tracery, while the ends of the hammer beams are richly carved, often with allegorical

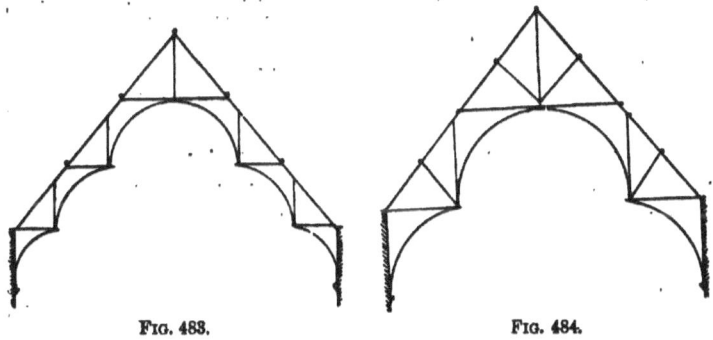

FIG. 483.   FIG. 484.

Line Diagrams of Gothic Roof Trusses.

figures. This is sometimes done to such an extent that the main timbers of the roof are scarcely discernible.

Such roofs, being subject to considerable wind stress, are often braced from truss to truss in the plane of the roof. An alternative plan is to insert straight or curved braces from the purlins to the trusses, as shown on the right hand side of Fig. 481.

Pyramid or Turret Roofs.—These vary much in size; they may have a triangular, square, polygonal, or circular base, and may be straight or curved in section; they may be large enough to require supporting by heavy framed and braced trusses, which form the main structure; or the framing together may be a very small matter. The guiding principles of roof and truss construction generally apply, and their detailed consideration is only necessary because they present good examples of the application of practical geometry to roof construction.

246   A MANUAL OF CARPENTRY AND JOINERY.

Applied Geometry in Roof Construction.—The determination of the lengths and end-bevels of roof timbers affords good examples of the application of geometry to the carpentry of roof construction. The difficulties which may occur in such work will be obvious from an examination of Fig. 485, which illustrates a hipped roof.

A **hip** is the ridge formed when a roof, instead of ending at a gable as at A (Fig. 414), is returned round the end of a building as at B. It may also be defined as the ridge formed when two sloping roof surfaces meet in a line inclined to the horizontal. A **valley** is the line in which two sloping roof surfaces meet to form an internal angle.

It is clear that the lengths and end-bevels of the various timbers will depend upon:

(1) the inclination of the roof surfaces;
(2) the angles at which the different walls of the building meet each other.

In order to obtain these lengths and bevels on scale drawings, it is necessary to apply the principles of projection explained in Chap. III. In the following examples, the lengths of members are in most cases measured along the centre lines. In all cases, the widest surfaces of the member are referred to as its *sides*, while the surfaces at right angles to the sides are called *edges*.

Lengths and Bevels of Common Rafters.—A vertical cross section through a roof with the walls and ridge-piece in position shows at a glance the lengths and end-bevels of the common rafters. In each of the Figs. 485 to 487, A indicates the bevel,—*i.e.* the angle of the side-cut—at the upper end, and B the bevel at the lower end, of each common rafter. It will be seen that these two angles together are always equal to a right angle, the edge of the common rafter being the hypotenuse of a right-angled triangle. If the lower ends of the common rafters overhang the wall, then that end-bevel will be the same as at A, to enable the fascia board or gutter to be fixed against it. The edge-cut at both ends of the common rafters is "square," *i.e.* at right angles to the length.

It is plain that with ridged roofs all the common rafters will have the same length and end-bevels only when the side walls are of equal height and parallel, and the ridge is central in position. In all other cases, the length and end-bevels of the

ROOF BEVELS.

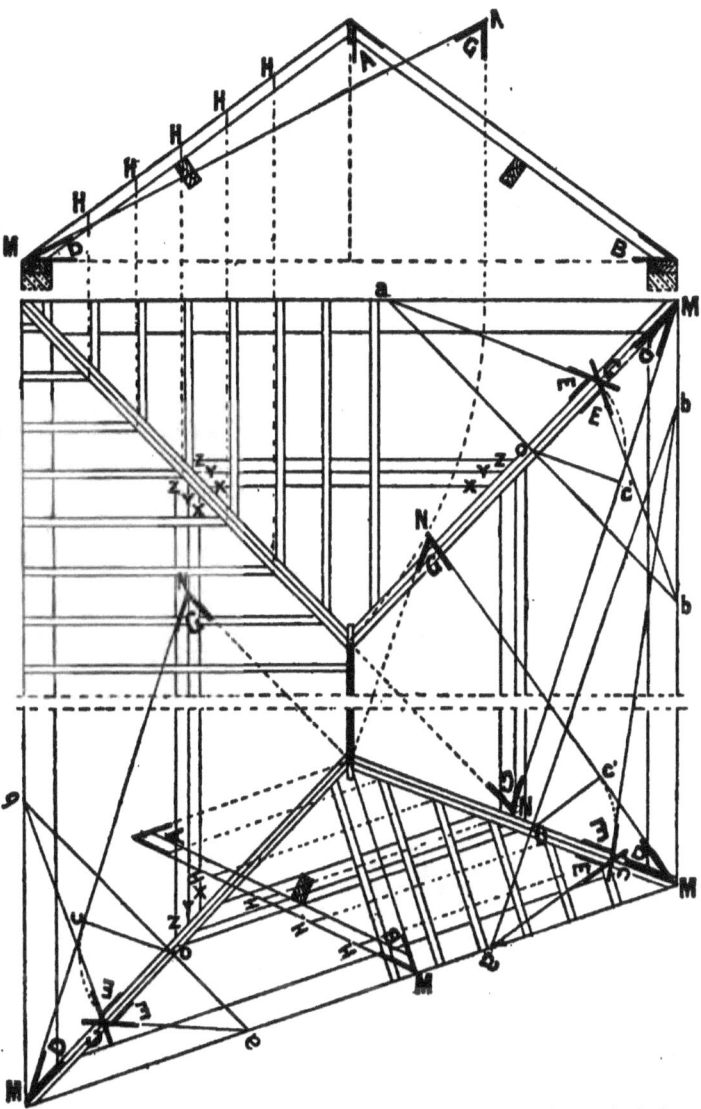

FIG. 485.—Plan and sectional elevation of Roof showing the method of obtaining the Lengths and Bevels of the different Members.

    AB. Length and Bevels of Common Rafter.
    MN. Length of Hip Rafter.
    G. Bevel for side cut at upper end of Hip Rafter.
    D. Bevel for side cut at lower end of Hip Rafter.
    E. Bevel for backing of upper edge of Hip Rafter.
    MH. Length of Jack Rafters.

(G in this illustration corresponds to C in Figs. 486 and 487.)

248   A MANUAL OF CARPENTRY AND JOINERY.

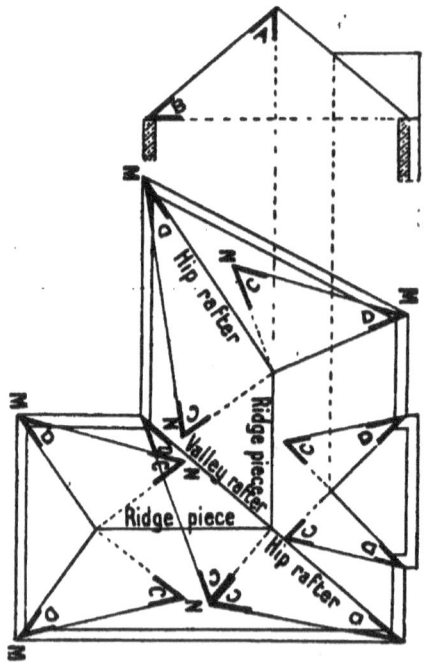

FIG. 486.—Roof Bevels.

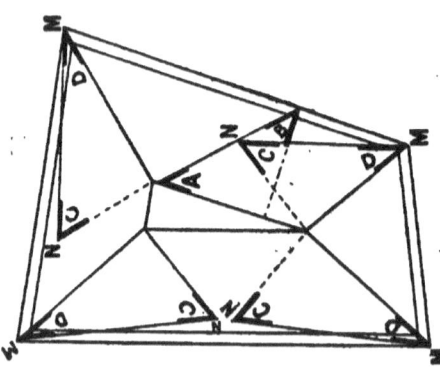

FIG. 487.—Roof Bevels.

AB. Length and Bevels of Common Rafters.
MN. Length of Hip Rafter.
  C. Bevel for side cut at upper end of Hip or Valley Rafter.
  D. Bevel for side cut at lower end of Hip or Valley Rafter.

rafters will vary; they may easily be determined by drawing a cross-section through the roof.

The Lengths and Bevels of Hip and Valley Rafters. — To obtain these, it is first necessary to draw the plan of the building, with the main roof timbers in position. If the inclinations of both sides, and of the end of the roof are the same, and if the end wall is at right angles to the side walls, then the plans of the hip rafters bisect the right angles, and the two hip rafters are of the same length, as shown in the upper part of the plan of Fig. 485. On the other hand, if the end-slope of the roof differs from the side-slopes, the plan of the hip rafter does not bisect the angle. Again, if the end is not at right angles to the side walls, then one of the hip rafters is longer than the other, as shown in Fig. 486.

ROOF BEVELS. 249

In obtaining the lengths of the hip rafters it is always best to work from the *centre lines* of the upper edges of the hip rafters and ridge piece. The length of the hip rafter is obtained by considering its plan as the base of a right-angled triangle,

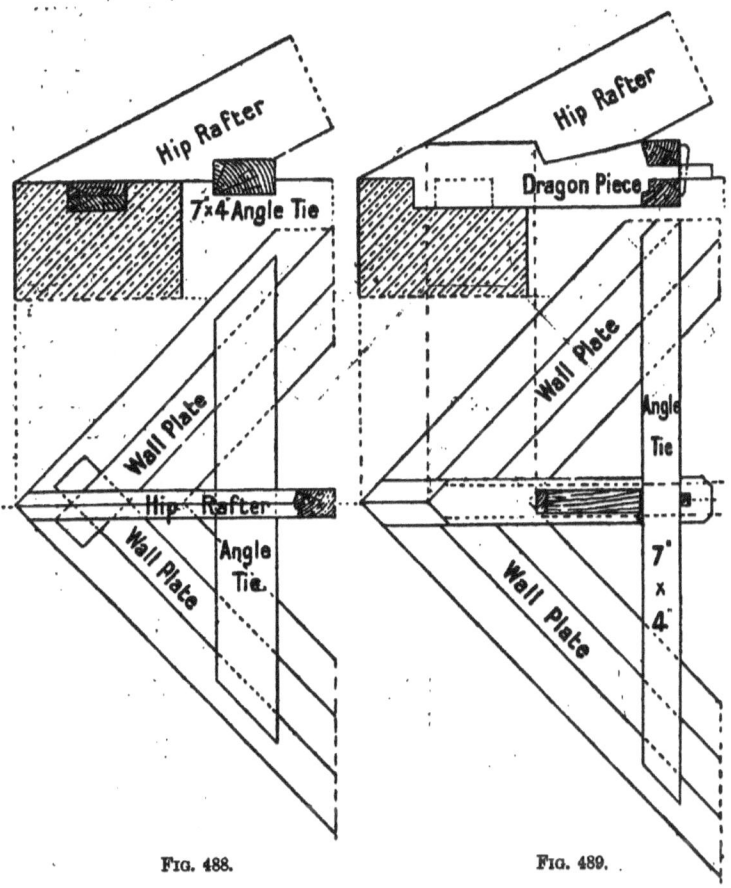

Fig. 488. Fig. 489.

Methods of Supporting lower end of Hip Rafter.

the hypotenuse of which is the true length, while the altitude is the height of the ridge above the wall level. In Figs. 485 to 487 MN is in each case the length of the hip or valley rafter.

The lower end of a hip rafter rests upon the wall, in the angle. It may be supported further by an **angle tie** (Fig. 488), or be provided with an **angle tie** and **dragon piece**, placed across the corner as shown in Fig. 489. The upper end generally abuts against the ridge, and is supported either by a division wall or by a roof truss. The angles of the side cuts (bevels for the ends of the hip rafter) —neglecting the special abutment required when a dragon piece is used (Fig. 489)— are together equal to a right angle. This is shown in Figs. 485, 486, 487, and 494, where the bevel at the upper end is in each case lettered C* and the bevel at the lower end D.

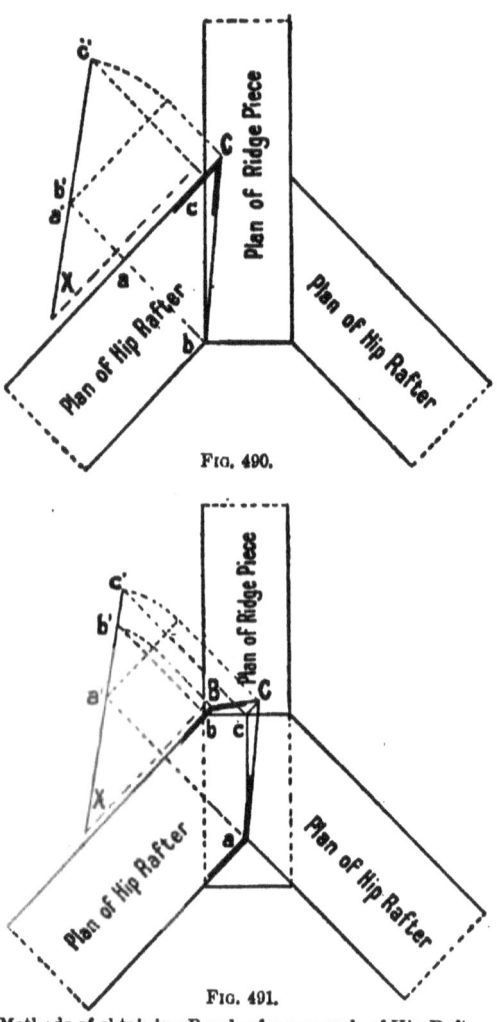

Fig. 490.

Fig. 491.

Methods of obtaining Bevels of upper ends of Hip Rafters abutting against Ridge Piece.

Figs. 490 and 491 show how to obtain the edge-cut at the upper end of the hip rafter. The rafter may fit against the side of the ridge (Fig. 490), or the ridge may be cut to form a seating on which the hip rafters are mitred to fit each other (Fig. 491). In either case the problem resolves itself into finding the true shape of a right-angled triangle, the plane of which is inclined,

*(G in Fig. 485.)

WOODEN ROOFS. 251

the inclination depending upon that of the hip rafter. If the hip rafter were horizontal—which is never the case—the plan of the vertical plane of intersection between it and the ridge would give the edge-cut. If the hip rafter is nearly vertical, then the same plan represents the plan of a triangle having the line *ab* horizontal and the point *C* much higher, as shown in Fig. 490. This true shape, which gives the angle for the edge-cut, is found by revolving the triangle until it is horizontal, the angle at *C* being the one required.

In Fig. 491, the hip rafters meet together upon the end of the ridge. The figure cut off above the horizontal line is in this example a four-sided one, and the same method of determining its true shape, and therefore the bevels to which the end must be cut, is adopted.

The lengths and bevels of valley rafters are obtained in the same manner as with hip rafters, the only difference being that there is no angle tie or dragon piece needed at the lower end.

It is often necessary to cut the upper edge of the hip rafter so that, from its centre

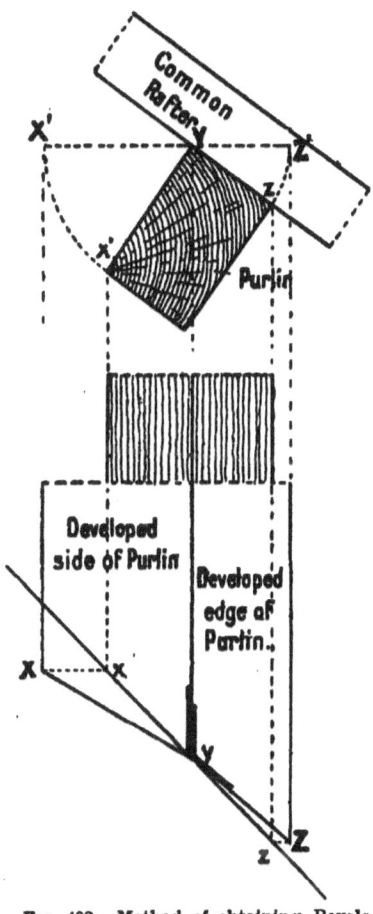

FIG. 492.—Method of obtaining Bevels at ends of Purlins abutting against Hip or Valley Rafters.

line, it is in the planes of the roof surfaces. This is technically termed "backing" the hip rafter. In Fig. 485, *E* shows in each case the bevels required in backing the hip rafter. To obtain these, draw any line *ab* at right angles to the plan of the hip rafter; where this line cuts the centre line of the hip as at o, draw a line oc' perpendicular to the elevation of the hip rafter. With o as centre and radius oc', cut off on the centre line of the hip rafter a length oC equal to the altitude oc'; join aC and bC. The angle aCb is the inclination of the roof surfaces to each other, and therefore of the "backed" upper surfaces of the rafter.

Bevels of Purlins against Hip Rafters.—The lengths of purlins—which are almost always horizontal—can be found from the plan, while the bevels to which the ends require cutting to fit against hip rafters are shown in plan when the purlins are fixed on edge—that is, with the side of the purlin vertical. With purlins in this position the side-cut is "square."

When the edge is parallel to the slope of the common rafter, the end-bevels present more difficulty. Fig. 492 shows how these bevels are obtained. A plan gives the true length of each edge of the purlin, and shows how much shorter xx is than yy, and how much longer zz is than yy (Fig. 485); but the plan does not show the exact width of either the side $xx\ yy$, or the edge $zz\ yy$. It is in the section that the true width of these surfaces is seen, the

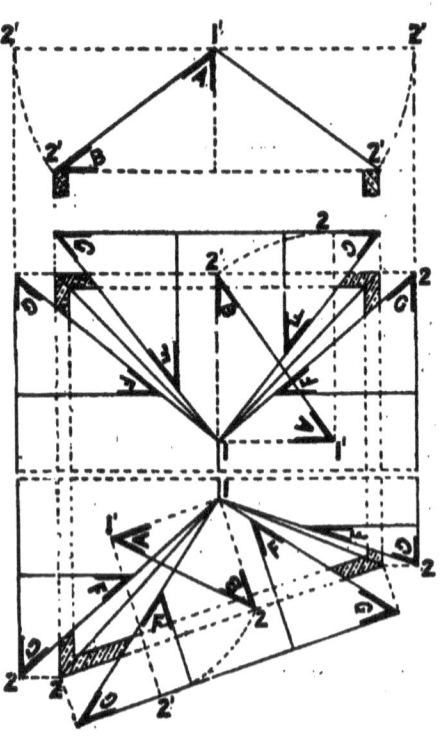

Fig. 493.—Showing Developed Roof Surface and Bevels of Jack Rafters.

A.B. Length and Bevels of Common Rafter.
A. Bevel for side cut at upper end of Jack Rafter.
B. Bevel for side cut at lower end of Jack Rafter.
F. Bevel for edge cut at upper end of Jack Rafter.
G. Bevel for side cut at ends of Roof Boarding mitred on Hip Rafter.

width of the plan depending upon the inclination of the roof. By "developing" or turning the widths as seen in section until they are horizontal, then projecting them to the plan, and carrying the points x and z to the projected lines, the bevels are obtained. An enlarged section of a purlin, with the plan showing the angle at which the end of the purlin meets the hip rafter, is shown in Fig. 492. By following this method it is possible to obtain the end-bevels of purlins without confusion, even with a roof having many differently inclined surfaces. In all cases, it is best to draw out to a large scale a cross-section of the common rafter and purlin in position; to project from these the plan of the purlin meeting the hip rafter—which may be shown by a single line—at the angle indicated in the "roof plan"; and to draw the developed surfaces as in Fig. 492.

Lengths and Bevels of Jack Rafters.—The side-cuts of jack rafters have the same bevels as those of the common rafters. If the hip rafter against which they abut bisects the angle, then the jack rafters on each side of this hip rafter are similar. The lengths are determined by projecting the plan of each to the section, as shown in Fig. 485 at MH. The edge-cut is found by developing the roof surfaces as shown in Fig. 493. In this figure each surface is turned about the ridge, and the angles marked F give the bevels for the edge-cut in each case.

It will also be seen that as these developed surfaces are the actual roof surfaces turned horizontally, the area of the surface of the roof will be obtained by measuring them. The end-bevels for the roof boarding are also shown at G.

Turret Roofs.—Fig. 494 shows the plan and sectional elevation of a small turret roof, the plan of which is a regular hexagon. On it are shown the lengths and bevels of the hip and jack rafters, the backing of the hip rafter, and the development of one triangular face. The same index letters are used as in the previous examples; the bevels will therefore be understood readily. Roofs of this description are used generally for ornamenting the corners of a building, or as roofs for ventilators. The exposed positions in which they are placed render it necessary that they should be well braced and anchored to the building. This latter necessity is provided for by passing long bolts through angle-ties at each corner to holdfasts driven into the wall several feet below the eaves level.

A turret roof having a curved roof surface is shown in plan and sectional elevation in Fig. 495. The outline of the jack rafters is shown in the sectional elevation. The shape of the hip rafter, which is also shown on the drawing, is obtained by taking a number of points 1' to 7' in the sectional elevation, projecting from these points to the plan, and from the plan of

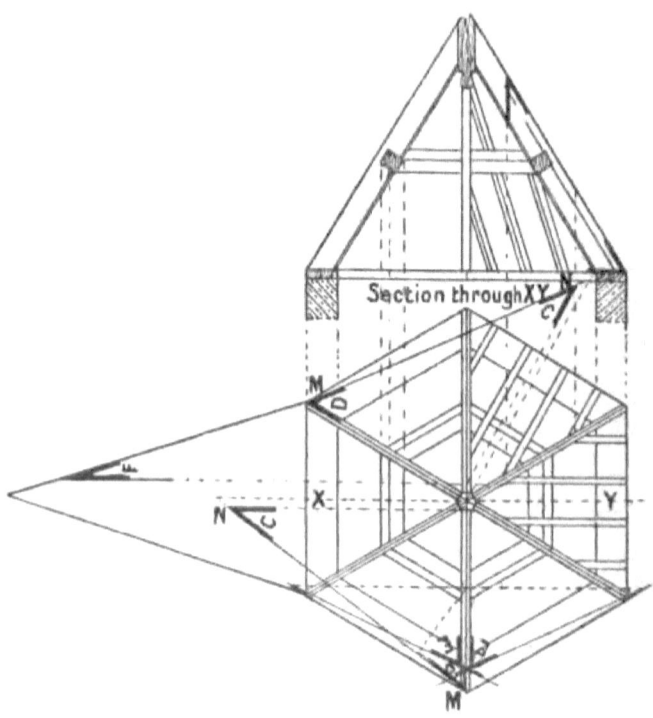

Fig. 494.—Plan and Section of a Pyramid Roof.   (Reference letters as in Fig. 485.)

one of the hip rafters cut by projectors from these points, erecting perpendicular lines on which corresponding heights 1' to 7' are taken. A freehand curve drawn through the points thus obtained gives the outline of the hip rafter.

The developed roof surface is obtained by taking the same points 1' to 7'—measured along the curved line in elevation— and drawing a "stretch-out" so that projectors from the same points in plan will give the width at the respective heights.

By drawing freehand curves through these points, the developed roof surface is obtained.

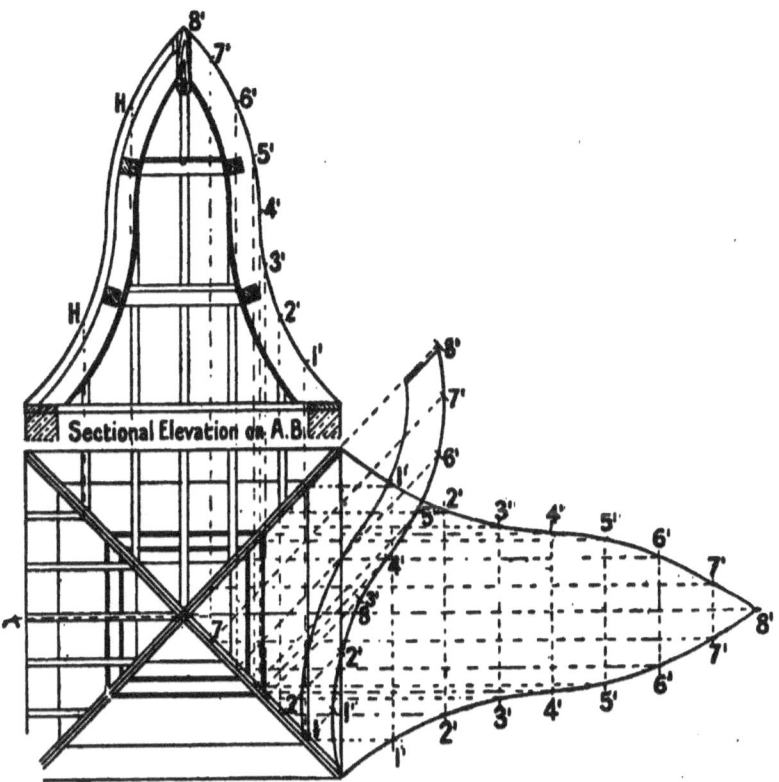

Fig. 495.—Plan and Section of a Turret Roof of Curved Outline, with the method of obtaining the Hip Rafter, and the development of one side.

Summary.

Wooden roofs may be *lean-to* or *ridged roofs*.

The **slates** or **tiles** of a sloping roof are carried by *common rafters* which rest on *purlins*. In dwelling-houses the inner walls are generally sufficiently near each other to support the purlins. In larger buildings the purlins are carried by *trusses* placed from 8 to 10 feet apart. Purlins should not be more than 8 feet apart, and when trusses are used they should be so designed as directly to support each purlin. The shape of the trusses varies according to the width between the walls and the outline of the roof. The principal types of trusses are named *collar-beam, King-post, Queen-post, combination* (wood and iron), *latticed, Mansard,* and *Gothic.*

All the **joints** in roof trusses should be so made as to be unaffected by shrinkage of the timber.

The **eaves** of the roof may overhang, or gutters of cast iron or lead may be formed behind parapet walls.

The **lengths** and **bevels** of the oblique cuts in hipped roofs may be obtained by applied practical geometry.

Flat roofs may be covered with *lead, zinc,* or some bituminous substance. Their construction is similar to that of a floor, with the exception of the slight "fall" required.

Questions on Chapter IX.

1. Make a line diagram and write the names of the parts of a collar-beam roof of 16 ft. span, and show by line diagrams the form of principal (truss) you would use for a 25 ft., 35 ft., and a 50 ft. span roof. Show the parts in compression by single lines, and those in tension by double lines. (C. and G. Ord., 1898.)

2. Make a drawing of rather more than half of a simple King-post truss for a roof, the span of which is 25 ft. Scale $\frac{1}{2}$ in. to 1 ft. (C. and G. Prel. 1904.)

3. Make a drawing of rather more than one-half elevation of a roof truss of 30 ft. span; scale $\frac{1}{2}$ in. to 1 ft. Dimension and name the parts, and make freehand sketches of the joints used. (C. and G. Ord., 1900.)

4. Draw to a scale of one and a half inches to a foot, three methods of forming the joint between a principal rafter and a tie-beam. (C. and G. Ord., 1896.)

5. Draw to a scale of one and a half inches to a foot, three methods of securing with iron the foot of a principal rafter to a tie-beam. (C. and G. Ord., 1896.)

6. It is required to cover a building 28 ft. by 42 ft. with a tiled roof. Show by plan, to scale $\frac{1}{8}$ inch to a foot, where you would place the roof trusses; and give to a scale of $\frac{1}{4}$ inch to a foot the elevation of half of one truss. (C. and G. Ord., 1896.)

7. It is required to cover a building 40 ft. wide with roof in one span and $\frac{1}{4}$ pitch. Give elevation of the truss you would use to scale 4 ft. to an inch. (C. and G. Ord., 1897.)

8. Give enlarged details of joints to the foregoing roof (Q. 7) in isometrical projection, showing the ironwork you would use. (C. and G. Ord., 1897.)

QUESTIONS ON CHAPTER IX.

9. Draw, to a scale of ⅜ in. to one foot, the elevation of about one-half of a roof truss for a building 30 ft. wide (inside measurement). The principal rafters and the collar beam are to be of wood, and the tie- and King-rods to be of iron. Give, to a scale of 1½ in. to one foot, the details of the joints.

10. Draw, to a scale of 1½ in. to one foot, alternative vertical cross sections through the eaves of a roof showing :
   (a) the eaves overhanging 18 in., and finished with fascia board, cast-iron gutter, and soffit boarding;
   (b) a parallel gutter behind a stone cornice and blocking course;
   (c) a tapering lead gutter behind a brick parapet wall;
   (d) a cast-iron gutter behind a brick parapet wall.

11. An open void in a roof is 7 ft. by 4 ft. Show how you would "trim" round it. (C. and G. Ord., 1901.)

12. Draw to a scale of ½ inch to a foot, a roof truss to a span of 20 ft. so as to form as large a room as possible in the roof. (C. and G. Ord., 1895.)

13. Make a half elevation of a Mansard roof truss of 38 ft. span; scale ¼ in. to the foot. Mark on the dimensions of the several parts, and make freehand sketches of the joints used in construction. (C. and G. Ord., 1899.)

14. Draw the elevation of a light roof-truss for a temporary building, the width to be 30 ft. in the clear, and the trusses to occur every 8 ft. to have a semi-circular built up rib, the springing being 7 ft. 6 in. above the floor. The roof may be covered with light boarding and corrugated iron. (C. and G. Hon., 1904.)

15. A public hall, 50 ft. wide, is to be roofed in one span by either a hammer-beam roof or a collar-beam roof. The whole roof is to be seen as part of the interior, and the ribs to be moulded, spandrels ornamented, etc. Draw to a scale of 4 ft. to 1 in. rather more than half the elevation of a suitable timber truss, and furnish sketches to a larger scale, or in perspective, of the joints, ironwork, and other details. The material to be pitch pine. (C. and G. Hon., 1903.)

16. Draw to scale of 1 in. to a foot the foot of a hammer-beam truss, 40 ft. span and ¼ pitch; dot outline of tenons and show the bolts and straps. The hammer-beam, with all work below it, and the ends of timbers framed above, to be shown. (C. and G. Hon., 1897.)

17. Draw rather more than half elevation of a hammer-beam roof of 35 ft. span. (C. and G. Hon., 1904.)

18. Draw to a scale of 1 in. to a foot, half (at least) of the elevation of a hammer-beam truss for the roof of a small church, to

be executed in oak. Show the joints and any ironwork introduced, by sketches, to a larger scale, or in perspective. (C. and G. Hon., 1901.)

19. Make drawings of a dragon tie. Show how you would determine the length of a hip rafter, the angle at the back of the hip rafter, and the bevels for purlins and jack rafters. (C. and G. Ord., 1904.)

20. Draw to a scale of 1½ in. to a foot plan and elevation of an angle tie and dragon piece, and show how you would obtain the bevels of hip rafter. (C. and G. Ord., 1897.)

21. A hipped roof is inclined at the angle of 30°. Find the angles necessary for cutting the hip rafters, purlins, and jack rafters. (C. and G. Ord., 1903.)

22. Make a drawing showing how you would find the different bevels for a valley rafter. (C. and G. Ord., 1900.)

23. Explain with sketches how you would construct the angle of a hipped mansard roof, and give the bevels for the various cuts. (C. and G. Ord., 1895.)

24. Make a drawing of sufficient of the plan and elevation of an octagonal dome 8 ft. in diameter boarded internally. All the applied geometry should be clearly shown in the drawings. (C. and G. Hon., 1900.)

25. Make the drawings of an octagonal pyramidal turret-shaped roof; span 45 ft., height 46 ft. All timbers to be shown and dimensioned, and the geometrical method of obtaining the angles of the backs of rafters, purlins, etc., should be shown. Part only of the plan, elevation and section should be drawn. (C. and G. Hon., 1901.)

CHAPTER X.

PARTITIONS AND WOODEN FRAMED BUILDINGS.

Partitions.—It is often inconvenient to have the upper rooms of a building of the same size and shape as the lower rooms. In such cases the walls which divide the lower rooms from each other cannot be carried upwards to form the divisions of the higher rooms. For various other reasons it may be undesirable to continue brick division-walls to the upper storeys. The rooms of the upper storeys may, however, be separated by **partitions** of wood and plaster.

A frequently adopted means of forming such partitions is to fix upright pieces of wood named **studs** in the same vertical plane at distances of from twelve to fifteen inches apart. **Wooden laths**, which carry the plaster, are nailed to both sides of these studs. As a further means of stiffening them, short horizontal pieces of wood, 3" by 1½", called **nogging pieces**, are fitted and nailed between the studs, in rows, at distances of about four feet in height. This method of arranging studs has, however, the disadvantage of throwing the whole of the weight of the partition on the floor on which it rests; and any settlement or "sagging" of the floor naturally strains the partition, and tends to crack the plaster.

As the studs and other pieces of timber used in framing are of section known as **quartering**, such partitions are known as **quartered partitions**. These partitions are usually from 3" to 4½" thick, and the studs used are generally 2" wide. It is necessary to have all the members of the same partition of the same thickness to enable both sides to be plastered evenly.

260 A MANUAL OF CARPENTRY AND JOINERY.

Framed and Trussed Partitions.—A better method than the above is to construct the partition as a framework, or truss, so arranged that the whole weight of the partition is directly transmitted to the walls. Fig. 496 is a line diagram of a framed partition without any doorway. Each member is shown by a single line. Fig. 497 shows the elevation of a framed partition with a central doorway, seven feet high and three feet wide, and

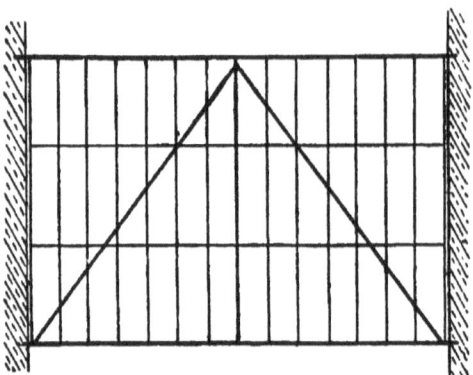

FIG. 496.—Line Diagram of a Framed Partition.

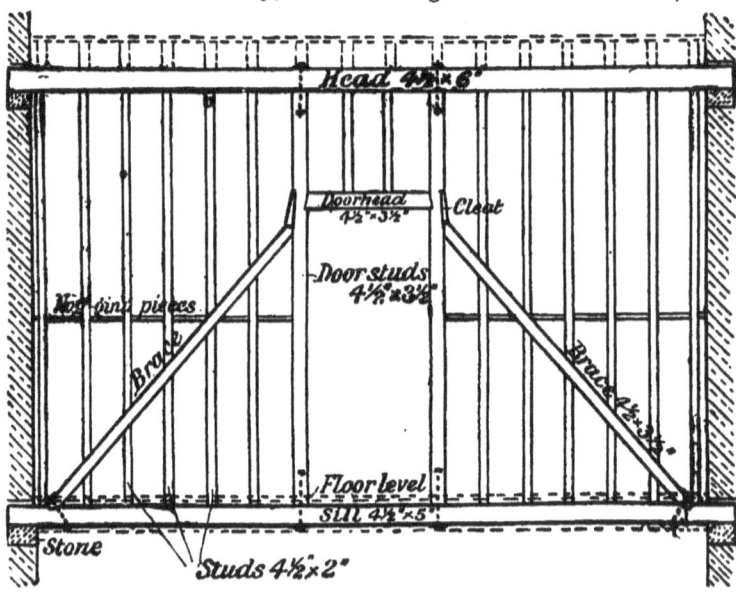

ELEVATION OF FRAMED PARTITION.
FIG. 497.

has the names of the various parts indicated. In this case the partition runs in the direction of the floor joists of the lower

PARTITIONS AND WOODEN FRAMED BUILDINGS. 261

floor, and the sill, which is in one length, is arranged between two joists. The upper floor joists are at right angles to the partition, and are supported by it.

The stronger members of these partitions—that is, the **head, sill, door-posts**, and **braces**—are first framed together, the joints being secured with iron bolts or straps; the intermediate spaces are then filled with studs placed from twelve to fifteen inches apart. Each brace should always be in one length, with the studs cut to fit on it. All the joints should be arranged so that they are as little as possible affected by shrinkage, and all

FIG. 498.

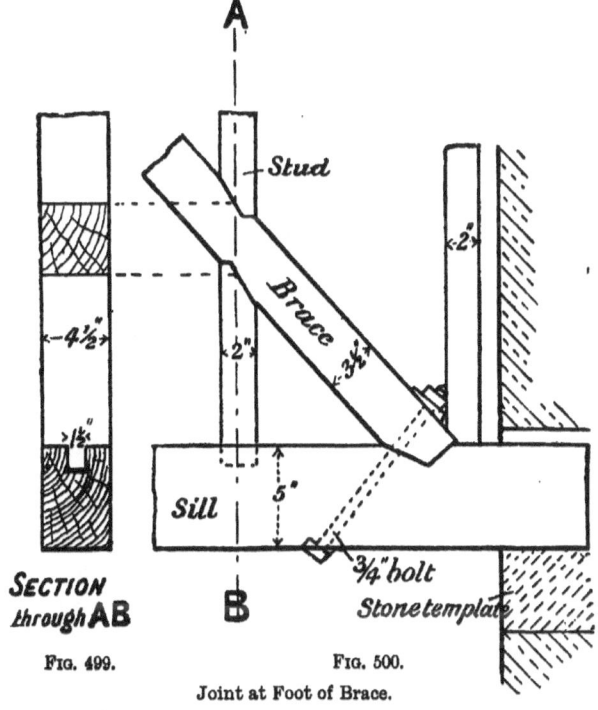

FIG. 499.   FIG. 500.
Joint at Foot of Brace.

the thicker members of the partition, such as door-posts, braces, etc., should have the corners taken off (Fig. 498). Seasoned timber should always be used in the construction of partitions, either red deal or white deal generally being used.

Joint at Foot of Brace.—Fig. 500 shows in elevation the joint at the foot of the brace. The joint may be **bridled**, as in Fig. 501, or may be **halved** on (Fig. 502). In either case a bolt is necessary to secure the connection.

 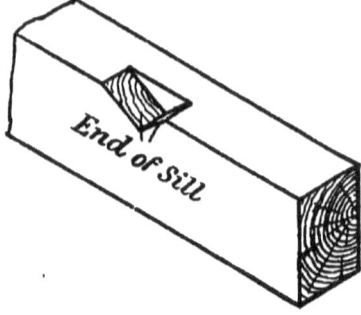

FIG. 501.—Bridle Joint.   FIG. 502.—Halved Joint.

Joint between Stud and Brace.—This joint may be simply cut to the required bevel and nailed (Fig. 503), or it may be cut as shown in Fig. 500.

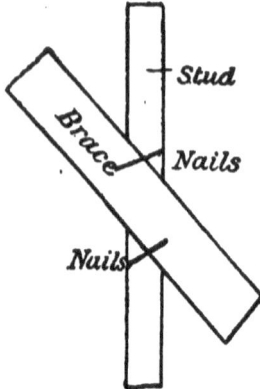

FIG. 503.—Joint between Stud and Brace.

Joint between Stud and Sill.—This joint is made by a short tenon (named a **stump tenon**) on the stud fitting into a corresponding mortise in the sill (Figs. 499 and 500). The ends of the door-posts, as well as the upper ends of the studs, are also stump-tenoned into the head or sill as the case may be.

Joint at Head of Brace.—In Fig. 505 the door-post is wider above the door-head to allow for the abutment of the brace. This arrangement necessitates increased labour as well as a waste of material. An alternative method is to let in a **cleat** and nail it to the door-post. The upper end of the brace abuts against this cleat (Figs. 497 and 504). The door-head is stump-tenoned into the door-post as shown in Figs. 504 and 505.

Joint at Head and Foot of Door-post.—When the sill runs "straight through" as in Figs. 497 and 510, the lower end of the door-post is stump-tenoned into it, and may be secured with

PARTITIONS AND WOODEN FRAMED BUILDINGS. 263

a joint bolt, as shown in elevation and section in Figs. 506 and 507. Or, it may have a wrought-iron strap to clip the

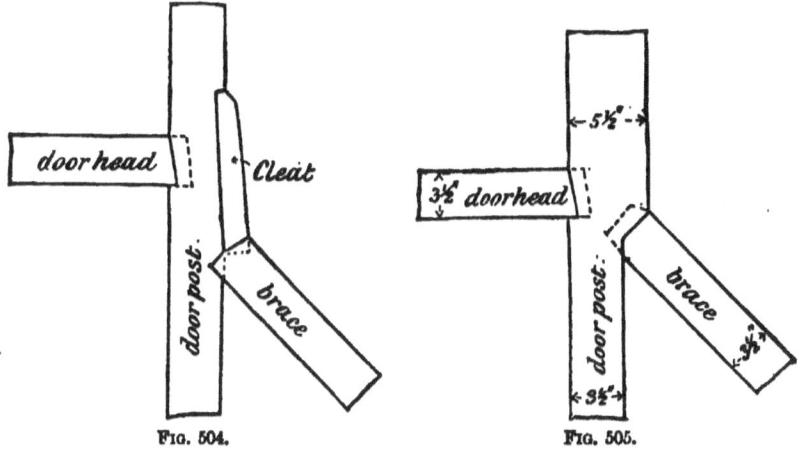

Alternative Joints at Head of Brace.

sill and door-posts, with bolts passing through to fasten the joint. The objection to this latter method is that the bolts are

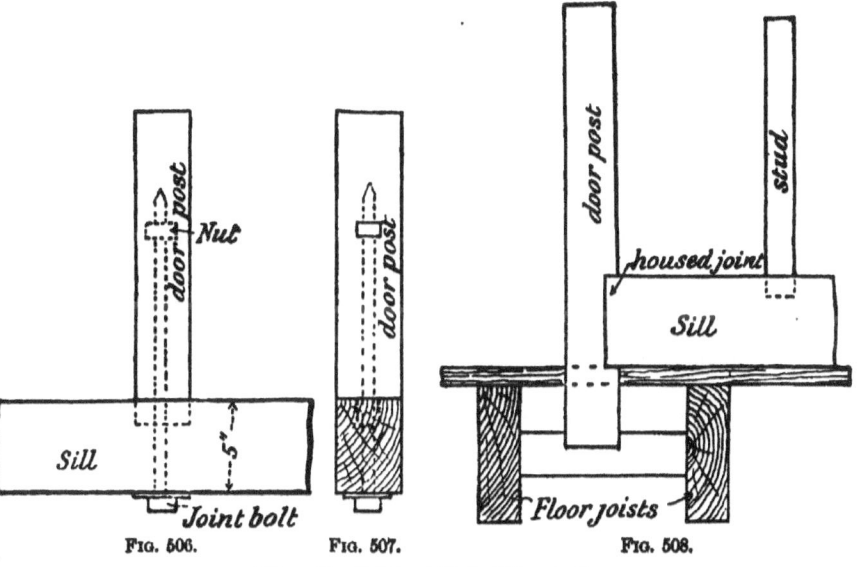

Alternative Joints at Foot of Door-post.

liable to be in the way of the laths and plaster. The stump-tenon and joint bolt are also used to secure the upper end of the door-post to the head (Fig. 497). When, as frequently happens, the partition runs across the joists of the lower floor, the sill cannot be continuous on account of the doorways (Figs. 509 and 512). In such circumstances the sill is sunk or housed into the door-posts, these latter going between the joists, as shown in Fig. 508.

Partition with Two Side Doorways.—Fig. 509 is the elevation of a partition with two side doorways. The horizontal

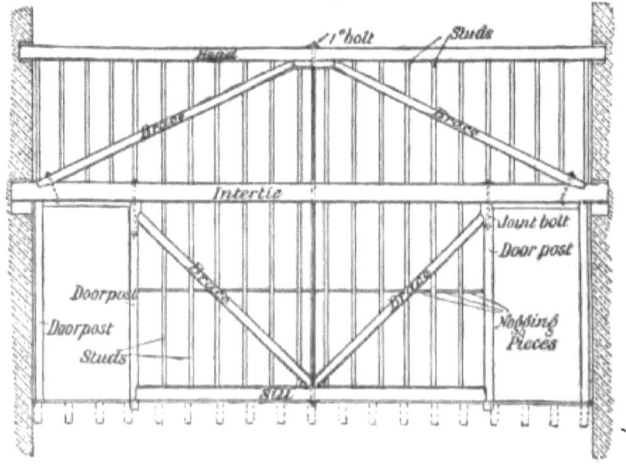

FIG. 509.—Partition with Two Side Doorways.

member, which is continuous and forms the door-head, is named an **intertie**, and acts in this example as the main support of the partition. A long wrought-iron bolt, one inch in diameter, and having a nut at each end for tightening up, passes through the centre of the partition, as shown in the illustration. A strong wooden member might be substituted for the bolt, with the ends stump-tenoned into the head and sill, and the joints secured with joint bolts in a manner similar to the joints shown at the head of the door-posts (Fig. 497).

Figs. 510 and 511 are diagrams of **other framed and braced partitions**. In these, the stronger framing is shown by double lines, while the studs and horizontal nogging pieces are indicated by single lines. These diagrams represent typical

PARTITIONS AND WOODEN FRAMED BUILDINGS. 265

examples of the manner in which partitions are framed. The size and arrangement of the framing are, of course, dependent upon the width of span between the walls, on the number, size,

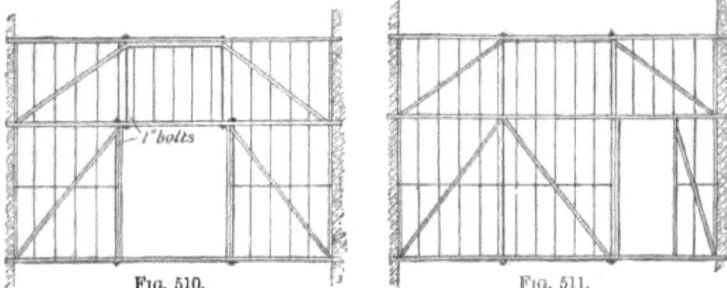

Fig. 510.   Fig. 511.
Line Diagrams of Framed and Trussed Partitions.

and position of doorways, and on the number, if any, of floors to be supported by the partition. Fig. 512 shows a partition extending through two storeys in height, with a wide central doorway in the upper part, and two smaller side doorways in the lower part. The joints of these partitions are arranged on the principles given in detail above, and therefore do not need further explanation.

Brick-nogging.—The timber partition, instead of having the studs placed to carry laths and plaster, may be fixed at intervals of from two feet three inches to three feet, and the intervening

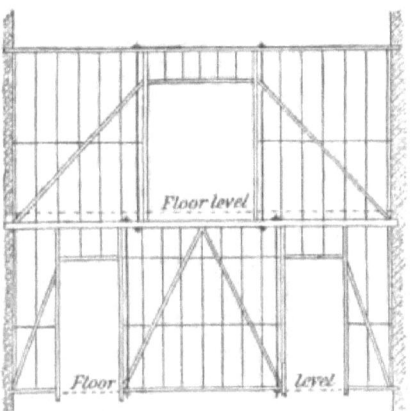

Fig. 512.—Two-storey Framed and Trussed Partition.

space filled with brickwork. Horizontal nogging pieces of wood, one inch thick, should be inserted at every third or fourth course. The usual thickness for brick-nogged partitions is four and a half inches, though often for the sake of economy, or to gain room, they are made three inches thick, in which case the bricks are laid on edge between the studs.

266   A MANUAL OF CARPENTRY AND JOINERY.

WOODEN FRAMED BUILDINGS.

Wooden framed structures of the kind just described are also much used instead of bricks or stone, to form the outside walls of buildings of a temporary character. The framework may be covered with either boards or corrugated iron. In various parts of the world, dwelling houses are constructed in this manner, but in this country wooden framed buildings are

FIG. 513.—Elevation of Cricket Pavilion

confined to such structures as small railway stations, exhibition buildings, portable workshops and sheds, temporary warehouses, cricket and football pavilions, etc.

General Principles of Construction.—The general arrangement, of course, depends upon special circumstances, while the dimensions of the framing and the methods of bracing it together are influenced by the size of the building, and the uses to which it is to be put. The usual arrangement of such timber structures is to have heavy square **angle posts**, with **intermediary**

WOODEN FRAMED BUILDINGS. 267

posts if necessary, and between these to insert **cross rails** and **diagonal braces**. The main braces should by preference be continuous, in order to brace the structure rigidly, any abutting cross-rails being cut to fit them. The joints used are similar to those already described, and include the mortise and tenon, the bridle, and halved joints, care being taken to arrange them so that they are least affected by shrinkage. Bolts, joint bolts, coach screws, iron straps, and wooden pins, are used as fastenings according to requirements. If the building is more than one storey high, it is necessary to make provision in the framing for supporting the upper floor. When window or door openings occur in such a building, it is advisable to have them directly over each other whenever possible.

Wooden structures of this description should always rest upon a foundation of brick or stone-work or concrete, so that

FIG. 514.—Tongued, Grooved and Beaded Battens.

all timber is at least 12 inches from the ground. A layer of some bituminous substance, which serves as a damp-proof course, will, when laid upon the foundation prevent the wood from absorbing moisture out of the earth. When a wooden ground-floor is used—as is often the case—every care should be taken to have a free circulation of air under the floor to prevent dry rot. When this class of building is to be of a portable nature, it may be built in sections, with the various parts fastened together with bolts, joint bolts, or screws. Temporary buildings are most economically constructed out of marketable sections of deals and battens. Heavy supporting posts may be formed by bolting two or three deals together.

Covering Materials.—As previously stated, the covering of the framework may be either **wood** or **corrugated galvanized iron**. When the framing is covered with wood, the covering boards may be fixed vertically with match-boarding joints, that is, either tongued, grooved and beaded (Fig. 514), or rebated (Fig. 515), or with square-edged joints covered by narrow laths or fillets of wood as shown in Fig. 516. Or, the boards may be placed horizontally with joints as shown in Figs. 519 and 520; this class of boarding is known as *weather boarding*. Corrugated galvanized iron sheets are used as a more permanent covering than wood; the sheets are secured to the framing with screws and washers.

In the inside of the building, the framing is either left exposed without covering, is boarded with match boarding, or

FIG. 515.—Rebated and V-jointed Battens.

is plastered, according to the finish required. Some such buildings, in addition to being lined inside with boards, have a layer of felt or "Willesden paper" behind the boarding as a means of warmth. The **roofs** of such buildings may be covered with boards, boards overlaid with **felt, corrugated iron, slates,** or **tiles,** and the construction follows the principles already explained in Chap. IX.

It is obvious that in such wooden buildings there is considerable scope for ornamental treatment in cases where an attractive

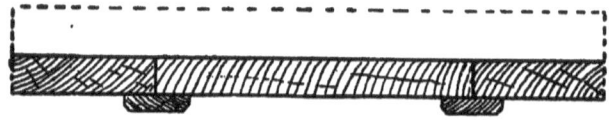

FIG. 516.—Square-edged Battens with Fillets over Joints.

appearance is of importance, as for example, in exhibition buildings, cricket pavilions (Fig. 513), etc. On the other hand, in warehouses (Fig. 517), workshops, and the like, decorative treatment is of small consequence, and strength and rigidity are the main considerations.

Half Timber Work.—A style of architecture which presents a picturesque appearance, and is frequently adopted in villas and country residences, is known as half timber work. Some of the older examples of this work show the walls of the building constructed entirely with wooden framing, the spaces between which are filled in with brickwork, to form slightly recessed

WOODEN FRAMED BUILDINGS.

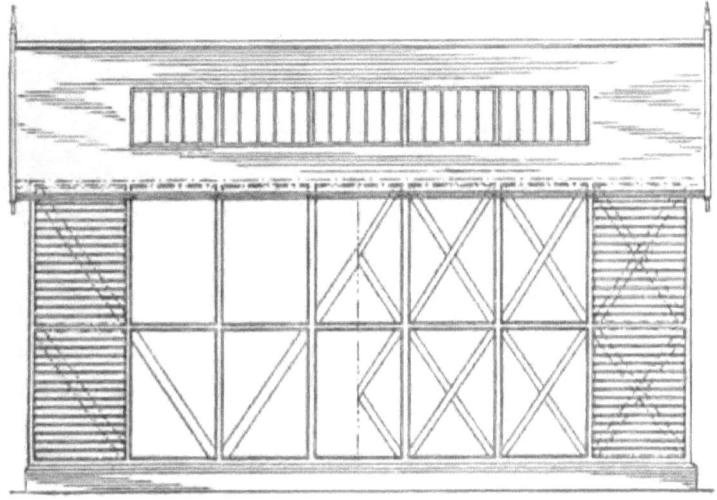

ELEVATION.

PLAN.

FIG. 517.—Wooden Framed Building.

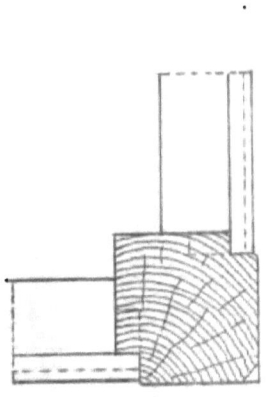

FIG. 518.—Plan of Corner-Post of Fig. 517.

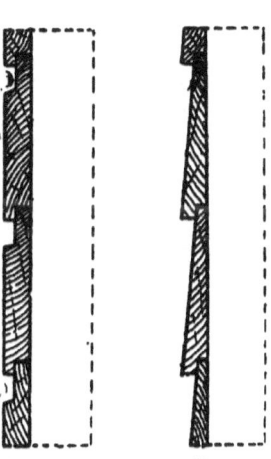

FIG. 519.   FIG. 520.
Types of Weather Boarding.

270   A MANUAL OF CARPENTRY AND JOINERY.

Fig. 521.

Fig. 522.

Examples of Half Timber Buildings.

panels, the surface of the brickwork generally being plastered. More modern examples have the lower storey built of stone or brick, with only the upper walls—or in some cases only the gables—of half timber work (Figs. 524 and 523).

In the best examples of half timber work it is usual to have stout corner posts of quartering, into which are framed the necessary head, sill, and cross-rails, with intermediate framing of the required design. The joints are chiefly mortise and

Fig. 523.   Fig. 524.
Examples of Half Timber Buildings.

tenon, held together with hard-wood pins (*trenails*). The spaces between the framing are filled in with brickwork, which is set back for about 1¼″ from the face of the framing so that when the surface of the brickwork is plastered it forms recessed panels about three-quarters of an inch deep. The finished surface of the plaster may be either smooth or rough cast. To obtain a sufficient thickness of wall, additional brickwork—bonded with the rest—is built behind the wooden framing.

The best timber for this work is oak, although pitch pine and red deal are also used. Red deal is better than pitch pine as it is not so liable to crack on exposure to the weather.

272   A MANUAL OF CARPENTRY AND JOINERY.

For the sake of economy, modifications of half timber work are often used which, although preserving the same outward appearance, have nothing to commend them but cheapness. One of these consists of using framing as described above and filling in the spaces with vertical studs and lath and plaster. Another method is to fix thin frames of timber, not more than $1\frac{1}{2}''$ thick, against the face of the brick wall, and to plaster the recessed panels as described above.

Summary.

Partitions of wood covered with laths and plaster often take the place of brick walls between upper-storey rooms. Such partitions are best framed into trusses directly transferring the weight to the walls.

The **framework** consists of horizontal members (*head*, *sill*, and *intertie*), vertical members (*door-posts* and *studs*), and of inclined *braces*. All the members of the same truss should be of the same *thickness* to enable both sides to be plastered evenly.

Horizontal *nogging pieces* are fixed at intervals to stiffen the studs. The joints mostly used for the framework of partitions are the *stump tenon* and the *bridle* joints, secured with bolts.

Brick-nogging consists of filling in the wooden framework with bricks.

Structures such as exhibition buildings, temporary workshops and warehouses, etc., often consist entirely of **wooden framing** covered with boards or corrugated galvanized iron. Such buildings should always rest upon a base of brickwork or concrete.

In **half timber** work the spaces between the exposed wooden framing are filled with brickwork, the surface of which is covered usually with cement plaster.

Questions on Chapter X.

1. Draw rather more than half the elevation of a framed and trussed partition, 16 ft. 6 in. by 12 ft. 6 in. in size, having a central door-opening 8 ft. 9 in. wide and 7 ft. 6 in. high. The partition is to be supported at its ends, and is to carry the weight of the floor above it. (C. and G. Ord., 1903.)

2. Draw a framed and braced partition supported only at the ends, the head carrying floor joists, to measure 17 ft. by 11 ft., with two door openings, each 3 ft. 3 in. by 6 ft. 9 in., and within 2 ft. 6 in.

of the end of the partition in each case. Figure scantlings. (C. and G. Ord., 1901.)

3. A framed and braced partition, 16 ft. 3 in. by 12 ft., has two door-openings, each 7 ft. by 3 ft. 2 in. One is in the centre of the partition and one at the end. The partition is supported at the ends and is to carry floor joists. Make a drawing of this partition and dimension the scantlings. (C. and G. Ord., 1902.)

4. Draw the elevation of rather more than half of a framed and trussed partition, showing the method of construction. The partition is 25 ft. by 12 ft., and contains three doorways, each 3 ft. by 7 ft. A doorway is to be placed 18 in. from each end, and one in the centre. The partition will be required to carry its own weight, together with the weight of the floor above. (C. and G. Ord., 1904.)

5. Draw out a quarter partition, 15 ft. long, going through two storeys, supported only at the ends of the lowest sill, and carrying two floors. The lowest storey is 11 ft. 6 in. in the clear, the upper one 9 ft. in the clear. There is an opening 9 ft. by 9 ft. in the lower storey, and there are two doorways, each 3 ft. 3 in. by 7 ft. in the upper storey. (C. and G. Hon., 1902.)

6. Give elevation to scale $\frac{1}{4}$ in. to a foot of a quarter partition 18 ft. wide and 24 ft. high, running through two storeys and self-supporting over the ground floor. On the first floor is a central doorway 6 ft. 6 in. wide by 7 ft. 6 in. high; on the second floor is a doorway 3 ft. wide and 6 ft. 6 in. high, 3 ft. 6 in. from one side-wall; and another 4 ft. wide and 6 ft. 6 in. high, 2 ft. from the other wall. Give details of joints, show all ironwork and figure scantlings. (C. and G. Hon., 1897.)

7. A temporary wooden building for a flower show is to occupy a space 40 ft. by 50 ft. It is to be roofed cheaply in one or two spans, chiefly using deals and battens, and covering the roof with felt. Draw a cross-section of the building, and part of a longitudinal one, with details. Scale not less than $\frac{1}{4}$ in. to a foot. (C. and G. Hon., 1903.)

8. A drill-shed, 40 ft. wide, is to be constructed in an extremely exposed situation, entirely of wood, the roof being slated. Draw the elevation of one end, the cross-section and the elevation of one bay, to not less than $\frac{1}{4}$ in. scale, showing how you would protect the shed from wind; height to wall plate, 10 ft. Accompany the drawing with a written description. (C. and G. Hon., 1902.)

CHAPTER XI.

MISCELLANEOUS CARPENTRY CONSTRUCTIONS.

SCAFFOLDING.

Scaffolds are temporary structures of wood, which serve as platforms upon which the workmen stand during the execution of any work which cannot be reached from the ground. Scaffolding is indispensable not only during the actual erection of buildings, bridges, etc., and during the

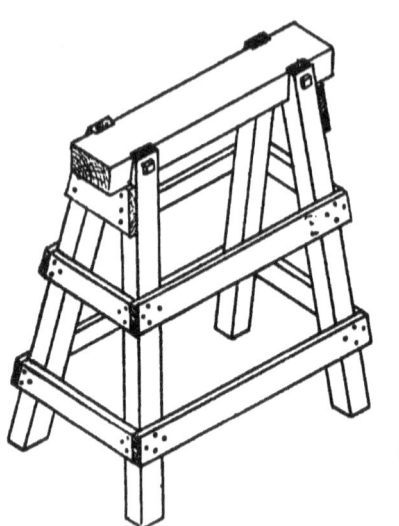

FIG. 525.—Scaffolding Trestle.   FIG. 526.—Folding Trestle.

construction of ships, but also for the subsequent work of the engineer, painter, etc. The extent to which scaffolding is required, and the method of constructing it, vary according to the use to which it is to be put: that is, whether it is to be used for supporting the workman only, or for carrying also large quantities of material.

Trestles.—For scaffolds of small height, wooden trestles of the shape shown in Fig. 525 are much used. They vary in height up to 10′; the larger ones are very clumsy, however, and are not in general use. Fig. 526 shows a folding trestle, which is much employed by painters.

Ladders.—Ladders are necessary for mounting the scaffolds. The sides of a ladder are usually made

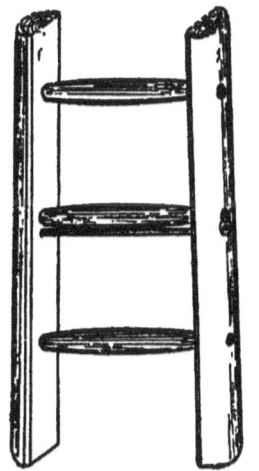

FIG. 527.—Three Rungs of a Ladder.   FIG. 528.—Four Rungs of a Ladder.

by cutting a larch, or spruce-fir, pole down the middle. The pole must be free from knots, shakes, and other defects, and while being straight, must not be too thick. Its thickness is determined by the length of the ladder required. It is possible to get a suitable pole from 40′ to 50′ long, the butt end of which is about 5″ in diameter, and the top end $2\frac{1}{2}$″ in diameter. The ladder **rungs** or **staves** are of hard wood, preferably oak. They should be *riven* (*i.e.* split), rather than sawn, to the required size; as sawn rungs are not infrequently cross-grained, and therefore untrustworthy. The rungs are placed at 9″ distances; they vary in length, being about 16″ long at the lower end, and 12″

276 A MANUAL OF CARPENTRY AND JOINERY.

at the upper end of the ladder; they are circular in section, being thinner at the ends, and the sides of the ladder are bored to receive them, the ends of the rungs being secured with paint and wedges.

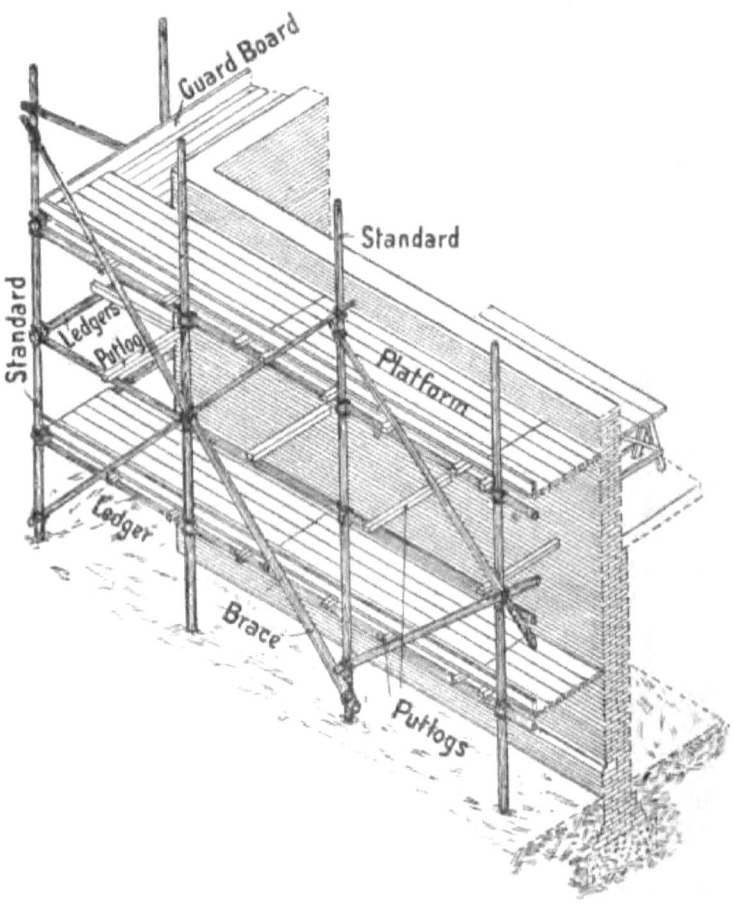

FIG. 529.—Sketch of a Bricklayers' Scaffold.

To strengthen the ladder still more, small bars of wrought iron, placed at intervals of six or eight rungs, are passed from side to side just under the rungs, and the ends are riveted over iron washers (Fig. 527). For access to high scaffolding, it is strongly advisable to use short ladders with frequent landings,

SCAFFOLDING.

rather than to employ long ladders, as the fatigue of constantly carrying up materials is thereby much lessened. In the construction of large buildings, inclined gangways are often used instead of ladders. When such gangways are more than one plank in width, the planks composing them are fastened together by cross ledges nailed to the under-sides.

Bricklayers' Scaffold.—In the erection of buildings the builder requires an elevated scaffold directly the work of building becomes too high to be reached from the ground. In work of small extent, the scaffold may simply consist of scaffold boards resting either upon trestles, or upon cross-bearers (putlogs) which are supported by short uprights (standards).

For larger buildings, scaffold-poles lashed together are almost invariably used in the construction of the scaffold. A scaffold of this description used for bricklayers' work is from 3' to 4' wide. As illustrated in Fig. 529, its main supports are vertical **standards** placed about 8' apart. The lower ends of the standards are either let into the ground for a short distance, or they are placed into barrels without ends which rest upon large slabs of stone, the barrels being filled with earth. In either case the earth is well rammed around the lower ends of the posts to keep them in position. Across the standards, horizontal poles called **ledgers** are placed at successive heights of about 5'—that is, at the height of each tier requiring a platform for the execution of the work. As scaffolding is of a temporary character, the various members are secured together with either hempen or steel cords lashed round the joinings. The cords are further tightened by the insertion of wedges (Fig. 530) between them. Resting with one end upon the ledgers, and with the other end upon the wall, are **putlogs,**—short pieces of timber (preferably of hard wood) about 3" thick, and from 3" to 5" wide. The putlogs are placed about 4' apart, and carry the **scaffold boards** which form the platform. It will be seen that the putlogs can only be placed in position as the work proceeds, whereas the same scaffold-boards are raised as required. The putlogs of each tier of scaffolding are left in position, with scaffold boards here and there, as an aid in stiffening the scaffold and holding it to the wall. The scaffold

Fig. 530.

boards are from 1½" to 3" thick, and should by preference be all the same length, and abut end to end, although they are often laid to overlap at the ends. Along the outer edges of the platform, vertical **guard boards**—9" to 12" deep—should be fixed, to prevent any material from falling off the platform. It is a wise precaution to fix also a **guard rail**—especially when a scaffold is very high—at a height of about 3' 6" above the platform level. To give the necessary rigidity to the scaffold, and prevent any rocking or giving way, diagonal **braces** are lashed to the standards and to the ledgers.

If the height of the building is so great that standards cannot be obtained long enough to reach to the top, additional poles may be lashed to the upper ends of the lower standards. If the height of the scaffold is considerable, or if it has to carry heavy weights, each standard may consist of two parallel series of poles lashed together with the joints of one series alternating with those of the other. Hempen cords are affected by the weather, and may in time become slack. It is therefore necessary to examine the lashings periodically.

Masons' Scaffold.—In stone buildings, especially those in which the walls are built of large stones, the scaffold is often constructed so that it is entirely separate from the building. This necessitates two separate frames of standards and ledgers, so that both ends of the putlogs are supported independently of the wall. The inner row of standards is fixed a few inches from the building line, to enable the stones to be put in position. As there is no tie to the wall in this scaffold, it is necessary to brace it in the direction of the width of the platform.

With the exception of the differences mentioned above, the arrangement is similar to the bricklayers' scaffold. As the building material used by the mason is generally heavier than that used by the bricklayer, however, the scaffold is usually made stronger by placing the standards and the putlogs nearer together, and by bracing the structure more firmly.

Gantries.—In large towns or in places where there is considerable street traffic, and a building is erected close to the footpath, limits of space render it advisable to erect, over the footpath, an elevated platform called a gantry. It consists of heavy frameworks of timber arranged in two parallel rows, one at the curb of the footpath, and the other near the building;

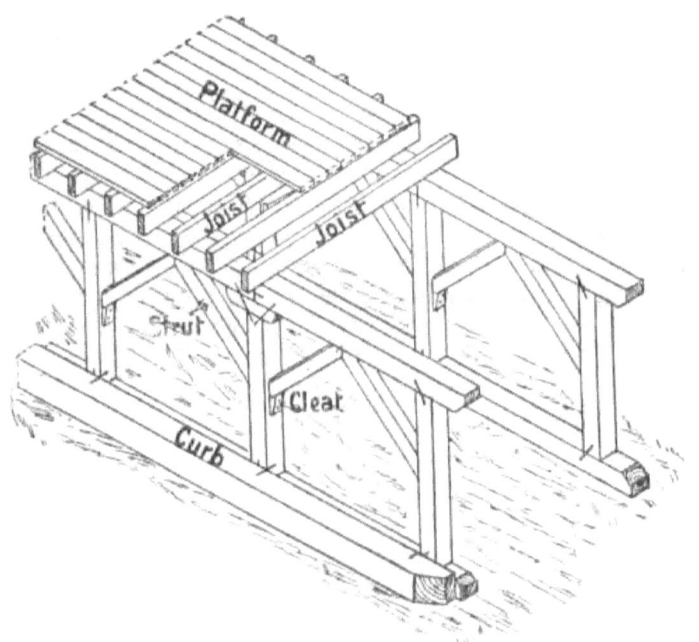

Fig. 531.—Sketch of part of a Gantry.

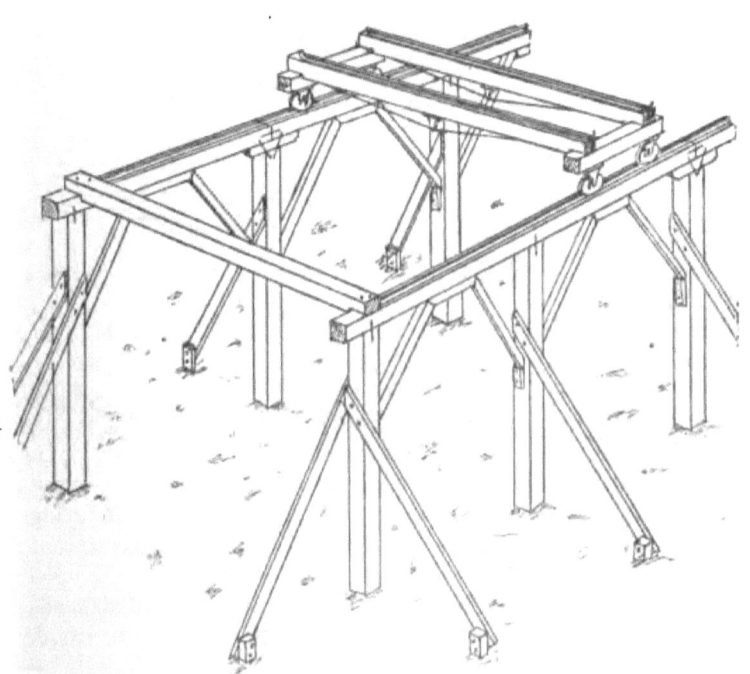

Fig. 532.—Sketch of a Gantry to carry a Travelling Crane.

280   A MANUAL OF CARPENTRY AND JOINERY.

these carry joists which support a sheeting of planks at a height of from 9' to 12'. The length of such a gantry depends upon the character of the work, as well as upon many other conditions. In the construction of a gantry of this description the main timbers are usually of large section, and the joints are made as simple as possible. The cleat, iron dog, bolts, and coach screws are the chief means of fastening the timbers together. A heavy wooden curb is necessary at the outer side of the gantry, to

FIG. 583.—Sketch of three Derrick Towers to carry a Jib Crane.

protect it from the street traffic. Fig. 531 shows a sketch of such a gantry.

The heavy timber structures which support the travelling cranes found in engineering works, in timber and stone yards, and wherever heavy weights have constantly to be carried from one place to another, are also named gantries. Fig. 532 shows the general construction of such a gantry with the supporting posts fixed in the ground. An alternative arrangement to that of fixing the posts into the ground is to have them resting upon heavy wooden curbs. The size of the timbers used depends upon the span of the *traveller*, and upon the weight to be lifted.

The main point for consideration is that the joints must have good abutments, and be properly braced and stayed in order to obtain a rigid structure.

Derrick Towers.—Yet another type of scaffold is required in the erection of large buildings, namely, that to carry an elevated jib crane fixed at an altitude sufficiently great to raise the various building materials to their respective positions. The platform is supported by 3 or 4 framed timber structures braced together in the manner shown in Figs. 533 and 534, and called **derrick towers.** The size and material of such towers depend on the height of the platform and the weights to be raised. The towers usually vary from 3' to 8' square.

In this type of scaffold there are generally three supporting towers as shown in the line-diagram sketch (Fig. 533). One of the towers (B) is directly beneath the mast or upright of the jib crane; the other two support the ends of the stays of the crane. The stays are usually anchored by means of chains or wire ropes down the middle of the towers, the bases at A being loaded with stones, bricks, or other heavy material. The tower supporting the mast of the crane is strengthened by an additional central post.

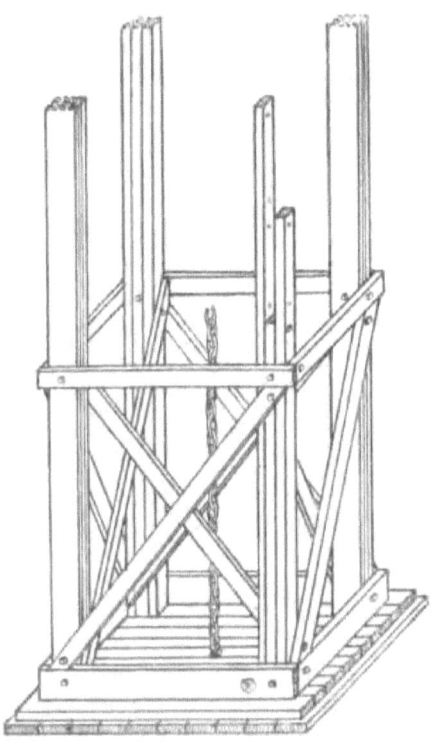

FIG. 534.—Detail of lower ends of Derrick Towers shown in Fig. 533.

TIMBERING FOR EXCAVATIONS.

When excavating deep trenches in soft ground, or constructing the puddle trenches for a reservoir, it is necessary to support (shore) the sides of the trenches to prevent them from giving way.

Timber is commonly employed to keep up the sides of the earth in excavations, and generally when the ground is such that it will not stand without support. Timber is also used

FIG. 535.—Sketch of Timber Shoring of a Trench in good ground.

to provide a temporary partition and to divert the water, where it is necessary to alter, repair, or reconstruct the banks of rivers, docks, waterways, etc.

Timbering or Shoring of Trenches.—The extent to which the timbering of trenches is necessary depends upon the nature of the earth which is being dug into, the depth to which the trench is carried, and the length of time the trench is left open.

With ground of a hard nature, and a depth of trench not exceeding 5 feet, it is often sufficient to place short vertical planks 7" to 9" wide and 2" to 3" thick, called **poling boards**, at distances of from 3 to 6 feet apart, with horizontal **struts** spanning the width of the trench and fixed between them as shown in Fig. 535. The size of the struts depends upon the width of the

TIMBERING FOR EXCAVATIONS.

trench; they are usually either square or round in section, and from 4" to 7" side or diameter.

An alternative method, applicable when the ground is loose, is shown in Fig. 536. It consists of fixing on each side of the trench a horizontal **sheeting** of planks from 12 to 14 feet long, close together, and held in position by vertical **waling pieces** and horizontal struts. The waling pieces are placed from 3 to 5 feet apart, with the sides of the trench cut with a slight "batter" (slope); and the struts are tightly driven between

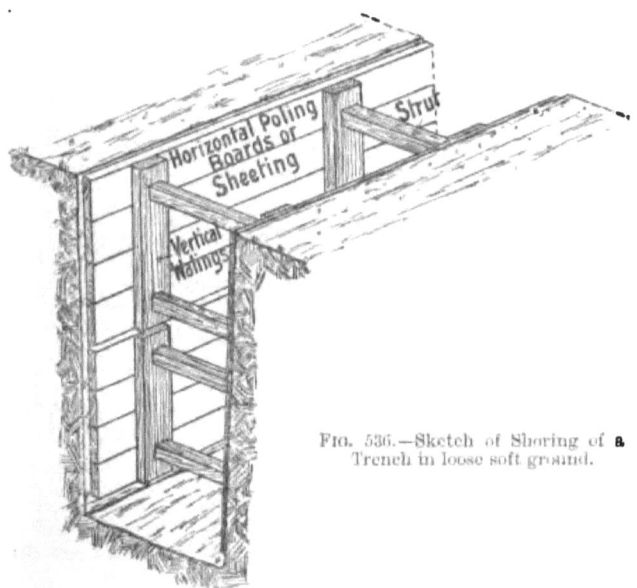

FIG. 536.—Sketch of Shoring of a Trench in loose soft ground.

the waling pieces. The sheeting is inserted in about 3 feet depths (*i.e.* four sheeting boards), and, as the depth of the trench increases, additional sheeting and supports are fixed in position.

Another method of timbering or shoring up the sides of a trench is to have vertical poling boards fixed behind horizontal waling pieces, which are held in position by horizontal struts spanning the trench (Fig. 537). If the ground is very bad, the poling boards are placed close together, and it is sometimes necessary to have the lower ends cut so that the poling boards can be driven into position behind the waling pieces as the excavation proceeds. When such a method of timbering is adopted, the poling boards are from 6 to 8 feet long; and as the depth of the trench increases, another layer of poling boards, with waling pieces and struts, is driven in front of and below those previously driven.

Figs. 535 to 537 illustrate typical examples of the shoring of trenches under ordinary conditions. It often happens that trenches have to be dug to a considerable depth in streets where there is a large amount of heavy traffic, or where large

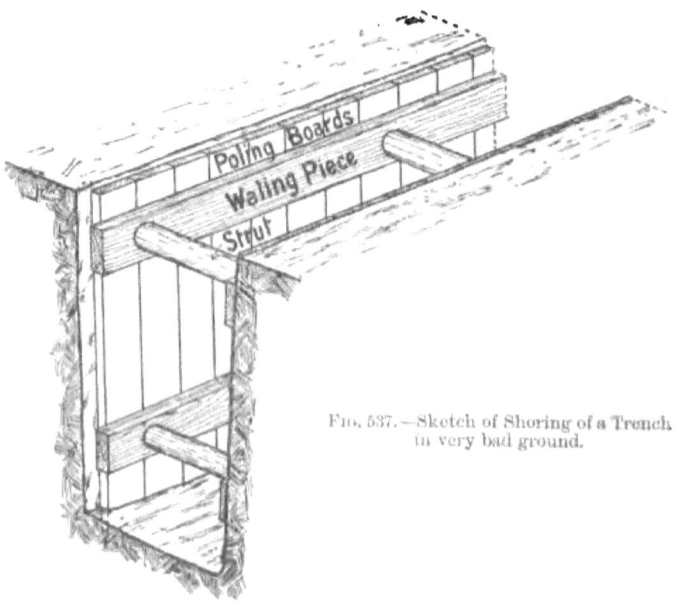

FIG. 537.—Sketch of Shoring of a Trench in very bad ground.

buildings abut against the street. It is not uncommon in such cases to have first of all to shore up the buildings on each side of a street, and also to use heavy struts to prevent the sides of the trench from giving way during the excavations.

With such trenches, platforms resting upon the struts are necessary to allow the excavated earth to be thrown out: for a workman cannot easily shovel earth higher than 6 feet.

The sides of very deep and extensive trenches such as the puddle trenches of reservoirs, etc., are supported usually by horizontal sheeting, vertical poling boards, and struts. All these timbers are much stronger than those used for the

TIMBERING FOR EXCAVATIONS.

narrower trenches, and the struts are braced together to prevent any giving way through unequal pressure.

The Timbering of Excavations.—If the earth forming the sides of deep excavations is fairly hard and compact, it may be temporarily supported by upright poling boards, held in position by either inclined or horizontal struts. If, on the other hand, the ground is such that it necessitates close sheeting, it may be necessary to drive stout **guide piles** into the ground at about 10 feet apart, to bolt to these horizontal waling pieces arranged in pairs, and between the waling pieces to insert **sheet piling** of planks driven close together. If the depth of excavation is considerable, the guide piles will require bracing or stiffening with struts.

Piling.—During the repair or reconstruction of waterway embankments, dock walls, river walls, promenades, etc., timbering is almost indispensable. As the object of the timbering is to provide a temporary partition which will divert the water and keep the scene of operations clear, it is necessary to arrange the timbers so that the partition will be practically water-tight.

One way in which this can be accomplished is to drive, into the bed of the river, guide piles of wood, shod at the foot with iron, and each having at the upper end an iron hoop (Fig. 538) to prevent it from splitting when being driven. These piles are placed in an upright position, from 8 to 12 feet apart, and are driven into position by means of a pile driver; and waling pieces arranged in pairs are then bolted to them, the space between the waling pieces being such that it allows of planks (sheet piles) being driven close together between them to fill up the space between the guide piles. The edges of the planks

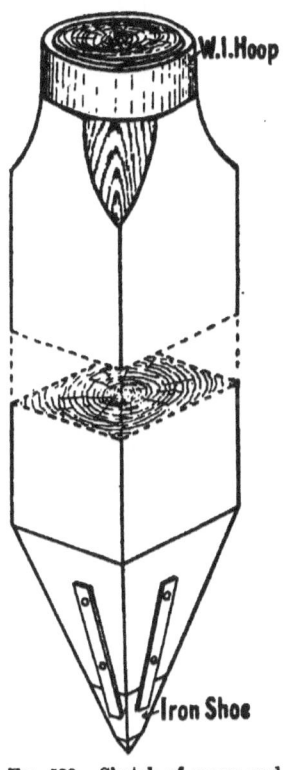

FIG. 538.—Sketch of upper and lower ends of a Wooden Pile.

forming the sheet piles are often either grooved and tongued (Fig. 540) or V-jointed (Fig. 541); and the lower ends of these

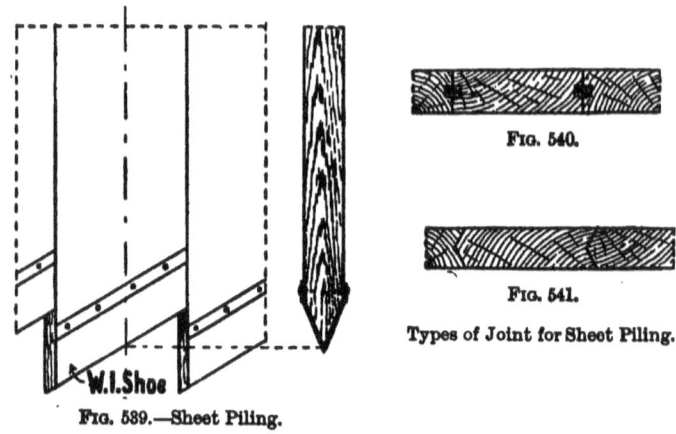

Fig. 539.—Sheet Piling.

Fig. 540.

Fig. 541.

Types of Joint for Sheet Piling.

piles are cut, as shown in Fig. 539, so that as they are driven they tend to close the joints between the piles. By this means a temporary partition, or **coffer-dam** (Fig. 542), is formed which,

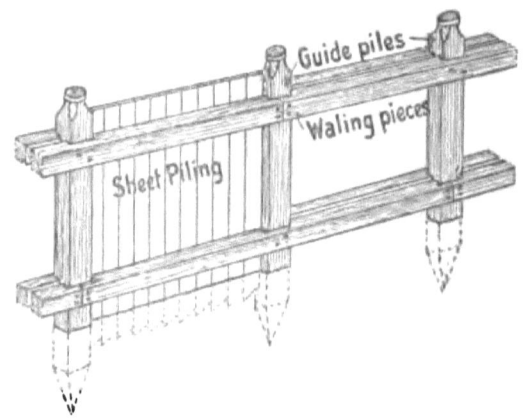

Fig. 542.—Sketch showing construction of a Coffer-dam.

with the aid of a pump, effectually excludes the water from the enclosed space. If the work is of large extent, or if the depth of water is considerable, the guide piles require stiffening by struts and braces.

A more effective way of making such partitions water proof is to arrange two rows of piles, about 18" apart, and then fill the space between them with clay puddle.

Piles similar to that shown in Fig. 538 are also much used in the foundations of large buildings, on sites where a layer of soft earth overlies firm ground but is too deep to excavate. Such piles are driven from 3 to 4 feet apart, and support cross timbers which are embedded in concrete. Elm is the best timber for piles which are to be left in position permanently.

SHORING OF BUILDINGS.

Necessity for Shoring.—Whenever a building shows signs of giving way, either through the failure of the foundations or from any other cause, it is necessary to support temporarily any bulged part with props of timber. These supports are called **shores**, and the method of arranging them is called **shoring**. Shoring is also required when structural alterations necessitate the taking down of some portion of a building, especially if parts on each side are to be left standing.

The shores of buildings may be divided into three different types:

(1) When shoring is required to keep up the corner or the sides of a building, inclined timbers called **raking shores** are placed to reach from the ground to the part of the building which requires supporting.

(2) Horizontal timbers (**flying shores**) and **inclined struts** are inserted between two buildings during the reconstruction of a building between them; these are also used when deep sewer trenches are being dug in narrow streets between large buildings.

(3) Vertical posts called **dead shores**, carrying crossbeams (**needles**) are used for supporting the upper part of a building when it is necessary to remove the lower part entirely.

Precautions to be adopted when Shoring.—The shoring of buildings needs great care and calls for special judgment. Any careless or insecure shoring may do more harm than good; in fact it may be fraught with great danger and possibly loss of life.

The timber for shoring must be sound and strong enough

to bear the stress put upon it. Since the work is temporary, and the material can afterwards be used for other purposes, it is usual to employ timbers of size and strength greater than are theoretically necessary. It should be noted, also, that the shores are in compression, and any weakness will give rise to buckling ; this tendency is best resisted by having timbers of square cross-section. Pitch-pine, owing to its being obtainable in long straight-grained lengths and free from large knots, is a very suitable wood for shoring. Care must be taken to examine the ground upon which the lower ends of the inclined or dead shores rest, to see that it is solid, free from old drains, and capable of withstanding the pressure to be placed upon it. All shores should be put in position with a minimum of knocking, which of necessity causes vibration. As they are generally used to prevent any further giving way, rather than as a means of forcing back any defective part, care should be taken not to overstress the wall in fixing the shores in position.

Raking Shores.—The best angle for raking shores is 45 degrees. Space will seldom allow of shores being fixed at this angle ; a more usual one for the top (longest) shore is from 60 to 70 degrees with the horizontal.

The lower ends of raking shores should rest upon a **sole-piece** or small platform of timber, to distribute the pressure over the ground surface. This sole-piece often consists of two or three thicknesses of planks crossing each other at right angles. The lower ends of raking shores should have a small notch cut into them, to enable a crowbar to be used in tightening them in position.

At the upper ends, a vertical **wall piece**—a plank about 11" by 3"—is fixed against the wall ; and **needles**—pieces of timber about 18" long by 4" square—pass through holes made in the wall piece, go into the wall for a distance of from 4" to 8", and project outside the wall piece, thus providing an abutment for the upper ends of the raking shores. The point of abutment should be a little below the floor level, the floor thus providing the necessary reaction. The needle is further strengthened by placing above it a cleat which may, with advantage, be housed into the wall piece for about half-an-inch. Fig. 543 shows a sketch of the upper end of a raking shore in position, abutting against a needle. The part of the needle which goes into the wall is usually cut so that it fits into a hole made by removing

SHORING OF BUILDINGS.

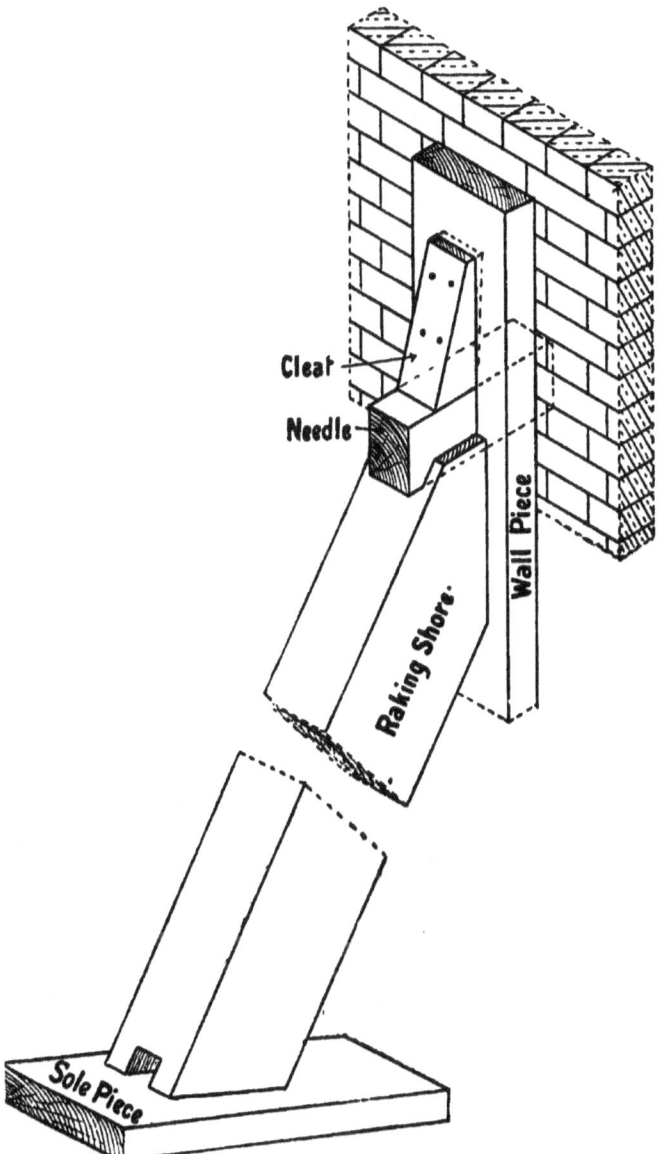

Fig. 543.—Sketch of upper and lower ends of a Raking Shore.

290 A MANUAL OF CARPENTRY AND JOINERY.

half a brick. It will be noticed that the upper end of the raking shore is bridled on to the needle to prevent it from getting out of position.

When a number of raking shores are in the same vertical plane, as, for example, in a building several storeys high (Fig. 544), the lower ends usually all rest upon the same sole piece, and may be fastened to it with iron dogs. The lower ends may be placed close to each other, or there may be a space of from 6" to 8" left between them to allow of either tightening a single shore, or removing it without disturbing the others. It is an advantage to have the wall pieces as long as possible, and, if practicable, to have the upper ends of all the raking shores in the same plane abutting against the same wall piece, with a needle going into the wall at the upper end of each shore. With high buildings it is sometimes convenient to have the longest shore in two lengths: the lower length resting upon the shore beneath it—which is accordingly arranged to be a little stronger. The upper length of this top shore is called a **rider**, and the shore underneath it is called the **back shore**. The rider shore is tightened by inserting folding wedges as at A (Fig. 544).

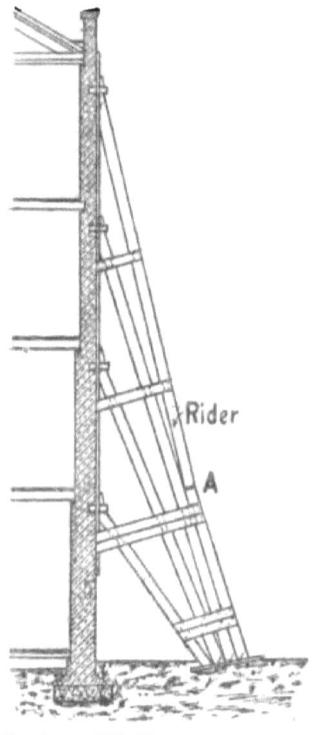

FIG. 544.—Side Elevation of Raking Shores.

Raking shores are stiffened by nailing braces consisting of boards from 1" to 2" thick to the sides, at different heights, as shown in Fig. 544. When several raking shores are placed with their lower ends close together, stout hoop-iron is often nailed round them with clout nails to bind them together.

Flying Shores.—Fig. 545 shows an example of the use of flying shores. These consist of horizontal timbers placed between two buildings when it is necessary to remove or

SHORING OF BUILDINGS.

reconstruct a building between them. They are also occasionally placed across a narrow street, from building to building, during the excavation of a deep trench for a sewer. Flying shores are better than raking shores, where they can be adopted, as they act more nearly at right angles to the pressure. Wall pieces are first fixed in position, with needles running through them and into the wall at the required heights for support. It is usual to have struts meeting on each side of the horizontal (flying) shore, and to have a straining piece between the struts.

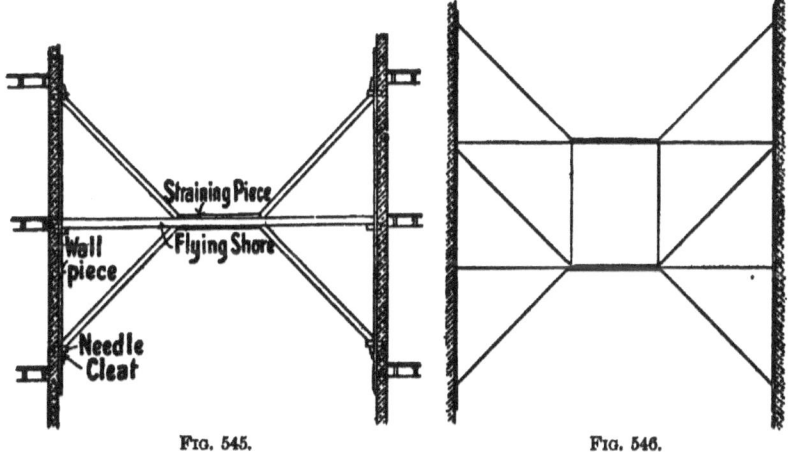

Fig. 545.   Fig. 546.

Methods of arranging Flying Shores.

The whole system is tightened when in position by inserting folding wedges. Figs. 545 and 546 show two different ways of arranging flying shores. If the struts are long they may be stiffened by nailing braces across them, as with raking shores.

Dead Shores are the vertical posts used to support **needle shores** when it is necessary to underpin a building to renew the foundation, or when the lower part of the front of a building is taken out, as, for example, during the conversion of a house into a shop with a large window opening (Fig. 547).

In this kind of shoring it is necessary to get the posts as nearly as possible underneath the structure they have to support. This plan shortens the bearing length of the needles, and consequently increases their strength. The outer posts should rest upon sleepers in order to distribute the weight over

292 A MANUAL OF CARPENTRY AND JOINERY.

a larger surface of the ground. The inner posts should also

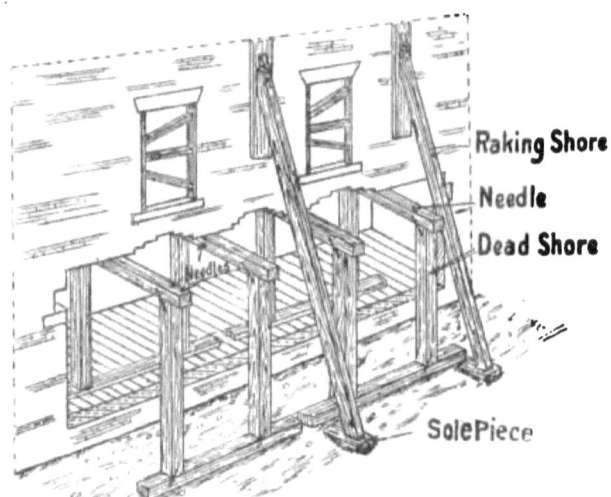

Fig. 547.—Sketch showing the method of Shoring a Building.

have a firm base; if the building has a basement it will be necessary either to pierce the floor or to fix posts from the floor in the basement directly underneath those required to support the needles. By this means a direct bearing from the ground is obtained.

When fixing shoring of this description, it is first necessary to make holes through the wall above the level at which the girder has to be inserted. These holes are placed in the best position for carrying the weight above, the needles are passed through them, and the dead shores are fixed in position, being tightened by means of folding wedges. When the

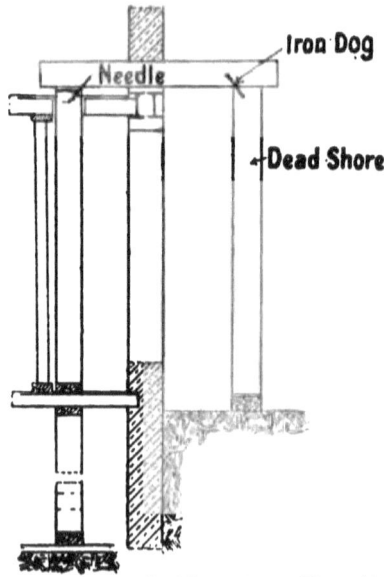

Fig. 548.—Detail of Dead Shores (Fig. 547).

weight is considerable, or when the needles cannot be supported at points nearly under the walls, and have consequently to be long, diagonal struts may be used, or the needles may be of wrought iron or steel. It is a wise precaution to brace the dead shores in a diagonal direction. Raking shores are often also necessary in such cases to keep the walls vertical; this is especially so at the corner of a building.

Whenever shoring is necessary, it is advisable to place struts between the reveals of all window or other openings in the walls, as shown in Fig. 547.

WOODEN CENTRES.

Whenever arches of brick, stone, or concrete are built, as for examples in the heads over window openings or doorways, in bridge construction, in groined work of roofs, etc., wooden structures are used temporarily for supporting the parts of the arch during the construction. These wooden structures are called **centres**. The upper surface of the centre corresponds in outline to that of the *soffit*, that is, the underside, of the arch.

Fixing the Centres.—All centres used for supporting arches should be fixed in position so that they can be lowered (eased) as soon as the construction of the arch is completed, and thus allow any slight irregularity in the brickwork to adjust itself before the mortar sets.

With the simpler types of centre this is provided for by resting the ends upon **vertical posts**, and by inserting **folding wedges** between the upper ends of the supporting posts and the ends of the centre. As soon as the arch is completed, these wooden wedges are slackened and the centre slightly dropped, to allow the arch to find its bearings. Hardwood—preferably teak—should be used for the wedges, they should be arranged either in pairs or three together, with the thin ends blunt so that they can be driven out easily.

With very large or complicated centres, special consideration needs to be given to the means of easing the centres.

Centres for Small Arches.—A centre, or turning piece, for a flat, or segmental, arch of not more than six feet span in a half-brick-thick or a thin stone wall is readily constructed by cutting to the required curvature one edge of a plank of 2" to 3" in thickness.

294 A MANUAL OF CARPENTRY AND JOINERY.

An alternative method of constructing such a centre is illustrated in Figs. 549 and 550. It consists of two parallel boards

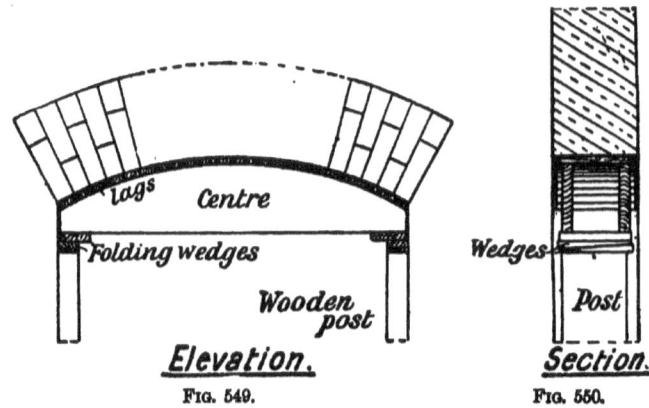

Fig. 549.   Fig. 550.

Wooden Centre for a Segmental Arch, showing some of the Arch-bricks in position.

(ribs), each one inch thick (Fig. 552, a and b), which have their upper edges cut to the required curvature, and are connected throughout their curved length by narrow wooden strips (lags)

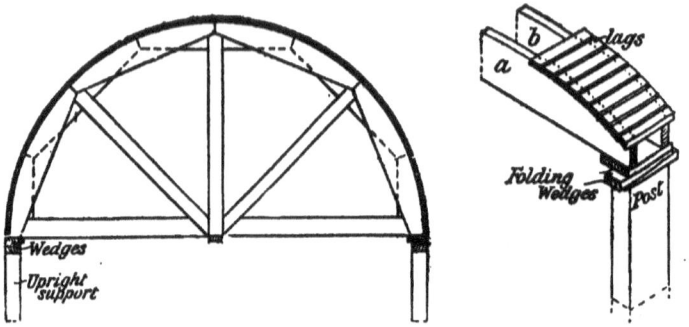

Fig. 551.—Elevation of Centre for a Semicircular Arch.

Fig. 552.—Sketch of part of Centre (Fig. 549) showing the method of supporting it.

for supporting the bricks of the arch. The size of the lags is from 1" to 2" wide, and about an inch thick; and they are placed about ¾" apart. Their length and the distance apart of the two ribs to which they are nailed depend upon the thickness of the wall. The length of each lag should be at least half an

WOODEN CENTRES. 295

inch less than the thickness of the wall, so that the bricklayers' "guide-line" may not be interfered with. The ribs are connected on the underside by a short **horizontal tie** at each end; this provides a seating for the folding wedges.

Setting out the Curve for a Segmental Arch.—In obtaining the curve of the wooden centre for a segmental arch, it is often difficult to find the "striking point," or geometrical centre, of the curve. When this point is inaccessible, and the width of the opening and the rise of the middle of the arch above the

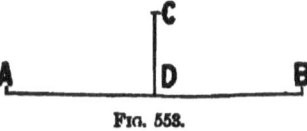

Fig. 553.

springing line are given, a practical way of determining the curve is as follows:—Drive three nails a, b, c, (Fig. 554) into a board such that ab is the span and cd is the rise. Obtain two laths, each double the length of ac, and nail them together so that they cross each other at c; let the outer edges of the laths rest against the nails a, b, c. Connect the laths by a third lath so that the angle acb will be fixed. Now remove the nail c, and

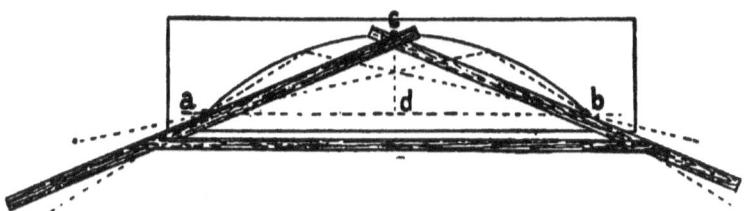

Fig. 554.—Method of obtaining the curved outline of a Wooden Centre.

substitute the pencil for it, and move the laths so that their edges remain in contact with a and b. The pencil will trace the segmental curve required.[1]

The method of calculating the radius of curvature for a segmental arch, when the width of opening and the rise in the middle are given, is as follows:

Square half the width of the opening, divide by the rise, add the rise, and divide by two, all in the same units.

Or (Fig. 553), $\quad \text{radius} = \dfrac{\left[\left(\dfrac{AB}{2}\right)^2 \div CD\right] + CD}{2}$.

---

[1] Students who have read Euclid will recognise that the method depends upon III. 34.

296 A MANUAL OF CARPENTRY AND JOINERY.

EXAMPLE.—*An arch has a span of six feet, and a rise of 8 inches. Find the radius of curvature.*

Half the width of span = 3 feet = 36 inches;

$$\therefore \text{radius} = \frac{(36^2 \div 8) + 8}{2} = \frac{(1296 \div 8) + 8}{2} = \frac{162 + 8}{2}.$$

$$= 1\tfrac{7}{2}0 = 85''.$$

∴ Radius of curvature = $85'' = 7'\ 1''$.

Graphically, the question resolves itself into determining the centre of a circle which passes through three given points (p. 26).

Centres for Larger Arches.—The centre for a segmental, semi-circular, or semi-elliptical arch, suitable for spans not

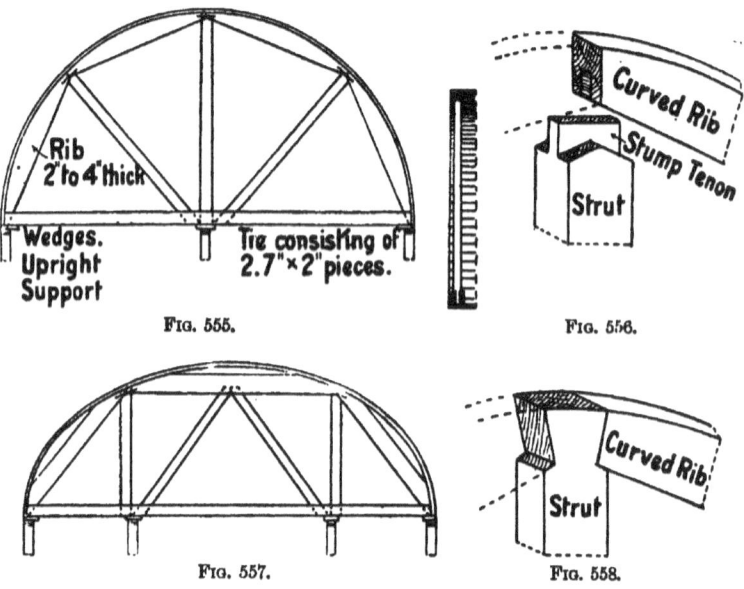

FIG. 555.   FIG. 556.

FIG. 557.   FIG. 558.

Types of Wooden Centres.

more than 12 feet wide, may have each of the curved ribs built up of two thicknesses of one-inch boards, nailed together with overlapping joints so that the joints of one layer are in the middle of the length of the boards of the other layer. The lower ends are kept from spreading by nailing or bolting across, at the springing level, a horizontal tie, 6" to 9" wide and 1" to 2" thick. The curved ribs are stiffened, and rigidity is

WOODEN CENTRES.

given to the centre, by adding **braces** of 4" or 5" by 1¼", as shown in elevation in Fig. 551. If the wall is a thin one, of not more than half-a-brick, or 6" of stone, one only of these ribs is required. If the wall is thicker than this, then two ribs, connected on their curved edges by lags, are required—the distance apart of the ribs and the length of the lags being governed by the thickness of the wall.

An alternative method of construction, and one which is applicable to openings of not more than 20 feet wide, is to make the centre out of thicker stuff, 2" to 4" thick, built up as shown in elevation in Fig. 555. The ribs of this type of centre may abut end to end and have stump tenons on the ends of the struts fitting into mortises made into the under side of the ribs (Fig. 556); or the struts may be arranged so that the ends go between the ribs as shown in Fig. 558. In either case it is necessary to secure the various members of the centre together by means of light **iron dogs** as shown in the drawings (Figs. 555 and 557).

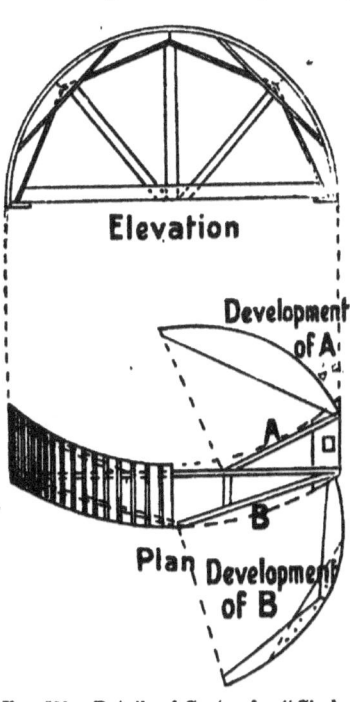

FIG. 559.—Details of Centre for "Circle-on-circle" Arch.

Many modifications may be made in the arrangement of the struts, to fulfil the requirements when the centre has to carry (i) a very heavy, or (ii) only a light arch, when (iii) the centre is to be supported at the ends only, or (iv) intermediate supports are also to be used. Figs. 555 and 557 are elevations of typical examples of wooden centres.

For centres used for supporting large bridges, etc., the framed ribs are built up to the required curvature, and are placed at from 3 to 4 feet apart, with a sheeting of battens or boards laid upon them.

298 A MANUAL OF CARPENTRY AND JOINERY.

The curves of arches for which centres are required vary widely. They may be segmental (*i.e.* arcs of circles) semi-elliptical, or even built up of arcs of circles of different radii, or be composed of other complex curves which cannot be considered here. In general the determination of the curve is a practical application of geometry.

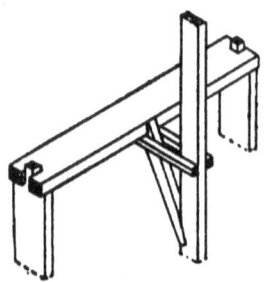

Fig. 560.—Framed Stand for supporting Centre (Fig. 559) in position.

The construction of centres for "circle-on-circle" arches, and for supporting groined arches, present other interesting examples of the application of practical geometry to carpentry. Fig. 559 shows the elevation and plan, with the development of the curvature of the ribs, of a centre for an arch which is semicircular in elevation

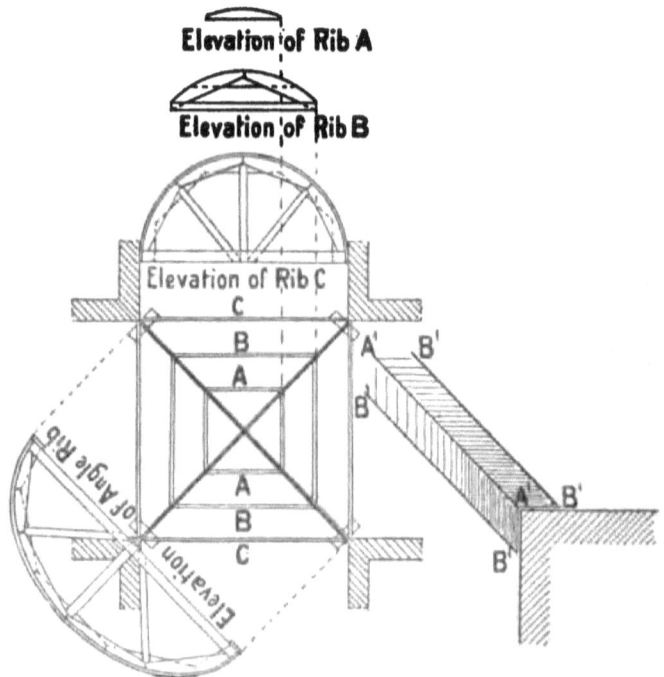

Fig. 561.—Details of Wooden Centres for intersecting semicircular Arches.

WOODEN CENTRES.

and segmental in plan. Fig. 560 is a sketch of the supporting frame for such a centre.

Fig. 561 shows the details of the centres required where four semi-circular arches of equal radii, and at right angles to each other, intersect at the same height. The angle ribs, which are built up of two thicknesses, require to be "backed" (as shown in plan in Fig. 561) to provide a seating for the sheeting. To obtain

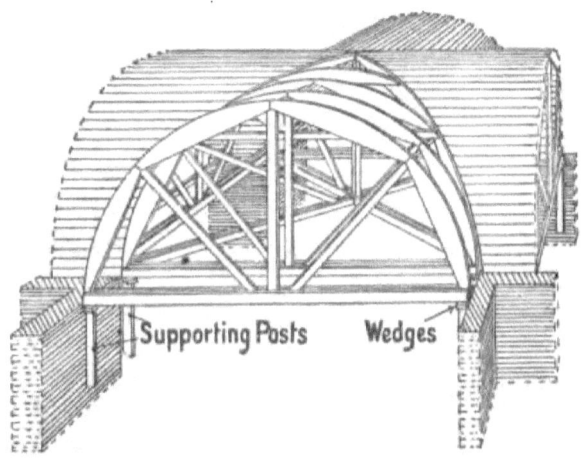

FIG. 562.—Sketch of Wooden Centres shown in detail in Fig. 561.

this backing it is necessary to have a template of the required outline of the angle ribs, and to slide it along the face of the centre for the distance shown at A' and B' (Fig. 561). Fig. 562 is a sketch of the centres just described, with part of the sheeting omitted to show the general arrangement.

SPECTATORS' STANDS.

For the purpose of witnessing field sports, cricket, or football matches, street processions, etc., elevated wooden **tiered stands** are much used. The construction of these varies according to whether they are of a temporary character only, or are to remain as permanent structures. Again, permanent spectators'-stands are often entirely or partly enclosed, in which case they become the galleried floor or floors of a building which may be, and often is, erected entirely of wood.

300 A MANUAL OF CARPENTRY AND JOINERY.

With stands of a temporary character, the construction is usually effected out of the common marketable sections (stock

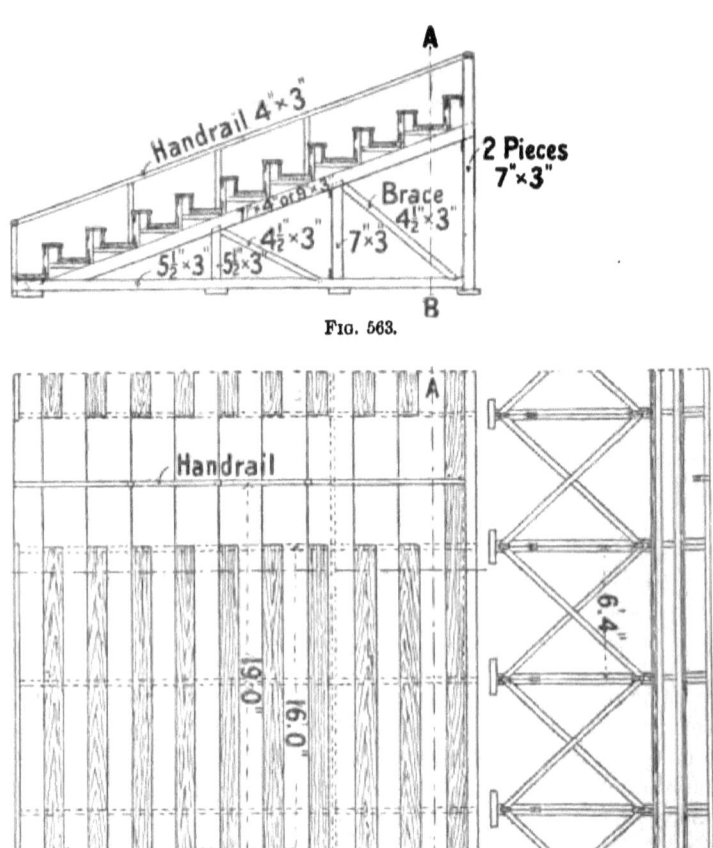

FIG. 563.

FIG. 564.

FIG. 565.—Section through AB.

Plan and Sections of a Spectators' Stand.

sizes) of planks and deals, the joints being made as simple as possible, with an extensive use of the cleat and iron dog as a means of fastening the various parts together. With the more permanent structures, accurate calculations may with advantage be employed to obtain the requisite sizes of the timbers, and the whole is framed together more rigidly.

Spectators' stands, when crowded with people who are likely to become excited, tend to swing, and therefore special care should be devoted to the bracing together of such structures to obtain rigidity. Especially when the stands are much elevated, the vertical supports should be strong and should be well braced in a diagonal direction, so that there is no possibility of giving way. The posts should also be placed upon large base stones or upon concrete blocks so that the lower ends are clear of the

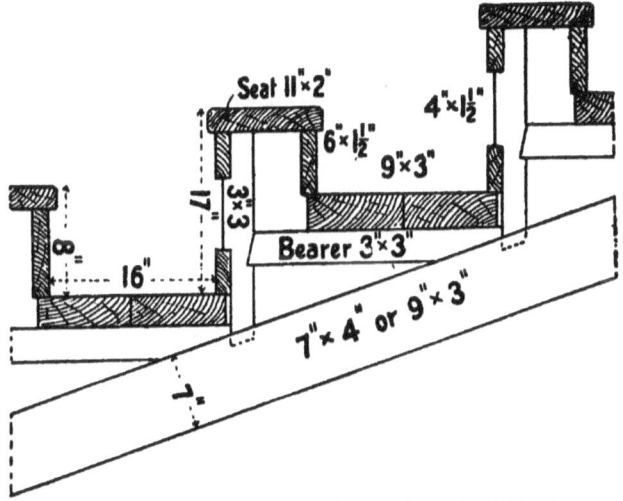

FIG. 566.—Detailed Section of Seats of Spectators' Stand.

damp ground. For temporary stands, rough sleepers of wood, or concrete piers may be laid for the timbers to rest upon. When the stand is of large area it is necessary to consider especially the means of egress in case of panic. To attain this object it is well to divide up the stand, by handrails, into lengths of from 15 to 20 feet, and also to divide into two—by a handrail up the middle—each passage which gives access to the upper part of the stand.

The accommodation of a stand depends upon whether the occupants require seating accommodation, or standing room only. This consideration also influences the general arrangement of the timbers. If seats are to be provided, the space required for each person is from 18 to 20 inches.

Figs. 563 to 565 show plan and two sections of a temporary stand constructed out of deals and quartering, with the main dimensions given. It consists of ten tiers in depth, each tier rising 8 inches above the one below it. The length of such a stand and also the number of tiers composing it will necessarily depend upon the accommodation required or upon the amount

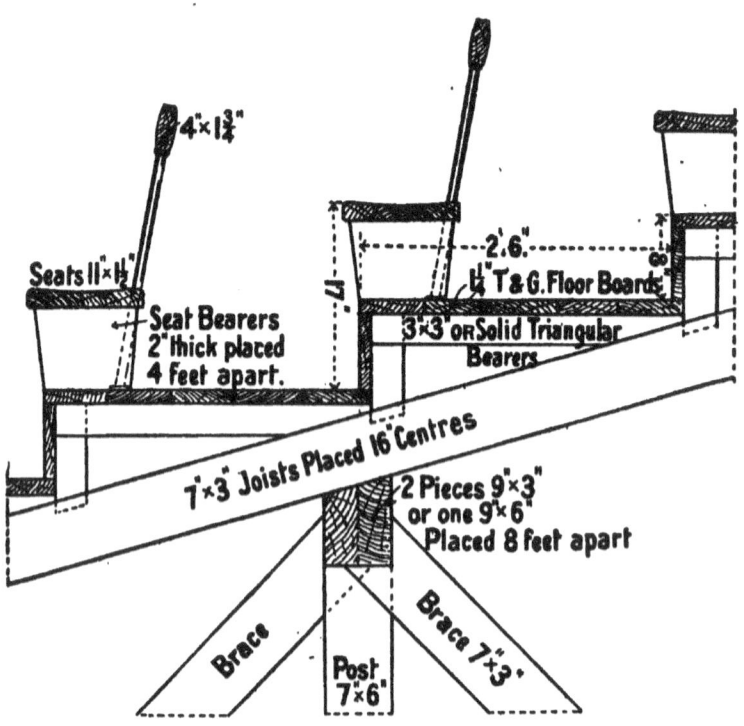

FIG. 567.—Detailed Section of Seats of Spectators' Stand.

of available space. In this example the length is divided into 19 feet distances, the approaches to the different sections are arranged in pairs, with a stout handrail between them, and a handrail is arranged midway between the lengths of the seats. Allowing for the thickness of this handrail, each section has ten seats, each 15 feet 10 inches long, which, allowing 19 inches for each person, provides accommodation for 100 spectators. Fig. 566 shows an enlarged dimensioned section through two tiers of this stand.

'SPECTATORS' STANDS. 303

An alternative method of construction, often adopted in permanent stands, is shown in section in Fig. 567. It consists of joists inclined to give the necessary difference in height of successive tiers (usually from 6" to 9"), and placed at from 15" to 18" apart. These joists are supported either upon heavy cross-beams and posts, or upon steel girders and cast-iron columns. The horizontal surfaces are obtained by lining up the upper edge of the joists with 3" by 3" quartering, upon which rest floor boards from 1" to $1\frac{1}{2}$" thick. The risers between one tier and the next are also boarded.

The seats on such a stand are placed at the front edge of each tier; they may be made more comfortable by fixing a back rest behind each row of seats. It will be seen that, whereas each tier is not more than 9 inches high, the seat will require to be 17 inches high; this arrangement will allow the feet of those on one seat to rest on the floor without interfering with the comfort of those seated in front of them.

Summary.

Scaffold boards are supported by *trestles*, or by a framework of *poles* fastened together by *cords* and *wedges*.

A **masons' scaffold** is so framed as to be independent of any support from the building itself, while one end of each *putlog* of the bricklayers' scaffold usually rests upon the wall being built.

A **gantry** is an elevated platform so built as to allow traffic to proceed beneath it. The heavy timber framing used to carry overhead travelling cranes is also called a gantry.

Derrick towers are framed timber structures carrying a platform used to support an elevated jib crane.

The sides of **excavations** for sewers, drains, and for deep foundations of buildings are temporarily supported (shored) by *struts*, *poling boards*, *waling pieces*, etc.

Piles are heavy, pointed beams driven into the ground either to form the main supports of the partitions used as water **coffer-dams**, or for foundations in soft earth.

Shoring is the arrangement of temporary wooden supports (shores) for parts of a building liable to give way during structural alterations. Shores may be arranged as *raking shores*, *flying shores*, or *dead shores*.

Wooden centres are frames upon which brick arches are supported during construction.

Spectators' stands may be temporary or permanent; they should be well braced together. For temporary stands the stock sizes of timber are used with simple connecting joints. Permanent stands are of more elaborate construction.

Questions on Chapter XI.

1. Make sketches of two types of scaffold trestle, and also of about six rungs at the lower end of a ladder. Dimension the sizes of the different parts of the ladder, and state the best materials for its construction.

2. Draw, to a scale of $\frac{1}{4}$ in. to one foot, the elevation and a vertical cross section of the bricklayers' scaffold required in the erection of a wall 24 feet long and 24 feet high. Name the various parts.

3. Draw a cross section of a gantry required for a stone building, which is to be built close against a public foot-path 10 ft. above pavement, and to have protecting rail; also draw elevation from roadway, showing rather more than one complete bay, the uprights being 10 ft. apart. Scale $\frac{1}{2}$ in. (C. and G. Hon., 1904.)

4. Make a sketch of a gantry to support a "traveller." Dimension the scantlings used. (C. and G. Hon., 1900.)

5. Draw, to a scale of $\frac{1}{2}$ in. to one foot, a plan and a vertical cross section of a sewer trench in bad ground, 10 ft. deep, and show all the timbering required to keep the sides intact. Name and dimension all the parts.

6. One of the banks of a river, the average depth of which is 3 ft., having shown signs of giving way for a length of about 30 ft., it is necessary to divert the course of the water to enable the bank to be repaired. Make sketches showing the timbering required for the purpose.

7. Draw a raking shore against a dwelling-house four storeys high. Figure the scantlings of the different timbers and give their names, and describe how such a shore is fixed in position. (C. and G. Ord., 1903.)

8. Make a sketch of the upper end of a raking shore abutting against a brick wall. Name and dimension the different parts.

9. Two houses of 18 ft. frontage each in a terrace have been pulled down, and shoring is required for supporting the adjoining houses on each side. Sketch to scale $\frac{1}{8}$ in. to a foot the shoring you would construct, and give details of the joints. (C. and G. Hon., 1897.)

QUESTIONS ON CHAPTER XI. 305

10. Two buildings are each three storeys high and 15 ft. 6 in. apart. Make a drawing showing how these buildings would be shored with flying shores. (C. and G. Ord., 1902.)

11. Describe and show in detail the mode of taking out the front wall of a ground storey to insert a shop front, with needful shoring. (C. and G. Hon., 1898.)

12. A centre is required for a segmental arch of 30 ft. span and 10 ft. rise. Make rather more than half elevation, and show how you would provide for striking such a centre. (C. and G. Ord., 1903.)

13. Make a drawing of a centre to carry a semicircular brick arch of 38 ft. span. (C. and G. Ord., 1902.)

14. A centre is required for an elliptical arch of stonework, having 25 ft. span and 10 ft. rise. Draw to a scale of $\frac{1}{4}$ in. to the foot such centering, and mark thereon scantlings of the timbers. (C. and G. Hon., 1898.)

15. (a) Draw a centre for a masonry elliptical arch, 20 ft. span, to be carried by the piers that will support the arch. Show how the centre is to be eased and struck.

[*Or*],

Sketch and describe, in writing, a gantry, 35 ft. high, to carry a steam crane for use on a large building. (C. and G. Hon., 1901.)

16. Make an elevation and section of the centre required for a pointed arch with a span of 16 ft., and with apex 15 ft. above springing, which is 12 ft. above the ground. The arch to be of stone, with flat soffit 18 in. wide. (C. and G. Hon., 1904.)

17. Draw to a scale of $\frac{1}{2}$ inch to a foot the centering for two semicircular brick arches intersecting at right angles to each other, the widths of arches 10 ft. and the rise 5 ft. Show the method of cutting the boarding accurately at the groins. (C. and G. Hon., 1895.)

18. A staging is required for persons to sit and view a procession, the front of the staging to abut on the street, the depth of the ground is 20 ft., the frontage is 22 ft., no support to the staging can be obtained at either end. Make plan and sections in pencil to a scale of $\frac{1}{2}$ in. to the foot. (C. and G. Hon., 1899.)

CHAPTER XII.

MECHANICS OF CARPENTRY.

It is well known that some members of a framed structure must be made stronger than others. The reason is that the weights or other forces acting on a truss differ from each other in magnitude and direction. It is obviously necessary, therefore, to be able to estimate the various forces acting, so that the members may be made of the required strength without undue waste of material. The general principles underlying the measurement of forces may with advantage now be considered briefly.

The Nature of Force.—Force may be defined as that which moves, or tends to move, a body at rest, or which changes, or tends to change, the direction or rate of motion of a body already moving. A familiar example of force is met with in gravitation, whereby an object has a tendency to fall to the ground. In order to support it, an upward force equal to the weight of the object must be exerted. The phrase "equal force" implies that forces can be measured. In this country they are usually measured in terms of weights in lbs., cwts., etc. Any one who has seen a pulley, or lever, at work knows that the direction of application of a force can be changed. Evidently, then, forces can be represented *graphically*. Lines drawn to scale are employed, and these can be arranged to exhibit at the same time both the magnitude and the direction of the forces. Thus, a weight of 10 lbs. acting vertically downwards can be represented by a vertical straight line 10 units in length. If the unit of length be $\frac{1}{8}''$, the line will measure ten times $\frac{1}{8}'' = 1\frac{1}{4}''$; whereas, if the unit of force be represented by a length of 1", the graphic representation of the force will be a vertical straight line 10" long.

Resultant of two or more Forces.—(1) When two or more forces together act at a point in the *same* direction and in the same straight line, the **resultant** force is equal to the sum of the **components**.

EXAMPLE.—(a) If two 10 lb. weights attached to a cord are hung upon the same nail, the resultant weight acting upon the nail is 10+10=20 lbs.

(2) If two equal forces together act at the same point in *opposite* directions, but in the same straight line, they neutralise each other, and the forces are said to be in **equilibrium**.

EXAMPLE.—A spring balance carries a weight of 6 lbs. The index finger of the balance shows that the spring exerts an upward force equal to the downward force —the weight ; and a state of equilibrium is obtained.

If the two unequal forces together act at the same point in opposite directions, but in the same straight line, the resultant force is equal to the difference between the forces, and is in the direction of the greater.

It is evident, then, that the directions of the forces, and therefore the angles they make with one another, must be considered in determining the forces acting at any given point.

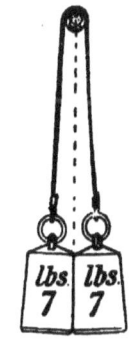

FIG. 568.—Two forces acting in the same direction.

If a flexible string be attached to a weight, and then passed over a frictionless pulley, there will be the same tension in every part of the string, irrespective of any change of direction caused by using the pulley.

To illustrate these facts clearly, suppose that two 7 lb. weights, connected by a cord, hang over a smooth peg as shown in Fig. 568. The total weight on the peg, neglecting the weight of the cord (which may thus be any length), is 14 lbs., the sum of the two weights.

Again, suppose three such pegs in a horizontal straight line, and the cord and weights to be passed over them as shown in Fig. 569. Evidently the weight on the central peg is nothing.

Now, suppose the outside pegs to be lowered slightly, as shown by dotted lines in the figure; the central peg will now carry a small proportion of the weight, and the more the outside pegs are lowered, the more weight will be thrown on the central peg, until, as shown in Fig. 568, it carries all the weight, *i.e.* 14 lbs. Therefore the weight upon the central peg varies according to the direction of the forces acting on it—from nothing in Fig. 569 to 14 lbs. in Fig. 568.

The magnitude and direction of the resultant force acting upon the central peg, and upon each of the outside pegs, can be determined by the parallelogram of forces.

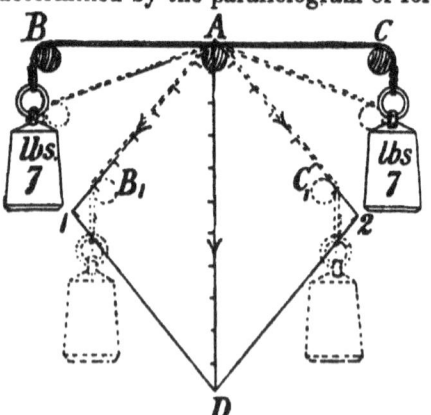
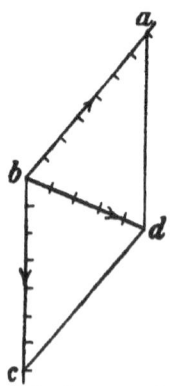

FIG. 569.—Arrangement of Weights with Cords passing over Pegs to illustrate the Parallelogram of Forces.

FIG. 570.—Diagram showing the Forces acting on the Peg B_1, Fig. 569.

The Parallelogram of Forces.—If two forces acting at a point be represented in magnitude and direction by the adjacent sides of a parallelogram, the resultant of these two forces will be represented in magnitude and direction by that diagonal of the parallelogram which passes through the point.

EXAMPLE 1.—*The angle at A, when the cord passes over the pegs B_1, A, C_1, shown by the dotted lines in Fig. 569, is given. Determine by the parallelogram of forces the stress on the peg A*, i.e. *the single force acting through the point A, which shall be equal in effect to the forces AB_1, AC_1 acting together.*

Produce AB_1 and AC_1, and mark off on each line 7 units, measuring from A. Then $A1$ and $A2$ represent in magnitude and direction the forces caused by the loads. Complete the parallelogram by drawing $1D$ parallel to $A2$, and $2D$ parallel to

MECHANICS OF CARPENTRY.

$A1$. The length of the diagonal AD, measured in the same units as the lines $A1$ and $A2$, represents the magnitude of the resultant force—*i.e.* the stress on the peg A. The direction of the force will obviously be downwards. A force represented in magnitude and direction by DA would evidently counterbalance the force AD, and would therefore counterbalance $A1$ and $A2$ acting together. **Forces which balance each other are said to be in equilibrium.**

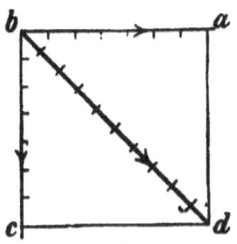

FIG. 571.—Diagram showing the Forces acting on the Peg B, Fig. 569.

EXAMPLE 2.—*Determine the magnitude and direction of the single force which will replace the two forces exerted by the cord and weight on the peg B_1 (Fig. 569).*

Draw ab 7 units long (Fig. 570) and parallel to the cord $A1$ in Fig. 569. From b draw bc also 7 units long and parallel to the cord below the peg B_1. Complete the parallelogram by drawing dc and ad parallel to ab and bc respectively. Then the diagonal bd gives the magnitude of the required force, the direction of which is from b to d.

EXAMPLE 3.—*Fig. 571 shows the application of the parallelogram of forces to determine the resultant force on the peg B.*

In the above examples no allowance has been made for the weight of the cord or for the friction on the pegs. It is assumed in each case that the forces are acting at the point of intersection of the straight lines produced.

EXAMPLE 4.—*Two forces of 10 and 6 lbs. respectively act from a point and in directions which are at right angles to each other. Determine the magnitude and direction of the single force which can replace the two forces.*

Let the line AB (Fig. 572) represent in magnitude a force of 10 lbs. acting at the point A in the direction indicated by the arrow, and AC a force of 6 lbs. acting at right angles to AB. Complete the parallelogram $ACDB$. Then the length of the diagonal AD represents the magnitude of the resultant force, and the direction in which it acts will be from the point A, as shown by the arrow.

It must be understood clearly that a resultant is a force which can take the place of, and will produce the same effect

310   A MANUAL OF CARPENTRY AND JOINERY.

as, two or more forces. To maintain equilibrium, the resultant force must be counterbalanced by an equal force acting in the opposite direction. The force so acting is called the **equilibrant**.

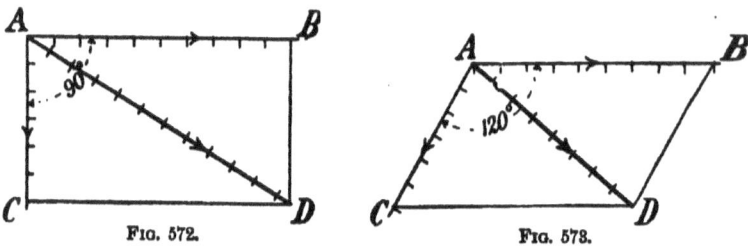

FIG. 572.   FIG. 573.

EXAMPLE 5.—*Figs. 573 and 574 show the magnitude and direction of the resultant force when forces of 9 and 6 lbs. respectively act at angles of (a) 120°, (b) 45°.*

The simple apparatus shown in Fig. 575 clearly illustrates the principle of the parallelogram of forces. On a vertical board

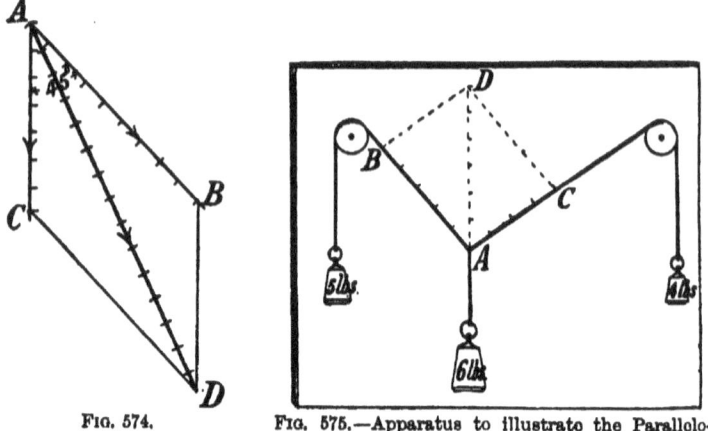

FIG. 574.   FIG. 575.—Apparatus to illustrate the Parallelogram of Forces.

are fixed two small pulleys by means of screws, so that they revolve with as little friction as possible. By making a three-way string, passing it over the two pulleys, and adding varying weights to each of the three ends of the string, it can be demonstrated clearly how the three forces act. In Fig. 575 the weights are respectively 5, 6, and 4 lbs. By drawing the parallelogram $ABDC$, such that AB equals 5 units in length, and AC equals 4 units, the diagonal DA is found to measure

MECHANICS OF CARPENTRY

6 units, and to represent the magnitude of the middle weight. If other weights are attached to the ends of the strings, different results will, of course, be obtained.

Triangle of Forces.—The triangle of forces is used to determine the magnitude and direction of any three forces which balance each other. The rule may be stated as follows : **If three forces acting at a point are in equilibrium they can be represented in magnitude and direction by the three sides of a triangle taken in order.**

EXAMPLE 1.—*The forces acting upon A (Fig. 575) are in equilibrium.*

Since the length of the line $AB = 5$ units, and the line BD is parallel and equal in length to $AC = 4$ units, and the diagonal DA is in a line with the direction of the middle vertical weight and equal in length to 6 units ; then the sides AB, BD, and DA of the triangle ABD represent both in magnitude and direction the forces acting at the point A.

To save confusion it is usual, however, to draw a separate triangle to illustrate these forces. A somewhat different system of lettering also simplifies the consideration of the examples. This is known as **Bow's notation**. In it the two letters denoting a force are placed one on each side of the line representing the force, that is, in the spaces between such lines. Thus in Fig. 576 the three forces acting at the point o are referred to as AB, BC, CA respectively.

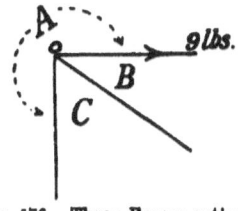
FIG. 576.—Three Forces acting at a Point.

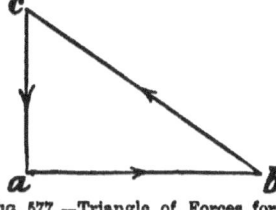
FIG. 577.—Triangle of Forces for Fig. 576.

EXAMPLE 2.—*Given the magnitude (9 lbs.) and the direction (indicated by the arrow) of AB, and the angles which the directions of the three forces make with each other, it is required to find the magnitude and direction of BC and CA when the forces are in equilibrium.*

Draw the line ab (Fig. 577) parallel to the direction of action of the force AB, 9 units long, and in the direction shown by the arrow. From b draw bc parallel to BC until it meets ac drawn parallel to CA. Then the triangle abc is the triangle of forces, and the direction of the forces BC and CA can be found by taking the sides of the triangle *in order*, viz. a to b, b to c, c to a; and these directions give also the directions of action of the forces represented by the lines parallel to ab, bc, and ca respectively. Thus AB acts *from* the joint o; BC acts *towards* o; and CA acts *from* o.

The following examples show the application of these principles to simple practical questions.

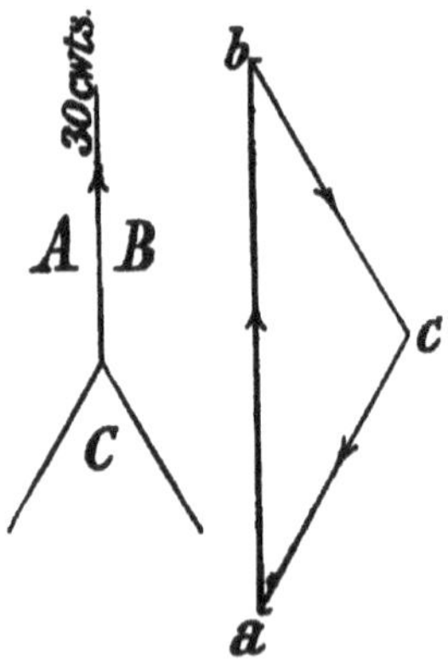

EXAMPLE 3.—*A rope bears a tensile stress (pull) of* 30 *cwts. Find the magnitude of the stress in each of two other ropes which make an angle of* 60° *with each other, and together balance the stress in the first rope, supposing the second and third ropes are equally stressed.*

Fig. 578 shows the application of the triangle of forces to the solution of this question, the answer giving the stress in each rope as 17·32 cwts.

FIG. 578.

By going round the sides of the triangle in order, it will be seen that the force in each of the three ropes acts *from* the joint.

EXAMPLE 4.—*A buckling-chain is used to raise heavy blocks of stone. What is the amount of stress in the links of the chain when raising a weight of one ton, if the buckling-chain is:*

(a) *pulled tightly as in Fig.* 579;

(b) *placed loosely round the stone as in Fig.* 580.

The correct solution of this question

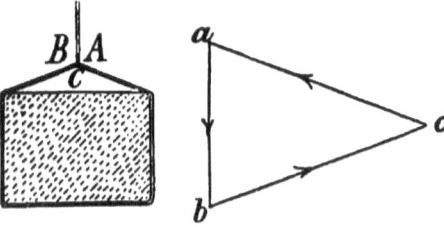

FIG. 579.—Stresses in a Buckling-chain when pulled tight.

depends on (1) the weight of the stone; (2) the angle between the forces AC and BC.

MECHANICS OF CARPENTRY.

The application of the triangle of forces in each case (Figs. 579 and 580) shows that the stresses AC and BC are more than twice as great when the chain is fixed as in Fig. 579 as they are with the arrangement in Fig. 580; or, the tighter the chain—*i.e.* the greater the angle between the forces BC and CA—the greater is the stress on the links.

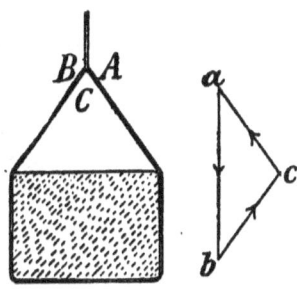

Fig. 580.—Stresses in a Buckling-chain when placed loosely round a load.

EXAMPLE 5.—*A triangular bracket fixed against a wall, as shown in Fig. 581, has a weight of 5 cwts. suspended from the outer end o. What is the nature and amount of stress in each of the members oA and oB?*

Fig. 582 is the triangle of forces used to determine these stresses, and is drawn as follows : $1_1 2_1$ is drawn parallel to and

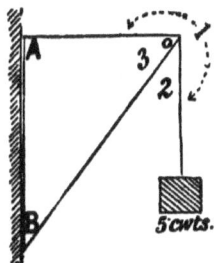

FIG. 581.—Line Diagram of Triangular Wall-bracket.

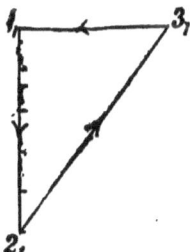

FIG. 582.—Stress Diagram for Fig. 581.

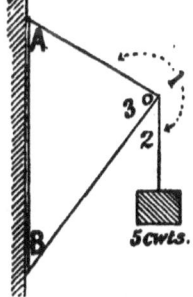

FIG. 583.

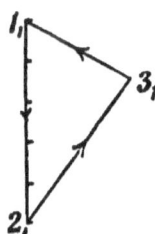

FIG. 584.

Another form of Wall-bracket with Stress Diagram.

represents the downward force (the weight of 5 cwts.) to scale. From 2_1 draw $2_1 3_1$ parallel to 2 3 in Fig. 581 until it meets $1_1 3_1$ drawn parallel to 1 3. Then the triangle $1_1 2_1 3_1$ represents the magnitude of the forces.

By going round the triangle in order as shown by the arrows, we find that 2 3 acts towards the joint o and is therefore a compression stress or *thrust*, and 3 1 acts from the joint and is therefore a tension stress or *pull*.

Fig. 583 shows a somewhat modified design of triangular wall-bracket, and Fig. 584 is the triangle of forces by which the stresses in the various members are ascertained.

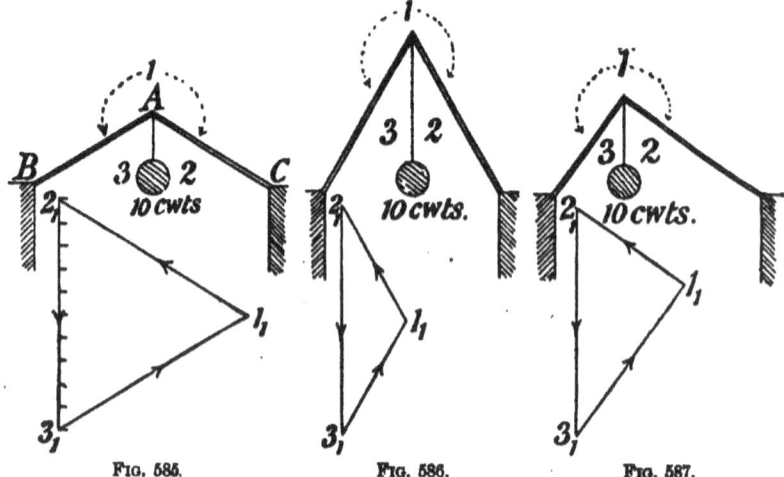

FIG. 585.   FIG. 586.   FIG. 587.

Examples typifying Simple Roof Trusses.

EXAMPLE 6.— *What is the nature and amount of stress in each of the members AB and AC (Fig. 585) caused by the weight of 10 cwts. acting as shown?*

This example may be taken as typifying a simple kind of roof-truss with the weight taking the place of the ridge piece. Re-letter or figure the diagram according to Bow's notation. Draw the vertical line $2_1 3_1$, equal in magnitude and direction to the weight 2 3. Complete the triangle by drawing lines parallel to the members AC and AB, from the points 2_1 and 3_1 respectively. These lines represent the amount of stress along the members AC and AB. On taking the sides of the triangle

MECHANICS OF CARPENTRY.

in order as shown by the arrows, it is seen that $2_1 3_1$ act downwards; $3_1 1_1$ acts towards the joint A, as does also $1_1 2_1$; therefore each member is subject to a compression stress (thrust).

Fig. 586 shows another example of this kind with a much smaller angle between the forces.

Fig. 587 illustrates a still further example, where the two sides are of unequal inclination.

Polygon of Forces.—The method of obtaining the resultant of any two forces acting at a point can be extended to three, four, or any number of forces.

EXAMPLE.—*OA, OB, OC, OD, OE, (Fig. 588) represent the magnitude and direction of five forces acting at the point O. Determine the magnitude and direction of the resultant force.*

This problem can be solved either by an application of the parallelogram of forces or by a direct construction.

(1) Determine by the parallelogram of forces, the resultant $O1$ of forces OA and OB (Fig. 589). Similarly, determine the resultant $O2$ of the forces $O1$ and OC. Again, $O3$ is the resultant of the forces $O2$ and OD; and finally $O4$ is the resultant of $O3$ and OE. Therefore, $O4$ is the resultant of *all* the original forces; or, in other words, a single force equal in magnitude and direction to the force $O4$ will have the same effect at the point O as the five forces have when acting together. Since a force $4O$ will balance $O4$, a force represented in magnitude and direction by the line $4O$ will, together with the five given forces, produce equilibrium at the point O.

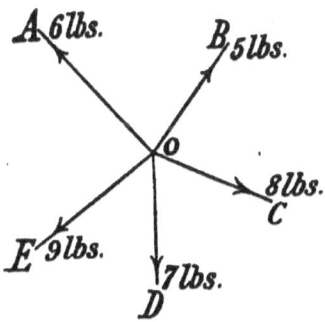

FIG. 588.—Five Forces acting at a Point.

(2) The same result may be obtained more simply as follows: Re-letter the forces as shown in italics (Fig. 589), and then, as in Fig. 590, draw a straight line $a'b'$ equal in magnitude and parallel to ab (Fig. 589). From b' draw $b'c'$ equal and parallel to bc; continue the process, taking the forces in order. It will be found by drawing the closing line of the polygon, that is, by joining x' to a', that $x'a'$ gives the magnitude and the direction

of the force required to produce equilibrium. Conversely, $a'x'$ is the *resultant* of all the original forces. By drawing the line $4O$ through the point O (Fig. 589) and indexing it to scale, the

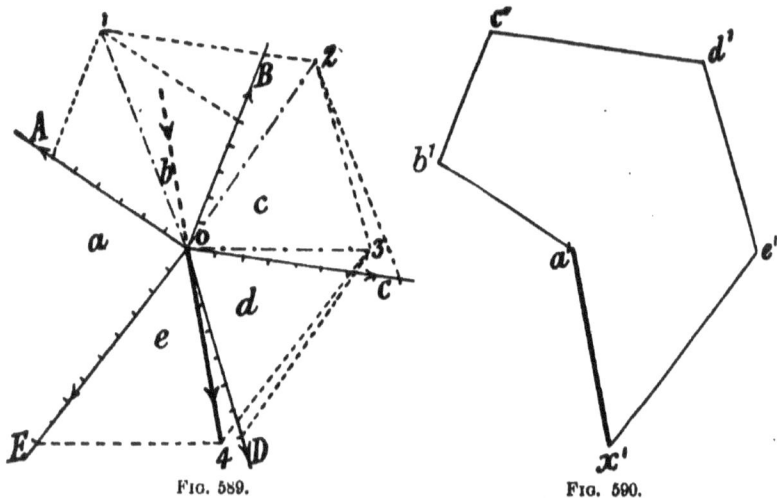

Fig. 589.   Fig. 590.

Alternate Stress Diagrams for Fig. 588.

required resultant—which corresponds with the one determined by the parallelogram of forces—is obtained. Its direction is indicated by the arrow.

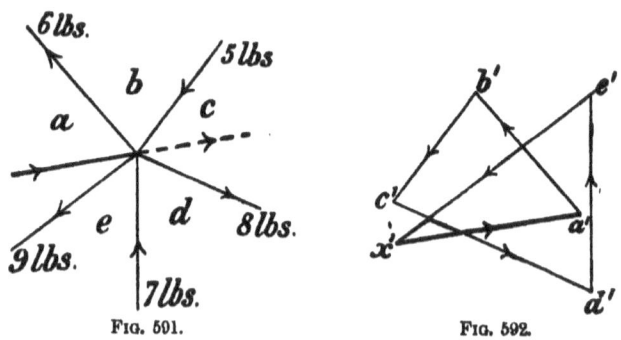

Fig. 591.   Fig. 592.

Examples showing the application of the Polygon of Forces.

Fig. 592 is the polygon of forces when two of the forces, bc and de, act towards the joint (Fig. 591), the magnitude of all the forces being as in the previous example. In this case the

MECHANICS OF CARPENTRY. 317

equilibrant is determined, and is shown by the thick line in Figs. 591 and 592.

Figs. 588 to 592 should be compared carefully.

The **polygon of forces** may be stated as follows: If two or more forces act at a point, then, if starting at any point a line be drawn to represent the magnitude and direction of the first force, and from the point thus obtained another line be drawn similarly to represent the second force, and so on until lines have been drawn representing each force,—the resultant of all these forces will be represented by a straight line drawn from the starting point to the point finally reached.

Polygons, parallelograms, or triangles, of forces, when used to determine either the resultant or the equilibrant of stresses acting at a point, are called **reciprocal diagrams**.

Inclined Forces in one Plane but not acting through one Point.—The foregoing examples deal only with forces which act at a single given point, and in these cases the resultant acts at the same point. When all the forces do not act at the same point, the magnitude and direction of the resultant is obtained as in previous examples, *i.e.* by drawing the reciprocal diagram; the line of action, however, still remains to be determined. To determine this line of action, it is necessary to draw what is known as the **funicular** or **link polygon**. The method is as follows:

EXAMPLE.—*Let X, Y, Z (Fig. 593) be three forces in the same plane and of the magnitude and direction shown. It is required to find the magnitude and the line of action of the resultant force.*

Re-letter the forces $abcd$ according to Bow's notation (p. 311), and draw the reciprocal diagram $a'b'c'd'$; the line $a'd'$ which closes the figure represents the magnitude of the resultant. To obtain the actual line of action of the resultant, take any point or pole O and join $a'O$, $b'O$, $c'O$, $d'O$. The figure thus obtained is called the **polar diagram**. The funicular polygon is now constructed by drawing—anywhere in the space b—a line 1 2 parallel to $b'O$ and intersecting the forces X and Y at 1 and 2 respectively. From 2 draw 2 3 parallel to $c'O$, intersecting the force Z in 3. Through 1 draw 1 4 parallel to $a'O$, and through 3 draw 3 4 parallel to $d'O$. Through the point of intersection 4, draw a line R parallel to $a'd'$. R is the required line of action of the resultant of the three given forces, and its magnitude is represented by the length of $a'd'$.

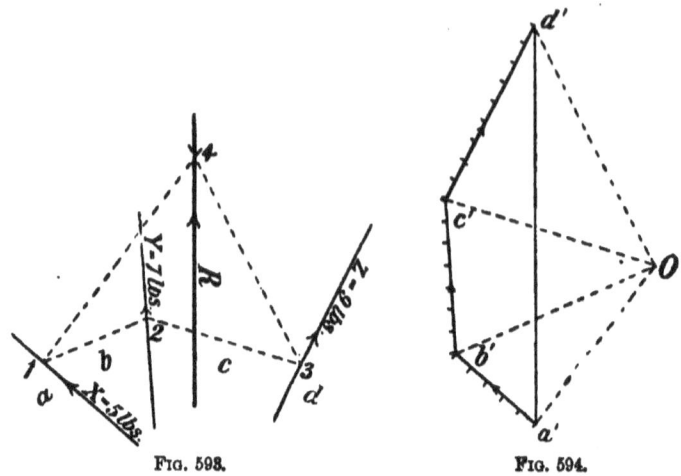

Fig. 593.   Fig. 594.

Method of determining the Resultant of three Forces which do not act at the same Point.

Parallel Forces.—In addition to forces acting in the ways already explained, it is necessary to consider a few examples of **parallel** forces. (These must not be mistaken for those dealt with by the parallelogram of forces, as they are entirely different.)

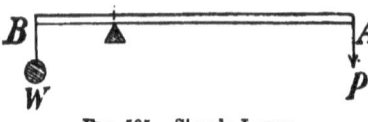

Fig. 595.—Simple Lever.

In all the examples of parallel forces now to be considered, the forces will act vertically. As these can be shown easily both graphically and arithmetically, each example will be worked out by both methods.

The simplest examples of the equilibrium of parallel forces are found in the use of **levers**. The lever shown in Fig. 595 is a straight bar resting on a triangular block, F, called a **fulcrum**. At the ends A and B of the lever, forces P and W respectively act vertically downwards. It is plain that forces P and W will tend to rotate the lever in opposite directions around the fixed point F. The tendency of either force to rotate the lever is called the **moment** of that force; it is measured by the product of the force into the perpendicular distance (called the **arm** of the force) of the fixed point from the line of action of the force. **When the two moments are equal the lever is in equilibrium.** The conditions of equilibrium therefore are:

$$P \times AF = W \times BF.$$

If AF be 6″, BF be 2″, and $W=9$ lbs, then P will require to be $\frac{9 \times 2}{6} = 3$ lbs.: the moment of each force being 18 inch-lbs.

Since moments are always expressed in terms of the product of a force and a length, both these factors enter into every statement of the magnitude of a moment. If the distances be expressed in feet, and the forces in cwts., the moments will, of course, be expressed in ft.-cwts., and so on.

EXAMPLE 1.—*A horizontal bar 3 ft. long has a weight of 2 lbs. at one end, and of 4 lbs. at the other end (Fig. 596). Find the point at which the bar must be supported so that it will rest horizontally. (Neglect the weight of the bar.)*

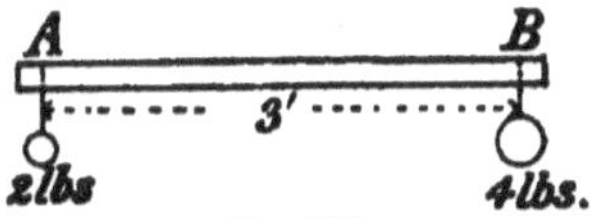

FIG. 596.

Arithmetically.—Since the lever is in equilibrium, the total downward force of 6 lbs. is balanced by an upward force (reaction) of 6 lbs. at the unknown point of support, and the moment of the upward reaction, about any point, is equal to the sum of the moments of the downward forces about the same point. Consider moments about A:

Moment of weight at A, about $A, = 2 \times 0$.
    ,,   ,,   ,,   ,, B ,, $A, = 4 \times AB$.
    ,, reaction about $A = (2+4) \times AX$.
$$\therefore \ 6 \times AX = (2 \times 0) + (4 \times AB);$$
$$\therefore \ 6AX = 0 + (4 \times 3);$$
$$\therefore \ AX = \tfrac{12}{6} = 2 \text{ feet}.$$

Graphically.—In the consideration of these forces graphically, the polygon of forces becomes a straight line. A polar diagram and a funicular polygon are required.

Fig. 597 shows the bar with the weights suspended. Letter the forces AB and BC. The polar diagram is drawn as follows: Draw to a suitable scale, a vertical line ac, 6 units long—equal to the sum of the weights. From any point O which may be at any convenient distance from ac, draw Oa, Ob, and Oc. To construct the funicular polygon, draw, in the space B, *1 2*

320   A MANUAL OF CARPENTRY AND JOINERY.

parallel to *bo*. From *1* draw *1 3* parallel to *aO*, and from *2* draw *2 3* parallel to *Oc*, and produce it to intersect *1 3* in *3*. Then the vertical line drawn through the point *3* will give the position of the fulcrum. If the distances from this point to the points of application of the weights be measured, it will be found that

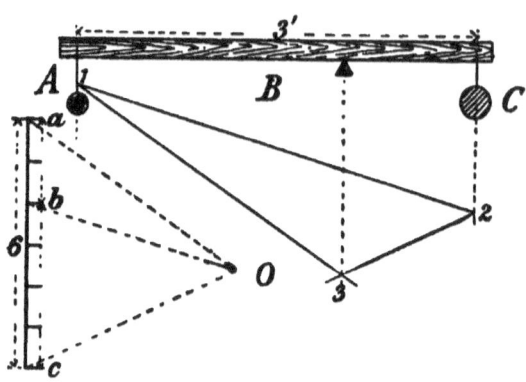

FIG. 597.—Loaded Beam, with Stress Diagrams.

they are in inverse proportion to the magnitudes of the weights, and that the weight on the right hand side of the fulcrum, multiplied by its arm of leverage, will be equal to the weight on the left hand side, multiplied by the arm of leverage on that side—the arms being one and two feet respectively.

EXAMPLE 2.—*Four weights of 2, 3, 6, and 4 lbs. respectively hang on a bar as shown in Fig.* 598. *Determine the point at which the bar must be supported to rest horizontally, the weight of the bar being neglected.*

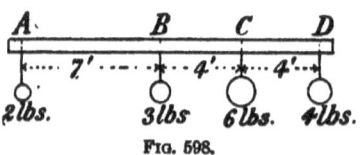

FIG. 598.

Arithmetically.—Let the required point of support be denoted by the letter X. When the bar is in equilibrium, the sum of the moments about A of the downward forces, must be equal to the moment, about A, of the upward reaction at the point of support.

∴ the downward moments about A

$= (2 \times 0) + (3 \times 7) + (6 \times 11) + (4 \times 15)$

$= \quad 0 \quad + \quad 21 \quad + \quad 66 \quad + \quad 60 \quad = 147.$

The moment about A of the upward reaction
= Sum of all the weights × AX
= $(2+3+6+4) \times AX = 15AX$;
∴ $15AX = 147$;
∴ $AX = \frac{147}{15} = 9\frac{4}{5}$ feet.

Graphically.—Draw the vertical line of loads ea, representing to scale the sum of the weights as shown (Fig. 599). Construct the polar diagram by drawing from any point O the lines eO, dO, cO, bO, and aO. To draw the funicular polygon, draw vertical lines under each weight, and—starting anywhere in

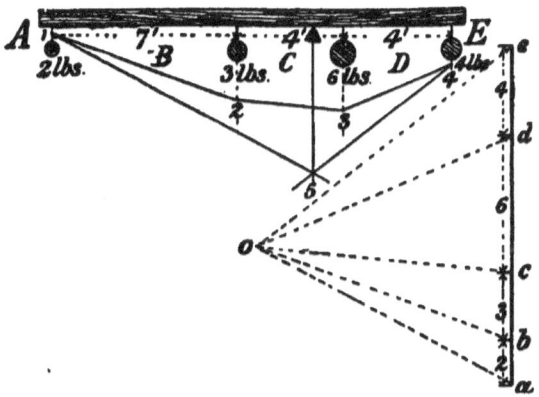

Fig. 599.—Loaded Beam with Stress Diagrams.

the line of the first weight as at 1—draw in the space B a line 1 2 parallel to Ob; in the space C draw 2 3 parallel to Oc; in the space D draw 3 4 parallel to Od. Through 4 draw 4 5 parallel to eO and through 1 draw 1 5 parallel to Oa. The vertical line drawn through the point 5, where these two lines meet, gives the position of the point of support.

Although the application of the lever as a tool or machine is an everyday occurrence with the workman in such appliances as the turning bar of the bench-vice and sash-cramp, the screw-driver, brace, pincers, claw-hammer, grindstone, treadle lathe, mortising-machine, etc., the detailed consideration of each of these cannot be entered into for want of space. The following examples involving the use of the crowbar will suffice further to illustrate the principles involved.

EXAMPLE 1.—*What force must be exerted at one end of a crowbar 6 ft. long, to raise a weight of 10 cwts. at the other end: the bar resting on a fulcrum 9" from the weight. (Neglect the weight of the crowbar.)*

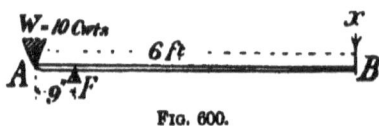

FIG. 600.

Let AB (Fig. 600) be the bar 6 ft. long, and F the fulcrum at 9" from A. Consider moments in inch-lbs. about F. Let x be the required force.

Moment of 10 cwts. about $F = 9 \times 10 \times 112$ inch-lbs.
Moment of x about $F = BF \times x = (72 - 9) \times x = 63 \times x$ inch-lbs.

$$\therefore x = \frac{9 \times 10 \times 112}{63} = 160 \text{ lbs.}$$

EXAMPLE 2.—*A man weighing 140 lbs. is using a crowbar 5 ft. long. What must be the position of the fulcrum to enable him to balance a weight of 1260 lbs. at the other end?*

Let AB be the length of the bar; F the position of the fulcrum; and x the length of the long arm in inches;
then $(60 - x)$ is the length of the short arm in inches.
Taking moments about F,

$$140x = 1260(60 - x) ;$$
$$140x = 75600 - 1260x ;$$
$$140x + 1260x = 75600 ;$$
$$1400x = 75600 ;$$
$$\therefore x = \frac{75600}{1400} = 54 \text{ inches} = 4' 6'' = \text{length of long arm.}$$

EXAMPLE 3.—*A lever 7 ft. long is used as shown in Fig. 601. If a force of 200 lbs. is applied at P in the direction of the arrow, what weight, placed at a point 12" from the fulcrum, can be raised?*

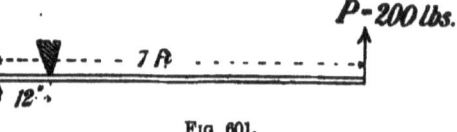

FIG 601.

Taking moments in ft.-lbs. about F,

$$W \times 1 = 200 \times 7 ;$$
$$\therefore W = 1400 \text{ lbs.}$$

Loaded Beams.—The determination of the proportion of the total weight carried by each support of a loaded beam—

MECHANICS OF CARPENTRY.

in other words, the upward reaction of each support which is necessary to maintain equilibrium—affords a good practical example of the theory of parallel forces.

EXAMPLE 1.—*A beam rests upon supports placed 8 feet apart. A weight of 12 lbs. is placed on the beam at a distance of 2 ft. from the right-hand support. What proportion of the weight is carried by each of the supports, the weight of the beam being neglected?*

Arithmetically.—In this case (Fig. 602) the downward force (weight) of 12 lbs. must be balanced by upward forces (re-

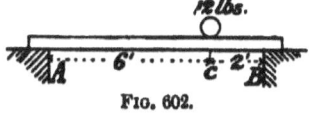

FIG. 602.

actions) at the points of support, respectively equal to the pressure at these points, and together equal to 12 lbs.; and the moments of the upward forces about the point c must be equal.

∴ Reaction at $A \times Ac$ = Reaction at $B \times Bc$,

i.e. Reaction at A : Reaction at B :: Bc : Ac,

or Reaction at A : $\dfrac{\text{Sum of reactions}}{\text{at } A \text{ and } B}$ :: Bc : $(Bc + Ac)$,*

i.e. Reaction at A : 12 lbs. :: Bc : AB.

This may be expressed in general terms as follows:

Pressure on one end that caused by any load : load :: Distance of that load from other end : Length between supports.

therefore   Pressure on A : 12 lbs. :: cB : AB ;

∴ Pressure on $A = \dfrac{12 \times cB}{AB} = \dfrac{12 \times 2}{8} = 3$ lbs.

Similarly, Pressure on $B = \dfrac{12 \times Ac}{AB} = \dfrac{12 \times 6}{8} = 9$ lbs.

Graphically.—Fig. 603 shows the beam and supports with the load in position. The polar diagram is drawn as follows: Draw a vertical line ab, representing the weight (12 lbs.) to a suitable scale. From any point O, which may be at any convenient distance from ab, draw the triangle Oab. Draw as in the figure a vertical line directly under the load, and one under each point of support, as Z, x, y. Letter the load AB, and the space between the supports C. These letters can now be used to

*(Euclid, Book V., Props. 18 and B.)

324 A MANUAL OF CARPENTRY AND JOINERY.

denote the reaction at each point of support—*i.e.* the upward force required to maintain equilibrium—which is equal and opposite to the pressure exerted on each support by the load. Anywhere in x, as from 1, draw, in the space A, a line 1 2, parallel to aO; from 2, in the space B, draw 2 3 parallel to bO. Join 1 3, and through the pole O, draw Oc parallel to 3 1. Then ac (on the vertical line of loads ab) represents to scale the pressure

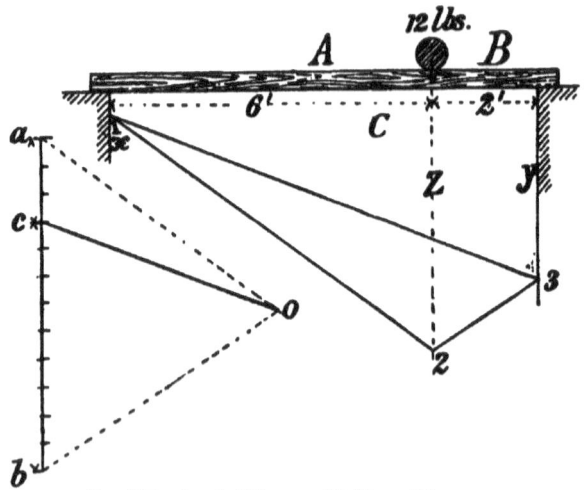

Fig. 603.—Loaded Beam, with Stress Diagrams.

on the left-hand support, and cb to the same scale represents the pressure on the right-hand support.

As the reaction at each end is equal in magnitude and opposite in direction to the pressure, ac gives the amount of the reaction AC, and bc gives the amount of the reaction BC; and the sum of the reactions—both acting upwards—is equal to the total weight (12 lbs).

EXAMPLE 2.—*A beam is loaded as shown in Fig. 604. Determine the reaction at each end, that is, the upward force required at each point of support to maintain equilibrium.*

Arithmetically :

$$\text{Reaction at } A \text{ due to weight at } C : \text{wt. at } C :: CB : AB ;$$

$$\therefore \frac{\text{Reaction at } A \text{ due}}{\text{to weight at } C} = \frac{\text{wt. at } C \times CB}{AB} = \frac{5 \times 13}{16}.$$

MECHANICS OF CARPENTRY.

Similarly,

$$\frac{\text{Reaction at } A \text{ due}}{\text{to weight at } D} = \frac{\text{wt. at } D \times DB}{AB} = \frac{7 \times 9}{16}.$$

Also

$$\frac{\text{Reaction at } A \text{ due}}{\text{to weight at } E} = \frac{\text{wt. at } E \times EB}{AB} = \frac{2 \times 2}{16}.$$

The total reaction at A is equal to the *sum* of the partial reactions as shown above; or it may be obtained directly thus:

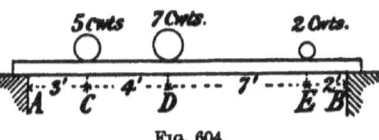

Fig. 604.

Total reaction at A

$$= \frac{(\text{wt. at } C \times CB) + (\text{wt. at } D \times DB) + (\text{wt. at } E \times EB)}{AB}$$

$$= \frac{(5 \times 13) + (7 \times 9) + (2 \times 2)}{16} = \frac{132}{16} = 8\tfrac{1}{4} \text{ cwts.}$$

Similarly,

Total reaction at B

$$= \frac{(\text{wt. at } C \times CA) + (\text{wt. at } D \times DA) + (\text{wt. at } E \times EA)}{AB}$$

$$= \frac{(5 \times 3) + (7 \times 7) + (2 \times 14)}{16} = \frac{92}{16} = 5\tfrac{3}{4} \text{ cwts.}$$

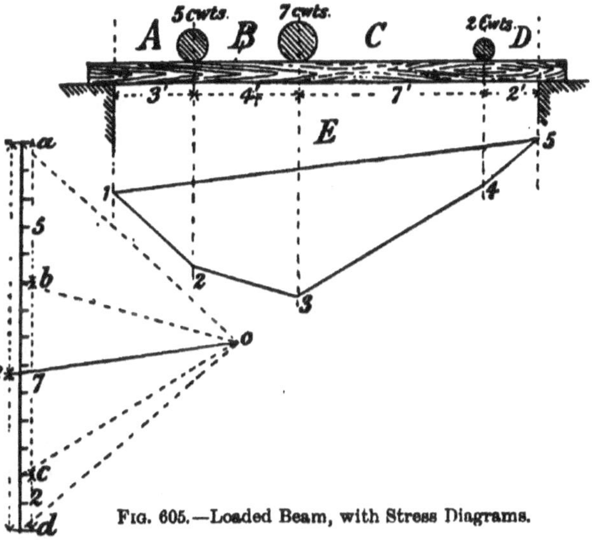

Fig. 605.—Loaded Beam, with Stress Diagrams.

Graphically.—Construct the vertical line of loads, representing to scale the sum of the weights as shown in Fig. 605. Fix the pole O, and draw the dotted lines Oa, Ob, Oc, Od. Letter the loads and draw a dotted vertical line directly under each load and under each support as shown. From any point in the first line, draw in the space A, a line 1 2 parallel to aO; from 2 draw 2 3 parallel to bO; from 3 draw 3 4 parallel to cO; and in the space D, from 4 draw 4 5 parallel to dO. Join 1 to 5, thus completing the funicular polygon. By drawing a line parallel to 5 1—the closing line of this polygon—through pole O, and meeting the vertical line of loads at e, it is found that ea equals the reaction EA, and ed equals the reaction ED; they are together equal to the sum of the weights in the beam.

EXAMPLE 3.—*A beam weighing 6 cwts. is loaded as shown in Fig. 606. Determine the reaction at each end necessary to produce equilibrium.*

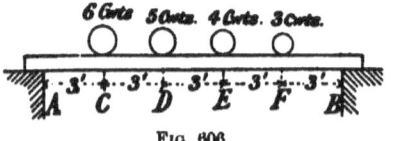

Fig. 606.

When the weight of a uniform beam is to be considered, it may be taken as acting half-way between the supports, and thus adding half its weight to each support. With this difference the method used is as in the previous example. Fig. 607 shows the graphical solution.

Stress Diagrams for Roof Trusses.—Figs. 608 to 617 show an application of the foregoing graphic methods to the determination of stresses in roof trusses. Fig. 608 is a line diagram of a king-post truss loaded in the usual way. It must be noticed that the lettering is arranged so that every member is indicated by a letter on each side. It is first necessary to determine the amount of weight carried by each point of support. This example is simplified by the symmetrical loading, as one half the weight is carried by each point of support. When this is not the case, the proportion of the weight carried by each support must be determined first, by a consideration of parallel forces, as in earlier examples.

It is usual when determining the stresses of such a truss, to draw the stress diagram, shown in Fig. 613. This diagram is a combination of Figs. 609 to 612, which are only drawn as separate figures to assist in understanding the question more clearly.

Fig. 609 is the polygon of forces for the joint (1) at the foot

MECHANICS OF CARPENTRY. 327

of the principal rafter on the left. Four forces act at the point: AB downwards, BN the principal rafter, NG the tie beam, and the upward force, AG—the reaction at the point of support. Of these four forces the amounts of two, AB and AG, are known; it is required to determine the nature and amounts of the stress of BN and of NG when acting at the angles given.

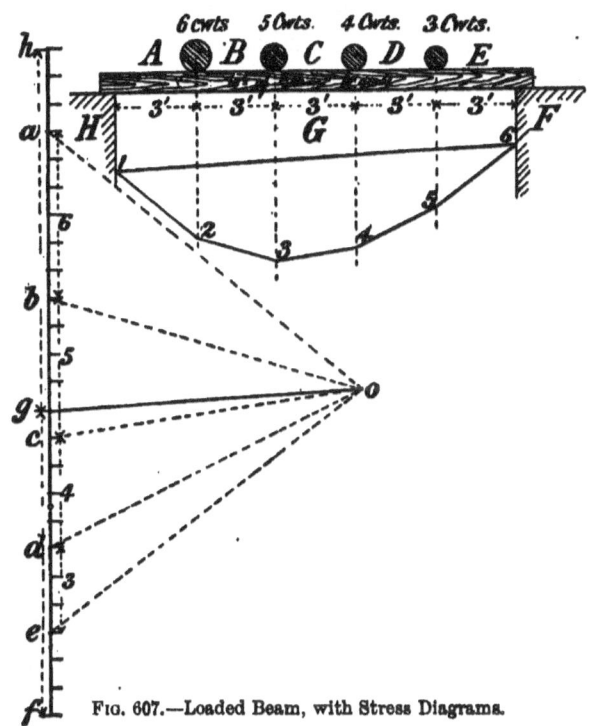

Fig. 607.—Loaded Beam, with Stress Diagrams.

Commence Fig. 609 by drawing ab equal to AB, and ag equal to AG, the upward force. As these two forces are in the same straight line, and in opposite directions, their resultant is the line bg. From b draw bn parallel to BN; and from g draw gn parallel to GN until bn and gn meet. Then bng is the polygon (a triangle in this case) of forces acting at the point; and bn and ng represent the *amount* of stress in the principal rafter and tie-beam respectively.

The *direction* of the stress is found by taking the forces in order: thus, gb acts upwards; bn acts towards the joint,

328 A MANUAL OF CARPENTRY AND JOINERY.

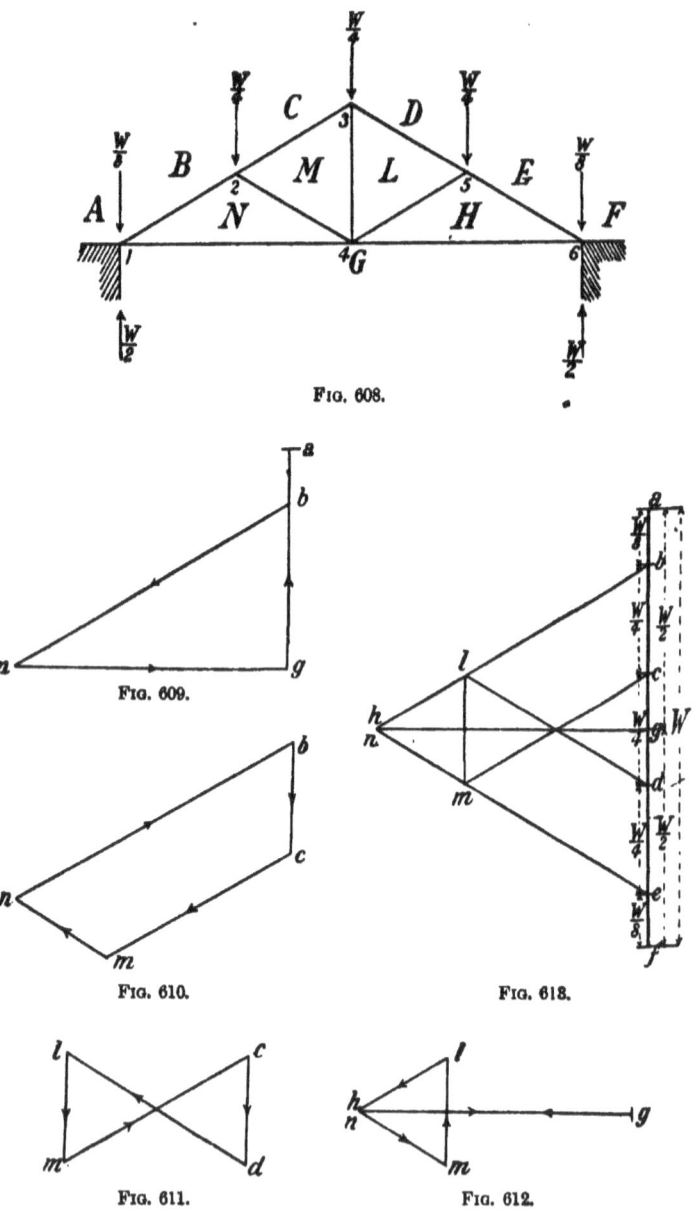

Fig. 608.

Fig. 609.

Fig. 610.

Fig. 611.

Fig. 613.

Fig. 612.

Line Diagram of King-post Truss, with Stress Diagrams.

MECHANICS OF CARPENTRY.   329

therefore this member is in compression; *ng* acts from the joint, which indicates that the tie-beam is in tension.

At joint (2), four forces act, namely, *BC*, *BN*, *CM*, and *NM*. The two known forces are *BC* acting downwards and *BN* towards the joint. For the magnitude of the stress on *BN* has already been found, and its direction of action at joint (2) is the opposite to its direction at joint (1). Fig. 610 shows the application of the polygon of forces to this joint. In it, *bc* and *bn* are drawn equal and parallel to *BC* and *BN* respectively; and, by drawing *nm* parallel to *NM* and *cm* parallel to *CM*, the stress diagram is obtained. This shows that the stress in *CM*, the upper part of the principal rafter, is much less than in *BN*, the lower part. By tracing the polygon, it is found that *bc* acts towards the joint, *cm* towards the joint (therefore *CM* is in compression), *mn* towards the joint (compression) and *nb* towards the joint (compression as in the previous figure).

At joint (3) there are four forces, *i.e.* *CM*, *CD*, *DL*, *ML*, acting as shown. Of these four forces the two *CM* and *CD* are known. Since the amount and nature of the stress in any member must be the same at any intermediate point between the joints, the stress in *CM* acting upon joint (3) must be as determined by the diagram for joint (2). Fig. 611 is the stress diagram; *cd* is drawn parallel and equal to *CD*; *cm* parallel and equal to *CM*; *ml* and *dl* are drawn parallel to *ML* and *LD* respectively until they meet. Taking these forces in order, *cd* is towards the joint, *DL* towards the joint (compression), *LM* is from the joint (tension), and *MC* towards the joint (compression).

The tension stress in *LM* is caused by the struts *MN* and *LH*, which transfer part of the loads *BC* and *DE* respectively to the foot of the king-post. If no struts existed in this truss there would be no stress in *ML*.

Joint (4) has five forces acting, each one of which has already been determined, since the stress diagrams for one side of the truss are in this example applicable to each side. For example, the diagrams showing the stresses in the joints (1) and (2) are applicable to (6) and (5) respectively. An examination of Fig. 612 will show that *gn* is parallel and equal to *GN*; *nm* is parallel and equal to *NM*; *lm* is parallel and equal to *LM*; and *lh* being drawn parallel to *LH* meets *mn* in *n*, whilst *hg* is equal to *ng*. The diagram therefore shows the stress in each of the five members.

330 A MANUAL OF CARPENTRY AND JOINERY.

In Fig. 613, which is the complete stress diagram for the members of the truss, the lettering is identical with that in each

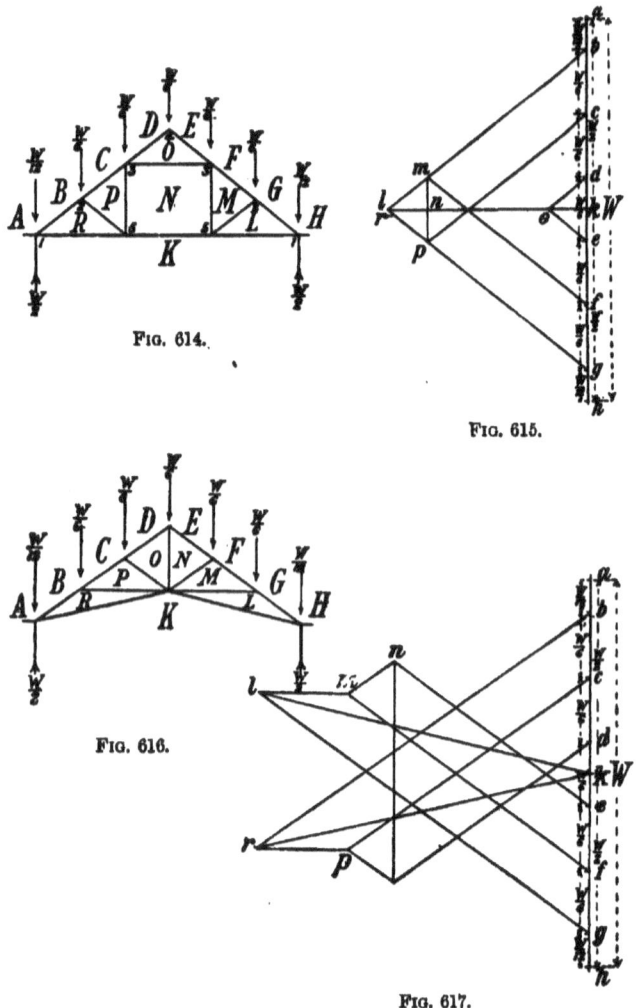

Fig. 614.

Fig. 615.

Fig. 616.

Fig. 617.

Types of Roof Truss, with Stress Diagrams.

of the separate Figs. 609 to 612, and will be easily understood from them.

Fig. 614 is a line diagram of a queen-post roof truss, and

MECHANICS OF CARPENTRY.

Fig. 615 is the stress diagram of this truss. Similarly, Figs. 616 and 617 are respectively the line diagram of and the stress diagram for, a composite roof truss, sometimes named a German truss. The detailed explanation already given will enable the figures to be understood.

STRENGTH OF WOODEN BEAMS.

For the purpose of calculating the carrying capacity of wooden beams, it is necessary to notice the nature of the stresses to which they are subjected, as well as the manner in which they are loaded, and the arrangement of the load.

Stress and Strain.—When a weight, or other force, acts upon a beam, it tends to change the shape and size of the beam. The force is technically called a **stress**, while the change in

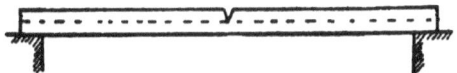

FIG. 618.—Beam cut to illustrate Stresses.

shape or size is called a **strain**. When a beam or girder, supported at both ends, is loaded, the upper part tends to shorten. The lower fibres, on the other hand, are in a state of tension, as they tend to stretch. The force acting on the upper fibres of such a beam is therefore a **compression stress**; that on the lower fibres is a **tension stress**.

The existence of these stresses may be made very apparent either by making a saw-cut across, or by actually cutting out a wedge-shaped piece from the middle of a beam of wood for half its depth, as shown in Fig. 618. On resting the beam on two supports with the cut edge uppermost, and then loading it, it will be seen that the saw-cut closes. This shows that the fibres on the upper side are in a state of compression. If the same beam is now turned over so that the saw-cut is on the lower side, and again loaded, the tendency is for the cut to open, thus showing that the fibres on the lower side are in a state of tension.

Shearing Stresses.—A shearing stress is one which gives the fibres of the wood a tendency to slide over one another. A shearing stress may be either in the direction of the fibres or at right angles to them. To illustrate a shearing stress in the direction of the fibres of a beam, imagine the beam cut into a number of boards; place these on the top of each other in the

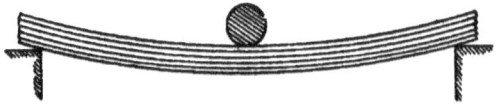

FIG. 619.—To illustrate Shearing Stress in the direction of the Fibres.

position of a beam resting upon supports at each end, and place a load in the middle. The result will be that the beam will bend, as shown in Fig. 619, and the boards will slide over each other. A shearing stress across the fibres of a loaded beam can be illustrated by taking a bar of soap, or some such soft material, resting it upon supports, and loading it. The result will be as shown in Fig. 620.

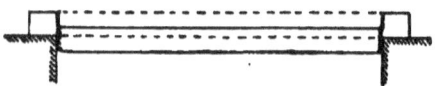

FIG. 620.—To illustrate Shearing Stress across the Fibres.

Methods of Arranging Beams.—The nature and amount of stress in the fibres of a loaded beam depend upon the way the beam is supported and on the arrangement of the load. Thus a **cantilever** is a beam with one end only secured upon a support, the other end overhanging. The load upon a cantilever may be a concentrated load at the outer end, as in Fig. 624, or the load may be anywhere between the outer end and the supported end; a number of loads of varying weights may be distributed over the length; the load may be a uniformly distributed one extending over the length of the beam, or it may be a combination of a concentrated load and a distributed load. A cantilever loaded in any of the ways just described has the fibres in the upper edge in a state of tension, those in the lower half being in compression (Fig. 621).

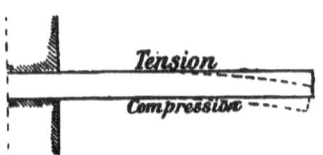

FIG. 621.—A beam fixed as a Cantilever.

A **beam supported at both ends** may be loaded in any of the ways described for the cantilever, with the result that the stresses will be as shown in Fig. 622; *i.e.* the upper part will be in compression, and the lower half in a state of tension. The stresses in the various parts of a loaded beam which has the **ends fixed** differ from those of the beam which simply rests upon supports. They are illustrated in Fig. 623, which shows that for a distance of about one-fourth from each end the beam takes the form of a cantilever, and has the fibres in the upper half in a state of tension and the lower fibres in compression. The remainder of the beam has the upper fibres

FIG. 622.—Beam supported at both ends.

in compression and the lower part in tension. The neutral axis of all these beams is in the centre of the depth. If a long beam has intermediate supports as in Fig. 623, it may be regarded as being "fixed" at the points of intermediate support.

Bending Moments.—For the purpose of making comparisons of the relative strengths of loaded beams, a further consideration of the "moment of a force" is necessary. Since the tendency

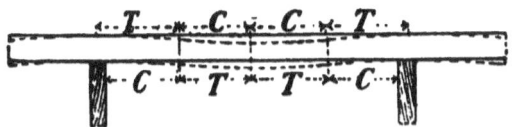

FIG. 623.— Beam fixed at the ends.

to bending, to which a given beam is subject at any point, depends upon the moments of the stresses about that point, it is obvious that the relative strengths of beams may be measured in terms of moments. **The bending moment at any given section is the algebraic sum of all the external forces acting on one side of the section.** Since it is at the point where the greatest bending moment occurs that the beam is subjected to the greatest stress, it follows that it is of some importance to be able to determine the bending moment of beams loaded under different conditions. The bending moment—like other moments—must always be expressed in terms of a length and a force.

334 A MANUAL OF CARPENTRY AND JOINERY.

EXAMPLE 1.—*A cantilever carries a load of 6 tons at its outer end, which is 5 ft. from the supporting wall. Determine the maximum bending moment, and also the bending moment at 2 ft. from the wall.*

The greatest tendency to bending will be at the point of support, *i.e.* at a distance of 5 ft. from the load.

∴ Maximum bending moment = 5 × 6 = 30 ft.-tons.

Bending moment at 2 ft. from the wall (*i.e.* 3 ft. from the load)
$$= 3 \times 6 = 18 \text{ ft.-tons.}$$

The bending moment at any distance from the load may be determined graphically by drawing, as in Fig. 624, a vertical line AB 30 units long (representing the maximum bending moment) under the point of support A (*i.e.* the point where the bending moment is a maximum), and joining BC. Then the bending moment at the point a will be represented by the length of ab drawn parallel to AB.

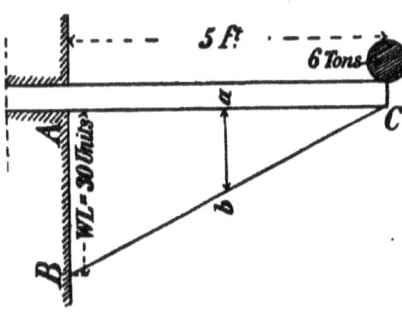

FIG. 624.—Side Elevation of a Cantilever with a Concentrated Load at the outer end.

EXAMPLE 2.—*A cantilever projects 4 ft. and carries a uniformly distributed load of 8 cwts. along the upper edge. Determine the maximum bending moment, and also draw a diagram from which the bending moment at any section along the length of the cantilever may be determined.*

A load arranged as shown in Fig. 625 is equivalent to a concentrated load of 8 cwts. acting in the middle of the length, *i.e.* 2 ft. from the point of support. The maximum bending moment will therefore be
$$8 \times 2 = 16 \text{ ft.-cwts.}$$

Fig. 625 is the diagram from which the bending moment at any section may be determined. The load is supposed divided into 4 equal parts, and the bending moment due to each part is drawn to scale on the vertical line AE. The weight of Z acts at 3' 6" from A, and the maximum bending moment due to $Z = 2 \times 3.5 = 7$ ft.-cwts. Draw AB 7 units long. Similarly, the maximum bending moment due to $Y = 2 \times 2{\cdot}5 = 5$ ft.-cwts., and is represented by BC; maximum bending moment due to $X = 2 \times 1{\cdot}5 = 3$ ft.-cwts., represented by CD; maximum bending moment due to $W = 2 \times 0{\cdot}5 = 1$ ft.-cwt., represented by DE. The maximum bending moment due to the *total* load is therefore $7 + 5 + 3 + 1 = 16$ ft.-cwts., and is represented by AE. Draw a vertical line through the centre of each part of the load, and complete the triangles AaB, BbC, CcD, DdE. Draw an even curve touching the lines Ed, Dc, Cb, Ba. This curve is a parabola. *The bending moment at any section P is represented by the length of the vertical line PQ cutting the parabola at Q.*

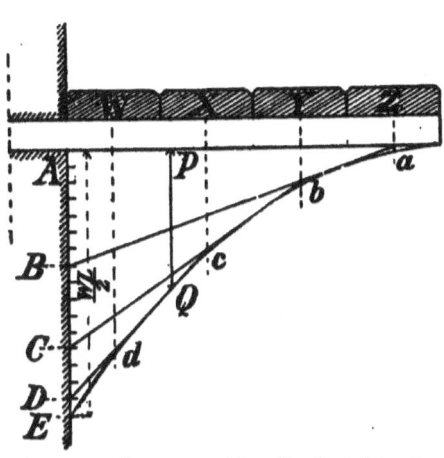

Fig. 625.—Cantilever with a distributed Load.

The following formulae are used for determining the relative bending moments (and therefore the relative strengths required) of beams loaded in various ways. In each case L = the length of the beam and W = the weight of the load.

	Maximum Bending Moment.	Relative Strength.
Cantilever fixed at one end and loaded at the other end (Fig. 624),	WL	1.
Cantilever fixed at one end and loaded with a uniformly distributed load,	$\dfrac{WL}{2}$	2.
Beam supported at both ends and loaded with a central load (Fig. 626),	$\dfrac{WL}{4}$	4.
Beam supported at both ends and loaded with a uniformly distributed load (Fig. 629),	$\dfrac{WL}{8}$	8.
Beam fixed at both ends and loaded with a central load (Fig. 628),	$\dfrac{WL}{8}$	8.
Beam fixed at both ends and loaded with a uniformly distributed load,	$\dfrac{WL}{12}$	12.

Figs. 626 to 629 show beams loaded in various ways, and serve to illustrate the method of determining graphically the bending moment at any section of the beam.

It will be noticed that the maximum bending moment of a beam supported at each end is in each case in the line of the load, and with a central or an evenly distributed load is at the middle of the length of the beam.

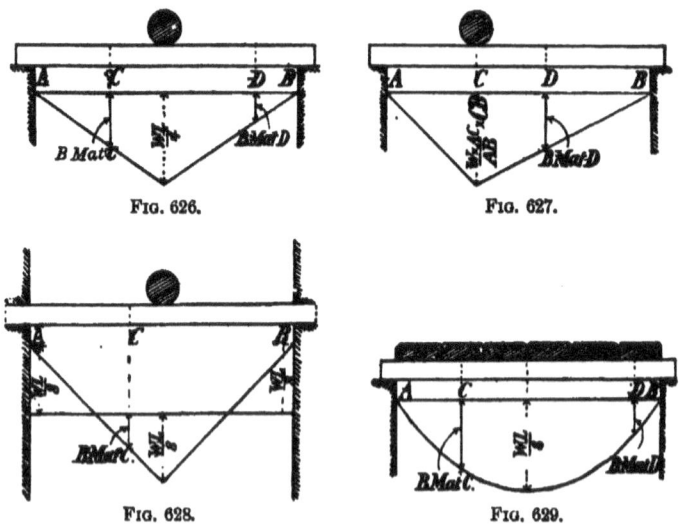

Examples of Loaded Beams, with Bending Moment Diagrams.

Calculation of the Transverse Strength of Wooden Beams.—Other things being equal, the strength of a rectangular wooden beam is directly proportional to the breadth in inches multiplied by the square of the depth in inches, and inversely proportional to the length in feet. Of course the nature of the material is also an important factor, since timber, even of the same kind, varies in strength to a considerable extent. Each beam therefore has what is called a natural **constant**, which must be considered in the calculation of its carrying capacity. To obtain this constant, it is usual to take a bar of similar wood, 1 inch square in section, and long enough to allow of its being placed on supports 1 foot apart. The constant is the weight of the central load, which is just sufficient to break the bar. The constant may be expressed

STRENGTH OF WOODEN BEAMS.

in lbs., cwts., tons, etc., and the carrying capacity will always be in the same terms. The following constants (in cwts.) may be adopted for the purposes of calculation: oak, ash and pitch pine, 5; red deal, red pine and beech, 4; white deal and yellow pine, 3.

Another important consideration is the ratio which the breaking load of a beam bears to the "safe" load. This ratio is called the **factor of safety,** and its value depends upon whether the load is a live—a constantly moving—load, or a dead (*i.e.*, a stationary) load. The factor of safety for a dead load is usually taken at 5, which means that the safe load upon a beam must not exceed one-fifth of the breaking load; the factor of safety for a live load is often taken at 10.

For beams supported at both ends the formula $W = \dfrac{bd^2c}{L}$ may be used for the purposes of calculation when:

W = breaking weight or maximum carrying capacity of a centrally loaded beam, expressed in the same terms as the constant,
b = breadth of the beam in inches,
d = depth of the beam in inches,
L = length of the beam in feet,
c = the constant, found by experiment as described above, and expressed in terms of lbs. or cwts.

To illustrate the above formula, take two pieces of the same kind of wood say 7 ft. long, 6 in. wide and 2 in. thick. Place one of these pieces flat, and the other one on edge, the distance between the supports in each case being 6 ft. As the constant is the same in both (say 5 cwts.), the carrying capacity of each will be expressed by the formula $W = \dfrac{bd^2c}{L}$;

for the flat beam, $W = \dfrac{6 \times 2 \times 2 \times 5}{6} = 20$,

for the one on edge, $W = \dfrac{2 \times 6 \times 6 \times 5}{6} = 60$;

and the relative strengths will be as 20 : 60 or as 1 : 3.

When it is necessary to find other terms than W, the equation $W = \dfrac{bd^2c}{L}$ may be expressed as follows:

$$L = \frac{bd^2c}{W}; \quad b = \frac{WL}{d^2c}; \quad d^2 = \frac{WL}{bc}; \quad d = \sqrt{\frac{WL}{bc}}; \quad c = \frac{WL}{bd^2}.$$

The value of W for a **distributed load** is twice that for a concentrated load, i.e. $W = \dfrac{2bd^2c}{L}$. When the ends are fixed the carrying capacity is increased by about one-half.

For safe central loads the formula $W = \dfrac{bd^2c}{LF}$ is used : F being the factor of safety.

EXAMPLE 1.—*Find the maximum carrying capacity of a centrally loaded wooden beam of pitch pine, 13 ft. long (12 ft. between the supports), 10 in. wide, and 6 in. thick, (1) when placed on edge; (2) when placed flat. Assume a constant of 5 cwts.*

Applying the formula

$W = \dfrac{bd^2c}{L}$, (1) $W = \dfrac{6 \times 10 \times 10 \times 5}{12} = 250$ cwts. when on edge.

(2) $W = \dfrac{10 \times 6 \times 6 \times 5}{12} = 150$ cwts. when placed flat.

EXAMPLE 2.—*What would be the maximum safe load to which the beam in Ex. 1 may be subjected (1) as a central load; (2) as a uniformly distributed load?*

Formula for safe central load using a factor of safety of 5, is

$$\text{Safe central load} = \dfrac{bd^2c}{LF}$$

$= \dfrac{6 \times 10 \times 10 \times 5}{12 \times 5} = 50$ cwts. for beam on edge,

or $= \dfrac{10 \times 6 \times 6 \times 5}{12 \times 5} = 30$ cwts. for beam placed flat.

Formula for safe uniformly distributed load, again using factor of safety of 5, is

$$\text{Safe distributed load} = \dfrac{2bd^2c}{LF}$$

$= \dfrac{2 \times 6 \times 10 \times 10 \times 5}{12 \times 5} = 100$ cwts. for beam on edge,

or $= \dfrac{2 \times 10 \times 6 \times 6 \times 5}{12 \times 5} = 60$ cwts. for beam placed flat.

EXAMPLE 3.—*Find the breadth of a beam of oak resting upon supports 18 feet apart, the beam being 12 in. deep, to carry safely a uniformly distributed load of 5 tons. Constant 5 cwts.*

Safe distributed load, $W = \dfrac{2bd^2c}{LF}$;

$\therefore b = \dfrac{WLF}{2d^2c} = \dfrac{(5 \times 20) \times 18 \times 5}{2 \times 12 \times 12 \times 5} = \dfrac{25}{4} = 6\tfrac{1}{4}$ inches,

STRENGTH OF WOODEN BEAMS.

EXAMPLE 4.—*A beam of red or yellow deal 20 ft. long (between supports), and 10 in. broad has to carry safely* (1) *a central load,* (2) *a distributed load of 4 tons. What must be the minimum depth of the beam in each case?* (*Constant* 4 *cwts.*)

With a central load $d^2 = \dfrac{WLF}{bc}$;

$$\therefore d = \sqrt{\dfrac{WLF}{bc}} = \sqrt{\dfrac{80 \times 20 \times 5}{10 \times 4}} = \sqrt{200} = 14\cdot14 \text{ inches.}$$

With a distributed load

$$d = \sqrt{\dfrac{WLF}{2bc}} = \sqrt{\dfrac{80 \times 20 \times 5}{2 \times 10 \times 4}} = \sqrt{100} = 10 \text{ inches.}$$

EXAMPLE 5.—*What size of beam is required to carry safely a central load of* 35 *cwts. over a* 10 *ft. span; the depth and breadth of the beam being in the proportion of* 7 : 5 ? (*Constant* 5 *cwts.*)

$$b = \tfrac{5}{7}d\ ;$$

$$d^2 b = \dfrac{WLF}{c}$$

i.e. $d^2 \cdot \dfrac{5}{7} d = \dfrac{WLF}{c}$

$$\dfrac{5d^3}{7} = \dfrac{WLF}{c}$$

$$d^3 = \dfrac{7\,WLF}{5c} = \dfrac{7 \times 35 \times 10 \times 5}{5 \times 5} = 490.$$

$$d = \sqrt[3]{490} = 7\cdot88'' = \text{nearly } 8''.$$

$$\therefore b = \dfrac{5 \times 7\cdot88}{7} = 5\cdot6 \text{ inches.}$$

The strength of flitched girders (p. 162) may be calculated by considering the wooden beam and iron flitch separately. The thickness of the flitch is usually about $\tfrac{1}{12}$ that of the wooden beam. The constant for wrought iron is 25 cwts.

Deflection.—In arranging beams it is necessary to consider not merely the strength of the beam, but also its liability or otherwise to be bent out of shape—or deflected—by the load placed upon it; since a beam which is overloaded and bent to a large extent has the fibres strained and therefore permanently weakened. The resistance which a beam offers to deflection is called its **stiffness.** It should be noticed that the "strongest" beam is not necessarily the "stiffest," nor the stiffest beam the strongest.

340   A MANUAL OF CARPENTRY AND JOINERY.

It is of importance to be able to determine the cross-sections of the strongest and the stiffest beams respectively which can be cut from a given log.

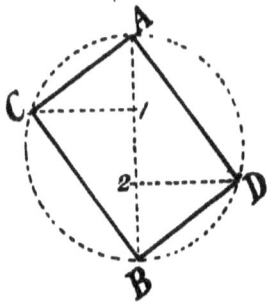

FIG. 630.—Strongest Beam from a given Circular Section.

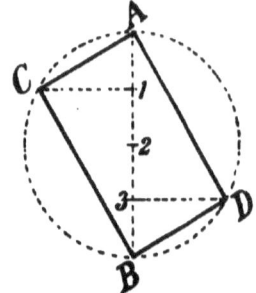

FIG. 631.—Stiffest Beam from a given Circular Section.

Suppose the log is of circular cross-section.

(a) *To find the cross-section of the strongest beam.*—Draw a diameter AB (Fig. 630) and divide it into 3 equal parts at 1

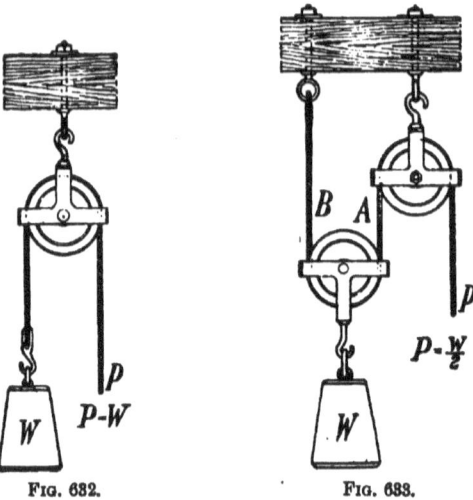

FIG. 632. FIG. 633.

Arrangements of Pulleys and Weights.

and 2. From 1 and 2 draw perpendiculars to AB cutting the circumference at C and D respectively. Join $ACBD$. The rectangle $ACBD$ is the section required.

(b) *To find the cross-section of the stiffest beam.*—Divide the

PULLEYS. 341

diameter AB (Fig. 631) into 4 equal parts at 1, 2, 3, and draw $1C$ and $3D$ perpendicular to AB, and cutting the circumference in C and D respectively. The rectangle $ACBD$ is the section required.

Since the strength of a beam is proportional to $\frac{bd^2}{L}$, and the value of this fraction increases as d increases when bd (i.e. the sectional area) remains constant, the strongest beam of any given sectional area would be that of greatest depth if the tendency to buckling could be avoided. In the case of floor joists the ratio of depth to breadth is often as 3 : 1 or even 4 : 1, and the tendency to buckling is overcome by strutting. The strongest beam is that which has the depth to the breadth as 7 : 5.

FIG. 634.—Two-Sheaved Pulley Block.   FIG. 635.—Three-Sheaved Pulley Block.

Pulleys.—It is necessary to consider one or two simple arrangements by which pulleys are used for hoisting purposes. In the following examples the friction will for the sake of simplicity be neglected, although in practice it must be taken into account. Fig. 632 illustrates the simplest application of the pulley. It is plain that when the forces acting on the pulley are in equilibrium they are equal, and the only advantage gained is in the change of direction of the force required to balance W. Therefore in this example $P = W$.

In Fig. 633 the force balancing P is the tension of the cord A, which is equal to that of B. The *sum* of these two equal tensions is plainly equal to the weight W. Therefore $P = \frac{W}{2}$, and the mechanical advantage is 2.

Figs. 634 and 635 are illustrations of a two- and a three-sheaved pulley block respectively. By arranging pulleys side by side in this manner, and using a combination of two similar blocks as in Fig. 636 a mechanical advantage equal to the number of pulleys around which the rope passes is obtained. In other words, the power required is equal to the weight raised divided by the number of pulleys around which the rope passes. Thus with 3 pulleys in each block there will be six cords, and the power required to balance a weight of 18 cwts. will be $18 \div 6 = 3$ cwts., *plus* the force required to overcome friction

Specific Gravity.—The specific gravity, or relative density, of a body is the ratio of the weight of that body to the weight of an equal volume of water. Thus a block of wood weighing 40 lbs. per cubic foot has a specific gravity of $\frac{40}{62 \cdot 5} = 0 \cdot 64$ (since a cubic foot of water weighs 62·5 lbs.).

When a body floats in water, and is therefore in equilibrium, the weight of the body is balanced by an equal upward reaction, the weight of the water displaced being equal to the total weight of the floating body.

EXAMPLE.—*A block of wood* $9'' \times 9'' \times 9''$, *floats in water with its upper surface* $2 \cdot 5''$ *above the surface of the water. Find its specific gravity.*

$\frac{6\frac{1}{2}}{9} = \frac{13}{18}$ of the block is submerged.

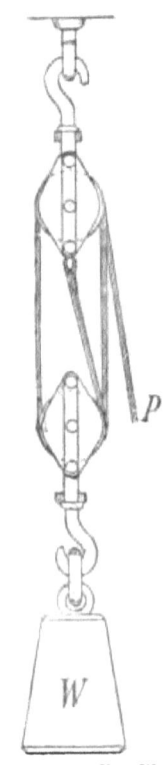

FIG. 636.—Pulley Blocks and Rope.

By definition, the specific gravity of the wood is the ratio of the weight of any portion of the block to the weight of an equal volume of water. Consider the part of the block below the surface of the water.

$$\text{Specific gravity} = \frac{\text{Weight of submerged part of wood}}{\text{Weight of displaced water}}$$

$$= \frac{\text{Weight of submerged part of wood}}{\text{Weight of whole block}}$$

$$= \frac{\text{Volume of submerged part of wood}}{\text{Volume of whole block}}$$

$$= \frac{13}{18} = 0 \cdot 72.$$

Questions on Chapter XII.

1. Two forces of 16 and 63 lbs. act upon a point at right angles to each other. Find their resultant. (C. and G. Prel., 1897.)

2. Represent graphically, to a scale of ¼ in. = 1 lb. the resultant of two forces of 9 and 13 lbs. respectively acting at the same point:
   (a) In the same straight line but in opposite directions.
   (b) In the same straight line and in the same direction.
   (c) At right angles to each other.
   (d) At an angle of 135° with each other.
   (e) At an angle of 60° with each other.

3. The spur of a field-gate abuts in the angle between the front post and the horizontal top rail, and is inclined at 30° to the horizontal. Determine the stress in the spur caused by a boy weighing 80 lbs. swinging on the outer end of the gate.

4. Two posts which meet at an angle are inclined to the horizontal at 30° and 60° respectively, and are in the same vertical plane. Determine the stress in each post caused by a load of two tons being suspended from the point of intersection.

5. Three equal poles meet at a point 12 feet high, their lower ends being at the angular points of an equilateral triangle of 8 feet side. Find graphically the stress in each pole when a load of 3 tons is suspended from the joined upper ends of the poles.

6. From a point draw six lines so that each line makes an angle of 60° with the next. Forces of 5, 6, 7, 8, 9, 10 lbs. respectively act from the point of intersection along the lines. Find graphically the magnitude and direction of the resultant force.

7. With the data of Q. 6 find the resultant if the directions of two of the forces, viz. those of 6 lbs. and 9 lbs., are reversed.

8. A king-post roof truss, 20 feet span and 10 feet in height, has a purlin on each side resting on the middle of principal rafters, under which are the struts. The load of each purlin is 5 cwts. Find, graphically, the strain on each part of the truss. (C. and G. Prel., 1897.)

9. Explain the "parallelogram of forces," and use it to find the strains on a king-post roof principal 24 ft. span, ¼ pitch, the trusses being 6 ft. apart. (C. and G. Hon., 1894.)

10. Draw line diagrams of the roof trusses shown in elevation in Figs. 438 and 448. Assuming a concentrated load of one ton at each of the purlins and at the ridge, draw, for each truss, the stress diagram.

11. A mason is trying to move a heavy stone by throwing all his weight on the end of an iron bar. He weighs 1 cwt. 2 qrs. 7 lb., and his bar is 6 ft. 6 in. long, fulcrum 1 ft. 6 in. from the end. How much force is he exerting upon the stone? (C. and G. Prel., 1903.)

12. A man weighing 175 lbs. has to move a block of stone weighing 1½ tons with a lever 7 ft. long. Determine the position of the fulcrum in order that the weight of the man may just move the stone. (C. and G. Prel., 1904.)

13. The handle of a mortising machine is 2 feet long. How much more pressure would you be able to exert, applying the same force, if the handle were made 1 foot longer? (C. and G. Prel., 1898.)

14. A beam 20 ft. long, supported at both ends, is loaded 6 ft. from one end with a weight of 15 cwts. Determine the pressure at each support, neglecting the weight of the beam. (C. and G. Prel., 1904.)

15. A beam 16 ft. long is supported at each end, and is loaded at a point 4 ft. from one end with a load of 12 tons. Make a sketch showing the weight carried by each support. (C. and G. Prel., 1902.)

16. A beam rests upon supports 12 feet apart. Loads of 2, 4, and 6 cwts. respectively are placed at 3 ft. distances. Determine both graphically and arithmetically the reaction required at each end to keep the beam in equilibrium. Neglect the weight of the beam.

17. A pitch pine beam, 12 in. by 8 in., and 17 feet long, rests upon supports 16 feet apart. Determine the maximum carrying capacity, the load being in the middle of the length, when the beam is placed (a) on edge; (b) laid flat. Also find the maximum safe distributed load which may be placed on the beam when (a) on edge; (b) laid flat.

18. An oak beam 12 inches deep spans an opening 20 feet wide. With a concentrated load of 9 tons in the middle of the length there are signs of fracture. Find the approximate breadth of the beam.

19. A beam of Memel fir, over an opening 16 feet in the clear, is broken in the centre with a load of 90 cwts. Required, the depth and breadth of the beam; the beam being proportioned as 5 to 7. (C. and G. Ord., 1892.)

20. A beam over an opening of 12 feet has a safe distributed load of 7 tons. What section should it be in Memel fir, and what if a flitched girder is used. (C. and G. Hon., 1892.)

21. A warehouse floor has to carry 3 cwts. to the foot super. What size beams would you use if the width is 20 ft. and the beams

are 10 ft. apart, centre to centre? If flitch beams were used, what would be their size and what the thickness of the flitch? (C. and G. Hon., 1895.)

22. A man sitting upon a board suspended from a single moveable pulley pulls downwards at one end of a rope, which passes under the moveable pulley and over a pulley fixed to a beam overhead, the other end of the rope being fixed to the same beam. What is the smallest proportion of his whole weight with which the man must pull in order to raise himself? (C. and G. Prel., 1897.)

23. Describe a simple arrangement of pulleys by which a man pulling with a force of a little over 50 lbs. might lift a body weighing 200 lbs. Why is it that with the arrangements proposed he must exert a force of more than 50 lbs. ?

24. How is the specific gravity of any kind of timber ascertained? (C. and G. Prel., 1903.)

25. What is meant by the density of timber? (C. and G. Prel., 1902.)

26. How would you ascertain that the density of oak is greater that that of fir? How would you determine the density of either? (C. and G. Prel., 1901.)

CHAPTER XIII.

DOORS AND OTHER PANELLED FRAMING.

Doors.—Doors may be either *ledged, framed and ledged*, or *framed and panelled*.

Ledged Doors.—Ledged doors are only used for out-buildings and temporary work. They consist of narrow **battens**, or boards securely nailed to **cross ledges**. Fig. 637 shows the back elevation and vertical section of a typical ledged door. The joints of the battens of which a ledged door is constructed may be either

(i.) Tongued and grooved ;
(ii.) Ploughed and tongued ;
(iii.) Rebated.

To relieve the monotony of the surface, and to hide any slight shrinkage that may take place, the edges of the battens may be either beaded or V-jointed (Figs. 639 and 640). The outer edges of the cross-ledges are usually chamfered as shown in Fig. 637.

Ledged and Braced Doors.—The ledged door above described has a tendency to droop at the outer edge. To prevent this drooping, and also to strengthen the door, it is customary to insert sloping **braces** between the ledges (Fig. 638). Each brace should slope upwards from the hinged edge. A door of this description is called a **ledged and braced door**.

Framed Doors.—These doors are formed by constructing **frames** of wood, and fitting between the frames thinner vertical narrow **battens** (in framed and ledged doors), or thin boards called **panels** (in framed and panelled doors). The object of using such a frame, either for doors, or for any similar panelled framing, is to obtain a structure in which the tendency to shrinkage, inseparable from the use of wide pieces of timber, is to a large extent obviated.

DOORS AND OTHER PANELLED FRAMING.   347

Terms used in describing Framed Doors.—The outer vertical members are called **styles**. During the construction of

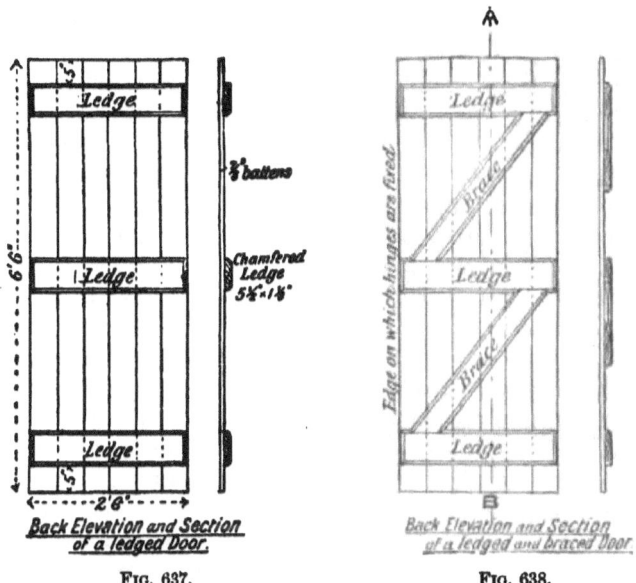

Fig. 637.   Fig. 638.

the door the styles are left about three inches longer than the finished door is intended to be. The projecting 1½ inches at each end of the style is called a horn. The projecting horns are left on the style to protect its corners until the door is finally fixed in position, at which time the horns are sawn off. The horizontal cross pieces of a framed door are known as **rails**. They have distinctive names according to their positions in the door, *e.g. top rail, frieze rail* (only used in panelled doors), *lock rail*, and *bottom rail*. The inclined members of a

Tongued, grooved & beaded battens

Fig. 639.

Ploughed, tongued & V-jointed battens

Fig. 640.

Rebated & V jointed battens

Fig. 641.

door—which are only used in framed and ledged doors—are called **braces**. The vertical members separating panels are known as **muntins**.

Joints used in Doors and other Panelled Framing.—(1) The **mortise and tenon joint** is used for connecting the frames together, the joints being secured with wedges and either glue or stiff paint. The *mortises* are cut into the styles, while the *tenons* are cut on the ends of the rails. The thickness of the tenon is from one-fourth to one-third the thickness of the framing. If a tenon is made very wide in proportion to its thickness, it is liable to buckle when being wedged, and subsequently to become loose if any slight shrinkage should take place. A tenon should therefore have a width of not more than five times its thickness. The mortise should, moreover, be a little wider at its outer edge, and thus allow for the insertion of the wedges by which the framing is secured.

(2) **Haunched Tenon.**—When part of a tenon is cut off, so as to make its width less than the width of the rail, it is known as a haunched tenon. Such haunching is necessary in the top and bottom rails to enable them to be wedged securely to the style. Haunching is also necessary in the lock rails (Figs. 642 and 643) and bottom rails, so that the proper proportion of the width of the tenon to its thickness may be obtained, as well as to enable it to be wedged firmly.

(3) **Bare-faced Tenon.**—This form of joint has one side of the tenon flush with one face of the rail (Fig. 642). Bare-faced tenons are used in the lower rails of a framed and ledged door (Figs. 644 to 647).

(4) **Stump or Stub Tenon.**—This term is used for short tenons such as those which occur, for example, on the end of a muntin. Stump tenons in door framing are usually about 2 inches long.

(5) **Double Tenon.**—A double tenon consists of two tenons cut side by side in the thickness of the rail as shown in Fig. 643. In doors not more than $2\frac{1}{2}$ inches thick, the double tenon is only used for the ends of lock rails, and then only in cases where the lock is fixed in the thickness of the door. A lock so fixed into the edge of the door is called a **mortise lock**. For thicker doors, double tenons may with advantage be used at all the joints.

Framed, Ledged and Braced Doors.—Figs. 644 to 647 show front and back elevations, together with horizontal and vertical sections, of this type of door. The names and dimensions of the

FRAMED, LEDGED, AND BRACED DOORS.

various parts are marked in the illustrations. The styles and top rail are of the same thickness; the lock rail, bottom rail,

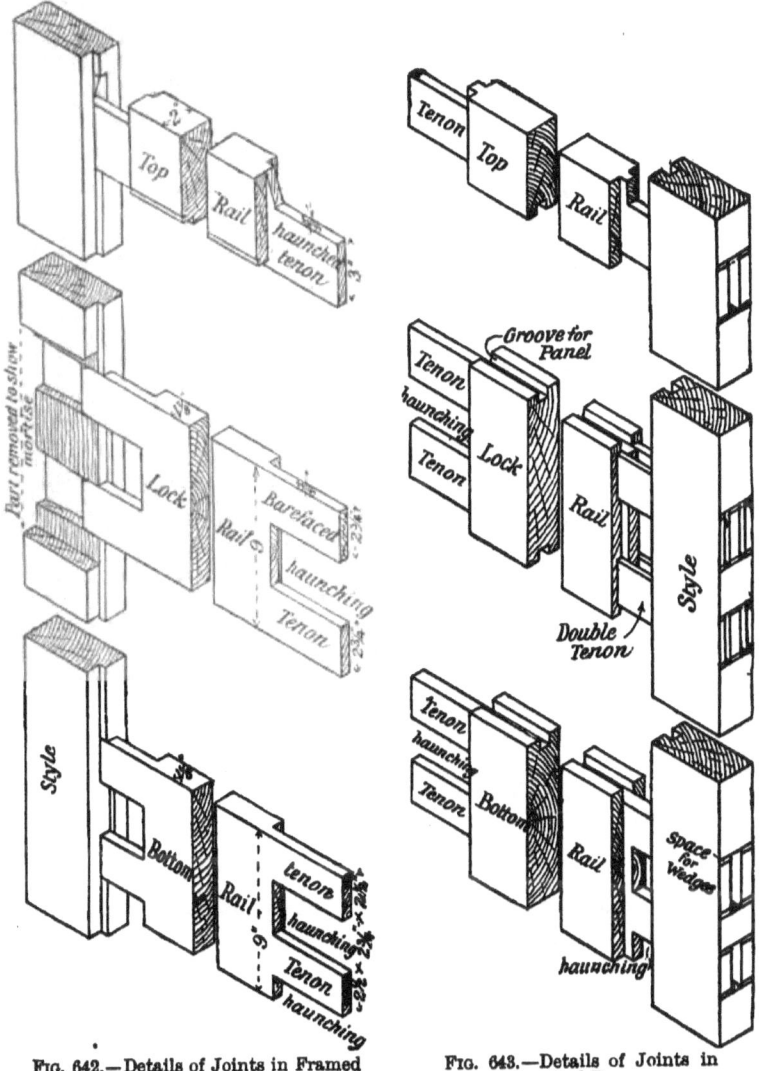

Fig. 642.—Details of Joints in Framed and Ledged Doors.

Fig. 643.—Details of Joints in Panelled Doors.

and braces are of less thickness than the styles, being thinner by the extent of the thickness of the battens. All the framework

350   A MANUAL OF CARPENTRY AND JOINERY.

is flush on the inner side. In Fig. 646 the framework is shown stop-chamfered on the inner face; such chamfering gives the door a lighter appearance. The rails and braces may be beaded, or moulded, as an alternative to stop-chamfering. The joints of the framing of the door under consideration are formed as shown in Fig. 642; the lock rail and bottom rail are there

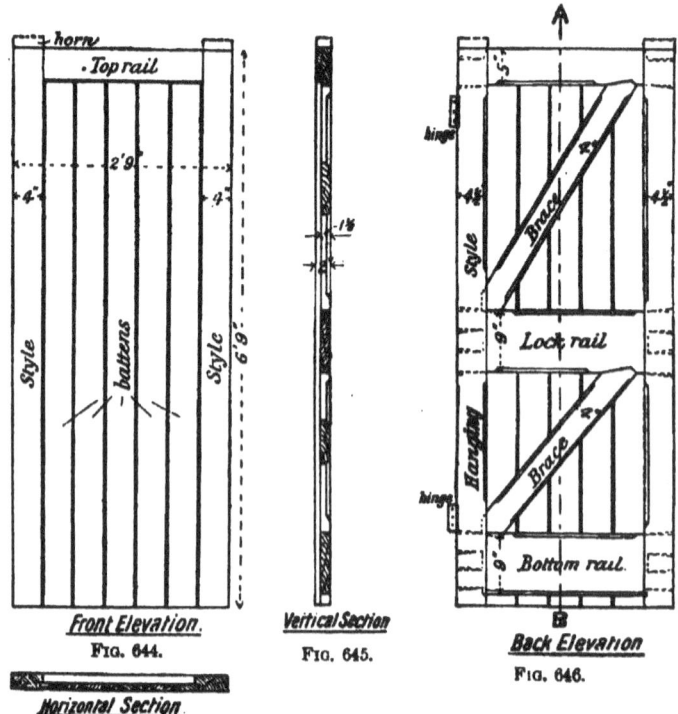

Framed, Ledged, and Braced Door.

seen to have bare-faced tenons. The edges of the styles are rebated, or grooved, to receive the edges of the battens. The edges of the battens may be:
  (i.) Tongued, grooved, and beaded (Fig. 639);
  (ii.) Ploughed, tongued, and V-jointed (Fig. 640); or they may be
  (iii.) Rebated as shown in Fig. 641.

In arranging the braces for such a door, the lower ends may be stump-tenoned into the style, but the upper ends should be

FRAMED, LEDGED, AND BRACED DOORS. 351

cut into the rail as shown in Fig. 646. If the upper end of the brace fits into the corner as the lower end does, it is liable to push off the joint between the rail and the style. Again, the brace must always be arranged to support the outer edge of the door, the lower end being against the hanging-style.

Framed, ledged, and braced doors are generally used for workshops, warehouses, mills, stables, the outbuildings of dwelling-houses, etc. The size and arrangement of the framing of the larger doors vary considerably, and depend upon the position and the method of hanging them. In wide doorways, the door is often made in halves, hung folding, with a rebated joint between the meeting styles. Fig. 648 shows the elevation of a door of this class.

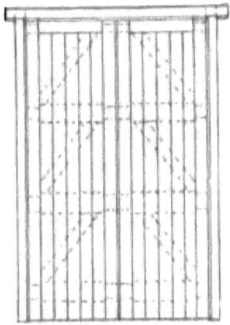

FIG. 648.—Elevation of Framed and Braced Doors hung folding.

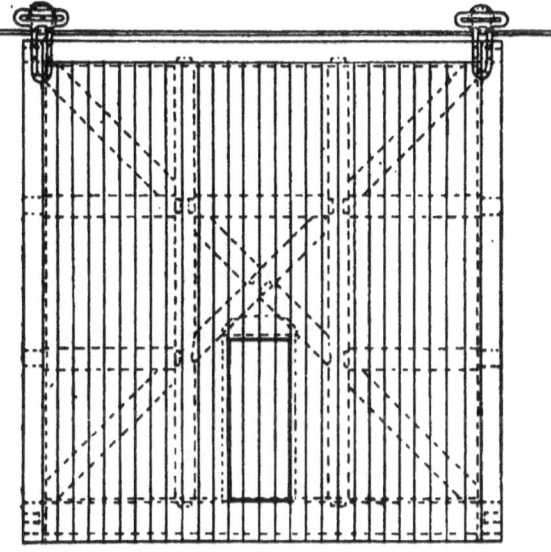

FIG. 649.—Elevation of a Sliding Door.

Fig. 650 shows a high doorway usually found in warehouses. In this doorway two pairs of doors, arranged in two heights with rebated joints, are shown.

Fig. 652 shows the elevation of a stable door arranged in two heights, with a ventilator constructed in the upper door. The

FIG. 650.—Framed and Braced Doors in two heights.

FIG. 651.—Section on AB.

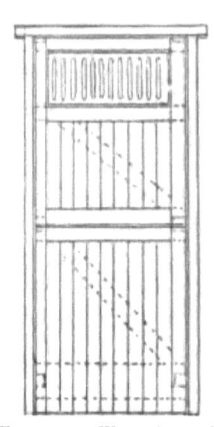

FIG. 652.—Elevation of a Stable Door.

elevation of a very large door, suitable for the entrance to a mill yard, warehouse, or other works is shown in Fig. 649. Such a door is often framed together so that it allows for the insertion of a smaller wicket-door as shown in the drawing. The doorways of Gothic buildings—especially churches—almost invariably have framed, ledged, and braced doors. Fig. 653 is the elevation of a door of this class.

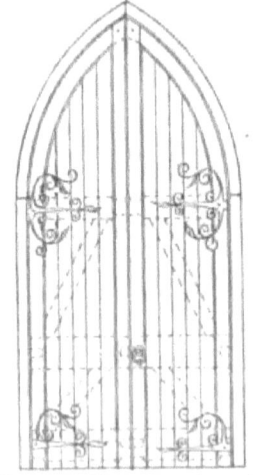

FIG. 653.—Elevation of a pair of Church Doors.

When framed, ledged, and braced doors are fixed as outside doors, or in exposed positions, it is very necessary that the upper edges of all rails and braces be chamfered ("weathered") to throw off rain water; and the joints, both of the framework and at the edges of the battens, as well as

PANELLED DOORS.

the backs of the rails, should be well painted before the doors are put together.

Panelled Doors.—The framing of panelled doors differs from that of framed and ledged doors in that the **panels**—

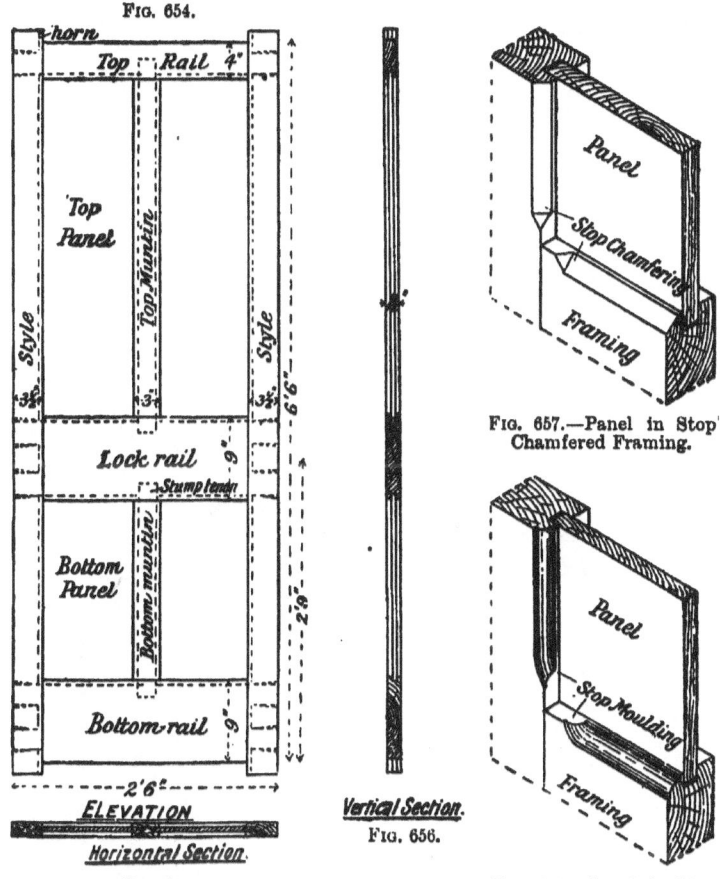

Fig. 654.

Fig. 655.—Elevation and Sections of a Four-panelled Door.

Fig. 656.—Vertical Section.

Fig. 657.—Panel in Stop Chamfered Framing.

Fig. 658.—Panel in Stop Moulded Framing.

which are usually about one-third the thickness of the door—fit into grooves in the middle of the framing. In framed and ledged doors the framing is put together, wedged up, and finished before the battens are nailed on; whereas in panelled work the panels are inserted in the grooves as the framing is

354   A MANUAL OF CARPENTRY AND JOINERY.

put together. The grooves also affect the width of the mortises; an allowance must therefore be made for the reduced width of the tenons which results from the grooving.

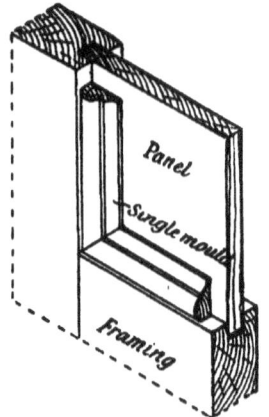

FIG. 659.—Panelled Framing "Single Moulded."

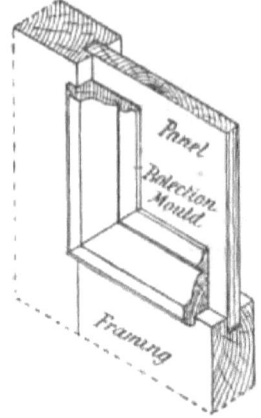

FIG. 660.—Panelled Framing "Bolection Moulded."

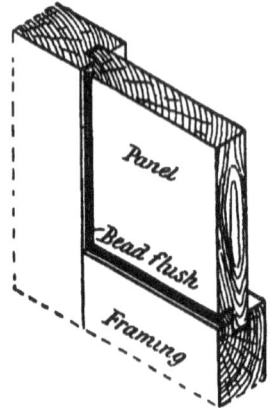

FIG. 661.—Framing with Bead-flush Panel.

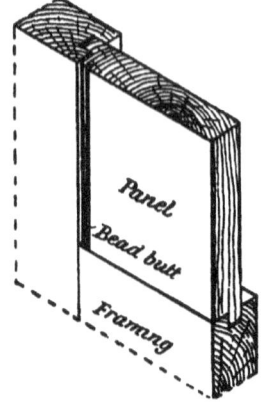

FIG. 662.—Framing with Bead-butt Panel.

Proportions of Panelled Doors.—Since doors vary considerably in size, arrangement, the number of panels, and the method of their treatment, no hard and fast rule can be laid down as to the proportions suitable. For an ordinary dwelling-house door, however, the dimensions indicated on Figs. 654

TREATMENT OF PANELLED FRAMING.

and 667 may be taken as typical. It is important to notice that the height of the centre of the lock rail is usually about 2' 9" from the floor; this height is considered the most suitable for a lock or other door-fastener.

Treatment of Framing.—When door framing or other panelled work is left square, and the panels are plain, and one-third the thickness of the material of the framing, the method of finishing is named **square and flat** (Fig. 654). Square and flat is, however, improved upon by **stop-chamfering** (Fig. 657), **stuck stop moulding** (Fig. 658), **single moulding** (Fig. 659) or **bolection moulding** (Fig. 660). In the two last-named an almost endless variety of sections is in use. The treatment of the framework around the panels on the same side of the same door is of course similar. In outer doors, the thickness of the lower panels is frequently made equal to two-thirds the thickness of the door. In such a case one surface of the panel is flush with the surface of the framing. Figs. 661 and 662 show two methods of treating such a panel. In Fig. 661 the bead runs round the panel; this treatment is known as **bead flush**.

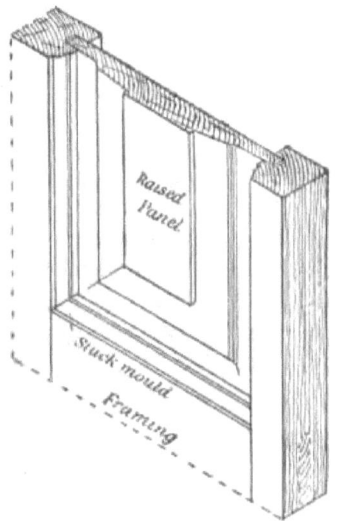

FIG. 663.—Solid-moulded Framing with Raised Panel.

If the vertical edges only of the panel are beaded, it is named **bead butt**. When the panel is thicker in the middle than at the edges, so that the middle part is above the general surface, it is known as a **raised** or **fielded panel**. Fig. 663 shows an example of a raised panel. The framework here shown is solid-moulded, that is, the mould is stuck on the arris of the framing, whereas in single moulding and bolection moulding the mould is "planted in" after the framing is put together. An important difference is necessary in the preparation of framing where the mould is to be stuck on the framing—as compared with square framing, which afterwards has the moulds planted in—because allowance has to be made, in the setting out and cutting of the shoulders of the tenons, for the depth of the stuck moulding. Moulds planted in are almost invariably **mitred** at the angles ; but with stuck moulds a better plan, wherever possible, is to **scribe** the joint.

Scribing consists of cutting the shoulders of the rails to the profile of the mould ; it allows slight shrinkage to take place without visible effect.

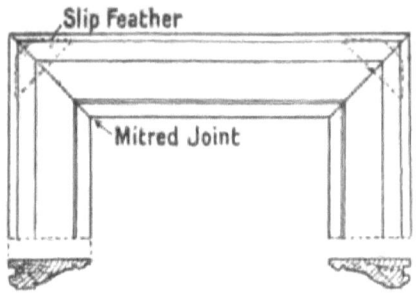

Fig. 664.—Method of securing the Mitred Angles of Moulding.

In general, when moulds are planted in framing, as either single or bolection moulds, they are **bradded**, that is, fixed by nails (brads) passing through the mould into the framing. As, however, the nail-holes are objectionable in superior framing, the moulds, if not stuck on the framing, are first mitred together with **slip feathers** at the angles (Fig. 664), and are provided with projecting tongues at the outer edges which fit into grooves prepared in the framing.

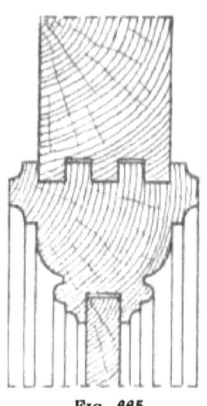
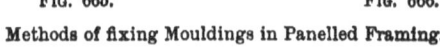
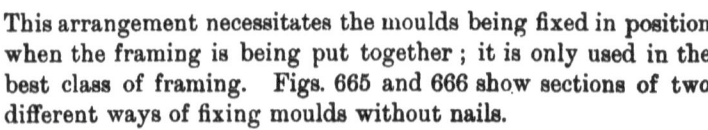

Fig. 665.   Fig. 666.

Methods of fixing Mouldings in Panelled Framing.

This arrangement necessitates the moulds being fixed in position when the framing is being put together ; it is only used in the best class of framing. Figs. 665 and 666 show sections of two different ways of fixing moulds without nails.

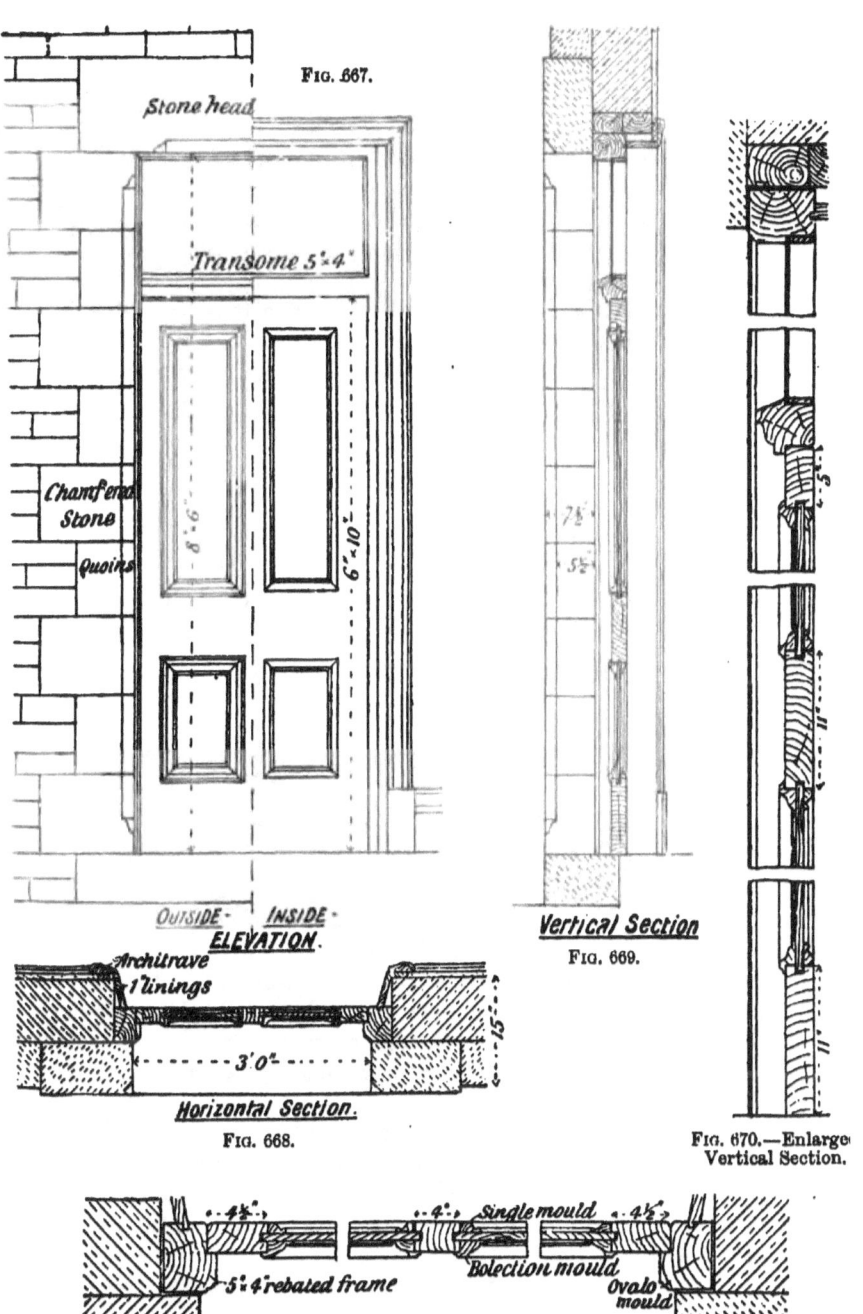

Fig. 671.—Enlarged Horizontal Section.

Details of a Four-panelled Outer Door in a Stone Wall.

Folding Doors.—When doors exceed 3′ 6″ in width, and are hung with hinges, it is often advisable to have them "hung folding," that is, to have the door in two parts—each a little more than half the width of the opening; the joint where they meet is rebated. The meeting styles are usually made a little narrower than the hanging styles. Figs. 680 and 687 show examples of such folding doors.

Double Margin Doors.—A double margin door (Fig. 673) is one which imitates a pair of folding doors but opens as a single door. It is made either as a single door having a very

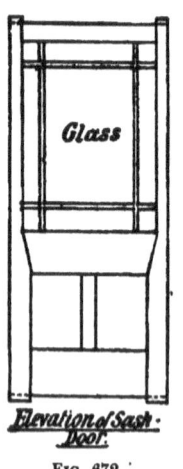

Fig. 672.

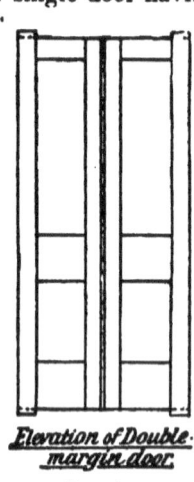

Fig. 673.

wide muntin, or as two narrow doors fastened together with hardwood folding wedges, and strengthened by wrought-iron bars, which are fixed into the top and bottom rails. In either case it has a bead running down the middle of the door. Such a bead is named a **double quirked** or **centre bead**. A double margin door is often used for improving the appearance of a wide low doorway.

Sash Doors.—Sash doors are those which have the upper part prepared for glass panels. The upper portions of the styles are generally narrower than the lower parts. Such styles are named **diminishing** or **gun-stock styles**. In the upper part of the door the framework is rebated to receive the glass; while in the lower part it is grooved to receive the wooden panels. To hold the glass in position, small moulded wooden

PANELLED DOORS.

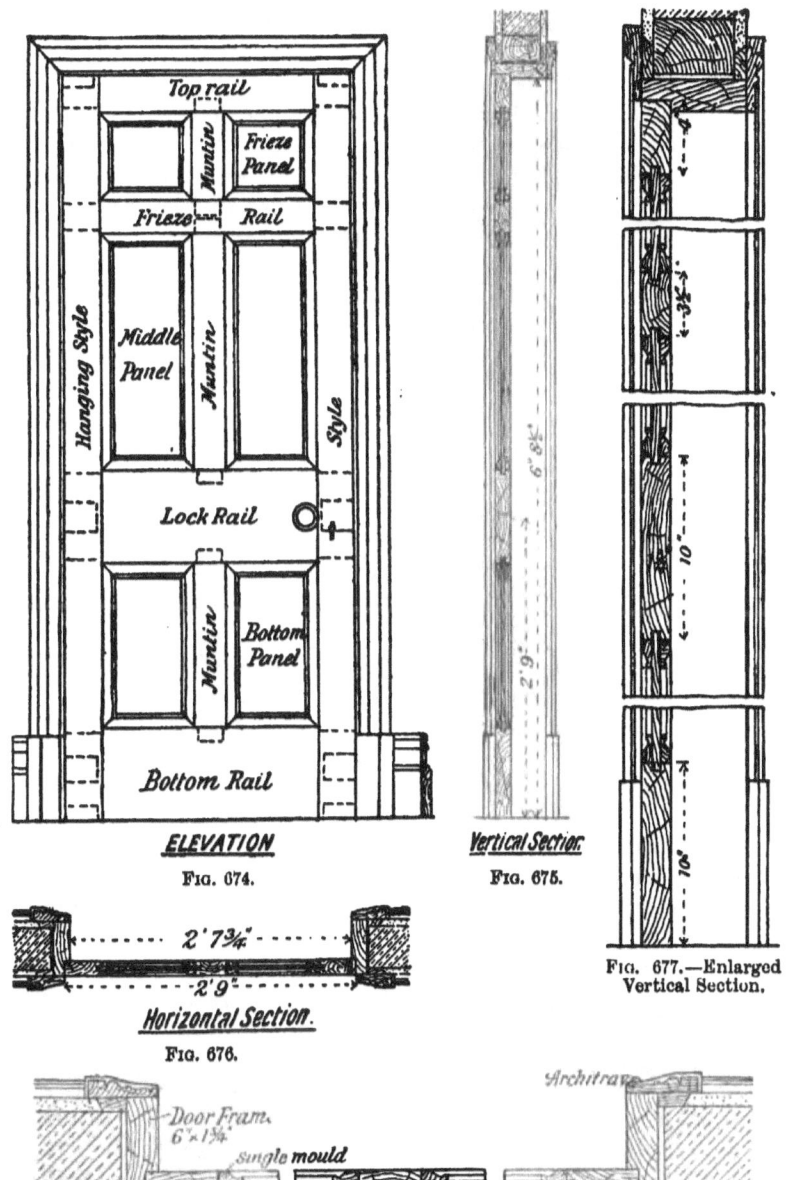

FIG. 674.—Elevation.
FIG. 675.—Vertical Section.
FIG. 676.—Horizontal Section.
FIG. 677.—Enlarged Vertical Section.
FIG. 678.—Enlarged Horizontal Section.
Details of a Six-panelled Inside Door in a 4½" Brick Wall.

fillets are bradded into the rebate in such a manner that they can easily be removed when it is necessary to replace broken glass.

Sash doors are in general use as the outer doors of shops; as inside doors wherever it is desirable either to have additional light or to see from one room to an adjacent room; and as vestibule doors.

A **vestibule** door is a door arranged in the hall or passage of a dwelling house or public building. It may consist of a sash door hung to a rebated frame, and have a width nearly equal to the width of the passage; it may have side-framing to match the door when the width of the passage is more than the width of the door, as illustrated in Fig. 691; or, as in the case of public buildings, it may consist of a pair of folding or swing doors with fixed sidelights and a fanlight above. The design, as well as the treatment of the framing, of such doors varies considerably, and is often of an ornamental character. Fig. 697 shows a pair of swing doors with fixed sidelights and fanlight; they are suitable for the entrance to a school, bank, hotel, or similar building having a wide entrance hall.

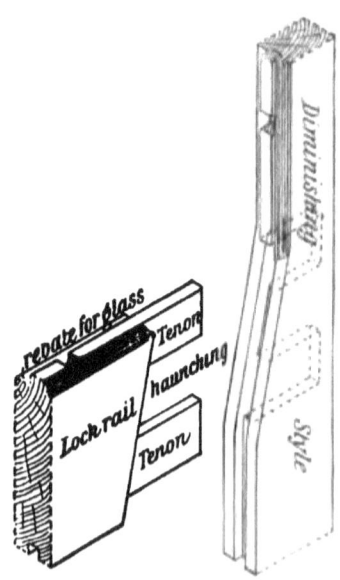

FIG. 679.—Joint between Lock Rail and Style of a Sash Door.

An arrangement of vestibule doors, suitable for banks, hotels, etc., is shown in plan in Fig. 685. The doors are arranged at right angles to each other, and revolve around a vertical axis like a turn-stile. Curved side frames, each a little wider than a quarter of a circle, are fixed on each side of the doorway. A suitable width for the doors is 3' 6". The advantages of such an arrangement is that it is noiseless and draughtproof, the latter feature being obtained by having an india-rubber tongue fixed in the outer edge of each door. The doors are so hung that alternate doors can be folded back against the adjacent

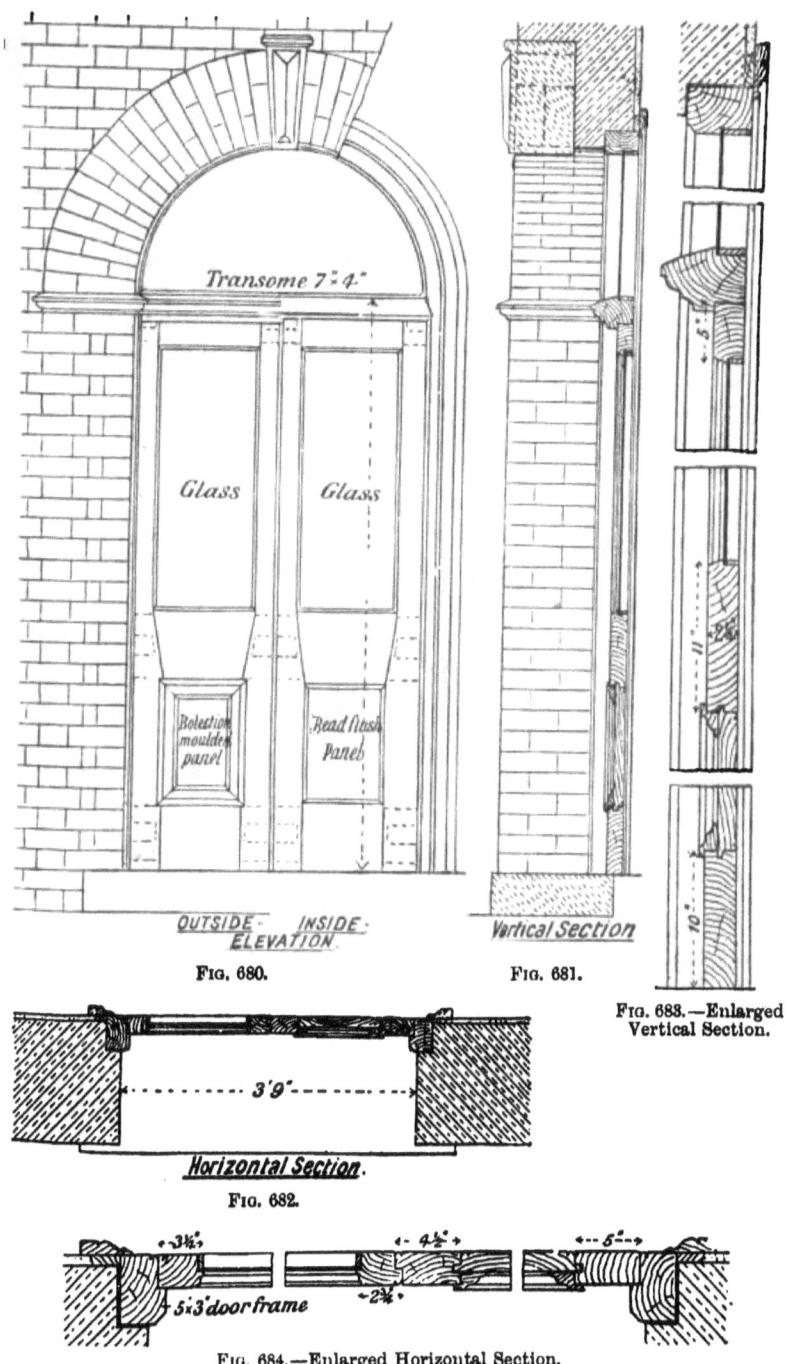

Fig. 680. — Outside / Inside Elevation. Transome 7' 4".

Fig. 681. — Vertical Section.

Fig. 683. — Enlarged Vertical Section.

Fig. 682. — Horizontal Section. 3' 9".

Fig. 684. — Enlarged Horizontal Section.

Details of a pair of Folding Doors (with Upper Panels of Glass) in an 18" Brick Wall.

362 A MANUAL OF CARPENTRY AND JOINERY.

ones (Fig. 686), and thus give an uninterrupted passage when required.

Other Panelled Framing.—Framework filled in entirely with wooden panels, or with wooden panels in the lower part and glass in the upper part, is also required in the fittings for offices, for school partitions, and for screens in churches, business premises, etc. The arrangement of the framing is similar to that of doors, and the same terms are used to describe the various parts, the only difference being the proportions of height and width; these are, of course, governed by special requirements. The setting-out of panelled framing is dealt with in Chap. XVII.

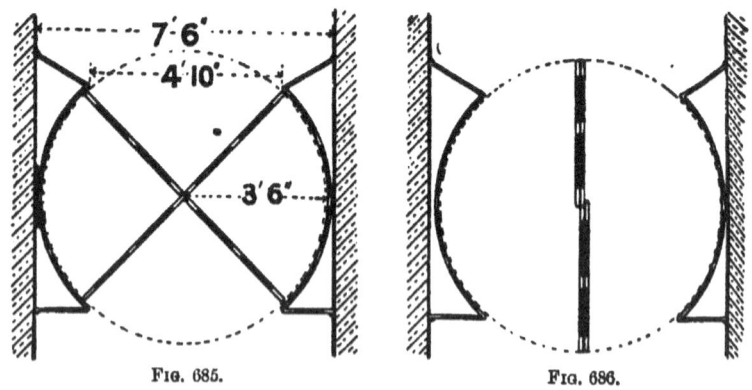

FIG. 685.   FIG. 686.
Plans of Revolving Vestibule Doors.

Superior Doors.—In superior work, where the doors and surrounding framework are made of ornamental hardwood, it is often necessary to construct a door which shall be of one kind of wood on one side of the door and an entirely different kind on the other side. This would be necessary, for example, with a door opening from an entrance hall fitted entirely with oak into a room, the fittings of which must all be of walnut or mahogany. Such a door may be constructed in two thicknesses, each of the respective kind of wood, and each of a thickness equal to one-half of that of the finished door. The two parts are then secured together by tapering dovetailed keys, and the edges of the door are afterwards veneered to match the side of the door to which they correspond. Figs. 701 to 703 give details of this kind of door.

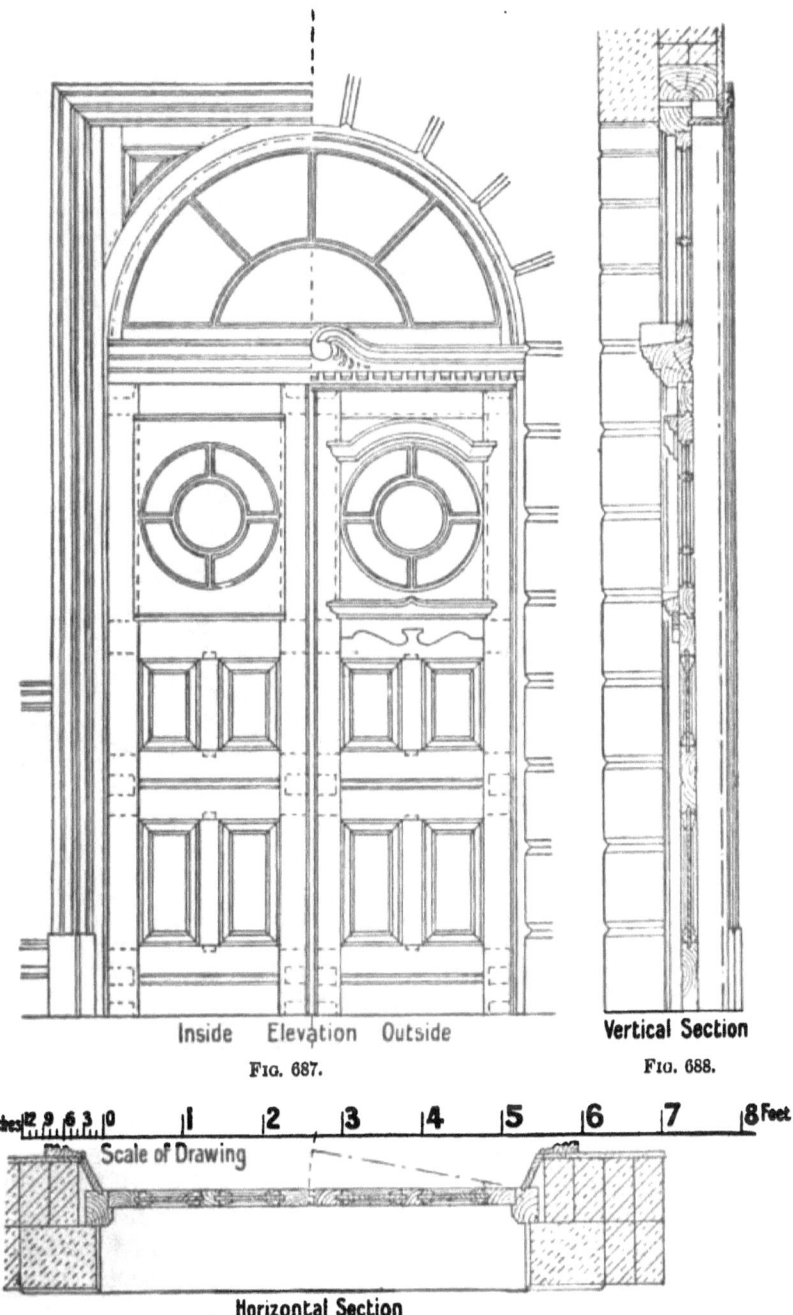

Fig. 687. Inside Elevation Outside
Fig. 688. Vertical Section
Fig. 689. Horizontal Section

Elevation and Sections of a pair of Superior Entrance Doors.

364 A MANUAL OF CARPENTRY AND JOINERY.

The doors of **cupboards**, and similar framing, being generally smaller, are made thinner and lighter than ordinary doors. They are arranged either as single doors or as a pair of doors hung folding, according to their width. With this exception, the construction and treatment of the framing do not materially differ from those already described.

A **jib door** is a door arranged in the side of a wall in such a manner that it is not readily seen. The surface of such a door

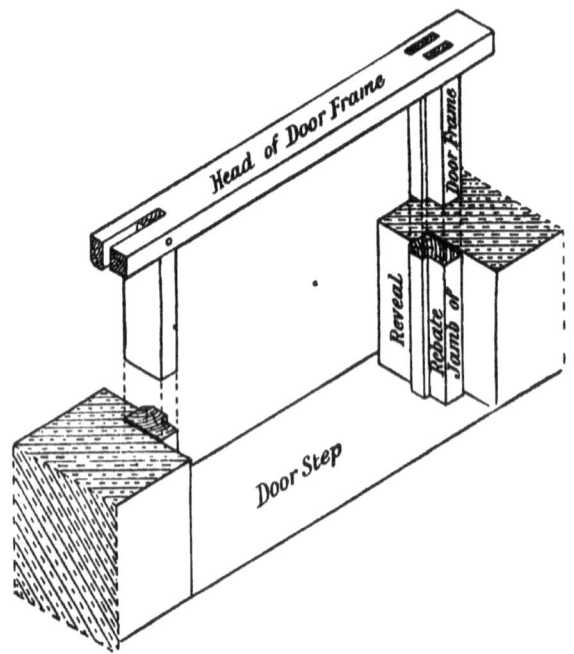

Fig. 690.—Door Frame fixed in Revealed Opening.

is flush with the wall surface, and is treated in the same way as the wall of the room. Its position can only be detected by a careful examination, as only the joints between the edges of the door and the wall are visible.

Door Frames.—There are many ways of fixing doors. An outer door for a dwelling-house has generally a **solid wooden frame**, which fits into the recess formed in the wall. This frame consists of two uprights named **jambs** and a cross piece or **head** into which the jambs are tenoned. As the door

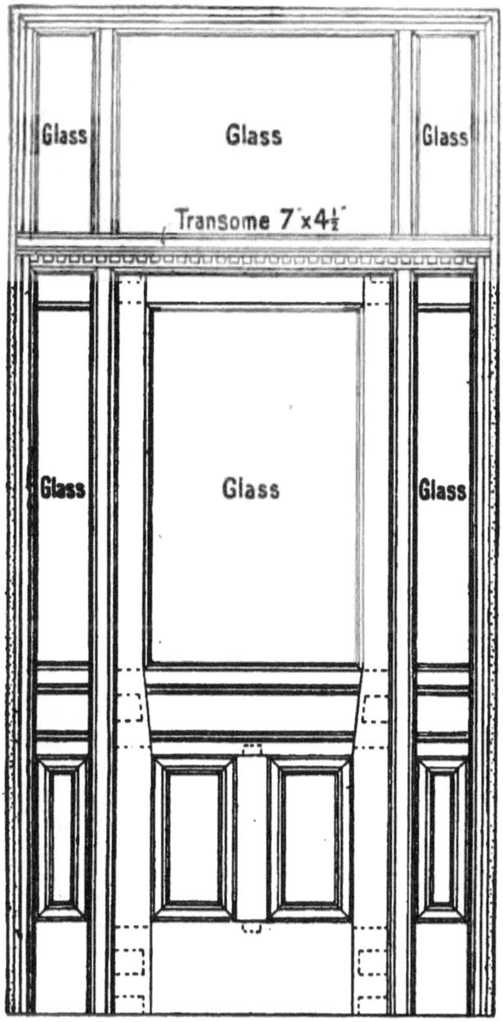

Elevation

FIG. 691.

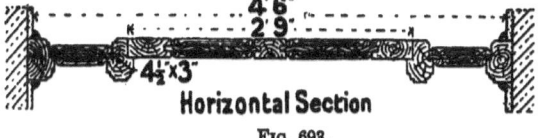

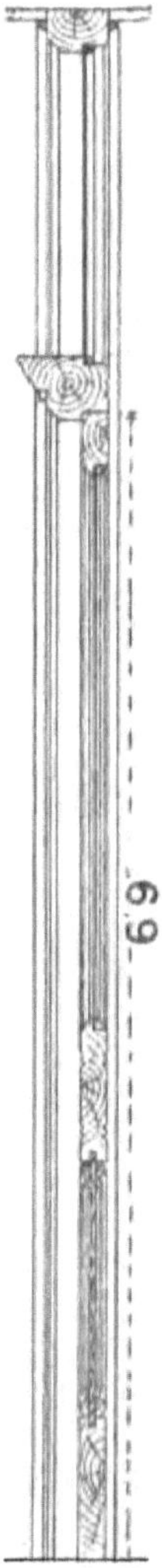

Vertical Section

FIG. 692.

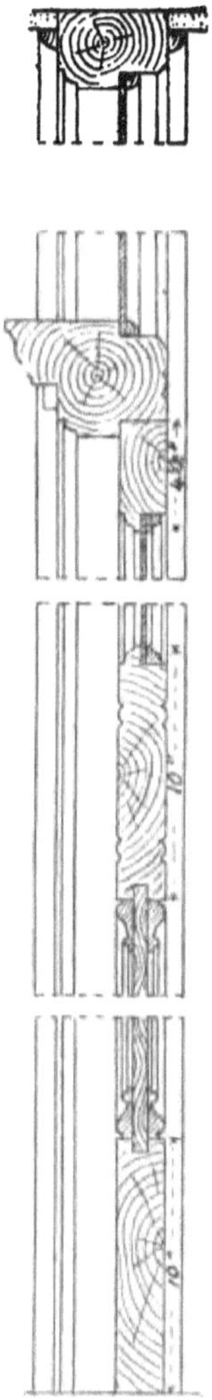

FIG. 694.—Enlarged Vertical Section.

Horizontal Section

FIG. 693.

Elevation and Sections of a Vestibule Door and Frame.

almost invariably opens inwards, the frame is rebated on the inner side to receive the door (Fig. 690). The door frame may either be built in as the brickwork proceeds, or it may be afterwards fixed by nailing it to **wooden bricks** or slips built into the wall; or the nailing may be to **wooden plugs** driven into the joints. If the doorway is of stone, as in Fig. 695, the frames are secured by means of iron holdfasts named **split-bills**, or by **rag-bolts** secured to the stone by lead or brimstone. The lower

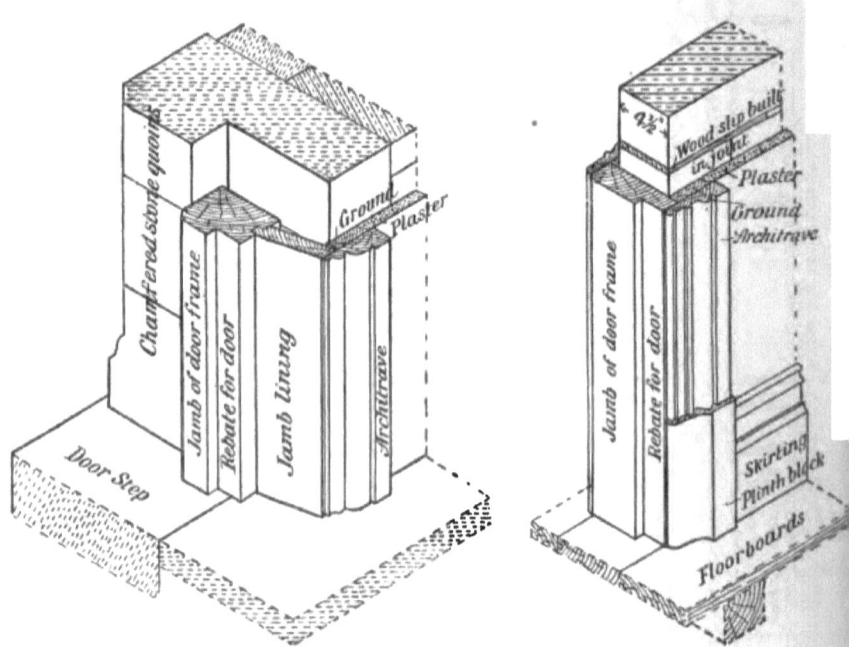

Fig. 695.—Sketch of lower part of Outer Door Frame, etc., fixed in Stone Wall.

Fig. 696.—Sketch of lower part of Door Frame fixed in a thin Inside Wall.

ends of the jambs may be secured additionally by **iron dowels**, which fit into holes in the doorstep; or they may be secured similarly to stone door-blocks, which are rebated and keep the door frame several inches above the step.

The doorway is often higher than the door, and a cross-rail called a **transom** is placed across the doorway at the height of the top of the door. Above this transom is a window called a **fanlight**. The fanlight may be simply a sheet of glass secured by fillets into the rebate of the door frame, or it may have

SUPERIOR PANELLED DOORS. 367

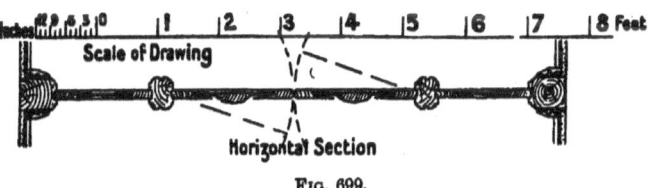

Elevation
Fig. 697.

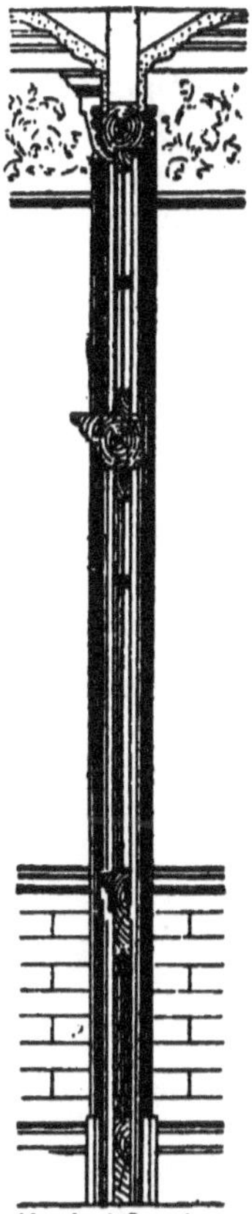

Vertical Section
Fig. 698.

Fig. 699.

Details of a pair of Vestibule Doors with Side-lights.

a separate frame hinged to the door frame so that it can be opened for ventilation. The outer arris of the door frame may be **chamfered** (Fig. 684), **beaded** (Fig. 695), or **moulded** (Fig. 700).

Linings.—The door frame is seldom of sufficient thickness of itself to come flush with the inside face of the wall, but usually requires to be supplemented by **linings**, *i.e.* by boards about an inch thick and wide enough to project beyond the inner surface of the wall for a distance of three quarters of an inch (the usual thickness of the plaster). The linings are tongued on one edge to fit into a groove in the door frame, and are generally **splayed**, that is, fitted at an oblique angle, as shown in Fig. 695. The joint between the lining and the plaster is covered with a mould, named according to its shape a **band mould** or **single architrave**, or a **double-faced architrave**. The architrave is fixed around the inside of door and window openings to give a finished appearance to the whole. When the wall is very thick, forming a deep recess, the linings, instead of being plain, wide boards, are framed, panelled, and moulded to match the door. Fig. 700 shows a horizontal cross-section through one side of a doorway, into which is fitted a door-frame with a panelled jamb-lining.

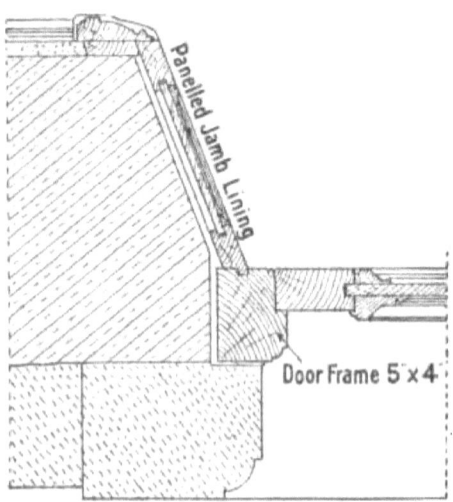

FIG. 700.—Horizontal Section through one side of an Outer Doorway in a thick Wall, showing Door Frame and Panelled Jamb Lining.

Inside Door Frames.—Inside doors require frames, the width of which is equal to that of the wall *plus* the thickness of the plaster on both sides. They are fixed to wooden fillets or to plugs, much as outer door frames are fixed. Fig. 696 is a sketch of a door frame for a half-brick-thick wall. In superior buildings having thick inside walls, the door frames are

SUPERIOR PANELLED DOORS. 369

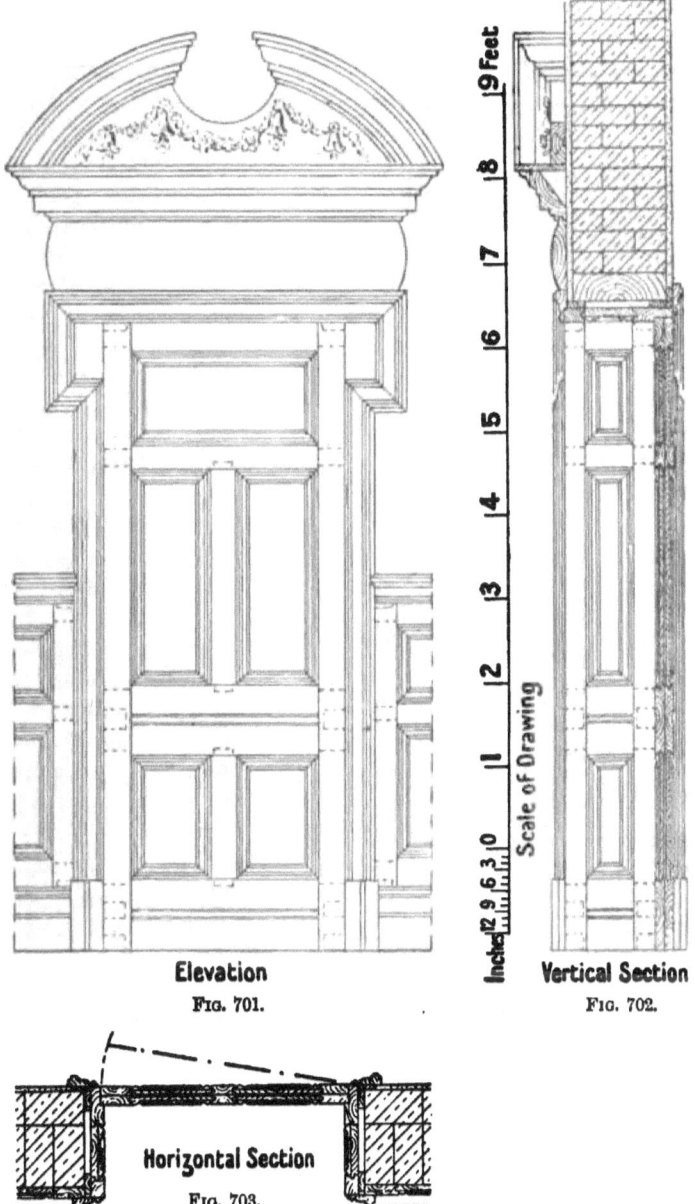

Elevation
Fig. 701.

Vertical Section
Fig. 702.

Horizontal Section
Fig. 703.

Elevation and Sections of a Superior Inside Door and Frame.
M.C.J. 2 A

panelled and moulded to match the door, and are rebated generally on both edges (Fig. 704).

Grounds.—The architraves surrounding an opening are nailed to the lining, or where possible to the frame. In the best class of work, however, it is usual not to fix the door frames until the plastering is finished. Rough wooden battens or **grounds**, of thickness equal to that of the plaster, are fixed to the walls around all door and window openings. These serve as a guide to the plasterer, and the door frames and the surrounding architraves are secured to them. When it is not desirable to have any nail holes visible in the finished surfaces, the door frames and architraves are fixed by screws.

The fixing of the architraves around such a doorway affords a good example of **fixing by secret screwing**.

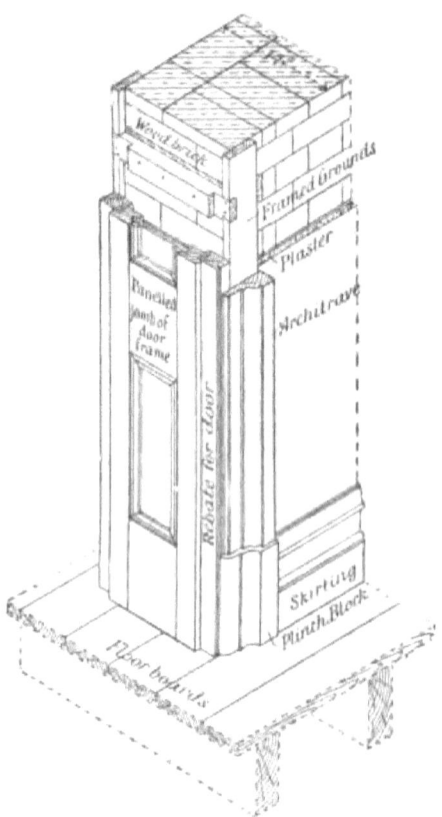

FIG. 704.—Sketch of lower part of Panelled Door Frame fixed in a 14″ Inside Wall.

The mitres of the architraves are first glued and secured with dovetail keys or slip feathers. Stout screws are turned into the grounds about 12″ apart, being left so that the head of the screw projects about half-an-inch in front of the surface. On the back side of the architrave, exactly opposite the screw heads, small holes—equal to the size of the *shanks* of the screws—are bored; and about three-quarters of an inch below these, larger holes—of size equal to the *heads* of the screws—are bored. Each small hole is connected to the large one adjacent to it by a slot, the depth of which is slightly greater than the projection of the screws. The architrave is fixed by placing it against the wall with the larger holes fitting on the screws, and then carefully driving it down so that the heads of the screws hook into the fibres behind the slots. By placing the screws so that they are slightly inclined, the tendency is to draw the architrave closer to the wall. Fig. 705 shows the explanatory detail.

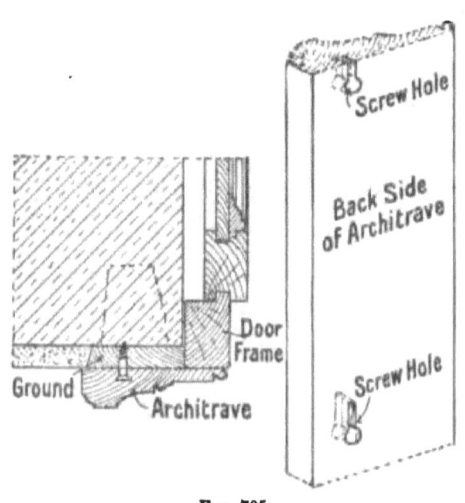

Fig. 705.

The above remarks upon door frames, linings, etc., apply especially to the doors of dwelling-houses. Door frames for warehouses, workshops, outbuildings, etc., do not as a rule require linings or architraves, a small fillet being nailed into the angle between the door frame and the wall instead. Vestibule doors are often hung to swing both ways, and the door frames have a hollow rebate or groove in the middle of the width of the frame, to receive the rounded edge of the door (Fig. 699). Many of the heavier kinds of framed and ledged doors are not provided with wooden frames, but are hung with bands and gudgeons, or arranged to run on pulleys as described below.

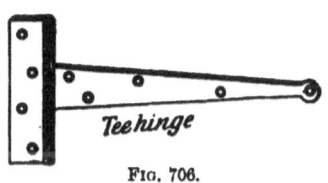

Fig. 706.

Hinges.—**Tee** or **cross garnet** hinges (Fig. 706) are used for the commoner kinds of ledged doors. They are screwed on the surface of the door and frame.

H and **HL** hinges (Figs. 707 and 708) are also hinges, used for special purposes, which are screwed on the surface.

Butt hinges (Fig. 709) are used for framed doors generally, two or three hinges being used for each door, according to its size and weight. Usually one-half of the hinge is let into the edge of the door, while the other half is let into the frame (Fig. 712). When the arris of either the door or the frame is

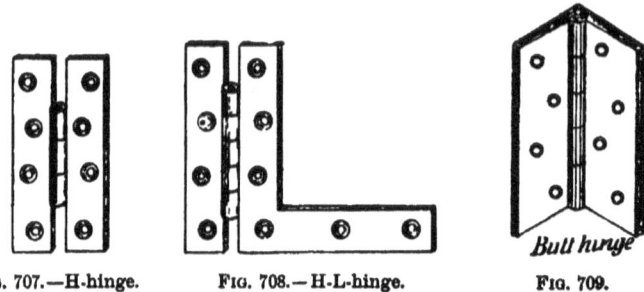

FIG. 707.—H-hinge.   FIG. 708.—H-L-hinge.   FIG. 709.

beaded, it is desirable to have the "knuckle" of the hinge in line with the bead. In this case the hinge is let in, as shown in Fig. 711. Butt hinges are of cast iron, wrought iron, steel, or brass; they are secured by screws.

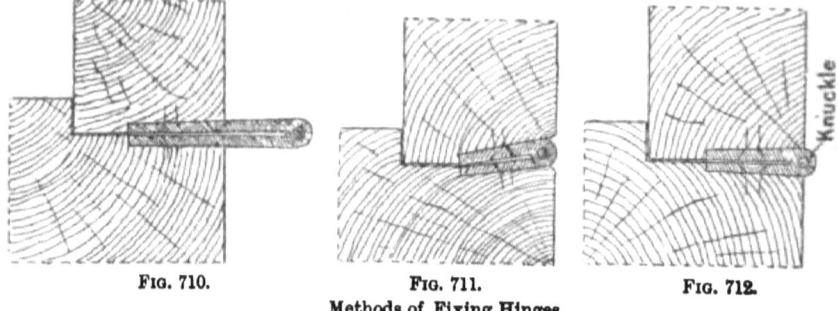

FIG. 710.   FIG. 711.   FIG. 712.
Methods of Fixing Hinges.

Rising butt hinges (Fig. 713) have a helical knuckle joint which causes the door to rise upon being opened. They are generally used when the floor is irregular, and a door hung with ordinary butts would not open without rubbing on the floor or carpet.

Projecting butt hinges (Fig. 714) are used when the door has to open quite back and to clear an architrave or other projection. The method of fixing is shown in Fig. 710.

Parliament hinges (Fig. 715) are another kind of hinge, a little stronger than projecting butts. They are used for the

Fig. 713 —Rising Butt Hinge.

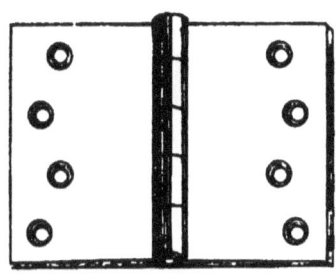

Fig. 714.—Projecting Butt Hinge.

same purpose, and for shutters—fixed in revealed openings—which are required to open clear of the reveal.

Pew or **egg-joint** hinges (Fig. 716) are a type of projecting hinge used, as the name implies, for the pew doors of churches,

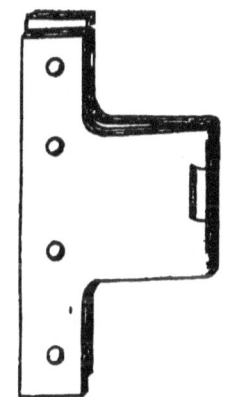

Fig. 715.—Parliament Hinge.

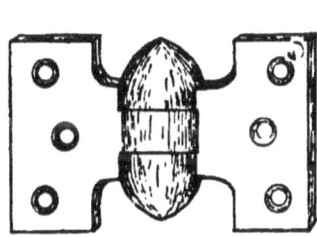

Fig. 716.—Pew or Egg-joint Hinge.

etc. The projection allows the door to fold back clear of any projecting moulding.

Back-flap hinges (Fig. 717) are somewhat similar to projecting butts, but are lighter in make. Whereas butt hinges are generally screwed on the edge of the door or framing, the back-flap hinge is usually screwed on the surface. Boxed window-shutters with rebated joints (Fig. 792), are usually hung together with back-flap hinges. These hinges are also used for hingeing

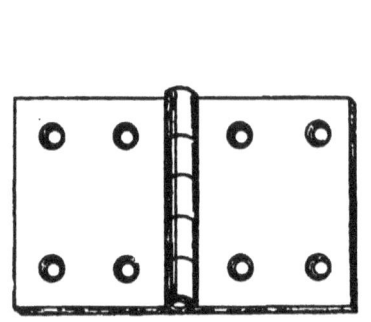

Fig. 717.—Back-flap Hinge.

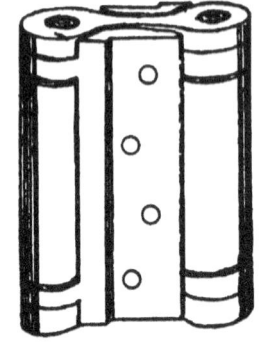

Fig. 718.—Helical Spring Hinge.

together the framing required to fold round an angle. When the joint is arranged as in Fig. 793, it is called a **rule joint.**

Spring hinges.—Spring hinges are often used when it is desirable to have a self-closing door. The **helical hinge** (Fig. 718) affords a good example of a spring hinge for screwing on

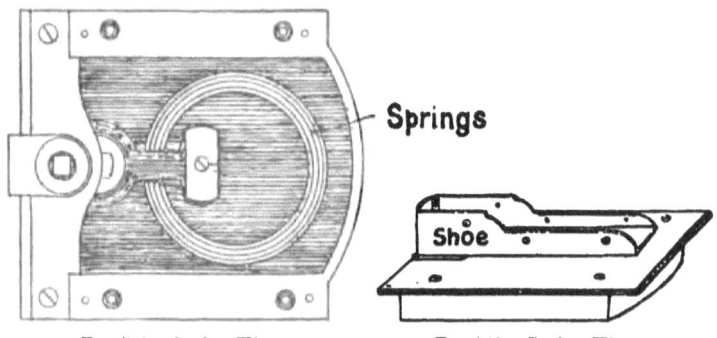

Fig. 719.—Spring Hinge.   Fig. 720.—Spring Hinge.

the edge of a door. One only of the hinges on each door contains a spring, the other being known as a *blank hinge*. Such hinges are single or double according to whether the door closes into a rebate or swings both ways. Other types of spring hinges, especially applicable for vestibule doors which are to

BANDS AND GUDGEONS.

swing both ways, are those which are let into the floor and contain mechanism in the shape of springs which are acted upon when the door is opened (Fig. 719). A shoe (Fig. 720) is fitted on the bottom corner of the door; this fits on a pin which acts upon the springs in the box. A centre-pin holds the upper end of the door in position.

Bands and gudgeons.—For the heavier kinds of framed, ledged, and braced doors, stronger hinges are required than those above described. These hinges, which are made of

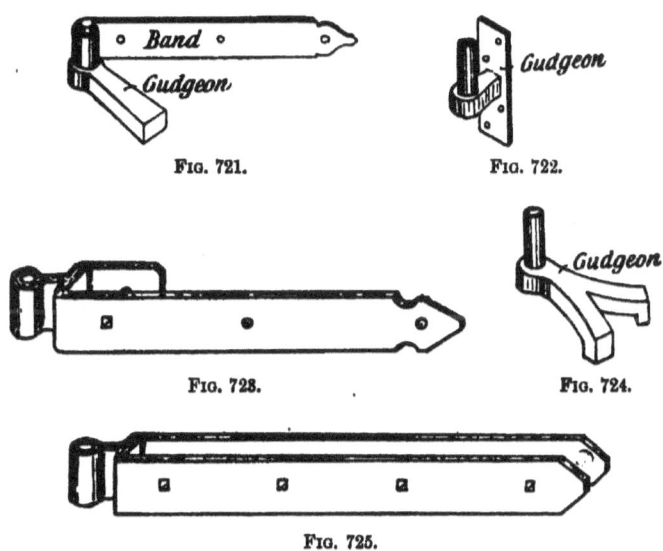

Types of Band and Gudgeon.

wrought iron, are known as **bands** and **gudgeons** or as **hook and eye** hinges. The gudgeon has a projecting pin upon which the band swivels. This allows of the door upon which the bands are screwed or bolted being easily detached from its swinging position. The gudgeons may be so made that they can be screwed to the frame (Fig. 722), although in the heavier kinds of doors the frame is dispensed with, and the gudgeons are so shaped that they can be fixed securely by lead or brimstone to large *gudgeon stones* built into the wall. Figs. 721 and 724 show two different shapes of gudgeons for stones. The bands may be as single straps bolted to one side of the

376 A MANUAL OF CARPENTRY AND JOINERY.

door (Fig. 721), or they may be made to clip the door, in which case they will be shaped as shown in Figs. 723 or 725. They may be plain, or they may be of an ornamental shape (Fig. 653). The size of such hinges differs widely and depends upon the size and weight of the door.

Sliding Doors.—When the door is a very large one, or where space will not allow conveniently of a hinged door to open

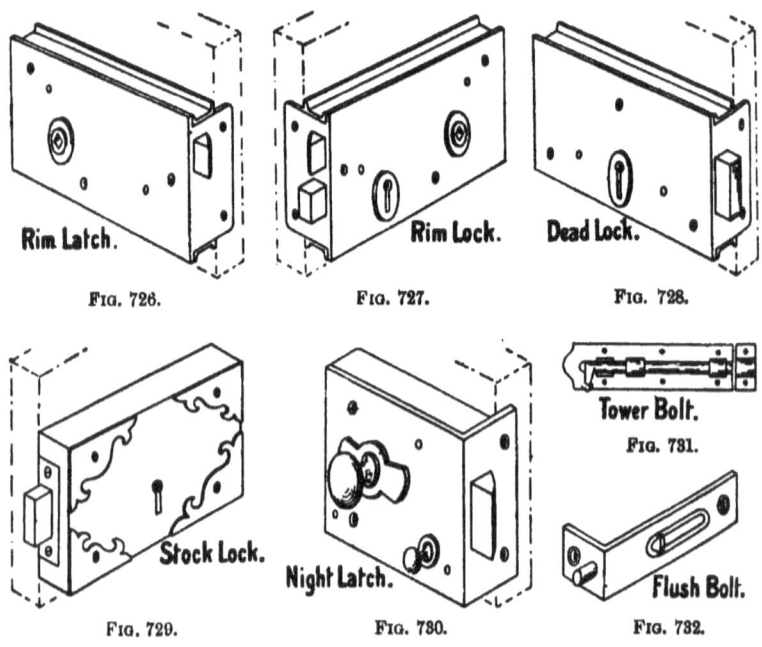

Types of Door Fasteners.

radially, the door may be made to slide by means of pulleys running upon an iron bar. The pulleys may be placed either at the top or at the bottom of the door. The door may slide in a slot constructed in the middle of the thickness of the wall, or it may slide on the outside surface, or be arranged to slide against the inner face of the wall as is most convenient. Fig. 649 shows a door fitted with pulleys at the upper end.

Fastenings.—The fastenings for a door comprise **thumb latches, rim latches, bars, bolts, locks,** etc. To enumerate these in detail would be beyond the scope of this book, as they vary

DOOR FASTENINGS.

considerably. It should be remembered, however, that careful selection of the door-fastenings is necessary to obtain good results. Figs. 726 to 733 illustrate different locks, latches, and other fastenings with their distinctive names appended. It will be noticed that a rim latch differs from a lock in that it is self-fastening, and is released by turning the knob. A rim lock is a latch and lock combined in the same case. The best locks are fitted with levers. These levers are kept in position by springs, and require to be raised to different heights to allow the bolt to slide. The more levers a lock contains, the more difficult it is to open it with any key which has not been fitted to it. Many locks contain pivoted weights instead of levers. It has already been mentioned that a mortise lock is so called because it is fixed into a mortise made in the edge of the door. Mortise latches and locks are always used in superior work.

FIG. 733.—Mortise Lock.

Summary.

Doors are classed as *ledged, ledged and braced, framed ledged and braced,* and *panelled.* The two last-named consist of frames filled in with thinner battens and panels respectively.

The **mortise and tenon** joint is used in the construction of framed doors. The **tenon** is *bare-faced, haunched, stump,* or *double,* according to its position in the door.

The **battens** of "framed and ledged" and "ledged" doors have either *tongued and grooved, ploughed and tongued,* or *rebated* joints. The edge joints of the battens are *beaded* or *V-jointed.*

The **frame** of a door consists of *styles, rails, braces* (in ledged and braced doors), and *muntins* (in panelled doors).

Panelled framing is finished *square and flat, stop-chamfered, single moulded, bolection moulded, bead flush, bead butt,* or *raised (fielded).*

Folding doors are used for wide doorways.

A **double margin** door is one door made to imitate folding doors.

Sash doors have the upper panels of glass.

The joints and general treatment of panelled doors are also applicable to other kinds of panelled framing.

Door frames.—Outer doors are hung to solid rebated frames fixed in reveals in the wall. *Linings* are required when the door frame is not as wide as the recess. *Inside* door frames must be wider, by the thickness of the plaster, than the thickness of the wall. *Architraves* surround the inner sides of outer doorways and both sides of inner doorways. *Grounds* fastened to the wall by wooden plugs are necessary for securing wide architraves.

Hinges.—*Tee* hinges, *butt* hinges, *spring* hinges, and *bands and gudgeons* are commonly used for hanging doors.

Heavy doors are often hung to large gudgeon-stones by means of bands and gudgeons, or are constructed to slide with pulleys. Wooden frames are then not required.

Questions on Chapter XIII.

1. Give the ordinary dimensions of various kinds of door, with the sizes of the following parts of a common four-panel door: styles, top rail, middle rail, bottom rail, muntin; also state the proper height of the middle rail to suit the handle or lock. (C. and G. Ord., 1894.)

2. Draw in isometrical projection, quarter full size, the mortise and tenon to the bottom rail of a 2-inch door, the parts being separated. (C. and G. Prel., 1897.)

3. Make detailed drawings of the following:
   (1) Framing moulded on the solid, with raised panel.
   (2) Bead and butt panel.
   (3) Bead and flush panel.
   (4) An arrangement for fixing moulding in squared framing panelled. No nails or screws are to be visible when the work is finished. (C. and G. Ord., 1902.)

4. Make an elevation and sections of a 2-in. framed, braced, and battened door, 3 ft. 3 in. by 6 ft. 6 in.; show all construction by dotted lines. Scale 1½ in. to the foot. State in what situation such a door would be most suitable. (C. and G. Ord., 1901.)

5. Draw plan and elevation to ½ in. scale of framed, ledged, and braced door, in two heights, with fanlight over and solid fir wrought, rebated and beaded frame in opening 4 ft. by 9 ft. (C. and G. Ord., 1897.)

6. Make the elevation of rather more than half of a six-panelled door, 7 ft. high and 3 ft. 2 in. wide; and a vertical section, scale 1 in. to the foot. All the parts should be fully dimensioned. Make to scale ½ full size a detailed section through the panel and moulding. (C. and G. Ord., 1898.)

QUESTIONS ON CHAPTER XIII.

7. Make isometric drawings of the joint at the lock-rail of the door in the preceding question (6), and also of the joint at the bottom rail of the door, with double tenons. (C. and G. Ord., 1898.)

8. Make elevation, horizontal, and vertical sections of a 2 in. 6-panelled door, 7 ft. high and 3 ft. 5 in. wide, with framed jamb linings and raised panels, moulded on the solid, grounds and architraves. All construction to be shown in dotted lines. The thickness of the wall is 27 in. Describe how you would make and fix this door and fittings, presuming all to be first-class work. (C. and G. Hon., 1902.)

9. Give detail drawings, and describe how you would make and fix a set of plain jamb linings, grounds and architraves for an internal doorway. Thickness of wall, 14 in. (C. and G. Ord., 1904.)

10. Draw plan and elevation to ½ in. scale of a pair of 2¼ in. folding doors, each leaf five-panel bolection moulded, with raised (or fielded) panels. Size of opening 6 ft. by 7 ft. 6 in. (C. and G. Ord., 1897.)

11. Show the linings and finishings, with details of grounds and backings, necessary to the above door (Q. 10) in a 14 in. wall. (C. and G. Ord., 1897.)

12. Make detailed drawing, scale ¼ full size, of the joints of a 2 in. sash door, 6 ft. 6 in. high and 3 ft. wide. The styles are to be diminished, and one prepared for a lock. The upper portion of the door is to be moulded and rebated for glass. (C. and G. Ord., 1902.)

13. A door, such as that referred to in the foregoing question, is to be hung in a solid frame 3½ in. by 4½ in. Make a drawing of this frame and describe how you would make it in a shop without machinery. (C. and G. Ord., 1902.)

14. Draw to a scale of one inch to a foot, plan, section and elevation of a pair of 2½ in. swing doors, 5 ft. 6 in. wide, upper part framed for glass, bolection moulded below, and hung to solid frame. (C. and G. Ord., 1895.)

15. Draw rather more than half the horizontal section through an internal doorway, wall 1 ft. 6 in. thick. Show framed jamb-linings, grounds and architrave, and the method of fixing same. The door to be 2 in. thick, with raised panels and mouldings. Scale 3 in. to 1 ft. (C. and G. Ord., 1900.)

16. A front doorway to a mansion is 7 ft. 6 in. wide and 9 ft. 6 in. high. Design a frame and door for this opening. The door is required to be double margined with a fanlight over it. Make

rather more than half elevation, and the necessary sections. All details are to be shown by dotted lines. (C. and G. Hon., 1901.)

17. A screen 15 ft. wide and 10 ft. high is required for a public office. It is to be fitted with a door 3 ft. by 6 ft. 9 in., and to be made of mahogany, and well finished. Draw as much of the elevation as is necessary to show the construction, and give details. Describe the process of manufacture in a good workshop well provided with machinery. (C. and G. Hon., 1900.)

CHAPTER XIV.

WINDOWS.

Size and Position.—The sizes and positions of window openings are influenced by the size of the rooms, and the purposes for which the building is used. For the sake of ventilation, and also to secure good lighting, the windows should be placed at as great a height as the construction of the room will allow. In dwelling-houses the height of the sill is usually about 2' 6" above the inside floor level.

Construction.—The framework holding the glass of the window may be fixed or movable. It must be so prepared that the glass can be replaced easily when necessary. In warehouses, workshops, and similar buildings, the frames holding the glass are often fixed as **fast sheets** (Fig. 734). As however, this arrangement affords no means of ventilation, it is more usual to have the glass fixed in lighter frames called **sashes**. If the sashes are hung to solid rebated frames, and open as doors do, the windows are called **casement sashes**. If they slide vertically and are balanced by weights or by each other, the window is a **sash and frame window**. Other methods of arranging sashes, either hinged, pivoted, or made to slide past each other, are described in detail later.

Sashes.—The terms used for the various parts of sashes and fast sheets are somewhat similar to those employed in describing doors. Thus, the **styles** are the outer uprights, and the **rails** are the main horizontal cross-pieces: *top rails, meeting rails,* and *bottom rails* being distinguished. Any intermediate members, whether vertical or horizontal, are named **bars**.

Sashes are from 1½ to 3 inches thick. The inner edge of the outer face is **rebated** to receive the glass. The inner face is left

382   A MANUAL OF CARPENTRY AND JOINERY.

either square, chamfered, or moulded; two common forms of moulding are *lamb's-tongue* (Fig. 736) and *ovolo* (Fig. 737).

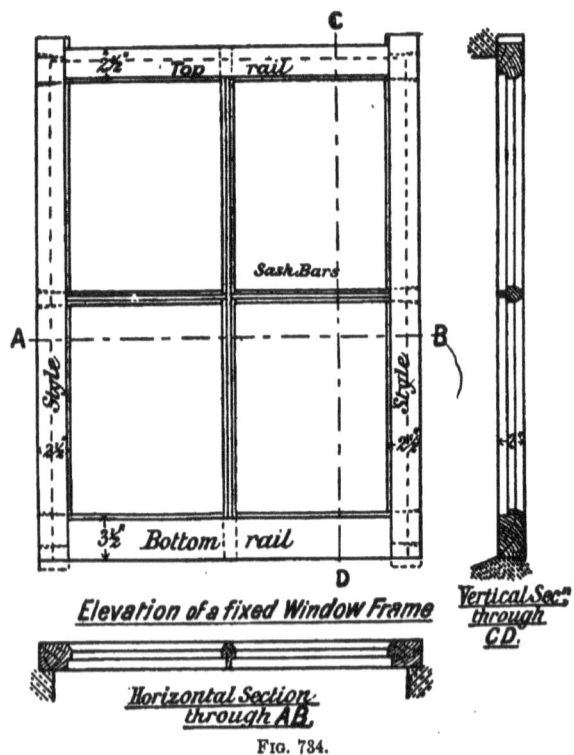

FIG. 734.

The size of the rebate is indicated in Fig. 735; it varies with the thickness of the sash, its depth being always a little more

FIG. 735.   FIG. 736.   FIG. 737.   FIG. 738.
Alternative Sections of Sash Framing.

than one-third this thickness. The width of the rebate varies from a quarter of an inch to half an inch, and the mould is usually sunk the same depth as the rebate. This last fact is of some importance, as it affects the shoulder lines; and with

WINDOWS. 383

hand work it influences the amount of labour in the making of the sashes.

As little material as possible is used in the sashes, in order that the light shall not be interfered with. In general, the styles and top rail are square in section before being rebated and moulded. In casement sashes, however, it is often advisable to have the outer styles a little wider than the thickness, especially when they are tongued into the frame. The width of the bottom rail is from one and a half to twice the thickness of the sash. Sash bars, which require rebating and moulding on both sides, should be as narrow as possible, in order not to interrupt the light. They are usually from five-eighths of an inch to one and a quarter inches wide.

Joints of Sashes.—The sashes are framed together by means of the **mortise and tenon joint** (Fig. 739). The remarks made on p. 348 respecting the proportions of the thickness and width of tenons, haunched tenons, etc., are to a large extent applicable here also. Hardwood cross-tongues are sometimes inserted to strengthen the joints (Fig. 302), while thick sashes should have **double tenons** (Fig. 782). The best joint for connecting sash bars is shown in Fig. 740; this method is known as **halving.** An alternative to halving in sash bars is to arrange that the bar which is subjected to the greater stress—as for example, the vertical bars in sliding sashes, and the horizontal bars in hinged casement sashes—shall be continuous; this continuous bar is mortised to receive the other, which is scribed, *i.e.*, cut to fit the first, and on which the short tenons are left. This method is called **franking the sash bars**, and is illustrated in Fig. 741.

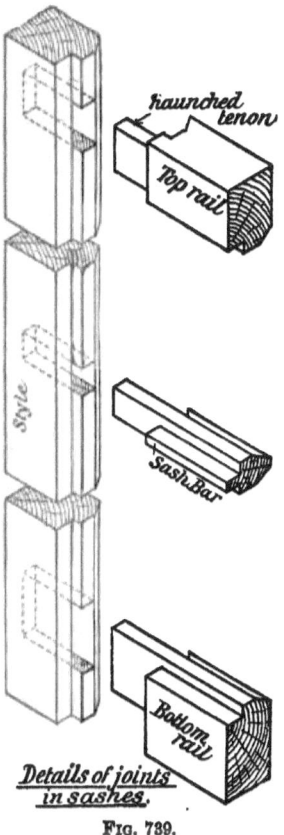

Details of joints in sashes.

FIG. 739.

Casement Windows.—Casement windows may be hinged in such a manner that they open either inwards or outwards. They may consist either of one sash, or of folding sashes, and are hung with butt hinges to solid rebated frames. These frames consist of jambs, head, and sill. The head and sill "run through," and are mortised near the ends to receive tenons formed on the ends of the jambs. The upper surface of the sill is weathered to throw off rain water. Casement windows which reach to the floor are usually called **French casements.** Their sashes require an extra depth of bottom rail.

Casement Sashes opening Inwards.—Figs. 742 to 745 show the elevation and vertical and horizontal sections, of a window opening in a 14" brick wall fitted with a casement

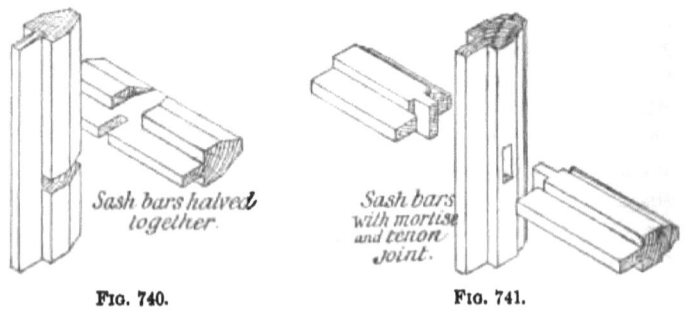

FIG. 740.   FIG. 741.

window having folding sashes to open inwards. In this class of window the frame is rebated for the sashes on the inner side. Each sash has, on the outer edge of the outer style, a semi-circular tongue, which fits into a corresponding groove in the jamb of the frame. This tongue renders the vertical joint between the sash and frame more likely to be weather proof; it is to provide for the tongue that the extra width of style already referred to is necessary. The tongue, however, is often omitted, as in Fig. 746. It will be seen readily that, if the sash were in one width, it would be impossible to have a tongue on more than one edge of it. With casement sashes opening inwards, the greatest difficulty is found, however, in making a water-tight joint between the bottom rail of the sash and the sill of the frame. Figs. 746 and 747 show two methods by which this may be accomplished. An essential feature of all these sashes is a small groove or

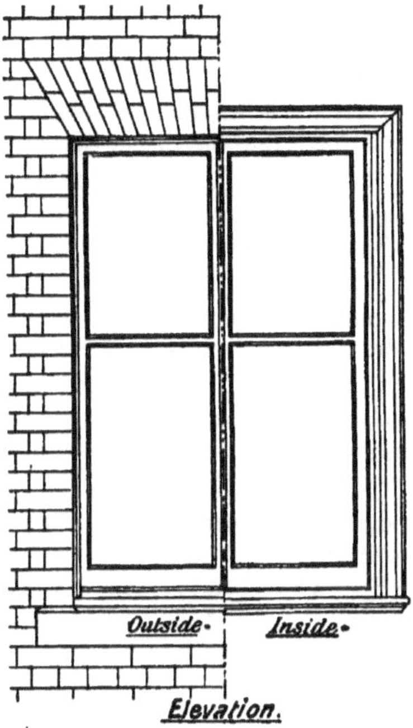

Outside.
Inside.
Elevation.

FIG. 742.

Vertical Section

FIG. 743.

2¼"
½"
4"
Enlarged Vertical Section.

FIG. 744.

2¼"
4½×3"
2"
2"
2¼"
Enlarged Horizontal Section.

FIG. 745.

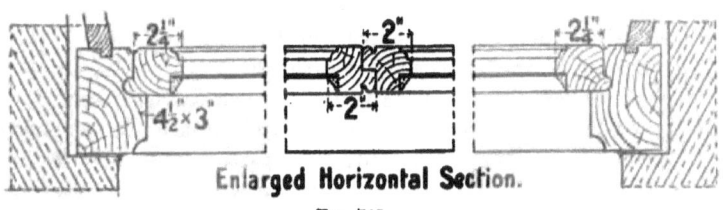

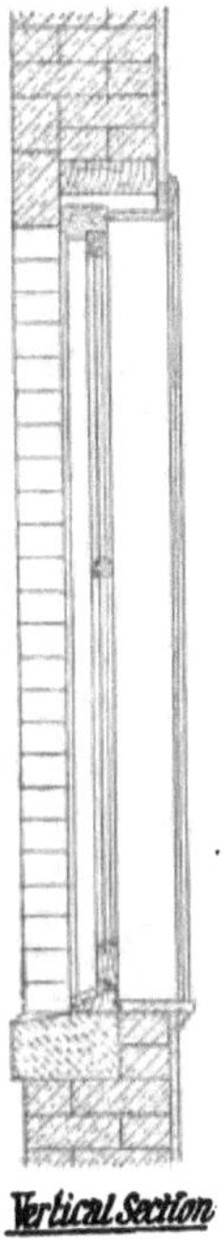

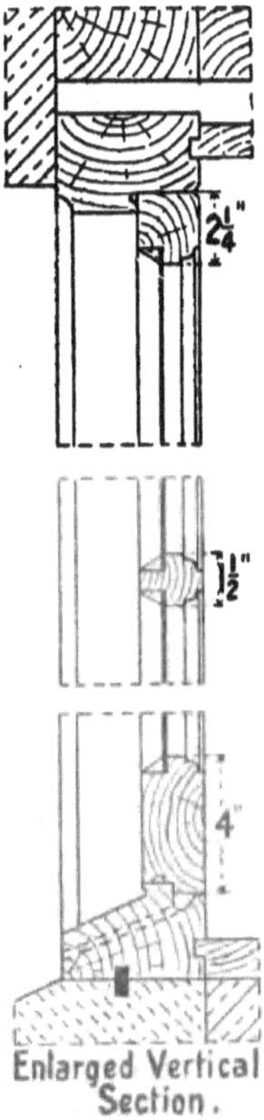

Details of a Casement Window with Sashes opening inwards.

throating on the under edge of the bottom rail; this prevents the water from getting through. The groove in the rebate of the sill (Fig. 747) is provided to collect any water that may drive through the joint. This water escapes through the hole bored in the centre of the sill.

When casement sashes are hung after the manner of folding doors, the vertical joint between the meeting styles is rebated. Alternative methods of rebating are shown in Figs. 748 and 749. Fig. 749 is known as a **hook joint** and is the better one.

Casement Sashes opening Outwards.—These are more easily made weather proof than inward-opening sashes. The chief objections to their adoption are that they are not easily accessible for cleaning the outside, especially in upper rooms, and that they are also liable, when left open, to be damaged by high winds and to let in the rain during a storm. Fig. 750 is a sketch of one corner of such a window. It will be noticed that these frames, like door frames, have the exposed arrises moulded in various ways, and that the sashes may either be hung flush with one face of the frame, as in Figs. 745 and 746, or fit in the thickness of the frame (Figs. 747 and 750). The sill in Fig. 749 is shown to be **double sunk**, *i.e.* to have the upper surface—upon which the bottom rail of the sash fits—rebated with two slopes (weatherings).

Other Hinged Sashes.—Various different methods of arranging—in solid rebated frames—sashes which can be opened for purposes of ventilation, etc., though they may be in positions difficult of access, are shown in Figs. 751 to 754. Fig. 751 is the elevation of a window, the lower sash of which is fixed in the frame, the upper sash being hinged on the bottom rail to open **inwards**. The bottom rail is rebated to fit the **transom** (the intermediate horizontal member of the window frame); the upper side of the transom is weathered and double sunk, as shown in enlarged section (Fig. 752). Such an arrangement is also applicable to a fanlight over a door, where the sash may be made conveniently to fit into the rebate of the door-frame. Fig. 754 is a section through a similar window with the sash hung on the top rail. A sash so hung must of necessity open **outwards**, to keep out the rain, etc.

Pivoted or Swing Sash.—Another method of arranging the sash is shown in section in Fig. 753. Here the sash swings on iron pins or **pivots** (Fig. 797). The pivots are placed a little

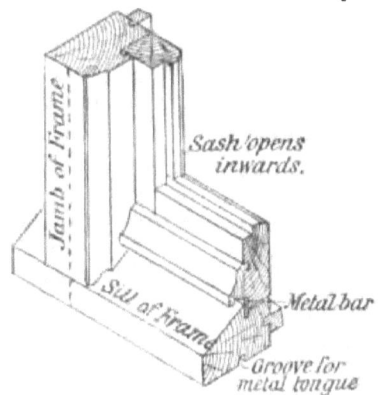

Fig. 746.

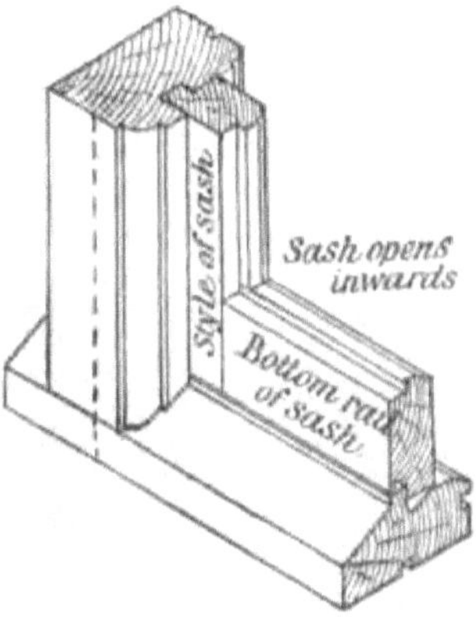

Fig. 747. 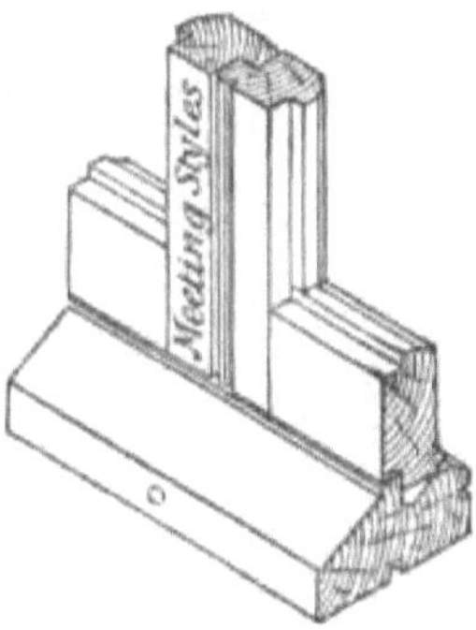 Fig. 748.

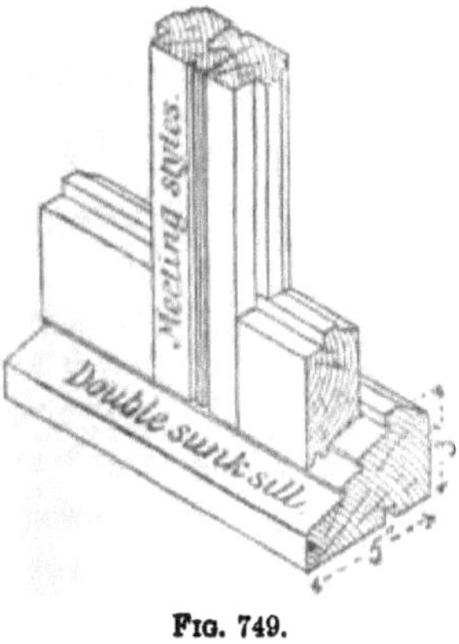

Fig. 749. 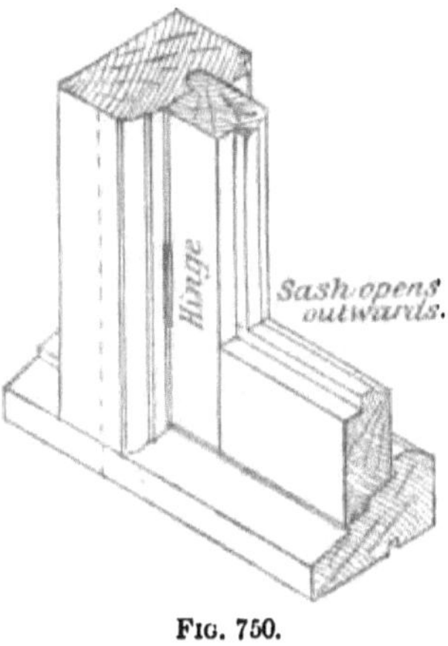 Fig. 750.

Sketches showing Alternative Methods of arranging Casement Sashes in the Frames.

above the middle of the sash, so that the lower part (which always swings outwards) is heavier than the upper. This facilitates the closing of the window. The rebate on the lower part of the frame must of necessity be inside, and the rebate of the upper part must be outside. To secure uniformity of

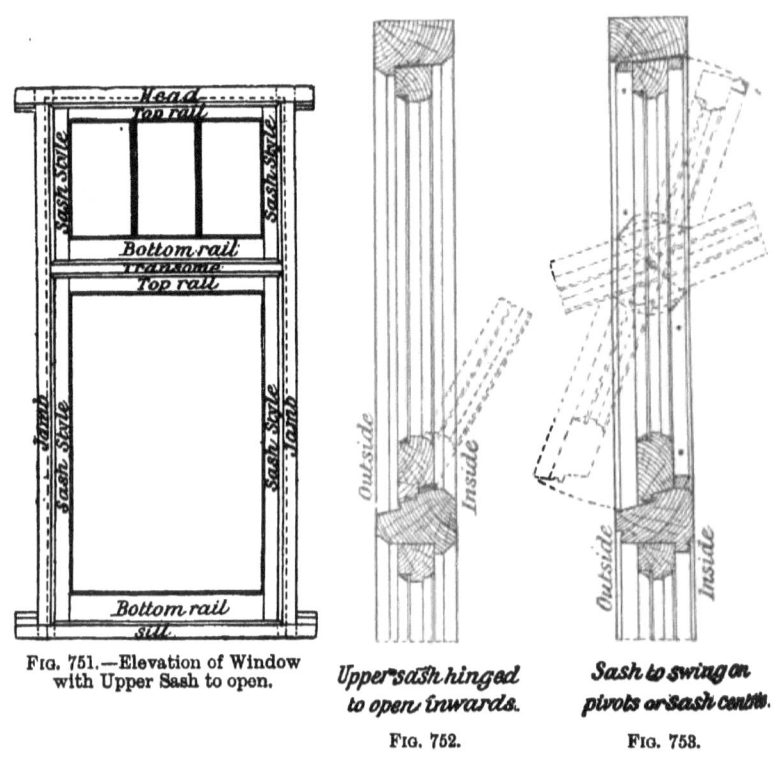

FIG. 751.—Elevation of Window with Upper Sash to open.

Upper sash hinged to open inwards.
FIG. 752.

Sash to swing on pivots or sash centres.
FIG. 753.

Alternative Sections through Upper Sash of Fig. 751.

appearance, a bead is run round the sash along both styles and top rail, and on each side of the sash. It is therefore necessary to have the lower part of the outside bead, and the upper part of the inside bead, *fixed to the sash*. These points will be clear from a careful inspection of Fig. 753. Occasionally the styles of the sash and the jambs of the frame are rebated "out of the solid." This, however, involves increased labour, and is seldom done.

SASH AND FRAME WINDOWS.

Sashes Sliding Horizontally.—It is often necessary to have two sashes fitted into a solid frame so that one or both of the sashes may slide horizontally. The sashes are constructed in the ordinary way, and are often provided with metal shoes or pulleys at the bottom corners, to enable them to slide smoothly. Figs. 755 to 757 are the elevation and two sections of this type of window arranged for both the sashes to slide. If only one sash slides, and the other sash is fixed, the window is sometimes called a **Yorkshire light**. Such windows are often used as basement windows. The glass doors of show-cases in shops are commonly constructed to slide in this manner.

Sash and Frame Window.—In this class of window, which is by far the most common, because it is easily made weatherproof, there are **two sashes**, which slide past each other in vertical grooves, and are usually balanced by iron or leaden **weights**. As will be seen from Fig. 760 the frames form cases or boxes in which the weights are suspended. They are hence called **cased frames**. **Pulley styles** (Fig. 765) take the place of the solid rebated jambs of casement windows. The pulley styles, **outside** and **inside linings**, and **back lining** (Fig. 760) together form a box which is subdivided by a vertical **parting slip** suspended as shown in Fig. 760. In superior window frames of this kind, the pulley styles and linings are tongued and grooved together as shown in Fig. 761. In commoner work the tongues and grooves are often omitted. The frame must be so constructed that the sashes can be removed easily for the purpose of replacing broken sash-lines. To enable this to be done, the edge of the inside lining is either made flush with the face of the pulley style (Fig. 761), or it is rebated slightly as shown in Fig. 774. The edge of the outside lining projects for a distance of about three-quarters of an inch beyond the face of the pulley style, to form a rebate against which the outer (upper) sash slides.

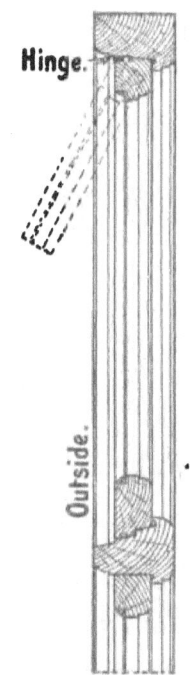

FIG. 754.—Upper Sash hinged to open outwards.

390 A MANUAL OF CARPENTRY AND JOINERY.

The outer sash is kept in position by the **parting lath** (Fig. 760) which fits into a groove in the pulley style. The groove for the inner (lower) sash is formed by the parting lath and a **staff bead** or **stop bead** which is secured by screws. The staff bead on the sill is often made from two to three inches deep, to allow the lower sash to be raised sufficiently for ventilation

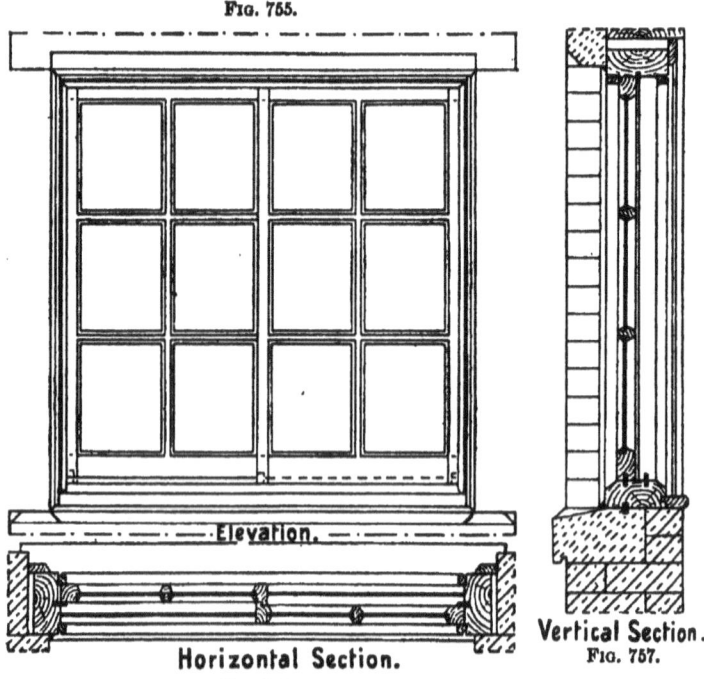

Fig. 755.

Elevation.

Horizontal Section.
Fig. 756.

Vertical Section.
Fig. 757.

Details of a Window with Sashes sliding horizontally.

at the meeting rails without causing a draught at the bottom (Fig. 791).

A vertical section through the head of the frame is similar to a horizontal section across the pulley style, except that the back lining and parting slip are of course absent (Fig. 759).

The sill of the frame is solid and weathered, and should always be of hardwood, preferably oak or teak. The sill has a width equal to the full thickness of the frame. When the weathering has two steppings, it is known as a **double**

SASH AND FRAME WINDOWS. 391

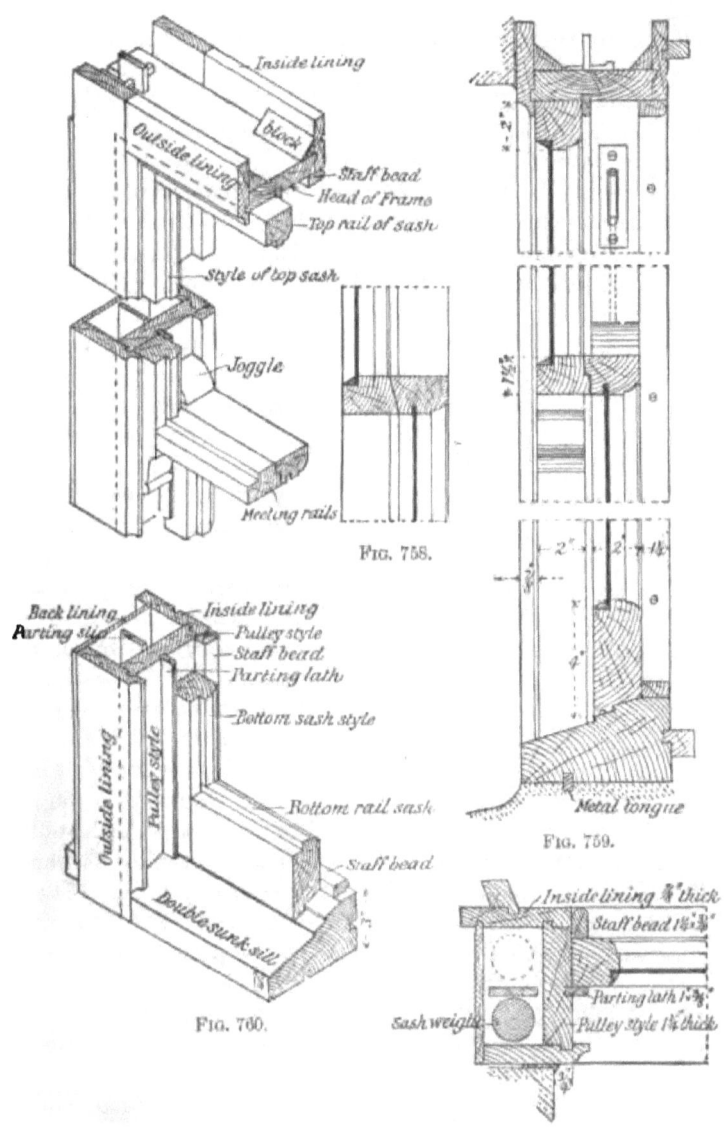

Fig. 758.
Fig. 759.
Fig. 760.
Fig. 761.

Details of a Sash and Frame Window.

sunk sill. An alternative to the plan of having the width of the sill the full thickness of the frame, is to arrange it so that the outside edge is flush with the outside face of the bottom sash, as shown in Fig. 762. With a sill arranged in this manner, and double sunk, there is less danger of water driving through the joint between the sash and the sill than with a sill the full thickness of the frame. In order to render watertight the joint between the wooden and stone sills of window frames, a metal tongue is often fixed into corresponding grooves cut into the under side of the wooden sill and the upper surface of the stone sill. A rebated joint between the two sills serves the same purpose as the metal tongue.

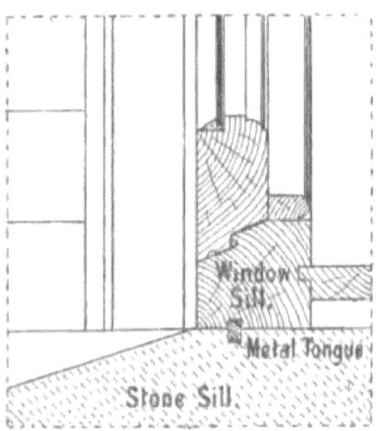

FIG. 762.—Section through the lower part of a Sash and Frame Window.

Fig. 765 shows the methods of fixing the pulley style into the head and sill respectively, when the width of the sill is equal to the full thickness of the frame. The **pulleys** on which the sash lines run—sash or axle pulleys (Fig. 800)—are fixed in mortises near the upper ends of the pulley styles. It is also necessary to have a removable piece in the lower part of each pulley style, to allow of access to the weights. This piece is named the **pocket piece.** It may be cut as shown in Fig. 764 ; its position is then behind the lower sash, and it is hidden from view when the window is closed. Or, the pocket piece may be in the middle of the pulley style as shown in Fig. 763 ; the vertical joints between the pocket piece and the pulley style are then **V**-shaped to prevent damage to the paint in case of removal.

Sashes.—The only difference between the joints of sliding sashes and those of the casement sashes already described is in the construction of the meeting rails. Each of the meeting rails is made thicker than the sash to the extent of the thickness of the parting lath ; otherwise there would be a space between them

SASH AND FRAME WINDOWS.

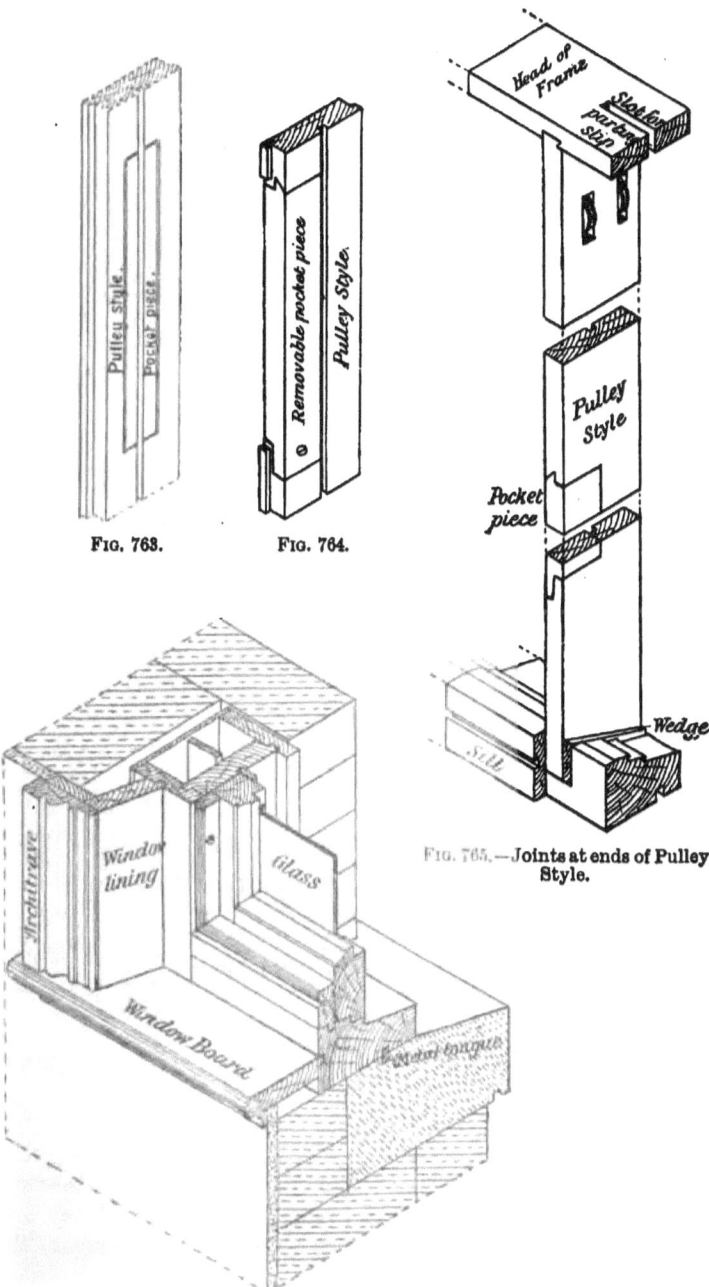

Fig. 763.

Fig. 764.

Fig. 765.—Joints at ends of Pulley Style.

Fig. 766.—Sketch of one corner of a Sash and Frame Window.

equal to the thickness of the parting lath. The joint between them may be rebated (Fig. 759) or splayed (Fig. 758). The

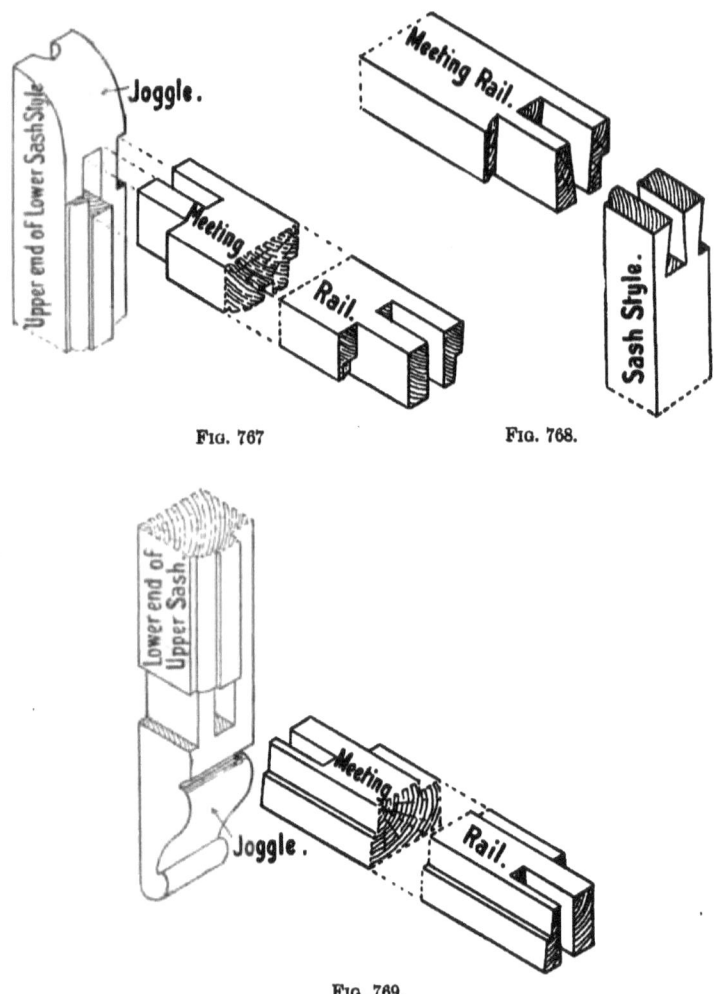

Fig. 767. Fig. 768.

Fig. 769.

Details of Joints of Sashes.

angle joints between the ends of the sash styles and the meeting rails are often dovetailed as shown in Fig. 768. They are, however, stronger if the styles are made a little longer, the projecting part being moulded, and mortise and tenon joints used as shown in Figs. 767 and 769. The projecting ends of the

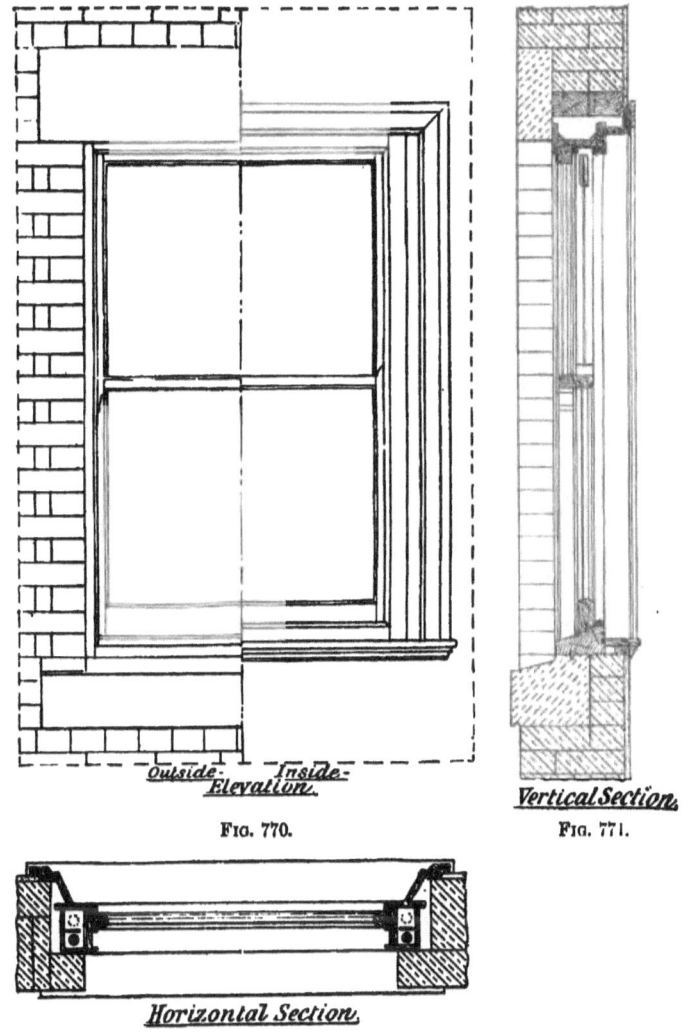

Fig. 770. — Outside Elevation. Inside Elevation.

Fig. 771. — Vertical Section.

Fig. 772. — Horizontal Section.

Elevation and Sections of a Sash and Frame Window, fixed in a 14 in. Brick Wall.

styles are called **joggles**; they assist in enabling the sashes, especially in wide windows, to slide more freely. When, as is usually the case, both sashes slide and are balanced by weights, the window is known as a **double-hung** sash and frame window. If one sash only slides, and the other is fixed in the frame, the window is **single-hung**. Figs. 770 to 772 show the details of a sash and frame window fixed in a one-and-a-half-brick-thick wall and having a stone head and sill.

For the sake of appearance, or when it is required to have wider windows than can be arranged with one pair of sashes, two or three pairs of sashes are often constructed side by side in the same frame. When three pairs of sashes are used, it is usual to have the middle pair wider than the others; such a combination (Fig. 773) is named a **Venetian window**. The vertical divisions between adjacent pairs of sashes are called **mullions**. These mullions may be constructed in several different ways. If the middle pair of sashes only is required to slide, the mullions may be solid, from $1\frac{1}{4}''$ to $2''$ thick, and the sash-cord conducted by means of additional pulleys to the boxes, which are at the outer edges of the frame. Figs. 775 and 777 show this arrangement. If it is desirable to have all the sashes to slide, the mullions must be hollow to provide room for the weights. Figs. 776 and 778 show details of a mullion with provision made for one weight to balance the two sashes adjacent to it. With this arrangement the sash-cord passes round a pulley fixed into the upper end of the weight. If stone mullions are used in the window opening, separate boxings may be made so that each pair of sashes is hung independently as shown in Fig. 774, and the window becomes, as it were, two or three—as the case may be—separate window frames, with the sill and head each in one length for the sake of strength.

Hospital Lights.—A type of window specially suitable for hospitals, and also much used in schools and other buildings, is shown in Fig. 779. It consists of a sash and frame window in the lower part, with, in the upper, a hinged sash hung on the bottom rail to open inwards. By opening this upper sash, ventilation without draught is obtained at the highest part of the window.

The Hanging of Vertical Sliding Sashes.—As shown in numerous illustrations already given, the sashes of sash and frame windows are balanced by cast-iron or leaden weights. The best hempen cord is employed for hanging sashes of ordinary size, while for very heavy sashes the sash lines are

SASH AND FRAME WINDOWS. 397

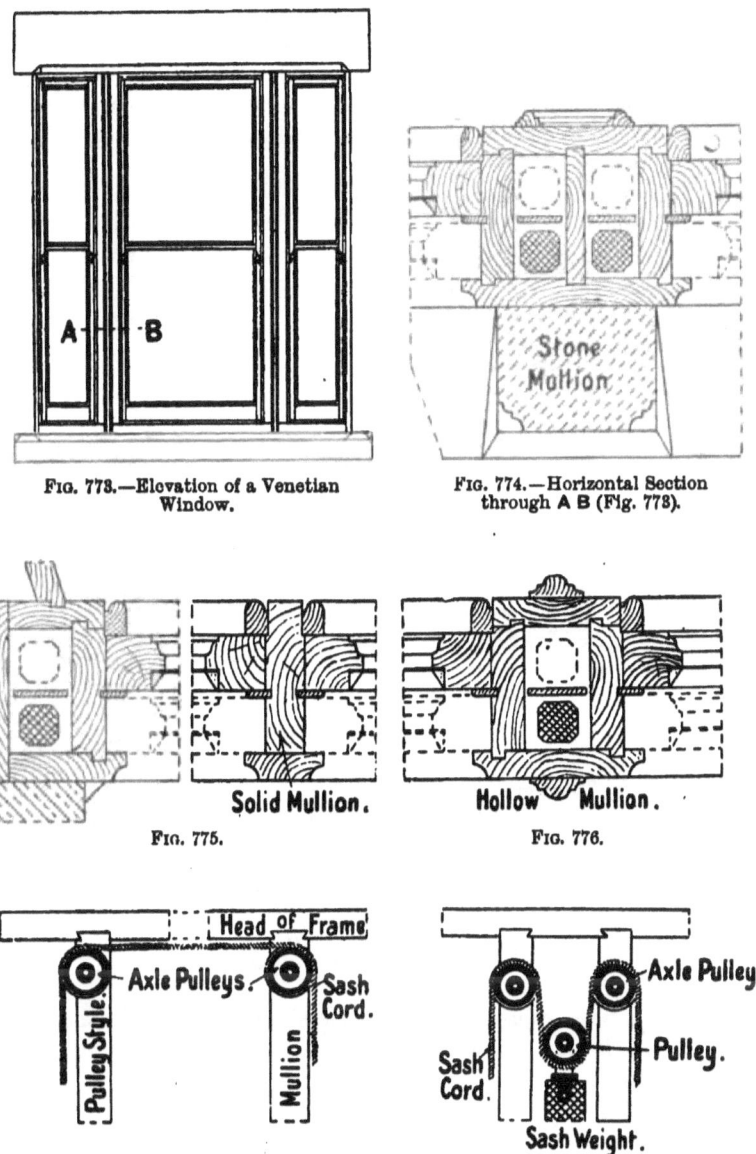

Fig. 773.—Elevation of a Venetian Window.

Fig. 774.—Horizontal Section through A B (Fig. 773).

Solid Mullion.   Hollow Mullion.

Fig. 775.   Fig. 776.

Fig. 777.   Fig. 778.

Alternative Sections through A B (Fig. 773), with details of hanging arrangements.

398 A MANUAL OF CARPENTRY AND JOINERY.

often of steel or copper. The staff bead and parting lath having been removed, the cords are passed over the axle pulleys (which are best of brass to prevent corrosion) and are tied to the upper ends of the weights. The weights are passed through the pocket holes and suspended in the boxes. The pocket pieces

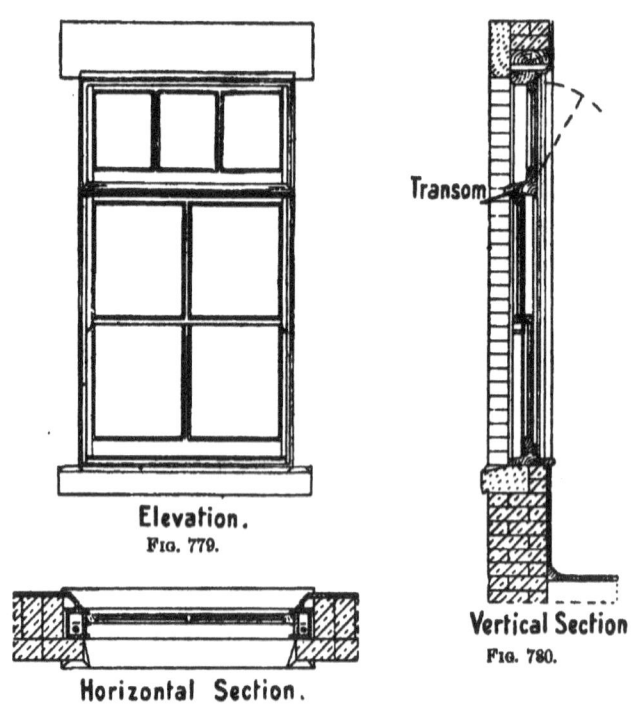

Elevation.
FIG. 779.

Horizontal Section.
FIG. 781.

Vertical Section
FIG. 780.

Elevation and Sections of a Window with Vertical Sliding Sashes in the lower part, and Hinged Sash above.

having been replaced, the upper sash, which slides in the outer groove, is hung first, the free ends of the cords being either nailed into grooves in the outer edges of the sash (Fig. 783) or secured by knotting the ends after passing them through holes bored into the styles of the sash (Fig. 782). The upper sash having been hung, the parting laths are fixed into the grooves in the pulley styles, and the lower (inner) sash is hung in a similar manner, after which the staff beads are screwed in position. Care should be taken to have the cords of the right lengths: if the cords for the upper sash are too long the weights will touch the bottom of the frame, and cease to balance the weight of the sash before the latter is closed. If the cords for the lower sash are too short, the weights will come in contact with the axle pulleys, and thus prevent it from closing. Several different devices for hanging sashes—the objects of which are either to render unnecessary the use of weights or to facilitate the cleaning of the outside of the window—have been patented,

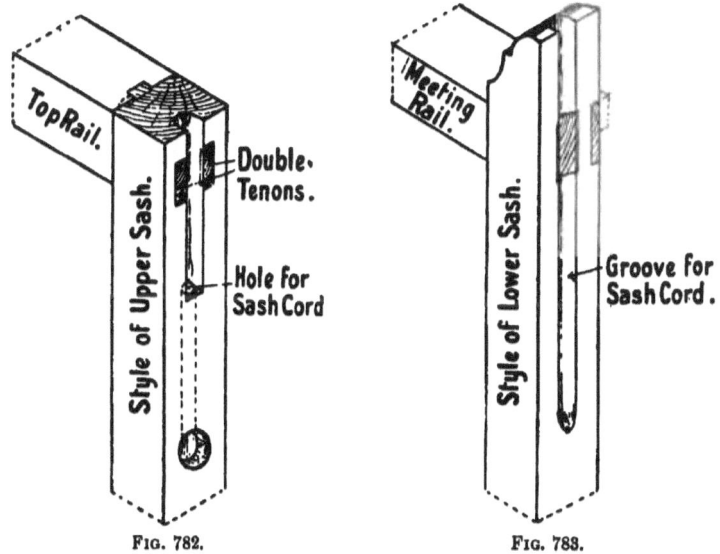

FIG. 782. FIG. 783.
Methods of fixing Sash Cords in Vertically Sliding Sashes.

and are in more or less general use. A detailed description of these is, however, beyond the scope of this book.

Bay Windows.—A bay window is one that projects beyond the face of the wall. The side lights may be either splayed or at right angles to the front. The window openings may be formed by having stone or brick mullions or piers at the angles, against which the window frames are fixed, or the wooden framework of the window may be complete in itself. When the latter is the case, it is usual to have stone or brick work to the sill level, as shown in Fig. 784. Bay windows naturally lend themselves to decorative treatment. With the

Front Elevation.
FIG. 784.

Vertical Section.
FIG. 785.

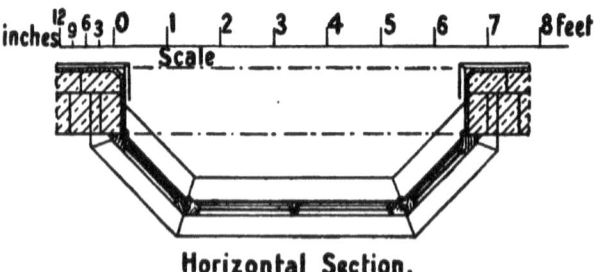

Horizontal Section.
FIG. 786.

Elevation and Sections of a Bay Window.

WINDOWS.

addition of masonry or brickwork they often assume a massive and bold appearance. When constructed of wood the framework is surmounted usually by a wooden cornice, and the wooden roof is covered with lead, slates or tiles. The window frames may be arranged as fixed lights, sash and frame, or casements. The most usual arrangement is to have the lower lights fixed, and the upper ones as sashes hinged to open for ventilating purposes. Figs. 784 to 786 show the details of a bay window with splayed side lights, the upper side lights being hinged on the transom to open inwards.

Windows with Curved Heads.—When a window opening is surmounted by an arch, the top of the window frame requires to be of the same curvature as the under side (soffit) of the arch. In the case of fixed sashes, or of solid frames with casement sashes, the head of the frame is "cut out of the solid." A head which, owing to the size of the curve, cannot easily be obtained in one piece, is built up of segments, the joints being radial to the curve, and secured by hardwood keys.

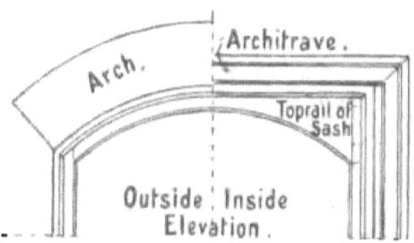

FIG. 787.—Elevation of upper part of a Window having Curved Head.

As an alternative method, the head may be built up of two thicknesses—with overlapping joints—and secured together by screws.

A sash and frame window in such an opening may have only the outside lining cut to the curve of the arch, the inner side of the frame being left square. The upper sash will then require a top rail with a straight upper edge and a curved lower edge, as shown in Fig. 787.

When the head of the frame has to be curved, it may

(1) be built up of two thicknesses with overlapping joints, and secured by screws; it may

(2) be formed of three thicknesses of thin material, bent upon a block of the correct radius, and well glued and screwed together; or

(3) the head may be of the same thickness as the pulley styles, with trenches cut out of the back (upper) side, leaving

only a veneer on the face-side under the trenches. Wooden keys are glued and driven into the trenches after the head has been bent upon a block to the required shape.

A strip of stout canvas glued over the upper side will strengthen the whole materially. The outside and inside linings are in such a case cut to the required curvature, and when nailed in position hold the head in shape. The end joints of the linings may have hardwood cross-tongues.

Shop Windows.—The main object in view in the construction of shop windows is to admit the maximum of light, and to give opportunity for an effective display of the goods. The glass is in large sheets, and therefore is specially thick to secure the necessary strength. Shop windows are usually arranged as fast sheets, with provision for ventilation at the top. The glass is held in position by wooden fillets, and is fixed from the inner side. The chief constructional variations are found in the pilasters, cornice, provision for sign-board, sun-blind, and the arrangement of the side windows. Figs. 788 to 790 show the details of a typical example.

The Fixing of Window Frames.—Window frames may be built into the wall—which has usually a recessed opening to receive them—as the brickwork proceeds, or they may be fixed later. In the former case, the ends of the sill and head project and form **horns**, which are built into the brickwork and help to secure the frame. Wooden bricks or slips may also be built into the wall, the frames being nailed to them.

In the latter case, the frames are secured by wooden **wedges**, which are driven tightly between the frame and the wall. These wedges should be inserted only at the ends of the head and sill and directly above the jambs; otherwise the frame might be so strained as to interfere with the sliding of the sashes. Window frames as well as door frames should be bedded against a layer of hair-mortar placed in the recess.

Linings.—When window frames are not of sufficient thickness to come flush with the inner face of the wall, the plaster may be returned round the brickwork and finished against the frame, or a narrow fillet of wood may be scribed to the wall and nailed to the frame as shown in Fig. 756. In dwelling-houses, however, the more usual way is to fix linings similar to those used for outer door frames (p. 368). The width of the linings depends upon the thickness of the wall; they should project

WINDOWS.

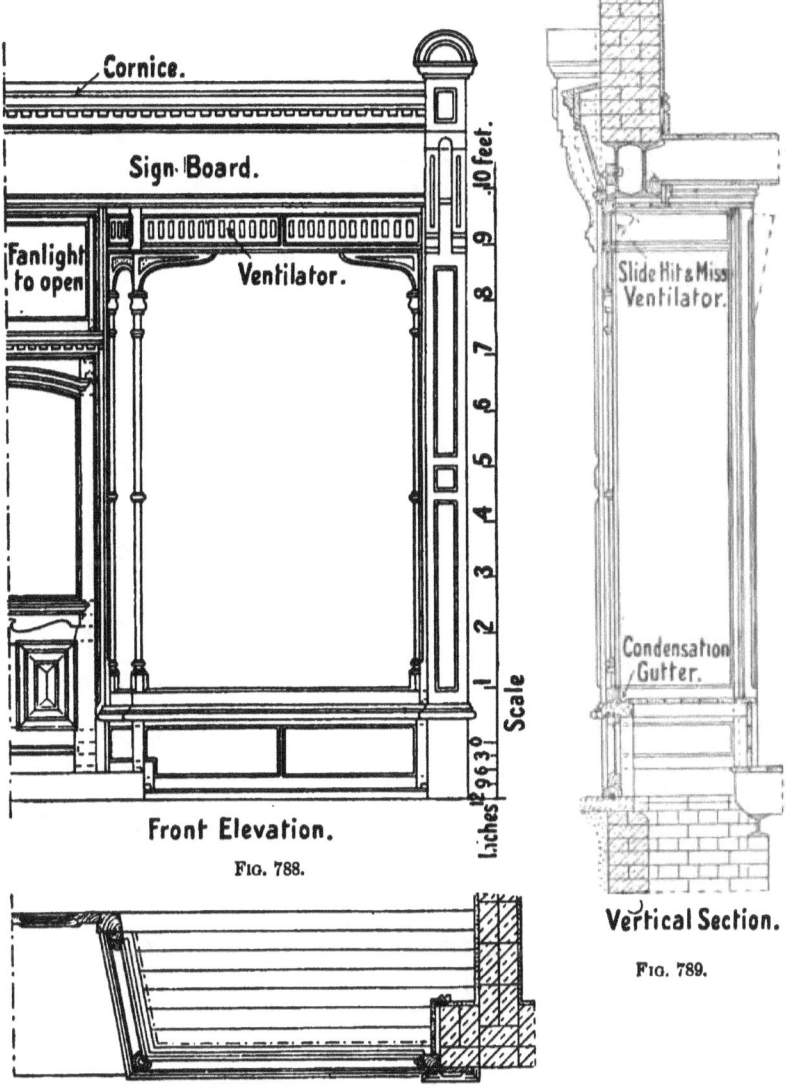

Front Elevation.
Fig. 788.

Horizontal Section.
Fig. 790.

Vertical Section.
Fig. 789.

Elevation and Sections of a Shop Window.

beyond the inner face of the wall for a distance equal to the thickness of the plaster, and are usually splayed so that they will not interfere with the admission of light. The inside of

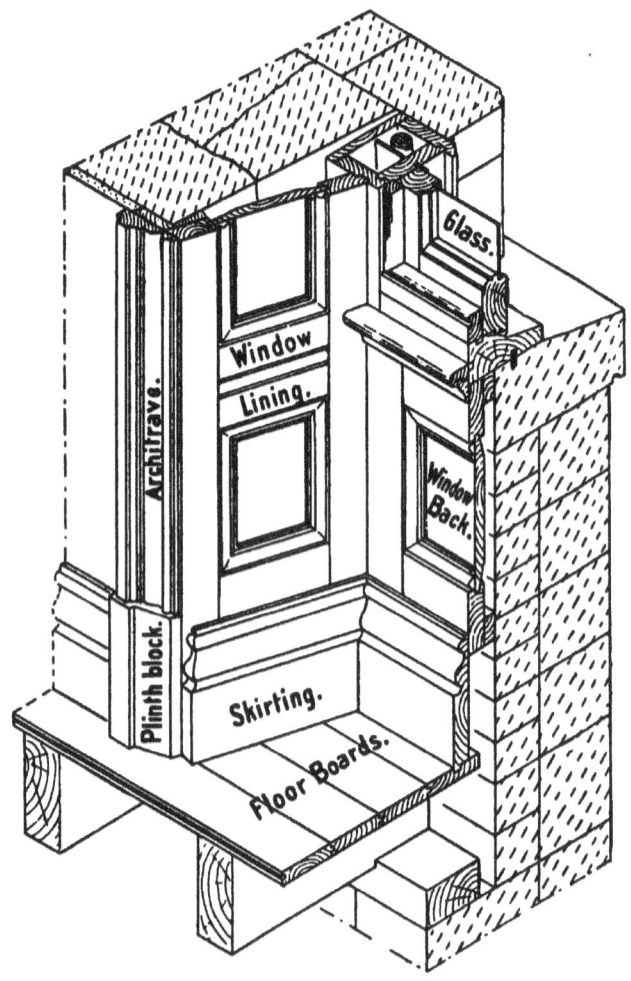

FIG. 791.—Sketch of part of a Sash and Frame Window, showing Panelled and Moulded Jamb-lining, etc.

window and door openings usually are finished similarly; thus, the **architrave**, or **band moulding**, which is secured to the edge of the linings and to rough wooden **grounds**, is fixed along the sides and top in both cases. The bottom of the window opening is finished with a **window board** which is tongued into the sill of the frame. The board is about 1¼ inches thick, and is made wide enough to project beyond the surface of the plaster for a distance of about 18 inches. The projecting edge is nosed (rounded) or moulded. It is longer than the opening, to allow the lower ends of the architrave to rest upon it.

When the walls are thick, the linings are often framed and panelled. Such linings may terminate on a window board at the sill level, or the inner side of the wall may be recessed

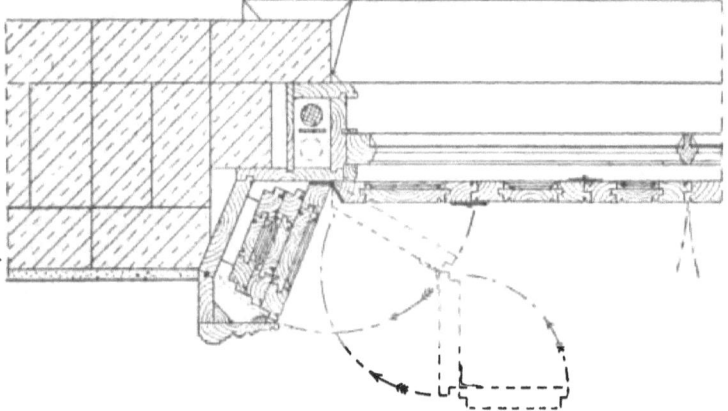

FIG. 792.—Horizontal Section through one side of a Sash and Frame Window, showing Box Shutters.

below the sill level and the linings carried to the floor as shown in Fig. 791.

Window Shutters.—Although not used to the same extent as formerly, wooden window shutters are fitted occasionally to close up the window opening. Window shutters, which are arranged generally on the inner side of the window, may be hinged as box shutters, or may be vertically sliding shutters.

Box shutters consist of a number of leaves or narrow frames which are rebated and hinged together, an equal number being on each side of the window opening, the outer ones on each side being hung to the window frame. When closed they together fill the width of the window-space, and when open they fold behind each other so that the front one forms the

406 A MANUAL OF CARPENTRY AND JOINERY.

jamb lining of the window frame. If the walls are thick, the shutters can be arranged to fold in the thickness of the wall; if the wall is a thin one it is necessary to construct projecting boxes into which the shutters fold. The nature of the framing of the shutters depends upon the surrounding work; it is usual to have the outer surface framed and moulded, and the inside finished bead-flush. The arrangement of box shutters requires that the shutters on the same side shall vary in width so that they will fold into the boxes on each side of the window, the outermost shutter (which is the widest) then acting as the window lining. Fig. 792 shows a horizontal section through one side of a window, showing hinged shutters folding so that a splayed

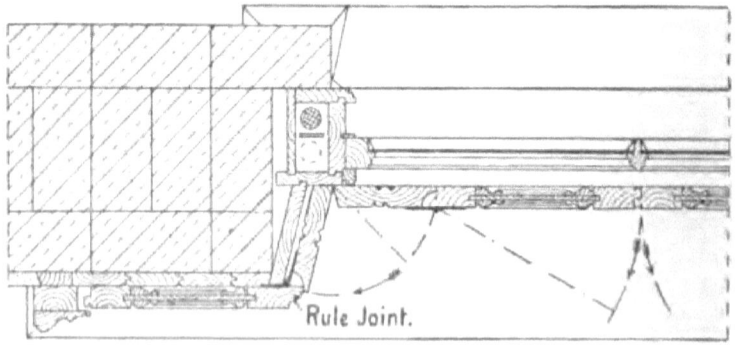

FIG. 793.—Horizontal Section through part of a Sash and Frame Window, showing Hinged Shutters.

lining is obtained. Fig. 793 shows hinged shutters consisting of one narrow and one wide shutter on each side of the opening. This arrangement is suitable for a thin wall, where it is undesirable to have boxes for the shutters projecting beyond the face of the wall. For hanging window shutters it is usual to use back-flap hinges (Fig. 717); the joint at the corner of the shutters in Fig. 793 is named a rule joint.

Sliding shutters, working in vertical grooves and balanced by weights, are sometimes used. They require that the wall under the window sill shall be recessed; the floor also often needs trimming to allow space for them to slide sufficiently low. To hide the grooves in which the shutters slide, thin vertical flaps are hung to the window frame, and the window board is also hinged at the front edge to allow the shutters to slide

WINDOWS.

FIG. 794.—Vertical Cross Section through a Sash and Frame Window, showing Vertically Sliding Sashes.

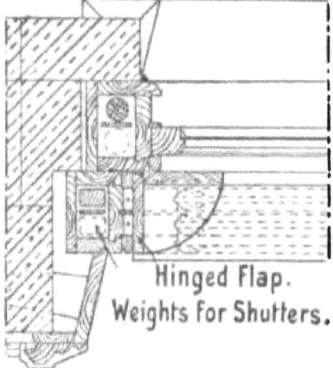

FIG. 795.—Horizontal Section through one side of a Sash and Frame Window, showing Vertically Sliding Shutters.

below the sill. Figs. 794 and 795 are sections of vertical sliding shutters.

Window Fittings and Fasteners.—For casement and hinged sashes, **butt hinges** are used. These should be strong enough for the purpose, preferably of brass, and they should, whenever possible, have one wing of the hinge let into the frame, and the other one into the sash. There are many types of metal **water bar** suitable for use for the joint between the bottom rail and sill of casement windows, and these materially assist in making the joint waterproof. Hinged casement sashes may, when closed, be fastened by **tower bolts** (Fig. 731), **flush bolts** (Fig. 732), or **casement fasteners** (Fig. 779). Many special casement-fasteners are obtainable, among which one of the most serviceable is an **Espagnolette bolt**. It consists of two long bars or bolts, which are so arranged that by turning a handle to which they are connected, both bolts

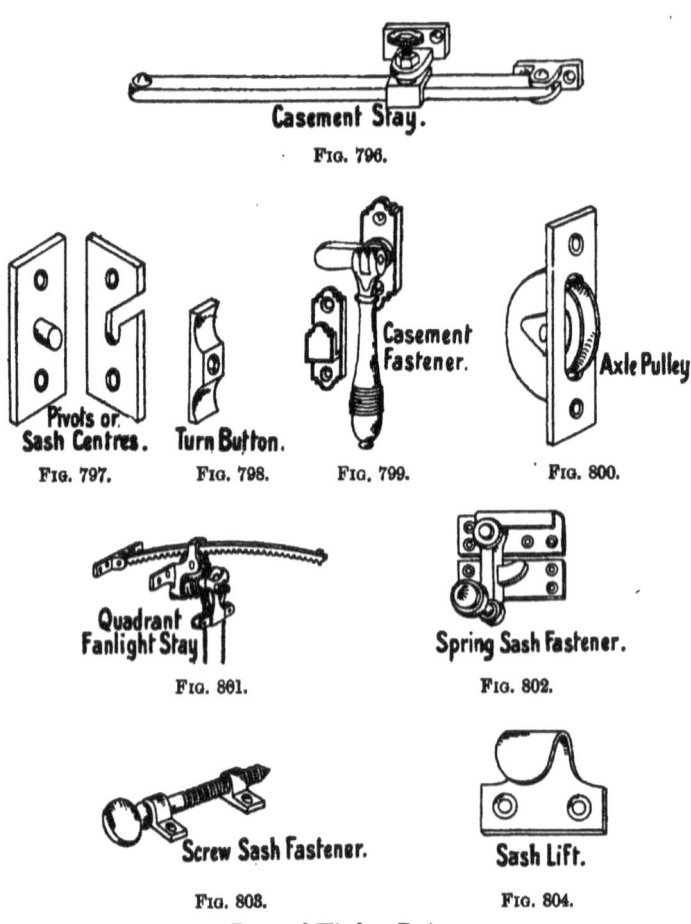

Types of Window Fastener.

are shot forward at the same time, and fasten the window effectively at both top and bottom. Casement sashes are held in any required position when open, by using a **casement stay** (Fig. 796), one part of which is screwed to the sash and the other part to the frame. **Iron quadrants** are used generally for regulating the opening of fanlights, *i.e.* sashes that are hung as shown in Figs. 752 and 754. Fig. 797 shows the **pivots** or **sash centres** used for pivoted sashes. The opening and closing of such sashes is effected either by a quadrant, or by means of cords passing over pulleys. Vertical sliding sashes are secured by a **sash fastener** screwed on the meeting rails. Figs. 802 and 803 show two kinds of sash fastener. The lower sash of such a window should always be provided with **sash lifts** (Fig. 804) for raising and lowering.

Summary.

Windows may be either fixed or made to open. Those which open consist of a **frame** and movable **sashes**, which are rebated to hold the glass.

In **casement windows** the sashes open like doors. They may open inwards or outwards. The frame is solid and rebated.

In **sash and frame windows** the sashes slide vertically alongside each other, and are balanced by weights. The upper sash always slides in the outer groove. The frame consists of several parts which together form on each side a box or case in which the weights are suspended.

Sashes **hinged** on the bottom rail to open inwards, and sashes **swinging on pivots**, are sometimes used, especially in positions not easily accessible.

Sashes are framed together with **mortise and tenon** joints.

Linings and **architraves** are required with thick walls, to obtain a finished internal appearance.

Bay windows project beyond the face of the wall; they may be arranged as fast sheets, as casements to open, or with vertical sliding sashes.

Window shutters may either consist of a number of leaves hinged together and folding into boxes at each side of the window (box shutters), or two shutters may slide vertically past each other and be balanced by weights.

Questions on Chapter XIV.

1. Draw full-size section through the sill of a casement window opening inwards. (C. and G. Ord., 1896.)

2. Draw sections through the sill, head, and the styles of a casement window to open outwards. Scale $\frac{1}{4}$ full size.

3. Make one half horizontal and a vertical section through a window frame 7 ft. 4 in. high and 4 ft. 3 in. wide, fitted with a pair of French casements to open inwards. Scale 2 in. to the foot; give details to a larger scale. (C. and G. Ord., 1902.)

4. Draw to a scale of one inch to a foot, plan and section of an ordinary French casement window to open inwards. Show the linings for a 14 in. wall, and give full-size sections of devices for excluding the weather. (C. and G. Ord., 1895.)

5. Draw plan and section to scale $1\frac{1}{2}$ in. to a foot of a three-light casement with solid frame and mullions. Size of opening 5 ft. 6 in. by 3 ft. Give section through sill $\frac{1}{4}$ full size. (C. and G. Ord., 1897.)

6. Make vertical and horizontal sections of a solid window frame with a 2 in. sash hung on pivots, and show how the beads are cut. The size of the window opening is 4 ft. high and 2 ft. 9 in. wide. Scale 2 in. to the foot. (C. and G. Ord., 1902.)

7. Draw a section, one-quarter full size, through the oak sill and lower portion of a 2 in. double hung sash, showing the method you would adopt to prevent the admission of water; also similar sections through a transom with opening fanlight, and the lower portion of a French casement to open inwards in an exposed position. (C. and G. Ord., 1894.)

8. Draw out, full size, a horizontal section through one of the jambs of a window in a brick reveal, having the usual cased frame and 2 in. deal ovolo sashes. Draw also a vertical section through the same sashes at the meeting rail. (C. and G. Prel., 1900.)

9. Draw half horizontal and vertical sections (scale 2 in. to 1 ft.) of 2 in. double-hung sashes with cased frame, opening 3 ft. by 5 ft., adapted to exposed positions. (C. and G. Ord., 1899.)

10. Draw $\frac{1}{4}$ full-size sections through head, sill, jamb, and meeting rails of an ordinary double-hung sash window in a 14 inch wall. (C. and G. Ord., 1896.)

11. Make half elevation, plan, and vertical section of a pair of 2 in. double-hung sashes and cased frame with semicircular head; width of opening 4 ft.; height to "springing line" 5 ft. Give details to show the best method of constructing the head of the frame. Scale $1\frac{1}{2}$ in. to 1 foot. (C. and G. Ord., 1903.)

12. Make rather more than half elevation, vertical and horizontal sections of a boxed Venetian window-frame, 6 ft. 6 in. wide and 5 ft. high. (C. and G. Hon., 1904.)

13. Draw plan, elevation and section of a double-boxed Venetian window of three lights, to occupy an opening in a wall two bricks

thick; opening to be 10 ft. wide by 7 ft. 6 in. high in the clear. Scale for the general drawings, ½ in. to a foot; details not less than ¼ full size. (C. and G. Hon., 1903.)

14. Draw plan and section to scale of ½ in. to a foot of a shop front, showing arrangement for giving light to basement. Frontage 18 ft.; height from floor to ceiling, 13 ft. (C. and G. Hon., 1897.)

15. Draw, in plan, elevation and section, an ordinary shop front, to occupy 16 ft. There is to be a light to the basement under the shop-board. Scale ½ inch to a foot; with details to 1 inch to a foot.

16. An ordinary sash window set in an opening 5 ft. wide by 8 ft. 6 in. high in the brickwork, in a brick and a half wall, is to have folding shutters. Draw the plan of the shutter boxing and architrave, taking in half the window, to a scale of not less than 1 in. to 1 ft., or larger than 1½ in. to 1 ft. Show the grounds or other fixing. (C. and G. Hon., 1900.)

17. A window has a 6 ft. opening. It is to be fitted with splayed folding boxing shutters. The soffit is framed. Write a brief description of the method of fixing the various parts. (C. and G. Hon., 1898.)

18. Draw, to a scale of 2 ins. to one foot, a horizontal section through one side of a double hung sash and frame window in a 14 in. brick wall showing hinged shutters arranged to open back against the inside face of the wall. Width of opening 3 ft. 6 in.

19. Describe back flap, rule joint, and give illustrations of their use. (C. and G. Ord., 1898.)

20. Give a plan and section, ¾ inch to the foot scale, of lifting shutters to a properly cased sash frame 3 feet 6 inches wide, fixed 4½ inches in reveal (wall 1 foot 10½ inches thick) and show the splayed, moulded, and panelled linings, window backs, architraves, etc., complete. (C. and G. Hon., 1892.)

CHAPTER XV.

ROOF-LIGHTS AND CONSERVATORIES.

IN many buildings it is necessary to have the top rooms lighted by windows in the plane of the roof or slightly elevated above the roof surface. Such windows are called **roof-lights** or **skylights**. They may either be "fixed" into the roof, or be constructed to allow of being opened for purposes of ventilation. The chief difference between the frames of roof-lights and the sashes described in Chap. XIV. is that in the former, cross bars are not used, and the bottom rail is thinner by the depth of the rebate than the other parts of the sash. These modifications are necessary, as will be seen from the illustrations, to allow the free escape of rainwater.

Owing to their exposed positions, it is specially necessary that the timber used for all roof-lights shall be of the best quality, well seasoned, and entirely free from sapwood, shakes, loose knots, and other defects. Red deal is in general the best wood for this purpose. Further, all the joints should be well **painted** with lead paint before the framework is put together, and the framework itself requires re-painting periodically.

There are many different methods of arrangement, some of which are described below.

Fixed Skylights.—The simplest roof-light, and one that is specially applicable to large sheds of the warehouse type, is constructed by placing, on each common rafter, a double rebated bar, from 3 to 5 feet long, as shown in Fig. 805. In the rebates of these bars the squares of glass are fixed. At its upper end the glass fits into a grooved cross rail, and the slates or lead flashings overhang this. At the lower end, the glass is so arranged that it overlaps the slates, or sheet lead may be used to make a watertight joint.

An alternative method is to "trim" the common rafters, so that a rectangular space, equal in size to the required skylight, is obtained. The frame of the light consists of **two styles**, a **top rail** of the same thickness as the styles, and a **bottom rail** the thickness of which is less than the thickness of the other parts by the depth of the rebate. Intermediate **bars** parallel to the styles, and in the same direction as the slope of the roof, are placed at from 12 to 16

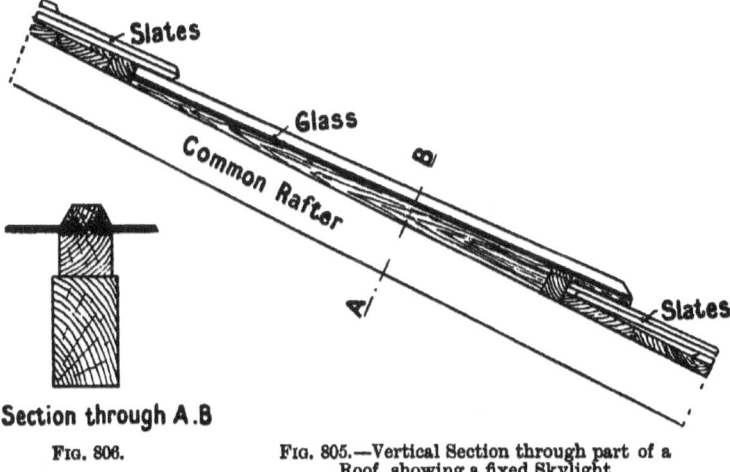

Section through A.B

Fig. 806.

Fig. 805.—Vertical Section through part of a Roof, showing a fixed Skylight.

inches apart, as it is not advisable to have the sheets of glass more than that width. As these lights are in the slope of the roof, there are no cross bars, therefore the sheets of glass should be as long as possible. As the glass used for glazing such lights is thicker than in ordinary windows, it is necessary to have the bars thicker than in ordinary sashes, and a rebate at least one inch deep is required. The thickness of the frame depends upon its size, but should never be less than $2\frac{1}{4}$ inches.

Glass may be fixed in wooden frames either by means of small brads and putty, or by wooden fillets. When putty is used, it is essential that the rebates, which are to hold the glass, be previously painted or "primed." The paint prevents the wood from absorbing the oil of the putty. Special provision is also needed for the removal of **condensed water**, which is invariably found where skylights are used. The condensation is most marked in rooms, such as mills, in which the air is hot and moist. To provide channels for the condensed water, grooves are cut along the sides of the bars (Fig. 809) and styles. Sinkings are also made upon the upper side of the bottom rail, as shown in Fig. 815, to prevent the water from being drawn by capillary attraction between the glass and the rail.

The **joints** between the sides of the light and the roofing material—slates or tiles—are made watertight by sheet lead flashings which overlap the woodwork of the frame. Fig. 807

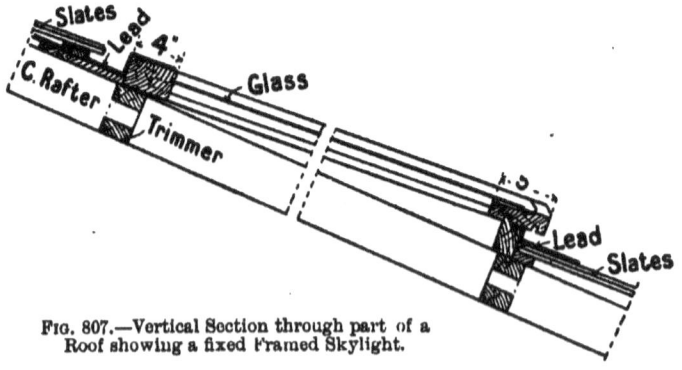

Fig. 807.—Vertical Section through part of a Roof showing a fixed Framed Skylight.

is a section showing a framed roof-light resting on the common rafters. The bottom rail overlaps the slates or tiles, and this joint is also made watertight with sheet lead as shown in section in the illustration.

Fig. 808 shows in section an elevated skylight fixed upon a "curb" near the ridge of a roof. Fig. 810 is a section through a fixed skylight in a shed-roof.

Hinged Skylights.—Skylights which are hinged to open are fitted upon the upper edge of a **curb** or frame fixed in the plane of the roof, the common rafters being "trimmed" to the required size to receive the curb. The curb is made from material $1\frac{1}{4}$ to 2 inches thick, and of width such that its upper edge stands from 4 to 6 inches above the plane of the roof. The **angle joints** of the curb may be dovetailed or tongued and nailed. The **sash frame** rests upon the upper edge of the curb; it is from 2 to 2½ inches thick, and consists of styles and top rail of the same thickness, and a bottom rail which

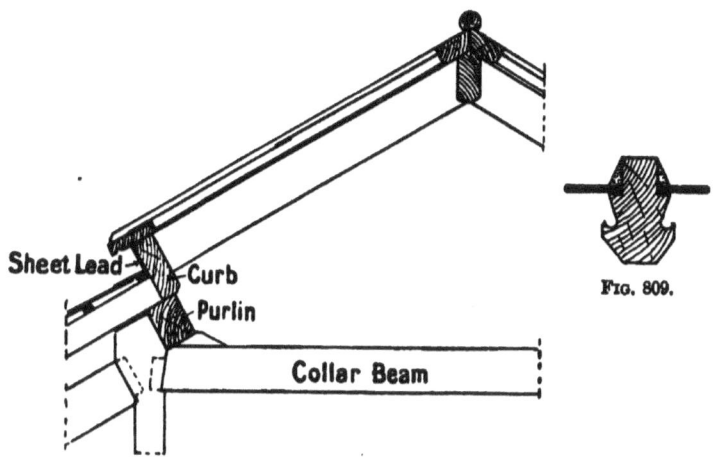

Fig. 808.—Section through an Elevated Skylight fixed at the Ridge.

(because the glass overlaps it) is thinner than the styles by the depth of the rebate. Bars are inserted in the direction

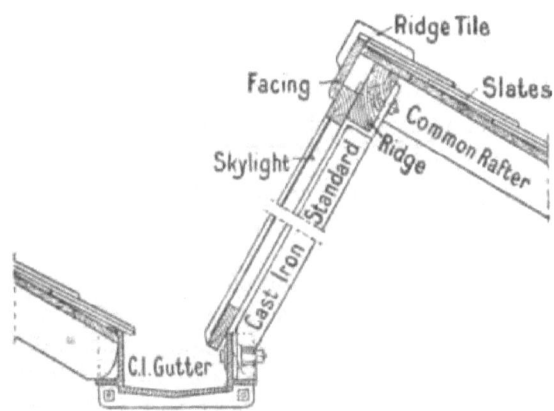

Fig. 810.—Section through part of a Shed-roof, showing a fixed Skylight.

of the slope of the roof, and the butt hinges used for hanging the sash are invariably fixed on the underside of the top rail.

416   A MANUAL OF CARPENTRY AND JOINERY.

Considerable care is required to make the joint between the sash and the curb watertight. Fig. 814 shows the upper edge of the curb rebated to form a tongue which fits into a corresponding groove cut in the underside of the sash. Another way is to have the edge of the curb square, and to fix a tongued fillet around the underside of the sash so that it overlaps the curb as shown in Fig. 813. This type of skylight is extensively

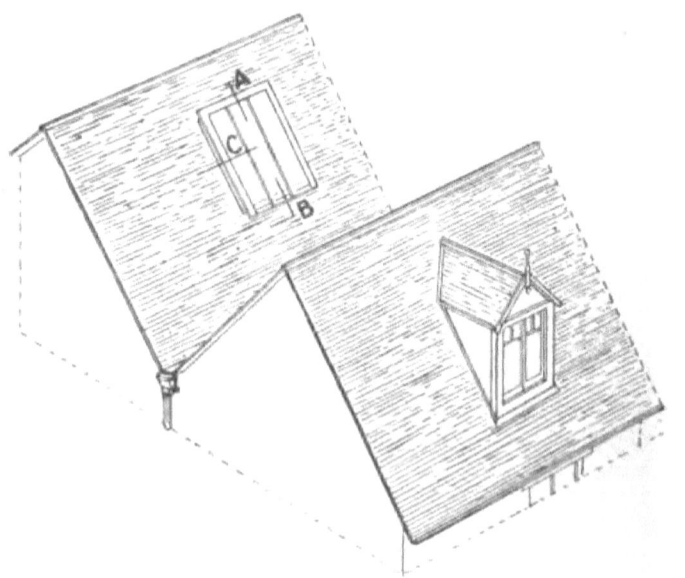

FIG. 811.—Sketch of part of the Roof of a Building, showing a Hinged Skylight and a Dormer Window.

used for lighting attics and staircases of dwelling-houses. Figs. 812 to 814 show sections of such a skylight with the main dimensions indicated thereon.

The joints between the curb and the roofing slates or tiles are made weatherproof with sheet lead. At the upper end—the back of the curb—a small **lead gutter** is formed, with the lead going underneath the slates and overlapping the upper edge of the curb. The sides of the curb may be flashed with soakers—short lengths of sheet lead which are worked in between the slates—or the joint may be made with one strip of lead forming a small gutter down the side of the curb. In either case the lead overlaps the upper edge of the curb. At

ROOF-LIGHTS AND CONSERVATORIES.

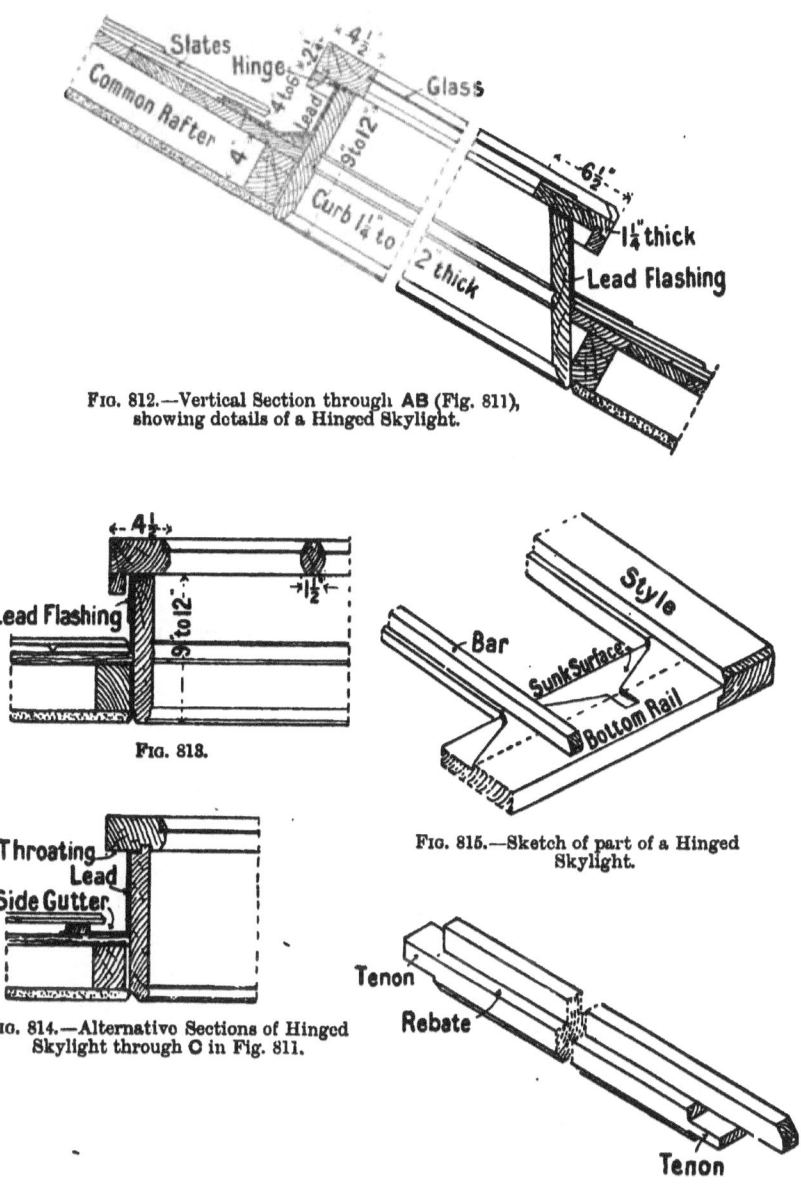

FIG. 812.—Vertical Section through AB (Fig. 811), showing details of a Hinged Skylight.

FIG. 813.

FIG. 814.—Alternative Sections of Hinged Skylight through C in Fig. 811.

FIG. 815.—Sketch of part of a Hinged Skylight.

FIG. 816.—Sketch of one of the Bars of a Skylight.

the lower end of the curb, the lead overlaps the slates. To prevent water from rising between the glass and the upper side of the bottom rail, sinkings are cut into the rail as shown in Fig. 815.

Dormer Windows.—Instead of having the light in or parallel to the plane of the roof, it affords a more artistic treatment of the roof, and often gives a better result in lighting, if the window is fixed vertically. The general arrangement of the framing, as well as of the sashes, depends upon the kind of roof, the width of the window required, and the general style of architecture of the building.

The construction of a dormer window necessitates trimming of the rafters, and the arrangement of projecting framework, the front of which consists of **corner posts** and **crossrails**—rebated to receive hinged sashes—which are connected to the main roof by other crossrails and by **braces**. This framework is surmounted by a **roof** which may be either ridged, of curved outline, or flat. By arranging a ridged roof to overhang, and adding suitable **barge boards** and **finial** (Fig. 819), a dormer window may be made to improve the general appearance of the roof of a building. The sides of the dormer may be either boarded and covered with the same kind of material as the roof, or they may be framed for sidelights.

As dormer windows are generally in exposed positions, and the sashes are arranged as casements to open, their efficiency depends largely upon the perfection of the joints between the sashes and the frame. The methods of arranging these joints are explained in detail in Chap. XIV. to which reference should be made. It ought to be mentioned, however, that with sashes hung folding, semicircular tongues on their hanging styles (Fig. 745) are by far the best. Figs 817 and 818 give the details of a dormer window, with sidelights, fixed in a roof of ordinary pitch. The sashes, which are hung folding, open inwards. The roof may be boarded and covered with lead, or it may be covered with slates or tiles. The joints between the roofing slates of the main roof, and the roof and sides of the dormer, are made weather-proof with sheet-lead flashings. Figs. 819 and 820 show a dormer window fixed in a Mansard roof ; in this example there are no side lights. Figs. 821 and 822 show a three-light dormer, of which the middle sash only is hinged to open. The roof in this case is flat, and is

ROOF-LIGHTS AND CONSERVATORIES.

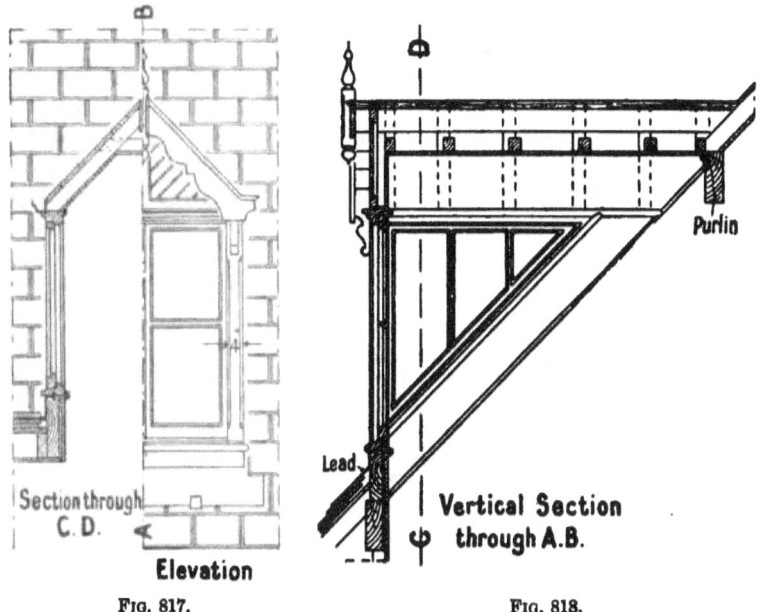

Fig. 817.   Fig. 818.

Details of a Dormer Window in a Slated Roof of ordinary Pitch.

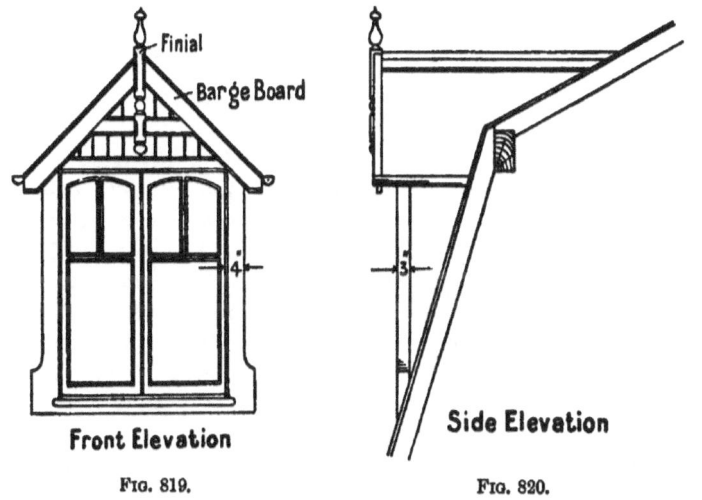

Fig. 819.   Fig. 820.

Dormer Window in a Mansard Roof.

420   A MANUAL OF CARPENTRY AND JOINERY.

covered with lead; it has a wooden cornice around the upper edges.

Large Skylights and Lantern Lights.—For lighting the well of a large staircase, or a room which, for some reason, cannot be lighted with side windows, specially large skylights are often necessary. These are of more elaborate construction than the skylights already described; they vary considerably in size, shape, and design; the plan may be rectangular, polygonal, circular, or elliptical, and the outline may be pyramidal, conical, or spherical. The framework may be of

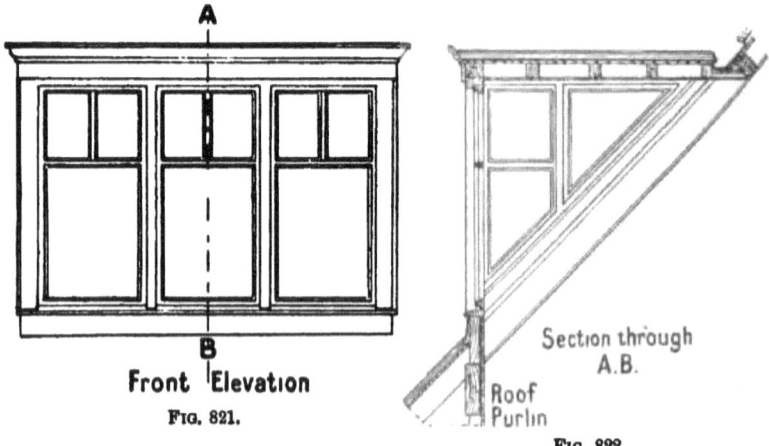

Three-light Dormer Window with a Flat Roof.

either wood or iron. To support such a skylight, a strong wooden curb is framed into the roof, and projects from 6 to 9 inches above the roof surface. The joints between the curb and the roof are made watertight with sheet lead. The framework of the skylight may consist of rebated quartering, with separate lights which fit into the rebates of the framing; or the sashes themselves may be constructed with strong angle styles, which are mitred together, and provided with either a hardwood tongue inserted in the joint, or with a wooden roll on the top to keep out water.

With skylights of this description, channels for condensed water should always be provided. These are placed at the upper inner edge of the curb, the remainder of the inside face

ROOF-LIGHTS AND CONSERVATORIES. 421

of the curb being covered by either panelled framing or match boarding.

Figs. 823 and 824 give details of a skylight having the form of a square pyramid. In this example the four triangular lights are mitred at the angles, and have wooden rolls over the

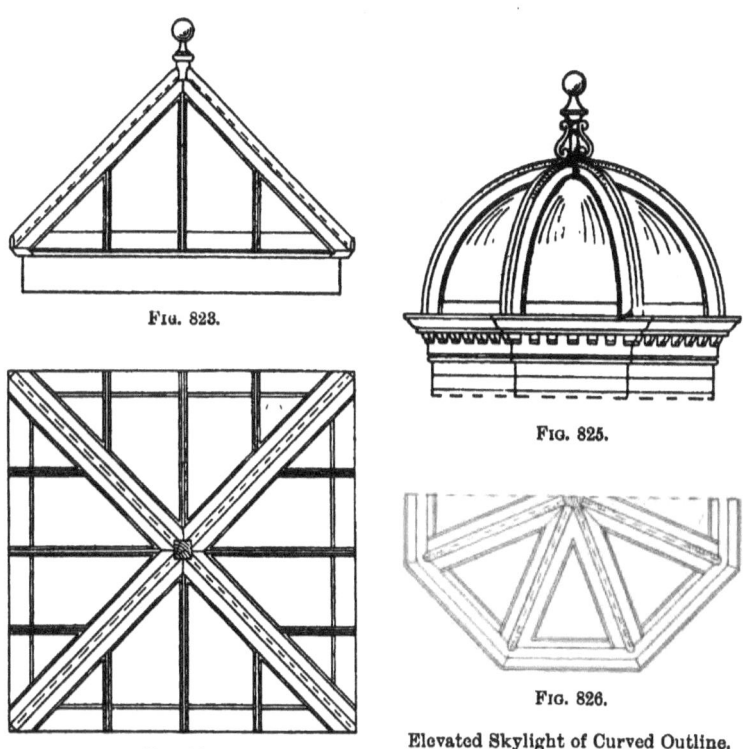

Fig. 823.

Fig. 825.

Fig. 826.

Elevated Skylight of Curved Outline.

Fig. 824.

Elevated Pyramidal Skylight.

joints. Figs. 825 and 826 show elevation and part plan of a skylight with a curved roof surface.

A **lantern light** differs from the skylights just described in having, in addition, vertical **sidelights**. The sidelights consist of sashes, which, by being hinged or pivoted, are often available for ventilation. As they are in exposed positions, the greatest care is required in order to obtain watertight joints, the detailed construction of which is considered in Chap. XIV.

When the sidelights are hinged on the bottom rail, as in Fig. 827, they open inwards; when on the top rail (Fig. 828), they open outwards. When they are hung on pivots, the pivots are fixed slightly above the middle of the sash, which opens in the manner shown in Fig. 829. Figs. 830 to 833 show details of a rectangular opening surmounted by a lantern light which is hipped (p. 216) at both ends, and has sidelights arranged to open inwards.

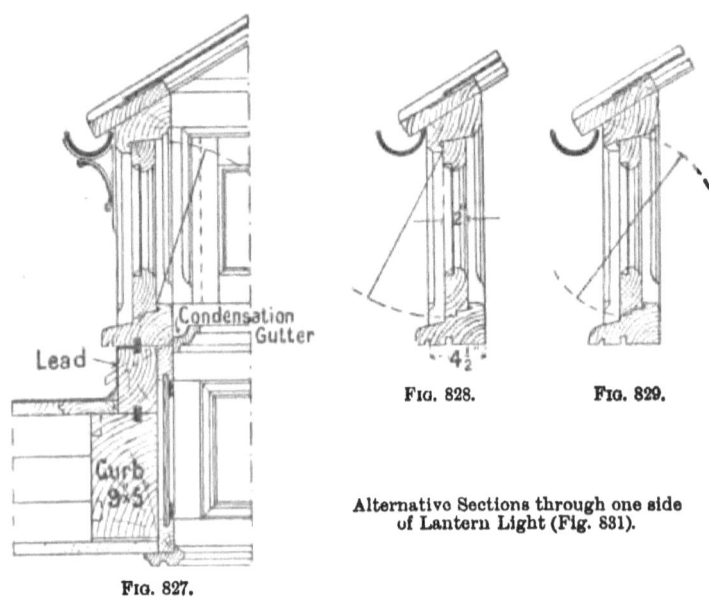

Fig. 827.

Fig. 828.   Fig. 829.

Alternative Sections through one side of Lantern Light (Fig. 831).

The construction of skylights and lantern lights affords good examples of the application of geometry to practical work as described in Chap. III. When the roof-lights are pyramidal as shown in Figs. 824 and 831, and a separate frame is constructed as shown in Fig. 831, the methods of obtaining the lengths and bevels of the hip rafters are similar to those described in Chap. IX., p. 248. When the roof-lights mitre against one another, the sizes of the lights and the bevels of the angle-styles which mitre together are obtained as shown at **X** in Fig. 833. With lights of curved outline, the shapes of the hip rafters or angle-styles, as well as the developed surfaces, are obtained as explained on p. 255.

ROOF-LIGHTS AND CONSERVATORIES.

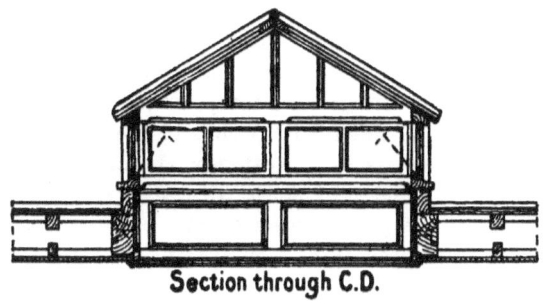

Section through C.D.
Fig. 880.

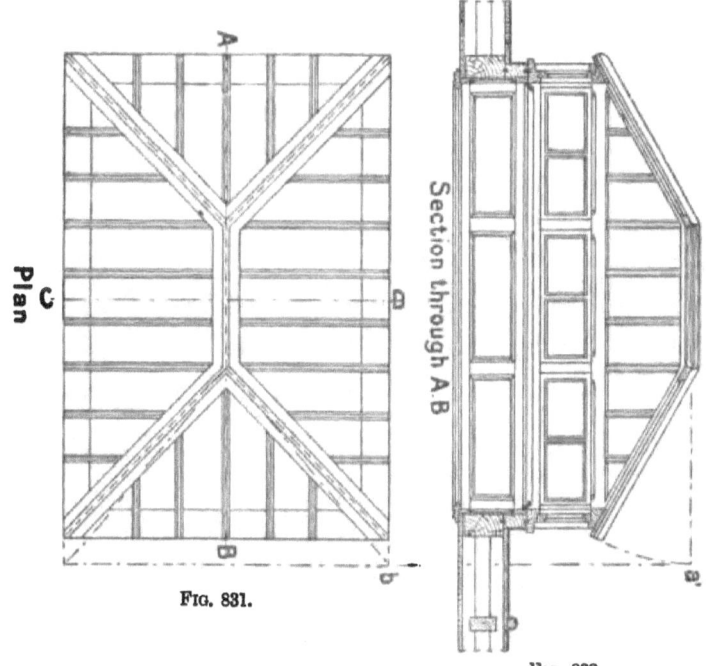

Fig. 831.

Fig. 882.

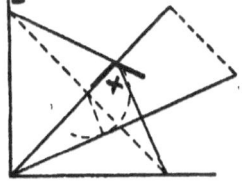

Fig. 833.

Plan and Sections of a Lantern Light fixed on a Flat Roof.

424 A MANUAL OF CARPENTRY AND JOINERY.

Lay-lights.—At the ceiling level of roof-lights used for staircase wells, or in similar positions, it is often considered advisable, for the sake of appearance, to have a horizontal second light called a lay-light. This consists of a sash,—or if the space is large, a number of sashes—fixed into frames in the ceiling. The chief feature of lay-lights is in the attempt at decoration by arranging the bars in some ornamental design (Figs. 834 and 835). The lay-lights are often glazed with ornamental glass, which, although it improves the appearance, diminishes the amount of light transmitted.

FIG. 834.   FIG. 835.
Designs for Lay-lights.

Greenhouses and Conservatories.—In this type of building, which is largely constructed of wood and glass, the framework is usually of moulded and rebated quartering, with side sashes fixed in the rebates. As in the case of skylights, the roof-lights, which in this case reach from the ridge to the eaves, have no cross bars, since these would impede the flow of water running down the slope of the roof. Care should be taken to have the bars strong enough to carry the glass without sagging; and it is well to remember that when a roof is of flat pitch a heavy snowstorm will throw a large additional weight upon it, while with a steep roof the wind has much power. The distance apart of the bars which carry the glass ranges from 12 to 18 inches, and the lengths of the sheets of glass should be as great as possible, so as to diminish the number of cross-joints, since these allow of accumulations of dirt which cannot be removed easily. These roof-lights are constructed in exactly the same manner as skylights; they are, however, often much larger, and require to be thicker, unless purlins are placed to support them. When, as is often the case, part of the roof-light is

FIG. 836.—Sketch of Conservatory.

made to open, this part—often a narrow strip at the highest part of the roof (Fig. 836)—is made as a separate light, which overlaps the upper edge of the fixed lower light. Additional ventilation is secured by arranging the side sashes to open.

The above description is intended merely to outline the broad principles of the construction of conservatories, but it should be remembered that the details, while conforming to casement and roof-light construction generally, lend themselves to considerable variation in design and arrangement. Three typical examples are illustrated in Figs. 836, 837, and 838. Many patented systems of glazing, which simplify the fixing

Fig. 837.—Sketch of Conservatory.

Fig. 838.—Sketch of Conservatory.

ROOF-LIGHTS AND CONSERVATORIES.

and replacing of glass, are in use. It is, however, beyond the scope of this book to deal with such.

Fasteners.—Because roof-lights are fixed at the highest parts of a building, they are useful for purposes of ventilation. On the other hand, their position renders them difficult of access, so that the means of opening and regulating the sashes requires special consideration.

Pivoted rods, pulleys and cords, quadrants, levers, etc., are among the devices used for this purpose. The position and the method of hanging the sash, the general style of the building, the cost, and other considerations will of course decide which particular type of regulator is most suitable.

Summary.

Roof-lights may be fixed or they may be arranged to open. They may be in the plane of the roof or elevated above its surface.

Lead flashings are required to render watertight the joints between roof-lights and slates or tiles.

A **dormer** window is an arrangement of vertical lights on a sloping roof surface. The construction of the projecting roofed framework necessitates trimming of the rafters. The lights often open as casements.

Large elevated skylights are supported by strong wooden curbs framed into the roof. **Lantern lights** have in addition vertical side lights.

A horizontal light fixed at the ceiling-level directly below a roof light is called a **lay light.**

The principles governing the construction of window framing and roof-lights are applicable also to wooden framed greenhouses and conservatories.

Questions on Chapter XV.

1. Draw, to a scale of 3 in. to one foot, cross sections to show fully alternative methods of constructing the fixed skylight shown in the roof of the building illustrated in Fig. 517.

2. The lighting of a large shed is effected by fixing roof-lights arranged as shown in Fig. 810. Draw the complete details, showing the construction of the roof-lights, to a scale of 2 in. to one foot.

428 A MANUAL OF CARPENTRY AND JOINERY.

3. A skylight is to be placed in a sloping roof. Give sketches showing the construction of the skylight, and how you would trim around the opening. The void is to be finished internally with linings. (C. and G. Ord., 1904.)

4. Draw to scale of 1½ inches to one foot, a plan and two vertical sections of the hinged skylight shown in Fig. 811. Show all the details of the carpenters' and the plumbers' work. Size of opening (between common rafters) 4 ft. 6 in. by 3 ft.

5. Make a drawing of a small skylight, to be fixed in a flat roof, and give details to show how the weather is kept out. (C. and G. Ord., 1898.)

6. Draw all the details of a dormer window fixed in a slated roof which is inclined at 45° to the horizontal. Show fixed side-lights, and casement sashes hung folding to open inwards in the front part. Scale 2 in. to one foot.

7. Give a section through a Mansard roof 30 feet span, showing all details connected with gutter behind, the parapet in front, and a skylight in upper front slope of roof. (C. and G. Ord., 1892.)

8. Make plan, elevation, and section of a dormer window, 8 ft. wide over all, divided into three lights, one fixed, the others on centres, the openings for lights to be 3 ft. high. The dormer to be in the slope of a roof at 45° pitch, and to be covered with a lead flat. Show the method of trimming the opening and the details of framing, and all precautions to be taken for keeping water out and getting rid of condensation, and describe the materials to be used. (C. and G. Hon., 1904.)

9. Draw to scale ¼ inch to a foot, section through a skylight over a billiard room, the clear width being 8 ft. (C. and G. Hon., 1896.)

10. A lantern light, 8 ft. by 5 ft., is to be fitted to a billiard room, covered with a lead flat. Draw rather more than quarter of plan and half the vertical section of the light. Any necessary details may be drawn to a larger scale. Show clearly how you would keep it watertight, and provide for ventilation. (C. and G. Hon., 1901.)

11. It is proposed to cover a space, 12 ft. by 6 ft., in an exposed situation with a lantern light. Give a plan and longitudinal section of same to a scale of half an inch to a foot. Also give details, quarter full size, of sections of upper part of light and lower part of sash and junction with roof. The light is to be made to open. (C. and G. Hon., 1894.)

12. Draw to a scale of ¼ inch to a foot the construction of a flat lead-covered roof over a room 20 ft. by 18 ft., showing the

arrangement for a lantern light 10 ft. by 9 ft., and give details, one-eighth full size, through rolls, gutter, and one side of skylight. (C. and G. Ord., 1895.)

13. Draw to scale of ½ in. to a foot a lantern light, elliptical on plan, 7 ft. long, 4 ft. wide, and 3 ft. 6 in. high internal dimensions. Show how you would get cuts or bevels of bars at top and bottom. (C. and G. Hon., 1897.)

CHAPTER XVI.

STAIRCASE WORK AND HANDRAILING.

Definition of Terms.—As a means of obtaining access to the upper rooms of a building it is usual to provide a space in which is arranged a series of steps. This space is named the **staircase**, and the combination of steps is named a **flight of stairs**.

Wooden stairs consist of horizontal **treads**, generally supported by vertical **risers** placed under the front edges of the treads; and **string boards** which support the ends of the treads and risers. The front edge of each tread usually overhangs the riser under it, and is nosed or moulded. **The line of nosings** is an imaginary line parallel to the edges of the string boards and touching the nosing of each tread in a flight.

The **going** of a stair is the horizontal distance from the face of the lowest riser to the face of the highest riser in the same flight. The **width of the tread** is measured from the face of one riser to the face of the next, any overhanging nosing not being taken into account. The **total rise** is the height from floor to floor, although the word "rise" usually refers to the height from the top of one tread to the top of the next one above it. Parallel rectangular treads in a flight are named **fliers**; when it is necessary to change the direction of a flight of stairs, say through a right angle, either **winders** (triangular treads) or a square landing called a **quarter-space landing** must be used. The middle tread of three winders is four-sided (kite shaped), and is named the **kite winder**. When the width of the staircase is at least double the width of the stairs, and the stairs are arranged in two flights running in opposite directions, the change of direction (through two right angles) may be obtained by winders only, by winders and a quarter-space landing

(Fig. 841), or by a landing extending the width of the staircase, and called a **half-space landing**. It is sometimes necessary to have treads which are a little wider at one end than at the other, as shown in Fig. 880; these treads are named **balancing** or **dancing**

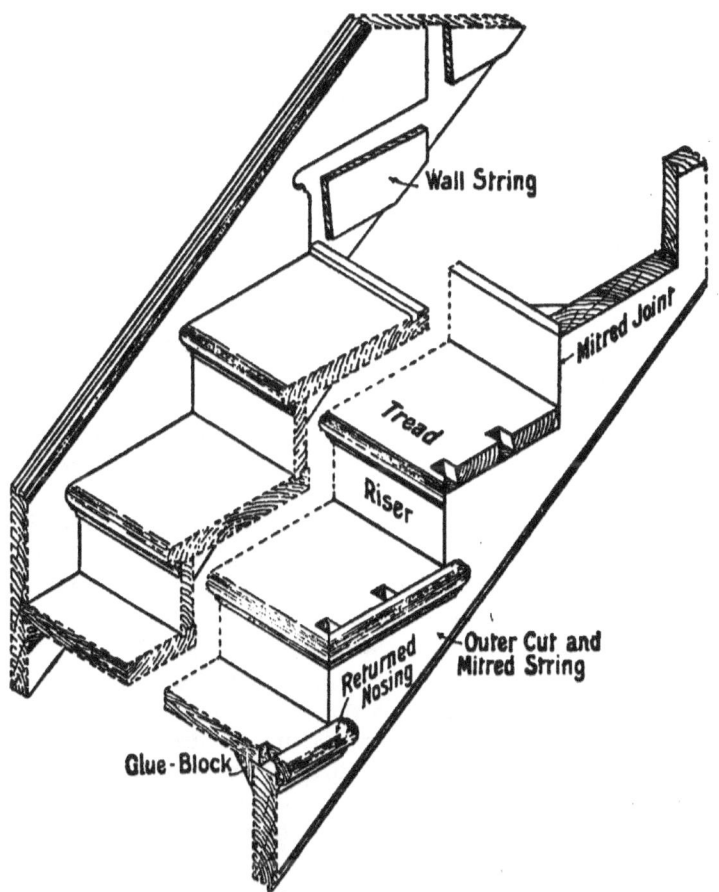

FIG. 839.—Sketch of part of a Flight of Stairs, showing Constructional Details.

treads. The lowest tread, or sometimes two of the treads at the bottom of a flight, may be of different shape from the fliers, to allow of additional room, or to improve the appearance of the stairs. A step which has a curved front edge, as shown in Fig. 880, is named a **commode step**. A step with its outer corner rounded to a quadrant is a **bullnose step**; if the end of the step is semicircular it is a **round-ended step**, while if the curved end is somewhat of a scroll the step is called a **curtail step**.

Distinctive names are given to the string boards. For example, a string board with parallel edges, which is trenched to receive the ends of the treads and risers, and has therefore part of its width above the steps, is called a **close string**: it is either the *wall string* or the *outer (well) string*, according to its position. The outer string has, in some types of stairs, the upper edge cut to the profile of the treads and risers, and is then named a **cut string**. With a cut string, the ends of the treads overhang, and have mitred and returned nosings (Fig. 839); the risers under these treads may have the ends mitred to the string boards, or thin, shaped brackets may be mitred against the ends of the risers, the object being in either case to avoid showing the end of the riser. The former of these cut strings is called a **cut and mitred string**, and the latter a **bracketed string** (Fig. 848). With some types of stairs it is necessary to have the outer string constructed to turn through an angle at the change of direction of the stairs; such a string is named a **wreathed string**.

Stairs more than 3 feet wide should be supported upon inclined wooden **carriages** consisting of rough quartering. Triangular blocks placed upon the upper edge, or rough cleats nailed to the sides of these carriages, support the treads; the plasterers' laths are nailed to the under sides when a plastered soffit is required.

When all the treads are rectangular and of the same size, the stairs constitute a **straight flight**. When winders are used to turn through a right angle, the stairs are described as **winder stairs**. When the change of direction extends through two right angles, with a landing between the two flights, the upper flight is named the **return flight**. Stairs having return flights are called **dog-legged** when the width of each flight is equal to half the width of the staircase, and the outer strings of the two flights are in the same vertical plane. When, on the other hand, the width of the staircase is more than double the width of the stairs, it allows of an open space between successive flights; this space is called the **well**. When there are posts (newel posts) at the angles, the stairs are called **open newel stairs**. Where there are no newel posts, and the outer string and the handrail are continuous from bottom to top, the stairs are said to be

geometrical. Geometrical stairs may be arranged in either a rectangular, polygonal, circular, or elliptical staircase, and are usually named accordingly.

The triangular framing placed under the outer string of a flight of stairs is called the **spandrel framing.**

General Principles of Stair Construction.—In superior dwelling-houses and in public buildings it is usual to make a special feature of the staircase and stairs. In cottages, however, the space is generally too limited to allow much scope in this respect. In planning the stairs the following important points need attention. The staircase should be well lighted. The stairs should be arranged in straight flights of not more than twelve steps each, and all steps in the same flight must have an equal rise. If the height from floor to floor renders more than twelve steps necessary, there should be a landing between successive flights. A single step, or a combination of two steps only, between adjacent flights is objectionable; winders should be avoided as far as possible, although by their use a saving in space can be effected. When winders must be used, they should be arranged so that in the middle of their length in narrow stairs, and at about 18 inches from the handrail in wide stairs, the width of tread is equal to that of a flier. It is usual, however, to arrange three winders to turn through a right angle (Fig. 873).

To economise space on the landing of the upper floor, the floor joists are trimmed so that part of the floor overhangs the lower flight of stairs. In arranging the trimming joists it is necessary to provide **headroom**, that is, sufficient space between the stairs and the under side of the upper floor to allow persons to ascend and descend the stairs without stooping. A usual distance to allow for headroom is about 6' 6", measured vertically in line with the face of the risers. Special consideration needs to be given to the positions of doorways and windows—on both the upper and lower floors—as they often introduce difficulties in the planning of the stairs. As the space beneath the stairs is almost invariably used, either as an approach to the cellar or as a storage room, any landing between two flights should be high enough to allow of a passage under it.

Proportion of Tread and Riser.—The width of the tread, the amount of rise, and the proportions between these are of paramount importance. A good proportion for an easy-going stair is to have a tread 11 inches wide (neglecting any overhanging nosing) and a rise of 6 inches. These dimensions when multiplied together equal 66 ; it will be found a satisfactory guide to take this number as a constant, and the following formula can be used :—

$$tread \times rise = 66.$$

From this it will be seen that a $5\frac{1}{2}$ inch rise will need a 12 inch tread, while a rise of 7 inches will require a tread $9\frac{3}{7}$ inches wide.

Another rule, which also gives satisfactory results, is to make the width of the tread, *plus* twice the height of rise, equal to 23 inches. This can be expressed as follows :—If $T =$ width of tread in inches, $R =$ height of rise in inches, then

$$T + 2R = 23 \text{ inches.}$$

Although limitations of space often prevent the construction of an ideal stair, care should be taken to make the best of the available space, especially as a badly designed and proportioned stair is not only fatiguing, but a serious danger to the safety of old people and young children. For a dwelling-house the stairs should be from 2′ 6″ to 3′ wide, with a rise of from $6\frac{1}{2}$ to 8 inches, and a proportionate width of tread. For public buildings, the width of the stairs varies from 3 feet to 6 or even 8 feet, and the rise is from 5 to 7 inches.

The Setting-out of Stairs.—It is reasonable to assume that the type and general arrangement of the stairs, with the positions of start and finish, landings, winders (if any), adjacent doorways, etc., have all been considered during the preparation of the designs and general plans of the building. It is the joiner's duty to "set out" and construct the stairs from drawings supplied to him which embody the points just mentioned. The first thing to do in the construction of a flight of stairs is accurately to measure the staircase, test the angles, and to draw to scale a plan showing the amount of space available and the exact positions of any doorways or windows in close proximity.

The plan of the staircase having been drawn, it will be necessary to determine the number of steps required to ascend from the lower to the higher floor-level. To do this, the height from floor to floor must be obtained. It is usual to employ for this purpose a **storey rod**, that is, a rod about $1\frac{1}{2}$ inches square

STAIRCASE WORK AND HANDRAILING.   435

and long enough to reach from floor to floor. It must be borne in mind that in each flight there is one more riser than tread, owing to the landing on the upper floor serving the purpose of a tread. By applying the rule previously given of the proportion of tread to riser, it remains to be decided what the rise shall be. For example, if the height from floor to floor measures 10′ 6″, and there is plenty of "going space" in the staircase, a

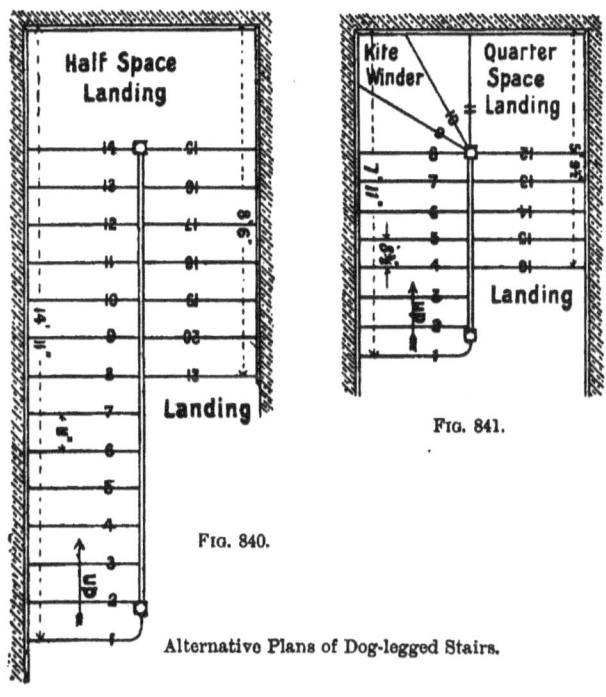

Fig. 840.

Fig. 841.

Alternative Plans of Dog-legged Stairs.

rise of 6 inches—which would give an easy stair—might be adopted: this would require 21 risers, and 20 treads each 11 inches wide. On the other hand, assuming that the going space is more limited, while the height is still 10′ 6″, a greater rise and a narrower tread will be necessary. A rise of more than 8 inches is not desirable, so that it is necessary to find a height between 6 and 8 inches which will divide without remainder into the total height (10′ 6″). The number of risers thus obtained will obviously lie between $\frac{126}{6}$ (*i.e.* 21) and $\frac{126}{8}$ (*i.e.* 15¾). It may be 16, 17, 18, 19, or 20, with corresponding rises of $\frac{126}{16} = 7\frac{7}{8}″$;

$\frac{126}{17} = 7\frac{7}{17}''$; $\frac{126}{18} = 7''$, etc. Although the rise of $7\frac{7}{8}''$ does not give a very easy stair it is often adopted where space is limited. The rise having been decided upon, the width of tread is found by the rule given on p. 434. With a rise of $7\frac{7}{8}''$ the tread will be $\frac{66}{7\frac{7}{8}} = 8\frac{8}{21}''$ (approximately $8\frac{3}{8}''$). Figs. 840 and 841 show plans of

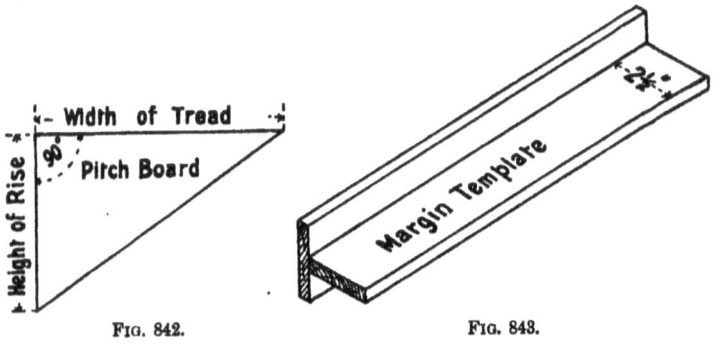

FIG. 842. FIG. 843.

the two stairs just described. In the former, 21 risers are shown, the stairs being in two flights with a half-space landing. In the latter, winders and a quarter-space landing are shown at the change of direction. These two illustrations are introduced mainly to show the difference in the space occupied, with what

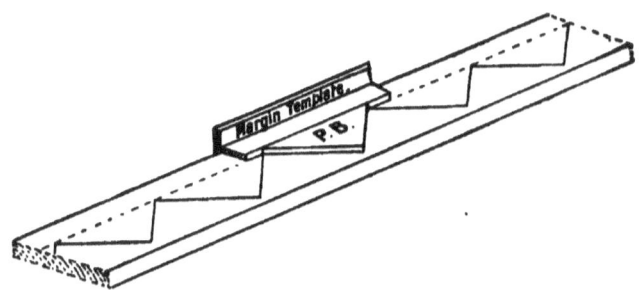

FIG. 844.—Method of "setting-out" a String Board.

may be considered the two extremes of rise for the stairs of dwelling-houses.

The plan of the stairs having been completed, it is necessary to prepare a **pitch board** and **three templates**. A pitch board is a thin triangular board; two of the sides of the triangle contain a right angle, and are of length equal to the rise and the width

STAIRCASE WORK AND HANDRAILING

of the tread respectively (Fig. 842). The **margin template** (Fig. 843) is used along with the pitch board in marking out upon the string-boards the positions of the trenches for the treads and risers as indicated in Fig. 844. The other templates (Figs. 845 and 846) are used for marking the widths of the trenches for the treads and risers respectively. With close strings, the distance of

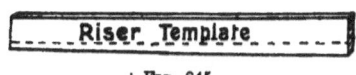

FIG. 845.

the line of nosings (p. 430) from the upper edge of the string is from 2½" to 3½", and the setting out of the trenches is done from the upper edge. The width of the string varies from 9 to 12 inches; it is governed by the inclination of the stairs. It should be noticed that the two strings for the same flight must be set out in pairs, and in setting out winders, the direction in which the stairs turn must be borne in mind.

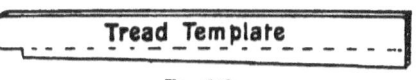

FIG. 846.

When winders are used it is well to draw a full-sized plan of these, in order to obtain the exact widths of the ends of the winder treads; and as they are wider than the fliers, the wall -strings supporting them require to be wider than in the remaining part of the stairs, as shown in Figs. 869 to 873.

Joints between Treads and Risers.—The **edge joints** between the treads and risers may be square, or they may be tongued and grooved. It is only in the commoner kinds of stairs that the edge joints are square as shown in Fig. 847, since square joints allow of dirt getting through them. Fig. 862 shows the lower edge of the riser tongued to fit into a groove in the upper side of

FIG. 847.—Section through Tread and Riser.

the tread. The upper edge of the riser is square, and fits against a rebate formed by having a moulded fillet tongued into the underside of the nosing edge of the tread. Fig. 863 shows an alternative method of arranging the joints between the treads and risers. These joints are not so good as those shown in Fig. 862; it will be seen that the groove on the lower edge of the riser is a source of weakness. The joints

438 A MANUAL OF CARPENTRY AND JOINERY.

are secured by nailing or screwing them together; they are further strengthened by glueing wooden blocks in the angles (Fig. 864).

Types of String-board.—When **close string-boards** are used, the ends of the treads and risers are housed for about half

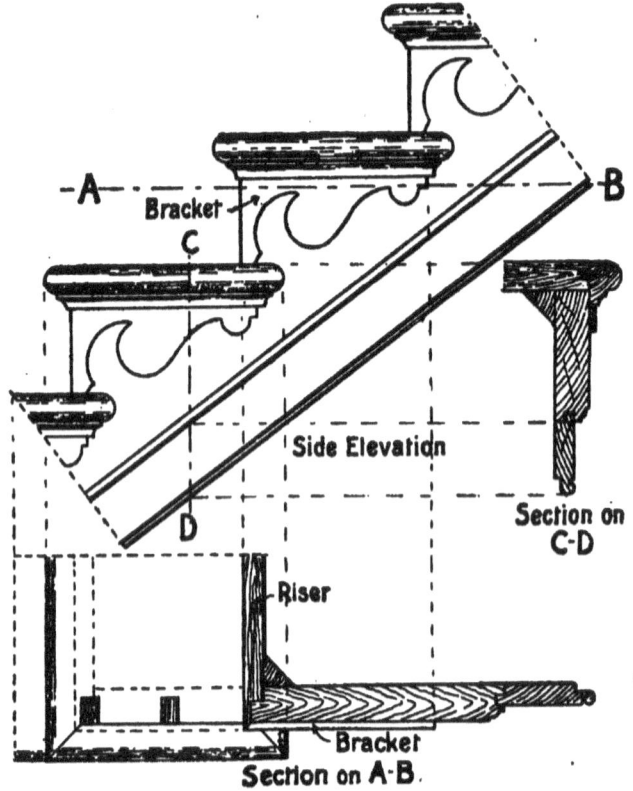

FIG. 848.—Details of part of a Bracketed Stair.

an inch into trenches cut into the face of the strings (Fig. 864). These trenches are cut wider than the thickness of the treads and risers to allow of the insertion of tapering wedges, which are glued and driven in at the back, and hold the stairs together. Nails are often driven through the wall strings into the ends of the treads and risers, and in addition glue-blocks are placed in all the angles on the under side of the stairs.

STAIRCASE WORK AND HANDRAILING.

Although the wall strings are almost invariably close strings, the outer string—especially in geometrical stairs—is either **cut and mitred**, or **cut and bracketed**. When close strings are used for both sides of the stairs, the treads (fliers) and the risers under them are all cut to the same length and the ends left square. With a cut string, the outer ends of the treads are mitred, and a narrow nosing is returned around the end (Fig. 839). If the risers are mitred to the string, they are cut as shown in Fig. 839. Fig. 848 shows the details of the ends of two steps which are finished with brackets and returned treads. It will be noticed that the ends of the risers are mitred to the brackets, the object being to avoid showing the end grain of the wood. The lower ends of the vertical balusters which support the handrail rest upon the ends of the treads, and are secured by being dovetailed into them as shown in Fig. 839.

The outer strings in newelled stairs have the ends tenoned into the newel posts as shown in Fig. 849. The newel post may extend to the floor, and thus act as a support, or it may finish a little below the ceiling level of the stairs, with a turned or carved terminal called a **drop**. Any treads or risers which abut on the newel posts are generally housed into the posts as shown in Fig. 849. The angle joints of wall strings are tongued and grooved, and the upper and lower ends are "eased" to correspond in width with the skirting board (Figs. 869 and 870); the mould of the skirting being continued along the upper edge of the string-board. A close outer string is usually surmounted by a moulded capping, upon which the lower ends

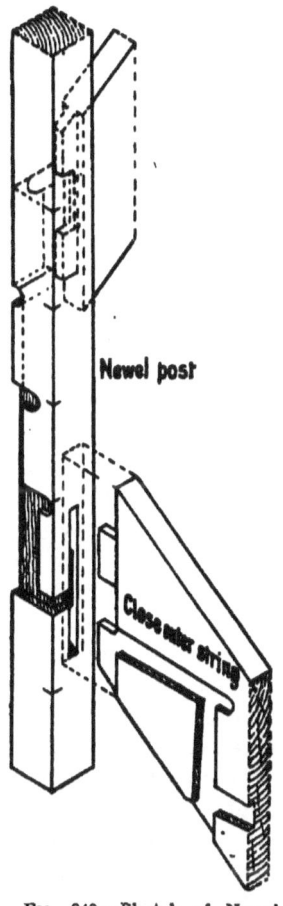

FIG. 849.—Sketch of Newel Post cut to receive Strings, Treads, Risers, etc.

of the balusters are fixed (Fig. 875), and the outer side of this string may be panelled or ornamented by sunk mouldings.

A **wreathed string** (the outer string of a geometrical stair) may have the curved part constructed in several different ways. When the well is of small radius and the outer surface of the string has deep sunk mouldings, the curved part of the string may be built up by glueing together narrow pieces with cross-tongues in the joints, as shown in Fig. 850; this construction is known as a *staved well*. Another way is to reduce the thickness of the curved part of the string to a veneer, and block the back side of the veneer with ribs, the grain of which is vertical (Fig. 851).

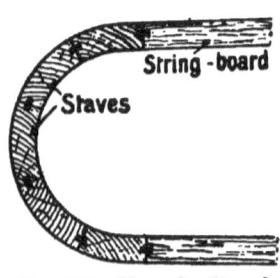

FIG. 850.—Plan of a Staved String Board.

Stout canvas glued on the ribs is an additional source of strength. Such a *veneered string* is generally considered better than a staved string. With wells of large radii, or in stairs the strings of which form a continuous curve (*e.g.* geometrical stairs, either circular or elliptical), the outer strings are usually built up by glueing and screwing together several layers (laminae) of thin boards with overlapping joints. The resulting string is called a *laminated string*. The two methods last named require a semi-cylindrical block (or, in the case of a circular well, a complete cylinder) of radius equal to the radius of the well of the stairs, round which the veneer or thin layers are bent and temporarily held until the glue has set.

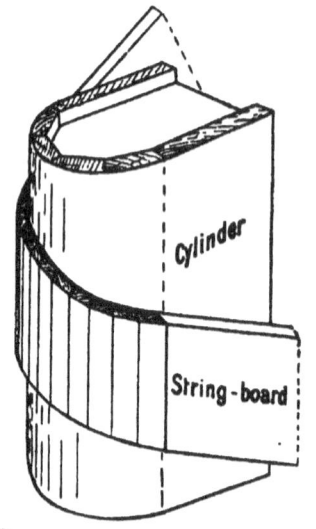

FIG. 851.—Sketch of a Veneered String Board bent round a Cylinder.

The method of ascertaining the shape to which the veneer for a wreathed string must be cut is shown in Figs. 852 to 855.

STAIRCASE WORK AND HANDRAILING. 441

The plan of the curved part of the string is first drawn *full size*, and on it are marked the intersections of the veneer and the faces of all the risers. The next thing to be done is to draw the "stretch-out" (development) of the curved surface represented in plan. The length of the curved lines A, B, C, etc.

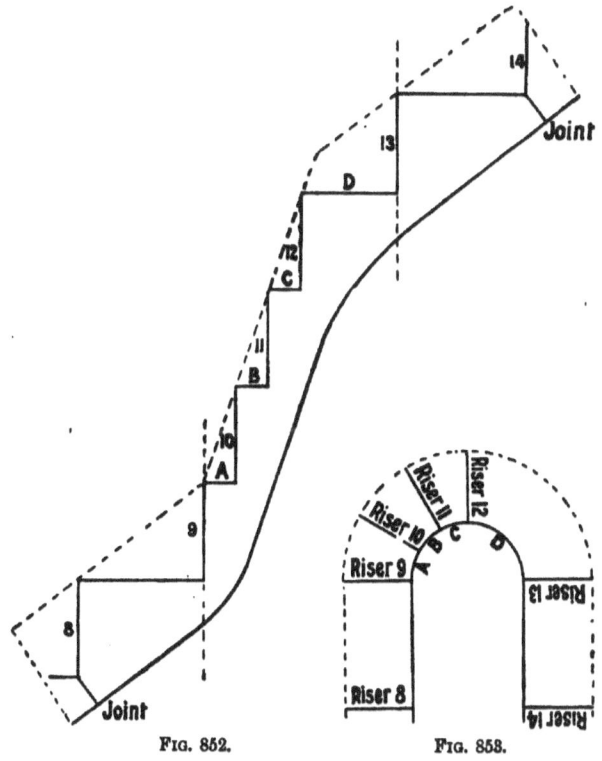

Fig. 852.   Fig. 853.

Method of development of a Veneered String Board.

(Fig. 853), are of course the widths of the treads where these intersect the veneer. The risers are all equal. The soffit curve of the veneer is drawn parallel to the line of nosings. Fig. 854 shows the development of the veneer for the wreathed string of a geometrical stair with six winders used to turn through two right angles, as shown in Fig. 883.

Construction of Steps with Bent Risers.—The risers of bull-nose, round-ended, and curtail steps have curved

442 A MANUAL OF CARPENTRY AND JOINERY.

surfaces. A general method of construction is to cut the risers out of a board of the same thickness as the other risers, and reduce to a veneer the part which has to be bent round the curved surface. A solid block of the required curvature, built up of several thicknesses of material, with the grain crossing, is prepared, round which the riser is bent and secured with

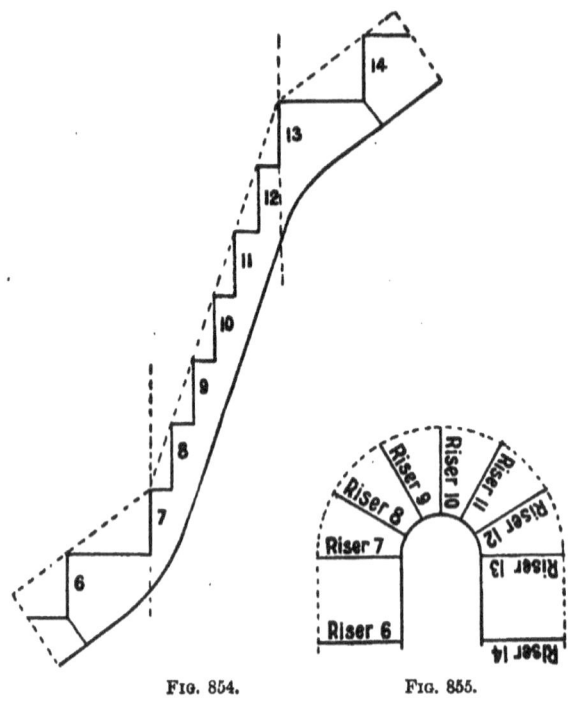

FIG. 854.   FIG. 855.

Method of development of a Veneered String Board.

glue, wedges, and screws. Figs. 856 and 857 show a **bull-nose** step; Figs. 858 and 859 show a **round-ended** step; and Figs. 860 and 861 show the method of construction for a **curtail** step. The outline for a curtail tread corresponds to that of the handrail scroll above it (Fig. 880). It will be noticed that the small mould under the nosing of the tread is worked out of the solid, and is placed between the tread and the upper edge of the riser (Fig. 861), thus reducing the width of the latter. This method gives much better results than would be obtained from

STAIRCASE WORK AND HANDRAILING. 443

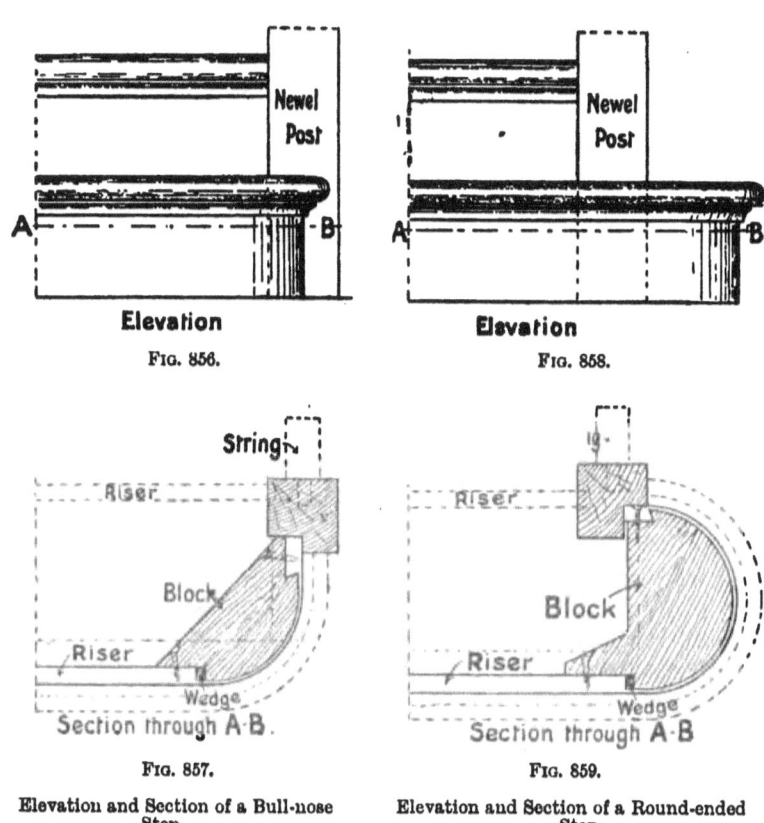

Fig. 856. — Elevation

Fig. 858. — Elevation

Fig. 857. — Elevation and Section of a Bull-nose Step.

Fig. 859. — Elevation and Section of a Round-ended Step.

Fig. 860. — Plan of Riser

Fig. 861.

Details of a Curtail Step.

an attempt to bend the small mould round the curve. The riser for a **commode** step, the whole length of which is curved (Fig. 880), may either be constructed out of an inch board having saw-cuts in the back side to allow of bending (p. 471); or it may consist of a thin veneer which is glued and screwed to shaped blocks.

Landings and Carriages.—A **quarter** or **half-space landing** for stairs is constructed as a small floor, as much support as possible being obtained by building the ends of the joists into the wall. These joists being of short bearing, do not require to be so strong as ordinary floor joists; they are usually from 4 to 6 inches deep, and 3 inches thick. The tusk-tenon joint is the best joint to use at the ends of all joists abutting against the trimmer. Additional support is often given to the outer corner of a quarter-space landing, by allowing the newel post to extend to the floor. The same support may be obtained by having a strong corner-post against the spandrel framing; this post often serves as part of the door framing when a door is placed adjacent to the spandrel framing.

For stairs more than three feet wide, it is advisable to have **rough carriages** as an additional means of support. These carriages are about 5 inches deep and 3 inches thick. They extend from the floor to the landing, and forward to the upper floor, and are inclined so that the steps rest upon them. By securing them to the floor and to the landings, additional strength is given to the latter, while the treads receive further support by **cleats** nailed to the sides of the carriages, as shown in Fig. 862. With some types of geometrical stair considerable skill is required to arrange the carriages in the best positions. An alternative to the carriages above described is to have **triangular blocks**, from 2 to 3 inches thick, glued and screwed together in a continuous line under the middle of the treads as shown in Fig. 863.

The trimming joists of an upper floor landing, which form the sides of the well, require facing to match the stairs. This may be done with either plain or panelled facing-boards. The boards used must be a little wider than the joists, so that their lower edges finish flush with the plaster ceiling. Such facing-boards are called **apron linings**.

Erection of Stairs.—The actual putting together of a flight of stairs is done as far as possible in the workshop. Straight

STAIRCASE WORK AND HANDRAILING. 445

flights present no difficulty in this respect; with stairs having winders, however, their bulkiness when completed, and often the limited space in which they are to be placed, renders it

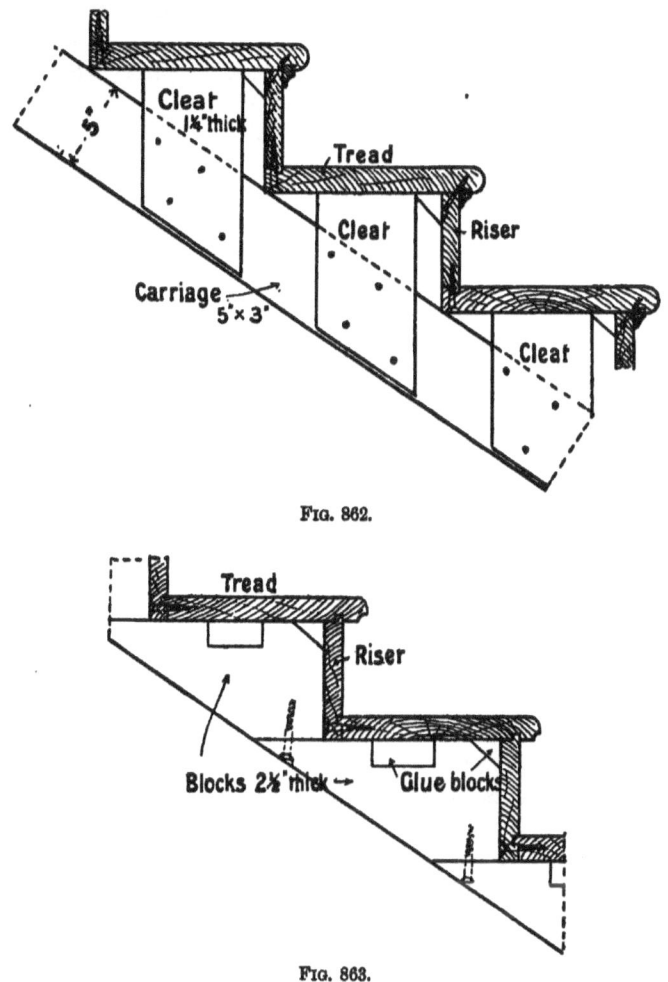

Fig. 862.

Fig. 863.

Sections through the Steps of Stairs.

necessary to fix the winders after the straight parts have been fixed in position.

Assuming that the string boards have all been trenched,

446 A MANUAL OF CARPENTRY AND JOINERY.

with the necessary easings along the edges; that the treads and risers have been trued up, nosed, tongued and grooved, and smoothed off: it is usual first to fasten the treads and risers together in pairs. A handy workshop appliance called a cradle is used for this purpose. The steps are then fitted into the trenches in the strings and numbered, and are finally put together with the aid of specially devised cramps. The tapering wedges which are used for securing the ends of the steps are then glued and driven into position. It will be noticed

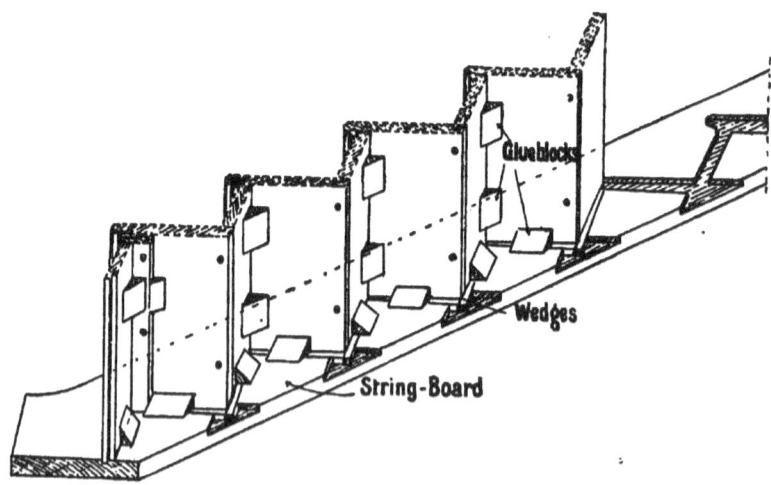

FIG. 864.—Sketch of part of a Flight of Stairs, showing the method of Wedging and Blocking together the various parts.

that these wedges are driven in at the back sides of the treads and risers (Fig. 864), and that as they are driven they tend to close all the joints between the face of the string and the steps, and also the joints between the edges of the treads and risers. The edge joints are also screwed together and glue blocks inserted in all internal angles on the under side of the stairs.

TYPES OF STAIRS.

The foregoing description of stairs is of general application, and covers the work to a considerable extent. As, however, each different arrangement has peculiarities of its own, it will now be well to glance at these in detail.

TYPES OF STAIRS.

Straight Flight.—The simplest kind of stairs is one much used in warehouses, workshops, etc., where the available space is very limited. These stairs have **no risers**. The ends of the treads are tightly housed into the string boards, and are secured by nailing. The stairs are strengthened by passing bolts through the strings from side to side, just under every fifth or sixth tread. Both the treads and the string boards—often

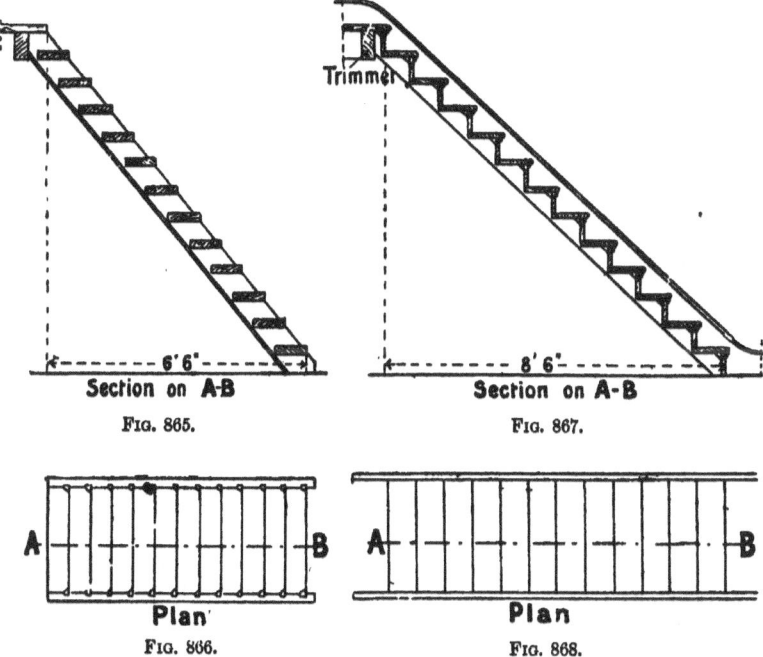

Types of Straight Flights of Stairs.

called *notch boards* in such stairs—are thicker than those of stairs which have risers. Figs. 865 and 866 show sectional elevation and plan of such stairs. It will be seen that the front edge of each tread overhangs part of the next tread below it; by this means a considerable amount of going space is saved. This type of stair is improved by boarding the back or underside of the notch boards with tongued and grooved match boarding.

Figs. 867 and 868 show sectional elevation and plan of a

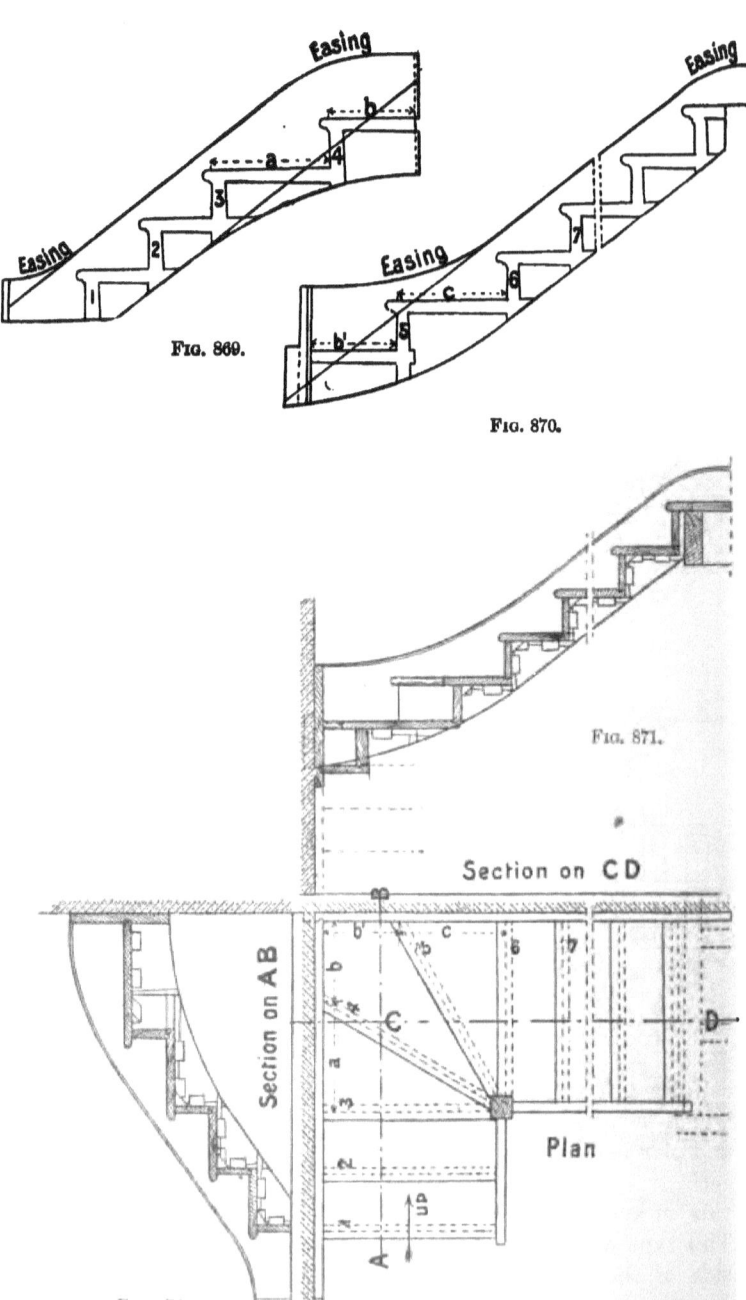

Details of Winder Stairs to turn through a right angle.

straight flight of stairs **with treads and risers,** the rise being the same as in Fig. 865. A comparison of the two examples shows that much more horizontal distance (going space) is necessary in Fig. 867 than in Fig. 865.

Stairs with Winders.—Figs. 869 to 873 illustrate details of part of a flight of stairs often found in cottages and other small dwelling-houses. The arrangement shows three winders used to turn through a right angle to the right. The outer angle is supported by a newel post which extends from floor to floor ; it is mortised to receive the ends of the outer strings, and trenched for the abutting treads and risers as shown in Fig. 849. Such stairs are often enclosed by fixing one-inch tongued and grooved match boarding against the sides of the outer strings, vertically in line with the newel post. Figs. 869 and 870 show the wall strings for these stairs with the trenches and joint-lines marked thereon. The lengths of the trenches for the ends of the winder treads are obtained from the plan, as shown in Fig. 873. In this type of stairs close strings are used on both sides. The ends of the wall strings which fit together have a tongued and grooved joint, are nailed together at the angle, and are secured to the wall by being nailed to plugs driven into the joints of the brickwork. It gives additional security if a joggle, left upon the end of the upper string, fits into a hole cut in the corner of the wall.

Dog-legged Stairs.—As previously stated, a dog-legged stair is one in which the change of direction is through two right angles, and the outer strings are in the same vertical plane. Although the change of direction may be effected by using winders only, such a construction is not advisable, and should be adopted only where the space is very limited. Figs. 840 and 841 are plans of two examples of this type of stair, and Figs. 874 and 875 show details of a similar stair with a half-space landing between the two flights. The landing is placed at a convenient height to allow of access to a room under the stairs. The width of the landing is equal to the width of the stairs, the arrangement of the joists of the landing and the carriages being as shown in the plan.

Open Newel Stairs.—This type of stair has a well, and a newel post at each angle. Fig. 876 shows the plan of an open newel stair where the staircase is a little wider than double the width of the stair, and winders and a quarter-space landing are

450   A MANUAL OF CARPENTRY AND JOINERY.

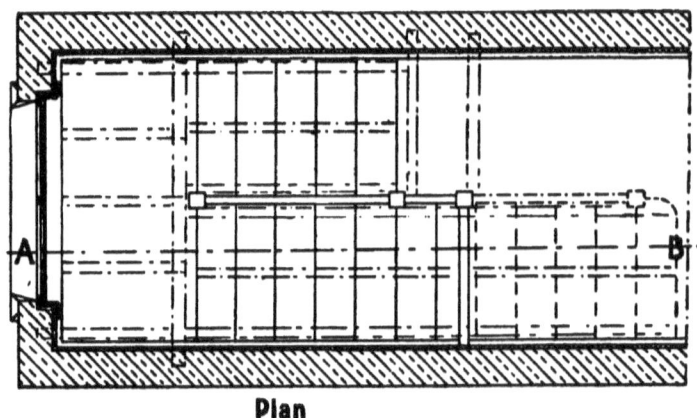

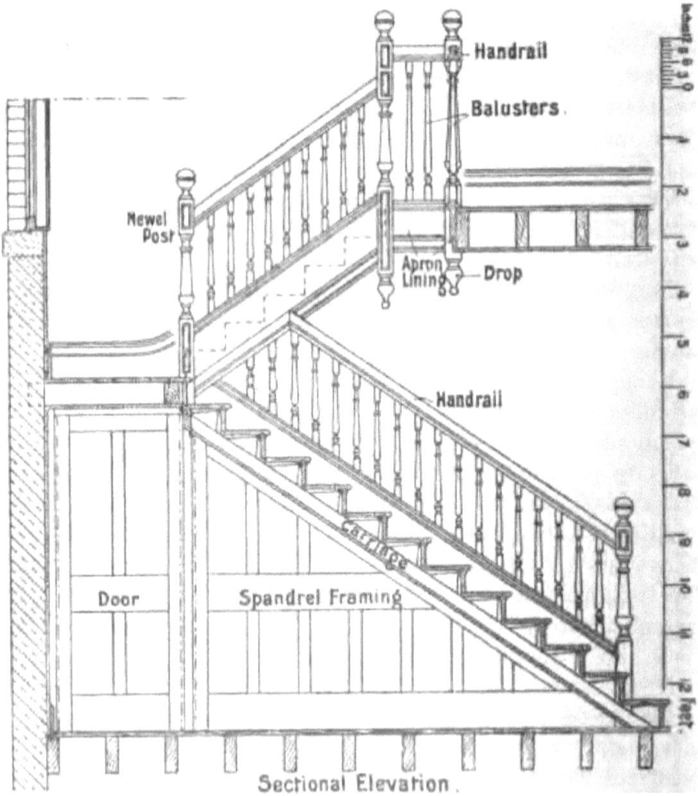

Fig. 875.

Plan and Sectional Elevation of a Dog-legged Stair.

TYPES OF STAIRS.

used. Figs. 877 and 878 are respectively the plan and sectional elevation of an open newel stair in a rectangular staircase, arranged to allow of ascent being made in easy stages of short flights with quarter-space landings between them. The close outer strings are in this example shown panelled: they have the ends tenoned into the newel posts, and are further supported by the panelled spandrel framing; the carriages and the landings are all framed together as shown.

Geometrical Stairs.

—A geometrical stair is one in which the direction is through one or more right angles: it has a continuous outer string, as well as a continuous handrail without any newel-posts.

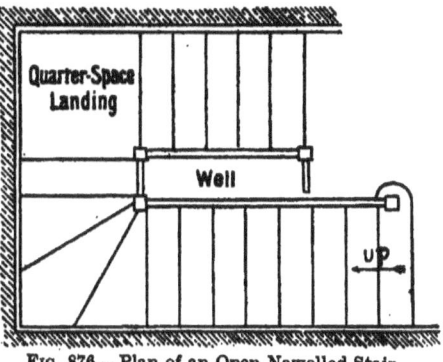

FIG. 876.—Plan of an Open Newelled Stair.

This type of stair lends itself to considerable variation of treatment, being applicable to any shape of staircase, and even to the construction of self-supporting stairs. A circular geometrical stair takes up less space than any other, and is often constructed in stone as well as of iron. The construction of a circular geometrical stair involves a large amount of labour, as the string boards are all wreathed. Figs. 879 and 880 show sectional elevation and plan of a geometrical stair with a half-space landing. The outer string is cut with mitred and returned treads and brackets. A number of the lowest treads are arranged as balancing treads: the two nearest the bottom are commode steps. The brackets under the outer ends of the balancing treads are narrower than those under the fliers. Fig. 881 shows a method of finding the shape of these diminished brackets by what are known as radial ordinates. Figs. 882 and 883 show plans of different arrangements of geometrical stairs.

Handrails.

—The **handrail** is a rail fixed directly over the outer string board; sometimes also against the wall. Its object is twofold: to act as a protective fence and as an aid to persons ascending or descending the stairs. A handrail fixed against a wall is generally supported by **iron wall brackets**, which are screwed to plugs in the wall. A handrail over the string

452   A MANUAL OF CARPENTRY AND JOINERY.

Fig. 877.

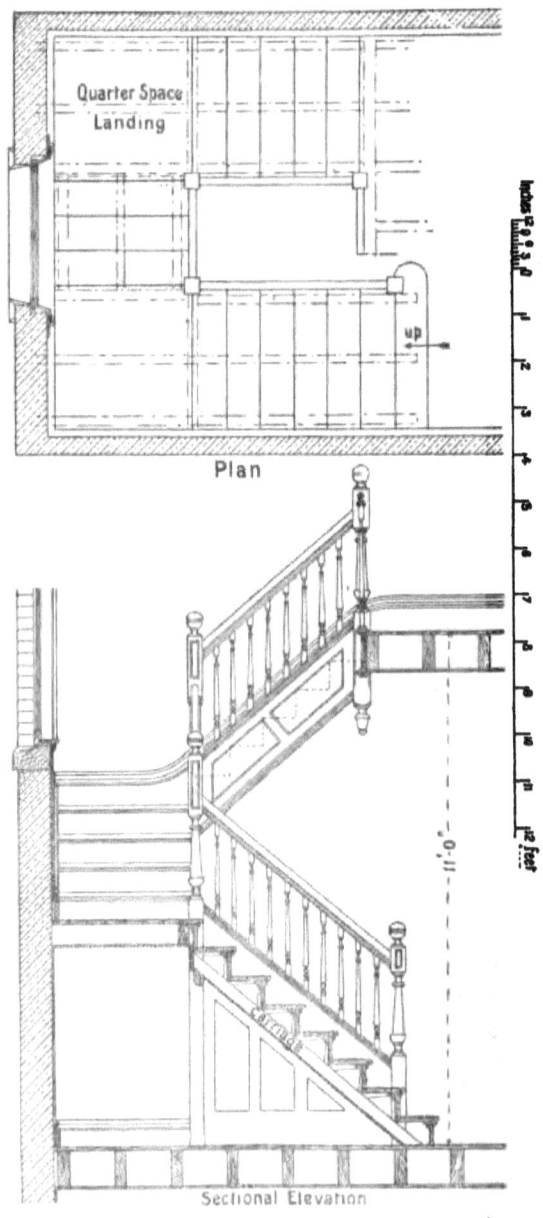

Fig. 878.

Details of an Open Newelled Stair

TYPES OF STAIRS. 453

Fig. 879.

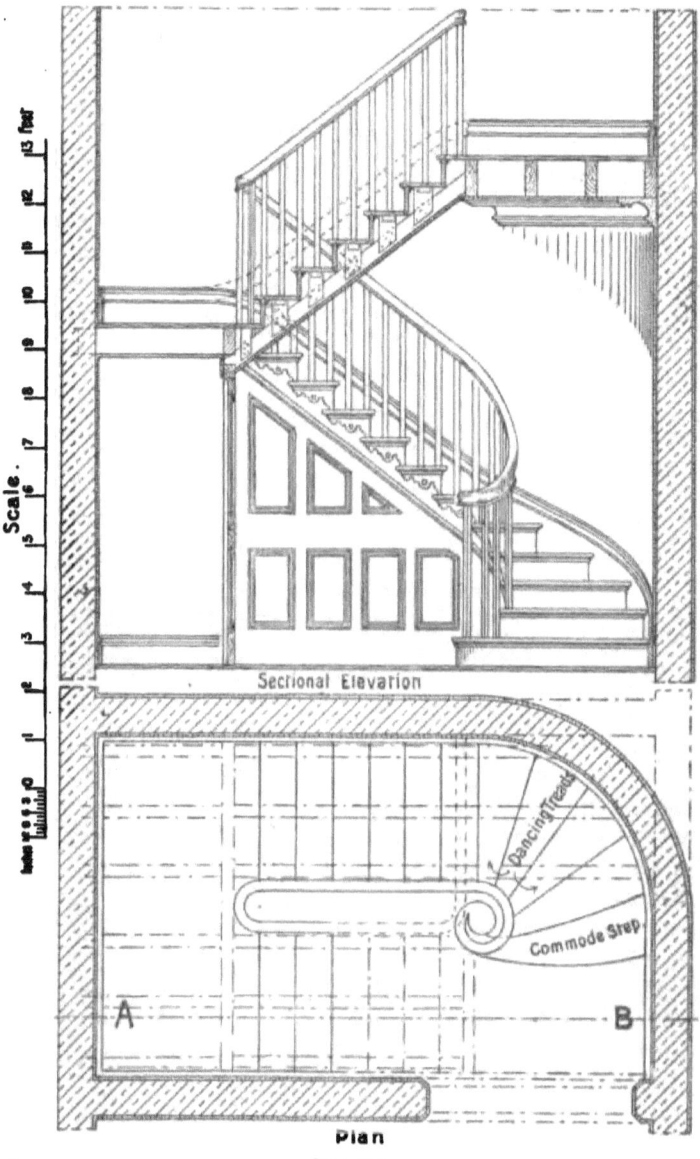

Fig. 880.

Plan and Sectional Elevation of a Geometrical Stair.

454   A MANUAL OF CARPENTRY AND JOINERY.

board has the ends tenoned into the newel-posts, and is further supported by balusters, as shown in Figs. 884 to 887. The balusters may be square, moulded, or turned. The newel-posts may be moulded, turned, or otherwise ornamented by being carved. Considerable variation exists in the size and designs of newel-posts and balusters, as will be seen from an observation of every-day examples. The line of the handrail is parallel to the

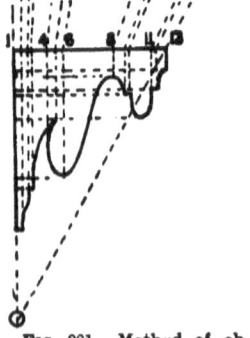

Fig. 881.—Method of obtaining shape of Brackets for Wells, etc.

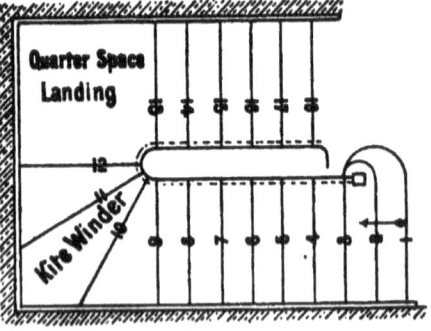

Fig. 882.

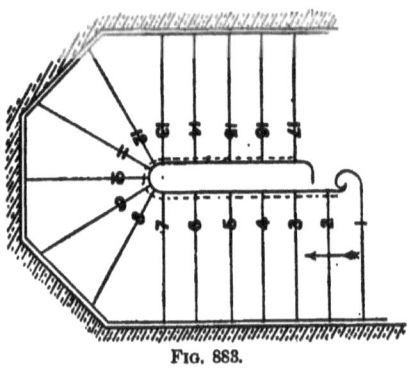

Fig. 883.

Plans of Geometrical Stairs.

line of nosings, and is placed at a height above it of about 2′ 7½″ (measured vertically in line with the face of the riser). The handrails of dog-legged and open newel stairs are generally in straight lengths, with the ends tenoned into the newel-posts. A handrail should be of such a section that it can be easily grasped. Figs. 888 to 891 are typical sections of handrails. In the best work the underside of the handrail is grooved, and an iron bar

TYPES OF STAIRS.

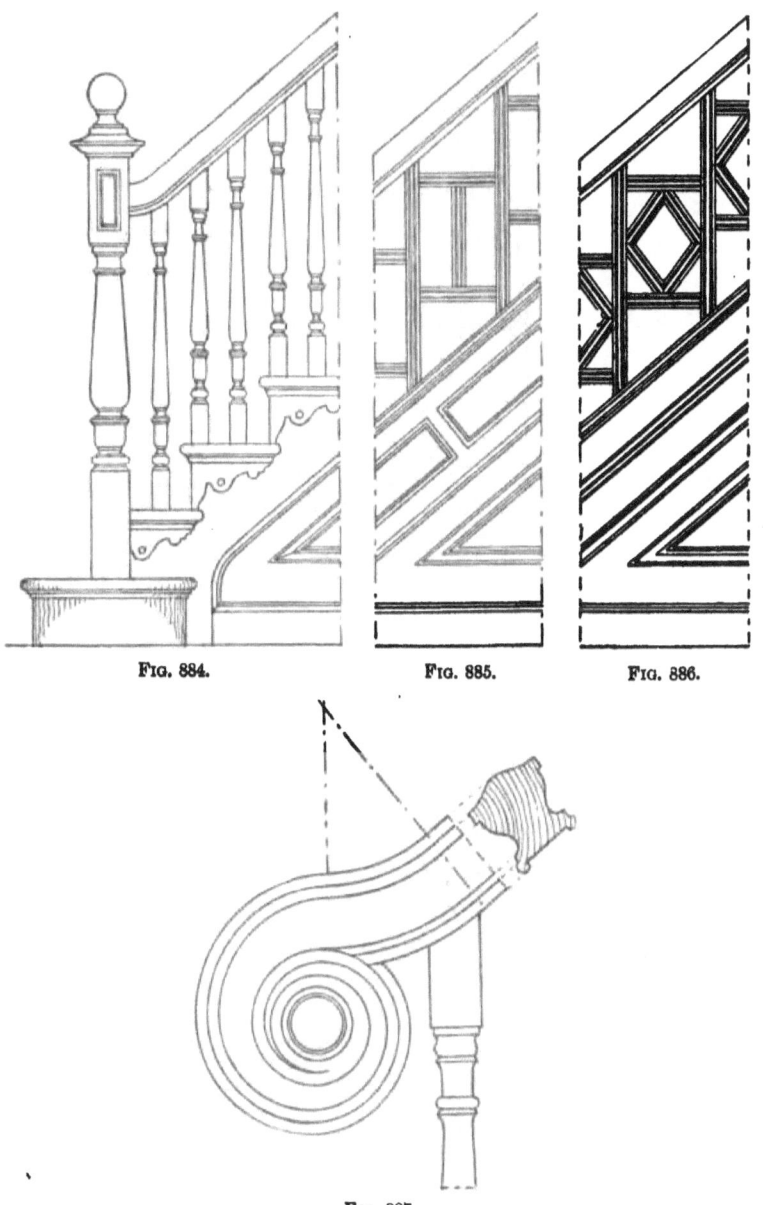

Fig. 884.   Fig. 885.   Fig. 886.

Fig. 887.

Elevations of different types of String-board, Balusters, etc.

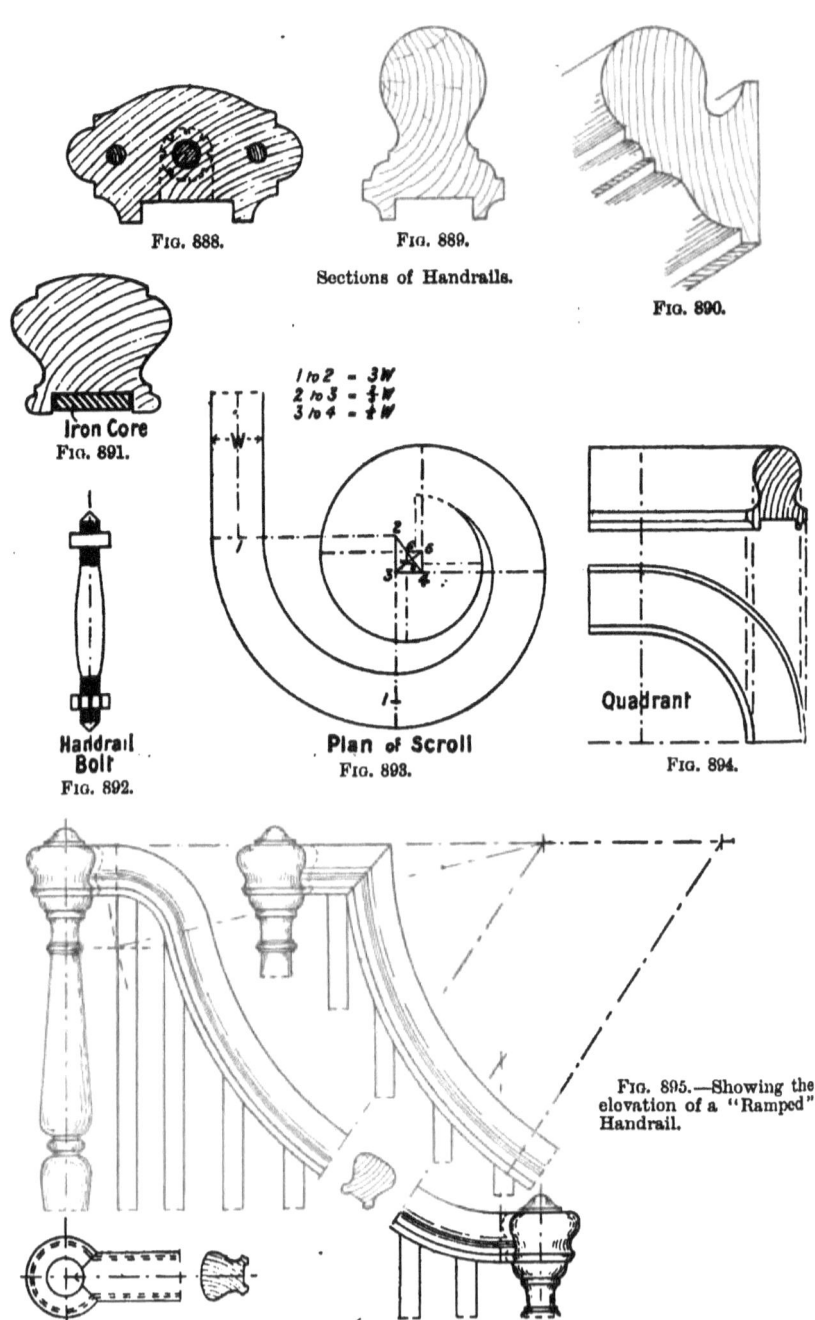

Fig. 888.

Fig. 889.

Sections of Handrails.

Fig. 890.

Iron Core
Fig. 891.

Handrail Bolt
Fig. 892.

Plan of Scroll
Fig. 893.

Quadrant
Fig. 894.

Fig. 895.—Showing the elevation of a "Ramped" Handrail.

Fig. 896.—Elevation of a Curved Handrail, the upper end being known as a "Swan-neck."

TYPES OF STAIRS. 457

placed in the groove; this bar is screwed to the upper ends of the balusters and to the underside of the handrail. Iron balusters are often inserted—one in every seven—as a means of giving additional rigidity to the rail. The handrail is often curved at the angles of upper landings, when turned into a wall, or against a newel-post. Figs. 893 to 896 show some of these curves with their distinctive names appended.

The **height of the handrail at a landing** should be greater by about half a riser, than at the inclined part of the stairs. In geometrical stairs, where it is continuous, the handrail requires to be "wreathed" at the change of direction. The preparation of these wreaths is the most difficult part of the stair-builder's work, and is generally deputed to the specialist. Satisfactorily to explain the construction of wreaths in handrailing would require more space than is here available. Any cursory treatment would be unsatisfactory, and will therefore not be attempted. It remains to be mentioned that any joints in handrails are made with dowels and handrail bolts as shown in Figs. 888 and 892.

Summary.

Wooden stairs consist of *string boards* supporting horizontal *treads* and vertical *risers*.

String boards may be *close* (having parallel edges) or *cut* (with the upper edge cut to the profile of the steps).

A **cut string** may be *cut and mitred* or *cut and bracketed*.

The outer curved string of a geometrical stair is called a **wreathed string**.

The triangular framing under the outer string is named **spandrel framing**.

When the successive flights of a stair are not in the same straight line, the change of direction is obtained by **winders** or by **landings**—*quarter-space* or *half-space* according to the angle between the flights.

Wide stairs require further supporting by rough **wooden carriages** upon which are nailed *cleats* or triangular *brackets*.

Useful relative dimensions (in inches) of the *width* of tread and *height* of rise are given by the formulae:

$$T \times R = 66, \text{ or } T + 2R = 23.$$

The principal types of stairs are **straight flight, stairs with winders, dog-legged, open newel,** and **geometrical.** The two last named are arranged around a space called the **well.**

A **handrail** is supported by vertical **balusters,** and in newelled stairs has its ends tenoned into **newel posts.**

Questions on Chapter XVI.

1. Give sketches $\frac{1}{8}$ full size of the various methods used in the joint between riser and tread. Also explain with plan (scale $\frac{1}{2}$ in. to the foot) the use and meaning of the term "balancing treads." (C. and G. Ord., 1892.)

2. (a) Make a drawing of the end of a curtail step. (b) How are treads and risers secured to the strings in the case of both cut string and close string? (C. and G. Ord., 1899.)

3. Explain the following kinds of stair: Dog-legged; newel; geometrical; dancing. (C. and G. Ord., 1896.)

4. The stairs of a cottage have to be arranged, with winders, to turn through a right angle to the right when ascending. On the lower floor there is a doorway 4 ft. 9 in. from the corner. The stairs are to be 2 ft. 9 in. wide, and are to be enclosed with 1-inch vertical tongued and grooved match-boarding. The height from floor to floor is 9 ft. 9 in. Make all the necessary working drawings; scale, for plan and section $\frac{1}{2}$ in. to one foot, for enlarged details 1$\frac{1}{2}$ in. to one foot.

5. Explain, with sketches, the meaning of the terms wall string, well string, close string, cut string, mitred string, bracket string, wreathed string. Make a plan and section of a dog-legged staircase; all construction to be shown. (C. and G. Ord., 1903.)

6. Draw the plan and sectional elevation of a dog-legged stair in a staircase 6 ft. wide. The height from floor to floor is 11 ft. Arrange a quarter-space landing and winders above it at such a height that headroom for a passage under the landing is obtained. Scale $\frac{3}{4}$ inch to one foot.

7. Make plan and section of an open newel stair, having winders. All details, such as strings and carriage pieces, are to be shown. (C. and G. Ord., 1902.)

8. Draw, to a scale of $\frac{1}{2}$ in. to a foot, a plan of a newel staircase, 3 ft. 6 in. wide; height, floor to floor 12 ft.; in a hall 9 ft. wide. Explain the method of setting out this stair, and how you would determine the proper proportion of tread to risers. (C. and G. Ord., 1898.)

9. Draw, to a scale of ½ inch to a foot, in plan and section, a newel staircase, to rise 12 ft. from floor to floor, to be 3 ft. wide, and to be contained in a space 8 ft. by 8 ft. (C. and G. Ord., 1893.)

10. Draw a plan and sectional elevation, with all details necessary to show the construction, of a geometrical stair 3 ft. 6 in. wide, in a staircase 7 ft. 9 in. between the walls. The height from floor to floor is 12 ft. Show a half-space landing at about 8 feet from the lower floor level. Scale $\frac{1}{12}$ and (for details) ½ full size.

11. Make a drawing of a geometrical staircase; all details should be shown. (C. and G. Hon., 1904.)

12. Draw a plan of a geometrical stair, scale 1 in. to the foot, and give full details of the construction of the curtailed step. (C. and G. Ord., 1901.)

13. Show how you would make the internal string of a geometrical stair. The well hole to be 2 ft. 4 in. in the clear. (C. and G. Hon., 1901.)

14. A geometrical staircase has a veneered string. It has three winders and a quarter-space landing at one part. Well hole 12 inches in the clear. Work out to a large scale, the development of the veneer round the well hole, and show by dotted lines the construction. (C. and G. Hon., 1892.)

15. Draw the plan and show the construction of a commode step for a geometrical stair; show also the method of developing the inside string, and give a description of the process of preparing it. (C. and G. Hon., 1903.)

16. Draw a plan and section to ½ in. scale, showing the construction of circular geometrical stairs 3 ft. 9 in. wide, in a circular space 10 ft. in diameter, the stairs to rise to a landing 9 ft. from floor to floor. (C. and G. Hon., 1893.)

17. Make the drawing of a scroll wreath for a curtail step. (C. and G. Hon., 1903.)

CHAPTER XVII.

WORKSHOP PRACTICE AND SPECIAL CONSTRUCTIONS.

THE detailed consideration of the methods of preparing and fixing the varied work upon which the carpenter and joiner are engaged will now be considered briefly. Although the preceding chapters give detailed information of the several branches under distinctive headings, there are many points of importance which demand further attention.

Arrangement of Workshop.—Although the arrangement of the workshop is of some importance, there is evidence to show that in a large number of cases it does not receive the amount of consideration which it merits. An up-to-date workshop is arranged so that there is abundance of light, an economical utilisation of space, with sufficient room to undertake the different kinds of work that come to hand, and convenience for transference of the work to and from the machines and the benches.

Benches are usually from 9 to 12 feet long; they may be single or double, according to the space available, or the manner of lighting the room. When the workshop is in an upper storey, as is often the case, special attention should be given to the strength of the floor, in order to minimise vibration. It is economical to have each bench fitted with an instantaneous-grip vice, and a tail vice will also be found useful. The space between the benches will depend upon the available accommodation, but at least 2 feet is required for the bench-way between single and 3 feet between double benches. When much machinery is in general use, it is better to have separate rooms for machinery and benches, as the dust which is unavoidable in the machine-room will interfere with the cleanliness of the finished work, and the noise and vibration often detract from the accuracy necessary at the benches. It is essential that the workshop be kept clean and well ventilated, and it should be provided with artificial heat in the winter months, as well for the comfort of the workman as for the sake of the material. Side lights are much better for lighting the workshop than roof lights, and the benches should be arranged with the head ends to the light. When, as is often the case, the machine-room is below the workshop, a trap door in the floor of the latter will be found a necessity, while easily-ascended stairs are indispensable. The artificial lighting of the room, the arrangement for heating the glue, the position of the grindstone, and the storage arrangements for templates, cramps, and sundry appliances in occasional use, all demand careful consideration.

"**Trueing-up**" **of Material.**—As has been explained in Chapter VI., machinery is used very extensively for cutting up and preparing material. Not only is machinery commonly used to "dress" (plane) to the exact size all the "stuff" required, but any grooving of the edges, or rebating or moulding of the arrises is also done by machinery, and mortising and tenoning machines are used for cutting mortises and tenons ; so that in addition to the setting-out of the work, it is only necessary, in the mass of ordinary framing, for the workman to examine and, when necessary, to trim, the joints, and to put the framing together and smooth it off.

When the trueing-up of the material for framing is carried out entirely by hand labour, care must be taken to have each separate piece planed **perfectly true**, with the edges straight and at right angles to the sides. Unless this is done the resulting framing will have a " twisted " surface. In sawing out material which has to be hand dressed, it is necessary to allow, over the finished sizes, about one eighth of an inch in both width and thickness for planing.

In dressing the material, the workman uses distinctive marks for what he considers the best side and edge of each piece. These marks are named **face marks**, and they play an important part in guiding the several operations through which each piece has to go. He first examines the piece and selects its best side, dresses this side until a truly plane surface (which is tested with the winding strips (p. 108) and straight edge) is obtained, and then puts on the face-side mark ⌽ which points towards the best edge. He then planes the best edge until it is straight and at right angles to the face side, and then puts on the face-edge mark ∧. The material is next gauged with the marking gauge (p. 109) to the required width, and planed to this width ; after which it is gauged to the required thickness and planed to this thickness. Of course, the above description of trueing-up work applies only to stuff which is required to be of definite finished size, such as the panelled framing of doors, dado-framing, bath and lavatory fittings, office screens, the framing of sashes, etc. Other material often needs only to have the surfaces dressed, with no particular care as to straightness or exact size.

Setting-out.—The setting out of framing consists of marking the shoulder lines for the joints, and the exact lengths of the various members to be fitted together. The nature of the work is so varied, and—as previous chapters have shown—the number of suitable joints for different purposes is so great, that only a few typical examples can be illustrated, although the explanation given is generally applicable.

The setting-out of the work is undoubtedly its most important side, and is a test of the efficiency of the craftsman. He must have a thorough knowledge of geometrical projection to be able clearly to understand the drawings of the architect or designer, and a practical knowledge of detail to be able to set out all the intricate framework with which he may have to deal. It may happen that some impossible method of construction is being attempted, and it is the business of the craftsman to detect this when setting out his work.

The foreman of the workshop generally undertakes the duty of setting-out, and of solving any difficulties which may arise, although he often deputes part of this work to the most trustworthy of his workmen.

For the mass of ordinary panelled and sash framing it is usual first to draw out, to full size, a horizontal and a vertical section upon a rod or thin board (the setting-out rod), showing the shoulder lines, mortises, tenons, and any grooving, rebating or moulding which occurs, and then to transfer as many of these lines as are necessary to the different members of the framework. It is impossible to give more than a general idea of how this is done, since custom varies in different workshops, and the opinions of various craftsmen differ as to what is necessary.

With rectangular framing, the sections supply all the data necessary, but if there are curved surfaces, such as circular-headed panels, curved heads to window frames, or triangular spandrel or irregular-shaped framing, an elevation also is needed.

When a number of rails of the same dimensions and having the same thickness of tenon are cut with a tenoning machine, it is only necessary to set out one rail. This rail can then be used as a template, and one setting of adjustable fences on the machine will serve for the cutting of all the remaining rails. A similar remark applies to any tenoning of a number of pieces (*e.g.* muntins) of the same size, but not to the cutting of mortises.

It must be remembered that a tenon should not have a width of more than five times its thickness (p. 170) and that haunched tenons (p. 170) are necessary at the corners of panelled framing. When the edges of the framing are grooved, as in nearly all kinds of panelled work, it is necessary to allow for the grooves since they reduce the width of the tenons. When the framing is rebated, as in sash framing and the upper part of sash doors, the depth of the rebate has to be allowed for in marking the shoulder lines. When the inner arrises of the sashes or other framework are beaded or moulded, this fact must be taken into consideration and allowed for in the setting out of the work.

The **setting-out rod** may be square in section (about $1\frac{1}{2}''$ side), or a thin board of from 7 to 11 inches wide may be used, the surface of which has been covered with a thin coating of powdered whitening mixed with very thin glue size, and afterwards sand-papered down until fairly smooth.

Fig. 897 shows a rod upon which are details for the door illustrated in Figs. 674 to 678. It will be seen that from this rod the lengths and widths of all the members of the framing, the exact sizes of all the panels, the lengths between the shoulder lines of all rails and muntins, and the sizes of all mortises, can be obtained. It is advisable, when transferring shoulder lines from the setting-out rod to such members as muntins, to allow for slight shrinkage of the wide rails during second seasoning (p. 7). Fig. 898 illustrates the

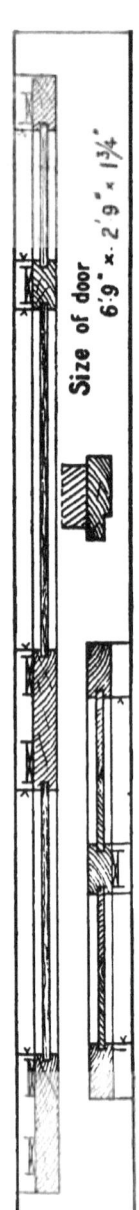
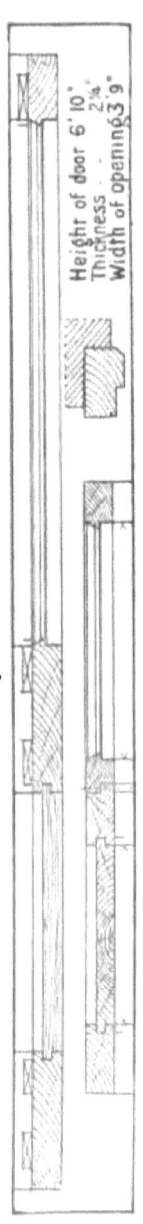
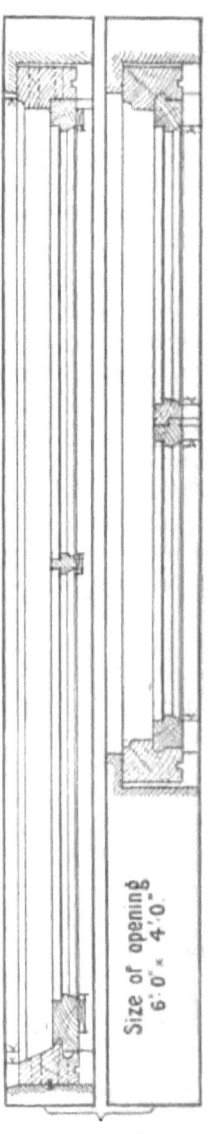

FIG. 897.—Setting-out Rod for the Door illustrated in Figs. 674 to 678.

FIG. 898.—Setting out Rod for the Sash Doors illustrated in Figs. 680 to 684.

FIG. 899.—Setting-out Rod for the Casement Window illustrated in Figs. 742 to 745.

setting-out rod for the pair of sash doors of Fig 680, the upper parts of which are of glass. It is usual in such a case to set out one half of the horizontal section to show the lower part of the doors with the panelled framing, and to have upon the other half the upper part which shows the moulded arrises and the rebate for the glass.

Fig. 899 shows a rod upon which are set out all the details required for the casement window illustrated in Figs. 742 to 745; and Fig. 900 shows a similar rod with the setting-out lines for the sash and frame window given in elevation and sections in Figs. 770 to 772. It will be noticed that on each of these rods the vertical section is drawn on one side and the horizontal section upon the other side of the rod, that the mortises are indicated by the diagonal lines, and that an arrow head is placed at each of the shoulder lines. It is a wise precaution at all times to confirm, by measuring, the sizes of all openings in brick or stone walls before setting out the rods for the window or door frames.

Such framing as movable panelled and glazed partitions, office screens, dado framing, church, chapel and assembly-room fittings, and in fact all kinds of panelled or other framing, needs setting out by drawing upon rods vertical and horizontal sections to full size, and then transferring the lines for the shoulders and the mortises to the material composing the framing. With complicated framing the difficulties increase and more care is needed, and it will be readily understood that in such hard wood as oak,

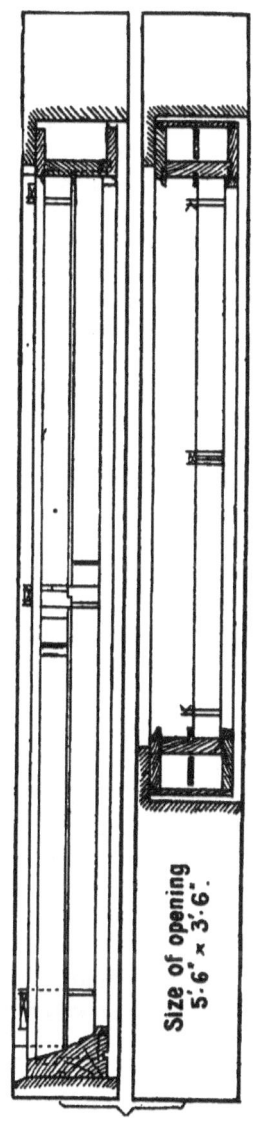

FIG. 900.—Setting-out Rod for the Sash and Frame Window illustrated in Figs. 770 to 772.

mahogany, walnut, etc., greater care is needed in execution than with the mass of work done in soft woods.

The Putting Together of Framing.—After the setting-out comes the mortising and tenoning, which in hand work is done before any grooving, rebating, or moulding. When the mortises and tenons are machine-cut, they require subsequent examination, and, often, cleaning up by the workman. When these operations have been completed it is necessary, before putting the framing together, to smooth all parts that cannot be smoothed afterwards. In panelled work the panels must be inserted as the framing is put together; after which it is glued, cramped together, wedged and smoothed off.

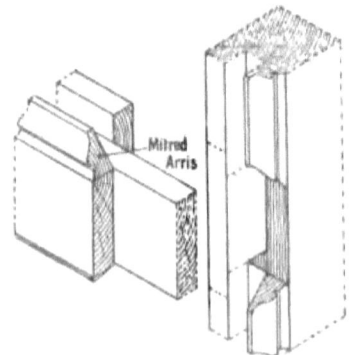

FIG. 901.—Solid Moulded Framing with Mitred Joint.

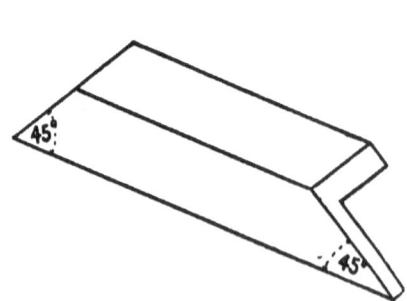

FIG. 902.—Mitre Template.

When the framing is solid moulded, the moulded arrises need to be fitted together unless the mouldings are stopped at each of the joints as shown in Fig. 658. The joint can be made by **mitring** each of the members of the framing as shown in Fig. 901, or—which is better because it does not show any slight shrinkage that may possibly take place—the members may be **scribed** as shown in Fig. 357. When mitring is resorted to, a **mitre template** (Fig. 902) is used.

When the mouldings are "planted-in," which is the case with the bulk of panelled framing, a **mitre block** (for small mouldings) or a **mitre box** (for larger mouldings) is used in cutting the ends of all the mouldings that fit into rectangular framing. Figs. 903 and 904 show a mitre block and mitre box respectively; it will be seen that each has saw grooves cut at an angle of 45° to the sides—this being the angle to which the ends of mouldings meeting at a right angle are cut. In nailing the mouldings in position, care must be taken to drive the nails so that they pierce the solid framing and not the panel; this leaves the

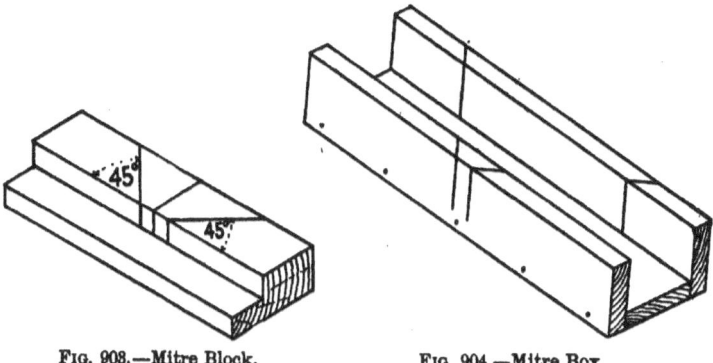

FIG. 903.—Mitre Block.   FIG. 904.—Mitre Box.

edges of the panel free for slight shrinkage. When the angles of the framing are not right angles, the mitre bisects the angle. Fig. 905 shows part of a piece of panelled framing suitable for the soffit of a deeply recessed shop doorway, or the soffit of a bay window, in which some of the edges of the

FIG. 905.—Irregular shaped Panelled and Moulded Framing.

framing are curved. When the mouldings of such framing are to be planted-in, some of the mouldings will be curved, and the mitres of these require special attention. In some cases (Fig. 905) the mitres are curved surfaces. The method of obtaining the intersecting mitre, when a straight moulding meets a curved one (as at A in Fig. 905) or when two curved mouldings intersect (as at B in Fig. 905) is shown in detail in Fig. 906. The mitre line $O\,4$ is an even curve drawn through the points of intersection of the pairs of equidistant parallels to AO and BO respectively. It will be seen from Fig. 905 at C that in certain circumstances the intersection of two curved mouldings, or a curved and a straight one, may be a plane or "straight" mitre.

Raking Mouldings and Angle Bars.—In Chapter II., Figs. 79 and 80 show methods of enlarging and diminishing mouldings. A modification of this geometrical principle is to be found when a moulding, fixed against a vertical wall in an inclined (raking) position, intersects a horizontal moulding against a wall at right angles to the first one. Fig. 907 shows

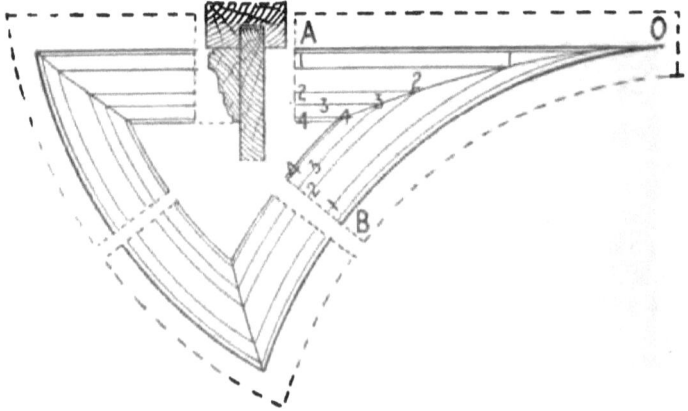

FIG. 906.—Enlarged detail of Panel (x) in Fig. 905, showing Mitres of Moulding.

how to obtain the shape of the horizontal moulding on the upper edge of a skirting board which has to mitre into the inclined skirting board of the given cross section. To obtain a true intersection at the angle, the horizontal moulding is necessarily of different shape from the raking moulding. Fig. 908 shows another type of raking moulding with the shapes of horizontal returns at both the upper and the lower ends. The return in each case is upon a vertical surface and through a right angle. The projection of the various members beyond the face of the wall is the same in each case, as indicated by the corresponding numbers. Fig. 909 shows the method of obtaining the shape of a moulded angle-bar for a shop window or some similar framing.

WORKSHOP PRACTICE. 469

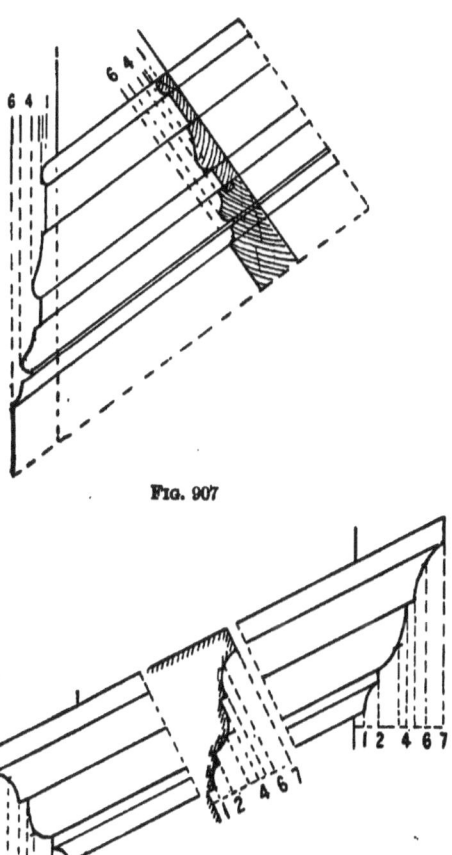

Fig. 907.

Fig. 908.

Methods of obtaining the shapes of Intersecting Raking Mouldings.

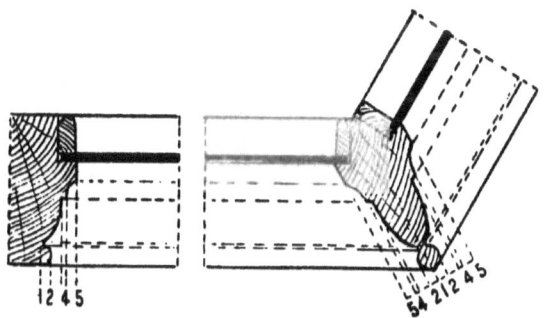

Fig. 909.—Method of obtaining the shape of a Moulded Angle Bar.

Angle Brackets.—The ceilings of rooms are often relieved by having plaster cornice-moulds run in the angle between the ceiling and the vertical walls. When the cornice is large, the plasterers' laths supporting it are carried by rough wooden

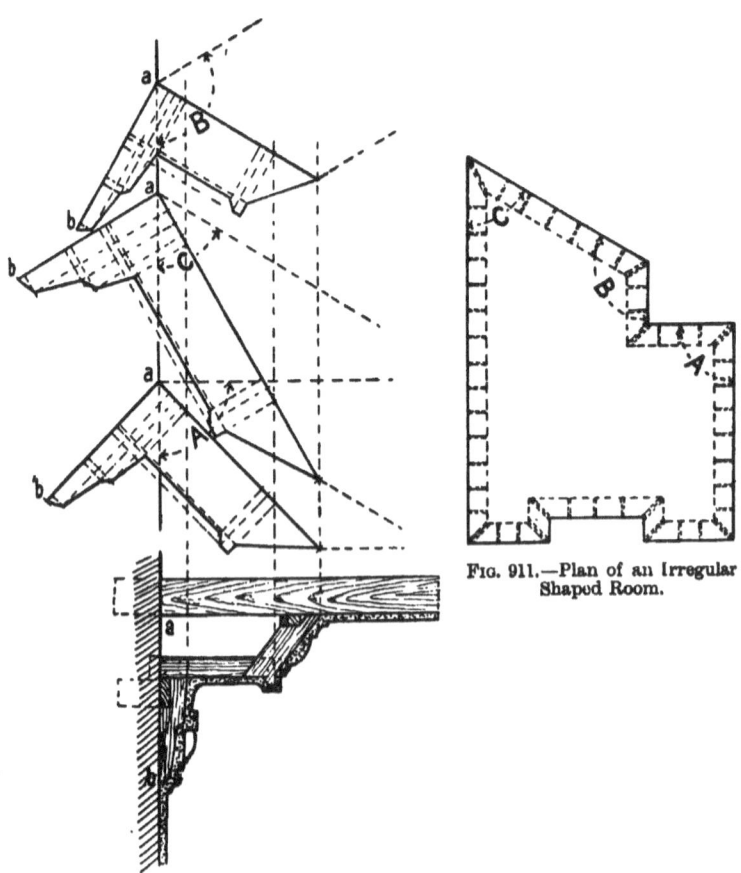

Fig. 911.—Plan of an Irregular Shaped Room.

Fig. 910.—Methods of obtaining shapes of Angle Brackets in Fig. 911.

brackets (**angle brackets**) placed about 15 inches apart along the intersection of the wall and the ceiling. These brackets are cut approximately to the shape of the section of the cornice as shown in Fig. 910. Specially shaped brackets are needed for the support of the ends of the laths at the corners of the room.

The method of determining the shape of such **corner brackets** is an excellent example of geometrical projection, and is shown in detail in Fig. 910. Fig. 911 shows the plan of a peculiarly shaped room, purposely selected to give variety of corners. The reference letters of Figs. 910 and 911 are identical, and Fig. 910 shows the outline of the corner brackets at A, B, and C. In cutting out these corner brackets it is necessary first to prepare a template of the required shape. The template is then applied to the surface of the material, and—as the edges of the corner brackets are not at right angles to their vertical plane, but must be cut so that they are in line with the other brackets as shown in Fig. 911—the bevels to which the edges are cut must be obtained from the plan of the room. The template must be applied to both sides of the material to

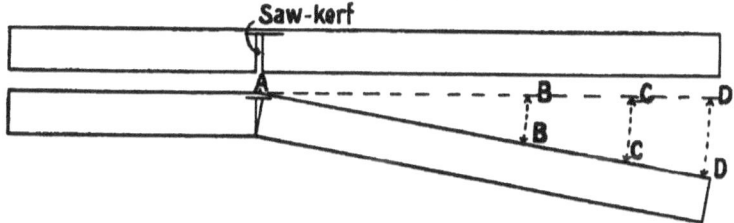

Fig. 912.—Method of finding the distances apart of the Saw-Kerfs when bending boards.

correspond to the edge bevel required. A similar construction is applicable wherever large wooden moulded cornices meet at an angle and have to be supported by wooden brackets.

Saw-Kerfing.—Curved surfaces are often "cut out of the solid" and dressed to the required curvature. It is occasionally necessary, however, to bend a board to obtain a curved surface. In addition to the methods already explained of bending boards (pp. 401 and 440), a method often adopted is to make saw-cuts (**kerfs**) in the side which is to be concave, at such distances apart that in order to close the kerfs the board must be bent to the required curvature.

A ready appliance for obtaining the exact distances apart of the saw-kerfs is illustrated in Fig. 912. It consists of a lath of exactly the same thickness as the board to be bent. About the middle of the length of this lath a saw-kerf is made. The lath is then bent until the kerf closes, and the angle through which it has been turned from the straight line is obtained. An arc of a circle is then struck (Fig. 912) with A as centre and a radius equal to the radius of the curve required. The chord BB of the arc is the distance apart of the kerfs to be cut in the board to be bent. Similarly, with a curve of radius AC, CC gives the distance apart of the saw-kerfs; and, again, DD would be the distance apart of kerfs required for curvature of

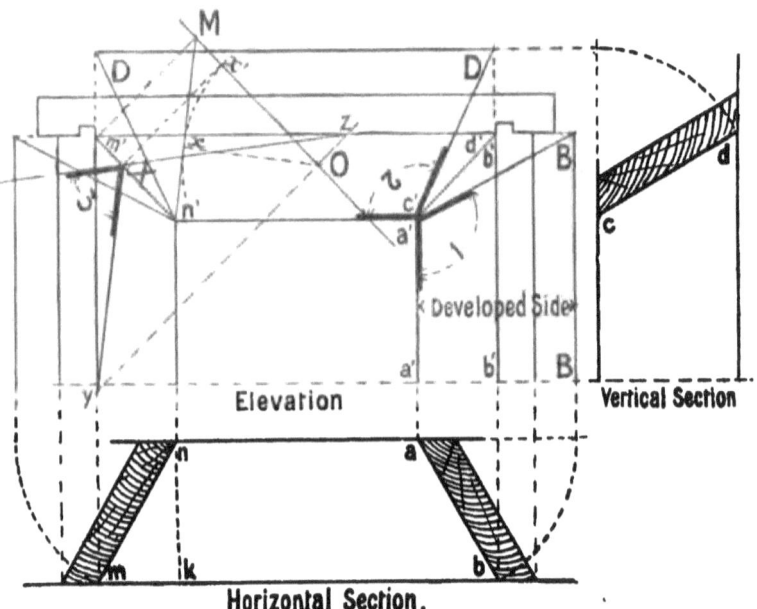

Fig. 913.—Method of obtaining the Bevels at the ends of Splayed Linings around a door or window opening.

radius AD. The following precautions must be carefully attended to:

(1) The lath must be of exactly the same thickness as the board to be bent.

(2) All the saw-kerfs must be made with the same saw, *i.e.* the saw used for cutting the lath.

(3) The depths of all the kerfs must be equal, and deep enough to allow of bending without breaking the fibres on the convex side of the board.

Splayed Linings.—Fig. 913 shows the upper part of the

WORKSHOP PRACTICE.

elevation, a horizontal section, and a vertical section of the inside linings of a window or door frame, where both the jamb and head linings are "splayed." To obtain the lines of intersection of the oblique (splayed) planes, it is necessary to draw out the appearance of each when the two have been rotated into the same plane. In Fig. 913 ab is the horizontal section and $a'a'$, $b'b'$ the elevation of the front face of the jamb-lining on the right-hand side. The line ab is rotated on a as centre, and the true shape of the front face thus developed is seen to be $a'a'$ BB; while angle 1 gives the bevel for the side cut. Similarly, by rotating the line cd on centre c, the development $Dn'c'D$ of

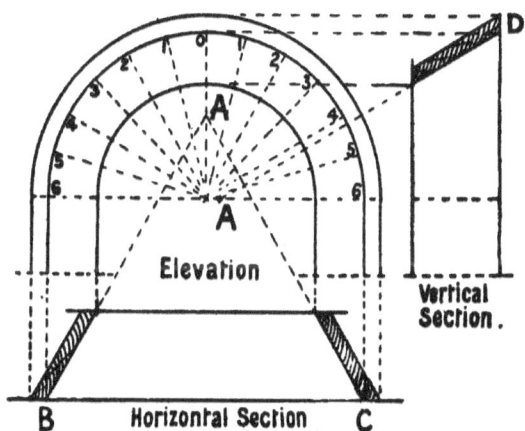

FIG. 914.—Splayed Linings around a semi-circular opening.

the head is obtained: the bevel of the head at its intersection with the jamb being given by the angle 2.

The method of obtaining the angle (marked 3) which the edge cut makes with the face of the jamb-lining is shown on the left-hand side of the drawing. As a geometrical problem it is the determination of the angle between two planes, *i.e.* the faces of the vertical jamb-lining and the head-lining. $m'n'$ is the elevation of the line of intersection of these two planes, and Mn' shows its true length, because Mm' is equal to nk in the horizontal section. Through M draw MO parallel to $m'n'$. From any point O in MO draw Ox perpendicular to Mn', and through O draw yz perpendicular to $m'n'$. Make Ox' equal to Ox and draw Xx' perpendicular to $m'n'$. Join Xy and Xz. The angle

474   A MANUAL OF CARPENTRY AND JOINERY.

yXz is the angle between the two planes, and its complement 3 is the angle of the edge cut.

The principles involved in this exercise are applicable also to the construction of hoppers, triangular louvre ventilators, and to splayed work generally.

Fig. 914 shows splayed linings for an opening with a semicircular head. Fig. 915 shows the development of the circular part, which is a portion of the stretch-out of a cone. The numbering indicates corresponding points on the two drawings.

Circle-on-Circle Work.—Circle-on-circle work, as the name implies, involves the construction of framing which is circular in

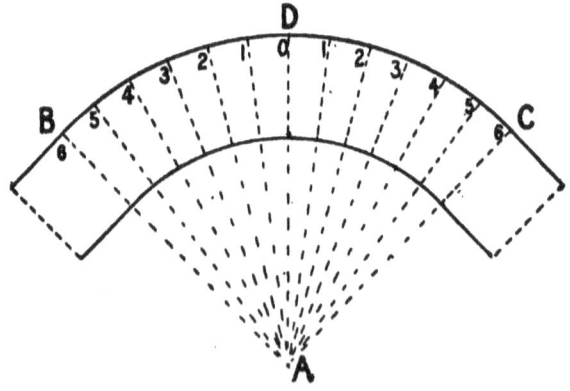

FIG. 915.—Development of the curved part of the Splayed Lining in Fig. 914.

both plan and elevation. It generally occurs in door or window frames which are segmental in plan, and have the upper part (head) semicircular in elevation. Fig. 916 is an illustration of a typical example with "radiating" jambs. The curved part of such frames is usually built up of two, three, or more members, according to size. As the curved members are of necessity worked out of rectangular pieces, and have the joints prepared before the curved surfaces are worked, the determination of the minimum size of material required, and of the bevels to which the ends must be cut, needs careful consideration. In Fig. 916 the minimum thickness of the material is the perpendicular distance between MN and PQ. The face joints are shown at X and Y, the point x being obtained by drawing through o perpendicular to PQ. The edge joint at the lower end is perpendicular to the face side, and the bevel for the edge joint at the upper end is shown at Z. The **face moulds** are templates

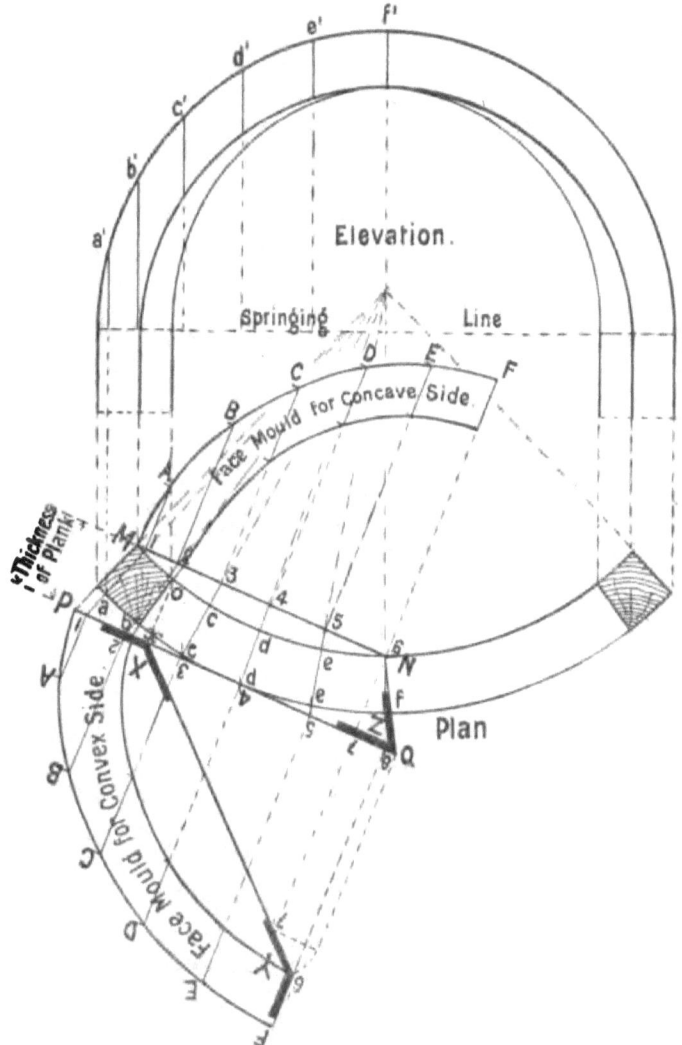

Fig. 916.—Circle-on-Circle Framing with Radiating Jambs.

for marking out the curvature of the upper and lower faces. They are obtained by developing the vertical plane PQ for the

476 A MANUAL OF CARPENTRY AND JOINERY.

outer (convex) side, and the vertical plane MN for the inner (concave) side. The development is in each case an even curve drawn through points obtained by measuring, from PQ and

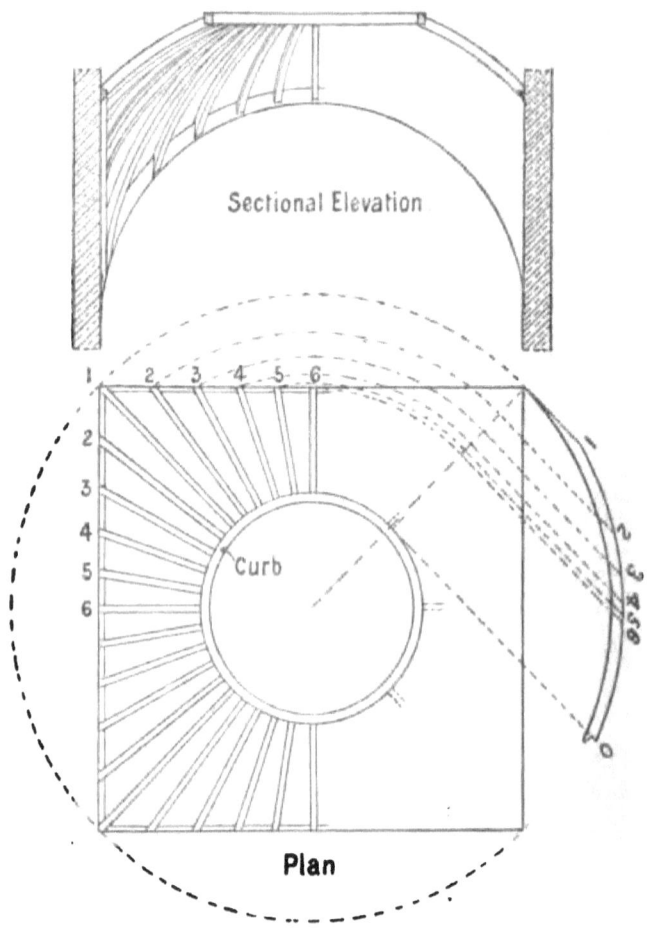

FIG. 917.—Hemispherical Pendentive Cradling.

MN respectively, ordinates equal in length to corresponding ordinates projected from the elevation. After working these curved surfaces, the lines to which to cut the vertical curved surfaces are obtained by transferring the horizontal radiating lines 1 1, 2 2, 3 3, etc., to the upper and lower surfaces, and measuring along these lines the points *cc*, *dd*, *ee*, etc., from the faces *PQ* and *MN* respectively. Even curves drawn through these points give the lines required. Any rebating or moulding of the arrises may be done easily by working parallel to the curved surfaces. Joints in circle-on-circle work usually abut normally to the curve, and are secured with hammer-headed keys (Fig. 368) or handrail bolts (Fig. 892) and dowels.

Pendentives.—When a room is lighted from the ceiling, as in art galleries, museums, etc., the ceiling of the room often takes the shape of a dome. With such a construction the wooden curb (p. 420) which carries the roof-light is supported, as is also the plastered ceiling, by rough wooden brackets or cradling. Such a treatment is said to be pendentive, and the rough wooden framework is known as **pendentive cradling**. The ceiling may have either circular or elliptical curved ribs, and the curb upon which the lantern light rests may be square, polygonal, circular, or elliptical. If the curved ribs are long, they may be built up of two or three thicknesses nailed together with overlapping joints. Fig. 917 shows the details of the pendentive cradling for a ceiling the shape of which is hemispherical; it supports a circular curb.

FIXING OF JOINERS' WORK.

If the finished wrought woodwork is, after being properly seasoned, fixed in position in a new building before the walls and the plaster are dry, it will absorb moisture and swell, and, after drying, it will be apparent that the joints have been strained. On this account, therefore, all finished work should, as far as possible, be left unfixed until the building is quite dry. The method of fixing depends upon the class of building and the character of the finished work. The usual plan is to fix wooden battens called **grounds** to the walls around all doorways, window openings, and along the walls for the upper edges of skirting boards, dado framing, and in fact generally where finished woodwork has to be secured to the wall. These grounds are nailed either to slips which have been built into the wall, or to plugs driven into the joints between the bricks. The grounds around doorways and window openings are framed at the angles, and it is necessary to arrange that all the

478　A MANUAL OF CARPENTRY AND JOINERY.

grounds on the same wall shall be in the same vertical plane, so that, as the plasterer uses them for a guide when plastering the surface, he will be able to obtain true surfaces. Iron

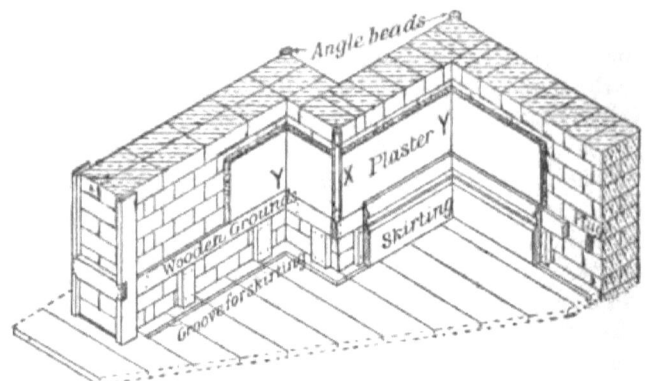

Fig. 918.—Angles in a room showing method of fixing Skirting, Grounds, Angle Beads, etc.

holdfasts are sometimes used for securing such grounds, especially around chimney flues. Fig. 918 shows how the grounds are fixed in part of a doorway, and also behind the skirting boards. In the mass of ordinary work the finished material is nailed or screwed to the grounds, with the nails punched below the surface and the nail-holes afterwards puttied-up by the painter. In superior work, where such material as oak, mahogany, etc., is used, and where the finished surface is afterwards polished, any visible nail-holes or screws would be objectionable, secret screwing is largely resorted to. In addition to this, the material is so constructed that tongued and grooved joints and glue blocks are largely used as fastenings. Fig. 919 illustrates a method which may occasionally be used with advantage. It consists of cutting a narrow chase of small depth into the face of the board, raising carefully the part cut, driving a nail or a screw into

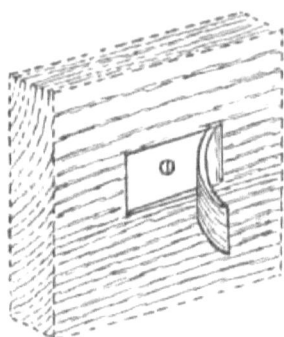

Fig. 919.—Method of Secret Screwing or Secret Nailing.

position, and then gluing the raised portion into its original position.

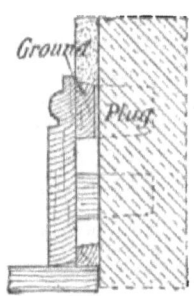

FIG. 920.—Section through Torus Moulded Skirting.

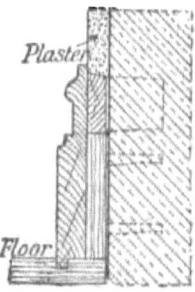

FIG. 921.—Moulded Skirting tongued to the Floor.

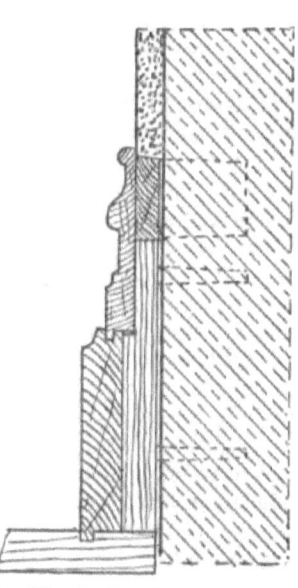

FIG. 922.—Section through a double-faced Skirting.

Figs. 920, 921, and 922 are sections through three different forms of skirting boards, with their names attached. In the best class of work the lower edge of the skirting is tongued into the floor.

Angle Beads.—When an external angle occurs in a room, as at X in Fig. 918, an angle or staff bead is fixed by means of wooden plugs to the wall as a guide for the plasterer, as well as to protect the angle. Fig. 923 is a horizontal section of an angle bead. The bead is sometimes dispensed with, and the plasterer works the angle in cement.

FIG. 923.

Summary.

A **workshop** should have abundance of light, be properly heated in winter, and have special regard paid to the arrangement of the benches, machinery, storage arrangement, artificial lighting, etc.

In the preparation of framing by **hand labour**, both the "trueing-up" of the material, and the systematic testing for straightness and size call for great care.

The ability to "**set out**" all kinds of wooden framing is one of the surest tests of the skill of the craftsman. The setting out is usually first done on rods, the measurements being afterwards transferred from these rods to the various members of the framing.

Panelled framing may have the mouldings worked on the arrises, or they may be "planted in." The **mitre block** or **mitre box** is often used for mouldings which are **mitred**. In certain cases the mitre of two intersecting mouldings is a curved surface.

When a **raking moulding** intersects a horizontal moulding at an angle between two planes, the two mouldings are of different shape.

A board can be bent to almost any radius by cutting equidistant **saw-kerfs** on one face. The distance apart of the kerfs depends upon (1) the radius of curvature; (2) the thickness of the board to be bent; and (3) the thickness of the saw used.

In **splayed linings**, **circle-on-circle** work, and **pendentive cradling**, the practical application of geometrical principles of projection is necessary for the determination of the sizes of the material, and the bevels of the joints.

Finished woodwork is fixed to **grounds** plugged to the walls of the building. It should never be taken to the building until the walls and the plaster are dry.

Questions on Chapter XVII.

1. Show how you would set out on a rod for an inside four-panelled door and frame. Size of door 7 ft. by 3 ft. by 2 in.

2. Show how you would set out a rod for a window-frame fitted with a pair of French casements. (C. and G. Hon., 1898.)

3. Make a drawing of a piece of irregular-shaped panelled and moulded framing, some of the panels of which have curved edges, and determine the shapes of all the mitres of the mouldings, assuming them to be planted in.

4. (a) Give an illustration of the method of diminishing the section of a moulding. (b) Show how you find the section of a

QUESTIONS ON CHAPTER XVII. 481

raking moulding, such as is used in the angle of a shop front. (C. and G. Ord., 1899.)

5. Show how you would determine the section of an angle bar of a shop front, also how the bar is connected to the top and bottom rails and how the rails are joined at the angles. (C. and G. Ord., 1904.)

6. Show and explain fully the method of obtaining the moulds for angle brackets for finishing the moulded bottom of an oriel bay window, half octagon on plan. (C. and G. Ord., 1895.)

7. It is required to run a bracketed plaster cornice (24 inches girth) round a room, one angle of which is 75 degrees on plan. Give a plan and section (1 inch scale to the foot) of the cornice, showing the brackets and also an elevation of the angle bracket. (C. and G. Ord., 1892.)

8. Describe some different methods of bending wood for circular work other than steaming, also some ways of joining desk framing at angles. (C. and G. Ord., 1895.)

9. The inside linings of a window opening are 9 in. wide, and are (including the head) splayed to the extent of 3 in. Determine the bevels to which the upper ends of the jambs must be cut.

10. Explain fully how you would get out and put together the head of a sash, circular on plan and segmental in elevation. (C. and G. Hon., 1894.)

11. Describe the method of framing up a sash circular on plan and in elevation, showing, by drawing, the lines for getting out the moulds, etc. (C. and G. Hon., 1893.)

12. Show the method for obtaining the face mould of a solid door frame head "circle-on-circle." (C. and G. Hon., 1899.)

13. A square lantern light, 6 feet internally, has in the centre an opening 1 foot 6 inches in diameter, octagonal on plan. The hips are moulded to the same section as the mouldings round the opening. Show by scale sketches how you would obtain the intersection of the mouldings. (C. and G. Hon., 1892.)

14. Make a drawing of sufficient of the plan and elevation of an octagonal dome 8 ft. in diameter boarded internally. All the applied geometry should be clearly shown in the drawings. (C. and G. Hon., 1900.)

15. Draw the construction of a small hemispherical dome 12 ft. in diameter, to be formed in the flat roof of a billiard room measuring 20 ft. by 30 ft. Show the necessary trimming for supporting the dome, and the timber, etc., of the dome itself. (C. and G. Hon., 1900.)

16. Draw to ½ inch scale, section through a room panelled in wood, with ¼ full size details of cornice, chair rail and skirting. Height of room 12 ft. (C. and G. Hon., 1896.)

17. A room, 20 ft. by 15 ft. has a bay window, fireplace, and two doorways. Describe the method of fixing the grounds to receive the skirtings, architraves, etc. (C. and G. Ord., 1898.)

CITY AND GUILDS OF LONDON INSTITUTE.

DEPARTMENT OF TECHNOLOGY.

TECHNOLOGICAL EXAMINATIONS, 1905.

CARPENTRY AND JOINERY.

PRELIMINARY EXAMINATION.

Instructions.

Candidates may take the Ordinary Grade without having passed the Preliminary Examination; or both Examinations may be taken in the same year.

A sheet of drawing paper is supplied to each Candidate.

Three hours are allowed for this paper.

Not more than ten questions to be attempted.

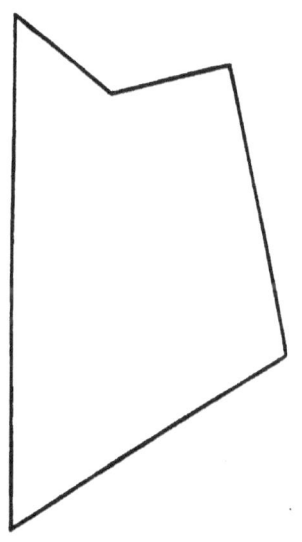

1. A metre = 39·37079 ins. What is the area, in metres, of a room 31 ft. 6 ins. by 12 ft. 6 ins.? (30 *marks.*)

2. Divide a line 4½ ins. long into tenths, and subdivide one such part into sixths; dividers not to be used. (25.)

3. Make an oblong equal in area to the given figure. (30.)

484 A MANUAL OF CARPENTRY AND JOINERY.

4. The side of a circular tank, 7 ft. 6 ins. diameter and 3 ft. 9 ins. high, has to be covered externally with matchboard. How many square feet are required? (35.)

5. Calculate the superficial area of the wall surface shown upon the diagram. (30.)

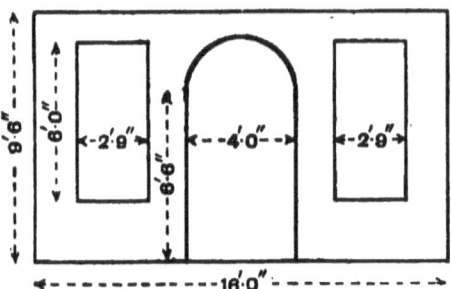

6. The dimensioned sketch shows plan and section of a roof; it has to be boarded. What will be the superficial area of boarding required? (30.)

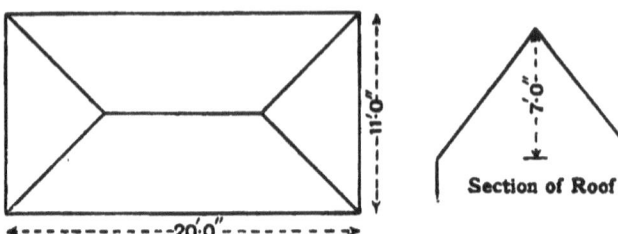

7. A piece of timber is 20 ins. square at one end and 11 ins. square at the other, its length is 16 ft. 6 ins., weight 74 lbs. per cubic foot. Find the cubic contents and the weight. (40.)

8. A window is 4 ft. 3 ins. wide; it has an elliptic arch rising 10 ins. from the springing line. Make a drawing of the centre for the arch. (25.)

9. Draw the plan and elevation of a cylinder 3 ins. diameter, 4 ins. axis, standing on one end. The axis is cut by a plane inclined at 60° to the axis. Draw the section. (35.)

10. Represent in isometric or oblique projection the following joints, and dimension the parts:
    (1) Haunched mortise and tenon.
    (2) Groove and tongue for skirting.
    (3) Tusk tenon joint.
    (4) Mitre bridle joint. (30.)

11. Make the drawings of a solid door frame, rebated and beaded, to receive a 2-in. door 3 ft. wide, 6 ft. 3 ins. high. (35.)

12. A cubic foot of timber floating in water is submerged to a depth of $9\frac{1}{2}$ inches. What is its specific gravity? What weight placed on the top of the timber will suffice to just submerge it? (40.)

13. A beam 25 ft. long, weighing 15 cwt., is supported on two walls; it carries a load of 6 cwt. 12 ft. from one end, and 2 cwt. 4 ft. from the other end. Find the pressures on the two walls. (40.)

14. Give a short description of the undermentioned saws, and the reason for the various shapes of the teeth:
              Dovetail saw.
              Tenon ,,
              Hand ,,
              Rip ,,
              Bow ,, (25.)

15. Give a short description of the following timbers, and the uses to which they may be put: Mahogany, pitch pine, yellow deal. Also state the countries from which they are obtained. (25.)

16. Make a drawing of a collar beam roof, 16-ft. span.
Or,
Make a drawing of a dwarf cupboard front. (30.)

Instructions.

The Candidate must confine himself to one grade only, the Ordinary or Honours, and must state at the top of his paper of answers which grade he has selected. He must *not* answer questions in more than one grade.

If he has already passed in this subject, in the first class of the Ordinary Grade, he must select his questions from those of the Honours Grade.

A sheet of drawing paper is supplied to each Candidate.

Drawing instruments to be used in this Examination.

Four hours allowed for this paper.

486 A MANUAL OF CARPENTRY AND JOINERY.

ORDINARY GRADE.

Not more than TEN *questions to be attempted.*

1. (*a*) Make sketches to show how oak logs are converted to obtain (1) timber of the maximum strength, and (2) boards for joiners' work.

   (*b*) What is water seasoning? How does it affect timber as compared with other forms of seasoning? (25 *marks*.)

2. Some planes are fitted with pairs of irons, others with single irons. Why is this? Give sketches to illustrate your answer. (25.)

3. Make the elevation, vertical and horizontal section of a 2-in. sash door, 3 ft. 3 ins. wide, and 6 ft. 9 ins. high, the bottom panels to be moulded. All construction to be shown by dotted lines, and the drawings to be fully dimensioned. Scale, 1 in. to ft. (40.)

4. What would be the sectional area of an oak beam to carry a distributed load of 6 tons on a span of 10 ft.? (35.)

5. Make a plan to ½-in. scale of an open newel staircase to fit the space shown; the height from floor to floor is 10 ft. 3 ins. Going to be 10 ins., rise not more than 6½ ins., no winders. Number steps, and show all bearers and carriages. Make a section ¼ full size of one tread and riser, showing framing and housing into string. (50.)

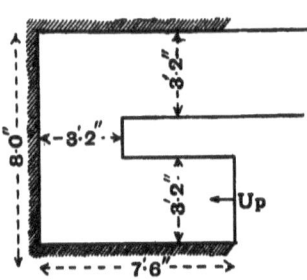

6. Make drawing to show how a fireplace in a single floor would be trimmed round. Scale, 1½ ins. to 1 ft. (25.)

7. Make sketches of the following joints: Secret dovetail, mortise and tenon for the lockrail of a door, two forms of scarfing joints, the meeting styles of French casements. (30.)

8. The sketch shows a *brick* arch in elevation and section; make to a scale of 1 in. to 1 ft. an elevation and cross section of the

necessary centre for its construction. How would you fix and strike the centre? The springing of the arch is assumed to be 10 ft. from the ground. (35.)

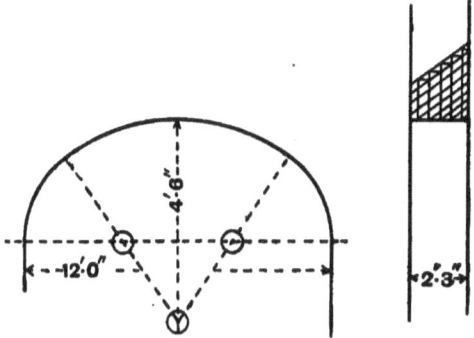

9. Make a drawing, showing rather more than half elevation, and vertical section of a solid door frame, with transom beaded on one edge, rebated and beaded on the other, to receive a 2in. door and a fanlight over door. Also make a sketch to show the joint at the head of the frame; width of opening, 3 ft. 2 ins.; height, 9 ft. (30.)

10. Make detail drawings of a "box gutter" 9 ins. wide, and "cesspool" 6 ins. deep, showing how the work is prepared for the plumber. State what fall the gutter should be given, and how far apart the drips should be. (40.)

11. Draw rather more than half elevation of a framed and trussed partition, 18 ft. wide, 11 ft. 6 ins. high; the partition to have an opening in the centre for a pair of folding doors 7 ft. wide and 7 ft. 3 ins. in height. The partition has to carry its own weight and that of the floor above. Fully dimension the scantlings used. Scale, ½ in. to 1 ft. (40.)

12. The roof of an attic storey has a slope of 60 degrees, and the storey is 9 ft. high in the clear. The sill of a dormer window is 3 ft. 6 ins. above the floor; the window is 3 ft. wide, and as high as possible. Make elevation and section, or an isometric sketch, to a scale of ½ in. to a foot, showing the framing required to form the window, including cheeks and roof and all trimming. No joinery need be shown. (35.)

13. A solid window-frame, 3 ft. 6 ins. wide and 2 ft. 3 ins. high, is fitted with a pair of 2 in. sashes hung with butts to open externally. Make vertical and horizontal sections, showing how the wet would be kept out. Choose your own scale. (30.)

488 A MANUAL OF CARPENTRY AND JOINERY.

14. A roof has a span of 42 ft. Make a drawing of rather more than half elevation of the truss. Fully dimension the scantlings used. Scale, ½ in. to 1 ft. Also make sketches of the joints of the truss, about ¼ full size. (40.)

15. A framed dado is 2 ft. 9 ins. high. Make drawing of the frame showing the construction and fixing, and how the external and internal angles would be secured. Scale, 1½ ins. to 1 ft. (40.)

HONOURS GRADE.

WRITTEN EXAMINATION.

Candidates for Honours must have previously passed in the Ordinary Grade, and must have already forwarded to the Institute a specimen of their Practical Work. They are also required to attend an approved centre for a Practical Test.

Not more than TEN questions to be attempted.

1. Make half elevation, and vertical and horizontal sections of a circular-headed cased sash-frame, fitted with 2-in. double-hung sashes. Show two methods of constructing the head of frame. (35 marks.)

2. Make a plan of the timbers of a double-framed floor for the room shown, to a scale of ¼ inch to 1 ft. Girders to be 10 ft. apart, and 14 ins. by 10 ins.; binders, 10 ins. by 7 ins. Show all other timbers and figure sizes. Give section of girder ¼ full size, showing framing of binders and bridging and ceiling joists. (35.)

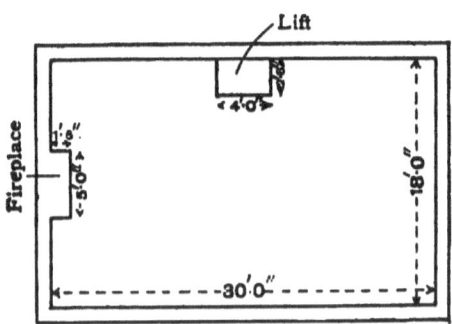

3. Make half elevation, a vertical and horizontal section of a window fitted with a pair of French casements with fanlight over.

Width of opening, 4 ft. 6 ins. ; height, 9 ft. 6 ins. Scale, 1 in. to 1 ft. (30.)

4. A shop front, 14 ft. long, exclusive of any door, is to be arranged so as to light a basement storey by means of a glazed stall board 3 ft. high from pavement. The shop floor is 6 ins. above pavement, and 10 ins. thick. Make a section through stall board and sill of front, showing bulkhead in shop, and give elevation of bulkhead from shop, one half to show framing, the other half the finishing. Scale, ½ in. to 1 ft. (45.)

5. Make drawing sufficient to show the construction of a pair of swing doors and frame, such as are used in first-class office fittings. Scale, 1 in. to 1 ft. (35.)

6. A geometrical staircase has a veneered string. Show how the development of the string is obtained. Take any size of well-hole you please. (30.)

7. Make an elevation, showing the framing of one of a pair of yard gates for an opening 12 ft. wide. Each gate to be 7 ft. 6 ins. high at meeting style, 9 ft. at hanging style, and to be hung with strap hinges, and to have a moulded capping. The gate shown to have a wicket door, not less than 2 ft. 3 ins. by 5 ft. 6 ins., formed in it. Scale, 1 in. to 1 ft. (35.)

8. A stepped gallery extends across one end of a church 50 ft. wide ; the front of the gallery is fixed at each end to the external walls, and carried by two columns, each 12 ft. from the wall. Draw a cross-section through the gallery ; make provision for four rows of pews. The pews need not be shown. (35.)

9. Draw a section and an elevation of a portion of the gallery front in the foregoing question sufficient to show the construction. The front has to provide a book-rest. (30.)

10. The sketch indicates the front of a detached house, without a basement ; it is proposed to take out the whole of the ground-floor wall, and to insert a girder on piers or stanchions with a view to forming a shop. Make an elevation and section to ¼ in. scale. Show the positions

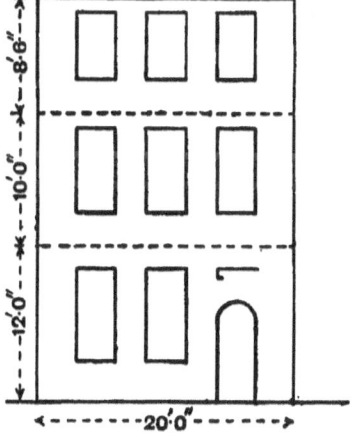

of all dead and raking shores and struts, and name all parts of the shore. Make a drawing ⅛th full size of the head of a raking shore. (45.)

11. The sketch shown below is the plan of a chamber covered by brick vaulting. Make drawing, showing how the centring is made, and provision for striking the same. All geometrical work to be shown. (45.)

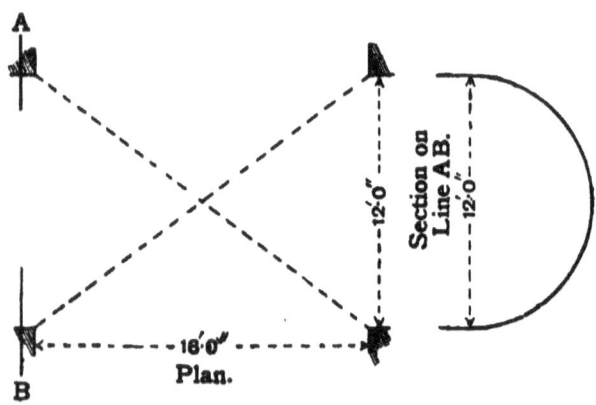

12. A staircase has an open string. The two steps at the foot of the staircase, through which the newel is mortised, are "bull-nosed." Make a plan and elevation, showing the fixing of the string to the steps; also the fixing for the balusters and newel. (40.)

13. A fluted circular column, 18 ins. diameter at base, has a moulded base and carved capital. Make a sketch to show how the base is built up, and how to joint up the column. Also make a smaller drawing to show how to diminish the column. (40.)

14. Make a drawing of about one-half of a mansard roof; span, 24 ft.; trusses, 10 ft. apart. The lower part of the roof to have an inclination of 60 degrees, the upper part ¼ pitch. The tie-beam to carry a floor of 7-in. by 2-in. joists; the underside of collar to be 8 ft. above the floor. Indicate all ironwork necessary for the roof. Scale, 1 in. to 1 ft. (45.)

15. What is the cause of "dry rot"? If a building is attacked by it, what steps should be taken? (25.)

ANSWERS

Chapter IV. (p. 105).

1. 35·56 cms. 2. 3716 sq. cms. 3. 17. 61. 264.
4. 17 ft. nearly. 5. 6·24 ft. = 6 ft. 3 in. nearly.
6. 7 ft. 2½ in. 10 ft. 7½ in. 20 ft. 6 in. 29 ft. 4⅛ in.
7. 161·45 sq. ft. 8. 6 sq. metres. 10. 405⅞ sq. ft.
11. 43·45 sq. ft. 13. 10 ft. 14. 4 ft. 11½ in.
15. 137·47 sq. ft. 16. 105⅝ cub. ft.
17. 25⅝ cub. ft. £2 10s. 7½d. 18. 103¼ cub. ft.
19. 163·67 cub. ft. 20. 17·3 cub. ft.

Chapter XII. (p. 343).

11. 5 cwts. 23¼ lbs. 12. 4·16 inches from one end. 13. 50% more.
14. 10½ cwts. at end nearest load, 4¼ cwts. at the other end.
15. 9 tons at one end, 3 tons at the other end.
16. 7 cwts. at one end, 5 cwts. at the other end.
17. Maximum carrying capacity (a) 360 cwts., (b) 240 cwts. Safe distributed load (a) 144 cwts., (b) 96 cwts.
18. 5 inches broad.
19. 5·9 inches deep by 8·26 inches broad, or 7·4 inches deep by 5·3 inches broad.
20. 10½ inches deep by 7½ inches broad, or 9 inches deep by 7½ inches broad with a W.I. flitch 8 inches by ⅜ inch thick.
21. 20 inches deep by 15 inches broad, or 18 inches deep by 13 inches broad with a 17 inches by 1¼ inches W.I. flitch.
22. Slightly more than one-half.

INDEX

Acute angle, 23, 28.
Adze, 121.
Angle, acute, 23, 28; bars, 468-9; beads, 479; brackets, 470; dovetail joint, 185; joints, 168, 183-4; measurement of an, 22, 108; obtuse, 23, 28; right, 23, 28; tie, 249.
Annual rings, 2.
Applied geometry in roof construction, 246-55.
Apron linings, 444.
Arch, brick trimmer, 197-9; coach-headed trimmer, 200.
Architrave, 368, 404.
Area of, a circle, 97; an ellipse, 99; a polygon, 94; a rectilineal figure, 90; a square, 90; a triangle, 91.
Arrangement of workshop, 460.
Ash, 18.
Astragal bead, 181.
Auger brace bit, 123-4.
Axe, 121.

Back or tenon saw, 113.
Backflap hinge, 373.
Back-iron of a plane iron, 115.
Backing of hip rafter, 251.
Back shore, 290.
Balancing treads, 431, 453.
Balusters, 454-6.
Band and gudgeon, 375.
Band moulding, 368.
Band saws, 135-7.
Bare-faced tenon joint, 170, 348.
Barge boards, 240, 418.

Bars, angle, 468-9.
Basswood, 19.
Bay window, 399-401.
Beech, 18.
Bead, angle, 479; astragal, 181; cock, 182; flush, 181; plane, 119; staff, 181.
Beams, lengthening of, 163; strength of wooden, 331, 336; stresses in, 160.
Bench, vice, 124; holdfast, 126.
Benches, 460.
Bending moment, 333; diagram, 334-6.
Bevels at ends of, hip and valley rafters, 248; jack rafters, 253; purlins, 252.
Birch, 18.
Bird's-mouth joint, 220.
Block, mitre, 467.
Boards, edge joints for wide, 187; floor, 210-2; match, 186, 267; skirting, 478.
Bolts, as fastenings, 175; handrail, 183, 456, 477; joint, 176, 183; lewis or rag, 177, 366.
Boucherie's system of seasoning, 12.
Bow or turning saw, 114.
Bow's notation, 311, 317.
Bow-string roof truss, 241.
Box gutter, 234.
Box shutters, 405.
Box, mitre, 467.
Brace, 122; bits, 122-4.
Braces, 261, 278.
Bracketed stair, 438.

Bracketed string, 432, 439.
Brackets, angle, 470.
Brad awl, 122.
Brads, 179, 211.
Bressummer, 162.
Brick, nogging, 265; trimmer arch, 197-9.
Bricklayers' scaffold, 276-7.
Bridging, joists, 194; herring bone, 200.
Bridle joint, 174, 262.
British and metric methods of measurement, 86.
Bullnose, step, 432, 442-3; plane, 118.
Burnett's process of seasoning, 12.
Butt hinges, 372.

Calculations, 85.
Calculating, measurement of timber, 100; strength of wooden beams, 336.
Cambium, 1.
Canadian red pine, 16.
Canary wood, 19.
Cantilever, 332.
Carriages, rough stair, 444-5.
Casement windows, 384; fasteners for, 408; to open inwards, 384-6; to open outwards, 386.
Cast iron, columns, 204-5; gutters, 234; struts, 230-2.
Ceiling joists, 193, 195, 202, 218, 232.
Cement concrete, 208.
Centre bit, 123.
Centres, for arches, 293-9.
Chalked line, 110.
Chariot plane, 119.
Charring of timber, 11.
Chase mortise joint, 173, 203.
Chestnut, 18.
Chisels, 120.
Chord of a circle, 24.
Circle, 23; area of a, 97; periphery of a, 25.
Circle-on-circle, centre for arch, 297-8; framing of, 474-5.
Circles, concentric, 25.
Circular saws, 138-41.

Circumscribed figures, 36.
Clamped joint, 189.
Clasp nails, 178; cut, 179; wrought, 179.
Classification of joints, 159.
Cleat, 174-5, 280.
Close string board, 432, 438.
Clout nails, 179.
Coach screws, 175, 280.
Coach-headed trimmer arch, 200.
Cock bead, 182.
Coffer-dam, 286.
Cogged joint, 174, 202, 220.
Collar beam, 219, 226.
Collar beam roof, 219.
Columns, cast iron, 204-5.
Commode step, 431, 444, 453.
Common rafters, 215, 217; lengths and bevels of, 246-7.
Compass, saw, 114; plane, 117.
Compasses, 109.
Component forces, 297-8, 307.
Composite roof truss, 229-31.
Compression stress, 331.
Concrete, 208.
Conifers, 1.
Conservatories, 424-7.
Construction of joints, principles governing, 158.
Converting of timber, 4.
Co-ordinate planes, 50.
Corbelling, 196.
Couple roof, 216-7.
Cradling, pendentive, 476-7.
Cramp, floor, 126, 212; G., 126; sash, 125.
Creosote oil, 11.
Cross-cut saw, 112, 133, 135.
Cross-grooving, 185.
Cross-tongue, 171-183.
Cube, 51.
Cubic or solid measure, 100-5.
Cup shakes, 9.
Curtail step, 432, 442-3.
Cut string, 432, 439.
Cutting gauge, 109.
Cutting tools, 111-21.
Cylinder, 52.

Dancing or balancing treads, 431, 453.
Dead shores, 287, 291-2.

Deal, red, 14, 211 ; white, 14, 211 ; yellow, 14, 211.
Deal frame saws, 130, 132-3.
Defects of timber, 8.
Deflection, 339.
Derrick towers, 280-1.
Desiccation of timber, 8.
Development of solids, 77-82.
Diagram, bending moment, 334-6; polar, 317 ; reciprocal, 317.
Dimensions of floor boards, 210.
Diminishing figures, 46.
Doatiness, 10.
Dog, iron, 174, 280, 297.
Doglegged stairs, 433, 435, 449, 450.
Door, fastenings, 376 ; frames, 364-71 ; framing, 348-9 ; setting out of framing for, 463.
Doors, 346-80 ; double margin, 358 ; framed, ledged and braced, 346-52 ; folding, 358 ; ledged, 346-7 ; ledged and braced, 346-7 ; panelled, 353-69 ; sash, 358 ; superior, 369 ; vestibule, 360, 365, 367.
Dormer windows, 418-20.
Dovetail, angle joints, 185 ; halved joint, 220 ; keys, 188 ; saw, 113 ; tenon joint, 173.
Double floor, 193, 201-3.
Double margin door, 358.
Double tenon joint, 171.
Double quirked bead, 181.
Dragon piece, 249.
Draw boring, 177.
Draw knife, 121.
Drawing instruments, 21.
Druxiness, 9.
Dry rot, 10, 195.

Eaves, of a roof, 215, 232 ; gutter, 232 ; overhanging, 233.
Edge joints, 186.
Electric seasoning, 12.
Ellipse, 73.
Encasing of girders, 208.
Enlarging and diminishing figures, 46.
Equilateral triangle, 28.
Equilibrant of forces, 310.
Equilibrium of forces, 307-8, 319.

Expanding brace bit, 124.
Excavations, timbering of, 285.

Face marks, 461.
Face mould, 475.
Fanlight, 366.
Fascia board, 233.
Fasteners, window, 407 ; sash, 408.
Fastenings for carpenters' joints, 174.
Felling of trees, 4.
Fillets, 203.
Fillister, sash, 119.
Fir, Scotch, 14 ; spruce, 14.
Fireclay blocks, 209.
Fire-resisting floors, 208.
Firmer chisel, 120.
Fished joint, 164.
Fixed skylights, 412-4.
Fixing of, joiners' work, 477 ; window frames, 402.
Flitched girders, 162.
Flight of stairs, 430.
Floor board joints, 210-1.
Floor cramps, 126, 212.
Floor joists, 193.
Floors, double, 193-201 ; fire-resisting, 208 ; framed, 193, 203 ; method of laying, 211 ; single, 193-4 ; wooden block, 209.
Flush bead, 182.
Fluting, 182.
Flying shores, 287, 290.
Folding doors, 358.
Force, nature of a, 306.
Forces, parallel, 318-27 ; parallelogram of, 308 ; polygon of, 315-7 ; triangle of, 311.
Formula for wooden beams, 337.
Forstner brace bit, 124.
Fox-wedging, 172.
Foxiness, 10.
Framed floors, 193, 203.
Framed, ledged and braced doors, 346-52.
Framed and panelled doors, 353-69.
Framed roof trusses, 216, 220.
Framed and trussed partitions, 260-5.

INDEX.

Framed wooden buildings, 266-72.
Frames, door, 364-71; window, 402.
Fulcrum, 318.
Funicular or link polygon, 317.

G-cramp, 126.
Gables, 240.
Gantries, 278-9.
Gauge, cutting, 109; marking, 108; mortise, 108; thumb, 109.
General joiner, 152-6.
Geometrical definitions, 23.
Geometrical stairs, 433, 451, 453-4.
Geometry, solid, 49.
Gibs and cotters, 223-4.
Gimlet, 122.
Girders, encasing of, 208; flitched, 161-2, 204; trussed, 162-3; wrought iron and steel, 206-7.
Glue, 187, 189.
Glue-blocks, 189-90.
Gothic roof truss, 242-5.
Gouges, 120.
Graphic determination of areas, 92.
Gravity, specific, 342.
Greenheart, 19.
Greenhouses, 424-7.
Ground line, 50.
Grounds, 370, 477.
Guard boards, 278.
Guard rails, 278.
Gudgeons, bands and, 375.
Guide piles, 285-6.
Gutter, behind chimney, 239; behind parapet wall, 234; cast iron, 234; eaves, 232; lead, 234; parallel, 234; tapering, 234, 236-7.

H-hinges, 371.
Half timber work, 269-72.
Half-space landing, 431, 435, 444.
Halved joints, 182, 262.
Halved and cogged joint, 220.
Halving, 166-8.
Hammer-headed roof truss, 245.

Hammer-headed key, 167, 188.
Handrail bolt, 183, 456.
Handrails, 451; ramped, 456; swan-neck in, 456.
Hanging of sashes, 396-9.
Hardwood trees, 4.
Haunched tenon joint, 170, 348.
Heading joints, 183, 211.
Heart shakes, 9.
Heartwood, 2.
Heptagon, 35.
Herring-bone bridging, 200.
Hexagon, 34.
Hinged skylight, 414-8.
Hinges, backflap, 373; bands and gudgeons, 375; butt, 372; parliament, 373; pew or egg-joint, 373; projecting butt, 372; rising butt, 372; spring, 374.
Hip, 216, 246.
Hip rafters, 216; backing of, 251; lengths and bevels of, 248-9.
Holdfast, bench, 126.
Hollow-ground saws, 142.
Horizontal log frame saws, 132, 134.
Horizontal trace, 62.
Hospital light, 396, 398.
Hot-air seasoning, 8.
Housed joint, 68-9, 198.
Hyperbola, 76-7.

Inclined forces, 317.
Inclined planes, 62.
Injury caused by animals, 10.
Inscribed figures, 36.
Inside door frames, 368.
Instruments, drawing, 21.
Intertie, 264.
Iron, bolts, 222; columns, 204-5; dowels, 366; dog, 174, 212, 280, 297; girders, 206; planes, 117; purlins, 218.
Isosceles triangle, 28

Jack plane, 115.
Jack rafter, 216; lengths and bevels of, 253.
Jarrah wood, 19.
Jib crane, 281.

Joiners' work, fixing of, 477.
Joint, angle, 184; between king post and tie-beam, 223; between tread and riser, 437; bird's-mouth, 220; bridle, 262; butt, 183; chase mortise, 203; clamped, 189; cogged, 202, 220; dovetail, 185, 220; at foot of principal rafter, 221; halved, 182, 220, 262; at head of principal rafter, 222; at head of queen post, 226; mortise and tenon, 169, 180, 348, 463; rule, 188, 374; stump tenon, 262, 348; tusk-tenon, 171, 198, 225.
Joint bolt, 176, 183, 223-4.
Jointing plane, 117.
Joints and fastenings, 158, 174.
Joints, classification of, 159; floor board, 210; heading, 183; housed, 184, 198; in door framing, 348-9; keyed, 188-9; lengthening, 182; mitred, 184, 467-8; scarfed, 182; scribed, 185.
Joists, bridging, 194; ceiling, 193, 195, 202, 218, 232; dimensions of, 193; trimming, 197.

Key, hammer-headed, 182, 188.
Keyed joint, 167, 188-9.
King-bolt, 229.
King post truss, 221.
Knots, 8.
Kyan's process of seasoning timber, 12.

Ladders, 275.
Laminated string, 440.
Lantern lights, 420.
Lap dovetail joint, 185.
Lapped joints, 164, 169.
Larch, 16.
Latches, door, 376.
Lay lights, 424.
Laying floors, method of, 211.
Lead, covered roofs, 240; drip, 238; gutter, 234; roll, 238.
Lean-to roof, 216.
Ledged and braced doors, 346-7.

Ledgers, 277.
Lengths and bevels of, common rafters, 246-7; hip and valley rafters, 248-9; jack rafters, 253.
Lengthening joints, 163, 182.
Levers, 318.
Lewis or rag bolt, 177.
Line of nosings, 430.
Linings, apron, 444; jamb, 368; splayed, 472-3.
Loaded beams with stress diagrams, 319-27.
Locks, door, 376; mortise, 377.
Log frame saw, horizontal, 132-4; vertical, 129-31.

Machines, band saw, 135-7; circular saw, 138-41; cross-cut saw, 133-5; deal frame saw, 130, 132-3; horizontal log frame, 132-4; mortising, 151-3; moulding, 148; panel planing, 146; planing, 144-7; saw sharpening, 142-4; surface planing, 145; tenoning, 150; thicknessing, 146; vertical log frame, 129-31; vertical spindle moulding, 148.
Mahogany, 17.
Mansard roof truss, 242.
Maple, 18.
Margin template, 436-7.
Marking gauge, 108.
Masons' scaffold, 278.
Match boarding, 186.
Measurement of, angles, 22, 108; length, 22.
Measuring and testing tools, 107-11.
Mechanics of carpentry, 306-45.
Medullary rays, 2.
Mensuration, 85-106.
Method of, calculating timber, 100; laying floors, 211.
Metric measurement, 22, 85.
Mitre, block, 467; box, 467; template, 466.
Mitred joint, 184-5, 356, 467-8.
Mitring, 466.
Moulding, raking, 468-9.
Mouldings, 181; band, 368, 404.

INDEX.

Nails, 179.
Natural seasoning, 7.
Needle shores, 287-9.
Newel post, 439, 450, 452, 455.
Noden Bretenneau method of seasoning timber, 12.
Nogging, brick, 265.
Northern pine, 14.
Nose bit, 123.
Nosings, line of, 430.
Notch boards, 447.

Oak, 16.
Oblique planes, 62-9.
Obtuse, angle, 23; angled triangle, 28.
Octagon, 35.
Octahedron, 52.
Offsets, 196.
Oilstone, 119.
Open newel stairs, 432, 449, 451-2.
Oregon pine, 16.
Overhanging eaves, 233.
Oversailing courses, 196.

Pad saw, 114.
Paint, 11.
Panel, plane, 117; planer, 146; saw, 112.
Panelled doors, 353-69.
Parabola, 76-7.
Parallel forces, 318.
Parallel gutter, 234.
Parallelogram, 32.
Parallelogram of forces, 308.
Parapet wall, gutter behind a, 234.
Paring chisel, 120.
Parliament hinge, 373.
Pendentive cradling, 476-7.
Periphery of a circle, 25.
Pew or egg-joint hinge, 373.
Piles, 285-6.
Pillars, cast-iron, 204.
Pitch board, 436.
Pitch pine, 15, 211.
Pivoted or swing sash, 386-8.
Plane geometry, 21.
Plane iron, 115.
Planes, inclined, 62; oblique, 62-9.

Planing machine, 144-7.
Plough, 118.
Plugs, wooden, 178.
Plumb, bob, 110; line, 110; rule, 110.
Polar diagram, 317.
Pole plate, 234-5.
Poling boards, 282.
Polygon, 33; area of a, 94.
Preservation of timber, 11.
Princess post, 227.
Principal rafter, 221, 226.
Principles governing the construction of joints, 158.
Prism, 51.
Projecting butt hinges, 372-3.
Projection, of lines, 58-61; of solids, 53-7; orthographic, 50.
Proportion, 41.
Proportion of tread to riser, 433-4.
Protractor, 23.
Pugging, 201.
Pulleys, 240-2.
Purlins, 216-8; iron, 218.
Putlogs, 277.
Pyramid, 52.
Pyramid roof, 246.

Quadrilateral figures, 32.
Quadrants, 408, 427.
Qualities of good timber, 13.
Quarter space landing, 430, 435, 444, 451, 454.
Queen-post roof truss, 225-8.
Quirked bead, 181.

Rafter, common, 215, 217, 246-7; hip, 216, 246, 248-9; jack, 216, 253; principal, 221-2, 246; valley, 216, 246, 248-9.
Rag or lewis bolt, 177, 366.
Raking, mouldings, 468-9; shores, 287.
Ramped handrail, 456.
Rebate plane, 118.
Reciprocal diagram, 317.
Rectangle, 33.
Red deal, 14, 211.
Reeding, 182.
Relative density, 342.
Resultant of forces, 307.

Rider shore, 290.
Ridge, 215.
Ridge piece or tree, 215.
Right angled triangle, 28.
Right angles, 23.
Rindgalls, 10.
Rings, annual, 2.
Rip saw, 111-2.
Rising butt hinges, 372.
Rod, setting out, 462-5.
Roof, applied geometry in the construction of a, 246; couple, 216; lean-to, 216; lead covered, 240; lights, 412; pyramid, 245; turret, 245, 253-5; zinc covered, 240.
Roof truss, collar beam, 219; framed, 216-20; Gothic, 242-5; hammer beam, 245; king post, 221; lattice or bow-string, 241; Mansard, 242; queen post, 225-8.
Rosewood, 19.
Rot, dry, 10, 195.
Rough carriages, 444-5.
Round-ended step, 432, 442-3.
Router, 119.
Rule joint, 188, 374.

Sapwood, 2.
Sash and frame window, 389-96.
Sash, cramp, 125; doors, 358; fasteners, 408-9; fillister, 119; lifts, 408-9; pivoted or swing, 386-8.
Sashes, 381, 392; casement, 384-6; horizontal sliding, 389.
Saw-kerfing, 471.
Saw-set, 113.
Saw-sharpening machine, 142-4.
Saw-teeth, 112, 141.
Saws, 111-4; machine, 129-42.
Scaffold, 274; bricklayers', 276-7; boards, 277; masons', 278.
Scaffolding trestle, 274-5.
Scalene triangle, 28.
Scales, 42.
Scarfed joint, 165, 182.
Scotch fir, 14.
Screws, 180.
Screws, coach, 175, 280.
Scribed joint, 185.

Scribing, 184, 356, 466.
Seasoning of timber, 5-8; chemical, 12.
Second seasoning, 7.
Secret dovetail joint, 185.
Secret nailing, 478.
Secret screwing, 370-1, 478.
Sections, 69-77.
Sector of a circle, 25.
Segment of a circle, 24.
Sequoia pine, 16.
Set on a saw, 112.
Set squares, 21.
Setting out, curve for segmental arch, 295; door framing, 463; panelled framing, 462; of stairs, 434; rod, 462, 464-5; window frames, 465.
Shakes in timber, 9.
Sharpening, of saws, 114; of planes, 119.
Shearing stress, 161, 331.
Shed roof, 228.
Sheeting, 283.
Sheet piles, 285-6.
Shell bit, 123.
Shop window, 402-3.
Shoring, 287-92.
Shrinkage of timber, 4.
Shutters, window, 405.
Silver grain, 2, 5, 17.
Single floor, 193-4.
Skids, 7.
Skirting boards, 478-9.
Skylights, 412-8.
Sleeper walls, 195.
Sliding bevel, 108.
Sliding window shutters, 406.
Slip feathers, 356.
Smoothing plane, 116.
Snipe bill, 177.
Snow boards, 240.
Socketed chisels, 121.
Soffit boarding, 234.
Soft wood trees, 4.
Solid geometry, 49.
Solid or cubic measurement, 100-5.
Solids, development of, 77-82.
Sound boarding, 201.
Spandrel framing, 433, 444.
Spars, 215.

Specific gravity, 342.
Spectators' stands, 299-303.
Sphere, 52.
Spikes, 178.
Spirit level, 109.
Splayed linings, 472-3.
Split bill, 177, 366.
Spokeshave, 119.
Sprigs, 179.
Spring hinges, 374.
Square, 33.
Square root, 88.
Staff bead, 181.
Staircase work, 430-59.
Stairs, doglegged, 432, 449-50; erection of, 444; flight of, 430; geometrical, 433, 451, 453-4; open newel, 432, 449, 451-2; well of, 432; winder, 432, 448-9.
Stirrup iron, 204, 223.
Stone template, 207.
Storey rod, 434.
Straight edge, 108.
Straining, beam, 226; sill, 226.
Straps, iron, 175.
Strength of wooden beams, 331.
Stress, in buckling chain, 312-3; compression, 331; in wall bracket, 313-4; shearing, 161, 331-2; tension, 331.
Stress and strain, 160, 331.
Stress diagram, for loaded beams, 319-27; for roof truss, 326-31.
Stresses in beams, 160, 331.
String board, 432-9; bracketed, 432; close, 432; cut and mitred, 432; laminated, 440; staved, 440; veneered, 440-2.
Struts, 163, 221, 282.
Strutting, 200.
Studs, 259.
Stump tenon joint, 174, 262, 348.
Superior doors, 362, 369.
Surface planer, 145.
Swage saw, 142.
Swan neck in handrail, 456.
Swiss bit, 123.
Sycamore, 18.

Table or rule joint, 188.
Tacks, 179.

Tangent, 25.
Tapering gutter, 234, 236-7.
Tarring, 11.
Teak, 17.
Tee or cross garnet hinges, 371.
Tee square, 21.
Teeth, saw, 112, 141.
Template, margin, 436-7; mitre, 466; stone, 207.
Tenon saw, 113.
Tenoning machine, 150.
Tension stress, 331.
Teredo navalis, 10.
Termites, 11.
Testing tools, 108.
Tetrahedron, 52.
Thicknessing machine, 146.
Thumb gauge, 109.
Timber, crossgrained, 9; defects of, 8; methods of calculating, 100; preservation of, 11; seasoning of, 5, 6; shrinkage of, 4; varieties of, 13.
Timbering of, excavations, 285; trenches, 282-4.
Tools, 107-28; boring, 122-4; cutting, 111-21; testing, 108-11.
Torus moulding, 182.
Traces of a plane, 62.
Trammel pins, 109.
Trapezoid, 33.
Trapezium, 33.
Traveller, 280.
Tread and riser, joint between, 437; proportions of, 433-4.
Trees, 1, 4.
Trenails, 177, 271.
Triangle of forces, 311.
Triangles, 28; area of, 91.
Trimmer, 197.
Trimmer arch, 197-9.
Trimming of floor joists, 197.
Trimming of roofs, 240.
Trueing-up of material, 461.
Truss, composite, 229-31; Gothic, 242-5; hammer beam, 245; king-post, 221; latticed or bow-string, 241; Mansard, 242; queen-post, 225-28.
Trussed girders, 162.
Trying plane, 116.

Try square, 108.
Turret roofs, 245, 253-5.
Tusk tenon joint, 171, 198, 204.
Twisted fibres, 9.

Units, British and metric, 86.
Units of length, 85.
Upsets, 10.

Valley rafter, 216, 246.
Varieties of timber, 13.
Veneered string, 440-2.
Venetian window, 396-7.
Vertical log frame saw, 129-31.
Vertical spindle, 148.
Vertical trace, 62.
Vestibule doors, 360, 365, 367.

Waling pieces, 283.
Wall piece, 288.
Wall plates, 195-6, 215
Walls, sleeper, 195.
Walnut, 18.
Water seasoning, 8.
Wedging, 176; folding, 212, 293; fox, 172.
Well of stairs, 432.
Wet rot, 10.
White deal, 14, 211.
Winder stairs, 432, 448-9.

Winders, 430.
Winding strips, 108.
Window, fastenings, 407; linings, 402; shutters, 405-6.
Window frames, fixing of, 402.
Windows, 381-411; bay, 399-401; casement, 384-6; dormer, 418-20; sash and frame, 389-96; shop, 402-3; setting out of, 465; Venetian, 396-7.
Wire nails, 179.
Wooden, block floors, 209; centres, 293-9; floors, 193-214; framed buildings, 266; pins, 176; plugs, 178, 366; roofs, 215-58.
Wooden beams, strength of, 331.
Wood-working machinery, 129.
Workshop, arrangement of, 460; practice, 460.
Wreathed string, 432, 40.
Wrought, clasp nails, 179; clout nails, 179; iron girders, 206; iron straps, 222-4.

Yellow deal, 14, 211.
Yellow pine, 15.

Zinc covered roofs, 240.